Comparative
Environmental and
Natural Resources Law

Comparative Environmental and Natural Resources Law

Sandra Zellmer

University of Nebraska College of Law

Carolina Academic Press

Durham, North Carolina

Library of Congress Cataloging-in-Publication Data

Zellmer, Sandra Beth.
Comparative environmental and natural resources law / Sandra Zellmer.
    pages cm
Includes bibliographical references and index.

ISBN 978-1-59460-780-6 (alk. paper)

1. Environmental law. 2. Conservation of natural resources--Law and
legislation. I. Title.

K3585.Z45 2013

344.04'6--dc23

2013001211

Carolina Academic Press
700 Kent Street
Durham, North Carolina 27701
Telephone (919) 489-7486
Fax (919) 493-5668
www.cap-press.com

Printed in the United States of America

Contents

Preface

This book provides a comparative study of the laws and policies governing environmental degradation, environmental impact assessments, environmental human rights, and the management of water quality, wildlife, and habitat. It focuses on five nations, specifically, the United States, Canada, New Zealand, England, and India. The first four have been chosen for comparative analysis because of their common origins, which enables the reader to trace the evolution of environmental law and policy from some of the earliest judicial and administrative materials available, and because of their relatively common cultural influences yet divergent modern environmental problems and strategies. The fifth nation, India, represents yet another country deeply influenced by England but charting its own course as an emerging economic giant, whose growth poses significant implications for global climate change and other environmental concerns.

There is an exceedingly practical reason for choosing these countries as well. English is the common language of all but India, and legal materials are readily available in English in India. Studying law across cultural and jurisdictional lines is challenging enough without adding language barriers to the mix. English-speaking lawyers and judges who fail to "exercise extreme caution in using comparative materials from foreign language systems" run the risk of getting "lost in translation." Jane Stapleton, *Benefits of Comparative Tort Reasoning: Lost in Translation*, 1 J. Tort L. 6 (2007). This book strives to avoid that potential pitfall. Even so, scholars and lawyers from outside of the United States may wince at the citation form utilized throughout the book, which takes a distinctly American approach. Hopefully, all citations are sufficient to enable readers to locate the primary source without difficulty.

Choosing cases and other materials for inclusion is a challenging prospect. Rather than selecting the most "cutting edge" cases or the most spectacular environmental catastrophes in each nation, cases, statutes, regulations, and articles are chosen because they are representative of a particular country's approach or because they add unique insights into the country or the environmental topic at hand. In an effort to keep this book relatively concise and manageable for teachers, students, and other readers, it may at times seem like the coverage is incredibly broad ("a mile wide and an inch deep," as we say in the western United States about some of our rivers). Other topics, however, are covered in minute detail. In all instances, the choice of materials is intended to aid the reader in comparing or contrasting the laws of various nations, and in assessing the relative efficacy of any given legal doctrine or theory for achieving environmentally sustainable outcomes.

Comparative Environmental and Natural Resources Law is suitable as a text for law school classes and seminars as well as graduate courses in environmental and international studies. Students need not have taken a domestic environmental law course prior to studying this subject.

My own fascination with Comparative Environmental and Natural Resources Law began in Greece, when I taught a seminar on the Comparative Law of the Marine Environment for Tulane Law School. I subsequently taught Comparative Water Law as a seminar in New Zealand and Comparative Environmental Law in Portland, Oregon. I am grateful to the students of Tulane, the University of Auckland, and Lewis and Clark law schools, who responded to early versions of these materials with good cheer as well as insightful questions and comments. I am also grateful to research assistants Tanya Nodlinski, Joslyn VanCleave Luedtke, Samantha Pelster, and Samantha Staley for their diligent work on the book.

Acknowledgments

Chapter 1

Michael G. Faure and Jason S. Johnston, in The Law and Economics of Environmental Federalism: Europe and the United States Compared, 27 Virginia Environmental Law Journal 205 (2009).

Kathryn A. Perales, It Works Fine in Europe, So Why Not Here? Comparative Law and Constitutional Federalism, 23 Vermont Law Review 885 (1999).

Mathias Reimann, Stepping Out of the European Shadow: Why Comparative Law in the United States Must Develop its Own Agenda, 6 American Journal of Comparative Law 637 (1998).

Chapter 2

Paul A. Barresi, Mobilizing the Public Trust Doctrine in Support of Publicly Owned Forests as Carbon Dioxide Sinks in India and the United States, 23 Colorado Journal of International Environmental Law & Policy 39 (2012).

Albert C. Lin, Beyond Tort: Compensating Victims of Environmental Toxic Injury, 78 Southern California Law Review 1439 (2005) reprinted with permission of the Southern California Law Review.

Chapter 3

Sarah Michaels and Owen J. Furuseth, Innovation in Environmental Policy: The National Environmental Policy Act of the US and the Resource Management Act of New Zealand, 17 The Environmentalist 181 (1997).

Ravi Singhania and Sunayna Jaimini, Lafarge Decision—Light at the End of the Tunnel?, 2 Indian Law News 18 (American Bar Association Section of International Law Newsletter 2011). © Copyright 2011 by the American Bar Association.

William A. Tilleman, Public Participation In The Environmental Impact Assessment Process: A Comparative Study of Impact Assessment in Canada, The United States and the European Community, 33 Columbia Journal of Transnational Law 337 (1995).

Mary Williams Walsh, Environmental Law in Canada Comes of Age, Los Angeles Times F1, April 8, 1990. Copyright © 1990 Los Angeles Times.

Christopher Wood, Environmental Impact Assessment: A Comparative Review (2nd ed. 2003). © Copyright 2003 Pearson Education, Harlow, UK.

Chapter 4

Peter Bernard and Andrew P. Mayer, A Tale of Two Sovereigns: Canada, The United States, and Trans-Border Pollution Issues, 13 U.S. Maritime Law Journal 125 (2000–2001).

Michael J. Robinson-Dorn, The Trail Smelter, Is What's Past Prologue? EPA Blazes a New Trail for CERCLA, 14 N.Y.U. Environmental Law Journal 233 (2006).

William Howarth, Water Quality and Land Use Regulation Under the Water Framework Directive, 23 Pace Environmental Law Review 351 (2006).

M.C. Mehta, The Accountability Principle: Legal Solutions to Break Corruption's Impact on India's Environment, 21 Journal of Environmental Law & Litigation 141 (2006).

Chapter 5

Joshua Walters and Shi-Ling Shu, Saving the Northern Spotted Owl in British Columbia (2008), at www.law.ubc.ca/files/pdf/enlaw/SpottedOwlCase04_20_09.pdf.

Shalini Bhutani and Ashish Kothari, The Biodiversity Rights of Developing Nations: A Perspective From India, 32 Golden Gate Law Review 587 (2002).

Owen Furuseth and Chris Cocklin, An Institutional Framework For Sustainable Resource Management: The New Zealand Model, 35 Natural Resources Journal 243 (1995).

Oliver A. Houck, Tales from a Troubled Marriage: Science and Law in Environmental Policy, 17 Tulane Environmental Law Journal 163 (2003). Reprinted with permission of the Tulane Environmental Law Journal, which holds the copyright.

Michael Stockdale, English and American Wildlife Law: Lessons from the Past, 47 Proc. Annual Conf. Southeast Assoc. Fish and Wildlife Agencies 732 (1993).

Mitsuhiko A. Takahashi, Are the Kiwis Taking a Leap? Learning from the Biosecurity Policy of New Zealand, 24 Temple Journal of Science, Technology & Environmental Law 461 (2005).

Chapter 6

Benjamin A. Kahn, The Legal Framework Surrounding Maori Claims to Water Resources In New Zealand: In Contrast to the American Indian Experience, 35 Stanford Journal of International Law 49 (1999).

Peter Manus, Indigenous Peoples' Environmental Rights: Evolving Common Law Perspectives in Canada, Australia, and the United States, 33 B.C. Environmental Affairs Law Review 1 (2006).

James Salzman, Thirst: A Short History of Drinking Water, 18 Yale Journal of Law and Humanities 94 (2006).

Introduction

Prior to the 1960s, concerns about the state of the environment were rarely raised in court or even in the media. Most disputes about pollution or the loss of wildlife were private ones, tested and resolved by private property or tort law. But by the time the first Earth Day was celebrated in April 1970, communities across the globe demonstrated that they would no longer be content with governments, corporations, and landowners that treated pollution and habitat destruction as merely an economic dispute to be resolved behind closed doors. Accordingly, the right to a quality environment was proclaimed at the United Nations Conference on the Human Environment in the 1972 Stockholm Declaration, and a vast body of environmental law grew from that foundation. *See* John Bonine and Svitlana Kravchenko, Human Rights and Environment 1 (2008); Kate O'Neill, *The Comparative Study of Environmental Movements*, in Comparative Environmental Politics 119 (2012) (eds. Steinberg and VanDeveer).

Perhaps most importantly, the Rio Declaration was adopted in 1992 at the conclusion of the United Nations Conference on Environment and Development (UNCED) (the Earth Summit), in Rio de Janeiro, Brazil. There, countries adopted Agenda 21—a blueprint for sustainable development. Through the Rio Declaration and Agenda 21, signatories committed to rethink economic growth, advance social equity, and ensure environmental protection.

In June 2012, twenty years after Rio, world leaders gathered in Brazil at the Rio+20 conference. The official discussions focused on two main themes: how to build a green economy to achieve sustainable development and lift people out of poverty, including support for developing countries that will allow them to find a green path for development; and how to improve international coordination for sustainable development. According to the United Nations, Rio+20 was the largest U.N. conference ever held. Over 100 governments were represented at the Head of State level. Additionally, 487 Ministers attended. Significant outcomes included:

- Over $513 billion was mobilized in commitments for sustainable development in the areas of energy, transport, green economy, disaster reduction, desertification, water, forests, and agriculture.

- Governments, business, civil society groups, universities, and others registered 692 voluntary commitments for sustainable development.

UN Conference on Sustainable Development, *Rio+20 By the Numbers* (June 23, 2012), at http://www.uncsd2012.org/index.php?page=view&nr=1304&type=230&menu=38.

Some say that not enough progress has been made, however, since 1992. NGOs and community groups are criticising a deal "dangerously lacking" in ambition, urgency, and political will. "[A] sober, unambitious mood prevailed as negotiators produced what critics called a watered-down document that makes few advances on protecting the environment." Christian Science Monitor, *Economy Casts Shadow on Rio+20 Environmental*

Summit, June 20, 2012. According to Friends of the Earth, world leaders have responded to the global environmental crisis by sticking their heads in the sand. "World leaders are understandably concerned about the broken economy—but until they stop treating it separately from our social and environmental problems it will never be fixed." Friends of the Earth U.K., Climate Change News, June 23, 2012, http://www.foe.co.uk/news/rio20_outcome_36239.html. Environmental groups are pressuring governments to invest in clean energy from the sun, wind, and water and to end fossil fuel subsidies.

International declarations, such as the Stockholm and Rio Declarations, are considered "soft law." International "hard law," by contrast, is comprised of treaties, conventions, and customary international law. Implementing the objectives and policies of soft law declarations often falls to bi- or multi-lateral agreements, such as the 1988 Protocol to the American Convention on Human Rights in the Area of Economic, Social, and Cultural Rights (San Salvador Protocol), which provides that "Everyone shall have the right to live in a healthy environment and to have access to basic public services." O.A.S. Treaty Series No. 69, Inter-Am. C.H.R., OEA/Ser.L.V/II.82 doc.6 rev.1 (1992). The Protocol was ratified by 14 nations in the Americas (but not the United States and Canada). Parties to the Protocol and other international or regional agreements and treaties typically adopt domestic legislation to implement the international provisions. Accordingly, a critical means of effectuating the objectives and policies of international law is national (domestic) law adopted and enforced within each concerned nation.

Numerous casebooks and courses are devoted to international environmental law, which includes international, multi-lateral, and bi-lateral declarations and agreements. The focus of this course is *not* international environmental law but rather a comparative look at environmental laws adopted within selected nations. Of course, domestic legislation and caselaw is sometimes shaped by international agreements and norms, and influential agreements and norms are addressed in this book. Professor Pervical's remark is certainly apropos: "globalization is affecting the field of environmental law in a way that is blurring traditional distinctions between domestic law and international law." Robert V. Percival, *The Globalization of Environmental Law,* 26 Pace Envl. L. Rev. 451, 451 (2009).

Comparative law is "the study of the similarities and differences between the laws of two or more countries, or between two or more legal systems." Morris Cohen, Robert Berring and Kent Olson, *How to Find the Law* 565 (9th ed. 1989). It is *not* a system of law or a body of rules in and of itself, but rather a method of legal analysis and a means of assessing the strengths and weaknesses of different legal systems.

Determining which countries to compare is a daunting task. As noted in the *Preface,* this book singles out five: the United States; Canada; New Zealand; England; and India. The United States and Canada are close neighbors, geographically speaking, while New Zealand is about as far away as you can get on this planet. Yet these countries share a common heritage—the English language and the common law. In terms of their approaches to environmental law, four of these countries—the U.S., Canada, England, and India—have taken media-specific, and therefore somewhat fragmented, approaches to air, water, waste, wildlife, and land conservation issues. In contrast, New Zealand has made path-breaking efforts to adopt a more holistic, ecological approach to pollution prevention and sustainable development in its Resource Management Act of 1991.

In addition, the U.S., Canada, New Zealand, and England, are industrialized (rather than developing) countries. India has many large industries and produces and exports a vast array of goods as well, but its economy and its culture provide a sharp contrast, in many ways, to the other four countries. Despite its differences, India's legal system is heavily influenced by British overtones, too. These five countries also share certain physical characteristics—hundreds of miles of coastlines and inland waters; hardwood and softwood forests; and both exceedingly large cities and less populated rural areas.

These parallels enhance the ability to draw meaningful comparisons among the legal systems and environmental policies of these five countries. The jurisdictional and cultural divides are significant, but those differences can teach us something about our own legal systems. A far greater contrast in approaches would emerge if we were to add civil law countries or developing countries to the mix. A few such comparisons are sprinkled here and there throughout the book in hopes of stimulating creative thinking and new insights.

Determining which subjects to compare is an equally daunting task. The book strives for broad enough coverage of environmental laws and policies to enable the reader to get a feel for the legal landscape of the five nations. It covers environmental federalism, common law liability, environmental impact assessment, water quality and pollution, biological diversity, and environmental human rights. Two major topics within environmental law are addressed only in relation to these delineated subjects: air and solid waste. Each of these would warrant lengthy chapters in and of themselves, and if the reader wishes to pursue them, the multi-volume treatise on Comparative Environmental Law is an excellent starting point: Nicholas Robinson, et al. (eds.), Comparative Environmental Law and Regulation (2011–12). There are a number of useful books on point as well, *e.g.,* Noga Morag-Levine, Chasing the Wind: Regulating Air Pollution in the Common Law State (2005); Michael Bowman and Alan Boyle (eds.), Environmental Damage in International and Comparative Law: Problems of Definition and Valuation (2002); René J.G.H. Seerden, Michiel A. Heldeweg, Kurt R. Deketelaere, Public Environmental Law in European Union and US: A Comparative Analysis (2002).

The book is organized as follows. The first part examines the benefits of studying comparative law and, more specifically, learning about diverse approaches to resolving environmental problems. Second, in Chapter 2, the book covers negligence, nuisance, and other common law responses to environmental issues. This chapter also looks at the public trust doctrine as a tool for addressing climate change. Chapter 3 considers landmark laws governing environmental decisionmaking, beginning with the U.S. National Environmental Policy Act, widely considered the "grandfather" of environmental assessment requirements, and then comparing the objectives, requirements, and enforcement of similar statutes in Canada, New Zealand, England (and, by extension, the European Union), and India. In Chapter 4, keystone environmental statutes governing water quality and pollution are covered. Chapter 5 explores approaches to biological diversity, wildlife management, and land preservation. In the final part of the book, Chapter 6, environmental human rights in these five nations and beyond are addressed. Case studies on specific environmental controversies are provided throughout the book to enable readers to take a "hands on" problem-solving approach to environmental and natural resources law and policy, and to compare outcomes under the laws of various nations.

Comparative
Environmental and
Natural Resources Law

Chapter I

Why Study Comparative Law?

Why should lawyers and law students study the legal systems of other nations? This chapter explores that question and describes how comparative analysis can be useful to someone who intends to practice in domestic or international venues, and how comparative law might inform and influence advocates, legislators, judges, and other decisionmakers.

A. Comparative Legal Studies: Pro and Con

Justice Richard Posner once observed, "just as our states are laboratories for social experiments from which other states and the federal government can learn, so are foreign nations laboratories from whose legal experiments we can learn." Richard Posner, *No Thanks, We Already Have Our Own Laws*, Leg. Aff., July–Aug. 2004, http://www.legalaffairs.org/issues/July-August-2004/feature_posner_julaug04.msp. But those who venture into comparative law would do well to proceed with caution and a dose of humility.

> Comparative law can be a treacherous enterprise. Because law is so entwined with national culture, politics and history, a legal scholar who attempts to understand and contribute to a legal development in a foreign country is always at high risk of misunderstanding and misinterpreting.
>
> On the other hand, comparative law can be a wonderful tool for obtaining new perspectives on the law at home. A foreign legal development can cast new light on long-accepted doctrines of one's domestic law and, sometimes, cause one to think about them in new and different ways.

Steven L. Willborn, *Laval, Viking, and American Labor Law*, 32 Comp. Labor L. & Pol'y J. 1079, 1079 (2011).

Viewed through a narrow lens, legislation, executive proclamations or regulations, and judicial decisions from other countries provide an opportunity to consider domestic legal problems with a fresh perspective. An examination of foreign sources "may tell us something about the cross-cutting currents that contribute to the development of law." *Id.* at 1096. Viewed more broadly, situations where comparative law is relevant to the outcome of a case are likely to be "more common, contentious, and important as the world becomes more globalized and competitive." *Id.*

As the President of the American Association of Law Schools (AALS) observed:

> We must not suppose that we in this part of the western world have seen the fullest flowering, the final state of perfection, of the modern legal system. We have a lot to learn from each other.

John Garvey, *The President's Message, Internationalism and Pluralism*, 2008-3 AALS News 1, 4 (2008).

So far so good, but scholars debate whether comparative legal studies can realistically offer functional solutions to legal problems.

> Functionalism is historically one of the most influential approaches to the study of comparative law, and perhaps the most controversial. According to functionalism, comparative legal scholars should understand different countries' laws as solutions to similar social problems.... Perhaps the most widely criticized characteristic of the functional method of comparative law is its emphasis on the improvement of legal solutions to social problems. This so-called "better solutions" impulse flows from the principle of functionality.... Zweigert and Kötz assert that "the legal system of every society faces essentially the same problems" and argue that the object of comparison should be diverse legal solutions to those societal problems. Thus, functionalist analysis involves two preliminary steps: problem definition and solution identification....
>
> The principle of functionality not only provides methodological guidance for comparative legal scholars, but also ... attempts to provide advice on legal policy by "suggest[ing] how a specific problem can most appropriately be solved under the given social and economic circumstances." Zweigert and Kötz see comparative law as leading to "the discovery of models for preventing or resolving social conflicts," therefore provid[ing] a much richer range of model solutions than a legal science devoted to a single nation, simply because the different systems of the world can offer a greater variety of solutions than could be thought up in a lifetime by even the most imaginative jurist who was corralled in his own system.... Comparative law ... extends and enriches the "supply of solutions" and offers the scholar of critical capacity the opportunity of finding the "better solution" for his time and place.

Christopher A. Whytock, *Legal Origins, Functionalism, and the Future of Comparative Law*, 2009 B.Y.U. L. Rev. 1879, 1881–83, citing Konrad Zweigert & Hein Kötz, Introduction to Comparative Law 15, 34 (3d ed. 1998). Whytock cautions:

> [F]uture functionalist scholarship must respond to the claim that functionalism has a tendency to exaggerate the extent to which different societies face similar problems and to imply the ability to make objective claims about which solutions are better.... Future functionalist scholarship should also strive to take law's context seriously. Legal institutions are likely to interact with country-specific cultural, economic, political, and social factors. Without considering these factors, the causal inferences upon which functionalism relies are unlikely to be reliable, and legal solutions based on functional analysis are likely to lead to unintended consequences.

Id. at 1904. In short, context counts, and comparative law scholars and practitioners should "strive for a more sophisticated understanding of how legal institutions interact with contextual factors." *Id.* at 1905.

When is comparative legal analysis *not* helpful? For one thing, "the mere fact that a domestic lawyer can show that a party in a comparable suit prevailed in another jurisdiction provides no weight for his client's claim ... law should not turn on head counts." Jane Stapleton, *Benefits of Comparative Tort Reasoning: Lost in Translation*, 1 J. Tort L. 6, 8 (2007). For another, legal principles that turn on community norms cannot be lifted from one jurisdiction to another, quite different one. For example, "an acceptable lifestyle choice in one sub-community (loud music, scanty or otherwise revealing attire, religious calls to prayer, cooking odours, or slaughter of cows) is a gross nuisance in another." *Id.* at 10.

The following article examines the role of comparative legal analysis in the United States and in Europe.

Mathias Reimann, Stepping Out of the European Shadow: Why Comparative Law in the United States Must Develop its Own Agenda

6 American Journal of Comparative Law 637 (1998)

In the United States today, comparative law does not play nearly as prominent a role in teaching, scholarship, and practice as one would expect in our allegedly cosmopolitan age. Perhaps the discipline is not in an outright crisis but it surely does not occupy a prominent place in the American legal universe either. It is quite common to blame the parochial attitude and lack of international sophistication of American lawyers for the marginal role of comparative law. But, as a matter of fact, interest in international legal subjects, ranging from human rights to foreign trade law and international litigation, is currently high and growing fast. Course offerings in these and other specialized areas have mushroomed, the number of international journals is staggering, and in January 1998 the AALS held yet another annual meeting trumpeting the globalization of law. Only classic comparative law, it seems, has somehow missed the boat....

A major reason for this failure is that the product in its current form is not nearly as attractive as we would like to think. In large part, this is because the design of the product is badly flawed. It is essentially a copy of a foreign model which suffers from two fundamental ills: It is hopelessly out of date and it was never fashioned to fit either global or American needs. As a result, comparative law in the United States is both behind the times and far off the mark....

The "Classical Edifice"—It is often said that comparative law in the United States lacks common ground. This is not true. While the label of comparative law is attached to a multitude of diverse research projects and law school courses, there is nonetheless a common tradition to which the majority of comparatists adhere in one way or another, at least in their teaching and often in the direction of their scholarship. I will borrow Michael Ansaldi's felicitous phrase and call this tradition the "Classical Edifice". This "Classical Edifice" is known to every comparatist in America but it is not easily described in general terms. It is perhaps best characterized as the sum of the features shared by the major comparative law works in use in the United States.... [T]hey have at least four elements in common.

First, as far as substantive rules are concerned, their main emphasis is on private law. It is true that none of them is strictly limited to this area, but the private law perspective is particularly strong in all of them, albeit to varying degrees. Second, the main focus is on comparisons between the systems of the common law and the civil law. Again, this is not to say that there is nothing else, but the centrality of the traditional dichotomy is pervasive. Third, they rest on the assumption that the important legal sources are codification, legislation, and case law. Some look beyond that but only rarely and never far. Finally, they introduce the reader ... to foreign legal systems for the sake of certain educational and practical goals of which there is a fairly standard list....

The pervasiveness of these features is of course no accident. It is the result of common parentage. The works mentioned above are all the offspring of Western European ideas.... The heavy dose of the European perspective in all these books is symptomatic of the general state of comparative law in the United States: the whole discipline is dominated by Western European influences. This, again, is not surprising. The subject ... remains by and large in the hands of scholars who either come from Western Europe (mainly Germany, France, and, more recently, Italy) or have at least studied, researched, or taught there. As a result, the "Classical Edifice" of comparative law in the United States is of essentially European design.

In our (justified) gratefulness to the European founders, we have generally overlooked the fact that this European design is no longer a blessing but has become a curse. It is responsible for many of the discipline's problems and failures on this side of the Atlantic. A closer look at the design's three main features shows how poorly they fit general global conditions and particular American needs.

Private Law Orientation—The more recent tradition of comparative law in Western Europe, which dates back to the turn of the century, is heavily oriented toward private law.... When [Europeans] came to the United States, they brought their private law bias with them and shaped the American version of their discipline accordingly.... This private law focus was appropriate in turn-of-the-century Europe. As a basis for late twentieth century American comparative law, which must respond to worldwide as well as American realities, it has become largely dysfunctional.

On a global level, private law no longer enjoys dominant status. Virtually everywhere, the rise of the modern administrative and regulatory state, and of constitutionalism, not to mention international trade and treaties, means that public law at least rivals, if not overshadows, the importance of private entitlements.

In the United States in particular, this focus on private law has become inappropriate. Here, the days when contract, tort, and property were the unchallenged centerpieces of the legal system have been gone for at least half a century. Constitutional questions, procedure, regulatory regimes, and criminal law have become strong, if not superior, rivals. As a result, American legal discourse in the last few decades has been primarily concerned with judicial review and basic rights, courts and administrative agencies—with welfare, labor, and health law, environmental protection, and immigration issues not far behind. It is no surprise then that the comparative study of the traditional common law topics has generated so little interest lately....

Fortunately, the discipline has already begun to break out of the European mold. For some time, comparative law in the United States has gradually turned to constitutional, procedural, and criminal law. In fact, studies in these very areas have generated most of the current interest in the field—simply because they have touched on problems about which students, lawyers, and the public are concerned. This proves that comparative law needs to tackle current issues such as abortion or administrative regulation instead of clinging to old hats like cause and consideration....

Civil Law and Common Law—... While fundamental differences remain with regard to the styles of reasoning and the interpretation of legal materials, the two systems have been mixing and converging on several levels (sources of law, legal education, importance of administrative law, adjustment to supranational norms, etc.). This is especially true since England has joined the European Community while the United States has pursued a more isolationist course. Second, the dichotomy has become less plausible. As areas other than private law enter the picture, it becomes apparent that the grouping of legal systems depends very much on the particular context. It is not generally true that England and the United States are more closely related legal systems than, say, England and France (neither has full-fledged constitutional review) or the United States and Germany (both are federal states). Finally, as we take an increasingly global view, we must recognize that most legal systems in the world do not neatly fit either of the traditional European pigeonholes. Most are hybrids of one sort or another and many reflect indigenous, often non-Western traditions.

From the American point of view, the focus on the traditional civil v. common law dichotomy was, just like the private law bias, never as plausible as it was and still is in Europe. There, the two systems constituted the two major parts of the European tradition, existed in close geographic proximity, and are now both part of the European Community. Thus, from a continental European perspective, the common law is the most plausible object of comparison.

The American situation is markedly different. America is not part of Europe, but a world apart. It is true that strong transatlantic ties make the study of continental civil law relevant and intriguing, but the United States has strong historical, political, social, and economic ties to many other parts of the globe as well, notably to Latin America and, increasingly, Asia. Moreover, the United States is not a pure common law system but is itself a mixture of various English, continental (especially French, Spanish, and German), and other ingredients. Thus, from an American perspective, continental civil law is just one among several relevant foreign legal cultures.

None of this means, of course, that we should completely eradicate the traditional common v. civil law dichotomy in comparative law even in the United States. It continues to be an important step in every historical introduction as well as a useful heuristic and didactic device. But we should employ it only as a (non-mandatory) starting point for our endeavors, not as an overarching framework that dominates the analysis from beginning to end....

The Sources of Law—Tied up with the focus on private law and with the civil v. common law dichotomy is our continuing obsession with the traditional categories of legal sources. From the European point of view of a few decades ago, it actually made sense to think primarily about codification versus common law statutes and legislation versus case law. We are woefully slow in recognizing, however, that these categories are no longer sufficient.

While it is now widely acknowledged that there is much convergence as to the significance and use of these sources in the various legal systems, we fail to recognize that these traditional categories leave out huge areas of legal materials that are highly important in the today's legal world. They range from administrative regulations and executive guidelines to semi-private regimes such as commercial arbitration rules ... not to mention international treaties and conventions.

Particularly from an American point of view, the traditional categories make limited sense. The lines between code and statute are blurred, legislation and case law interact in complex ways, and the interplay between state and federal law presents special problems in its own right. In practice, executive orders, administrative guidelines, and public ordinances are ubiquitous. And a discipline concerned with international perspectives cannot afford to ignore conflict of laws rules ... or NAFTA and the WTO as legal sources of primary importance....

The Goals and Uses of Comparative Law—Perhaps the greatest burden imposed upon comparative law in this country by the European heritage is the traditional list of goals and uses which the discipline claims for itself. It is a list compiled many decades ago under European conditions. Few of its components make much sense from our present point of view.

The trouble starts with the general assertions that law can only be a science if it is studied comparatively, that its aim is simply to generate knowledge, and that it turns its students into more educated lawyers. In the context of the more academically oriented European tradition, these assertions are plausible and perhaps even attractive. In the United States, they seem lofty and vague. Here, the idea of law as a science has been dead for at least half a century. Americans are not idealists who seek knowledge pure and simple but pragmatists who want to accomplish something with it. And their desire simply to become more educated is often weak because they tend to regard legal knowledge not so much as a matter of general enlightenment but as a professional skill, particularly as graduate students in a professional school.

The professed jurisprudential goals do not fare much better. To be sure, comparative law does demonstrate that law is not a monolithic and universal body, that it consists of more than positive, blackletter rules, and that it is variously shaped by historical, social, political, and economic influences. For continental European jurists, these are indeed highly valuable messages because their legal education has traditionally portrayed law as a universal, positivist, and abstract body of rules. But for American lawyers these insights add little to what they have already learned in their first year of law school. They see the diversity of law within their federal system, constantly look beyond blackletter rules, and in our post-realist world inevitably come to see law as contingent on historical developments, socio-economic conditions, and political choices. In a sense, they already study and practice comparative law on a domestic level all the time....

Finally, even the avowed practical uses of comparative law are dubious from an American point of view. While the discipline's value for domestic lawmaking and law reform is significant in Europe, it is negligible in the United States where legislators and judges have paid scant attention to foreign ideas. There are exceptions but they are rare and most of them lie even further in the past than Karl Llewellyn's work on the Uniform Commercial Code half a century ago. In Europe (and many other parts of the world), the role of comparative law in the international harmonization and unification of law has been enormous and continues to grow but the United States has participated in these efforts too hesitatingly and sparingly to make comparative studies worthwhile on these grounds. Last, but not least, there is the alleged contribution to the education of the practicing lawyer in our age of international legal business. Again, this aspect is quite significant in Europe where lawyers have to deal with foreign legal systems all the time, especially as European integration proceeds. But in this country, it is far less important than is widely assumed. The vast majority of graduates, at least those from non-elite schools, have too little need for knowledge of foreign legal systems to make their study worthwhile as a professional matter. This is particularly true since much international business follows American patterns and special needs are usually fulfilled by a highly sophisticated international bar. In a sense, foreign legal systems are like a foreign language and, in practical terms, it is much more important for Europeans to learn English than for most Americans to learn any of the European tongues.

None of this means that the benefits of comparative law in the United States are so negligible that we should abandon it altogether. It does bring in new ideas, mainly through scholarship, and many of these ideas matter, whether as bases for criticism or simply because they expand our intellectual horizons.... We want broadly educated lawyers since many of them will hold key positions in public life or the private sector. But in order to introduce new ideas and educate lawyers broadly, we must first reach our audience....

What Needs to Be Done—It is time to acknowledge that the major features of the "Classical Edifice" of comparative law which we have imported from Europe are largely out of date and dysfunctional both in the general global context and in the specific American situation. We should make a conscious effort to overcome the limitations they have imposed.... In short, we need to develop new agendas for the future.... As far as teaching is concerned, I find three goals plausible. Comparative law can help students understand their own legal system better by providing an outside perspective on it. It enables them to overcome the parochialism that is often deeply ingrained in the American mind by demonstrating that there are plausible alternatives to the American way. And it can foster cultural tolerance as well as communication across boundaries by showing why these alternatives might make sense in their own right. In order to achieve these goals, however, our teaching must venture beyond rules and institutions. We must inculcate understanding of the foreign *mentalité*; i.e. the cultural dispositions, expectations, and values underlying other legal systems—something to which the traditional European model pays far too little attention. I also consider it important that we convey this understanding not only to the small and select group of students who enroll in a course in comparative law, but to the majority of future American lawyers as well. As I have suggested elsewhere, we should thus consider abandoning a separate course and teaching comparative perspectives in an integrated fashion, i.e., in small, manageable doses, throughout the curriculum.

[C]omparative legal scholarship ... can develop critiques of domestic institutions by introducing foreign alternatives.... It can further our understanding of how legal systems work, e.g., of the interplay between professional training and decision-making, political economies and legal institutions, cultural predispositions and procedural designs.... Comparative law can draw on, and cooperate with, other disciplines, such as comparative anthropology, linguistics, or politics.... Let us step out of the European shadow so that we can pursue new ideas with fresh energy and open minds.

Notes and Questions

1. Professor Reimann observes that the public law of constitutional questions and regulatory regimes has become a "strong, if not superior, rival" to private law tort- and property-based theories. This is especially true when it comes to environmental law, which involves a vast array of statutes and administrative regulations and procedures. You'll find that his point hits the mark when you read Chapters 3–6, *infra*, on environmental assessment, water quality, biological diversity, and environmental human rights.

2. Reimann argues that, in Europe, "the role of comparative law in the international harmonization and unification of law has been enormous and continues to grow," but that the value of comparative studies in the United States may be somewhat "negligible." Why? One rationale is that American lawyers and law students do not view law as a science and do not "seek knowledge pure and simple," but instead they are "pragmatists who want to accomplish something with it." Do you agree? And, if so, is there anything wrong with being pragmatic about the practice of law anyway?

3. What does Reimann's article suggest about the value of comparative legal analysis for other countries and regions, outside of the U.S. and Europe? What about India, which has the most distinct legal and political roots of the five countries covered in this book?

> The Union of India came into existence in 1947, with the expulsion of the British. Two years later, the new federal government had developed a constitution drawn from models of British, American and Australian law, which became effective

in 1950. The new constitution incorporated many of the checks and balances of the American system, with three branches of government and a parliamentary system, including a president and a prime minister.

Susan D. Susman, *Distant Voices in the Courts of India Transformation of Standing in Public Interest Litigation*, 13 Wis. Int'l L.J. 57, 60 (1994). In light of the commonalities in constitutional structure, it might seem safe to assume that Indian lawyers and courts would be fairly comfortable referring to, and even relying on, British, American, and Australian precedents. But then again, given the differences in the Indian judicial system and even more significant differences in Indian culture, perhaps the precedents of those other nations are not terribly useful after all. Consider the composition and function of Indian courts.

> Beginning with five justices in 1950, the [Indian Supreme Court] expanded to its current membership of twenty-six by constitutional amendment in 1986. The justices are selected in closed proceedings by the President in consultation with the current Chief Justice who, by tradition but not law, is the person who has served longest. As a matter of practice, the justices represent some of the diversity of the Indian population in terms of geography and religious community (mainly Hindu, with a few justices of Muslim or occasionally Christian background), but they are primarily from the upper castes....

> The [Supreme Court of India] generally decides the same sorts of issues presented to the U.S. Supreme Court: interpreting federal and state laws in light of the Constitution, resolving disputes among states and those between states and the central government, and deciding appeals on criminal and private law matters sent up from the states' High Courts. In addition, under Article 32 of the Constitution, the Court has original jurisdiction over all cases concerning "Fundamental Rights"....

> In the United States, constitutional law often focuses on individual rights as against the state.... The Indian focus, while acknowledging individual rights, emphasizes the group: society and its component communities.... The insistence on ... [pluralistic, unifying] goals carries forward the efforts begun with the transformation of standing, opening the doors of the court to India's dispossessed and to the possibility of justice as a means of strengthening society's weave....

Id. at 61, 100, citing Bandhua Mukti Morcha v. Union of India, 1984 A.I.R. (S.C). 802. Do these distinctions strengthen or diminish the utility of comparing and contrasting Indian laws and legal systems with those of other nations? Would you expect Indian citizens to have greater or more restricted access to the courts than, for example, American citizens?

   4. Should the United States and Canada, which are quite similar in historic, political, and cultural aspects, borrow judicial precedents from each other?

> One would think ... examples of regional borrowing would have occurred frequently. This is particularly so because most of English Canada began with the influx of the Loyalists who were on the losing side of the American Revolution. United States statutes were freely adopted in the new colonies, and many of the early lawyers and judges had American training.

Gerard V. La Forest, *The Use of American Precedents in Canadian Courts*, 46 Me. L. Rev. 211, 211 (1994). According to La Forest, a Canadian Supreme Court Justice from 1985–1997, Canadian judges have been open-minded from the beginning.

> The expansive use of foreign precedents by Canadian courts has deep roots in Canada's formal and informal connections to the traditions of Britain and of

France…. What ensured the continued influence of British material was the continued direct links to the English system even after the union of the British North American colonies at Confederation in 1867. Established in 1875, the Judicial Committee of the Privy Council in Britain, rather than the Supreme Court of Canada, remained the final court of appeal for Canada until 1949…. [T]he historical link to English traditions had generated a continued willingness to use English precedents. It was, in part, a function of familiarity, aided and abetted by the relatively undeveloped state of Canadian law schools, which, like the practitioners, relied heavily on English precedents and textbooks. These influences were also strengthened by the fact that a significant number of the leading lawyers were trained abroad. In light of this environment, it is not surprising that foreign material worked its way into the courts in Canada. It was a function of necessity flowing from the fact that Canada was then a small society with a relatively short legal tradition…. [However,] until recent years the use of American materials was infrequent, sometimes shallow, and definitely overshadowed by the use of English and, in Quebec, French precedents.

Id. at 212. Justice La Forest explains that things have changed fairly significantly in the last few decades, with Canadian courts increasingly turning to American legal materials, due in part to the number of Canadian legal scholars who attended law school in the United States but also to Canada's overall "cosmopolitan approach to law." *Id.* at 213. He adds, "Canada is now a larger, more influential society, with its own fairly lengthy legal tradition. Necessity has been replaced by a sincere outward-looking interest in the views of other societies, especially those with traditions similar to ours." *Id.* Other scholars have taken note of Canada's "earnest search for lessons from the experience of others." *Id.* at 219, citing John Fleming, *Economic Loss in Canada*, The Tort Law Review 68, 74 (1993).

Substantively, the adoption of the Canadian Charter of Rights and Freedoms in 1982 made the "American experience in constitutional interpretation … of more than passing interest." *Id.,* citing Law Society of Upper Canada v. Skapinker, [1984] 1 S.C.R. 357, 367. Even so, American jurisprudence is not to be "slavishly followed." But where does one draw the limits?

Although there are parallels between the constitutions of Canada and the United States, their provisions, even within the somewhat similar Canadian Charter and U.S. Bill of Rights, are not direct analogues. The Charter reflects Canada's "greater communitarian, less individualistic traditions" than does the U.S. Bill of Rights. La Forest, *supra,* at 214. More specifically, Section 1 of the Charter guarantees individual rights only insofar as they comport with "such reasonable limits prescribed by law as can be demonstrably justified in a free and democratic society." *Id.* at 215. There is no equivalent in the U.S. Constitution or Bill of Rights.

5. What weight should American courts give to Canadian precedents? In practice, very little, it seems.

One recent article on the criminal law jurisprudence under our Charter concluded on the pessimistic note that, although Canadian courts were referring to United States precedents with increasing sophistication, American jurists have yet to show a similar interest in Canadian criminal jurisprudence. Similarly, at a seminar with American judges on international human rights last year, I was amazed to find that American courts rarely make reference to international agreements on the subject, whereas one scholar has counted nearly 150 Canadian cases that made reference to international documents on human rights law from the enactment of the Charter in 1982 to 1990.

Id. at 218, citing Robert Harvie and Hamor Foster, *Different Drummers, Different Drums: The Supreme Court of Canada, American Jurisprudence and the Continuing Revision of Criminal Law Under the Charter*, 24 Ottawa L. Rev. 39, 112 (1992). Does the relative wealth or sophistication of the United States and its legal profession explain this difference? Or is it symptomatic of isolationism and elitism on the part of the U.S.?

6. Canadian courts have analyzed U.S. legal materials on a variety of legal subjects, including insurance, labor law, and retirement benefits. They tend to refer to both European and U.S. sources, though, with regard to economic integration, tort liability, and contracts. *Id.* at 217. Why might these subjects be treated differently? How should fundamental issues of justiciability (e.g., the political question doctrine and standing) be approached? *See* Justice Marshall Rothstein, *Address to the American Bar Association Section of Administrative Law and Regulatory Practice*, 63 Admin. L. Rev. 961 (2011) (describing Canadian courts' evolving view of the political question doctrine and drawing comparisons to Marbury v. Madison, 5 U.S. (1 Cranch) 137 (1803)). Should environmental law be added to the list of appropriate subjects for comparative analysis? If so, does it make more sense for Canada to consider U.S. or European environmental jurisprudence? Keep these questions in mind as you read the next section and the remaining chapters in this book.

B. Comparative Governmental and Political Foundations

Several of the countries included in this book have adopted a federalist governmental structure. Basically, this means that these countries—the United States, Canada, and to a large extent India—follow "a mode of political organization that unites separate states or other polities within an overarching political system in such a way as to allow each to maintain its own fundamental political integrity." Encyclopedia Britannica, *Federalism*, http://www.britannica.com/EBchecked/topic/203491/federalism (visited June 15, 2012). "The political principles that animate federal systems emphasize the primacy of bargaining and negotiated coordination among several power centres; they stress the virtues of dispersed power centres as a means for safeguarding individual and local liberties." *Id.* In other words, in federalist countries, sovereignty is constitutionally divided between a central governing authority and constituent political units (such as states or provinces). Nearly half of the world's population lives in federalist or quasi-federalist systems. Jenna Bednar, The Robust Federation: Principles of Design 2 (2009).

By contrast, the United Kingdom and New Zealand are unitary states with parliamentary democracies. A unitary state is governed as a single unit, where the central government is supreme and subnational units exercise only those powers that the central government chooses to delegate. The United Kingdom is governed under a parliamentary system, with a constitutional monarchy. The U.K. is comprised of England, Scotland, Wales, and Northern Ireland, each of which have some degree of autonomous devolved power as delegated by the central government. *Overview of the U.K. System of Government* (updated July 15, 2011), http://www.direct.gov.uk/en/governmentcitizensandrights/ukgovernment/centralgovernmentandthemonarchy/dg_073438. Although New Zealand is fully independent, the head of state is Queen Elizabeth II. The Queen's representative in the country of New Zealand is the Governor-General, who holds all the powers of the Queen in relation to New Zealand. New Zealand also has sub-national elected bodies, including territorial local authorities, and district health boards. John Wilson, *Nation and Government,* Te Ara — The Encyclopedia of New Zealand (updated Oct. 25, 2011), available at http://www.TeAra.govt.nz/en/nation-and-government.

When it comes to comparative law and politics, federalism is a major theme. Federalist concepts trace back to the ancient Greeks, but federalist governance is dynamic, "as some of the rules for division of authority and responsibility change and as new areas of policy are added to the system (such as poverty alleviation, healthcare access and delivery, and natural resources conservation or pollution regulation)." Henrik Selin and Stacy VanDeveer, *Federalism, Multilevel Governance, and Climate Change Politics Across the Atlantic,* in Comparative Environmental Politics 349 (2012) (Paul F. Steinberg and Stacy D. VanDeveer, eds).

Although federalist systems evolve, they "do not necessarily change in similar ways over time. Some increase centralization on some issues, and others may decentralize authority on similar issues." *Id.* Thus, "[d]imensions for comparative analysis include similarities or differences across countries in policy practices and the allocation of authority, as well as on explaining variation across time and across issue areas." *Id.*

Federalism concerns have become increasingly notable in environmental law. "As the diversity of environmental issues and policy instruments has increased, and as states and societies have grappled with questions about the centralization or decentralization of regulatory and decision-making authority, a scholarly subfield of environmental federalism has emerged." *Id.* at 350. In particular, federalism structures may explain, at least in part, the differences in European and North American approaches to climate change mitigation and adaptation, despite their relatively similar levels of economic development. In the United States and in several other federalist nations, such as Australia, there has been a pattern of "federal-level hostility and inaction on GHG (greenhouse gas) emissions, [in contrast to] active state-level policy making and interstate collaboration...." *Id.* at 362. Similarly, in Canada, "climate change politics are characterized by contentious debates between the federal government and provinces over issues of policy-making jurisdiction and responsibilities to take action." *Id.* at 363.

The following article considers the role of comparative analysis in judicial interpretation of federalism provisions.

Kathryn A. Perales, It Works Fine in Europe, So Why Not Here? Comparative Law and Constitutional Federalism
23 Vermont Law Review 885 (1999)

In 1993 the United States Congress enacted the Brady Gun Control Act which required state and local officials to use reasonable efforts to investigate potential gun purchasers.[1] Two local sheriffs from Arizona and Montana challenged the constitutionality of the Act on grounds that the federal government usurped too much power from state and local governments.[4] ... Justice Scalia, in his majority opinion, held that the federal government had overreached the limits of federalism by requiring local officials to perform duties without compensation or choice. The Court therefore found the Brady Gun Control Act to be unconstitutional. The case expanded *New York v. United States*[7] and continued the

---

1. Brady Handgun Violence Prevention Act § 102(a)(1), 18 U.S.C. § 922(s)(2) (1997).

4. Printz v. United States, 117 S. Ct. 2365 (1997).

7. *See* New York v. United States, 505 U.S. 144, 188 (1992) (holding in part that the national government cannot command a state government to enact regulations).

Court's recent trend of overruling federal laws which it considers to encroach on state sovereignty. Therefore, *Printz v. United States* also simultaneously diminished the federal government's power.

However, Justice Breyer, in his dissent, argued that in several European countries with similarly structured federal governments, local governments implement laws handed down by the national government. The local governments view this as less intrusive than the national government implementing the law itself. Justice Breyer asked: Why, in the United States, do we take the position that it is less intrusive for the federal government to implement a law than for the states to expend their own resources?

Justice Breyer's invocation of European examples of federalism is out of the ordinary in a United States Supreme Court opinion. Justice Scalia addressed Justice Breyer's dissent in a footnote, saying "such comparative analysis [is] inappropriate to the task of interpreting a constitution, though it was of course quite relevant to the task of writing one." According to Justice Scalia, comparing the United States' form of federalism to the governmental structure in other countries is inappropriate and irrelevant, since the relationship of the national government to the states is both uniquely American and fixed in the Constitution.

Justice Scalia's view makes sense as an instinctive reaction—how could foreign laws or policies be relevant in interpreting our own Constitution, especially when the issue involves the national government's relationship to the states? Some scholars argue that comparative studies are both relevant and valuable in considering any internal legal question, because of the potential for learning from others' experiences. Perhaps it is overly xenophobic or provincial to assume that we have nothing to learn from other countries, especially when studying something as vaguely worded and in need of interpretation as the United States Constitution ...

Lawmakers, legal scholars, and courts have studied and compared foreign laws with their own laws since ancient times.... For example, when Solon drafted the original laws for Athens, in the sixth or seventh century B.C., he studied laws from dozens of other Greek cities. Legislators and courts around the world continue to look to other nations and societies to formulate, interpret, and understand their own laws.

Using Comparative Law in Creating Constitutions—When people create a new constitution, they often look to other established constitutions for ideas. "Constitutions do not emerge in a political vacuum. Countries naturally borrow from each other, and borrow heavily during transitional periods when new political entities are emerging." This statement was true for the first written constitution and continues to hold true today. During the United States Constitutional Convention in 1787, the Framers often looked to other countries, hoping to avoid earlier mistakes, and to learn from laws and practices that worked well. For example, to choose between a confederacy and a federal system with dual sovereignty, the Framers scrutinized many other nations that had tried the confederate form of government, from the Amphyctrionic League in ancient Greece to contemporary Switzerland....

More recently, ... [t]he Estonian Constitution, adopted in 1992, contains procedural features from both the German and French Constitutions, such as the President's power to dissolve Parliament in certain situations and the "motion of confidence." When creating a new legal system and constitution, study of foreign law is commonplace and expected. This is compatible with Justice Scalia's textualist view that comparative analysis is valid and helpful in writing—as opposed to interpreting—a constitution.

Using Comparative Law in Drafting Statutes — Once the Constitution was in place, United States legislators often examined foreign law in the early years to help them create the many statutes needed to run the new United States. "The post-revolutionary period ... was marked by an intensive use of international comparative law." However, "[i]n the later period of the nineteenth century the use of international comparison declined." Scholars attribute this retreat from comparative law to a strong sense of nationalism.

Legislators in countries other than the United States commonly perform comparative research. For example, in 1932 the British parliament surveyed other European laws while drafting new liquor reform legislation. Today, "in the most advanced countries of continental Europe it is standard practice to survey pertinent foreign legislation before an important and innovative bill is submitted to parliament."

Though comparative research may not be standard practice for United States legislators today, it is not uncommon. United States lawmakers do consult foreign law, especially in researching an "innovative bill." Senators and Representatives who are preparing to introduce legislation frequently request comparative law information from the Congressional Research Service. For example, the Federal Workmen's Compensation statutes, enacted in 1908, "were based on the German model and this has been appropriately described as a triumph of comparative law." ...

Courts' Use of Comparative Law in Interpreting Statutes — Ever since colonial times, courts have interpreted and extrapolated from the Constitution and statutes. Those sources still do not cover all situations which may arise. It took time for a sufficient number of state and federal statutes to pass, and for enough case law to develop in order to effectively govern. Until then, courts consulted relevant established law, usually from England. For example, Chief Justice James Kent of the New York Supreme Court wrote, in an 1804 opinion, "[w]e must decide this question by the common law of England."

Courts in the early years of the United States also studied civil law from European countries. Justice Kent introduced a large amount of foreign law into his New York court. In his opinions, he "referred frequently to civilian sources and advocated with fervor their use." In *Pierson v. Post*, the famous property law "fox" case, another New York court examined not only English, but also Roman and German law, and created the United States common law rule of capture.[43]

By the end of the nineteenth century, the climate had changed — courts, like legislators, no longer routinely cited foreign law. Scholars attribute the retreat from comparative law to nationalism and to the ready availability of West Publishing Company reporters and digests of United States law. Since the turn of the twentieth century, however, courts have occasionally investigated foreign law to interpret United States law. ...

Courts seem to consult law from other countries when the applicable United States law is outdated or when a gap exists in the current law. Lawyers often use comparative law persuasively in questions of constitutional due process. "Counsel, seeking to uphold the constitutionality of a statute which is attacked as allegedly violating due process, often have made effective use of the fact that a number of other civilized countries have statutes similar to the one under attack."

---

43. *See* Pierson v. Post, 3 Cai. R. 175 (N.Y. Sup. Ct. 1805) (holding that in order to have title of a wild animal, one must completely capture or kill it; mere pursuit is not enough).

Constitutional framers invariably study comparative law. Legislators sometimes survey comparative law. However, the question … remains: should courts use comparative law in their decisions, especially to address questions of federalism?

The Development of United States Federalism—… One definition of [American] federalism is: "[t]he relationship and distribution of power between the individual states and the national government." … The judiciary is a very powerful instrument to develop the relationship between the states and the national government through its interpretation of the Constitution and its power of judicial review.[55]

The ambiguous phraseology of some sections of the Constitution, which enabled the Supreme Court in the early years to play the role of interpreter, also secured the role as reviser for the Court in subsequent years. Armed with the power to interpret the Constitution, the Supreme Court has been allowed, even encouraged in some circles, to reinterpret the Constitution in order to meet changing social, economic, and political conditions.… The continuation of the debate over whether the Justices should determine the Framers' intent, however, is evidence of the lack of consensus on this issue.… The shifts from dual federalism to cooperative federalism to creative federalism have been upheld by a Supreme Court restructuring intergovernmental relations to fit current needs. Recently, the Supreme Court has effected yet another shift, this time back toward dual federalism—"a system for dividing functions between the state and national governments that left each considerable autonomy within its own areas of jurisdiction." Federalism has come full circle.

The relationship between the states and national government of the new United States of America was a major topic of discussion during the Constitutional Convention, and in the pages of The Federalist. The Framers debated two options: the New Jersey Plan, where the states would remain in a confederate relationship and have more real power than the national government; and the Virginia Plan, where the national government would have at least as much power as the states.…

Ultimately, the Framers chose a structure closer to the Virginia Plan: though the national government's powers would be limited, its law would be supreme over the states.[66] The structure of government would not be a confederacy but a new style of federal state, with both the state and national governments exercising checks and balances on each other.

Since the states existed as colonies long before the national government was born, the states started out with more power in the federal relationship. People thought of themselves as state citizens first, and Americans second. From 1801 to 1835, when Chief Justice John Marshall dominated the United States Supreme Court, the Court tried to give the national government the upper hand in the federal relationship. The Court frequently allowed federal statutes to stand, though states may have felt that the statutes were usurping their power. Until the Civil War, "the Court attempted to shift the pendulum back towards the states to offset the pro-national Marshall Court decisions" by striking down federal statutes that encroached upon the states.…

Until the New Deal, the relationship between state and national governments can be characterized as dual federalism, with both state and national governments retaining autonomy. After the New Deal, cooperative federalism appeared, with power centralized in the national government.… From the time of the New Deal until … 1976, the federal

---

55. *See* Marbury v. Madison, 5 U.S. 137 (1803) (holding that the Supreme Court has the power of judicial review and can overrule federal statutes that violate the Constitution).

66. U.S. Const. art. VI, cl. 2 (the Supremacy Clause).

government increasingly gained power over the states. Congress often invoked the Commerce Clause to justify its growing power.[76]

Congress also increased its power by using its spending power to entice the states to do its bidding—it conditioned grants of federal funds on behavior by the states. This relationship started as cooperative federalism, but sometimes evolved into creative federalism. In situations of cooperative federalism, state and national government have the same goals. The national government provides funds and the state or local governments implement the law. In situations of creative federalism, however, the national government uses its spending power to promote goals of uniformity and social change, which are goals that states may not share.... One example of creative federalism is the federal law that requires each state to raise its drinking age to twenty-one in order to receive five percent of that state's federal highway grant funds. This statute was upheld in 1987....

The national government exercised its power to the greatest extent in 1985, in *Garcia v. San Antonio Metropolitan Transit Authority (SAMTA)*. The Court stated that it would no longer limit or consider Congress' authority to regulate local matters and would allow the political process to provide checks and balances on the national power. The Court in effect gave Congress free reign. In response to Garcia, a critic wrote, "Because the taxing, spending, and commerce powers are as a practical matter limitless, the Tenth Amendment is a kind of false promise.... In short, the reason that federalism is a dead or dying doctrine is that the Constitution as presently drafted consigns it to that fate." The Court would soon agree with critics of creative federalism, and the tidal wave of the national government would start to recede from the shore of the states.

The trend of the Court to check the national government's expanding power over the states ... continued with *New York v. United States*, where the Supreme Court used the Tenth Amendment as a source of state power for the second time in sixty years, and held that Congress may not compel state governments to enact legislation.[94] Three years later, the Court limited Congress' commerce power for the first time in sixty years in *United States v. Lopez*,[95] holding that a statute prohibiting guns near schools was not valid under the commerce power. *Printz v. United States*, holding that Congress may not compel state or local officials to carry out federal programs, took another step in the trend towards reducing national power over the states.[96] ...

In a study of the ebbs and flows of the power relationship between state and national governments, the only clear conclusion is that the relationship constantly changes. One theory as to why this happens is that when conservative ideology prevails, the states gain power.[99] Conversely, when the country is more liberal, the national government gains power.

---

76. *See* U.S. Const. art. I, § 8, cl. 3. "The Congress shall have Power ... [t]o regulate Commerce ... among the several States...."; *see also* American Power & Light Co. v. SEC, 329 U.S. 90, 104 (1946). "[T]he federal commerce power is as broad as the economic needs of the nation."

94. New York v. United States, 505 U.S. 144, 188 (1992).

95. United States v. Lopez, 514 U.S. 549 (1995). "[E]ven where Congress has the authority under the Constitution to pass laws requiring or prohibiting certain acts, it lacks the power directly to compel the States to require or prohibit those acts." New York v. United States, 505 U.S. at 166.

96. Printz v. United States, 117 S. Ct. 2365, 2404 (1997).

99. *See* Richard P. Nathan, Defining Modern Federalism, in North American & Comparative Federalism: Essays for the 1990s 89, 93 (Harry N. Scheiber ed., 1992).

> I see the U.S. situation and that of other modern federal countries as ... cyclical. The history of U.S. federalism ... involves the rising role of the states in periods when the overall role of government in the society on the whole has been reduced. In these conservative periods in U.S. history—the 1880s, 1920s, and 1980s—initiative and innovation ... has occurred at the state level.... in liberal or more expansive periods of our history, prior initiatives

Federalism is so dynamic because of, as Justice Breyer puts it, "the silence of our Constitution" on the issue.[100] The language of the Constitution does not pin the relationship down, but allows—indeed, forces—Congress and the courts to wrestle with the boundaries of the relationship....

Arguments Against Courts' Use of Comparative Law—Judges who use a textualist approach, like Justice Scalia, rely primarily on the actual text of a statute or constitution, and derive a reasonable construction from the words in the text itself. When the words are vague and susceptible to multiple meanings, as are many clauses in the United States Constitution, a textualist may investigate beyond the text for guidance to interpret the original meaning of the text. The Federalist Papers and records of the Constitutional Convention contain evidence of the "original meaning of the text" of the Constitution, as understood and intended by the Framers and their contemporaries.

Legislative intent is another method of statutory interpretation. On a spectrum describing statutory interpretation where the variable is the amount of judicial discretion, the textualist method occupies the end of least discretion, with the legislative intent method near the middle and natural law falling at the most discretionary end. On its face, the legislative intent method seems similar to textualism. "The best way to interpret law is to explore the intention of the lawgiver at the time the law was made, says Blackstone...." However, courts exploring legislative intent go beyond the text, trying to infer what the legislators meant the law to do, rather than what they intended the words to mean. For example, when Congress enacted the Fourteenth Amendment in 1868, the Framers of the Equal Protection Clause certainly did not intend to outlaw school segregation. A textualist sees equal protection as an abstract principle, capable of being interpreted differently by different people, whereas a student of legislative intent concentrates on what the Framers meant the Equal Protection Clause to do....

The natural law method of interpretation is the furthest from textualism, as it allows a court to ignore the text of a written law if it violates the court's notion of natural law and justice. Courts using the natural law method have used the morals and views of the present day to create rights which are not literally in the text of the Constitution. An example is the right to have an abortion....

Since a textualist restricts himself to only studying the words and meaning of the law as written, he would never look to law from other countries. Modern law from distant places can have nothing to do with the words that the Framers wrote, as they understood them. As Justice Scalia wrote from his textualist perspective, "[W]e think such comparative analysis [of modern European law] inappropriate to the task of interpreting a constitution...."

The role of the federal government's judicial branch is to interpret the law by deciding "all Cases, in Law and Equity, arising under this Constitution, the Laws of the United States, and Treaties made ... under their authority...."[111] The judiciary may not create law—that power belongs to the legislature.... In other words, if courts consider anything other than the meaning of the actual words in the statute, they have stepped over the line into lawmaking.

---

on the part of the leading states (e.g., Wisconsin, New York, California, Minnesota) have become generalized in the country through national action in a way that can be seen as having "ratcheted up" the role and spending of government overall and over time in the society.

100. *Printz*, 117 S. Ct. at 2404 (Breyer, J., dissenting).

111. U.S. Const. art. III, § 2, cl. 1.

The independent roles of the legislature and the judiciary are important, both for separation of powers issues and the integrity of the republican form of government.... The Executive Branch appoints all federal judges for life; the people do not elect them.... Since federal judges hold office for life, they are not accountable to the public, and therefore should not have the power to make law.

Can it be mere interpretation when a court looks to foreign law in order to interpret a purely internal United States law, or does it go too far? Looking outside of the United States strays farther from the text than mere research of legislative history, perhaps even beyond interpretation and into the realm of creation. If a court creates law, it may be unconstitutionally usurping legislative powers from Congress.

Even if consulting foreign law is an acceptable method of statutory or constitutional interpretation, foreign law is arguably irrelevant to a study of United States law. As an English scholar asked, "[W]hy bother with foreign cases when we have so much material of our own?" United States lawmakers have built a highly developed legal system for over 200 years, so the argument goes, leaving few gaping holes that courts might attempt to patch by looking to law from other countries.

Many United States lawyers might feel the same way as English lawyers once did: "[i]t was an almost universal article of faith that English law and legal institutions were without peer in the world with very little to be usefully learned from others...." Americans in general believe that anything American is the best in the world.[122] Following this logic, American lawyers would then believe that there is nothing to be gained from investigating inferior foreign laws.

Not only may the comparative law method be irrelevant, but it also contains two major pitfalls for the unwary: the difficulty of fully understanding a foreign legal principle and the inability to know whether a successful legal solution is transplantable to a different country or culture.... Language barriers, problems of translation and cultural differences could make it easy for a student to misinterpret the purpose or effect of a foreign law. In addition, real understanding of a foreign legal system "requires a knowledge not only of the foreign law, but also of its social, and above all its political, context."

Having mastered an understanding of a foreign law, the question remains whether a legal solution that works in one country will work in another....

Arguments For Courts' Use of Comparative Law — It is curious that the study of law is normally so bounded by the borders of a nation. For scholars of literature, science, economics, music, art, engineering or medicine, the national origin of a piece of knowledge, book or experiment does not matter. National parochialism would artificially hamper the quest for knowledge in all these fields. When scholars and reformers ignore all legal information except that of their own nations, the study and reform of law is similarly hampered....

Comparative scholars' main argument for the study of comparative law is that people should learn from the experiences and mistakes of others in order to avoid the same mistakes themselves. "Comparative law ... can enlighten the understanding of the place and significance of law by drawing upon the experience of all nations;" "is useful in gaining a better understanding of one's own national law and in the work of improving it;" and "broadens the perspective of those seeking ways to bring about its improvement by inviting them to consider new ideas."....

---

122. *See, e.g.,* Robert D. Hess & Judith v. Torney, The Development of Political Attitudes in Children 26–27 (1967) (Nearly all schoolchildren interviewed agreed that "America is the best country in the world.").

Several examples of one country learning from another were ... workers' compensation laws, liquor reform legislation, and the doctrine of quasi-contract. Examples of bad law also exist due to a lack of consulting foreign sources. For instance, Friedrich Juenger attributes the muddled doctrine of United States personal jurisdiction to numerous courts' insistence on adhering to confusing precedent, and their refusal to consider much simpler rules from other legal systems, like the European Union. It makes perfect sense to examine other legal systems, especially those similar to our own, in order to avoid wastefully repeating others' mistakes....

Learning from the mistakes and successes of other countries is a very pragmatic way to avoid our own mistakes. The figurative shrinking of the world in the past century has made it easier than ever to be informed about foreign countries, and quick transportation and instant communication allow close economic links. Parties from opposite ends of the globe may have a difficult time striking a business deal, not only due to language and cultural differences, but because of dissimilar legal concepts. If a scholar urged legislators to study comparative law sixty-five years ago to facilitate economic relationships, today it must be essential.

Law and economics scholars like Judge Posner and Justice Breyer are champions of pragmatism; they approve of comparative law study, perhaps because it makes law simpler and more uniform. For example, Judge Posner finds it more practical to survey other countries for evidence of a modern universal view on cruel and unusual punishment than to reexamine the Framers' eighteenth century view.

With foreign businesses and citizens so intricately connected to all aspects of the United States and the continued influx of immigrants in great numbers, exploring foreign law makes sense when reforming our own law....

John Locke and the Framers of the United States Constitution shared the view that "the essence of law is not will but reason." In other words, the people should not adhere to the law simply because a sovereign wills it, but rather because it is logical, moral and just. Natural law draws on what is intrinsically good and intrinsically bad, and is "the universal moral principals of which positive laws are but declaratory." ... Since "[n]atural law is the outcome of man's quest for an absolute standard of justice," it is logical to scrutinize other countries' laws. People in other countries also search for the best and most just legal rules, and if several countries have adopted the same rule, perhaps they are closer than the U.S. is to finding the "absolute standard of justice."

Comparative Law and Constitutional Issues of Federalism — A Resolution — Justice Breyer's position, as stated in his *Printz* dissent, is the correct conclusion.... While the petitioner, Printz, argued that the statute unconstitutionally violated United States principles of state autonomy and federalism, Justice Breyer pointed out:

> [t]he federal systems of Switzerland, Germany, and the European Union, for example, all provide that constituent states, not federal bureaucracies, will themselves implement many of the laws, rules, regulations, or decrees enacted by the central "federal" body.... They do so in part because they believe that such a system interferes less, not more, with the independent authority of the "state," member nation, or other subsidiary government, and helps to safeguard individual liberty as well.

Justice Breyer cites the other countries' experiences as successful ways to structure the federal-state relationship.... Though other countries' governmental structures are different, "their experience may nonetheless cast an empirical light on the consequences of different solutions to a common legal problem—in this case the problem of reconciling central authority with the need to preserve the liberty—enhancing autonomy of a smaller constituent governmental entity."

Justice Breyer's comparative law approach makes sense for a number of reasons. First, Congress has changed the relationship between the national and state governments frequently over the past 220 years with the U.S. Supreme Court's approval. "[T]he nature and evaluation of federalism remains a matter of contention, unabated since the debate between federalists and anti-federalists in the late eighteenth century." The constant changing, along with the lack of guidance in the Constitution itself and the records of the time, implies that federalism, like equal protection, is one of those aspects of the government that can be interpreted differently over time. Examining what works in other countries provides guidance....

Second, "[e]xperience is the oracle of truth; and where its responses are unequivocal, they ought to be conclusive and sacred." In this quote from The Federalist, Hamilton and Madison were referring to the experiences of other confederacies and federations, such as the United Netherlands, Poland, Germany and ancient Greece. Their comment suggests that it is always best to learn from others' mistakes in order to make the most informed decision. Their advice seems as logical today as it did in 1787....

Third, the federalist form of government is becoming so common around the world that perhaps there is a universal natural law element to it.... In 1987, fifty-eight nations had some sort of federalist government. "According to one estimate, 'nearly 40 percent of the world's population now lives within polities that are formally federal; another third live in polities that apply federal arrangements in some way.'" If almost three quarters of the people in the world live under similar governmental systems that they have chosen (we must assume), maybe there is a "just" governmental system that works the best. Therefore, the federal system is a kind of natural law itself....

If the real purpose and underlying principle of federalism is for the national, state and local governments to each feel that they retain some autonomy, neither the Constitution, the records of the Federal Convention of 1787, nor The Federalist dictate how exactly this should be accomplished. "[T]he text of the Constitution provides the beginning rather than the final answer to every inquiry into questions of federalism...." Since the details of the relationship require interpretation with only an underlying principle as guidance, we should be practical and let the judiciary construct its interpretation and gather ideas as it thinks best from any available source. If the judiciary chooses to look to comparative law and learn from others' experiences, so much the better since "[e]xperience is the oracle of truth...."[166]

Notes and Questions

1. Is it appropriate to "let the judiciary construct its interpretation and gather ideas as it thinks best from any available source"? Perales, *supra*. What are the comparative advantages and disadvantages? Does it matter whether judges are considering cases involving federalism, cruel and unusual punishment, due process, workplace safety, environmental harm, or other types of issues?

2. When it comes to federalism concerns, who do you find more convincing on the issue of comparative law's usefulness to American courts, Justice Scalia or Justices Breyer and Posner? Note that Scalia can call upon at least a few European luminaries to support his

---

166. The Federalist No. 20, at 97 (Alexander Hamilton & James Madison).

view, including French Enlightenment figure Charles de Secondat, Baron de Montesquieu. While most famous for his views on the separation of powers, Montesquieu believed that "only in the most exceptional cases [could] the institutions of one country ... serve those of another." Perales, *supra,* at 901 n. 124.

3. If it makes sense to explore foreign law in considering questions of federalism, how much weight should a foreign country's experience and its body of law have? And are there some countries that warrant more extensive study, and others that warrant none at all?

4. Like the United States Constitution, the Canadian Constitution spells out national powers with some precision, including a few related to environmental issues.

> The most relevant of these national powers was the authority to legislate on navigation, fisheries, and federal lands. Constitution Act, 1867, 30 & 31 Vict. Ch. 3 (U.K.), *as reprinted in* R.S.C., No. 5, pt. VI, § 92 (App. 1985) (describing Exclusive Powers of Provincial Legislatures). At the same time, the Constitution gave the provinces exclusive powers over, among other things, public works, property, and the "development of natural resources," including the production of electrical energy. Constitution Act, 1867, 30 & 31 Vict. Ch. 3 (U.K.), *as reprinted in* R.S.C., No. 5, pt. VI, § 92A (App. 1985).... While the Canadian government had some foundation for passing laws to protect the fishery, and perhaps even to prevent its contamination by pollution, it was on thin ice when it came to enacting general environmental law. And the first of the new environmental laws to sweep the United States, Canada, and the rest of the world were very general indeed: environmental impact review....

> The federal government in Ottawa was small, underpowered, and far away from nearly every activity in Canada that impacted the environment. Environmental protection in the 1970s had acquired some cachet, but it had also acquired some strong opponents including, for openers, a Who's Who of U.S. and Canadian industry. On thin ice constitutionally and looked on with suspicion by provincial governments jealous to retain their own autonomy, Ottawa's caution towards imposing environmental impact requirements was heightened by its perception of what was unfolding south of the border, where environmentalists had taken the same requirements to court to challenge government programs with alarming success. The American lawsuits led to delays and injunctions while new impact statements were written and their often-embarrassing contents were exposed to the press.

Oliver A. Houck, *O Canada!: The Story of Rafferty, Oldman, and the Great* Whale, 29 B.C. Intl. Comp. L. Rev. 175, 185–186 (2006). Professor Houck observes, "Federal environmental authority in the Canadian constitutional framework was, and remains, one of the hottest questions in Canadian environmental law." *Id.,* citing *Oldman River II,* 1 S.C.R. at 62–63. Canadian provisions on environmental impact assessment are covered in Chapter 3.B, *infra.*

5. It is often said that the states within the U.S. are "laboratories of democracy," where innovations can be tried out without jeopardizing the stability of the nation as a whole. Do the checks and balances found in a federalism structure like that of the U.S. advance or hinder the ability to take advantage of experimentation for purposes of effective environmental management? Are subnational units in unitary governments like England and New Zealand equally likely to experiment in ways that might be beneficial to the entire nation?

6. Are the U.S. and Canadian federal-state models more efficient and/or more equitable than unitary models such as that found in the United Kingdom and New Zealand? In comparing regulatory approaches to health care, one analyst observed:

> [A]symmetries in size, history, culture, and fiscal capacity between the four constituent nations [of the United Kingdom] have long created pressure for at least some devolution of authority.... These pressures eventually resulted in 1999 in a formal devolution of significant authority to Scotland, Wales, and Northern Ireland under which these constituent governments were, among other things, given increased discretion to set health care policy.... [Ironically,] this trend toward devolution is occurring at precisely the same moment that the European Union seems to be encouraging greater centralization of the health care systems in Europe.

Michael S. Sparer, *Inching Toward Incrementalism: Federalism, Devolution, and Health Policy in the United States and the United Kingdom*, 36 J. Health Pol. Pol'y & L. 33, 35–36 (2011). Are approaches to environmental problems likely to follow similar trends? Does centralization make sense for all types of environmental problems, or just transboundary problems?

7. In comparing the environmental federalism of Europe and the United States, Michael G. Faure and Jason S. Johnston, in *The Law and Economics of Environmental Federalism: Europe and the United States Compared*, 27 Va. Envtl. L.J. 205 (2009), discovered "a striking paradox." They found that, although there are significant differences, in both systems "centralized environmental regulation has been adopted not as a solution for transboundary pollution (interjurisdictional externalities), but rather for pollution that is primarily local." *Id.* at 205. But when environmental externalities like pollution cross state borders, isn't it all the more important "to shift powers to a regulatory level which has jurisdiction over a territory large enough to adequately deal with the problem"? *Id.* at 272. Federalism seems to be a double-edged sword when it comes to environmental laws.

> [I]n both Europe and in the U.S., the courts have struck down as unconstitutional (or as violating the European Treaty) state (or national Member state) environmental laws that impose too large a burden on interstate trade.... [B]y promoting the market for transboundary shipment of waste,[1] the Supreme Court and the ECJ have made it more difficult for states (or Member States) to pursue the goal of becoming self-sufficient in waste production and disposal....
>
> The pro-federalization stance of the U.S. courts creates another adverse consequence: By broadly implying the pre-emption of state and local environmental laws by federal environmental laws, the U.S. federal courts have created a situation where, when federal regulations are not adequately enforced, there is no longer the possibility of state and local regulators bridging the gap. In the EU, the reverse problem exists: since the EU has no EPA with enforcement powers, it is dependent upon Member States to implement and enforce European law. Therefore, the danger in Europe is not so much that Europe would pre-empt national law, but rather that Member States would (for a variety of reasons) decide not to implement or enforce European law. The fact that European laws' effectiveness depends on enforcement by the Member States is considered by

---

1. [Ed.] *See, e.g.,* C&A Carbone, Inc. v. Town of Clarkstown, 511 U.S. 383 (1994) (invalidating state laws that limited the importation of solid waste into the state, along with local laws that required local disposal of locally generated waste, because such laws created barriers to the interstate solid waste market in violation of the Dormant Commerce Clause).

many to be their most significant weakness today. This feature contrasts sharply with the U.S., where the federal EPA has direct enforcement power and can (at least in theory) directly control environmental quality in the states if necessary....

Especially in the U.S., capital, labor and residency are highly mobile, and there may well be ... a considerable risk of a *race to the bottom*, which may both explain and justify to some extent centralization in the U.S. The story in Europe appears to be more complicated: cultural, linguistic and (at least in the past) legal and institutional barriers largely prevented inter-jurisdictional mobility of capital, labor and residency. European industry in Western and Nordic countries like Denmark (and to some extent) Germany and the Netherlands may have been confronted with a median voter requiring a high level of environmental protection. Where possibilities for capital mobility were traditionally low in Europe, industry did not have the option (as in the U.S.) to move to a jurisdiction where the demand for environmental protection would be lower. Hence, this lower capital mobility also leads to a lower risk of a regulatory race to the bottom in Europe. At the same time, industry in countries with a high demand for environmental protection would lobby to impose tough standards on competitors in other jurisdictions, thus benefiting from their higher levels of environmental regulation by effectively creating barriers to entry.

Id. at 272–273 (emphasis added). The authors hypothesize that centralized environmental regulation focuses on localized pollution "due to inherent pressures for regional protectionism and redistribution within a (federalized) political system." *Id.* at 205. But they note that this may be changing in the EU due to "the enlargement of the EU in 2004 and a continuing increase in interjurisdictional mobility of at least capital and labor...."

Facing tough environmental standards in traditional Member States, industry could now benefit from increased inter-jurisdictional mobility, for example, by moving to Eastern Europe. Even though Eastern European Member States are formally required to comply with the same environmental *acquis communautaires*,[2] practical enforcement of environmental law may be less thorough than in the older fifteen EU Member States. If this were the case, one could expect a decrease of lobbying activities in favor of centralization at the European level — industry would now favor decentralization to take advantage of less stringent environmental standards in the East. Paradoxically, perhaps, EU enlargement may mean that the increasing Europeanization of environmental law is coming to an end.

Id. at 273–74. Where should regulatory power lie in order to counter the potential for a "race to the bottom," where economic competition motivates states and/or local governments to relax their environmental regulation in hopes of attracting and retaining industry? For opposing views, see Daniel C. Esty, *Revitalizing Environmental Federalism*, 95 Mich. L. Rev. 570 (1996) (explaining that centralized environmental regulations will generate better outcomes than decentralized "regulatory competition"), and Richard L. Revesz, *Rehabilitating Interstate Competition: Rethinking the "Race-to-the-Bottom" Ratio-*

---

2. [Ed.] *Acquis communautaire* is "the cumulative body of European Community laws, comprising the EC's objectives, substantive rules, policies and, in particular, the primary and secondary legislation and case law ... includ[ing] all the treaties, regulations and directives passed by the European institutions, as well as judgements laid down by the European Court of Justice." Eurofound Industrial Relations Dictionary (2007), at http://www.eurofound.europa.eu/areas/industrialrelations/dictionary/index.htm. All Member States are bound to comply with *acquis communautaire*.

nale for Federal Environmental Regulation, 67 N.Y.U. L. Rev. 1210 (1992) (arguing that competition among states yields the most promising innovations).

8. For in-depth analysis of environmental federalism in Europe, Canada, and the U.S., see Blake Hudson, *Fail-Safe Federalism and Climate Change: The Case of U.S. and Canadian Forest Policy*, 44 Conn. L. Rev. 925 (2012); Alastair R. Lucas, *Mythology, Fantasy and Federalism: Canadian Climate Change Policy and Law*, 20 Pac. McGeorge Global Bus. & Dev. L.J. 41 (2007); R. Daniel Kelemen, *Environmental Federalism in the U.S. and the European Union*, in Green Giants? Environmental Policies of the U.S. and the European Union 113 (Norman Vig & Michael Faure, eds.) (2004); Neil Hawke, *Canadian Federalism and Environmental Protection*, 14 J. Envtl. L. 185 (2002).

9. Where does the Indian government, and its relationship with the 28 states and seven territories within India, fall? The Central government was established by the Constitution of India, enacted in 1950, and it is the governing authority of the union. India has characteristics of both a federation and a unitary system, and is sometimes described as a quasi-federal state, with a strong bias toward the Central government. Subjects of national importance include the usual subjects of national defense and foreign affairs but also include atomic energy and banking. The constitution—one of the longest in the world—lists nearly 100 subjects within the Central government's power. By contrast, the constitution lists only about 70 topics of state authority, such as policing, commerce, and agriculture. Education, criminal and civil procedure, trade unions, and forty-some other topics are on a "concurrent" list, meaning that both Central and state governments have authority over them, but if conflict arises, Central law prevails. During emergencies, power shifts to the Central government.

> The legal system in India ... was, and still is, dealing with a mix of the colonial past, the Nehruvian idea of socialism, the Gandhian ideals of village self-rule and the written Constitution of Independent India. The Constitution of India is the fountain of law in the country. As the Supreme Court of India has held: "the Constitution is not only the paramount law of the land, but it is the source and sustenance of all laws. Its provisions are conceived in public interest and are intended to serve a public purpose."

Shalini Bhutani and Ashish Kothari, *The Biodiversity Rights of Developing Nations: A Perspective From India*, 32 Golden Gate U. L. Rev. 587, 605 (2002), citing Olga Tellis v. Municipal Corporation of Greater Bombay, AIR 1986 SC 180. For insights on authority over environmental affairs, see Armin Rosencranz and Kathleen D. Yurchak, *Progress on the Environmental Front: The Regulation of Industry and Development in India*, 19 Hastings Int'l & Comp. L. Rev. 489 (1996).

Among all of the jurisdictions considered in this book, India is perhaps the most open to borrowing good ideas from foreign sources. Indeed, "Indian Supreme Court Justices often reference U.S. case law in their decisions." Cyra Akila Choudhury, *Between Tradition and Progress: A Comparative Perspective on Polygamy in the U.S. and India*, 83 U. Colo. L. Rev. 963, 965 (2012), citing Rekha v. State of Tamil Nadu, (2011) 4 S.C.J. 637 (India) (referencing Joint Anti-Fascist Refugee Comm. v. McGrath, 341 U.S. 123 (1951)), and Narayan Dutt v. State of Punjab, (2011) 3 S.C.J. 845 (India) (referencing Ex parte Wells, 59 U.S. (18 How.) 307 (1855)). A survey of Indian Supreme Court cases from 1950–2004 revealed that 24.6% of them used foreign law on subjects ranging from the right to a fair trial to freedom of the press and other topics. Adam M. Smith, *Making Itself at Home: Understanding Foreign Law in Domestic Jurisprudence: The Indian Case,* 24 Berkeley J. Int'l L. 218, 239–40 Table 1 (2006).

C. Common Law Systems

The common law is the foundation of the legal systems of the United Kingdom, Northern Ireland, the United States (both federal and state, with the exception of Louisiana state law), Canada (both federal and state, with the exception of Quebec), New Zealand, and India (India's system of common law is a mixture of English law and Hindu law). The common law is also followed in Australia (both federal and individual states), Malaysia, Brunei, Pakistan, Singapore, Hong Kong, and many other English-speaking or Commonwealth countries.

"Common law" is law developed incrementally through decisions of courts and similar tribunals. In common law systems, law is created and refined by judges. (ROSCOE POUND, THE SPIRIT OF THE COMMON LAW xi–xiv, 174–75 (1921)). A decision in the case currently pending depends on decisions in previous cases and in turn affects the law to be applied in future cases. According to Karl Llewellyn's classic description, "the common law court deals not only with the particular decision, but with the rule which is to become a precedent and guide the future." (KARL N. LLEWELLYN, JURISPRUDENCE: REALISM IN THEORY AND PRACTICE 301 (Transaction Publishers 2008) (1962)).

If a similar dispute has been resolved in the past by an authoritative court, the court is bound to follow the reasoning used in the prior decision (*stare decisis*). *Stare decisis*, the principle that similar cases be decided according to similar rules, lies at the heart of all common law systems. In most common law jurisdictions, decisions by appellate courts are binding on lower courts in the same jurisdiction and on future decisions of the same appellate court.

Despite the binding nature of precedent, according to one English judge, common law systems are inherently flexible:

> The object of the common law is to solve difficulties and adjust relations in social and commercial life. It must meet, in so far as it can, sets of fact abnormal as well as usual. It must grow with the development of the nation. It must face and deal with changing or novel circumstances. Unless it can do that, it fails in its function and declines in its dignity. An expanding society demands an expanding common law.

Prager v. Blatspiel, Stamp and Heacock Ltd., 1 K.B. 566, 570 (McCardie, J.) (1924). While flexibility can be advantageous in resolving novel disputes, it can also foster uncertainty and confusion: "As a system of legal thought the common law … is inherently incomplete, vague and fluid…." Brian Simpson, *The Common Law and Legal Theory*, in LEGAL THEORY AND COMMON LAW 8, 17 (Wm. Twining ed. 1986).

As Professor Reimann noted in his article, *supra,* the main alternative to the common law system is the civil law system, which is used in Continental Europe and most of the rest of the world.

> In the civil law tradition, all law flows from a coherent set of legal principles contained in a written code provided or enacted by the sovereign…. The courts interpret the code and legislation but decisions of judges are not law. Consequently, the principle of *stare decisis* does not exist and courts are not bound to apply precedents contained in prior case law.

Nicholas Karambelas, *Civil Law Jurisdictions,* 1 Ltd. Liab. Co.: L., Prac. & Forms § 22:2 (2011).

The distinction between civil law and common law legal systems has become increasingly blurred as disputes about environmental protection, health care, occupational safety and compensation, and other matters become ever more complex. "The law of the common law systems is becoming more statutory. The law of the civil law systems is being made increasingly in judicial decisions and interpretations of civil code provisions and statutes." *Id.*

Notes and Questions

1. In contrast to the common law approach, civil law began as a collection of rules drawn from Roman law, as well as ecclesiastical and customary laws. *See* David Alan Sklansky, *Anti-Inquisitorialism*, 122 Harv. L. Rev. 1634, 1672 (2009). Modern civil law systems rely on comprehensive compilations of statutes that regulate a broad range of activities. "The theoretical foundation ... is that the principles of neutrality, consistency and predictability of the law are most effectively implemented by codification and legislation rather by the discretionary power of the judiciary." Karambelas, *supra*, § 22:2. Do you agree?

2. Some observers describe civil law traditions as "anything that is not permitted is prohibited," and common law traditions as "anything that is not prohibited is permitted." Karambelas, *supra*, § 22:2. What are the comparative advantages and disadvantages of the two systems? As you study the environmental laws described in the following chapters, consider whether either system makes more sense in the environmental context.

Chapter II

The Common Law as an Environmental Protection Tool

A. Comparative Tort Law

Personal injuries and property damage caused by pollution and other types of environmental harm have occurred around the globe. The following incidents are but a few notorious examples:

- *Bhopal, India*—Toxic gases leaked from a Union Carbide chemical plant in Bhopal in 1984, killing 3,000 people almost instantly, with many more dying later from the after effects of the gas, which was an ingredient in pesticides produced by the plant. Union Carbide paid a $470 million settlement, with each victim getting an average of $550. In 2010, eight former executives of the company were convicted of criminal negligence. Lydia Polgreen, *8 Former Executives Guilty in Bhopal Chemical Leak,* N.Y. Times, June 7, 2010.

- *Cumbria, England*—Britain's worst nuclear disaster occurred in 1957, when graphite rods used to control reactions in the Windscale nuclear plant's core reactor caught fire. The fire blazed out of control for two days, and sent a plume of caesium, iodine, and polonium across Great Britain and northern Europe. At one point workers used sledgehammers to try to knock the damaged, highly radioactive fuel rods out of the reactor before they eventually managed to extinguish the flames. After the fire, the government imposed a six-week ban on the consumption of milk from cows grazing within a 200-mile radius. The Windscale plant "was air-cooled, had no proper containment vessels and had insufficient monitoring of conditions in the core." Robin McKie, *Windscale Radiation 'Doubly Dangerous,'* The Observer, Oct. 6, 2007.

- *Gulf Coast, USA*—Over 200 million gallons of crude oil flowed from BP's well after an explosion at the Deepwater Horizon drilling platform on April 20, 2010. The blowout killed 11 workers and the oil spill contaminated the Gulf of Mexico and miles of its coastline. President Barack Obama called it America's worst environmental disaster. Coastal wetlands, deepwater corals, zooplankton, and insects continue to show signs of severe contamination, and dolphins are underweight, anaemic, and suffer from lung and liver disease and low hormone levels. BP has set aside $37 billion to pay for disaster-related costs. Although BP settled with the largest group of private claimants for $8 billion, the United States government is still pursuing a case against BP. Peter Beaumont, *Gulf's Dolphins Pay Heavy Price for Deepwater Oil Spill,* U.K. Guardian, Mar. 31, 2012.

- *North Island, New Zealand*—The Rena, a Greek-owned ship based in Ligeria, hit a reef off the coast of the Bay of Plenty in northern New Zealand in 2011. It was carrying 1,368 shipping containers, of which at least 22 contained hazardous goods. Extensive damage was caused when the ship's hull was drug along the reef by heavy winds and swells. Ruptures to the ship's tanks and the eventual break-up of the ship released 400 tonnes of fuel into the water, killing thousands of sea birds and polluting beaches up to 60 miles away. Maritime New Zealand charged the shipping company with discharging harmful substances. The ship's captain and second officer pleaded guilty to operating the ship in a dangerous manner, releasing toxic substances, and altering the ship's documents. Toby Manhire, *Oil Spill is NZ's Worst Maritime Disaster*, U.K. Guardian, Oct. 11, 2011. Losses to the tourism industry were estimated at $1.2 million a day. Affected businesses have filed a class-action lawsuit against the owners of the Rena. Jamie Morton, *Businesses Join Queue to Sue over Cost of Rena Wreck*, NZ Herald, June 15, 2012.

- *Ontario, Canada* — Drinking water supplies in Walkerton, Ontario were contaminated with E. coli in 2000, leaving seven people dead and inflicting several thousand with serious illnesses. The primary source of the contamination was manure that had been spread on a farm near one of the wells. A public inquiry identified government deregulation along with radical budget and manpower cuts to the Environment Ministry as key contributing factors to the contamination. The most serious case of water contamination in Canadian history could have been prevented by proper chlorination and monitoring of the drinking water well, according to the inquiry report. A class-action lawsuit was settled when the Ontario government agreed to provide a compensation fund to the victims. CBC News Online, *Walkerton Report Highlights*, Jan. 2002, at http://www.cbc.ca/news/background/walkerton/walkerton_report.html#one.

Common law tort claims can be powerful tools for addressing environmental harms like those described above.

> Tort law has seven characteristics relevant to its potential role in environmental protection: it is interpersonal, it focuses on bad outcomes, and its main concern is cure rather than prevention. Tort law is primarily a vehicle for reparation rather than punishment, and for reparation of harm to persons. It is not much concerned with risks as such, and tort liability is predominantly fault-based.

Peter Cane, *Using Tort Law to Enforce Environmental Regulations*, 41 Washburn L.J. 427, 448 (2002). While common law principles are no longer the predominant form of pollution control in the United States — comprehensive public law regulation has surpassed the common law in many ways — they are still relevant and in some cases may be the only way that victims can recover damages. Moreover, common law doctrines "still provide robust protection for water quality in rivers and streams in parts of England" and elsewhere. Jonathon H. Adler, *Free & Green: A New Approach to Environmental Protection*, 24 Harv. J.L. & Pub. Pol'y 653, 671 (2001).

Trespass, nuisance, negligence, and strict liability for abnormally dangerous activities are among the common law tort claims that may be brought for environmental harm. Gowling Lefleur Henderson, *Environmental Protection — Common Law*, 2 Transnational Jt Ventures § 24:172 (2012). All five of the countries included in this book have recognized these types of claims, at least to some extent. *See id.* (discussing all Canadian provinces except Quebec).

In Europe, "[e]nvironmental liability is among the most rapidly evolving areas of tort law." Gerrit Betlem & Michael Faure, *Environmental Toxic Torts in Europe: Some Trends in Recovery of Soil Clean-Up Costs and Damages for Personal Injury in the Netherlands,*

Belgium, England and Germany, 10 Geo. Int. Envtl. L. Rev. 855, 855 (1998). "Many classic questions that evoke discussion in the United States — including the balance between negligence and strict liability, the foreseeability requirement, and issues of proof and causation — have been discussed extensively in Europe as well." *Id.* Drawing comparisons is a challenge, however, because tort liability "is still subject to widely divergent systems in EU Member States." Mark Wilde, *Review,* Environmental Liability and Ecological Damage In European Law (ed. Monika Hinteregger) (2008), 21 J. Envtl. L. 377 (2009).

> It is clear that certain States continue to rely upon existing generally applicable legal principles, some have adopted specialist liability regimes for specific types of environmental damage, and a very limited number have adopted horizontal regimes for all types of environmental damage. The scope of environmental liability regimes varies widely in terms of the extent to which liability is strict, the rules on causality, standing, whether personal injury and property should be excluded from the definition of environmental damage and so forth.

Id. at 379. For an assessment of the main commonalities and differences in EU States, see Hinteregger, *supra,* Part III.

New Zealand has reformed its tort law system in a unique way. During the 1970s, New Zealand adopted an Accident Compensation Act, which replaced common law tort claims for accident-related personal injuries with a no-fault compensation system administered by a government Accident Compensation Corporation. Reformers hoped to counteract "the lottery-like nature of personal injury awards, the inadequacy of compensation under the existing workers' compensation system, and the limited availability of social security benefits." Albert C. Lin, *Beyond Tort: Compensating Victims of Environmental Toxic Injury,* 78 S. Cal. L. Rev. 1439, 1500 (2005). The Act has been amended several times over the years to address a variety of concerns. In particular:

> The Act made a limited attempt to link the premiums paid by those deemed responsible to the risks they caused.... But the flat-rate levy on privately owned automobiles and the industry-based levy on employers represented only a crude reflection of risk.... The perception that employers were being unfairly taxed for injuries occurring outside the employment context helped to fuel a backlash against the system.

Id. at 1503. In addition, the Act "only provided coverage for accidents and deliberately excluded coverage for illness, including environmental illness." *Id.* at 1502–03. By excluding environmental illnesses, does the New Zealand legislation create a disincentive for pollution control and deterrence? Professor Lin says yes, and argues that this is a "fundamental shortcoming" that ought to be fixed.

> Environmental illness would seem to be a prime candidate for inclusion in a compensation scheme premised on community responsibility given the disparate causes of these illnesses, the consequent difficulty of proving individual causation, and the universal vulnerability to disease-causing hazards in the environment.

> Like the Act, the administrative scheme proposed here is partial; it would only cover diseases caused by environmental exposure.... [I]t may appear unfair from a compensation perspective to distinguish between environmental injuries, for which compensation would be available, and hereditary diseases, for which no compensation would be available. The need to deter polluters, however, justifies a system that addresses the specific problem of environmental injury alone.

Id. at 1503–04.

Is an administrative compensation scheme of some sort preferable to common law judgments and awards? Professor Lin thinks so.

> Even if society had knowledge of every significant health effect of every major pollutant, the tort system would not fully compensate environmental tort plaintiffs. First, tort claims arise only when victims suffer harm. Therefore, problems associated with latency, such as insolvent defendants, faded memories, and lost or degraded evidence, will persist. Second, many potential tort plaintiffs will still face significant, even insurmountable, obstacles in proving specific causation. This is due to several factors: epidemiological limitations, difficulties handling probabilistic evidence, and requirements that both general and specific causation be proved by a preponderance of the evidence....

> [E]pidemiological studies describe only the excess risk from exposure to a substance; they do not pinpoint the actual source of disease in an individual case. Thus, where an environmental illness may be caused by multiple sources, epidemiology cannot demonstrate that exposure to a particular defendant's pollutants was the "but for" cause of the illness. For instance, a lung cancer victim may be unable to establish that the illness was caused by exposure to airborne carcinogens rather than smoking. Toxicogenomics offers the potential to identify chemical-specific genetic markers of disease processes. Even with this data, however, specific causation issues will bar recovery if there are multiple potential sources of a disease-causing chemical. This would likely occur in a significant number of cases. Given that regulations ban or limit the use of the most noxious chemicals, many environmental toxic tort injuries will likely involve low-level, long-term exposures to chemicals generated by multiple sources.

> Furthermore, a greater scientific understanding of causal relationships will not necessarily resolve the difficulties of environmental tort plaintiffs. The probabilistic nature of scientific evidence will hamper recovering in tort. Even if courts become more receptive to probabilistic evidence, plaintiffs may be unable to prove causation by a preponderance of the evidence. For example, plaintiffs would be unable to meet their burden whenever the added tortious risk is less than the background cumulative risk attributable to all other factors. Because most low-level exposures to toxic substances do not double the plaintiff's risk, many environmental tort victims will continue to be uncompensated, regardless of whether scientific research unearths significant relationships between chemical exposure and harm. The doubling of the risk threshold adopted by the tort system is not a necessary or particularly logical one. Compensation, deterrence, and fairness goals all argue for a lower threshold, which the proposed administrative system endorses.

> Finally, given the widespread exposure to chemical substances, the number of potential tort claims could overburden the courts.

Id. at 1511–13.

Regardless of your impression of the relative merits of an administrative compensation scheme versus common law tort cases and judicial remedies, how useful is New Zealand's Compensation Act to comparative law scholars, given that New Zealand is a "relatively homogeneous culture with a strong commitment to social welfare"? *Id.*

Apart from the New Zealand experience, what role can comparative analysis play in crafting legal arguments and resolving disputes or reform proposals involving common law tort claims?

[C]omparative tort law can enrich the palette of ideas, concerns, perceptions—in short, arguments—that a judge brings to bear on the matters in dispute, since "it is arguments that influence decisions." Moreover comparative law provides the insight that there is nothing inevitable about current domestic conceptual arrangements, and so can ease the path of the tort lawyer who is inviting a domestic court to alter those arrangements because it can show that others are at least intellectually viable.

Jane Stapleton, *Benefits of Comparative Tort Reasoning: Lost in Translation*, 1 J. Tort L. 6, 44 (2007). Stapleton notes that, in many English-speaking jurisdictions, "tort practitioners and courts have always regarded each other's national systems as an important source of readily accessible and intelligible ideas." *Id.* Not so, however, in the United States. Perhaps it is because there is a plethora of state and federal courts that handle tort claims in the U.S., providing a "sufficient diversity of arguments to oust a role for comparative non-U.S. English-language law given the practical constraints when practitioners advise and courts decide cases." *Id.* at 44.

When it comes to tort law, there are additional distinctions between the U.S. and other English-speaking countries. For one thing, mass tort litigation via class actions involving dozens, hundreds, or even thousands of plaintiffs tends to be more common in the United States than elsewhere. *See* David Wilkinson, *Mass Tort Treatment of Pharmaceutical Product Liability Cases in England*, 73 Def. Couns. J. 264, 264 (2006) ("The group action procedure is still in its infancy in England, and it is rarely used in contrast to … the United States."); S. Stuart Clark, *Thinking Locally, Suing Globally: The International Frontiers of Mass Tort Litigation in Australia*, 74 Def. Couns. J. 139, 139 (2007) (noting that, since legislative reforms in 1992, "much has changed … Australia is now the place outside North America where a corporation is most likely to find itself defending a class action"). For analysis of class actions in Canadian courts, see Patrick Hayes, *Exploring the Viability of Class Actions Arising from Environmental Toxic Torts: Overcoming Barriers to Certification*, 19 J. Env. L. & Prac.-Can. 189 (2009) (criticizing the courts' negative treatment of class certification due to the allegedly "individualized" nature of the causation inquiry "as generally, if not inherently, undesirable").

B. The Substantive Parameters of Environmental Torts

Trespass—The doctrine of trespass protects landowners' interests in exclusive possession of the land. Liability is imposed for intentional trespasses when there is an intrusion on another's property, even when it is harmless, while liability is imposed for negligent trespasses *only* when there has been harm to the property. To prove intent, it is sufficient to show that the actor knowingly enters the land of another without legal authority.

One of the earliest opinions to address whether invisible particles of air pollution can be grounds for a trespass action is Martin v. Reynolds Metals Co., 221 Or. 86, 342 P.2d 790 (1959), where plaintiffs brought a claim against an aluminum reduction factory that caused gas and fluoride compounds to become airborne and settle onto the plaintiff's land. The contaminated forage and water were unsuitable for plaintiff's livestock. The court adopted a new rule that materials invisible to the naked eye may form a trespass so long as there is some damage to the property; however, absent damage, there is no "entry" and therefore no trespass. Similarly, in Borland v. Sanders Lead Co., 369 So.2d 523, 530 (Ala. 1979), the court held that even microscopic materials can constitute a trespass if they harm the property, and in Bradley v. American Smelting & Refining Co., 635 F.Supp. 1154 (W.D. Wash. 1986), the court rejected a trespass claim where the plaintiff complained that imperceptible particles of cadmium and arsenic had come to rest on his property but failed to show "actual and substantial" damages. The *Bradley* court explained:

> No useful purpose would be served by sanctioning actions in trespass by every landowner within a hundred miles of a manufacturing plant. Manufacturers would be harassed and the litigious few would cause the escalation of costs to the detriment of many.

Id.; Bradley v. American Smelting & Refining Co., 104 Wash.2d 677, 709 P.2d 782, 791 (Wash. 1985).

Just because something is invisible to the naked eye doesn't mean it is innocuous. It does mean, however, that plaintiffs have the burden of proving that some sort of harm resulted from the invasion. In Mercer v. Rockwell Intern. Corp., 24 F.Supp.2d 735 (W.D. Ky. 1998), owners of riparian land (land located along a river) alleged that a manufacturing plant's discharge of polychlorinated biphenyls (PCBs) into a drainage system had caused damage to their property. The court held that plaintiffs must show that the PCBs had caused actual harm to property through the creation of health hazard to recover on a negligent trespass claim. Plaintiffs attempted to show harm by introducing evidence of a state-imposed fishing advisory for the river. The court was unmoved, and held that this evidence was insufficient to establish that the PCBs constituted a medical hazard, because the advisory was purely a government action and did not concern a condition of the plaintiffs' property. It noted that the amount of PCBs found on plaintiffs' property was "incredibly low" and that no witness had attempted to quantify the degree of risk or the increase of risk from the low levels of PCBs present on the property. *Id.* at 752.

With advances in science and in the ability to detect tiny amounts of hazardous pollutants, should trespass law be "modernized" to make *any* intentional invasion of another's property an unlawful trespass? If the plaintiff can show that some invasion has occurred, shouldn't she be able to recover nominal damages, at least, in addition to injunctive relief? In a case brought by landowners whose property was polluted by an immense spill of coal ash from a failed containment pond at a Tennessee Valley Authority (TVA) power plant, the court exhibited an open mind toward environmental trespass cases:

> [Pursuant to] the "modern" trend of trespass law, the Court finds that a common element in each of those cases is that a trespass claim may be premised upon the entry onto property of intangible particles.... [T]he Court agrees with plaintiffs that a trespass claim under Tennessee law may be premised upon the entry onto property of intangible particles and that there is no requirement of actual and substantial harm. This does not, however, obviate the requirement that plaintiffs must show causation, that particles from the ash spill, either tangible or intangible, entered plaintiffs' properties and would not have done so "but for" actionable conduct by TVA.

TVA Ash Spill Litigation, 805 F.Supp.2d 468, 484 (E.D. Tenn. 2011). Accordingly, the court denied the TVA's motion for summary judgment on plaintiffs' trespass claims.

For an account of the evolution of the torts of trespass and nuisance, see H. Marlow Green, *Common Law, Property Rights and the Environment: A Comparative Analysis of Historical Developments in the United States and England and a Model for the Future*, 30

Cornell Int'l L.J. 541, 552 (1997) (concluding that "the common law may still play a significant role in the modern environmental arena").

Nuisance—Generally speaking, private nuisance protects the use and enjoyment of private property from unreasonable interference by adjacent property owners. The plaintiff must have a legally recognized interest in the property at issue. In a landmark seventeenth century dispute, William Aldred's Case, 77 Eng. Rep. 816 (1611), the plaintiff brought an action to enjoin his neighbor's hog sty. The defendant argued that the social value of his sty was a defense to the plaintiff's nuisance action: because his activities were "necessary for the sustenance of man ... one ought not to have so delicate a nose." *Id.* at 817. The court rejected the argument and adopted the doctrine of *sic utere tuo ut alienum non laedas* ("one should use his own property in such a manner as not to injure that of another"). *Id.* at 821. *See* Green, *supra,* at 547; Jeff L. Lewin, *Boomer and the American Law of Nuisance: Past, Present, and Future,* 54 Alb. L. Rev. 189, 193 (1990) (describing the English origins of nuisance).

A single activity may be considered both a nuisance and a trespass. Hodas, *supra* 883 n.1, citing Miller v. Cudahy Co., 592 F.Supp. 976 (D. Kan.1984), *aff'd in part,* 858 F.2d 1449 (10th Cir.1988). In Friesen v. Forest Protection Ltd., 1978 CarswellNB 239 (New Brunswick S.Ct., Q.B. Div. 1978), landowners sought recovery for damages caused by government-sponsored pesticide spraying on an adjacent forest. Plaintiffs claimed injuries to their bees, livestock, and fruit trees and to their own health and wellbeing. The court held that the pesticide deposited on the plaintiffs' land was a foreign substance, and that its deposit disturbed the plaintiffs' enjoyment of their property. Is this enough to show that the defendant committed a *trespass* under the precedents described above? *See id.* para. 33 (yes). The court also found that the spraying constituted a private nuisance that caused damage to the plaintiffs' use or enjoyment of their land. Thus, the plaintiffs were entitled to compensation even though the defendant had not intended to harm the plaintiff and had not acted unreasonably. *Id.* para. 34, 48–51.

Environmental nuisances that affect members of the general public may be actionable as public nuisances. *See, e.g.,* Colour Quest Ltd and Others v. Total Downstream UK Plc and Others (Rev 1) [2009] EWHC 540 (Comm) (huge explosion at an oil depot, thought to be the largest explosion in peacetime Europe, caused widespread damage and injured 43 people); Corby Group Litigation v. Corby DC [2009] EWHC 1944 (contamination of air, soil, and water from failure to properly remediate a large industrial complex). A public nuisance is "the doing or the failure to do something that injuriously affects the safety, health or morals of the public, or works some substantial annoyance, inconvenience or injury to the public." Commonwealth v. South Covington Ry., 181 Ky. 459, 205 S.W. 581 (1918).

> A person is guilty of a public nuisance (also known as common nuisance) who (a) does an act not warranted by law, or (b) omits to discharge a legal duty, if the effect of the act or omission is to endanger the life, health, property, or comfort of the public, or to obstruct the public in the exercise or enjoyment of rights common to all Her Majesty's subjects.

Archbold, *Criminal Pleading, Evidence and Practice* (Sweet & Maxwell, London 2010) at paras 31–40. The above formulation is notoriously broad, and "[s]ince time immemorial the boundaries of nuisance have disturbed tidy-minded lawyers and jurists." John Pointing, *Public Nuisance: Beyond Highway 61 Revisited,* 13 Envtl. L. Rev. 25, 25 (2011). "Given its incredible breadth and lack of precision," renowned legal scholar Dean William Prosser described public nuisance as "a sort of legal garbage can." *Id.* at 27; *see* William Prosser, *Private Actions for Public Nuisance,* 52 Va. L. Rev. 997, 1001–02 (1966).

Generally speaking, a private plaintiff can bring an action for public nuisance only if the plaintiff can show particular, personal damage not shared in common with the rest of the public. David R. Hodas, *Private Actions for Public Nuisance: Common Law Citizen Suits for Relief from Environmental Harm,* 16 Eco. L. Q. 883, 884 (1989). Does this "special harm" rule still make sense in an era of "modern worries about an accident at a chemical plant that can kill thousands of persons, an oil spill that can spoil thousands of miles of beaches, riverbanks, or underwater areas, or the release of toxic substances that can contaminate the air, water, and land"? *Id.* Professor Hodas suggests that it does not, *id.* at 887, 907, and notes that, "[a]lthough these types of concerns prompted a revolution in statutory environmental law by the early 1970's, the common law public nuisance doctrine remained relatively unchanged." *Id.* at 885.

What if the defendant in a nuisance case has obtained a permit for the activity in question? Compliance with such a permit is not necessarily a defense to a common law nuisance claim. In Barr v. Biffa [2012] EWCA Civ 312, neighbors complained about odor from a waste tip (landfill) operated by the defendant in Hertfordshire. The UK court of appeal held that the claim should be governed by conventional principles of nuisance law—"a nuisance is caused by a person unduly interfering with his neighbor in the comfortable and convenient enjoyment of his land." Statutory authority or the receipt of a permit may be a defense, but only if permission to commit a nuisance is express or necessarily implied. "The latter will apply where a statute authorises the user of land in a way which will 'inevitably' involve a nuisance even if every reasonable precaution is taken." Justine Thornton, *Significant UK Environmental Cases: 2011–12,* 24 J. Env. L 371 (2012).

Negligence—Liability for negligence is imposed when a duty of due care is breached, causing foreseeable harm to the plaintiff. It is designed to protect against unreasonable risks of harm. Restatement (Second) of Torts §§ 281–282. The duty is typically defined as the reasonably prudent person's exercise of ordinary care and skill. Standards of care may be drawn from industry-wide practices or guidelines, as in the English case of Tutton v. A.D. Walter Ltd., [1985] 3 All E.R. 757, 766, [1986] Q.B. 61, 76, which found that a farmer had breached his duty to local beekeepers in applying an insecticide to his crop to control weevils. The bees' presence in the area was known, but the farmer failed to comply with published recommendations for spraying after flowering had occurred, and failed to provide an adequate warning to the beekeepers before he sprayed. *Id.* Arguably, the *Tutton* plaintiffs could have recovered for trespass as well, if the rule in the New Brunswick case, *Friesen v. Forest Protection Ltd., supra,* were applied.

Personal injuries in toxic tort cases may be addressed through negligence claims as well, if the defendant breached a duty to the plaintiff and if that breach was the proximate cause of plaintiff's injuries. For example, in Leibel v. South Qu'Appelle (Rural Municipality) (1943), [1944] 1 D.L.R. 369 (Sask. C.A.), a municipality was held liable for negligently allowing arsenic to escape into the environment and contaminate the plaintiff's well when its employee mixed up some arsenic-based bait to kill grasshoppers. The plaintiff became ill as a result of drinking contaminated water.

In a well-publicized case in England, Corby Group Litigation v. Corby DC [2009] EWHC 1944, a local authority was held liable for the negligent reclamation of an industrial site and for public nuisance. In the mid-1980s, the Corby Borough Council acquired contaminated land from the British Steel Corporation. Reclamation of the site caused the dispersal of toxic dust and volatile and toxic vapors and fluids. Over a dozen children were born with limb reduction defects, mainly missing fingers and clubbed feet. Their mothers lived near the site during their pregnancies between 1986 and 1999. The Council appealed the adverse judgment, arguing among other things that foreseeability was lacking. At the time of the reclamation, the Council had no notice or knowledge of any link between birth defects and its practices with respect to the types of contaminants at the site. Moreover, reclamation practices at other old industrial sites were similar to those undertaken at Corby, often on sites near residential areas. And although it had not yet been passed when cleanup began, the UK Environment Act 1995 obligates local authorities to survey their land to assess which land is contaminated and then to ensure that the land is remediated. EPA 1990, §§ 78B(1)(a), 78E.

The parties ultimately settled the case on confidential financial terms. The case has been dubbed "the British Erin Brockovich," in reference to a case made into a movie of the same name in the United States. Nick Britten, *Corby Birth Defect: Ten-year Struggle Ends in Victory that Echoes Erin Brockovich*, The Daily Telegraph, July 30, 2009. In that case, brought by Brockovich's law firm on behalf of hundreds of Hinkley, California, residents, Pacific Gas and Electric was held liable for contaminating groundwater with hexavalent chromium, which it had used to prevent corrosion at its Hinkley compressor station. The plaintiffs alleged that exposure caused increased rates of cancer and birth defects. The case settled in 1996 for over $330 million, the largest settlement ever paid in a direct action lawsuit in U.S. history. *See* Sedina Banks, *The "Erin Brockovich Effect": How Media Shapes Toxics Policy,* 26 Environs 219, 230 (2003).

Erin Brokovich notwithstanding, it is extremely difficult for plaintiffs to prove that toxic substances have caused latent diseases such as cancer, as the people of Woburn, Massachusetts discovered. During the 1970s and 1980s, residents were exposed to solvents and other contaminants in their drinking water. Many of them developed leukemia and other illnesses; some died. They were largely unsuccessful in their lawsuit against industries in the area because they could not establish that they were exposed to specific contaminants from specific industries, or that those contaminants ultimately caused their illnesses. *See* Anderson v. W.R. Grace & Co., 628 F.Supp. 1219 (D. Mass. 1986); JONATHAN HARR, A CIVIL ACTION (1996). Plaintiffs in England have experienced similar difficulties. *See* Reay and Hope v. BNFL [1994] Env LR 320 (dismissing a case brought by children whose fathers worked at the Sellafield Nuclear Plant for failure to prove that their leukemias were caused by radiation). For further analysis of international regimes governing toxic torts, see Mary Elliott Rolle, *Unraveling Accountability: Contesting Legal and Procedural Barriers in International Toxic Tort Cases,* 15 Geo. Int'l Envtl. L. Rev. 135 (2003).

Strict Liability — Strict liability — or liability without fault — has been imposed by common law courts for several types of activities or injuries. One of the earliest forms of strict liability arose in the context of riparian water law. Under the English "natural flow" theory, persons who owned real property that adjoined a body of water were entitled to its uninterrupted flow *no matter what. See* Leahy v. North Sydney, 1906 CarswellNS 230 (Canada S. Ct. 1906); John Young & Co. v. Bankier Distillery Co, A.C. 691, 698 (House of Lords 1893); Bellinger v. New York Central R.R., 23 N.Y. 42 (1861); Miller v. Miller, 9 Pa. 74 (1858). Anyone diverting or otherwise reducing the natural flow was automatically held liable for violating the rights of riparian users, regardless of the social value of the defendant's activity or the amount of care exercised by the defendant. Moreover, the plaintiff need not prove harm; damage was presumed once interference with a riparian right was shown. *Cf.* Mehta v. Nath [(1997) 1 S.C.C. 388, at 17, 26 (characterizing a developer's "illegal constructions and callous interference with the natural flow of river Beas" as an unlawful environmental degradation and a violation of India's public trust doctrine). Eventually, the natural flow doctrine evolved into a rule of "reasonable use" to accommodate the needs of a more industrialized economy. *See* Merrifield v. Worcester, 110

Mass. 219 (1872); Carol M. Rose, *Energy and Efficiency in the Realignment of Common-Law Water Rights*, 19 J. Legal Stud. 261 (1990). However, a few common law countries appear to retain the natural flow doctrine in some form. *See Mehta v. Nath, supra.*

The doctrine of strict liability for abnormally dangerous conditions and activities arose out of an 1868 English case, Rylands v. Fletcher, L.R. 3 H.L. 330. Mill owners in the coal mining area of Lancashire constructed a reservoir on their land. The water broke through the shaft of an abandoned mine and flooded adjacent passageways into the plaintiff's active mine. The trial court found that the mill owners were not negligent and dismissed the plaintiff's claim. On appeal, the Exchequer Chamber reversed the lower court and imposed strict liability on the defendants: "The person who for his own purposes brings on his lands and collects and keeps there anything likely to do mischief if it escapes, must keep it in at his peril, and, if he does not do so, is Prima Facie answerable for all the damage which is the natural consequence of its escape." The House of Lords affirmed the ruling but crafted a more limited rule of strict liability, which applied only to a "nonnatural" use of the defendant's land, as distinguished from "any purpose for which it might in the ordinary course of the enjoyment of land be used." The court emphasized the abnormal and inappropriate character of the defendant's reservoir in coal mining country. Thus, the basis of liability is the creation of an extraordinary risk. Blasting and crop dusting with toxic pesticides, for example, create unusual and unacceptable risks in the midst of a city, but may not in a remote, rural area.

The United States, Canada, and India have adopted strict liability for abnormally dangerous things and activities, but each jurisdiction has added its own nuances. The following cases are representative examples:

- *In re Hanford Nuclear Reservation Litig., 350 F. Supp. 2d 871 (E.D. Wash. 2004)*—The chemical separation process that occurred in the production of plutonium at a nuclear reactor was an "abnormally dangerous activity," even though the reactor operators may have exercised all reasonable care. Thus, plaintiffs were entitled for partial summary judgment on the issue of whether defendants could be held strictly liable for plaintiffs' thyroid diseases allegedly caused by exposure to radioactive substances.

- *Tock v. St. John's (City) Metropolitan Area Board, 1989 CarswellNfld 21 (Canada S.Ct. 1989)*—A storm sewer system maintained by a municipality became obstructed following an extraordinary rainstorm, and overflowed and flooded the basement of the plaintiffs' house. The rule in *Rylands v. Fletcher* applies only when damage occurs due to "non-natural use" of land, that is, a use inappropriate to the place where it is maintained. Thus, the rule did not apply to the municipality, which constructed and operated the sewer system pursuant to statutory authority. "It would be difficult to conceive of a use of land falling more squarely within those that may be said to be ordinary and proper for the general benefit of the community." *Id.* para. 59.

- *M.C. Mehta v. Union of India, WP 12739/1985, AIR 1987 SC 1086 (Oleum Gas Leak Case) (1987)*—A gas leak from Shriram Food and Fertilisers Ltd. Chemical complex in Delhi killed one person and hospitalized others. If an enterprise is engaged in a hazardous or inherently dangerous activity and harm results to anyone on account of an accident in the operation of such an activity, the enterprise is strictly liable to compensate all those who are affected, even if manufacturers of chemicals and fertilisers are engaged in activities that are fundamental to society. "[A]n enterprise which is engaged in a hazardous or inherently dangerous industry which poses a potential threat to the health and safety of the persons working in the factory and residing in the surrounding areas owes an absolute and non-delegable duty to the community to ensure that no harm results to anyone on account of the hazardous or inherently dangerous nature of the activity which it has undertaken.... [I]f any harm results on account of such activity, the enterprise must be absolutely liable to compensate for such harm and it should be no answer to the enterprise to say that it had taken all reasonable care." *Id.* para. 31.

Of these, the India Supreme Court added a unique wrinkle to the doctrine of strict liability by holding that the measure of compensation is not limited to the plaintiff's actual damages, such as medical expenses, lost wages, and the like, but rather "must be correlated to the magnitude and capacity of the enterprise because such compensation must have a deterrent effect. The larger and more prosperous the enterprise, greater must be the amount of compensation payable by it for the harm...." *Id.* para. 32. (Note that other jurisdictions may allow punitive damages in addition to compensatory damages; punitive damages are addressed below).

New Zealand courts have recognized *Rylands* as a viable legal theory, but have added a foreseeability requirement, making it quite difficult for plaintiffs to succeed on strict liability claims. In Hamilton v. Papakura Dist. Council, UKPC 9, 146 S.J.L.B. 75 (Privy Council 2002), the Hamiltons sued the defendant, a water supplier, for alleged damage caused to their tomato crops by the herbicide triclopyr. The Hamiltons claimed that the spraying of gorse had contaminated a lake from which the water supply was obtained, and that it, in turn, had caused their crops to be contaminated. The lower court rejected the negligence, nuisance, and strict liability claims. As for the latter, the Hamiltons argued that the defendant was liable under *Rylands v. Fletcher* because it had brought a hormonal herbicide onto the land, which was likely to cause damage if it escaped. The Privy Council affirmed the decision against the Hamiltons on all counts:

> The High Court rejected [the nuisance and strict liability claims] ... on the basis that, as it had already held in relation to the negligence claim, Watercare "had no reason to foresee harm to Mr. and Mrs. Hamilton's tomatoes growing as they were from the occasional occurrence of hormone herbicides in the concentration shown by the tests." The requirement of foreseeability as a matter of law under this head of claim was questioned in the Court of Appeal which concluded however that it must now be taken as clear that foreseeability is an element necessary to establish liability under *Rylands v. Fletcher* as under nuisance. The ... Court was correct in deciding that the damage complained of was not reasonably foreseeable as required to establish liability in negligence. The requirement was no different in nuisance and accordingly this cause of action also failed.

Id. para. 47. The Privy Council observed that "to require that [defendants] ... ensure that the town water supply had a zero level of triclopyr contamination would be unrealistic in this country with its agricultural based economy." *Id.* para. 31.

According to New Zealand's Justice Robert Chambers, the foreseeability requirement means that "there will never be a case where a plaintiff will succeed in *Rylands v. Fletcher* without also succeeding in nuisance.... [and] [t]here will rarely be a case where a plaintiff would succeed in nuisance without also succeeding in negligence." Negligence, Nuisance and *Rylands v. Fletcher*: The Struggle for Simplicity Continues 2 (2000), at http://www.nzila.org/conferences/docs/auckland/Justice_Chambers_negligence_and_nuisance.pdf.

New Zealand appears to follow closely on the heels of England when it comes to the modern application of strict liability. In Cambridge Water Co. v. Eastern Counties Leather,

1 All E.R. 53 (H.L. 1993), the court found that the defendants could not have reasonably foreseen that the seepage of chlorinated solvent at its tannery would migrate to Cambridge's well, situated over a mile from the tannery, causing the water to be unfit for human consumption. It held: (1) foreseeability of harm of the relevant type by the defendant was a prerequisite of the recovery of damages both in nuisance and under the *Rylands* rule; and (2) although the storage of the solvent constituted a non-natural use of the land, plaintiff's failure to establish that the pollution was foreseeable under the circumstances meant that the claims must fail.

Causation — Regardless of the type of tort claim asserted, the challenges facing a plaintiff in an environmental lawsuit are daunting, particularly when it comes to proof of causation.

> Adjudicating toxic tort suits is uniquely challenging. Toxic substances and the harms they cause have certain traits that make evaluating victims' claims of injury particularly difficult. By necessity, courts and juries rely on the opinion testimony of experts, testimony that is itself often drawn from "the frontiers of existing scientific knowledge." Legal institutions designed to prevent and redress harms caused by these substances are frequently strained as they are called upon to apply doctrines of causation and evidentiary sufficiency to such testimony. Assessing the evidentiary value of expert scientific testimony by attempting to fit its assertions into these legal categories has many inherent risks, not the least of which is the potential for non-specialists to apply naïve norms of reasoning to scientific data and, in this way, to arrive at mistaken conclusions concerning the weight, sufficiency and correctness of the evidence being presented. When judges and juries make such a mistake, the legal consequences can be disturbingly severe. A victim who was harmed (perhaps gravely) by a toxic substance may be uncompensated for that injury, while the manufacturer of the substance will be allowed to profit by externalizing social costs of its profit-seeking activities; or else damages may be paid to a plaintiff whose injuries were not attributable to the substance, and manufacturers will be subject to incorrect economic incentives in their production of a substance with beneficial uses.

Devin Brennan, *Book Note, Toxic Torts: Science, Law, and the Possibility of Justice, by Carl F. Cranor*, 30 Harv. Envtl. L. Rev. 565, 565 (2006).

Modern environmental statutes relax some of these burdens, but plaintiffs seeking monetary damages for environmental harm, personal injury, property damage, or other types of losses have little choice but to proceed with common law claims, because most citizens' suit statutory provisions allow only *injunctive,* not monetary, relief, to successful claimants. Although some citizens' suit provisions authorize a court to impose penalties on the polluter, penalties typically go to the government rather than to the citizen plaintiff. *See, e.g.,* Clean Water Act, 33 U.S.C. § 1365(a).

Remedies for successful tort claims include injunctive relief to stop or abate the pollution, as well as monetary damages to compensate for personal injury, property damage, and lost business, and, occasionally, punitive (or exemplary) damages. Punitive damages caused by reckless or willful conduct have been awarded in cases involving pesticide use, oil spills, and a variety of other types of environmental harms. A punitive damages claim against Exxon-Mobil for the wreck of the *Exxon-Valdez* is described in Chapter 4.A, *infra.*

Even so, common law claims "fall well short of providing comprehensive and systematic environmental protection." Paul Muldoon et al., An Introduction to Envi-

RONMENTAL LAW AND POLICY IN CANADA 46 (2009). Might there be some advantages to common law claims versus regulatory action? Those who oppose "big government" and "command and control" approaches to pollution control say so. At least in theory, private tort litigation might "enhance environmental protection without sacrificing individual rights or economic liberty, … safeguard environmental values without expanding government control of Americans' lives, and … find solutions grounded in market institutions, not regulatory bureaucracies." Adler, *supra,* at 656.

Notes and Questions

1. Imagine a scenario where your neighbor, a coal-fired power plant, emits various air pollutants, including particulate matter (dust), sulfur dioxide (acid rain), and mercury, along with carbon dioxide and other greenhouse gases, from its facilities. Your house is a mile or so away from the plant, but some of the pollutants from the plant disperse and then fall onto the roof of your house, your garden, and even onto your body when you are outdoors. Occasionally, you see fine brown dust on the hood of your car that you suspect may be from the power plant, and sometimes you have a sore throat from the dust, but otherwise you can't see, smell, or feel the air pollutants. Your youngest daughter has developed a severe case of asthma, but to your knowledge no one else in your family has ever had this problem. Meanwhile, the summer temperatures have risen significantly over the course of the past few years and precipitation has fallen off dramatically, and you are no longer able to grow as many vegetables as before. Newspaper reports quote scientists who attribute these changes to global warming. How useful will any of the tort theories described above be in a lawsuit against the power company? Can you think of other types of claims that might be asserted? With respect to damages caused by climate change, see Section C, below.

2. When it comes to common law tort claims, if you or your client suffered an environmental harm such as personal injury or property damage, what type of claim would suit you best? What if instead you or your client were accused of causing an environmental harm?

C. Climate Change and the Public Trust Doctrine

Parties seeking to combat climate change through common law claims have had an especially difficult time in court. In Alec L. v. Jackson, ___ F. Supp.3d ___, 2012 WL 1951969 (D.D.C. May 31, 2012), a United States district court dismissed a lawsuit alleging that federal agencies had violated their fiduciary duties to protect the atmosphere as a common resource under the public trust doctrine. The court held that the plaintiffs' public trust claims did not present a federal question over which the court had jurisdiction. It cited the U.S. Supreme Court's decision in American Elec. Power Co. v. Connecticut, 131 S. Ct. 2527 (2011), which held that federal common law nuisance claims seeking to enjoin greenhouse gas emissions were non-justiciable under the political question doctrine. Notably, in *AEP*, the Court did not reach the issue of whether *state* common law claims would also be barred.

What is the public trust doctrine anyway, and how likely are other Commonwealth countries to support public trust claims to curtail greenhouse gas emissions or otherwise address climate change? The doctrine is typically invoked to ensure access to navigable rivers and tidal lands, *see* Illinois Central R.R. Co. v. Illinois, 146 U.S. 387 (1892), but there is a historic basis for expanding its parameters. Professor Barresi explains:

> The public trust doctrine is an invention of the English common law, but with roots in the Roman civil law's concept of res communis. In the sixth century C.E., the Institutes of Justinian restated the Roman rule as follows: "By the law of nature these things are common to mankind—the air, running water, the sea, and consequently the shores of the sea." The public acquired certain usufructuary rights in these resources by virtue of its common property interest in them. For example, all rivers and ports were public such that everyone had a right to fish in them ... Finally, everyone had a right to navigate rivers ...
>
> By the thirteenth century, the English common law had absorbed the Roman concept, but added to it the idea that the Crown owned the property in question, at least insofar as it was comprised of the beds of navigable waters ... Moreover, the common law prohibited the Crown from alienating these lands ... The common law thus transformed the Roman concept of common property to which the public had certain usufructuary rights into an English concept of a public trust that prohibited the Crown from alienating royal lands so as to impair certain types of public uses of them.
>
> Despite the later spread of the English common law tradition throughout the British Empire, few former British colonies have embraced the common law public trust doctrine with much enthusiasm, although some have adopted constitutional or statutory provisions that impose on the state trust or other obligations with respect to natural resources, the environment generally, or other matters. India and the United States are notable exceptions to this pattern. Both have developed robust bodies of case law interpreting and elaborating on the public trust doctrine.

Paul A. Barresi, *Mobilizing the Public Trust Doctrine in Support of Publicly Owned Forests as Carbon Dioxide Sinks in India and the United States,* 23 Colo. J. Int'l Envtl. L. & Pol'y 39, 47–50 (2012).

If the United States is one of few countries with a "robust" body of public trust law, the *Alec L.* case cited above must be highly discouraging to climate change plaintiffs. Indeed, relying upon the doctrine to impose a duty on governments to combat climate change, whether in the U.S. or elsewhere, significantly stretches the doctrine beyond its historic roots. But Professor Barresi argues that such arguments might gain traction in India, citing the *Mehta v. Nath* case, which is described above.

> No Indian court has considered whether the protection of public trust resources for their favorable impacts on climate is a protected public use. What the Indian Supreme Court has done, however, is manifest a clear concern for the ecological value of public trust resources, including forests, as well as a general willingness to expand the universe of protected public uses far beyond its traditional bounds. In holding in *Mehta v. Nath* [(1997) 1 S.C.C. 388, at 22, 36] that the State of Himachal Pradesh had violated the public trust doctrine by leasing protected forest land to a private company [to build a motel resort], the court repeatedly emphasized the forest's ecological fragility, and in dicta clearly contemplated that the Indian public trust doctrine would apply to all "ecologically fragile lands." In doing so, the court argued that ecological factors—apparently including ecologically defined public uses—should be used to identify which public resources are subject to the public trust doctrine in the first place. More-

over, in declaring in *Reliance Industries* [SCC Civ. App. No. 4273, at 16–21 (2010)] that the public trust doctrine applies to natural gas, the Court defined the public use value of the gas solely in economic and development terms, which is well outside the universe of public uses traditionally protected by the doctrine. If the Indian Supreme Court is willing to recognize mere economic or development value as a protected public use of a public trust resource, then there is little reason to believe that it would refuse to do the same with respect to CO2 sequestration by forests as a means of mitigating climate change in appropriate circumstances.

Id. at 73–74. Remarkably, in the *Mehta v. Nath* case, the Indian Supreme Court not only invalidated the offending leases as a breach of the public trust, it also ordered the company to pay for the ecological restoration of the leased land as well as adjacent lands adversely affected by the company's efforts to protect its leased land from flooding. *Id.* at 57.

To date, Indian courts have not decided a case based exclusively on climate change damages. "[W]hilst there have been a number of actions [in India], based on constitutional rights to life, addressing the effects of air pollution, there has not yet been litigation focused on [greenhouse gas] emissions or climate change, although there is the potential." Tracy D. Hester, *Private Claims for a Global Climate: U.S. and Indian Litigation Approaches to Climate Change and Environmental Harm*, International Seminar on Global Environment and Disaster Management: Law and Society, New Delhi, India, July 23, 2011.

For in-depth analysis of the "atmospheric public trust," see Mary C. Wood, Nature's Trust: Environmental Law for a New Ecological Age (forthcoming 2013). For perspectives on how the public trust doctrine can assist efforts to adapt to a changing climate, see Robin Kundis Craig, *Adapting to Climate Change: The Potential Role of State Common-Law Public Trust Doctrines*, 34 Vt. L. Rev. 781 (2010). And for discussion of the public trust doctrine in Canadian water law, see Ralph Pentland, *Public Trust Doctrine—Potential in Canadian Water and Environmental Management* 2 (2009), available at http://poliswaterproject.org/sites/default/files/public_trust_doctrine.pdf (noting that Canadians have been slow to embrace the concept).

Other than the public trust doctrine, can other types of common law claims be effective in combating climate change or in obtaining remedies for resources lost to a changing climate? Plaintiffs alleging negligence and/or nuisance against power companies or large manufacturing plants due to emissions of gases from their factories or other facilities have not fared terribly well in American courts, as the following cases illustrate:

- *American Elec. Power Co., Inc. v. Connecticut, 131 S.Ct. 2527 (2011)*—The U.S. Supreme Court held that the federal Clean Air Act, which authorizes the Environmental Protection Agency (EPA) to place limits on carbon dioxide emissions from power plants, displaces any federal common law right to seek abatement of emissions.

- *Comer v. Murphy Oil USA, Inc., 839 F.Supp.2d 849 (S.D. Miss. 2012)*—Mississippi property owners sued several of the largest oil, coal, and chemical companies, asserting public and private nuisance, trespass, and negligence claims based on companies' release of greenhouse gases, which allegedly led to development of conditions that formed hurricanes, caused sea levels to rise, and resulted in higher insurance premiums. The court held that the plaintiffs lacked standing and that the companies' emissions were too remote to be proximate cause of owners' damages.

- *Native Village of Kivalina v. ExxonMobil Corp., 663 F. Supp. 2d 863, 881 (N.D. Cal. 2009) aff'd on other gds., 696 F. 3d 849 (2012)* — A Native Alaskan village sued oil, energy, and utility companies for public nuisance, alleging that the defendants' emissions of greenhouses gases contributed to global warming, which in turn caused melting and erosion of Arctic sea ice, which in turn threatened to inundate the village. The court found that plaintiffs lacked standing to bring suit, because global warming phenomenon dated back centuries and was the result of emissions of gases by many different sources. Standing requires proof of a substantial likelihood that the defendant's conduct caused plaintiff's injury in fact, but the plaintiffs' claim "was dependent on a series of events far removed both in space and time from the defendants' alleged discharge of greenhouse gases."

- *Barasich v. Columbia Gulf Transmission Co., 467 F. Supp. 2d 676 (E.D. La. 2006)* — Plaintiffs' class action alleged that oil and gas producers and pipeline companies contributed to two hurricanes' destructive effects on the Gulf Coast. The court held that the plaintiffs were not entitled to recovery under La. Civ. Code Ann. art. 667, which codified nuisance law by limiting the use of one's property where it damages neighboring property. The court reasoned that the statute was intended to impose obligations on owners of properties that lay physically close to one another, but not on parties whose properties were hundreds of miles apart. As for the negligence claims, the court found that the plaintiffs would be unable to show that the defendants owed a duty to hundreds of thousands of plaintiffs to protect them from the results of coastal erosion allegedly caused by actions that were physically and proximately remote from the plaintiffs and their property, nor would the plaintiffs be able to show that the defendants' conduct was a cause-in-fact of their injuries.

Similarly, Canadian climate change claimants will likely have a difficult time proving a breach of the duty of care owed to the plaintiff as well as causation. Canadian courts typically adhere to the "but for" test of causation. With respect to harm stemming from greenhouse gases, it is very difficult to attribute harm to a single defendant or even a specific industrial sector. Canadian courts may apply a "material contribution" test, but only under limited circumstances. In Resurface Corp. v. Hanke, 2007 SCC 7 at para 25, the Canadian Supreme Court stated that the "but for" approach is not applicable only if it is "impossible for the plaintiffs to prove that the defendant's negligence caused the plaintiff's injury using the but for test … due to factors outside the plaintiff's control." Further, "it must be clear that the defendant breached a duty of care owed to the plaintiff … exposing [the plaintiff] to unreasonable risk of injury," and that the plaintiff suffered from that injury. Canadian plaintiffs may have an equally difficult time relying on the "market share" theory of causation. Although the doctrine has been legislatively adopted, no court has applied the theory. *See* Shi-Ling Hsu, *A Realistic Evaluation of Climate Change Litigation Through the Lens of a Hypothetical Lawsuit*, 79 U. Colo. L. Rev. 701 (2008). The following cases are instructive:

- *Gariepy v. Shell Oil Co., 51 O.R. (3d) 181, 1 C.P.C. (5th) 120 (2000); Insurance Corp. of British Columbia v. Leland, B.C.J. No. 2073 (1999).* These cases briefly discuss the "market-share" theory of causation but do not adopt it.

- *Hollick v. Toronto, 3 S.C.R. 158, 2001 SCC 68.* The Supreme Court of Canada upheld a decision not to certify the class action of 30,000 people living near a City of Toronto landfill.

- *Pearson v. Inco, O.J. No. 4918 (C.A.) (2005).* The Ontario Court of Appeal certified a class action in relation to alleged environmental damages caused by long-term emissions from a nickel refinery in the Port Colborne area. The case was initially brought against municipal, regional, and provincial governments along with corporate defendant Inco, alleging both health and property impacts. The plaintiff withdrew the claims and brought the case again with fewer claimants and focusing on property devaluation alone.

- *Hickey v. Electric Reduction Co., 21 D.L.R. (3d) 368 (Nfld. S.C.) (1970).* A fishermen's group brought suit for a toxic spill that polluted waters, killing the fish that the plaintiffs relied upon. The court dismissed the case finding that, because fishing was a right enjoyed by all, the plaintiffs failed to show an injury that was different in kind to support a public nuisance theory. The court further required plaintiffs' injuries to be a "direct and not consequential" result of the defendants' actions.

How might a plaintiff or group of plaintiffs get around the jurisdictional and substantive defenses, particularly lack of causation, given this line of precedent? Is the pursuit of common law climate change claims completely hopeless? Perhaps plaintiffs will have better luck in Europe.

> The regulatory response to climate change in Europe is nothing if not diverse, including market mechanisms, information mechanisms and command-and-control type regulation. At present, administrative liability mechanisms have not been shaped by or for climate change, and background civil liability laws are little explored. … [A]ll too obvious limits to the administrative regulation of climate change, in terms of both ambition and achievement, turn attention to individualised forms of law, via tort forms of liability. … Liability is not just "the question to what extent victims of climate change could use the liability system to obtain compensation for damages resulting from climate change (the more traditional liability setting) but equally the question of to what extent civil liability and the courts in general may be useful to force potential polluters (or governmental authorities) to take measures to reduce (the effects of) climate change."

Maria Lee, *Book Review*, 24 J. Env. L. 385, 387 (2012), quoting Michael Faure and Marjan Peeters, Climate Change Liability (2011).

D. The Alien Tort Claims Act

The Alien Tort Claims Act, originally enacted by the U.S. Congress as part of the Judiciary Act of 1789, is a possible vehicle for international plaintiffs seeking redress for environmental harms in U.S. courts. Judiciary Act of 1789, ch. 29, §9, 1 Stat. 73, 77 (current version codified at 28 U.S.C. §1350). The ATCA initially made no assertions about legal rights, stating only that "the district courts shall have original jurisdiction of any civil action by an alien for a tort only, committed in violation of the law of nations or a treaty of the United States." 28 U.S.C. §1350.

Prior to the 1980s, the ATCA saw little action. Filartiga v. Pena-Irala, 630 F.2d 876 (2d Cir. 1980), opened the door for wider use when the court held that a violation of universally accepted norms of international human rights law constitutes a violation of the domestic law of the United States, thus giving rise to a claim under the ATCA whenever the perpetrator is properly served within the United States. *Id* at 886–887 & n. 21.

To bring a claim under ATCA, often called the Alien Tort Act (ATA) plaintiffs must satisfy three elements: (1) they are aliens, (2) suing for a tort, and (3) the tort violates the law of nations or a treaty of the United States. What is an "alien" for purposes of the

ATCA? *See* Al-Aulaqi v. Obama, 727 F.Supp.2d 1 (D.D.C. 2010) (holding that a Yemeni father was not authorized to bring a claim on behalf of his son, who was a U.S. citizen allegedly targeted for killing by the U.S. as a suspected terrorist, as the son was not within the class of persons who could have sued under the Act).

Absent an applicable treaty provision, the third element of the ATCA, in particular, causes hurdles for plaintiffs. *See* Pauline Abadie, *A New Story of David and Goliath: The Alien Tort Claims Act Gives Victims of Environmental Injustice in the Developing World A Viable Claim Against Multinational Corporations*, 34 Golden Gate U. L. Rev. 745 (2004). Courts have required that for a norm to be actionable under the ATCA it must be specific or definable, universal, and obligatory. *See, e.g.,* In re Estate of Ferdinand Marcos Human Rights Litig., 25 F.3d 1467, 1475 (9th Cir. 1994); Tel-Oren v. Libyan Arab Republic, 726 F.2d 774, 781 (D.C. Cir. 1984) (Edwards, J., concurring); Beanal v. Freeport-McMoran, Inc., 969 F. Supp. 362, 370, 383 (E.D. La. 1997). What might be considered definable and universal? The Supreme Court construed these concepts narrowly in Sosa v. Alvarez-Machain, 542 U.S. 692 (2004), which held that the customary international norms utilized in an ATCA suit must be comparable to the international law rules recognized at the time the ATCA was enacted. *See id.* at 732 (stating that, in the absence of a treaty or applicable legislative act or judicial decision, "federal courts should not recognize private claims under federal common law for violations of any international law norm with less definite content and acceptance among civilized nations than the historical paradigms familiar when § 1350 was enacted").

Environmental claims tend to take either of two directions under the ATCA. First, the claim may be brought under the norms of international environmental law, which includes the entirety of public and private international law that is relevant to environmental issues. *See* Kathleen Jaeger, *Environmental Claims Under the Alien Tort Statute*, 28 Berkeley J. Int'l L. 519, 523 (2010). Second, the claim may be based on international human rights law. *Id.* at 524. Plaintiffs have had somewhat more success using the latter approach, but either way it is an uphill battle, as the following cases illustrate:

- *Amlon Metals, Inc. v. FMC Corp, 775 F. Supp. 668 (S.D.N.Y. 1991).* Plaintiffs alleged that defendants had failed to ensure that copper residue shipped to England was free from harmful impurities and was not toxic to transport. Bringing suit under the ATCA, plaintiffs relied on Principle 21 of the Stockholm Declaration, which grants States the right to "exploit their own resources pursuant to their own environmental policies" but also imposes the "responsibility to ensure the activities within their jurisdiction or control do not cause damage to the environment of other States or of areas beyond the limits of national jurisdiction." *Id.* at 671 (quoting Report of the U.N. Conference on the Human Env't, Stockholm, Swed., June 5–16, 1972, Declaration of Principles [Stockholm Declaration], principle 21, U.N. Doc. A/CONF.48/14, reprinted in 11 I.L.M. 1416 (1972)). The court ruled that the Principles were not sufficiently specific to base an ATCA cause of action, stating they "do not set forth any specific proscriptions, but rather refer only in a general sense to the responsibility of nations to insure that activities within their jurisdictions do not cause damage to the environment beyond their borders." *Id.* at 671.

- *Aguinda v. Texaco Inc., 945 F. Supp. 635 (S.D.N.Y. 1996), vacated by Jota v. Texaco, Inc., 157 F.3d 153 (2d Cir. 1998), aff'd Aguinda v. Texaco Inc. 303 F.3d 470 (2d Cir. 2002).* This case arose out of Texaco's oil explorations in Equador, where plaintiffs alleged the company disposed of inadequately treated hazardous waste resulting in the destruction of tropical rain forest and causing harm to local forest dwellers. The cases were dismissed on three separate grounds: (1) forum non conveniens; (2) international comity; (3) the plaintiffs' failure to join other indispensable parties. The court remarked, "[P]laintiffs' imaginative view of this Court's power must face the reality that United States district courts are courts of limited jurisdiction. While their power within those limits is substantial, it does not include a general writ to right the world's wrongs." 945 F.Supp. at 628.

- *Beanal v. Freeport-McMoran, Inc., 969 F. Supp. 362 (E.D. La. 1997), aff'd, 197 F.3d. 161 (5th Cir. 1999).* Plaintiff accused a mine operator of committing environmental torts, cultural genocide, and other human rights abuses by causing "pollution, alteration, and contamination of natural waterways," deforestation, and destruction of physical surroundings. The court rejected plaintiff's reliance on three broad international principles (the Polluter Pays Principle, the Precautionary Principle, and the Proximity Principle), stating they "do not constitute international torts for which there is universal consensus in the international community as to their binding status and their content." The court went a step further and specified that the principles applied only to members of the international community, and that non-state corporations could only be bound to the principles by treaty. *Id.* at 384. The decision was affirmed by the Court of Appeals, which noted "federal courts should exercise caution when adjudicating environmental claims under international law to insure that environmental policies of the United States do not displace the environmental policies of other governments." 197 F. 3d at 167.

- *Sarei v. Rio Tinto PLC and Rio Tinto Ltd., 221 F. Supp. 2d 116 (C.D. Cal. 2002), aff'd in part, 456 F. 3d 1069 (9th Cir. 2006), aff'd in part, reversed in part, 487 F.3d 1193 (9th Cir. 2007), rehearing en banc, 550 F.3d 822 (9th Cir. 2008), on remand, 650 F.Supp. 2d 1004 (C.D. Cal. 2009), aff'd, 671 F.3d 736 (9th Cir. 2011).* Residents of Papua New Guinea sued Rio Tinto, an international mining group, for dumping tailings into the local water system and destroying the island's environment. The plaintiffs also alleged that Rio Tinto ordered the government to quash indigenous opposition to its copper mine, and provided the military with helicopters and other equipment to use against locals. "Violence, displacement, and a devastating economic blockade of the island reportedly killed about 10,000 residents." *Sarei,* 671 F.3d at 744. The court found that plaintiffs' claims of rights to life and to health were insufficiently specific to support a claim under the ATCA because of a lack of universal consensus that perpetrating environmental harm could violate these rights. The court did agree, however, that plaintiffs had a viable ATCA claim that environmental harm violated the principle of sustainable development and the United Nations Law of the Sea (UNCLOS). *Id* at 160. The district court's decision on UNCLOS as a basis for an ATCA claim was upheld by a three-judge panel, 487 F.3d at 1196–1197, but the case was remanded on rehearing en banc on an exhaustion of remedies defense. On remand, the district court found that the plaintiffs need not exhaust remedies and had adequately stated claims based on crimes against humanity amounting to genocide and on violations of the international law of war and the Geneva Convention, but not international environmental law. *See Sarei,* 650 F.Supp. 2d at 1031 ("Individuals have an interest in obtaining a remedy for such injustices and the United States has an interest in punishing the '*hostis humani generis,* an enemy of all mankind.'").

Notes and Questions

1. For commentary on *Sarei v. Rio Tinto,* see Kari Lydersen, *Pacific Rim and Beyond: Global Mining, Global Resistance and International Law,* 23 Colo. J. Int'l Envtl. L. & Pol'y

367, 373–78 (2012) (discussing *Sarei* and other international mining disputes); Chelsea M. Keeton, *Sharing Sustainability: Preventing International Environmental Injustice in an Age of Regulation*, 48 Hous. L. Rev. 1167, 1193 (2012) (stating that the *Sarei* case, by "only granting recovery for Rio Tinto's human rights abuses, ... denies the true environmental context of the plaintiffs' harms"); Jaeger, *supra*, at 520 (concluding that "environmental law norms are not yet part of 'the law of nations' and presently environmental harm may only be addressed in an [ATCA] case where human rights abuses and environmental wrongs overlap").

2. The ATCA cases described above indicate that courts are wary of using broad environmental principles to impose specific obligations on private actors under international customary law. Is this wariness justified? Is the desire to respect the sovereign prerogatives of host nations toward development and industry a compelling reason to dismiss cases alleging environmental harm? Are there any good reasons why courts should be more skeptical of cases alleging environmental harm than those alleging torture or discrimination?

3. In *Kiobel v. Royal Dutch Petroleum Co.*, 621 F.3d 111 (2nd Cir. 2010), the court rejected claims by victims of torture, false imprisonment, and extrajudicial executions on the ground that corporations could not be held liable. According to the court, "corporate liability has not attained a discernable, much less universal, acceptance among nations of the world ... and it cannot form the basis of a suit under the ATS...." *Id.* at 148.

> [The] States of the world, in their relations with one another, have determined that moral and legal responsibility for heinous crimes should rest on the individual whose conduct makes him or her "'*hostis humani generis,* an enemy of all mankind.'"... Nothing in this opinion limits or forecloses suits under the ATS against a corporation's employees, managers, officers, directors, or any other person who commits, or purposefully aids and abets, violations of international law. Moreover, nothing in this opinion limits or forecloses corporate liability under any body of law *other than the ATS*—including the domestic statutes of other States....

Id. at 149 (emphasis supplied). The U.S. Supreme Court granted certiorari, 132 S.Ct. 472 (2011), and arguments were held in 2012. In an unusual move, the Court subsequently ordered that the case be reargued and requested supplemental briefs on "[w]hether and under what circumstances the Alien Tort Statute allows courts to recognize a cause of action for violations of the law of nations occurring within the territory of a sovereign other than the United States [*i.e.,* Nigeria]." 132 S.Ct. 1738 (2012). Notably, other U.S. courts have exercised remedial jurisdiction in extraterritorial cases. *See, e.g., Filartiga v. Pena-Irala,* 630 F. 2d 876 (2d Cir. 1980) (allowing suit by a Paraguayan against another Paraguayan for violations of international law that occurred in Paraguay when the alleged torturer was found and served with process within the U.S.) (cited with approval in *Sosa v. Alvarez-Machain,* 542 U.S. 692 (2004)).

Chapter III

Environmental Impact Assessment

In 1970, the United States Congress adopted a path-breaking new environmental law, the National Environmental Policy Act (NEPA), 42 U.S.C. §4331 *et seq.* NEPA requires federal agencies to study the environmental impacts of major federal actions and to compare the impacts of alternatives to the proposed action in an open and responsive manner. While these analyses are called environmental impact statements (EISs) in the United States, the NEPA model has been adopted by over 100 nations, many of which call their analyses Environmental Impact Assessments (EIAs). "Born in the United States, [the EIS/EIA requirement] was initially ignored, then (in turn) caused great disturbance and antagonism, began to change people's lives for the better, settled down and learned from experience, became respectable, and, eventually, was extensively imitated all over the world." Christopher Wood, Environmental Impact Assessment: A Comparative Review xvi (2nd ed. 2003).

The relatively rapid spread of the EIA phenomenon is unique, in that its "international codification took place unilaterally without the mandate of an explicit multilateral environmental agreement or treaty." Caleb W. Christopher, *Success by a Thousand Cuts: The Use of Environmental Impact Assessment in Addressing Climate Change*, 9 Vt. J. Envtl. L. 549, 553–54 (2008). As Mr. Christopher explains, "All EIA laws and regulations share the overarching goal of encouraging government agencies to 'stop, look and listen' to the environmental impacts of an action, approval or policy, and to consider the integration of environmental stewardship with their own development goals." *Id.* at 554. Not all EIA laws are equally effective, though. Some are relatively narrow in terms of their scope (who and what actions they cover), some (but not all) require adverse effects to be mitigated, some (but not all) require monitoring to ensure that the effects of the proposal turn out to be as expected, and some (but not all) provide multiple layers of public involvement and independent review. For a comprehensive assessment of EIA systems, see Wood, Environmental Impact Assessment, *supra*.

Sustainable development—a persistent theme in international environmental law—is a common goal of many if not most EIA requirements. The 1987 Brundtland Report, *Our Common Future,* defines sustainable development as "development that meets the needs of the present without compromising the ability of future generations to meet their own needs." World Commission on Environment and Development, Our Common Future 43 (Oxford 1987). In other words, "[s]ustainability is a relationship between dynamic human economic systems and larger, dynamic, but normally slower-changing ecological systems ... in which the effects of human activities remain within bounds so as not to destroy the health and integrity of self-organizing systems." Bryan G. Norton, *A New Paradigm for Environmental Management*, in Ecosystem Health 25 (1992).

A management philosophy based on sustainable development reorients the use and allocation of natural resources to ensure not just immediate returns for present generations but also their availability for future generations. Resource consumption occurs only in a time, place, and manner that allows regeneration and continuity into the future. The concept of sustainable development also strives for intergenerational equity and distributive justice in the access to essential resources among human communities, be they wealthy or impoverished. Sandra Zellmer, *A Preservation Paradox: Political Prestidigitation and an Enduring Resource of Wildness,* 34 Envtl. L. 1015, 1038 (2004).

The precautionary principle may be one way to address sustainability, particularly when it comes to decisions where the direct, indirect, long-term, and cumulative effects of the decision are not certain. The precautionary principle "requires decision makers to proceed with caution (or not at all) in the face of uncertainty." *Id.* This places the burden of proof on the development proponent, who must show that their proposed activity is benign over the long run or the activity may not proceed. The 1992 Rio Declaration adopts the principle in Article 15:

> Where there are threats of serious or irreversible damage, lack of full scientific certainty shall not be used as a reason for postponing cost-effective measures to prevent environmental degradation.

Rio Declaration of the United Nations Conference on Environment and Development (UNCED), 31 I.L.M. 874 (1992).

Since 1992, many countries have begun to embrace the precautionary principle in their approach to development. Members of the European Union, for example, follow the precautionary principle in their approach to genetically modified (GM) foods by imposing a moratorium on imports of new GM products and by adopting strict labeling requirements for GM products that are used within their jurisdiction. *See* John S. Applegate, *The Prometheus Principle: Using the Precautionary Principle to Harmonize the Regulation of Genetically Modified Organisms*, 9 Ind. J. Global L. S. 207 (2001). GM foods and crops are discussed in Chapter 5 (Biological Diversity), *infra.*

Other than the procedural requirements of NEPA, and its laws governing the protection of federally listed endangered species, the United States generally does not follow the precautionary principle in its federal environmental laws. Should it, perhaps as a legally binding component of a new, comprehensive, sustainable development statute? Instead, should it adopt the principle on a case-by-case basis addressing, for example, GM foods, toxic chemicals, climate change, or other issues? What are the advantages and disadvantages of applying the precautionary principle to environmental and natural resource management issues? Consider these questions as you read about NEPA and the EIA requirements of other countries and of regional and international agreements and guidelines.

This chapter begins with NEPA and explores the parameters of the EIS process in the United States. It then turns to the EIA requirements of Canada, New Zealand, India, and England. Finally, the chapter looks at international or regional agreements and guidelines with EIA-like provisions, and considers whether any of these provisions, or the domestic EIS/EIA legislation of the five countries, can be effective in addressing climate change mitigation and adaptation. Sustainable development is an overarching theme throughout this chapter, as is the role of informational requirements and public involvement as a catalyst for environmentally sustainable outcomes. Also, because EIA requirements apply to many different kinds of development projects, ranging from pollution permitting to deforestation and beyond, studying EIA law reveals much about each nation's approach to environmental law and policy across the board.

A. The National Environmental Policy Act of the United States[1]

1. Policies and Goals

The National Environmental Policy Act (NEPA) is the granddaddy of an extended family of federal environmental statutes enacted in the U.S. around 1970, which together became the cornerstone of a new environmental era. Judge Skelly Wright provided this early description of NEPA and its statutory cohorts:

> Several recently enacted environmental statutes attest to the commitment of the Government to control, at long last, the destructive engine of material "progress." ... NEPA, first of all, makes environmental protection a part of the mandate of every federal agency and department.... It takes the major step of requiring all federal agencies to consider values of environmental preservation in their spheres of activity, and it prescribes certain procedural measures to ensure that those values are in fact fully respected.

Calvert Cliffs' Coordinating Committee, Inc. v. U. S. Atomic Energy Commission, 449 F.2d 1109, 1111–12 (D.C. Cir. 1971).

NEPA sets forth remarkably ambitious statutory goals. Among other things, Congress declared "the continuing policy of the Federal Government ... to use all practicable means and measures ... in a manner calculated to foster and promote the general welfare, to create and maintain conditions under which *man and nature can exist in productive harmony*, and fulfill the social, economic, and other requirements of *present and future generations* of Americans." 42 U.S.C. §4331(a) (emphasis added). Congress also hinted at an enduring public trust responsibility for safeguarding the nation's natural resources:

> In order to carry out the policy set forth in this chapter, it is the continuing responsibility of the Federal Government to use all practicable means, consistent with other essential considerations of national policy, to improve and coordinate Federal plans, functions, programs, and resources to the end that the Nation may:

> (1) fulfill the responsibilities of each generation as trustee of the environment for succeeding generations....

Id. §4331(b). NEPA aims primarily at federal agencies, but its policies reach well beyond the federal government. In a provision that comes as close to an environmental right as anything in federal law, Congress "recognize[d] that each person should enjoy a healthful environment...." *Id.* §4331(c). So far, so good, but the same provision goes on to state that "each person has a *responsibility* to contribute to the preservation and enhancement of the environment." *Id.* (emphasis added). Imagine if this were taken to its logical extreme, or even taken very seriously. According to Worldwatch Institute, "[i]f we are going to reverse biodiversity loss, dampen the effects of global warming, and eliminate the scourge of persistent poverty, we need to reinvent ourselves—as individuals, as societies, as corporations, and as governments." State of the World 2003, http://www.worldwatch.org/node/1042 (visited Aug. 6, 2012). Does NEPA require each American to give

---

1. This section is derived in part from Laitos, Zellmer & Wood, Natural Resources Law, Ch. 4 (2nd ed. 2012).

up sport-utility vehicles and take mass transit, and to eradicate domestic waste by composting or recycling every scrap of leftover food, paper, plastic, and glass? Beyond that, what might be required in terms of environmental *enhancement*? Compliance would be tough, to be sure, and just imagine the challenges of enforcement.

2. The EIS Requirement

Section 4332 requires an environmental impact statement (EIS) on "every recommendation or report on proposals for legislation ... and other major federal actions significantly affecting the quality of the human environment." 42 U.S.C. §4332(2)(c). Do not let the seemingly straightforward nature of this statement mislead you. NEPA has become the favorite tool of opponents of government projects to delay, reshape, or even dismantle those projects. It is estimated that at least 40 percent of all environmental litigation brought against the federal government has involved NEPA. *See* Council on Environmental Quality (CEQ), *The 1997 Annual Report of the Council on Environmental Quality, Appendix—"NEPA Statistical Tables"* 355, Tbl.1 (1997), available at http://ceq. eh.doe.gov/nepa/reports/1997/appendix.pdf.

NEPA requires agencies to "look before they leap" by taking a "hard look" at the environmental effects and alternatives to their proposals. This can be an onerous duty, but it is a limited one in that it is wholly procedural. The Supreme Court has made it abundantly clear that NEPA mandates certain procedures, but does not force any particular substantive outcome. *See* Robertson v. Methow Valley Citizens Council, 490 U.S. 332 (1989) (Other statutes may impose substantive environmental obligations on federal agencies, but *NEPA merely prohibits uninformed—rather than unwise—agency action.*") (emphasis added)).

Rather than establishing enforceable standards to effectuate a substantive right to a healthy environment, NEPA has revolutionized the way governmental agencies do business by disseminating pertinent information about their activities in a very public fashion, thereby throwing open the doors of bureaucratic decisionmaking to citizen involvement and judicial review—no small feat.

Due largely to the EIS requirement, NEPA has taken on a dual personality over the years. It has been characterized as "the Magna Carta of U.S. environmental law," as well as the "most admired" environmental statute worldwide. *See* Ray Clark, NEPA: THE RATIONAL APPROACH TO CHANGE, IN ENVIRONMENTAL POLICY AND NEPA: PAST, PRESENT AND FUTURE 15 (Ray Clark & Larry Canter eds. 1997); William H. Rogers, Jr., *The Most Creative Moments in the History of Environmental Law: "The Whats"*, 2000 U. Ill. L. Rev. 1, 31. No one can deny that NEPA has opened governmental decisions "to an unprecedented level of public scrutiny, with consequent political implications that decisionmakers ignore only at their peril." Bradley C. Karkkainen, *Toward a Smarter NEPA: Monitoring and Managing Governments Environmental Performance*, 102 Colum. L. Rev. 903, 907 (2002).

At the same time, critics attack NEPA both for going too far and for not going far enough. Perhaps the most frequently heard complaint is that the EIS requirement is a "paper tiger" that forces cumbersome, time-consuming, and expensive procedures while providing only minimal environmental benefits. More specifically:

> [NEPA] places extreme demands on agency resources, often generates little useful information, and produces a work product too late in the decisionmaking

cycle to influence the agency's course of action. Agency managers therefore have strong incentives to avoid the NEPA-mandated environmental impact statement whenever possible, which proves to be most of the time. All these observed effects are traceable to the statute's misguided insistence on comprehensiveness and clairvoyance, and they are compounded by the ready availability of judicial review to force the agency to go back and do more if it fails to produce a sufficiently comprehensive study the first time around.

Id. at 907. Other critics take a different tack. They agree that NEPA's informational requirements are environmentally beneficial, but argue that Congress should have seized the opportunity provided by the pro-environmental sentiment that prevailed at the time of NEPA's enactment and imposed rigorous *substantive* standards to protect the environment.

Despite it all, NEPA has become the "most widely emulated of the major U.S. environmental laws" domestically and around the world. *Id.* at 905. As noted above, over 100 countries have adopted an EIA requirement of some sort. In fact, the International Court of Justice held that environmental impact assessments are now such standard practice that they can be considered "a requirement under general international law." Pulp Mills on the River Uruguay p.83 para. 204 (Arg. v. Uru.) (2010), available at http://www.icj-cij.org/docket/files/135/11235.pdf. The case, brought by Argentina, involved pulp mills on the River Uruguay. In 2005, over strenuous objections from Argentina, Uruguay authorized construction of one of the largest pulp mills in the world. The Court ruled that Uruguay was obligated by treaty to consult with Argentina before authorizing the pulp mills, and that Uruguay had breached this obligation. However, the Court noted that general international law does not prescribe the scope or content of environmental assessments, but that the "sustainable development" and "equitable and reasonable use" of transboundary watercourses would be resolved in this case with reference to the 1975 Uruguay-Argentina Statute of the River Uruguay. For analysis, see Cymie R. Payne, *Pulp Mills on the River Uruguay: The International Court of Justice Recognizes Environmental Impact Assessment as a Duty under International Law*, 14 ASIL Insight 9 (2010).

Ironically, while environmental assessment requirements have gained traction throughout the world, numerous proposals in the United States have been made to amend and "water down" the statute. Congress has taken no action, but during the administration of George W. Bush, a number of executive agencies used categorical exclusions and other exceptions quite aggressively to sidestep NEPA. *See* Robert Keiter, *Breaking Faith with Nature: The Bush Administration and Public Land Policy*, 27 J. Land Resources & Envtl. L. 195, 202 (2007) (under "the Bush administration's existing hyper-aggressive oil and gas leasing program," development decisions have been accelerated and many are "being made without careful analysis"); Joshua Nathaniel, *Forests on Fire: The Role of Judicial Oversight, Forest Service Discretion, and Environmental Regulations in a Time of Extraordinary Wildfire Danger*, 84 Denv. U. L. Rev. 923, 937 (2006) (the Administration's so-called Healthy Forest Initiative "effectively dissolved many NEPA requirements by adopting the CEQ's new categorical exclusions for fuel reduction thinning projects").

Through it all, though, NEPA has proven its durability, and several of the U.S.'s more recently enacted "second-generation" environmental laws have picked up on NEPA's information-disseminating theme as their *raison d'etre*, including the Environmental Planning and Community Right to Know Act of 1986, 42 U.S.C. §§ 11001, *et seq.*, which requires corporations to provide detailed information about their use and releases of toxic substances.

Certain threshold requirements must be present before an EIS will be required: (1) an agency; (2) a proposal; (3) major; (4) federal action; (5) significantly affecting the environment. *See* Figure 1, below.

Figure 1. NEPA Flow Chart

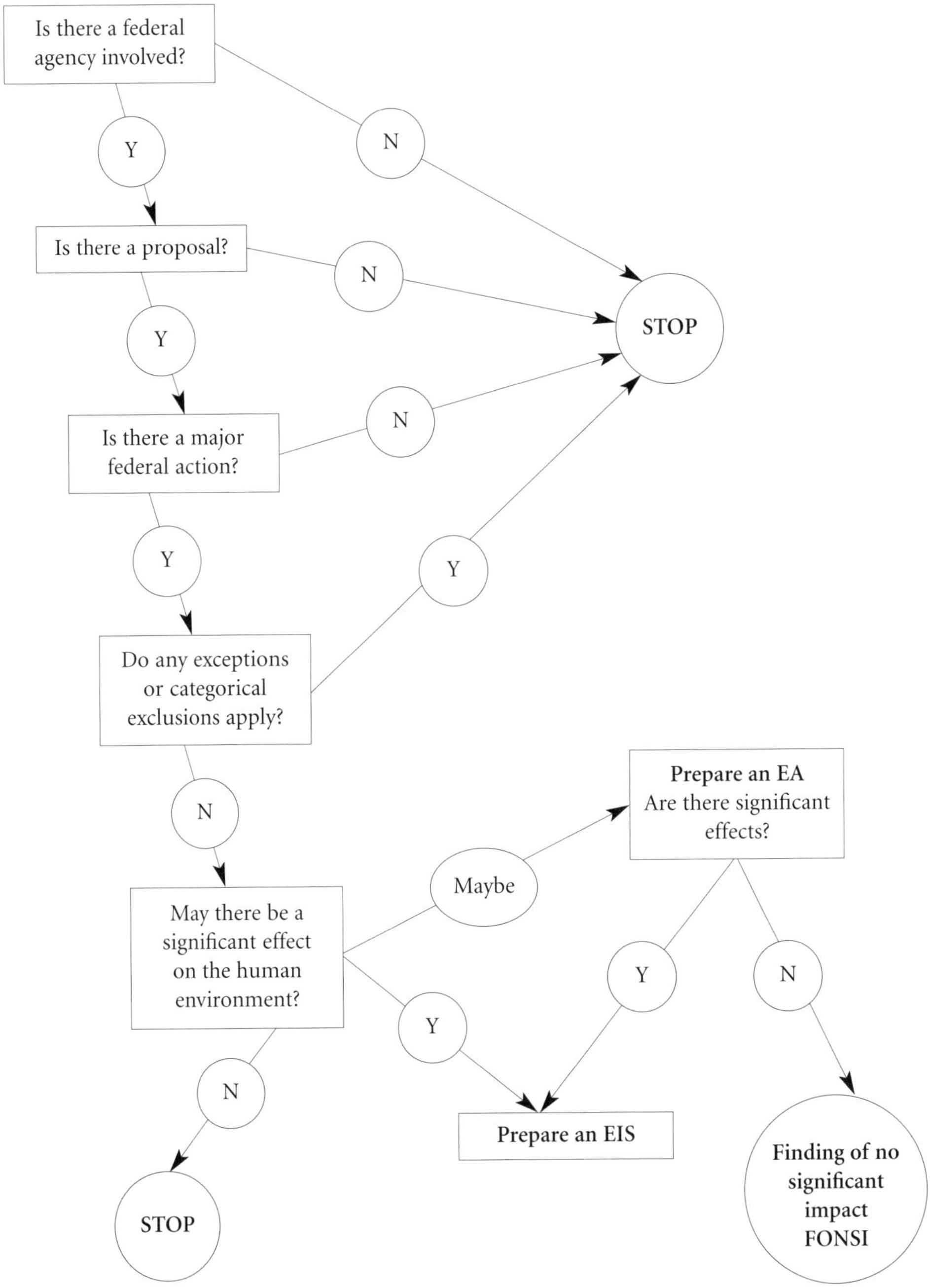

Is there a federal agency involved?

Y

N

Is there a proposal?

Y

N

Is there a major federal action?

Y

N

STOP

Do any exceptions or categorical exclusions apply?

Y

N

May there be a significant effect on the human environment?

N

Y

Maybe

Prepare an EA
Are there significant effects?

Y

N

Prepare an EIS

STOP

Finding of no significant impact
FONSI

Notes and Questions

1. NEPA is concerned with the "quality of the human environment." 42 U.S.C. §4332. The "environment," in this context, includes not only the physical environment—air, land, and water—but may also include aesthetic and socio-economic factors. *See* 40 C.F.R. §1508.14.

2. NEPA imposes responsibilities on "all agencies of the Federal Government." 42 U.S.C. §4332(C). Does it apply when the President, as chief of the executive branch and all its agencies, makes a decision? President Clinton designated dozens of new national monuments during his administration via executive order, including the Grand Staircase-Escalante National Monument in Utah (1.9 million acres), Kasha-Katuwe Tent Rocks, New Mexico (4,000 acres), and Buck Island Reef, The Virgin Islands (18,000 acres). As a result, millions of acres of federal public lands were effectively "off limits" for mining and oil and gas development. Not too surprisingly, many of the designations were highly controversial and encountered stiff local opposition. Plaintiffs sued to set certain designations aside on a variety of grounds, including NEPA. Was President Clinton required to issue an EIS for the designation of the Grand Staircase-Escalante or other national monuments? *See* Tulare County v. Bush, 185 F.Supp.2d 18, 28 (D.D.C. 2001), *aff'd,* Tulare County v. Bush, 306 F.3d 1138 (D.C. Cir. 2002), *cert. denied*, 540 U.S. 813, 124 S.Ct. 63, 157 L.Ed.2d 28 (2003).

3. NEPA is triggered by "major federal action." The CEQ regulations provide that this phrase covers actions "which are potentially subject to Federal control and responsibility." 40 C.F.R. §1508.18. Courts have construed this provision as requiring that a federal agency have some actual authority over the project. For example, in Mayaguezanos Por La Salud y El Ambiente v. United States, 198 F.3d 297 (1st Cir. 1999), the court concluded that private shipments of nuclear waste to Japan through the United States' Exclusive Economic Zone could not be considered a federal action for purposes of NEPA where the shippers voluntarily notified the Coast Guard of their transit but the Coast Guard had no authority to control the shipments under international or domestic law. And in Dep't of Transp. v. Pub. Citizen, 541 U.S. 752 (2004), the U.S. Supreme Court held that because the Federal Motor Carrier Safety Administration lacked discretion to prevent cross-border operations of Mexican trucks, NEPA did not apply. Likewise, if the federal involvement is limited to an advisory role, there is no federal action. *See* Ka Makani 'O Kohala Ohana Inc. v. Water Supply, 295 F.3d 955 (9th Cir. 2002) (concluding that the advisory actions of the U.S. Geological Survey and Department of Housing and Urban Development through the preliminary stages of a Hawaiian water transmission project did not constitute a "major Federal action").

Other circuits have agreed that the federal agency must have "actual power to control the project." *See* Ross v. Federal Highway Admin., 162 F.3d 1046, 1051 (10th Cir.1998). This will be found where "termination or modification of the agency involvement would terminate or significantly impact the project." Gettysburg Battlefield Preservation Ass'n v. Gettysburg College, 799 F.Supp. 1571, 1576 (M.D.Pa. 1992), *aff'd*, 989 F.2d 487 (3d Cir. 1993). In other words, non-federal projects will be considered "federal actions" if they cannot begin or continue without prior approval by a federal agency and the agency possesses authority over the outcome.

4. One potentially significant gap in statutory coverage involves extraterritorial activities. As a general rule, courts follow a presumption against the extraterritorial application of domestic statutes. That presumption does not apply, however, where the conduct regulated by the statute in question occurs primarily within the United States, so NEPA has been required for some federal actions that take place outside of the jurisdiction of the United States. In Environmental Defense Fund v. Massey, 986 F.2d 528, 532 (D.C. Cir. 1993), the court held that an EIS was required for a decision involving waste incineration in Antarctica, explaining that the federal agencies' decisionmaking processes were "uniquely domestic" as they took place almost exclusively in this country and involved the workings of the United States government. The court also found that the application of NEPA in

this particular context would not infringe on foreign policy or sovereignty because the United States enjoys a great deal of authority in Antarctica, which, like the high seas and outer space, lacks an independent sovereign. *Id.* at 534. *See* Executive Order 12114 § 2-3(a): Environmental Effects Abroad of Major Federal Actions, 44 Fed.Reg. 1957 (Jan. 4, 1979) (directing federal agencies to prepare environmental analyses for "major Federal actions significantly affecting the environment of the global commons outside the jurisdiction of any nation (e.g., the oceans or Antarctica)"). NEPA has been applied in a variety of other cases involving extra-territorial activities. *See* Sierra Club v. Adams, 578 F.2d 389 (D.C.Cir.1978) (applying NEPA without remarking on extraterritorial nature of Pan American highway project where the United States had two-thirds of the financial responsibility and control of the project); Natural Resources Defense Council Inc. v. U.S. Dept. of Navy, 2002 WL 32095131 (C.D.Cal. Sep 17, 2002) (NO. CV-01-07781 CAS-RZX) (applying NEPA to the Navy's sonar tests in the Exclusive Economic Zone, over which the United States had substantial legislative control).

5. Section 404 of the Clean Water Act, 33 U.S.C. § 1344, enacted in its present form only a few years after NEPA, requires mitigation when wetlands are destroyed by dredging or filling. Why doesn't NEPA require agencies to adopt mitigation plans when their projects will have adverse effects that could be avoided or mitigated, particularly if mitigation would be feasible and cost-effective? In *Methow Valley Citizens Council,* the Supreme Court concluded that NEPA doesn't require a mitigation plan, yet it does require a discussion of possible mitigation options. What good does it do to require a discussion of mitigation options if there's no compulsion to adopt them? *See Methow Valley Citizens Council,* 490 U.S. at 352; Neighbors of Cuddy Mountain v. U.S. Forest Service, 137 F.3d 1372, 1380 (9th Cir. 1998) (finding that a "perfunctory description" of mitigating measures for a timber sale was inadequate).

3. Findings of No Significant Impact, Supplements, and Exclusions

Many, if not most, NEPA lawsuits turn on the question of significance. Agencies must prepare an EIS when substantial questions are raised as to whether a project will have a significant impact on some human environmental factor. Otherwise, it may prepare a "short form" environmental assessment (EA) and Finding of No Significant Impact (FONSI) and proceed with the action without doing a full-blown EIS. To avoid preparing EISs, agencies are increasingly identifying measures to mitigate the effects of their actions and adopting those mitigation measures in their EAs, a phenomenon known as "mitigated FONSIs." *The National Environmental Policy Act: A Study Of Its Effectiveness After Twenty-Five Years* 19 (1997), available at http://ceq.eh.doe.gov/nepa/nepa25fn.pdf. This practice can save the agencies and project proponents significant time and money, and can even result in more environmentally beneficial decisions by identifying potential impacts and ways to avoid them earlier in the process. Professor Bradley Karkkainen argues that a mitigated FONSI offers an attractive bargain: in exchange for substantive measures that reduce anticipated environmental impacts below the threshold of "significance," an agency can bypass the burden of producing an EIS. Bradley C. Karkkainen, *Toward a Smarter NEPA: Monitoring and Managing Governments Environmental Performance,* 102 Colum. L. Rev. 903, 908 (2002). By the same token, however, mitigated FONSIs can erode trust in the community and result in less rigorous scientific analysis of both effects and viable alternatives.

The CEQ's definition of the term "significantly" requires considerations of both context and intensity. Significance might also be found if the action affects ecologically critical areas or other unique geographic characteristics or public health or safety. Smith v. United States Forest Serv., 33 F.3d 1072 (9th Cir. 1994). The question of significance is highly fact specific, but the regulations point out that both beneficial and adverse impacts can count as significant. Section 1508.27 provides further guidance.

40 C.F.R. § 1508.27 Significantly.

"Significantly" as used in NEPA requires considerations of both context and intensity …

(b) Intensity. This refers to the severity of impact … The following should be considered in evaluating intensity:

(1) Impacts that may be both beneficial and adverse. A significant effect may exist even if the Federal agency believes that on balance the effect will be beneficial.

(2) The degree to which the proposed action affects public health or safety.

(3) Unique characteristics of the geographic area such as proximity to historic or cultural resources, park lands, prime farmlands, wetlands, wild and scenic rivers, or ecologically critical areas.

(4) The degree to which the effects on the quality of the human environment are likely to be highly controversial.

(5) The degree to which the possible effects on the human environment are highly uncertain or involve unique or unknown risks.

(6) The degree to which the action may establish a precedent for future actions with significant effects or represents a decision in principle about a future consideration.

(7) Whether the action is related to other actions with individually insignificant but cumulatively significant impacts. Significance exists if it is reasonable to anticipate a cumulatively significant impact on the environment. Significance cannot be avoided by terming an action temporary or by breaking it down into small component parts.

(8) The degree to which the action may adversely affect districts, sites, highways, structures, or objects listed in or eligible for listing in the National Register of Historic Places or may cause loss or destruction of significant scientific, cultural, or historical resources.

(9) The degree to which the action may adversely affect an endangered or threatened species or its habitat that has been determined to be critical under the Endangered Species Act of 1973.

(10) Whether the action threatens a violation of Federal, State, or local law or requirements imposed for the protection of the environment.

Notes and Questions

1. Are the impacts of the following projects "significant" enough to require a full-blown EIS, which would provide detailed analysis of the effects of the proposal action as well as a full range of alternatives and their potential effects, or is an EA and FONSI sufficient? Why did the first case compel an EIS while the second one did not?

a. The U.S. Army Corps of Engineers issued a permit to construct an addition to an oil refinery dock at Cherry Point, a ten-mile stretch of coastline "of statewide significance" located in the Strait of Georgia in Puget Sound. The addition would double the berthing capacity for ships at the refinery. Potential environmental effects include those associated with the dock itself as well as the increased oil tanker traffic in the area. Ocean Advocates v. U.S. Army Corps of Engineers, 402 F.3d 846 (9th Cir. 2005).

b. The U.S. Corps of Engineers issued a permit for a mall development project located on wetlands in Florida. The Corps found that the wetlands were of "moderate quality" and were not unique or rare, and the permit required the developer to create and maintain substitute wetlands to mitigate adverse effects on bird species and other impacts. Sierra Club v. Van Antwerp, 661 F.3d 1147 (D.C. Cir. 2011), as amended (Jan. 30, 2012).

2. What if new information comes to light or circumstances change after an EA or EIS is issued but before the project is completed? In some cases, the federal agency may be required to prepare a supplemental analysis. The regulations require supplemental analyses when: (i) the agency makes substantial changes in the proposed action that are relevant to environmental concerns; or (ii) there are significant new circumstances or information relevant to environmental concerns and bearing on the proposed action or its impacts. 40 C.F.R. § 1502.9. Do the following circumstances trigger this requirement?

> In 1995, Glamis Corp. submitted a proposed plan of operations to the Bureau of Land Management (BLM) to construct and operate a huge gold mine on 1,570 acres of federal lands. The BLM prepared multiple analyses on the proposal over the course of the next few years, including a draft EIS, a supplement to the draft EIS, and a final EIS. The final EIS, which was issued in 2000, identified five alternatives of varying degrees of intensity, ranging from the actual proposal, for high intensity mining operations, to a no action (no mining) alternative. The high intensity proposal called for the removal of 450 million tons of rock and ore over the life of the project, along with three large open pits, a heap leach facility (consisting of a heap leach pad and processing ponds), a metal recovery plant, and multiple waste "tailings" piles up to 30 stories high. Numerous commentators, including the Quechan Indian Tribe, stated that the project's effects on historic, cultural, and natural resources in the area would be devastating and could not be mitigated. The BLM, in its final EIS, reviewed all of the public comments and concluded that the majority of them supported the no action alternative, i.e., denial of the proposal. Accordingly, toward the end of the Clinton Administration, the BLM denied the proposal. Several months later, after the newly elected Bush Administration took office, the BLM announced plans to adopt the high intensity proposal instead, citing political and legal concerns about denying the proposal.

For details about the case and its aftermath, see Jordan C. Kahn, *A Golden Opportunity for NAFTA*, 16 N.Y.U. Envtl. L.J. 380 (2008); Jordan C. Kahn, *Striking NAFTA Gold: Glamis Advances Investor-State Arbitration*, 33 Fordham Int'l L.J. 101 (2009)

3. Are there ever instances where federal agencies can avoid preparing an EA, FONSI, or EIS? In other words, when may they sidestep NEPA altogether? Agencies are authorized to adopt "categorical exclusions" (CEs) for certain categories of actions that normally do not have a significant impact on the environment. 40 C.F.R. § 1508.4. For example, in Help Alert Western Kentucky, Inc. v. Tennessee Valley Authority, 191 F.3d 452, 1999 WL 775931 (Table) (6th Cir.1999), the court upheld the Tennessee Valley Authority's decision to allow timber harvest without preparing an EA or EIS. The Authority (TVA) had

authorized a CE for "[m]inor non-TVA activities on TVA property authorized under contract or license … including … sale of miscellaneous … materials from TVA land." *Id.* at *3. It determined that the project in question, which consisted primarily of selective tree removal on 1.7 percent of the total acreage managed by the TVA, was a "minor" activity. Although the court found the TVA's conclusion "somewhat problematic," it deferred to the agency and allowed the project to go forward. Similarly, in Alaska Center for Environment v. U.S. Forest Service, 189 F.3d 851, 859 (9th Cir. 1999), the court upheld the Forest Service's application of its CE for "minor, short-term special uses of national forest lands" to the issuance and extension of annual permits for helicopter flights utilized in commercially-guided skiing and hiking tours.

When should a court reverse an agency's decision to invoke a CE? In Fund for Animals v. Babbitt, 89 F.3d 128, 133 (2nd Cir.1996), the U.S. Fish and Wildlife Service attempted to utilize a CE which covered non-destructive data collection, research, public safety, and education to justify its decision to authorize funding for a moose hunt in Vermont. The court held that the moose hunt, designed in large part to satisfy hunter demand, did not fit within the CE.

Was a CE warranted for the federal lease that resulted in the 2011 Deepwater Horizon explosion in the Gulf of Mexico? You may recall that eleven people died in the explosion and the Gulf was befouled with millions of barrels of oil. The NEPA analysis for oil exploration and development in the Gulf was "tiered"; in other words, there were nested layers of analysis, none of which, as it turns out, were adequate. In 2007, the federal government released two EISs: a programmatic EIS that purported to analyze the potential region-wide impacts associated with its 2007–2012 Outer Continental Shelf Oil and Gas Leasing (OCSLA) Program, and a final EIS (the Multi-Sale EIS) for eleven lease sales in the Gulf of Mexico Central Planning Area, which covered 80 million square miles, including the Deepwater Horizon site. A few months later, the government issued an EA for Lease Sale 206, which included the Deepwater Horizon project. The EA was accompanied by a FONSI, which concluded that because any potentially significant impacts associated with Lease Sale 206 had been addressed in the Multi-Sale EIS, no new or different impacts remained to be considered. In 2009, BP's drilling plan for the Deepwater Horizon project was approved without any environmental review whatsoever. The government stated that the plan was "categorically excluded" from NEPA because the danger of a blowout, and any potential environmental damage, was minimal or non-existent. Many observers disagree.

> The categorical exclusion used to approve BP's development and production plan appears in a Department of Interior manual … [which] largely endorses the use of tiering by excluding from NEPA analysis many agency actions that occur later in the OCSLA development program. The range of actions excluded by the manual is remarkable, from environmentally innocuous actions such as "approval of Sundry Notices and Reports on Wells" to those with the potential to create major environmental disruption, including "[a]pproval of an offshore lease or unit exploration, development/production plan or a Development Operation Coordination Document in the central or western Gulf of Mexico." The latter exclusion covered BP's plan….
>
> Even a cursory look at [the] invocation of the categorical exclusion for the Deepwater Horizon plan shows that … [it] is inappropriate in the context of approving drilling plans. Indeed, the [CEQ] guidance specifically uses … deepwater drilling as an example of when evolving conditions, the discovery of new risks, and the use of new technologies undercuts the justification for pre-existing cat-

egorical exclusion.... [The government] used the exclusion to sweep the potential risks of drilling a deepwater well under the rug.

Sandra Zellmer, Joel Mintz, and Robert Glicksman, *Throwing Precaution To The Wind: NEPA and the Deepwater Horizon Blowout*, 2 Geo. Wash. J. Energy & Env. L. 62, 67–68 (2011). Reform measures are being considered and some have been adopted since 2011. *See* Remarks of Michael R. Bromwich, Director of the Bureau of Ocean Energy Management, Regulation and Enforcement (Mar. 9, 2011), available at http://www.boemre.gov/ooc/press/2011/press0309.htm.

4. The CEQ may authorize streamlined NEPA procedures for emergency situations. *See* 40 C.F.R. § 1506.11. Federal disaster assistance, for example, may be covered by emergency procedures. *See* Linda Luther, CRS Report RL34650, *Implementing the National Environmental Policy Act (NEPA) for Disaster Response, Recovery, and Mitigation Projects* (2011) (describing the reconstruction of damaged levies and other rebuilding efforts in New Orleans after Hurricane Katrina, and noting that, in general, statutorily exempt and categorically excluded projects account for approximately 99% of all FEMA-funded projects undertaken annually). Although military objectives do not, standing alone, justify emergency treatment or otherwise warrant an exemption from NEPA's requirements, *see* Natural Resources Defense Council, Inc. v. Evans, 232 F.Supp.2d 1003 (N.D.Cal. 2002), the CEQ has treated Department of Defense proposals as emergencies in some cases. *See, e.g.,* Winter v. NRDC, *supra,* 555 U.S. 7 (2008) (considering the application of an emergency exemption to the Navy's mid-frequency active sonar training exercises).

5. NEPA is now over forty years old, and it "has become part of the U.S. environmental furniture." Wood, *supra,* at 359. Federal agencies have produced thousands of EISs and hundreds of thousands of EAs over the years. What has this mountain of paper accomplished? Project proponents might say that NEPA represents just one more layer of bureaucratic red tape. Although that may be true, by bringing adverse environmental effects to light and exposing them to the public, "NEPA has prevented inappropriate projects from being implemented...." *Id.* Would NEPA be more effective if it were amended to require mitigation before a proposed action could go forward? *See id.* (arguing that it would). Should post-implementation monitoring be required to ensure that the effects predicted in the EIS or EA turn out to be as predicted? What if the effects are different and more severe than anticipated in the EIS or EA? Who should pay for post-implementation monitoring and/or adaptation?

B. Environmental Assessment Requirements of Other Countries

The movement toward environmental planning and assessment has spread well beyond the boundaries of the United States. Many nations have adopted domestic laws modeled on NEPA, including Australia, Canada, Columbia, England, France, Ghana, India, Madagascar, Mexico, the Netherlands, New Zealand, South Africa, Thailand, Uganda, and Zambia. *See* Christopher Wood, Environmental Impact Assessment: A Comparative Review 3–4 (1995); UNEP/UNDP Joint Project on Envtl. Law and Inst. in Africa, Framework Laws and EIA Regulations (1996 ed. & Supp. 1998).

Although the precise application varies somewhat depending upon the jurisdiction, EIA applies to major government actions, such as the funding of an infrastructure project, adoption of an administrative rule or policy, or discretionary approval of a private development project. EIA generally requires agencies to first identify and study a wide variety of ecological and social impacts from proposed actions. Then agencies evaluate multiple alternative actions, and, to varying degrees of effectiveness, finalize an alternative that balances the agency's initial goals with environmental stewardship. While EIA may address environmental issues in a rote fashion long after decision-makers have reached consensus, it also holds the promise as a creative means of integrating conflicting public goals. An EIA's success, or failure, as a means to advance environmental goals is often rooted in the method and sincerity of its application....

EIA projects also evaluate, and sometimes implement, means of mitigating or minimizing significant environmental effects.

Christopher, *Success by a Thousand Cuts, supra,* at 555–56.

1. Canada

In 1973, just a few years after NEPA was enacted in the U.S., Canada adopted the Federal Environmental Assessment and Review Process (EARP). *See* Environmental Assessment and Review Process Guidelines Order, 188 C. Gaz. 2794 (Nov. 7, 1984) (Can.). EARP has since been revised and the relevant legislation is now known as the Canadian Environmental Assessment Act (CEAA), S.C. 1992, c. 37. The following excerpt provides the background of EARP and highlights provisions for public involvement in the assessment process. The author, Dr. William Tilleman, was appointed Judge of the Court of Queen's Bench in Alberta, Canada, in 2010.

William A. Tilleman, Public Participation in the Environmental Impact Assessment Process: A Comparative Study of Impact Assessment in Canada, the United States and the European Community
33 Colum. J. Transnat'l L. 337, 352–97, 432–35 (1995)

In Canada, the EARP ... Section 4(1)(b) states that the initiating department or agency "shall include" the concerns of the public in the consideration of environmental implication of proposals (mainly large projects affecting the government, or on government land). "Concerns of the public" can mean any environmental concern by individuals or by groups. Under EARP s 18(b), the Federal Environmental Assessment Review Office (FEARO, the Canadian CEQ-equivalent) has the responsibility of "assisting" the initiating department in the provision of information to the public, the solicitation of public response, and the publication of a summary of the public information provided to FEARO by the initiating department. This can lead to a requirement of mandatory screening.

Under EARP s 4(2), general socioeconomic effects, technology assessment, and the need for the proposal can be considered only after approval by the Minister of the Environment, in addition to the approval of the Minister of the initiating department. Under EARP s 10, the initiating department must subject the proposal to "an environmental screening or initial environmental evaluation" (IEE). The screening and IEE are chronologically equivalent to NEPA's preliminary EA.

EARP s 10(2) states that any further decisions which result from the screening or IEE, such as whether to proceed to an EIS or to exit via the FONSI, are made by the initiating department, and not delegated. More significantly, unlike NEPA, an EIS requirement never becomes a procedural requirement unless an EARP s 13 formal public hearing is called for by and through the discretion of the Minister of Environment. If the screening decision on the assessment of potentially adverse environmental effects concludes that there is no need for public review, then, under EARP s 13, regulators must further decide whether public concern is such that the proposal should still be referred for a formal public hearing, with the right of cross-examination. Before such a public hearing, the initiating department must also ensure that there is public access to the information and an opportunity to respond. In Canada, this is a lengthy process....

Federal In Canada, public review is the most prominent feature of environmental assessments. The Federal Environmental Assessment Review Process (EARP), Environmental Assessment and Review Process Guidelines Order, 188 C. Gaz. 2794 (Nov. 7, 1984) (Can.), which was inspired by NEPA, establishes federal environmental assessments for Canada:

> [The EARP is] a self assessment process under which the initiating department shall, as early in the planning process as possible and before irrevocable decisions are taken, ensure that the environmental implications of all proposals for which it is the decisionmaking authority are fully considered and where the implications are significant, refer the proposal to the Minister for public review by a Panel.

EARP applies to federal "initiating departments," which are federal departments responsible for proposals on activities for which the federal government has decisionmaking responsibility....

There are several public components in the federal process — both under the current EARP and the proposed Canadian Environmental Assessment Act. EARP requires public concerns to be incorporated into the federal departments' analysis of proposals. For initial assessments (screening), public reviews are required if the potential adverse environmental effects are significant or unknown, or where there is extensive public lobbying of the government, in which case public hearings are initiated at the discretion of the Minister.

Public review under EARP is conducted formally through review or hearing panels, comprised of members with special expertise and empowered to examine environmental effects and directly related social impacts. "Formal" hearings ... are conducted with the assistance of the Federal Environmental Assessment Review Office (FEARO), which is only partially analogous to the CEQ. FEARO, unlike the CEQ, is directly involved in federal environmental assessments in Canada and has substantially greater scope and power. For example, ... FEARO drafts the Terms of Reference for public hearings (when the hearings are ordered by the Minister).... Where there is a doubt between agencies about who is the lead ("initiating") agency, FEARO decides that question, too.

The Supreme Court of Canada recently held, in a challenge to a dam project, that the federal EARP (including public participation) was mandatory in nature, having been validly enacted pursuant to the federal Department of Environment Act. Friends of the Oldman River Society v. Canada, 7 C.E.L.R. (N.S.) 1 at 11–52 (S.C.C. 1992)....

Provincial Only a few provinces in Canada have passed EIA laws. Among these are Ontario (Environmental Assessment Act); Saskatchewan (Environmental Assessment Act); and recently, Alberta (Environmental Protection and Enhancement Act). Provincial mechanisms for public participation include the codification of the right to intervene formally and to receive advance funding. In Alberta, EIA review panels have adopted procedures whereby any interested party can appear and make submissions. Disgruntled parties have the right to appeal licences and permits which result from EIA approval decisions to the newly created Environmental Appeal Board.

Judicial Review In the United States, judicial review gives NEPA its significance.... Indeed, ... good arguments have been made that the successful implementation of NEPA requires a review of proper procedures by an independent institution such as the courts. The American standard of review for formal agency action (e.g., hearings) can depend on whether the review is based on factual or legal challenges.[253] Normally, when questions of fact are challenged, the matter is one of deference for the agency decision.... The most salient judicial statement on the matter is still found in *Citizens to Preserve Overton Park v. Volpe,* where the Supreme Court, referring to the only relevant statute of review, held that the court must consider "whether the decision was based on a consideration of the relevant factors and whether there has been a clear error of judgment." Any review must be based upon "the full administrative record that was before the Secretary at the time he made his decision." ...

In Canada, ... judicial review was until recently not available.... As a matter of law, judicial review is precluded in Canada unless all the administrative options are exhausted, and then only if the administrative body established to review the EIA committed an error of law or jurisdiction. This is quickly changing with the legislative mandate of new EIA Review Boards which will soon test the limits of EIA administrative findings.

Alternatives [In the U.S.,] alternatives must be considered.... [F]ederal agencies must not only study and describe, but "develop ... alternatives ... in proposals which involve ... unresolved conflicts concerning alternative uses of available resources." The Alternatives section is truly the heart of an EIS document ... "to ensure that each agency decision-maker has before him and takes into proper account all possible approaches to a particular project (including total abandonment of the project) which would alter the environmental impact and the cost-benefit analysis. Only in that fashion is it likely that the most intelligent, optimally beneficial decision will ultimately be made." Calvert Cliffs' Coordinating Comm., Inc. v. U.S. Atomic Energy Comm'n, 449 F.2d 1109, 1114 (D.C. Cir. 1971)....

In the United States, where the agency is ultimately responsible for the preparation of the EIS, one can look at agency procedures in determining the choice and effectuation of alternatives. Obviously, the agency does not "select" the best alternative, but it does approve or disapprove of a particular alternative. In Canada..., where the proponent is solely responsible for preparing the alternatives section, one expects to find bias in the choice of the best alternative, because the proponent who funds the project expects its choice of proposal to go forward. And, for private projects, one alternative, not several, is normally used in obtaining financing, appropriation of funds, and/or shareholder approval to proceed. This is the unfortunate reality of having private proponents not only select a proposal but also prepare the EIA documents without strong legal requirements for an objective scrutiny of alternatives to the proposal.

Thus, in Canada..., where there is no objective scrutiny of alternatives as a strict legal requirement, one does not expect to find a thorough analysis of proposals. Alternatives

---

253. The Administrative Procedure Act, 5 U.S.C. §706(2)(A), empowers a court to set aside agency actions that are arbitrary, capricious, an abuse of discretion, or otherwise not in accordance with law.

will not be scrutinized and balanced, because to do so requires more time and greater cost. Proponents can be expected to do no more than the law legally requires them to do. The result, unfortunately, is that the project which is built is not always the best environmental and economic choice....

How Government Systems Affect the EIA Process: A Look at Canada [I]t has taken many years for the Canadian EARP to become recognized as a significant procedural mechanism, and only recently did the Supreme Court of Canada uphold EARP as a valid legal process....

Although formal public hearings are common for large environmental projects in Canada, the Canadian legal system does not offer environmental law as an instrument to control arbitrary and capricious behaviour by agencies whose decisions are unlawful. Again, environmental statutes in Canada are not used as a basis for seeking injunctions or declarations, even when there is a prima facie case for relief based upon substantial evidence, and even when the challenge follows formal EARP hearings. Citizens' suits analogues, or the procedural "NEPA" mechanisms, do not yet exist in Canada. In fact ... [e]nvironmental assessment regulations, where they exist (provincially), seem to be established to advance the policy of the current government rather than to provide for procedural or substantive tools for industry, citizens, or the environmental bar. It is not surprising that in a country where freedom of information statutes are lacking, environmental laws have always been drafted to ensure broad and final ministerial discretion....

Since EARP is not a statute, and since ministerial discretion controls the decision, private complainants have great difficulty in challenging the procedural adequacy of an EIA. Although the Canadian Federal Courts have jurisdiction to entertain arguments about the proper application of federal legal matters, there is no judicial precedent that confirms the right to seek an injunction to stop projects until an EIS is prepared and reviewed—at least not without a substantial undertaking as to damages and compliance with a bond requirement. This is in contrast to the American situation, where there are environmental groups that can bring an action for a preliminary injunction to stop a project until the EIS, if required, is at least prepared. And, even though the American NEPA is not deemed to be substantive, this injunction will not be "released" in the United States until the EIS is prepared....

Conclusion Public participation may slow down the EIA process, but the real goal of EIA theory is to ensure sustainable development, no matter how long the EIA process takes.... NEPA and other EIA laws are consistent with sustainable development as long as these laws operate to force proper considerations of environmental impacts into the decisionmaking process.

Sustainable development should push—not pull—economic growth.... Today, the emphasis should be placed on promoting projects that are non-destructive and that do not deplete non-renewable resources. This "development" perspective is functional because sustainability and development are not mutually exclusive. These concepts merely suggest we promote projects based on a conservation ethic for today, balanced with the same ethic for tomorrow. Of course, this is not easy....

> In order for the sustainable development approach to be successful, individuals, the government and business must bring a new calculus to the decisionmaking table. The traditional priorities of short-run profits, quantitative growth and rational, left-brain dominance must give way to significantly modified priorities of sustainable development, increased quality of life and a better balance between right[-]brain feeling and intuition, on the one hand, and left-brain rationality, on the other. Each of us must balance environmental, social and economic interests in making decisions.

James P. Karp, *Sustainable Development: Toward a New Vision*, 13 Va. Envtl. L.J. 239, 253 (1994).

What this means is that we each need to reevaluate our development priorities, particularly from a global perspective. Internationally, we need to face the disparity in welfare between developed and less developed nations. Those countries with developed EIA laws and programs need to share their expertise and vision with the rest of the world.... Sustainable economic growth is needed in many countries; yet this economic growth need not be at war with environmental protection.

The goal of EIA laws is not to incur unreasonable environmental costs, nor is it to stop development. Instead, the goal of EIA laws in the United States, Canada, and the EC [European Community] is to promote sustainable development, but to do so carefully. This means project alternatives must be scrutinized, including the "no-go" alternative, as well as different-site and process-change alternatives. Countries that copy NEPA should therefore remember NEPA's primary goals: to prevent environmental damage, promote human health and welfare, and procedurally require detailed EIA studies that result in (and force) better government decisions relative to the proper project. The result should be sustainable economic growth....

Understandably, then, economic progress must still continue because it supports achievement of the world's environmental goals. This economic growth should be promoted only when it involves projects that improve poor countries and brings them to safer health, living and environmental standards.

Notes and Questions

1. In addition to Canada, Dr. Tilleman also addressed the EIA laws of the European Community in his article. Portions of the article relevant to the European Community, and in particular the U.K., are provided below in Section B.4, *infra.*

2. Is EIA a necessary component of sustainable development or is it too likely to be used to delay or obstruct important projects, such as necessary infrastructure for sewage treatment or drinking water supplies, through more bureaucratic red tape? Dr. Tilleman recognizes, "It is true that EIA laws stem from a policy encouraging preservation of the natural environment. However, these same laws do not foreclose an equitable balancing of economic interests." Do you agree?

3. In Canada, EIAs are reviewed by special review or hearing panels, "comprised of members with special expertise...." This function is performed by the Canadian Environmental Assessment Agency, described below. In the United States, the U.S. Environmental Protection Agency is empowered to review and "grade" EISs. If the EPA finds that the EIS is unsatisfactory, it is required by Section 309 of the Clean Air Act, 42 U.S.C. § 7609, to refer the matter to the CEQ. The EPA's findings are publicly available. *See* EPA, Environmental Impact Statement Database (updated June 25, 2012), at http://www.epa.gov/compliance/nepa/eisdata.html. The outcome of the EPA's review process is independent of any judicial review that may occur, but a negative rating could help challengers in litigation.

4. Just how important is judicial review in achieving the goals of NEPA and other EIA requirements? Should access to the courts be limited to those most directly affected by the EIS or EIA — project proponents — only? Or to environmentally friendly litigants only? Do you prefer the Canadian approach, described in the Tillman article, *supra,* or the more litigious American approach?

In the years since the Tilleman article was written, the EARP has been superseded by the Canadian Environmental Assessment Act (CEAA), which has been amended twice. In 2001, Bill C-19 was introduced in Parliament. It received royal assent in 2003 and the amendments took effect on October 30, 2003. On July 12, 2010, additional amendments to the Act took effect. The following are some of the key provisions of the CEAA as of mid-2012.

Canadian Environmental Assessment Act (S.C. 1992, c. 37)
Act current to 2012-06-10 and last amended on 2010-07-12

4. (1) The purposes of this Act are

> (a) to ensure that projects are considered in a careful and precautionary manner before federal authorities take action in connection with them, in order to ensure that such projects do not cause significant adverse environmental effects;

> (b) to encourage responsible authorities to take actions that promote sustainable development and thereby achieve or maintain a healthy environment and a healthy economy; ...

>> (b.2) to promote cooperation and coordinated action between federal and provincial governments with respect to environmental assessment processes for projects;

>> (b.3) to promote communication and cooperation between responsible authorities and Aboriginal peoples with respect to environmental assessment;....

> (d) to ensure that there be opportunities for timely and meaningful public participation throughout the environmental assessment process.

(2) In the administration of this Act, the Government of Canada, the Minister, the Agency and all bodies subject to the provisions of this Act, including federal authorities and responsible authorities, shall exercise their powers in a manner that protects the environment and human health and applies the precautionary principle....

5. (1) An environmental assessment of a project is required before a federal authority exercises one of the following powers or performs one of the following duties or functions in respect of a project, namely, where a federal authority

> (a) is the proponent of the project and does any act or thing that commits the federal authority to carrying out the project in whole or in part;

> (b) makes or authorizes payments or provides a guarantee for a loan or any other form of financial assistance to the proponent for the purpose of enabling the project to be carried out in whole or in part ... ;

> (c) has the administration of federal lands and sells, leases or otherwise disposes of those lands or any interests in those lands, or transfers the administration and control of those lands or interests to Her Majesty in right of a province, for the purpose of enabling the project to be carried out in whole or in part; or

> (d) under [certain circumstances to be described in regulations,] issues a permit or licence, grants an approval or takes any other action for the purpose of enabling the project to be carried out in whole or in part.

16. (1) Every screening or comprehensive study of a project and every mediation or assessment by a review panel shall include a consideration of the following factors:

> (a) the environmental effects of the project, including the environmental effects of malfunctions or accidents that may occur in connection with the project and

any cumulative environmental effects that are likely to result from the project in combination with other projects or activities that have been or will be carried out;

(b) the significance of the effects referred to in paragraph (a);

(c) comments from the public that are received in accordance with this Act and the regulations;

(d) measures that are technically and economically feasible and that would mitigate any significant adverse environmental effects of the project; and

(e) any other matter relevant to the screening, comprehensive study, mediation or assessment by a review panel, such as the need for the project and alternatives to the project, that the responsible authority or, except in the case of a screening, the Minister after consulting with the responsible authority, may require to be considered.

(2) In addition to the factors set out in subsection (1), every comprehensive study of a project and every mediation or assessment by a review panel shall include a consideration of the following factors:

(a) the purpose of the project;

(b) alternative means of carrying out the project that are technically and economically feasible and the environmental effects of any such alternative means;

(c) the need for, and the requirements of, any follow-up program in respect of the project; and

(d) the capacity of renewable resources that are likely to be significantly affected by the project to meet the needs of the present and those of the future....

(4) An environmental assessment of a project is not required to include a consideration of the environmental effects that could result from carrying out the project in response to a national emergency for which special temporary measures are taken under the Emergencies Act.

18. (1) Where a project is not described in the comprehensive study list or the exclusion list ... the responsible authority shall ensure that

(a) a screening of the project is conducted; and

(b) a screening report is prepared....

20. (1) The responsible authority shall take one of the following courses of action in respect of a project after taking into consideration the screening report and any [public] comments ... :

(a) subject to subparagraph (c)(iii), where, taking into account the implementation of any mitigation measures that the responsible authority considers appropriate, the project is not likely to cause significant adverse environmental effects, the responsible authority may exercise any power or perform any duty or function that would permit the project to be carried out in whole or in part;

(b) where, taking into account the implementation of any mitigation measures that the responsible authority considers appropriate, the project is likely to cause significant adverse environmental effects that cannot be justified in the circumstances, the responsible authority shall not exercise any power or perform any duty or function conferred on it by or under any Act of Parliament that would permit the project to be carried out in whole or in part; or

(c) where

(i) it is uncertain whether the project, taking into account the implementation of any mitigation measures that the responsible authority considers appropriate, is likely to cause significant adverse environmental effects,

(ii) the project, taking into account the implementation of any mitigation measures that the responsible authority considers appropriate, is likely to cause significant adverse environmental effects and paragraph (*b*) does not apply, or

(iii) public concerns warrant a reference to a mediator or a review panel,

the responsible authority shall refer the project to the Minister for a referral to a mediator or a review panel ...

21. If a project is described in the comprehensive study list, the responsible authority shall ensure that

(a) a comprehensive study of the project is conducted; and

(b) a comprehensive study report is prepared.

21.1 (1) Within 10 days after the inclusion on the Internet site of a notice of commencement of the comprehensive study, the responsible authority shall give a notice, in any manner that it considers appropriate, providing the public with an opportunity to comment on the project and the conduct of the comprehensive study....

21.2 The responsible authority shall ensure that the public is provided with an opportunity ... to participate in the comprehensive study ...

37. (1) ... [T]he responsible authority shall take one of the following courses of action in respect of a project after taking into consideration the report submitted by a mediator or a review panel or ... the comprehensive study report:

(a) where, taking into account the implementation of any mitigation measures that the responsible authority considers appropriate,

(i) the project is not likely to cause significant adverse environmental effects, or

(ii) the project is likely to cause significant adverse environmental effects that can be justified in the circumstances,

the responsible authority may exercise any power or perform any duty or function that would permit the project to be carried out in whole or in part; or

(b) where, taking into account the implementation of any mitigation measures that the responsible authority considers appropriate, the project is likely to cause significant adverse environmental effects that cannot be justified in the circumstances, the responsible authority shall not exercise any power or perform any duty or function conferred on it by or under any Act of Parliament that would permit the project to be carried out in whole or in part ...

(2) Where a responsible authority takes a course of action referred to in paragraph (1)(*a*), it shall...ensure that any mitigation measures referred to in that paragraph in respect of the project are implemented....

(3) Where the responsible authority takes a course of action referred to in paragraph (1)(b) in relation to a project, the responsible authority shall publish a notice of that course of action and ... no power, duty or function conferred by or under that Act or any regulation made under it shall be exercised or performed that would permit that project to be carried out in whole or in part ...

58. (1) For the purposes of this Act, the Minister [of Environment] may

(a) issue guidelines and codes of practice respecting the application of this Act and … establish criteria to determine whether a project, taking into account the implementation of any appropriate mitigation measures, is likely to cause significant adverse environmental effects or whether such effects are justified in the circumstances;

(b) establish research and advisory bodies;

(c) enter into agreements or arrangements with any jurisdiction … respecting assessments of environmental effects; …

(i) make regulations prescribing any project or class of projects for which a comprehensive study is required where the Minister is satisfied that the project or any project within that class is likely to have significant adverse environmental effects.

61. (1) There is hereby established an agency, to be called the Canadian Environmental Assessment Agency, which shall advise and assist the Minister in performing the duties and functions conferred on the Minister by this Act.

* * *

The Canadian Environmental Assessment Agency, a federal body established in 1994, describes its role in the EIA process as follows:

Our role is to provide Canadians with high-quality environmental assessments that contribute to informed decisionmaking, in support of sustainable development. The Agency plays a leadership role in the review of major projects assessed as comprehensive studies and those referred to review panels. We also coordinate the Government of Canada's Aboriginal consultation activities during the environmental assessment process.

Canadian Environmental Assessment Agency, Home, http://www.ceaa.gc.ca/ (visited Aug. 1, 2012). The Agency, which is accountable to the Minister of the Environment, has posted a citizens' guide for the public on its website.

When Does the Canadian Environmental Assessment Act Apply?

There are four questions to answer when determining whether an environmental assessment is required under the Act (see Figure 1).

What is a trigger?

The federal environmental assessment process is applied whenever a federal authority has a specified decision-making responsibility in relation to a project, also known as a "trigger" for an environmental assessment. Specifically, it is when a federal authority:

- proposes a project
- provides financial assistance to a proponent to enable a project to be carried out
- sells, leases, or otherwise transfers control or administration of federal land to enable a project to be carried out
- provides a license, permit or an approval that is listed in the *Law List Regulations* that enables a project to be carried out

Can a project be excluded?

A project may be exempted from an environmental assessment if it:

- is … likely to have insignificant environmental effects
- is to be carried out in response to a national emergency for which temporary special measures are being taken …

Figure 1. Determining if the Act Applies

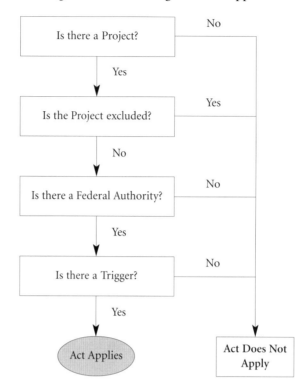

- is to be carried out in response to an emergency and the project is in the interest of preventing damage to property or the environment or is in the interest of public health or safety

Canadian Environmental Assessment Agency, *Frequently Asked Questions* (July 2, 2012), available at http://www.ceaa.gc.ca/.

Notes and Questions

1. If the EIA reveals that the project is likely to cause significant adverse effects, what must the responsible authority do? Does it depend whether the project will have positive economic effects? *See* CEAA §§ 20, 37 and Figure 1 and subsequent text, above. How does NEPA address this situation in the United States? Which approach is likely to be more effective in terms of ensuring sustainable development?

2. If the Deepwater Horizon blowout, described above in Section A.3, had occurred in Canadian waters, would the EIA have been required to include a "worst case analysis" of the potentially catastrophic effects of a major explosion or other accident? *See* CEAA § 16(1)(a). Would an EIA be required for the response to the blowout or to a similar disaster? *See* CEAA § 16(4).

3. The Agency lists the following four cases as "key court decisions" under the Act:

- *Rafferty-Alameda Dam (1989)*—Can. Wildlife Fed'n Inc. v. Canada (Minister of the Env't), [1989] 2 W.W.R. 69 (F.C.A. Can.).

The Federal Court of Appeal found EARP to be a law of general application, binding on the federal government. Accordingly, the Ministry of the Environment could not simply clear the project and issue a federal license for two dams on the Souris River based on the Saskatchewan provincial review process.

- *Friends of Oldman River Society v. Canada (1992)*—[1992] 1 S.C.R. 3.

An Alberta-based environmental group, Friends of Oldman River, sued to prevent Alberta from constructing a large dam on the Oldman River. Alberta needed to obtain a federal licence under the Navigable Waters Protection Act. The federal Minister of Transport issued the licence without conducting an environmental assessment. The Minister argued that the EARP Guidelines were not mandatory, and that, in any event, the project was a matter of provincial, not federal, concern. The Supreme Court found that the Guidelines were legally binding; EARP applies whenever the federal department has an "affirmative regulatory duty," such as its duties for navigation and fisheries.

As for the broader division of powers issue, the Court found that federal assessment of entire projects is constitutional so long as there is a federal trigger. The opinion "articulated a compelling theoretical and practical justification for dual federal-provincial jurisdiction over the 'environment' as a constitutional subject matter," Chris Tollefson, *Advancing an Agenda? A Reflection on Recent Developments in Canadian Public Interest Environmental Litigation*, 51 U.N.B. L.J. 175, 180 (2002): "The protection of the environment has become one of the major challenges of our time … [warranting a] wide variety of legislative schemes and administrative structures." The provinces have primary authority over natural resources development, but the federal government maintains control over the federal environmental review process.

- *Quebec (Attorney Gen.) v. Canada (Nat'l Energy Bd.) (1994)*—[1994] 1 S.C.R. 159, 189.

The case involved the authorization of transmission lines from a hydro-electric project. The Supreme Court held that the scope of the review under the CEAA would include not only the transmission lines carrying power out of Canada but also future construction of production facilities. In short, the Court took a broad view of federal capacity to assess the full scope of the project under review.

- *Mining Watch Canada v. Canada (2010)*—[2010] 1 S.C.R. 6.

Mining Watch, an environmental interest group, challenged the analysis for a proposal to operate a large open pit copper and gold mine in northern British Columbia under the CEAA. Comprehensive studies—extensive environmental assessment and public consultation process for projects that are likely to have significant adverse environmental effects—are required for such mines. *See* Comprehensive Study List Regulations, SOR/94-638. However, Fisheries and Oceans Canada, the federal agency involved, used the project's "scoping" provisions to exclude mine features that met the criteria listed in the Regulations in an attempt to redefine the "project" to allow a more limited type of screening level assessment.

Fisheries and Oceans argued that, as a "responsible authority" under the Act, it had discretion to define or "scope" projects as it deemed fit. The lower court held that the amendments to the CEAA in 2003 specified that the "project as proposed by the proponent"—the mining companies—determined the kind of analysis that was required. The Supreme Court agreed. The scope of the project for the purpose of environmental assessment must be the project as proposed, not as re-conceptualized by the government.

For background and analysis of the first three cases and their importance, see Oliver A. Houck, *O Canada!: The Story of Rafferty, Oldman, and the Great Whale*, 29 B.C. Intl. Comp. L. Rev. 175 (2006). As for *Mining Watch,* see Martin Z.P. Olszynski, *Adaptive Management in Canadian Environmental Assessment Law: Exploring Uses and Limitations*, 21 J. Env. L. & Prac. 1 (2010).

Case Study: Canada's Pulp Mills, Oil Sands, and Reform Proposals

Canada has a reputation for its beautiful, rugged environment. According to the Canadian Education Centre Network, a private non-profit entity, Canada is a great place to study:

> Canadians place a high value on their natural environment.... National parks are located in every province and territory, and some have been recognized as UN-ESCO World Heritage Sites.... Students who come to Canada will witness one of the most beautiful, natural environments in the world. Canada is also a country of diverse geography, and there is much to experience in its great outdoors: from the lush coastline of British Columbia, the majestic Rocky Mountains of Alberta, the big skies of the prairies, to the 'maple sugar country' in the Great Lakes and St. Lawrence and the rugged hills and picturesque coastline of the Atlantic provinces.

CEC Network, *Why Study in Canada* (2003), at http://www.studycanada.ca/english/why_study_in_canada.htm. Humans can't claim much credit for creating most of this beauty, but can those who implement and watchdog implementation of the environmental assessment process claim at least some credit for protecting it?

According to the *Canadian Geographer*, Canada's environmental strengths include lots of analysis — "land and resource analysis and mapping, institutional and procedural analyses, ... sustainable development, ... field and case study-based approaches addressing questions of how can we do things better both in Canada, and application of our expertise to resource and environmental management abroad." Scott D. Slocombe, *Resources, People and Places: Resource and Environmental Geography in Canada 1996–2000*, 44 Can. Geographer (Abstracts) 56 (2000). So far, so good, but American perspectives about Canada — and vice versa — have not always been so rosy, as illustrated in the following news article, notes, and questions.

Mary Williams Walsh, Environmental Law in Canada Comes of Age
Los Angeles Times, April 8, 1990, F1

ATHABASCA, Canada. Here in Alberta, the stands of aspens stretch as far as the eye can see, covering an area the size of Great Britain. With such vast boreal forests, with its emerald lakes and with its famously beautiful Canadian Rockies, Alberta is the stuff of tourist-poster fantasies ... But over the past few months, Alberta's pristine image has been tarnished. Critics have taken to calling the province an "environmental law-free zone." And Alberta citizens — generally a conservative, pro-development crowd — have accused provincial officials of signing away a good many of those whispering aspen trees to pulp-and-paper interests, without asking first.

The scene in Alberta reflects a number of changes on the Canadian environmental front, a ferment that calls to mind American environmentalism of the 1970s — the era of the renowned snail darter case, in which a tiny fish nearly halted construction of a huge dam.

"I don't think there's any question that there's an Americanization of Canadian environmental law going on," says Barry Rabe, an assistant professor of political science at the University of Michigan who has been comparing regulation in the two countries.... [But] differences of opinion on the subject highlight the sharp divergence of Canadian and American attitudes on the role of government in protecting society.

The assertion that America might have anything to teach Canadians about environmentalism would probably get a hoot from the average man on the street in this country. Ever since the U.S. Environmental Protection Agency, under President Ronald Reagan, backed away from bilateral talks on acid rain, Canadians have looked askance at Washington's professed concern for the air and water. "One of the things Canadians came to think was that we didn't have good laws," says Jean Hennessey, director of the Institute on Canada and the United States at Dartmouth University. In fact, she says, and other environmental analysts agree, America's laws are far stricter. "During the Reagan Administration, we just didn't enforce them," she explains.

Canada, meanwhile, has long had the luxury of a small population in a big, largely empty territory, and until lately it did not feel compelled to set American-style environmental standards on a federal level. For all its unspoiled wilderness, its sapphire skies and crystal rivers, Canada has no counterparts to America's laws prohibiting interstate transport of wildlife ... or controlling air and water quality nationwide. Fines slapped on polluters in Canada are generally lower than fines in the United States. And Canadian citizens who feel that they have been injured by industry have a much harder time suing than do their American neighbors.

Canada, on the other hand, tends to give provincial officials great power to negotiate environmental standards with industries, one on one. Lawyers on each side of the border see both good and bad in this. On the good side, the process is less adversarial, so there is less time and money wasted on courtroom stalling and maneuvering. On the negative side, by giving power to the provinces rather than Ottawa, Canada runs the risk that provincial officials will let their guard down for fear of losing industry.

Now, though, there are the beginnings of change. In Alberta, the stage was set for an environmental showdown in the mid-1980s, when provincial officials began to see in all those whispering aspens a magnificent way of diversifying the province's oil-reliant, boom-and-bust economy. They invited local and foreign forestry companies in for talks and offered incentives, including hundreds of millions of dollars in loan guarantees and infrastructure development. Before long, plans were under way for logging vast expanses of aspens, constructing seven new pulp mills and expanding three existing mills.

In the north-central Alberta town of Athabasca, local officials and business people saw what was coming to the province and lobbied hard for their share. They wanted the tax revenue. And in December, 1988, it seemed that they would be getting their wish: Alberta-Pacific Industries ... elected to build a $1.1-billion pulp mill just outside of town.... But as the proposal moved forward, and as approximately $2 billion in other pulp-and-paper investment began to take shape elsewhere across the province, the presumed beneficiaries—taxpaying Albertans—set up a howl of protest.

The Alberta-Pacific pulp mill was to be built in the hamlet of Prosperity, a clutch of about 30 farmhouses half an hour's drive from Athabasca.... The Athabasca River was to receive the effluent and carry it northward to the Arctic, into the Mackenzie River and finally into the Beaufort Sea. Prosperity grain and cattle farmer Emil Zachkewich lives just a mile from the proposed mill site. He studied the plans for the project and discovered that, based on the height of the smokestack, his home stood at the peak impact point for air emissions. Worse, he began to hear about other pulp mills leaking toxins into the soil and water. Bleached kraft pulp mills — the kind that Alberta-Pacific proposed to build — are particularly notorious for giving off organohalogens, a family of chemical compounds that includes dioxin [which] … promotes cancer. In neighboring British Columbia, Zachkewich learned, dioxin from pulp mills has turned up in such high concentrations along parts of the Pacific shoreline that the government has had to curtail crab, prawn and oyster fishing. Hundreds of seasonal fishermen were thrown out of work....

Alberta-Pacific argued that its milling techniques would be far cleaner than those of most existing pulp mills in Canada. But Zachkewich and others in Alberta … had no real way of spelling out their objections or finding out what was going on. For that is another way in which Canadian environmental law has differed from its U.S. counterpart: Until now, there have been no hard-and-fast nationwide requirements on environmental impact statements, even on huge developments such as billion-dollar pulp mills.

Canada has long had a federal "order in council" calling for such would-be polluters to submit to environmental impact assessments and offering guidelines, but no one saw how this order could be enforced. In practice, the federal government left the order to be carried out by the provinces, and the provinces haven't always lived up to federal ideals. In the case of Alberta's pulp mills, for instance, the developers were essentially permitted to write their own environmental impact statements. Alberta provincial officials say that does not mean that they caved in to industry or tried to keep secrets from the public....

"In U.S. law, there are prohibitions against people who have a conflict of interest writing the environmental impact statements," says John Bonine, a professor of environmental law at the University of Oregon.

"There was no public involvement in any land-use decisions," says Louis Schmitroth, a retired computer science professor who lives on a farm a few miles out of Athabasca. "This isn't the way you do things in a democratic society … Talk about banana republics!"

It was at this unhappy impasse that something happened in another province that changed everything for Alberta — and, perhaps in the end, for Canada. In an unrelated court case involving a dam under construction in Saskatchewan, a judge ruled that the builders had acted improperly in going ahead with the project without a full-fledged environmental impact statement meeting federal guidelines. It was a landmark decision for Canada, comparable, lawyers say, to American court cases of the early 1970s when judges began ruling that environmental impact statements were mandatory for all major federally licensed developments. Once the American judges had set this precedent, they say, groups rushed to file more suits and block other projects. Canadian lawyers now think that, for better or worse, something similar could happen here.

"Finally, animals and fishes are starting to shut projects down," Alberta environmental lawyer William Tilleman says. "This is routine in the United States, but in Canada, this was the first time."

… Environmentalists in Alberta saw their chance and filed suit against the federal government to force [Alberta-Pacific] to carry out a full-fledged assessment of a pulp mill it had planned. And in Edmonton, the provincial capital, environmental officials quickly set up a complete environmental impact assessment for the mill. The assessment may have come late, but it was extremely rigorous. A panel of experts heard public testimony for weeks, and the government even allocated funds to citizens who wanted to hire technical experts to represent them.

"That's a very admirable feature of Canadian law that is almost completely missing from environmental impact statements in the United States," Bonine says. In early March, the panel ruled that the Alberta-Pacific pulp mill should be shelved until extensive studies are done on the Athabasca River's ability to handle the effluent …

But other Canadians are less sanguine about the benefits of American-style legal actions.… A number of Canadian environmentalists perceive America, for all its stringent standards, as an excessively litigious place, and they wonder what might happen if America's adversarial spirit were to influence the Canadian way. Paul Griss, executive director of the Canadian Nature Federation, for one, says it would be "a nightmare" if Canada were to begin requiring full environmental impact statements for every new project. "The only people who would welcome that are lawyers," he says.

Notes and Questions

1. Whose perspective do you find most sympathetic? Is Canada's current environmental assessment law an appropriate and/or adequate response to the concerns raised in this news article?

2. Although Canada's environmental assessment law has been strengthened since this article was written in 1990, the fight over natural resources in Athabasca, Alberta, still rages. The most recent controversy involves oil tar sands in northern Alberta. The following notification was recently posted on the Canadian Environmental Assessment Agency's website:

> The Frontier Oil Sands Mine Project proposed by Teck Resources Ltd. would be a new 277,000-barrel-per-day oil sands mining operation located approximately 100 km north of Fort McMurray [located near the Athabasca Oil Sands]. The Project is a truck and shovel mine which includes three open pits, ore preparation plants, bitumen processing plants, tailings facilities, cogeneration facilities, support utilities, disposal and storage areas, river water intake, fish habitat compensation lake, roads, airfield, and camp. The project would have a disturbance area of 29,335 hectares [72,488 acres or 113 mi^2], resulting from four development phases. The proponent proposes to start producing oil in 2021. Mining operations would cease in 2057 with decommissioning and reclamation to be completed by 2068.

CEAA News Release, Mar. 9, 2012, available at http://www.ceaa-acee.gc.ca/050/document-eng.cfm?document=54658. What role will the public play in the review of this project? Are you confident that the environmental effects and possible alternatives will be fully vetted? Are you confident that the worst environmental effects will be avoided? Consider this 2008 report from Environmental Defence, a nonprofit group billed as "Canada's most effective environmental action organization":

> Few Canadians know that Canada is home to one of the world's largest dams and it is built to hold toxic waste from just one Tar Sands operation. Everything about the Tar Sands happens on a massive scale. The enormous toxics problems go hand-in-hand with massive global warming pollution and the impending destruction of a boreal forest the size of Florida.

> Because of sheer scale, all Canadians are impacted by the Tar Sands, no matter where they live. If you live downstream, your water is being polluted and

your fish and wildlife may be dangerous to eat. If you live in Saskatchewan you are a victim of acid rain. If you live in BC, "supertankers" may soon be plying your shoreline carrying Tar Sands oil to Asia. If you live in Ontario, you are exposed to harmful emissions from the refining of Tar Sands Oil. And the impacts do not stop at Canada's border — US refineries are re-tooling to handle the dirty oil from Alberta. Moreover, no matter where you live in Canada, your desire to tackle global warming is being held hostage to the Tar Sands. Instead of reducing greenhouse gas emissions, Canada is quickly increasing them, and fully half of that emissions growth is projected to come from the Tar Sands. Because Canada's elected officials refuse to clamp down on Tar Sands operators, they also refuse to clamp down on industry across Canada for fear of a double standard.

And it is just beginning. Approvals have already been given that will double the size of existing operations, and our leaders have been talking with the US government to grow the Tar Sands five-fold in a "short time span."

Environmental Defence, *Canada's Toxic Tar Sands, The Most Destructive Project on Earth* (2008), available at http://environmentaldefence.ca/reports/canadas-toxic-tar-sands-most-destructive-project-earth. A case study that focuses on the water-related impacts of Canadian tar sands development is provided in Chapter 4, *infra*.

3. Oil pipelines from Canada into the U.S. have proven to be equally controversial.

A Canadian company has come forward with a new application for the hotly debated Keystone XL pipeline, once again placing a crucial decision over jobs, energy and the environment in front of the Obama administration, which rejected an earlier bid to build the $7-billion structure. TransCanada filed its application with the U.S. State Department, which must determine whether the international pipeline — designed to bring diluted bitumen from the tar sands of Alberta, Canada, to a linking point in Steele City, Nebraska — is in the U.S. national interest.

Kim Murphy, Keystone XL pipeline: Canadian firm seeks U.S. permission, again, New York Times, May 4, 2012. How broadly must the geographic scope of the Canadian assessment for the pipeline extent under the CEAA? What role will NEPA play on the U.S. side of the border? Should the affected states and provinces have anything to say about the project? For a perspective from Nebraska, see Sandra Zellmer, *The Pipeline That Refuses to Die*, Feb. 16, 2012, and Sandra Zellmer, *Transcanada Says Nebraska Bill on Pipeline Routing is Unconstitutional: Here's Why They're Wrong*, Nov. 14, 2011. Both blogs are posted at http://www.progressivereform.org/CPRBlog.cfm (search Zellmer).

4. Professor Wood identifies several shortcomings of the CEAA, including its limited coverage of actions and of environmental effects, its lack of a means for ensuring that an EIA "centrally influences decisions," and its "lack of effective mechanism for ensuring compliance with mitigation and monitoring requirements." Wood, *supra*, at 362; *see* Figure 2, *infra*, p. 102. More specifically, he found:

The system is almost comprehensive but allows for the vast majority of federally controlled project EAs to be dealt with as screenings. The number of screenings in 1999–2000 was reported to be nearly 5,700. A small number of projects (less than 10 per annum) is subject to 'comprehensive study,' and an even smaller number (about two a year) to panel review, requiring the preparation of an EIS.

Id. at 71.

5. What are the relative strengths and weaknesses of the U.S. and Canadian approaches to environmental assessment? Which approach gives you the most confidence that all relevant environmental impacts of a large development project will be revealed and considered? What revisions to either system would you like to see?

6. As this book goes to press, it appears that significant changes in Canadian assessment law may be in the air. Recently, the Government of Canada proposed a new Canadian Environmental Assessment Act, 2012, "focused on improving timeliness, decreasing duplication, targeting projects with the most potential for significant adverse environmental effects and improving Aboriginal consultations." The Government explains the impetus behind its proposal:

> Government has been seeking to improve the environmental assessment process for several years as part of its broader initiative to reform the federal regulatory review process for major resource development projects. Initial steps were taken in 2010 when targeted amendments were made to the Act. Responsible Resource Development, the government's plan to further modernize the regulatory review and environmental assessment process, was announced in Budget 2012 and a new Canadian Environmental Assessment Act, 2012 was proposed as part of the Jobs, Growth and Long-term Prosperity Act.

Canadian Environmental Assessment Agency, *Government Response to the Report of the Standing Committee on Environment and Sustainable Development on the Statutory Review of the Canadian Environmental Assessment Act* (June 22, 2012), available at http://www.ceaa.gc.ca/default.asp?lang=En&xml=2F58D76C-DD91-437C-8681-6ACEEFC1236D. Some members of the public are worried about the proposed "streamlining" of the environment assessment process, particularly for energy development. "If this new CEAA becomes law, then for some types of environmental assessments, the public will still have a right to participate—but for others (notably pipeline projects)—the government may not want to hear from you unless the pipeline goes through your property or you have a degree (or other special qualifications or information)." *See* West Coast Environmental Law, *Who is Silenced under Canada's New Environmental Assessment Act?*, Apr. 27, 2012, at http://wcel.org/node/1501.

2. New Zealand

New Zealand is widely known for its dedication to sustainable development, and for its innovative, integrative Resource Management Act (RMA), Public Act 1991 No 69.

> New Zealand's domestic environmental policy framework has earned it recognition for its adoption of a holistic approach to environmental management. The Resource Management Act (RMA), 1991 is groundbreaking, comprehensive environmental legislation which has sustainable management as its cornerstone and concern over the effects of human activities as its linchpin. Wide sweeping in breadth, it replaced 59 previous resource and planning statutes, including major legislation on town and country planning and water and soil management.

Sarah Michaels and Owen J. Furuseth, Innovation in Environmental Policy: The National Environmental Policy Act of the US and the Resource Management Act of New Zealand, *The Environmentalist* 17, 181–190 (1997).

The purpose of the RMA is "to promote the sustainable management of natural and physical resources." RMA § 5.

[S]ustainable management means managing the use, development, and protection of natural and physical resources in a way, or at a rate, which enables people and communities to provide for their social, economic, and cultural well-being and for their health and safety while—

(a) sustaining the potential of natural and physical resources (excluding minerals) to meet the reasonably foreseeable needs of future generations; and

(b) safeguarding the life-supporting capacity of air, water, soil, and ecosystems; and

(c) avoiding, remedying, or mitigating any adverse effects of activities on the environment....

RMA § 5(2).

To ensure sustainable management and to facilitate an effects-based approach, the RMA requires proponents of public and private projects requiring permits (or consents) to submit an Assessment of Environmental Effects (AEE) to the permitting authority. RMA § 88(2)(b). AEEs should include the following topics:

(a) a description of the proposal:

(b) where it is likely that an activity will result in any significant adverse effect on the environment, a description of any possible alternative locations or methods for undertaking the activity; ...

(d) an assessment of the actual or potential effect on the environment of the proposed activity;

(e) where the activity includes the use of hazardous substances and installations, an assessment of any risks to the environment which are likely to arise from such use;

(f) where the activity includes the discharge of any contaminant, a description of—

(i) the nature of the discharge and the sensitivity of the proposed receiving environment to adverse effects; and

(ii)any possible alternative methods of discharge, including discharge into any other receiving environment;

(g) a description of the mitigation measures (safeguards and contingency plans where relevant) to be undertaken to help prevent or reduce the actual or potential effect;

(h) identification of the persons affected by the proposal, the consultation undertaken, if any, and any response to the views of any person consulted;

(i) where the scale or significance of the activity's effect are such that monitoring is required, a description of how, once the proposal is approved, effects will be monitored and by whom.

RMA § 88 Sched. 4(1). Several additional matters "should be considered" in an AEE:

(a) any effect on those in the neighbourhood and, where relevant, the wider community including any socio-economic and cultural effects;

(b) any physical effect on the locality, including any landscape and visual effects;

(c) any effect on ecosystems, including effects on plants or animals and any physical disturbance of habitats in the vicinity;

(d) any effect on natural and physical resources having aesthetic, recreational, scientific, historical, spiritual, or cultural, or other special value for present or future generations;

(e) any discharge of contaminants into the environment, including any unreasonable emission of noise and options for the treatment and disposal of contaminants;

(f) any risk to the neighbourhood, the wider community, or the environment through natural hazards or the use of hazardous substances or hazardous installations.

RMA § 88 Sched. 4(2).

Through these provisions, the RMA was designed to change the land use planning process in fundamental ways.

> The RMA has converted New Zealand land use planning processes into an 'assessment of environmental effects', allowing environmental impact assessment to become the key determinant. One of the consequences of introducing the RMA has been to reduce the significance of socio-economic considerations in determining whether a development should be granted resource consents, in favour of an 'environmental bottom-line' approach to sustainable development.

Tony Jackson, Jennifer Dixon, and Barbara Illsley, *Community and Land Use Planning: Scottish and New Zealand Perspectives,* 28th Annual Conference of the International Association for Impact Assessment, Perth Australia (2008). But just how innovative is the RMA? And what motivated its passage in 1991? The following article explores these issues. As you read it, you might refer back to the federalism dynamics explored in Chapter 1.B of this book, and consider the roles, responsibilities, and effectiveness of nested layers of government when it comes to environmental assessment.

Sarah Michaels and Owen J. Furuseth, Innovation in Environmental Policy: The National Environmental Policy Act of the US and the Resource Management Act of New Zealand
The Environmentalist 17, 181–190 (1997)

Signed into law on 1 January 1970, the National Environmental Policy Act (NEPA) of the US has been described ... as 'The keystone legislation of the thirty-year period from the sixties to the nineties'.... Both the NEPA and RMA are illustrative of policy change[s] [that] ... are a function of both macro-scale changes in society, economics and politics ... and the quest for more knowledgeable means of addressing [environmental problems.

In the US, the demand for pollution control resulted in a wave of new government regulations about air quality, water quality and solid waste management. However, just as importantly, it was a catalyst for the development of a national environmental policy, the NEPA. The impetus for the NEPA was widespread public dissatisfaction with increasing environmental pollution.... The public perception held that an environmental Armageddon was imminent.... NEPA was rare in US political history because the people led the Congress and the Congress, in turn, forced the President to act. The NEPA represented grass-roots-inspired political action....

In the 1960s and 1970s, New Zealand followed the US approach of having separate legislation for land, air and water. However, intractable problems arose when the same legislation did not extend to all the media. In reaction to this, the RMA allows for an in-tegrative approach to air, water and land which is coordinated between the levels of gov-ernment. This integration, combined with an emphasis on the environmental effects, empowers decision makers to deal with environmental issues that frustrate traditional environmental management regimes. Unlike previous legislation, the RMA makes the management of private property completely effects based rather than subject to a series of specific rules and regulations....

The RMA is by no means the definitive piece of environmental legislation. A utilitar-ian view of resources limits its relevance to the ecological dimension of environmental is-sues. It does not squarely address the social dimensions of environmental policy which are of great importance in the urban environment where most New Zealanders live.... How-ever, it does go further than any other national environmental policy instrument in adopt-ing the sustainable development framework set forth in the World Commission on Environment and Development Report (1987). Its introduction was not only highly vis-ible domestically, but has garnered international attention as potentially being a model for other countries.

While the NEPA and RMA have each received accolades for their innovativeness, until now little effort has been made to unpack the nature of their respective innovative qual-ities....

Policy innovation occurs for three reasons. First and most fundamentally, there is a cultural disposition towards applying rational thought to problems. The US and New Zealand, among many countries, have this in common. Second, the mechanisms for in-venting alternatives and communicating them to decision makers exist in both the New Zealand and US political systems. For example, both countries employ a professional-ized bureaucracy.... [However,] New Zealand does not have a national environmental regulatory agency comparable to the US Environmental Protection Agency (EPA)....

Third and worthy of particular emphasis here, the incentives are embodied in the po-litical system to seek out innovation. While this is true of both countries, how they play it is different because of the different forms of government. In the US more elected offi-cials have a political need to seek out innovation to enhance their power base. Routines which are a function of the separation of powers in the US generate a greater need for pol-icy innovation. True, both constitutions dictate routines associated with electoral cycles, but the British-style parliamentary basis dictates greater consistency between the head of the party and other members running for office. Members of the US Congress may cam-paign and carve out for themselves advocacy roles on particular substantive areas.... In New Zealand's parliamentary structure, these same opportunities do not exist. This is, in large part, a function of the cabinet being a subset of parliamentarians whose sub-stantive responsibilities are rotated and need not re-elect the expertise of the appointed minister.

Although both nations drew upon common colonial traditions, in New Zealand an extreme concentration of power was vested in central government. The governmental framework established in the US in 1789 took great care to restrict the power of the fed-eral government and its executive. The institutions of government are based on a writ-ten constitution that specifies powers and delegates functions to various levels and branches of government and the people. The powers of government are divided so that none can be independent and none can control the others....

The current institutional framework for environmental management in the US is far more fragmented than in New Zealand. Historically, the most progressive environmental policy initiatives and guidance have been developed in a top-down fashion, with central government directing state and local government actions affecting the environment. However, over the past decade, state governments have been given broader powers and authority in environmental quality management areas. The recent developments in environmental management are a function of federal government playing a reduced role, in part, as a backlash to the reliance on regulation to bring about compliance to national standards.... States with established progressive environmental policy systems, such as California, Oregon, Florida, Massachusetts, New York, New Jersey, Wisconsin, Washington, Michigan and Maryland, would be expected to use the flexibility and opportunity from decentralization of federal authority to craft policy innovations, whereas, a larger group of states, more concerned with short-term economic goals or fiscal conservatism, will probably retreat from formerly mandated environmental policy initiatives. The overall result over the near future will be a geographical patchwork of environmental standards and management outcomes, with little requirement for concordance or direction from the central government. The devolution of federal responsibility and leadership in developing environmental policy in the US will fragment, at best and regress, at worst the recent policy initiatives.

In theory, the creation of autonomous subnational governments to implement the RMA should facilitate ongoing policy innovation. Public choice theorists contend that such a form of decentralized political systems provides fora for policy experimentation. Their contention that decentralization enables comparison for evaluating different policy instruments ... may not hold fully in New Zealand where the central government has defined pivotal instruments such as regional policy statements and district plans. Still, at the least, distinctions are emerging in how local and regional councils are constructing and using policy instruments....

The form and structure of the government has been a profound force on environmental policy in New Zealand, but will past experience hold for the future? ... The consensus required in the future will make it highly improbable that a radical change in policy will take place at the rate experienced between 1984 and 1993.

... [C]risis can be a well-spring for innovation. It certainly was in the case of New Zealand. Economic reforms removed the government from business, removed subsidies which distorted environmental management and made public authorities more accountable. The institutional reforms downsized and rationalized both the central and local governments. The legislative reforms decentralized government programmes and coordinated environmental legislation for land, air and water. At the same time, intense lobbying was under way for such long-standing environmental concerns as the protection of indigenous forests, wild and scenic rivers and wetlands....

Both the NEPA and the RMA ... took advantage of the sentiment of their respective times in which they were introduced. The NEPA, in establishing action-forcing requirements, tapped into the concerns of the US public for greater accountability in the development of large projects. The RMA built upon the international as well as domestic spirit of employing a holistic approach to environmental management to base legislation on the concept of sustainable development.

One of the most important innovations associated with the NEPA was the impetus for ... EIA.... [T]he diffusion of what makes the RMA innovative is a more challenging undertaking. Still there are jurisdictions which are considering the applicability of the RMA to their own situations. For example, Tasmania, Australia's island state, is experimenting with formulating its own variation of the RMA ...

Thinking about the NEPA and RMA as successful innovative environmental policies highlights the importance of creating or taking advantage of political environments which are conducive to policy experimentation. Environmental policymakers need to strategize as to how they can foster a policy culture which is relatively free of political conflict and where there is agreement, preferably early on, about the need to act. Environmental managers with a technical orientation need to be particularly mindful of the primacy of political considerations.

Monument to one of NZ's most celebrated environmental victories, near Te Anau, NZ. Opposition to the Manapouri proposal fomented New Zealand's first mass environmental movement and awakened a "green consciousness." The debate "foreshadowed today's emphasis on sustainable management that has become enshrined in legislation such as the Resource Management Act ... [and] demonstrated that the power of public opinion could make a significant difference in the democratic process." N.Z. Forest and Bird, *Manapouri: A Green Awakening* (2008). *Photo cr: S. Zellmer.*

Under the RMA, decisionmakers must focus on environmental impacts as a primary factor in their decision. As Professor Birdsong explains, the "effects of the proposed activity are essential considerations for government authorities determining whether to subject a development application to public review and ultimately whether to grant the requested resource consent (permit)." Bret C. Birdsong, *Adjudicating Sustainability: New Zealand's Environment Court*, 29 Ecology L.Q. 1, 15 (2002), citing RMA § 94 (public notification), §§ 104 and 105 (considerations for granting consents).

A resource consent applicant must provide a statement of the "actual or potential effects that the activity may have on the environment, and the ways in which any adverse effects may be mitigated." RMA § 88(4)(b). If the primary decisionmaker does not have all of the relevant facts at their fingertips, "the authority should reject an application or seek more information if the submission is inadequate," but this does not always happen.

Birdsong, *supra,* at 48. In an early decision arising under the RMA, the Environment Court held that "reasonable compliance" with the requirement to provide an adequate assessment is sufficient. McFarland v. Napier City Council, [1993] 2 N.Z.R.M.A. 440.

The lack of public participation in the majority of resource consent applications exacerbates the problem of information gaps. Birdsong, *supra,* at 56. Compounding the problem is that only applicants, consent holders, and persons who make submissions to the consent authority have the right to appeal to the Environment Court. *Id.* at 57.

Dissatisfaction over inadequate consultations with a Maori tribe and a local community arose in a case involving geothermal energy development, *Contact Energy Ltd. v. The Waikato Regional Council and the Taupo District Council,* [2007] 14 ELRNZ 128 (HC). The following excerpt describes the proceedings in the Environment Court.

> [In] *Contact Energy Ltd. v. The Waikato Regional Council* ... a geothermal developer applied for a resource consent for three main purposes: (1) to extract 57,000 tons per day of geothermal fluids in the Wairakei and Tauhara geothermal fields; (2) to reinject discharged wastewater underground; and (3) to obtain a land-use consent to generate fifty megawatts of electricity at the Wairakei plant. The resource consent was refused by the Waikato Regional Council and the Taupo District Council in 1998 on two grounds: (1) that the Tauhara Hapu tribe sought exclusive and undisturbed possession of the geothermal resource because it was valued in the Maori culture; and (2) that businesses within the Waikato region would suffer because of the Wairakei plant's geothermal extraction of water resources.
>
> After the refusal by the Waikato Regional Council, Contact modified its proposal by reducing the extraction levels of geothermal fluids from 57,000 tons to 20,000 tons per day, which later became the main issue on appeal to the Environment Court. The Court considered the relationship between geothermal development and the Maori culture as a matter of "national importance" under RMA §6(e), which acknowledges the "relationship of Maori and their culture and traditions with their ancestral lands, water, sites, waahi tapu, and other taonga." ...
>
> Various environmental effects on water resources were identified [in the AEE required by RMA §88]..., including land subsidence, hydrothermal eruptions, and the continuity of supply of geothermal fluids for tourist facilities. For instance, the Lanecove Hotel uses geothermal fluids ... for heating spa pools, water supplies, and for space heating.... [T]he plant would result in a "material decline in the Waipahihi Springs."
>
> As the adverse effects of Contact's proposed plan were not subjected to a public consultation process, the nearby Taupo community [and the Tauhara Hapu tribe] argued that the quality of scientific information gathered by the developer was insufficient in assessing "actual and potential" effects on the environment.... [But] through expert witness testimony of engineers and geothermal scientists, Contact convinced the Environment Court that its modified geothermal plan would reduce the adverse effects on local communities through a series of mitigation measures such as reinjection of discharged water from the Wairakei plant, and a comprehensive monitoring program. The Environment Court thus granted a resource consent to Contact for the proposed geothermal power station near Taupo.

Kamaal R. Zaidi, *Environmental Mitigation Aspects of Water Resources in Geothermal Development: Using a Comparative Approach in Building a Law and Policy Framework for More Sustainable Water Management Practices in Canada,* 23 Geo. Int'l Envtl. L. Rev. 97,

133–34 (2010). On appeal, the High Court upheld the Environment Court's decision. Contact Energy Ltd. v. Waikato Regional Council [2007] 14 ELRNZ 128 (HC). Details on New Zealand's water quality laws are provided in Chapter 4.C, *infra*.

Despite shortcomings in consultation processes, New Zealand has become known for embracing the precautionary principle through the RMA's AEE provisions and other enactments. The Ministry for the Environment's "Environment 2010 Strategy" provides:

> The Precautionary Principle should be applied to resource management practice, where there is limited knowledge or understanding about the potential for adverse environmental effects or the risk of serious or irreversible environmental damage.... Where there is limited information available to decision makers, or limited understanding of the possible effects resulting from an activity and there are significant risks or uncertainties (for example, over the extent of environmental damage), a precautionary approach should be applied.

Ministry for the Environment, *Environment 2010 Strategy: A Statement of the Government's Strategy on the Environment* 14 (1995). The precautionary principle is featured in legislation dealing with the introduction of new organisms and hazardous substances:

> [In view of] the history of New Zealand's mistakes in that regard—the introduction of rabbits, wasps, gorse, and other species that have been disastrous—we believe that it is very important that we establish the principle that where there is significant doubt about technical or scientific issues, the new body to legislate in this area ... should take a cautious approach.

National Beekeepers v. Chief Executive of the Ministry of Agriculture [2007] NZCA 556, quoting Hansard: (19 December 1995) 552 NZPD 10763, on the Hazardous Substances and New Organisms (HSNO) Act of 1996. The HSNO Act is discussed in detail in Chapter 5.C, *infra*.

Although the RMA itself does not explicitly require "precaution" in decisionmaking, "the judiciary has shown itself willing to infer principles of precaution into the application of [the RMA]." Alexander Gillespie, *Precautionary New Zealand*, 24 N.Z.U. L. Rev. 364 (2011), citing Shirley Primary School v. Christchurch City Council [1999] NZRMA 66 (EnvC) at 69; Golden Bay Marine Farmers v. Tasman District Council EnvC Christchurch W42/2001, 27 April 2001 at [421]–[423].

> However, the courts have consistently pointed out: "[t]he weight to be given to the precautionary principle depends on the circumstances, including: the extent of scientific knowledge and the impact on otherwise permitted activities, the gravity of the effects and the statutory purpose of promoting sustainable management." ... In all instances, the scientific hypothesis proposing an effect must be exposed to testing and scrutinized to determine whether the hypothesis meets a basic threshold of reliability, so as to assist the tribunal to weigh the evidence and make a finding one way or the other. This was dealt with further in *Transpower v. Rodney District Council*, which considered the potential health effects of electrical and magnetic fields created by high-voltage electricity transmission lines. Here, the tribunal emphasized that when dealing with potential risk, "there needs to be some plausible basis, not mere suspicion or innuendo, for adopting that approach." Nevertheless, they accepted that some topics were of such "sufficient gravity" that they "deserve a higher standard of proof"—but not a standard of proof beyond reasonable doubt.

Id., citing Transpower New Zealand Ltd v. Rodney District Council, PT Auckland A85/94, 14 Nov. 1994 at 12. Regardless, the legal burden for obtaining a resource consent remains on the applicant, "[s]ince the ultimate issue in each case was always whether granting the resource consent would meet the single purpose of sustainable management." *Id.,* citing Shirley Primary School v. Christchurch City Council [1999] NZRMA 66 (EnvC) at 68.

Not everyone within the country embraces the principle. "[A] number of lobby groups and some government departments have come to argue that too much precaution may be unduly slowing down the economy, and policy makers should show restraint in the utilization of precaution." *Id.*

How does the precautionary principle play out in environmental assessments in New Zealand? In South Kaipara Harbour Environment Trust v. Auckland Regional Council A045/2006, *aff'd in relevant part sub nom,* Biomarine Ltd. v. Auckland Regional Council, Civ.2005-404-2495, 27 Nov. 2006, the Auckland Regional Council granted consent to allow construction of a mussel farm within a 30 hectare area in the Kaipara Harbour, citing economic, social, and cultural benefits and only minor impacts on marine ecology and birdlife. The Environment Court found that the shoreline in this area had a high degree of natural character, and that the proposed mussel farm would have significant adverse impacts on this natural character, would be intrusive on the landscape, and would deter public access and recreation by making the area less visually appealing. The resource consent was invalidated because these effects could not be prevented or adequately mitigated.

Similarly, in Infinity Group and Thorn v. Queenstown-Lakes District Council C10/2005, the court rejected a proposed variation to the district plan to incorporate a special zone to enable the development of up to 400 residential units. The development was to be located on a peninsula extending into Lake Wanaka, in an area mostly covered in pasture with a few pockets of trees and shrubs used for traditional medicinal purposes by Maori people. The court found that parts of the site were an Outstanding Natural Landscape (ONL) or a Visual Amenity Landscape (VAL). The court held that the potential adverse effects of the proposed development could not be adequately or appropriately avoided, remedied, or mitigated by restrictions on the construction of the buildings or by requirements to retain vegetation. *Id.* para. 148. In an expression of precaution, the Court questioned the effectiveness of mitigation in sensitive landscapes:

> While it remains alive in suitable locations and height, vegetation can hide, or at least soften the view of development. But hiding development, or softening its appearance, does not excuse providing for development that should not be provided for in an ONL, or a VAL where it would not have potential to absorb change without detraction from landscape values.... Further we do not have confidence that district plan requirements for retaining vegetation will necessarily be effective in the long term. As well as being vulnerable to fire, disease, and natural mortality, the continued life of vegetation may depend on the extent to which it is perceived to obstruct valued views.

Id. paras. 149–150. For detailed descriptions of these and other RMA cases, see Environmental Defence Society, Resource Management Act for the Community, http://www.rmaguide.org.nz/rma/keyissues/landscape.cfm?section=cases (visited July 12, 2012).

Notes and Questions

1. As detailed above in Section 1, *supra,* in the U.S., NEPA requires federal agencies to prepare environmental impact statements (EISs) for major federal actions having sig-

nificant effects on the environment. Direct federal action, as well as actions on federal land, federally funded actions, and federal permits trigger the NEPA obligation. EISs must consider a reasonable range of alternatives and all reasonably foreseeable direct and indirect effects. However, NEPA is wholly procedural, in other words, it does not require agencies to select the most environmentally friendly alternative. The AEE requirement of New Zealand's RMA, by contrast, imposes substantive duties for sustainable resource management. It also applied to both public and private action. Which approach do you prefer?

2. How do New Zealand courts discern whether a proposed project will meet the sustainable development goal of the RMA? In Genesis Power Ltd. v. Franklin Dist. Council, [2005] N.Z.R.M.A. 541 (Env. Court), Genesis Power appealed the denial of a resource consent for a wind farm south of Auckland on the Awhitu Peninsula. The District Council, citing the AEE for the project, argued that the proposal would not be a sustainable development because the local environmental impacts would be substantial while the benefits of reduced greenhouse emissions through alternative energy would be insignificant due to the small size of the farm.

The court weighed the positive and negative effects of the wind farm in assessing whether the proposal met the RMA's sustainable management purpose. With respect to the coastal area's landscape and natural character, the court held that the scale of the turbines was such that they would dominate the surrounding area and undermine the visual integrity of the natural character and landscape of the coastal environment. Even so, the court found that the visual and amenity effects on nearby properties and surrounding area would not be significant, and that the land on which the turbines were to be located was not situated within an outstanding landscape. Although the court recognized that there would be changes to the topography and vegetation due to the construction of the turbines and service roads, it concluded that these impacts would be adequately managed though consent conditions. Moreover, "to the extent that this proposal would provide for the generation of sustainable and renewable energy, it would assist New Zealanders to maintain the quality of their environment and, to some extent, enhance it by ... facilitating a move toward renewable energy and to reduce the emission of greenhouse gases." *Id.* para. [220(f)]. The court concluded:

> The ultimate question ... is whether the purpose of the RMA would be better served by granting consent or refusing it. We find that the proposal meets the sustainable management purpose of the RMA. Notwithstanding the effects on the coastal environment we consider the proposal to be appropriate in the circumstances of this case. We find that the benefits of the proposal, when seen in the national context, outweigh the site specific effects, and the effects on the local surrounding area. To grant consent would reflect the purpose of the Act as set out in Section 5.

Id. para [230]. The resource consent was granted subject to conditions.

3. Compare the role of government in NEPA, the RMA, and the Canadian Environmental Assessment Act (CEAA). What are the potential benefits and detriments of each system? What are the implications of the "devolution of federal responsibility" described by Michaels and Furuseth, *supra*?

4. Compare the role of the public in NEPA, the RMA, and the CEAA. What are the advantages and disadvantages of each system in terms of public participation and information-gathering?

> Public participation is important in the EIA process because increased participation can result in meeting public needs, better access to information, better de-

velopment decisions, and fewer court cases. Most importantly, increased participation can lead to the credibility of the entire EIA process because private and unsophisticated people speak to values rather than clouded issues lost in technical evidence. Participation avoids the intellectual vacuum of closed-door thinking....

Environmental assessments empower the public to participate in conflict resolution. Under this model, whether or not a proposed activity proceeds is the result of a competition between those for and those against a proposed activity. Arguably, decisionmaking is enhanced by providing such people an opportunity to argue publicly about different goals and objectives....

Environmental assessment is a process that relies on the expression of public communication. Discussion and dialogue are key. The process has merit as a therapy, or a relief valve to give voice to dissension among minorities and to expose differing opinions....

Tilleman, *supra,* at 337. Which nation seems to do the best job of fostering effective and timely public participation in the EIA process? Which provides the greatest access to the courts for members of the interested public?

3. India

In 1986, in the wake of the Bhopal gas leak, India adopted the Environment (Protection) Act (EPA), No. 29, Acts of Parliament 1986, with the goal of protecting and restoring the environment. "Environment" is defined broadly to include water, air, land, and the inter-relationships among them and with human beings and other living creatures. *Id.* § 2(a). Section 24 provides that the Act's provisions, and subordinate rules or orders issued pursuant to the Act, take precedence over any other law, including conflicting state laws. S. Jagannath v. Union of India (Shrimp Culture Case), AIR 1997 SC 811, 844.

EPA § 3 directs the central Indian government to take measures for "protecting and improving the quality of the environment and preventing, controlling and abating environmental pollution." The Ministry of Environment and Forests (MoEF) has primary responsibility over environmental regulations and enforcement. Sustainable development took prominence in 1994, when the MoEF issued the Environmental Impact Assessment Notification (EIA Notification), which requires proponents of new projects, or expanded or modernized projects, to prepare and submit an EIA report for approval to the impact assessment agency (the MoEF). India, Environment Impact Assessment Notification No. S.O. 60(E), para. 2(I)(a) (Jan. 27, 2004). Prior to this notification, developers of large projects needed only an "environmental clearance" from the central government. Julie A. Lemmer, *Cleaning Up Development: EIA in Two of the World's Largest and Most Rapidly Developing Countries,* 19 Geo. Int'l Envtl. L. Rev. 275 (2007). For background, see SHYAM DIVAN AND ARMIN ROSENCRANZ, ENVIRONMENTAL LAW AND POLICY IN INDIA 70 (2d ed. 2002).

Projects covered by the EIA Notification are limited to thirty-two categories of "Projects Requiring Environmental Clearance from the Central Government" as provided in Schedule I of the Notification. This includes major irrigation projects, harbors, ports, nuclear and thermal power plants, petro-chemical complexes, cement plants, and certain highway projects. However, Schedule I is not completely comprehensive:

[It] makes no specific provision for projects involving deforestation, human resettlement, land reclamation, weapons testing and manufacture of explosives, waste disposal sites and the transportation of hazardous and radioactive substances, or the building of major dams or levees. Furthermore, the legislation specifically excludes the building of major pipelines from the requirement of environmental assessment ... [despite the fact that] other countries have acknowledged these as significantly affecting the environment and have provided for them in their EIA legislation.

Lemmer, *supra,* at 296–97.

For projects that are covered by the Notification, proponents must describe the project's objectives and its land requirements, including the project's distance from the nearest National Park, Sanctuary, Biosphere Reserve, heritage site, or Reserve Forest, and "number of villages and population to be displaced" by the project. Notification Schedule II paras. 2–3, 10. Other topics to be covered include:

Climate and Air Quality:

(a) Wind rose at site:

(b) Max/Min/Mean annual temperature:

(c) Frequency of inversion:

(d) Frequency of cyclones/tornadoes/cloud burst:

(e) Ambient air quality data:

(f) Nature & concentration of gas emissions (CO, CO_2, NO_x, CH_n etc.) from the project ...

Water balance:

(a) Water balance at site:

(b) Lean season water availability ...

(c) Source to be tapped with competing users (River, Lake, Ground, Public supply):

(d) Water quality:

(e) Changes observed in quality and quantity of groundwater in the last years and present charging and extraction details:

(f) (i) The quantum of existing industrial effluents and domestic sewage with incremental load to be released in the receiving water body due to the proposed activities along with treatment details; (ii) The quantum and quality of water in the receiving water body before and after disposal of solid wastes including municipal solid wastes, industrial effluents and domestic sewage; (iii) The quantum of industrial effluents and domestic sewage to be released on land and type of land;

(g) (i) Details of reservoir water quality with necessary Catchment Treatment Plan ...

Solid wastes:

(a) Nature and quantity of solid wastes generated including municipal solid wastes, biomedical wastes, hazardous wastes and industrial wastes ...

(b) Solid waste disposal method ...

Power requirement indicating source of supply ...

Risk assessment report along with Disaster Management Plan....

Id. paras. 4–8, 11. The full text of the 1994 Notification can be accessed at Center for Environmental Law Education, Research, and Advocacy, *Important EIA Notifications,* http://www.ceeraindia.org/documents/lib_c3s2_EIAnoti_160300.htm#Notification II.

Persons "likely to be affected" must be given notice and an opportunity to participate at a public hearing and to provide oral or written suggestions. Notification, *supra,* Sched. IV(2). The authorities are given specific time limits for processing EIAs. "If no comments from the Impact Assessment Agency are received within the time limit, the project would be deemed to have been approved as proposed by project authorities." *Id.* para. 2(V). As described below, failure to comply with the public participation requirements may result in denial of environmental clearance.

> In 2001, the High Court of the state of Kerala ordered the proponent of a hydro-power generating project to comply with the public hearing requirements before environmental clearance would even be considered. Chithanya v. State of Kerala (Kerala H.C. 2001).... Considering that it had "a duty to ensure that the requirements of [India's environmental legislation] are strictly complied with," the court held that, "in the interest of [the] environment ... a public hearing cannot be dispensed with in respect of the grant of any clearance after the coming into force of the amended notification."

> While this court opinion is very encouraging in terms of strengthening public participation, EIA, and India's environmental law in general, it must be noted that Kerala has always been an atypical Indian state. Higher levels of education in the province have led to a broader public awareness and higher levels of public participation. These are characteristics that may be largely lacking in other parts of India. In fact, the High Court of Kerala itself acknowledged the "lack of concern or lukewarm attitude of the authorities towards environment and its protection." Scholars have pointed out that the Indian government's "use of law in maintaining environmental standards has been a failure" in large part because of its refusal to recognize public participation.

> Still, considering that India has only relatively recently articulated EIA as an important national environmental policy, it seems to be on the right path toward more effective implementation, particularly in the area of public participation. The Kerala High Court decision is evidence of this movement. Furthermore, community participation is a long-term process and it requires time and a lot of effort in addition to the government's willingness to incorporate it into the planning and implementation stages. The Indian government took the first step in this process by making public participation a mandatory part of EIA in 1997. The government should continue to recognize the importance of public participation in the EIA process and make implementation of public participation a priority.

Lemmer, *supra,* at 297–98.

As Lemmer notes, the Kerala High Court appears to be a favorable forum for environmental interests and public interest litigation; however, its jurisprudence may not be indicative of how other courts in India would resolve environmental conflicts. Although the Indian Supreme Court has had a reputation as an "activist" court, an "inherent pro-development bias" has been discernible in recent years. Armin Rosencranz, *Introduction To Environmental Law and Policy in India at the End of 2011,* 2 Indian Law News 1, 1 (ABA Section of Int'l Law 2011). According to Dr. Rosencranz, "The views expressed by judges in all environmental litigation concerning infrastructure projects have supported the government's assertion that it must carry out its development activities, such as dams and power plants, in the national interest." *Id.* at 2, citing, *e.g.,* Narmada Bachao Andolan v. Union of India (2000), 10 S.C.C. 664 (Narmada Dam).

The Narmada River Valley has been at the center of a prolonged struggle between government officials, who claim that dams and irrigation systems will bring much-needed electricity and water to drought-stricken areas of the country, and people's movements like the Narmada Bachao Andolan, who claim that the government "exaggerates the benefits and underestimates the costs ... [in terms of both] human suffering and environmental damage that comes with 'big dams.'" Talib N. Ellison, *The Sardar Sarovar Dam and Ethnic Conflict In India,* ICE Case Studies No. 153 (2005).

> These dams flood vast areas and displace hundreds of thousands, mostly peasants and adivasi (tribal/indigenous people) people, while promises of relocation and resources usually prove to be illusory. Just one of the dams, Sardar Sarovar, could uproot as many as a half-million people....
>
> As of 1983, the Sardar Sarovar Project (SSP) had not met the [MoEF] Regulations, and therefore was denied clearance for construction.... [But] construction of the SSP officially began in 1985 when the World Bank decided to provide financial support (to the tune of a $450 million USD loan) for the construction.... It was proclaimed by project coordinators and government officials that the Sardar Sarovar Dam was to benefit the greater well-being of the country by producing power sources and more widespread availability of electricity, and improving water management in general. In particular, the "SSP is intended to bring drinking water to Kutch and other drought-ridden regions of Gujarat," impounding water in a 455 foot high reservoir that will ultimately submerge 37,000 hectares of land in three states of Gujarat, Maharashrta and Madhya Pradesh. The dam will also divert 9.5 million acre feet of water into a canal and irrigation system. This canal, at 450 kilometers long, is the largest in the world, with the aggregate length of the distribution network being 75,000 kilometers....
>
> After six years of reports of violations of resettlement and environmental guidelines by developers and authorities, the World Bank formed an independent commission to review the project. This commission issued a report in 1992, describing the devastating effects of the dam and a harsh critique of the World Bank's negligent role in supporting the project in the face of so much negative evidence of the dam's impact. In its report, the commission came to the conclusion that "the SSP is flawed, that rehabilitation of all the people affected cannot be done within the allotted time, and that important data are missing in just about all areas." The World Bank did not immediately withdraw its funding, but rather provided the loan, conditionally....

Id., citing C. Alvares and R. Billorey, *Damning the Narmada: The Politics Behind the Destruction,* The Ecologist 12(2):62–73 (1987) (other citations omitted). The Indian government refused to comply with the loan conditions and ultimately gave up World Bank funding, but went forward with construction on its own. Molly More, *India's Lifeline or Man-Made Disaster?,* Wash. Post, Aug. 24, 1993, at A12. The Indian Supreme Court, in its 2000 decision on a challenge to the SSP, held that most of the plaintiffs' contentions could not be raised at this stage since the SSP "had already commenced and there had been a great deal of investment already undertaken in its execution." Madhav Khosla, *Addressing Judicial Activism in the Indian Supreme Court: Towards an Evolved Debate,* 32 Hastings Int'l & Comp. L. Rev. 55, 89–90 (2009), citing *Narmada,* (2000) 10 S.C.C. 664, ¶¶ 46–50.

The court went on to consider whether a violation of human rights, as guaranteed by Article 21 of the Indian Constitution, had occurred due to the forcible displacement of tribals from their land and the destruction of their sources of livelihood. Article 21 guarantees the right to life, which the courts have interpreted as including the right to a healthy environment. Plaintiffs argued that the Control Authority had "grossly underestimated the number of persons who would be displaced," and that "rehabilitation measures were only being undertaken for persons submerged by the project and not others affected by it." *Narmada*, 10 S.C.C. 664, paras. 134–35.

> Rejecting th[ese] argument[s], the Court held that the displacement of persons does not per se result in the violation of their fundamental rights. The appropriate test according to the Court, to determine such violation, was to examine the rehabilitation sites and compare them with the original habitation. On the question of whether the SSP had been comprehensively assessed by policy makers, the Court examined the history of the project in detail and arrived at the conclusion that the project had been duly considered by the government (i.e., there had been application of mind).… In sum, the Court rejected the arguments of the petitioner, emphasizing that courts would refrain from entering into questions of policy.

Khosla, *supra,* at 90–91, citing *Narmada*, 10 S.C.C. 664, paras. 62, 229.

The dissenting justice in *Narmada* explicitly recognized that the dam violated EIA guidelines and stated that it should not be built:

> 3.1. The environmental clearance was based on next to no data in regard to the environmental impact of the Project and was contrary to the terms of the then policy of the Union of India in regard to environmental clearances and, therefore, no clearance at all. [241-C]
>
> 3.2. Under its own policy, … the Union of India was bound to give environmental clearance only after, (a) all the necessary data in respect of the environmental impact of the Project had been collected and assessed; (b) the assessment showed that the Project could proceed; and (c) the environmental safeguard measures, and their cost, had been worked out.
>
> 3.3. The contemporaneous Notes prepared by the … Ministry of Environment and Forests leave no manner of doubt that the requisite data for assessment of the environment impact of the Project was not available when the environmental clearance thereof was granted …

With respect to the human rights issues, the dissent stated:

> 4. An adverse impact on the environment can have disastrous consequences for this generation and generations to come. This Court has in its judgments on Article 21 of the Constitution of India recognised this. This Court cannot place its seal of approval on the project without first ensuring that those best fitted to do so have had the opportunity of gathering all necessary data on the environmental impact of the Project and of assessing it. They must then decide if environmental clearance to the project can be given, and, if it can, what environmental safeguard measures have to be adopted, and their cost.

Narmada, 10 S.C.C. 664 (Bharucha, J., dissenting), paras. 3–4.

As *Naramada* indicates, regardless of how a reviewing court disposes of the issues, problems in EIA implementation begin at the agency level: "The central and state governments are inclined to grant clearances and approvals for projects which involve large investments by large Indian corporate houses and especially multinational companies due to the financial benefits at the cost of environment." Vandana Shroff and Ashish Jejurkar, *Environmental Law in India — Does it Lack Teeth?*, 2 Indian Law News, *supra*, at 10. However, from 2009–2011, during Jairam Ramesh's tenure as the Environment Minister, "hundreds of development projects" were denied clearance.

> For instance, the MoEF rejected the proposal for mining [bauxite for aluminum production] by Vedanta on grounds that the project would contravene various environmental laws and raised concerns on the livelihood related aspects of Dongria Kondh — a local tribe. This was followed by stalling construction of the ambitious Lavasa Housing Project at a [high elevation] hill station near Mumbai, on similar reasons of not securing the requisite environmental clearances.... [T]he tough stance ... taken by the [MoEF], in strictly scrutinizing projects prior to granting of clearances, is a step in the right direction.

Id. at 10–11.

Whatever happened to Minister Ramesh, viewed as "a hero among environmentalists who hailed his enforcement of the country's tough land-use laws," but "reviled in corporate circles where he was viewed as arbitrary and unfair"? Amol Sharma, *India Fires Environment Minister Who Held Up Projects*, WSJ, India News, July 13, 2011. It appears that Mr. Ramesh was "kicked upstairs" in the halls of government. The Wall Street Journal picked up the story:

> Indian Prime Minister Manmohan Singh removed a top environmental official who had held up several major industrial projects as part of a cabinet reshuffle, in a potentially positive sign for businesses frustrated by regulatory obstacles ... Mr. Singh removed Environment Minister Jairam Ramesh, who has held up several major industrial projects that many viewed as vital to India's economic development. Mr. Ramesh was promoted to cabinet rank as minister of rural development, which oversees several large-scale poverty alleviation programs. In his place, Mr. Singh installed Jayanthi Natarajan, a member of the upper house of Parliament and former spokeswoman for Mr. Singh's Congress Party....

Id. Although the reshuffling was not as extreme as some business interests had hoped, it was a bold move for "a government sidetracked for months by a corruption probe involving high-ranking public officials and growing concerns that the country's economy is veering off track." *Id.* Environmental groups did not seem too concerned: "some environmental groups expressed cautious optimism that Ms. Natarajan wouldn't veer far from Mr. Ramesh's path. 'There are lots of eyes watching the ministry. It will be hard to go back to business as usual,' said Divya Raghunandan, campaigns director for Greenpeace India." *Id.*

For its part, industry has long complained about delays and confusion caused by lack of coordination between various levels of governmental authorities. Too often, "developers were given the nod by one authority only to be stalled by another, sometimes even after the developers had commenced with the projects. Not only were the environmental clearances unnecessarily delayed, clearances — once granted — were also retracted by the authority after the lapse of a considerable time period." Ravi Singhania and Sunayna Jaimini, *Lafarge Decision — Light at the End of the Tunnel?*, 2 Indian Law News 18 (2011). The following article highlights one recent example, which resulted in a landmark case from the Indian Supreme Court in Lafarge Umiam Mining Private Limited v. Union of India, 2011 (7) SCALE 242.

Ravi Singhania and Sunayna Jaimini,
Lafarge Decision—Light at the End of the Tunnel?
2 Indian Law News 18–21 (2011)

In *LaFarge*, ... the Ministry of Environment and Forest ("MoEF") alleged that Lafarge Umiam Mining Private Ltd., a ... company that had leased mining rights in Meghalaya, misrepresented "forest land" to be infertile barren land to obtain environmental clearances. This gave rise to two issues before the Court—firstly, a determination of the nature of land in question, and secondly, an examination of whether the company had misrepresented the nature of the land in order to dishonestly obtain clearances from the Ministry....

In 1997, before commencing the project [Lafarge], through its subsidiary in India, namely Lum Mawshun Minerals Private Limited ("LMMPL"), began the process of obtaining the necessary environmental clearances from the MoEF. As a part of the application, LMMPL made representations that the limestone mines did not involve the diversion of "forest land." The LMMPL's representations were supported by two sources—firstly, the letters from the Khasi Hills Autonomous District Council ("KHADC"), the local authority with jurisdiction over the mines, and secondly, a certificate from the Divisional Forest Officer ("DFO") of the Khasi Hills Division stating that the mining site was not in a forest area. After several rounds of queries from the MoEF and consequent responses from LMMPL, the MoEF finally gave environmental clearance for the mines in 2001, and subsequently LMMPL commenced its mining operations.

In 2007, six years after the MoEF had already granted the appropriate clearances, MoEF asked Lafarge to stop all mining activity in the area. This step was taken after the Chief Conservator of Forests ("CCF") for Meghalaya informed the MoEF that Lafarge had misrepresented that the mining area was not a "forest land" and had diverted forest land for its mining activity without first obtaining the necessary forest clearance under section 2 of the Forest Conservation Act, 1980....

Ultimately, the court allowed the company to resume its mining operations in the region after taking into consideration that the MoEF had granted the forest clearance in April 2010 and that the Company had complied with the preconditions to the environmental clearance. In its determination, the Court placed great emphasis on the rights of locals to decide on the value of conservation of the environment. In addition, the Court observed that the KHADC's letters as well as the Court's subsequent findings revealed that the Lafarge project resulted in significant gains for the local community.

The *Lafarge* judgment is hailed for providing clarity on two important issues—firstly, for its clarification about the extent of judicial review in situations where environmental clearances have been granted but are later challenged with respect to the validity of the said process, and secondly, for laying down comprehensive guidelines for future projects that involve both forest and environmental clearances.

The Court also opined that the protection of the environment is an ongoing process and therefore "across-the-board" principles cannot be applied to all cases. Courts would have to examine the facts of each case on whether the project should be allowed or not....

On the question of the extent of judicial review, the Court held that the constitutional "doctrine of proportionality" should apply to environmental clearances. Therefore, decisions relating to utilization should be judged on well established principles of natural justice, such as whether all relevant factors were taken into account at the time of coming to the decision, whether the decision was influenced by extraneous circumstances, and whether the decision was in accordance with the legislative policy underlying the laws that governs the field. If these circumstances were satisfied, the decision of a government authority would not be questioned by the Court. The importance of this section of the judgment is that the Court lays down a clear principle that if a project developer complies with the specified procedure for obtaining environmental clearances and there is evidence on record that the entity granting the clearance had done so after due consideration, such clearances would not be reversed to the prejudice of the project developer. This provides some much needed stability to the environmental clearance process and both project developers and environmental activists would definitely benefit from this consistent approach....

In conclusion, the Court has taken bold steps to remove the various bottlenecks that plague development projects, while ensuring that the environmental agencies follow established directives and principles of protection of environment in granting environmental clearances....

Notes and Questions:

1. One of the "bold steps" taken by the Court was to order the Central Government to "appoint a National Regulator for appraising projects, enforcing environmental conditions for approvals and to impose penalties on polluters." The Court directed the MoEF to establish a dedicated body to issue forest and environmental clearances, and to report back to the court "within six months" on its progress. The objective of the National Regulator, according to the Court, is to streamline and make more transparent the process of granting environmental clearances. Bloomberg/BNA, *India's Supreme Court Orders Creation of New Body to Issue Environmental Licenses,* Int'l Env. Reporter, July 15, 2011. Is this an appropriate role for the Court to take? Can you imagine a federal court in the United States or Canada issuing such an order?

2. What penalties should be imposed on project proponents who misrepresent data to obtain consent from the Ministry? Does it matter if the data is something akin to a "trade secret"? What if the Ministry has independent means of obtaining the data?

4. England

In 1985, the European Community (EC) responded to the international drive for EIAs by adopting Council Directive 85/337/EEC, 1985 O.J. (L175), as amended by Directives 97/11/EC and 2003/35/EC. This EIA Directive aims to control development through environmental impact analysis, planning, and increased public consultation. The United Kingdom was concerned about implementing the EIA Directive because of the additional expense and the delays in project approval that could be caused by public participation. Tilleman, *supra,* at 339.

Dr. Tilleman provides additional context in the following excerpt. Other portions of this article are provided above in Section B.1 (Canada).

William A. Tilleman, Public Participation in the Environmental Impact Assessment Process: A Comparative Study of Impact Assessment in Canada, the United States and the European Community

33 Colum. J. Transnat'l L. 337, 372–376 (1995)

The EC found interest in EIAs due to the Community's desire to protect the environment and quality of life. The Treaty of Rome which had established the EC did not provide the European Community with the powers to achieve these environmental goals. The EC Member States concluded that the best environmental policy would be to prevent pollution at its source rather than deal with its effects at a later date. In view of the disparate EIA laws in force in the several Member States which could create unfavourable competition, the EC finally issued the Directive. EC Member States had to ensure that all measures necessary to comply with the Directive were completed by July 3, 1988, although members continue to have the latitude to "lay down stricter rules regarding scope and procedure when assessing environmental effects."

An international comparison should be made at this point. The American NEPA applies to major "federal actions." However private projects in the United States can invoke the NEPA whenever a private project needs federal approval (a license or permit). Several examples help to make the point. Consider, for example, a private project to build a dock adjacent to a river or a lake. This project requires a federal permit from the Corps of Engineers under the Rivers and Harbors Act of 1910, and the Corps of Engineers will have to do an EIS if the project is a major one.... The Canadian EARP (with similar prima facie requirements for federal undertakings) also applies to private projects as long as there is federal permitting authority, projects on federal land, or federal funds to support the project.

On the other hand, the EC EIA Directive avoids this confusion by specifying that this Directive applies to the assessment of all public and private projects likely to have a significant effect on the environment. Projects are defined in the Directive by reference to two Annexes. Annex I lists the classes of projects that are mandatory for assessments; the possible exception from this rule still requires members to make available to the public the information surrounding the granting of the exemption, with the reasons therefor. Annex II is more flexible; it only subjects projects to impact assessment if the Members States "consider that [project] characteristics so require."

The EC Directive incorporates public consultation concepts. First, where the Directive applies to projects found in the Annex, the developer has to provide broad information including the project description, measures to reduce significant effects, data required to assess impacts, and other information.... The public must be given an opportunity to express an opinion before the project is initiated. The ... EIS must ... identify, describe and assess in an appropriate manner, in the light of each individual case and in accordance with Articles 4 to 11, the direct and indirect effects of a project on the following factors:

- human beings, fauna and flora,
- soil, water, air, climate and the landscape,
- interactions between [environmental] factors ...
- material assets and the cultural heritage....

All of the information gathered during the consultation process must be considered in the development consent (approval) procedure.... An EIA document is then prepared including an outline of the main alternatives studied by the developer, a description of likely significant effects, mitigation measures, and a non-technical summary of all EIA information. The developer then presents the EIA documentation to the state "authorities" — a term not defined by the Directive — for approval, and must then notify the public of the proposal and present enough information to enable predecision participation to occur. Where a positive decision is made, the government authorities must inform the public of the decision and the conditions, if any, attached thereto ...

Member States that have implemented the Directive include Ireland, Netherlands, Spain, France, Germany, Belgium (Flanders and Walloon Regions), Greece, Italy, Portugal, Denmark, and the U.K. Despite delays, most Member States have now incorporated the EIA into national laws.

The remaining question of crucial importance is the effectiveness of public consultation in the EC, because unlike the U.S. where there is a well developed system of administrative law (with corresponding opportunities to challenge the decision if it is not satisfactory), the EC Directives are not binding in the Community unless internal or secondary legislation is passed and enforced. As a general rule, provisions made under the EEC Treaty for enforcement of obligations on Member States are weak. Although the Court of Justice has jurisdiction to rule on Member State failures to implement the Directives, no sanctions were provided to "compel states to fulfil their obligations." Nevertheless, the EC Directives may still create strong legal rights because certain Directives that are "unconditional and precise" enough are binding in that member states do have a legal obligation to eventually implement Directives....

In the EC, the review of EIA documents will primarily fall on the mechanisms adopted by each Member State as it adopts the Directive.... Several Member States have now adopted the Directive through implementing legislation, and each national law must be examined individually to determine the powers of review. Nevertheless, it is conceivable that the Court of Justice may be asked to intervene and review compliance with the EIA Directive if someone raises a claim of procedural failure by the developer to follow the terms of the Directive. However, it should be remembered that the EIA Directive alone does not guarantee a substantive result.... The Directive does not stop Member States from building projects where there are serious negative impacts. The Directive only requests that an EIA be made and, more importantly, that public consultation occur.... What the Directive has done, therefore, is to promote bilateral discussions between Member States....

Although the impact assessment law in the EC is hardly drafted in language that could meet the test of being "unconditional and precise" such that it is legally binding, some writers agree that the Directive will become de facto compulsory ... [This] means ... developers face the risk of their development being halted while Court actions are filed in the originating country to determine whether the approval was consistent with the EIA Directive and national laws. This legal challenge can be made after construction begins, or at least after significant financial resources are spent by the proponent.... Whether or not these challenges are successful, complaints can be filed with the EC Commission which can bring an action against the Member State for not implementing or applying EC law.

* * *

Basically, the EC Directive and subsequent regulations prohibit authorities from granting permission for "projects" that are "likely to have a significant effect" on the environment unless they have taken environmental information and public consultations into consideration. In England, the decisionmaker is the local planning authority, and England's regulations limit the planning authority's discretion for projects that require EIA. Town and Country Planning Regulations 1999, SI 1999/293 § 3(2). Such "projects" include developments, not exempted by the Secretary of State, that come within Schedule 1 or Schedule 2 of the regulations. *Id.* § 4(4).

> Schedule 1 projects, which correspond with Annex 1 projects identified in the [EIA] Directive, require a mandatory environmental assessment. Schedule 2 projects ... may require environmental assessments if they are likely to have significant environmental effects ... by virtue of factors such as its nature, size or location." Schedule 2 contains thresholds and criteria that indicate when a development will have significant impact. Entire categories of development may be included.

> When all of the development in a category is not included, the thresholds and criteria are usually quantitative. For example, the threshold criteria for urban development projects is when the area of development exceeds 0.5 hectare.... The significance of the environmental impact must be considered with respect to the environment widely, so a significant localized impact on individuals or individual amenity may not be significant for the purposes of the Directive.

Daniel R. Mandelker, NEPA Law and Litig. § 13:9 (2011), citing Town and Country Planning Regulations, (1999) SI 1999/293, Reg. § 2(1) (other citations omitted).

If a project requires EIA but an adequate assessment is not completed, permission may be revoked. Revocation is not mandatory, however, and permission may instead be granted with exceptions. Mandelker, *supra,* citing Case C-201/02 Regina (Delena Wells) v. Secretary of State for Transport, Local Government and the Regions [2004] 1 CMLR 31 (ECJ).

In Ardagh Glass Ltd. v. Chester City Council [2010] EWCA Civ. 172, an Irish manufacturer, Quinn Glass, began building one of the largest glass factories in Europe without planning permission. A competitor, Ardagh Glass, filed a complaint. Quinn applied for permission nearly a year after it began construction at its plant. The planning authority conducted a public inquiry and refused permission. According to the judge, Quinn had taken a "calculated risk" in building the facility without planning consent. The company then submitted a new application, along with an EIA, and the authority granted retrospective permission. The Court of Appeal held that the authority may grant retrospective permission, but only if the developer would gain no advantage by pre-emptive development, and only in exceptional circumstances. If retrospective permission is not granted, the development would have to be enjoined and removed. After a six-year legal battle, the Cheshire West and Chester Council Planning Committee ultimately granted approval for the Quinn plant, which employs around 600 staff.

Although *Ardagh Glass* dealt with a non-conforming project that sought after-the-fact approval, *id.* para. 25, the European Commission has provided guidance on the types of cases that may be considered "exceptional" and therefore altogether exempt:

> For a case to be considered as exceptional and qualify for the exemption [of Article 2(3)] all the following criteria would normally need to be met:
>
> • an urgent and substantial need for the project;
>
> • inability to undertake the project earlier;
>
> • inability to meet the full requirements of the Directive.

> The need for the project would have to be such that failure to proceed with it would be likely to present a serious threat, for example to life, health or human welfare; to the environment (*e.g.* contamination of land, water or air, or flooding); to political, administrative or economic stability; or to security. . . .

Clarification of the Application of Article 2(3) of the EIA Directive, paras. 2.9–2.10 (2006), at http://ec.europa.eu/environment/eia/pdf/eia_art2_3.pdf. Does it appear that Quinn Glass would satisfy the EC's criteria?

In addition to intensive industrial activities and major construction, "projects" also include "interventions in the natural surroundings and landscape." This means that agricultural activities may require EIAs. "The use of uncultivated land or semi-natural areas for intensive agricultural purpose" is specifically included in Schedule 2 as a type of project that may require EIA. Council Directive 85/337/EEC, Sch.2 para.1(a).

In England, however, agricultural development, for the most part, evaded legal scrutiny until fairly recently.

> The application of full planning control, with the public consultation and scrutiny of development projects that it entails, has in practice been reserved primarily for major building or operational work on farms. . . . Nevertheless, the assumption that all agricultural development should remain outside the ambit of legal scrutiny has been challenged in recent years by initiatives originating in European environmental law, aimed at minimising or eradicating the damage to the natural environment caused by intensive farming methods. Their impact on English law depends in large measure on the extent to which — and the circumstances in which — proposals for extensive land use changes to promote intensive agriculture come within the ambit of development control under the Town and Country Planning Act 1990. Not least, the characterisation of land use changes as 'development' or otherwise has important implications for the way in which tools of horizontal environmental regulation — such as Environmental Impact Assessment (EIA) — are implemented in domestic law. In this context the English courts have, in several recent cases, shown a willingness to extend the reach of development control into areas of agricultural land use that were hitherto assumed to be outside the planning system altogether.

Christopher Rodgers, *Environmental Impact Assessment: Mapping the Interface between Agriculture, Development and the Natural Environment,* 13 Envtl. L. Rev. 85, 86 (2011).

In R. (on the application of Wye Valley Action Association Ltd) v. Herefordshire Council [2011] EWCA Civ 20, the local authority granted planning permission for the erection of polytunnels (a type of greenhouse) for fruit production on existing farmland in an area of outstanding natural beauty. The lower court quashed the permission and determined that, since the site abutted a special conservation area (a site of special scientific interest), was overlooked by ancient monument, and was in an area of outstanding natural beauty, it came within the definition of "semi-natural" as a matter of law, and also that the development was a project for "intensive agricultural purposes." The Court of Appeal reversed, and held that the judge had overstepped.

> In determining whether development was in a "semi-natural area," it was necessary to ask whether the local authority correctly understood the meaning of the expression and, whether ... it reached a conclusion that was open to a rational decision-maker. In the instant case, the judge failed to distinguish sufficiently

between the two stages of that exercise and gave the appearance of substituting his decision for that of the primary decision-maker....

The local authority had plainly reached a rational decision and the judge was wrong to conclude that it had erred in law.... The reasons given in the local authority's screening opinion were adequate, though they could usefully have been fuller. The point being made in the opinion was that the extent of existing cultivation was such that the land did not come within the description "uncultivated land or semi-natural areas" in Sch.2 para.1(a).

Id. paras. 35–47. The *Wye Valley* case indicates that reviewing courts will give a great deal of deference to the planning authority's discretion, and also that, while the definition of "projects" subject to EIA "is very wide ... it is not indefinite in scope." Rodgers, *supra,* at 98.

Notes and Questions

1. In the United States, agricultural activities are rarely subjected to EIA requirements. For the most part, agriculture is a private endeavor, so NEPA does not apply. To the extent that planning requirements apply to land use changes (for example, conversion of farmland to residential development), those requirements are a matter of local or, at most, state concern. NEPA is triggered when a federal license, permit, or funding is at issue, 42 U.S.C. § 4322, but there are few such requirements for farming. NEPA may apply, however, when the farmer needs a Clean Water Act permit to drain wetlands to convert farmland to a new and different use. 33 U.S.C. § 1344(f)(2). But if impacts to wetlands occur during the course of normal farming operations, no federal permit is required, so no NEPA analysis is required. 33 U.S.C. § 1344(f)(1)(a). By contrast, the EIA Directive applies to both private and public activities, including agriculture, as discussed in the *Wye* case, above, and in R (Hall Hunter Partnership) v. Secretary of State [2006] EWHC 3482 (Admin), where the installation of a large number of polytunnels and dozens of caravans to house seasonal workers triggered the EIA requirement. EIA is also mandatory for livestock facilities engaged in the intensive rearing of pigs or poultry. Council Directive 85/337/EEC, Annex 1 para. 17. Concentrated animal feeding operations—or CAFOS, as they are known in the U.S.—require Clean Water Act permits, but the U.S. EPA's permitting decisions are statutorily exempt from NEPA. Cross Timbers Concerned Citizens v. Saginaw, 991 F.Supp. 563, 572 (N.D. Tex. 1997), citing 33 U.S.C. § 1371(c)(1). Environmental assessment requirements under the laws of individual states, however, may be triggered by state permitting decisions related to CAFOs. *See, e.g.,* Minn. Stat. Ann. § 116D.04 Subd.2.a(d). What are the arguments for and against requiring EIA analysis for agricultural activities?

2. The European Union is moving toward the concept of "integrating the environment into policy making" as a key principle of sustainable development. William Sheate, *The EC Directive on Strategic Environmental Assessment: A Much-Needed Boost for Environmental Integration*, 12 Eur. Envtl. L. Rev 341 (2003). How have England, the U.S., Canada, New Zealand, and India mirrored this concept (or not)? What advantages and disadvantages does environmental integration have for environmental protection? For timely and cost-effective development?

3. For an assessment of the effectiveness of the EIA process in the UK and throughout the EU, see Taking Stock of Environmental Assessment: Law, Policy and Practice (ed. Jane Holder and Donald McGillivray 2007). On the upside, "EA is now firmly established within the EU's legal and environmental governance framework with

a far-reaching jurisprudence at national and EU levels." Sharon Turner, *Review of* TAKING STOCK, *supra,* 20 J. Envtl. L. 323, 325 (2008). Yet critics claim that the EIA process has failed to deliver real, on-the-ground benefits to the environment: "there is no evidence that an EIA ever stopped an environmentally harmful project or led to significant changes." *Id.* (quoting Ludwig Krämer). Environmental groups criticize the UK as "not fully interpreting the spirit of the EIA directive." Friends of the Earth, EIA: A Campaigners Guide 3 (2005). Researchers have identified one reason:

> Previous survey research into screening for environmental impact assessment (EIA) in England has found that few local authorities have very much experience of dealing with EIA projects.... In the majority of [projects that fall within the ambit of the UK's EIA Regulations] examined ... they were not even screened to see if an EIA was required. This suggests that there is widespread misunderstanding of the EIA regulatory requirements by English local planning authorities. It is also suggested that there may be a culture of resistance to EIA among planners....

Joe Weston, *Screening for EIA Projects in England: What Screening?,* 29 Impact Assessment & Project Appraisal 90 (2011).

Another defect in the UK system is not unique to the UK, but can also be found in the U.S. and many other jurisdictions—a failure to monitor the EA process "and in particular ... to reflect on the impact and accuracy of mitigation measures." Turner, *supra,* at 326. In the EU, there may be an underlying political explanation: "the EU's constitutional and political context, which is focused fundamentally on supporting good relations between Member States, may not be capable of tolerating the hard edged battles that oversight of [EIA] requires." *Id.* (quoting Jonathan Wiener). Whatever the reasons, a reviewer of TAKING STOCK summed up the situation in bleak terms:

> Reading this collection it was difficult to resist the conclusion that EA in Europe has simply become an industry divorced from any sense of actual purpose.... In unpacking the dynamics underlying the law, policy and practice of EA, the collection also raises important questions about the environmental impact of embracing sustainable development as the fundamental organising principle of modern environmental law.... [U]nless the core function of EA is reconsidered, its credibility and ultimately its viability as a mechanism for evaluating the environmental impacts of policy making and regulation at either EU or national level is doubtful. If nothing else this collection clearly exposes the myth of sustainability appraisal when the core EA process—a totem of modern environmental governance—is floundering.

Id. at 328.

C. The Scope and Relative Effectiveness of EIA Requirements

The following two charts summarize the objectives, scope, and relative effectiveness of the EIA requirements of the U.S., Canada, New Zealand, India, and England. As you look at them, consider which framework you would prefer to be covered by if you represent (1) government, (2) environmental interest groups, or (3) developers and industry.

Figure 1. EIA Comparison

Country	Objective	Scope of EIA Requirement	Source
Canada	"[T]o ensure that projects are considered in a careful and pre-cautionary manner before federal authorities take action in connection with them, in order to ensure that such projects do not cause significant adverse environmental effects; [and] to encourage responsible authorities to take actions that promote sustainable development and thereby achieve or maintain a healthy environment and a healthy economy"	Federal projects and federal lands; federal financing and permits	S.C. 1992, c. 37
England	"Effects on the environment should be taken into account at the earliest possible stage in all the technical planning and decision-making processes" … "based on the precautionary principle and on the principles that preventive action should be taken, that environmental damage should, as a priority, be rectified at source and that the polluter should pay"	All types of development having significant environmental impacts; projects include construction works or other installations or schemes, and other interventions in the natural surroundings and landscape including the extraction of mineral resources	Directive 2011/92/EC of European Parliament and Council, 13 Dec. 2011, para. 2 and Art. 1(2)(a); The Town and Country Planning Regulations (England and Wales), 1999 No. 293
India	"[T]o achieve sustainable development and the prevention of long term adverse effects by incorporating suitable prevention and control measures"; "protecting and improving the quality of the environment and preventing, controlling and abating environmental pollution"	Any new "project" or the expansion of any existing project; projects include mining, nuclear energy, transportation, communication, construction, and tourism, but *not* pipelines	Environment Impact Assessment Notification, para. 2(I)(a) (2004); EPA § 3
New Zealand	"[T]o promote the sustainable management of natural and physical resources … while … avoiding, remedying, or mitigating any adverse effects of activities on the environment"	All plans, projects, and policies requiring "resource consent" approval by local authority; subject to "call in" by federal minister for issues of national significance	Resource Management Act of 1991, § 5 and Fourth Schedule
United States	"[T]o foster and promote the general welfare, to create and maintain conditions under which man and nature can exist in productive harmony, and fulfill the social, economic, and other requirements of present and future generations of Americans"	Major federal actions, including financing, permits, and management of public lands	42 U.S.C. §§ 4331–32

Figure 2. Overall Performance of EIA Systems

Evaluation criterion	Criterion met within jurisdiction				
	United States	UK	Canada	Australia	New Zealand
1. Legal basis	●	●	●	●	●
2. Coverage	◗	●	○	◗	●
3. Alternatives	●	◗	●	●	◗
4. Screening	●	●	●	●	●
5. Scoping	●	◗	●	●	◗
6. EIA report preparation	●	◗	◗	●	○
7. EIA report review	●	◗	◗	●	◗
8. Decision making	◗	◗	◗	◗	◗
9. Impact monitoring	○	○	◗	◗	○
10. Mitigation	●	●	●	●	●
11. Consultation and participation	●	◗	●	●	◗
12. System monitoring	◗	○	●	●	○
13. Benefits and costs	●	●	●	●	●
14. Strategic EA	●	◗	◗	◗	◗
● Yes ◗ Partially ○ No					

Christopher Wood, Environmental Impact Assessment, *supra*, p. 358.

D. International Agreements and Directives

1. Rio Declaration

The Rio Declaration on Environment and Development provides that EIA, "as a national instrument, shall be undertaken for proposed activities that are likely to have a significant adverse impact on the environment and are subject to a decision of a competent national authority." U.N. Conference on Environment and Development, *Report of the United Nations Conference on Environment and Development* ¶ 17, U.N. Doc. A/CONF.151/26 (Aug. 12, 1992). The Declaration specifically acknowledges "the universal importance of EIA as an environmental decision-making tool." Christopher, *supra*, at 553–54. Although the Declaration represents principles, or nonbinding norms, rather than enforceable "hard law" provisions, its principles are important "due to the breadth of participation in the summit and the global interest in its work product." Peter Manus, *Sovereignty, Self-Determination, and Environment-Based Cultures: The Emerging Voice of Indigenous Peoples in International Law*, 23 Wis. Int'l L.J. 553, 599 (2005).

2. Espoo and Aarhus

The United Nations Convention of Environmental Impact Assessment in a Transboundary Context, 30 I.L.M. 800 (1992), was conducted at Espoo, Finland, Feb. 25, 1991, and entered into force Sept. 10, 1997. As of July 2012, forty-five countries have ratified it. Most of them are European, but Serbia, the Ukraine, Slovakia, Slovenia, and Kazakhstan are also members. As its title suggests, the Convention focuses on projects with impacts that cross jurisdictional boundaries.

The EIA Convention, or Espoo, imposes a variety of obligations on the parties, including:

1) To take either individually or jointly "all appropriate and effective measures to prevent, reduce and control significant adverse transboundary environmental impact from proposed activities." *Id.* art. 2(1).

2) With respect to activities listed in Appendix I to the Convention (such as large oil refineries, steel smelters, dams, and power plants), parties shall ensure that "an environmental impact assessment is undertaken prior to a decision to authorize or undertake a proposed activity." *Id.* art. 2(3).

3) To monitor "compliance with the conditions as set out in the authorization or approval of the activity and the effectiveness of mitigation measures." *Id.* app. V(a).

To a large extent, the Convention parallels the EC EIA Directive, *supra* Section B.4. It is similar to the EIA requirements found in the United States and Canada, with one important distinction — it applies to public and private activities.

Espoo provides for international consultation, "even to the extent that the party of origin must furnish equal consultative opportunities to the affected (downstream) public in different countries," and comments must be solicited and incorporated into the final decision. Tilleman, *supra,* at 337.

The effectiveness of Espoo, however, may be hampered by its relatively weak enforcement mechanisms. Espoo encourages parties to resolve their differences through negotiations or arbitration. If all else fails, the parties retain the option to take their dispute to the International Court of Justice. *Id.* art. 15(2), at 318, 30 I.L.M. at 810.

In addition, it appears that the parties emphasize procedure over substance:

Despite the recent proliferation of transboundary EIA treaties [such as Espoo], states and scholars have paid relatively little attention to whether or how these agreements affect proposed projects. Because the treaties themselves prescribe only procedures, jurists tend to focus on whether the parties are conforming to that process instead of substantive compliance.... Of the fifty-six questions in the Espoo Convention's most recent [2008] survey on the treaty's implementation, only one dealt with the actual effect of EIA on the outcome of a project.... Furthermore, the success of EIA regimes is inherently difficult to judge; one cannot know whether a state's decision to modify a project resulted from the findings in an EIA or from some exogenous force, such as a change in policy priorities or a budget shortfall.

Charles M. Kersten, *Rethinking Transboundary Environmental Impact Assessment*, 34 Yale J. Int'l L. 173, 174 (2009). Kersten notes that the difficulty of measuring substantive success (or the lack of it) "is exacerbated by the lack of systematic record-keeping by states." *Id.*

What happens when a non-party believes it has been adversely affected by a party's failure to prepare an adequate transboundary EIA? A dispute between New Zealand (a non-party) and France (a party) is illustrative.

> In 1974, New Zealand ... petitioned the International Court of Justice after French atmospheric nuclear tests in the area caused radioactive fallout to reach New Zealand. Despite the French government's refusal to appear before the court and offer a defense, the court found evidence in public statements by the French government that France had agreed to hold no further atmospheric nuclear tests, which satisfied the petitioners' application. However, in 1995 New Zealand petitioned the court to reopen the case, alleging that France's shift to underground nuclear testing following the 1974 ruling still had harmful environmental consequences, and that New Zealand was entitled to the protection afforded by an environmental impact assessment. The majority of the court found that New Zealand had no procedural right to reopen the case. However, in a separate dissenting opinion, Judge Weeramanty addressed the question of an environmental impact assessment in this situation and stated:
>
>> [w]hen a matter is brought before [the ICJ] which raises serious environmental issues of global importance, and a prima facie case is made out of the possibility of environmental damage, the Court is entitled to take into account the Environmental Impact Assessment principle in determining its preliminary approach.

Jedidiah D. Vander Klok, *Transboundary Environmental Effects in World Bank Project Planning: Recommendations, Structure, and Policy,* 127 Banking L.J. 33 (2010), citing Nuclear Tests Case (N.Z. v. Fr.), 1995 I.C.J. 288, 342 (Sept. 22); Nuclear Tests (N.Z. v. Fr.), 1974 I.C.J. 457, 460 (Dec. 20). The EIA principle mentioned in the dissent refers to the UNEP Guidelines on "Goals and Principles of Environmental Impact Assessment," which state in Principle 1: "States (including their competent authorities) should not undertake or authorize activities without prior consideration, at an early stage, of their environmental effects." 1995 I.C.J. at 344, citing UNEP Guidelines, U.N. Doc. UNEP/GC. 14/17, Annex III, Pr. 1 (June 1987). Dissenting Judge Weeramanty continued:

> It is clear that on an issue of the magnitude of that which brings New Zealand before this Court the principle of Environmental Impact Assessment would prima facie be applicable in terms of the current state of international environmental law.... This Court, situated as it is at the apex of international tribunals, necessarily enjoys a position of special trust and responsibility in relation to the principles of environmental law, especially those relating to what is described in environmental law as the Global Commons.

Nuclear Tests Case, 1995 I.C.J. at 344. Over the next year, France completed its nuclear testing program, but it faced growing international pressure to complete an EIA before continuing the tests. Vander Klok, *supra,* at 33.

Espoo is complemented by the U.N. Economic Commission for Europe's Convention on Access to Information, Public Participation in Decision-Making, and Access to Justice in Environmental Matters (known as the Aarhus Convention), June 25, 1998, 38 I.L.M. 517 (entered into force Oct. 30, 2001). Aarhus is based on two fundamental principles: early and effective public participation. The Convention "ties environmental rights to human rights and links accountability of governments with environmental protection, focusing on the relationship between governmental authorities and the public." Yaser Khalaileh, *A Right to a Clean Environment in the Middle East: Opportunities to Embrace or Reject,* 42 Envtl. L. Rep. News & Analysis 10280, 10285 (2012). Although the Convention seems to have done a good job promoting access to information, "[p]ublic participation is still in its initial stages, ... [and it has done] little to advance the effort to protect the environment under the umbrella of human rights and environmental law, because it focused on the obligation of the States rather than the rights of the public." *Id.* Its popularity is spreading, though, and by 2009 it had been ratified by 41 countries, primarily European and Central Asian, and by the European Community.

> There is no more universal complaint by local communities than the lack of access to reliable, trusted information about the consequences of the process of change unleashed by development. The Aarhus Convention is being promoted widely as a framework for approaching this issue.

Luke J. Danielson, *Sustainable Development in the Natural Resource Industries: New Perspectives, New Rules, and New Opportunities,* 50 RMMLF-INST 14-1 (2004). For details, see Svitlana Kravchenko, *The Aarhus Convention and Innovations in Compliance with Multilateral Environmental Agreements Compliance Mechanisms,* 18 Colo. J. Int'l Envtl. L. & Pol'y 1, 10 (2007).

3. Other Regional Agreements and World Bank Guidelines

In North America, the Agreement on Environmental Cooperation, a side agreement to the North American Free Trade Agreement (NAFTA), established a Commission on Environmental Cooperation and charged it with developing recommendations for the assessment and mitigation of proposed projects likely to cause significant adverse transboundary impacts. North American Agreement on Environmental Cooperation, Sept. 14, 1993, 32 I.L.M. 1480 (1993) (entered into force Jan. 1, 1994). The parties have been slow to develop legally binding commitments on EIAs, however, in part because controversial border projects, such as the siting of a state-sponsored low-level radioactive waste facility in Texas, have contributed to deadlock between the parties. One of the major sticking points is whether to extend the EIA obligation to both federal and non-federal projects. Domestic law in Mexico requires EIAs for private hazardous waste facilities, but this would require a much broader commitment from the United States than is required by NEPA. The Agreement on Environmental Cooperation and other regional EIA commitments are addressed in Angela Z. Cassar & Carl. E. Bruch, *Transboundary Environmental Impact Assessment in International Watercourse Management,* 12 N.Y.U. Envtl. L. J. 169 (2003).

EIA requirements are also imposed on projects funded by the World Bank. According to former World Bank President Robert Zoellick, the Bank's purpose is "to assist countries to help themselves by catalyzing the capital and policies through a mix of ideas and experience, development of private market opportunities, and support for good governance and anti-corruption—spurred by our financial resources." Robert B. Zoellick, The National Press Club, Washington D.C., October 10, 2007.

The World Bank requires assessments for all projects or operations expected to have adverse environmental impacts that would be significant in terms of the project's type, location, sensitivity, or scale. *See* World Bank Operational Policy 4.01 (1999), available at http://www.worldbank.org. A dispute over the impacts of the Narmada dam in India resulted in the withdrawal of World Bank funds. *See* Ellison, *supra.* In other instances, World Bank funding for high-impact projects has gone forward despite adverse effects, prompting a call for reform:

> [T]he World Bank should pay greater attention to issues of transboundary environmental impact.... The Bank should expand its environmental safeguards to ensure the involvement in the project planning process of affected peoples outside the project's host country. The Bank's activities have a broad reach, and to improve the effectiveness of its programs the Bank should seek input from all stakeholders. Many of the Bank's programs require the involvement and support of local communities, and by involving all affected communities in the planning process the Bank can structure its program to the needs of the affected community and provide a greater assurance of its effectiveness. The Bank's environmental assessment procedures already require public disclosure of environmental assessment information and "meaningful consultation" with the borrower, non-governmental organizations, and other affected parties, but limit this to within the borders of the host country.

Jedidiah D. Vander Klok, *Transboundary Environmental Effects in World Bank Project Planning: Recommendations, Structure, and Policy*, 127 Banking L.J. 33, 52–53 (2010), citing Independent Evaluation Group, *Environmental Sustainability: An Evaluation of World Bank Group Support* 24–25 (2008). Are more rigorous environmental assessment and the denial of funding for high-impact environmental projects consistent with the Bank's mission of "catalyzing the capital and policies" of less developed countries?

E. EIAs and Climate Change

For the most part, EIAs are used to address relatively localized environmental impacts. According to critics, "EIA has had an increasing tendency to operate on autopilot, producing voluminous amounts of technical data, but often not taking advantage of the process as an opportunity for creative decision-making." Christopher, *Success by a Thousand Cuts, supra*, at 555–56.

Does this necessarily mean that EIAs cannot be an effective tool to address greenhouse gas emissions and climate change?

> The complex search for a universal solution to global climate change continues to perplex environmental policy experts.... Climate change is a nontraditional environmental topic demonstrated by immense volumes of cumulative contribution of pollutant gasses, but few, if any, major contributing sources responsible for a distinctive degree of environmental harm divisible from other sources....
>
> Never before has environmental law faced such a grave but distant challenge that cuts across so many levels of government and involves a multitude of political and socio-economic issues. Yet with all of the attention placed on creating a cooperative international solution, some of the most effective strategies for addressing climate change impacts may already exist in site-specific, localized decision tools such as EIA laws, which allow a government actor to weigh a variety of environmental impacts and alternatives to proposed action or con-

struction while also allowing both key stakeholders and the interested public to participate in the study and decision-making process.

Id. at 551, 555–56. That said, relatively few of the jurisdictions that have adopted EIA requirements analyze the implications and potential impacts of climate change as part of their EIA processes. *Id.* at 551. Should they? If so, how might they place reasonable, workable parameters on the analysis?

An example can be found in Genesis Power Ltd. v. Franklin Dist. Council, [2005] N.Z.R.M.A. 541 (Env. Court), *supra.* There, the court concluded that, on balance, a wind power project's national advantages through the reduction of greenhouse gas emissions would outweigh the adverse visual impacts on the local landscape, such that the project should be characterized as a sustainable development that complied with New Zealand's Resource Management Act. The court took note of the 2004 amendments to the Act that emphasized the importance of renewable energy and the need to combat climate change. *Id.* para. 4, [212(i)]. *See also* Meridian Energy Limited v. Wellington City Council & Wellington Regional Council, unreported, W031/07 (Env. Court 2007) (upholding a proposal to install seventy wind turbines on sensitive and difficult terrain in the Wellington region as an efficient use of a renewable resource).

How would you resolve the following dispute brought by an island nation concerned about one of Europe's largest coal-fired power plants, situated nearly 7,000 miles away?

> [T]he reconstruction of the biggest coal-burning power plant in the Czech Republic, Prunerov II, may have significant transboundary environmental impacts on the Federal Republic of Micronesia.... Micronesia ... alleges that the [Czech government's] EIA failed to assess all potential impacts and all possible alternatives to minimize the adverse impacts of the modernization of the power plant ... [*i.e.,*] that using outdated technology will result in an additional nine million tons of emitted CO2.... [It] identified four climate change phenomena which represent a significant threat to the well-being of the environment, among them, accelerated sea-level rise, El Niño effects, La Nina effects, and GHG emissions.

Svitlana Kravchenko, *Procedural Rights as a Crucial Tool to Combat Climate Change,* 38 Ga. J. Int'l & Comp. L. 613, 641–42 (2010). The Czech Republic is a party to the Espoo Convention, but Micronesia is not. Where should Micronesia assert its claim? (Recall the New Zealand v. France nuclear testing cases, described above.) What jurisdictional or causation issues might Micronesia encounter? In formulating your answer, keep in mind "that GHG emissions produced *solely* by Prunerov II will not directly cause sea-level rise ... and increased storms," but that "there are approximately only 5000 such power plants which contribute to total global CO2 emissions." *Id.* Note, too, that Micronesia already suffers from frequent flooding and destructive storms and tidal surges as a result of rising sea levels. Much of Micronesia, including at least one of its international airports, lies barely more than three feet above sea level. Experts predict that, unless climate change is addressed, sea levels will rise three feet by the end of this century. *Micronesia sues Czech Republic over Prunerov II Coal Plant Expansion,* PennEnergy, July 6, 2012.

Chapter IV

Keystone Environmental Laws Governing Water

In its broadest sense, water law addresses water quality as well as issues related to the conservation, use, and allocation of quantities of water. Although this chapter focuses primarily on the laws governing water quality and preventing pollution of water bodies, the diversion or consumption of water can have a tremendous impact on the quality of the source, too, as concentrations of pollutants might increase when water levels drop and salt-water and other contaminants leach into or otherwise intrude on depleted water bodies. Regimes for water quantity typically fall within the realm of property law, torts law, interstate or other regional or international agreements (contracts or treaties), and, increasingly, human rights laws (the latter is addressed in Chapter 6.A of this book). National security concerns may be implicated as well.

> Across the planet, water is an essential but unevenly distributed natural resource. A glance at a recent map of the world's water-stressed areas confirms that many of them lie in politically unstable and/or poor countries. In the past two decades, environmental degradation and resource conflict have been identified as national or regional security issues potentially as serious as armed conflict. Many water and security studies have drawn the normative conclusion that these stresses will result in internal and external conflicts over the use of limited water supplies and that these conflicts can lead to either military action or massive social unrest and political crises.

A. Dan Tarlock, *Four Challenges for International Water Law*, 23 Tulane Env. L. J. 369, 370 (2010). How might international and domestic law address these concerns?

> Access to clean water calls for a system of laws and responsibilities with the same features as those governing any other important matter: compliance with basic principles of the rule of law and democratic accountability, protection of citizens from the interference of others (including those who would pollute water and other common environmental resources), and protection of citizens' access to goods and services by means of competitive markets and freedom to choose. The rationale for [human] rights is not simply that water is important, but that the main threats to water can be alleviated by establishing certain principles for the way it is governed.

> Should water be free because it is essential and therefore priceless, or should it be expensive because it is essential and therefore valuable?

Bruce Pardy, *The Dark Irony of International Water Rights*, 28 Pace Envtl. L. Rev. 907, 917, 920 (2011). Professor Pardy acknowledges, "Governments have a legitimate role to play, protecting both quality and quantity, so that there is clean water available for the taking." *Id.* at 920. But he asserts that their role should be limited: "This role is as protector, not provider. All that is called for is to prevent pollution and depletion — not to actively provide water, but to protect the resource from interference from those who would impose environmental externalities upon it." *Id.* Do you agree? What should the government's role be when it comes to water management, conservation, and delivery?

Common law responses to water pollution are described in Chapter 2.B, *supra.* Common law claims and remedies are still relevant, but in the modern era the protection of water quality from pollutants is governed extensively by legislation and regulation. The remainder of this chapter addresses key provisions of water quality laws in the U.S., Canada, New Zealand, India, and England. The final section of the chapter covers international and transboundary provisions related to water, and provides a close look at a transboundary dispute between the U.S. and Canada over pollution from a smelter in British Columbia.

A. The U.S.

Prior to 1972, the federal government had adopted limited measures to protect navigable waterways from obstructions and refuse and had taken steps to assist the states with sewage treatment and other public health problems arising from contaminated water, but for the most part, it left water quality concerns to state and local governments. That changed when some of the nation's water bodies began to smolder, and images of burning rivers and oil-soaked seagulls became widely publicized, spurring the enactment of the United States' foundational environmental laws. One of these is the federal Clean Water Act (CWA) of 1972. *See* Richard J. Lazarus, *The Making of Environmental Law* 59 (2004).

The purposes of the CWA are to "restore and maintain the chemical, physical and biological integrity" of the nation's waters and to eliminate the discharge of water pollutants. South Florida Water Mgmt. Dist. v. Miccosukee Tribe, 541 U.S. 95, 102 (2004) (citing 33 U.S.C. § 1251(a)). To carry out these goals, Congress prohibited certain discharges except by permit. 33 U.S.C. § 1311 (a).

1. Discharges of Pollutants from Point Sources

The primary mechanism for accomplishing the CWA's objectives is Section 301, 33 U.S.C. § 1311, which prohibits the "discharge of any pollutant by any person" unless a permit is obtained. The CWA defines "discharge of pollutant" as "any addition of any pollutant to navigable waters from any point source." 33 U.S.C. § 1362(12). "Pollutants" include a variety of substances, including garbage, sewage, chemical wastes, biological materials, and even heat. The term "addition" looks relatively straightforward, but looks can be deceiving. Does it include cold water and fish moved from a deep reservoir through a dam into a warmer, shallower stream below the dam? *See* Nat'l Wildlife Fed'n v. Gorsuch, 693 F.2d 156 (D.C. Cir. 1982) (no). How about water pumped from a canal through a pumping station to a restored wetland utilized for stormwater impoundment? Note that water flowing through the canal and the pumping system contains more phosphorous than water in the wetlands. *See* S. Fla. Water Mgmt. Dist. v. Miccosukee Tribe of Indians, 541 U.S. 95 (2004) (pumping water between distinct water bodies may be an addition).

"Point source" is a term of art meaning "any discernible, confined and discrete conveyance, including but not limited to any pipe, ditch, channel, tunnel, conduit, well, ... concentrated animal feeding operation, or vessel or other floating craft, from which pollutants are or may be discharged." 33 U.S.C. § 1362(14). Congress crafted an exemption, however, for "agricultural stormwater discharges and return flows from irrigated agriculture." 33 U.S.C. § 1362(14).

The point source concept was developed so that pollution from simple erosion or run-off could be distinguished from pollution that has been collected or originates from confined systems. Run-off (non-point source pollution) is addressed largely through state and local efforts. However, it is not always easy to distinguish between point and non-point sources. *See* Northwest Envtl. Defense Center v. Brown, 640 F.3d 1063 (9th Cir. 2011) (finding that stormwater runoff that was collected in a system of ditches, culverts, and channels, and was then discharged from logging roads into streams, was a point source), *cert. granted*, Decker v. Northwest Envtl. Defense Center, No. 11-338, 2012 WL 2368685 (2012).

Are the following activities "discharges" from a "point source"?

- Pesticides sprayed from a nozzle on a tanker truck onto a field directly adjacent to a stream.

- Pesticides sprayed from a crop duster (airplane) onto a field a mile away from a stream.

- "Deep-ripping"—dragging a large heavy piece of equipment with fork-like tines—through saturated areas of a field to convert it from orchards to a vineyard.

- Ballast water pumped from a foreign flagged ship at a port in Detroit, Michigan, into Lake Michigan, resulting in the introduction of zebra mussels and other non-indigenous species.

- Mountain-top mining, where coal companies lop off the top of a mountain to reach the underlying seam of coal, pushing the overburden into the valley below. (*See* Perspective: Mountaintop Removal, *infra*.)

2. Waters of the U.S.

The geographic trigger for CWA jurisdiction is the "any addition of any pollutant *to navigable waters* from any point source." 33 U.S.C. § 1362(12) (emphasis added). The term "navigable waters," defined rather vaguely as "waters of the U.S.," 33 U.S.C. § 1362(7), has been the subject of extensive judicial attention in recent years. In U.S. v. Riverside Bayview Homes, 474 U.S. 121, 133 (1985), the Supreme Court upheld federal jurisdiction over wetlands adjacent to a navigable lake, stating that the term "navigable" was of "limited" importance in determining CWA jurisdiction. In 2001, however, Solid Waste Authority of Northern Cook County v. U.S. Army Corps of Engineers (SWANCC), 531 U.S. 159 (2001), narrowed the scope of waters regulated by the CWA. The Court refused to extend federal jurisdiction to a man-made lake with no connection to a navigable waterway, stating that to do so would "result in significant impingement of the States' traditional and primary power over land and water use." *Id.* at 174.

The Court's most recent word on the subject does little to dispel the confusion over the geographic scope of the CWA. In Rapanos v. United States, 574 U.S. 715 (2006), a split decision that gathered no clear majority, four justices expressed a view that would allow development of most non-adjacent wetlands as well as non-perennial streams. As in

SWANCC, the lead opinion by Justice Scalia stated that the CWA must be construed narrowly to preserve "primary state responsibility for ordinary land-use decisions." *Id.* at 756. Because it was a split opinion, the agencies and the lower courts have struggled to apply *Rapanos.* Many have followed Justice Kennedy's concurring opinion, which stated that, to come within federal protection, regulators must make a scientific determination that the tributary or wetland in question has a significant hydrological "nexus" to a navigable water body.

Commentators fear that *SWANCC* and *Rapanos* do not bode well for wetlands, birds, and overall environmental quality. The following editorial uses the 2006 World Cup, which was being played in Germany at the time, as a metaphor for the *Rapanos* opinion.

Sandra Zellmer, The World Cup of Environmental Law: The Supreme Court Takes Pot Shots at Each Other Over Wetlands
High Country News, June 26, 2006

In one of the most anxiously awaited decisions this session, the Supreme Court struck a blow against environmental protection by ruling for a couple of commercial developers. The issue in play in *Rapanos v. United States*: Can federal protection be extended to small tributaries and wetlands near, but not directly abutting, navigable waters? A lower court said yes, but the Supreme Court referees, in a 4–1–4 split decision, disagreed and vacated the judgments against the developers.

The lead opinion by Justice Scalia ... would clear the way for development of most wetlands and streams. According to the court's most conservative members, the regulation of non-perennial streams, wet meadows and arroyos under the federal Clean Water Act stretches the law's coverage "beyond parody."

But as the dissent by Justices Stevens, Souter, Ginsburg and Breyer noted, as the wetlands and their inhabitants go, so goes the entire watershed. The Scalia opinion, they argued, is nothing but blatant "antagonism to environmentalism."

Justice Scalia cavalierly dismissed the dissenters' concerns, saving his most heated rhetoric for Justice Kennedy [who opined, in his concurring opinion, that waters and wetlands come within federal protection only if there is a hydrological "nexus" to a navigable water body]. In a shot that would draw a "red card" in soccer, he accused Kennedy of misreading the court's prior decisions, hiding behind the statutory purpose of protecting water quality rather than adhering to the statute's plain language, and then bootstrapping his conclusion by claiming that anything that might affect waters of the United States bears a "significant nexus" to those waters and thus *is* those waters.

In a parting shot, Scalia disparaged Kennedy's logic as unsubstantiated "turtles all the way down." The turtle metaphor refers to a fictional exchange between an astronomer and a little old lady in a lecture hall. The astronomer described how the earth orbits around the sun. The lady remarked: "That's rubbish. The world is a flat plate supported on the back of a giant tortoise." When the astronomer, humoring her, asked what the tortoise was standing on, the lady replied, "Why, it's turtles all the way down."

The irony of Scalia's metaphor is palpable. According to Conservation International, 40 to 60 percent of all turtles in the world face extinction. United States' populations reflect this trend: Around half of our turtle species are imperiled ... and the primary culprit is habitat loss. In the last 200 years, the United States has lost over half of its original wetlands, the equivalent of 60 acres of wetlands every hour.

If Scalia had convinced … [just one more Justice] to join in his opinion, many—in fact, most—wetlands and streams would be excluded from federal protection. Many of the remaining wetlands are not adjacent to navigable waters, and the National Hydrology Dataset shows that nearly 60 percent of the total stream miles in the U.S. are non-perennial. In arid Western states like New Mexico and Arizona, the figure is much higher: 90 percent of assessed streams flow only in wet weather.

Although Justice Scalia expressed his concern for preserving "primary state responsibility for ordinary land-use decisions," 33 states and the District of Columbia filed "friend of the court" briefs on behalf of the United States, seeking to maintain broad federal jurisdiction over wetlands and tributaries. In their view, wetlands preservation—a political "hot potato" if ever there was one—is best accomplished by the feds.

Confusion reigns. As a result of the split, Justice Kennedy's concurring opinion has become the law of the land. Yes, it could have been worse for conservation interests. But the *Rapanos* decision places the burden of proving a "significant nexus" squarely on the shoulders of the U.S. Corps of Engineers, which itself is experiencing a crisis of legitimacy in the wake of Hurricane Katrina. It isn't unreasonable to question whether this beleaguered agency, subject to an array of contradictory statutory mandates, from wetlands protection to dredging navigational channels and constructing flood control levees, is up to the task of going toe-to-toe with well-heeled developers in this case-by-case fashion.

At least the U.S. soccer team could claim a tie, which kept its hopes alive in the World Cup (albeit briefly). Not so for the turtles, who swing in the balance while legal skirmishes continue.

Notes and Questions

1. After *Rapanos* was handed down, the Corps and the EPA issued Guidance on the scope of the CWA. *Draft Guidance on Identifying Waters Protected by the Clean Water Act* (2011), http://water.epa.gov/lawsregs/guidance/wetlands/upload/wous_guidance_4-2011.pdf. The Guidance urges reliance on Kennedy's "nexus" test coupled with a hydrologic function test. It delineates three classes of water:

> The first reaffirms categorical Clean Water Act jurisdiction over traditional navigable waters, interstate waters, wetlands adjacent to these waters, relatively permanent non-navigable tributaries and wetlands that directly abut permanent waters. The third equally identifies waters not generally protected such as artificially irrigated areas that would revert to upland if irrigation stopped. The most important … intermediate category subjects waters to jurisdiction under the nexus and hydrologic function tests. These waters include tributaries and adjacent wetlands and "other waters" … [*i.e.,*] "lakes, ponds, and other non-wetland waters that are bordering, contiguous, or neighboring to jurisdictional waters, including waters that are separated from jurisdictional waters by man-made dikes or barriers, natural river berms, beach dunes and the like."

A. Dan Tarlock, *L. of Water Rights and Resources* § 9:11 (2012), citing Draft Guidance at 19.

2. This area of the law remains murky (pardon the pun), and the courts have struggled to reach consistent results. Can the following cases be squared with each other and with the Guidance?

- Precon Development Corp. v. U.S. Army Corps of Engineers, 633 F.3d 278 (4th Cir. 2011)—There was no nexus between 448 acres of wetlands adjacent to two man-made ditches, which flowed at varying and unknown rates toward a river located several miles away.

- U.S. v. Donovan, 661 F.3d 174 (3rd Cir. 2011)—The CWA covered certain wetlands that contributed surface and ground water flows to a tidally influenced river, helped sequester pollutants, and contributed energy and carbon to downstream habitats, thereby affecting the "chemical, physical, and biological integrity" of navigable waters.

- U.S. v. Cundiff, 555 F.3d 200, 210 (6th Cir. 2009)—The CWA covered five acres of wetlands adjacent to two creeks that flowed into the Green River, a navigable tributary of the Ohio River. The government's expert testified, "the wetlands perform significant ecological functions in relation to the Green River and the two creeks, including: temporary and long-term water storage, filtering of the acid runoff and sediment from the nearby mine, and providing an important habitat for plants and wildlife." *Id.* at 211. The court found that the Cundiffs' alterations—unauthorized ditch digging, the mechanical clearing of land, and dredging material and using it as filler—had undermined the wetlands' ability to store water, which had affected the frequency and extent of flooding in the Green River. *Id.*

These and other cases indicate that the inquiry is highly fact-specific. In *Precon,* the court found that the Corps' administrative record, which included measures of the potential flow rates of the man-made ditches, without any indication of how much flow typically was in the ditches, did not establish the existence of a significant nexus between adjacent wetlands and a navigable river that was approximately seven miles away. It also indicated that information on the significance of the flow on the river's condition, such as on flooding or levels of nitrogen or sedimentation, was required to find CWA jurisdiction. Yet the court explicitly stated that, "the significant nexus test does not require laboratory tests or any particular quantitative measurements in order to establish significance." 633 F.3d at 294.

3. Discharge Permits

The Act has two major permit programs. First, the National Pollution Discharge Elimination System (NPDES) permit program found in Section 402 requires permits for "the discharge of any pollutant by any person." 33 U.S.C. § 1342. Section 402 permits must incorporate effluent limitations reflecting the best technology available. 33 U.S.C. § 1311(b)(2)(A). Today, around 100,000 facilities have obtained permits. Most permits are issued by state agencies with delegated authority from the U.S. EPA. Permit requirements may be enforced through injunctions, administrative, civil, and criminal penalties, and citizen suits. *See* 33 U.S.C. §§ 1319, 1365.

As a result of the NPDES program, chemical pollutants from point sources have been reduced significantly. Unfortunately, non-point source pollution remains virtually uncontrolled. Programs directed at non-point source pollution sources, which include a broad range of activities such as farming and construction run-off, are left to the states. Unlike the permitting provisions for point sources, EPA lacks direct regulatory authority over non-point sources. At most, EPA may withhold funding for delinquent states that do not take timely steps to address non-point pollution. Robert W. Adler, *The Clean Water Act Turns 30: Celebrating Its Past, Predicting Its Future,* 33 Envtl. L. 29, 47, 56 (2003).

States are required to establish water quality standards (WQS), which are comprised of designated uses for waterways within the state and numeric or narrative criteria sufficient to satisfy those uses. WQS also must include an anti-degradation program to protect Outstanding National Resource Waters and other streams with good water quality from being degraded or destroyed by development. 33 U.S.C. § 1313(c)-(d)(4)(B). *See* Sandra Zellmer and Robert Glicksman, *Using Public Natural Resource Management Laws to Improve Water Pollution Anti-degradation Policies,* G.W. J. E. & Env. Law (forthcoming 2012) (tracing the history of the anti-degradation policy, assessing its effectiveness, and suggesting reforms).

If the states fail to do so, EPA must promulgate legally enforceable WQS. 33 U.S.C. § 1313(c)(4); Raymond Proffitt Fnd v. EPA, 930 F. Supp. 2d 1088, 1098 (E.D. Pa. 1996). Waterways that do not meet WQS will be listed as impaired and total maximum daily loads (TMDLs) must be set. 33 U.S.C. § 1313(d).

TMDLs are applied to point sources through the NPDES permit program, but mechanisms for applying them to non-point sources are unclear. As a result, the track record for WQS implementation has been "less than stellar." Oliver A. Houck, The Clean Water Act TMDL Program: Law, Policy, and Implementation 5, 63 (2d ed. 2002).

> Large numbers of urban watersheds remain chemically impaired because of pathogens, phosphorus, insecticides, herbicides, and toxics from municipal and industrial sources; and many rural watersheds remain chemically impaired as a result of nutrients, sediment, and agricultural chemicals.... [A]quatic species are declining at a far more alarming rate than are terrestrial species.... Likewise, a recent assessment of riparian area health published by a committee of the National Research Council reported widespread hydrologic, geomorphic, and other impairment of riparian habitats, along with accompanying impacts to water quality and aquatic ecosystem health. The report documents as much as ninety-five percent loss of natural vegetation in some riparian areas, "indicating that riparian areas are some of the most severely altered landscapes in the country."

Adler, *supra,* at 47, 50.

The second CWA permit program is found in Section 404, which controls discharges of dredged or fill materials into waters of the United States. Section 404 has significant impacts for a variety of activities, including development that would fill wetlands. Wetlands act as buffers against flooding and as filters that trap pollutants. They also provide essential breeding, nesting and feeding grounds for countless migratory birds, fisheries, and wildlife species. Congress's recognition that wetlands provide a variety of ecosystem services worthy of protection is evident in CWA § 404, which authorizes the Corps of Engineers to issue permits "for the discharge of dredged or fill material into the navigable waters at specified disposal sites." 33 U.S.C. § 1344(a). The EPA retains oversight and veto power over permits if "unacceptable adverse effects" to the environment would result.

Individual 404 permits are evaluated on a case-by-case basis, while general or nationwide permits may be issued for categories of activities that are similar in nature and have only minimal impacts. To receive an individual permit, the project proponent must first demonstrate that there are no practical alternatives to the destruction of wetlands. Memorandum of Agreement Between the Environmental Protection Agency and the Department of the Army Concerning the Determination of Mitigation Under the Clean Water Act Section 404(b)(1) Guidelines, 55 Fed. Reg. 9210, 9212 (1990). The agencies presume that a practical alternative exists if the project is not water-dependent. Second, steps must be taken to minimize the adverse effects of development on the wetlands. 40 C.F.R

230.10(d). Finally, if damage to the wetlands cannot be avoided or minimized, the permittee must compensate for the damages.

The wetlands provisions of Section 404 is complemented by the Swampbuster program of the Food Security Act of 1985. Food Security Act of 1985, Pub. L. No. 99-198, 99 Stat. 1507, amended in the Farm Bill of 1990, 16 U.S.C. § 3821. These provisions remove previous federal incentives to drain wetlands by withholding federal subsidies from farmers who produce crops on converted wetlands.

Even with the protections of the CWA and Swampbuster in place, between 1986 and 1997, over 640,000 acres of U.S. wetlands were lost. Yet the rate of wetland loss has slowed from nearly 500,000 acres per year between the 1950s and 1970s to less than 60,000 acres per year from 1986 to 1997.

Some wetlands and small streams are found in the valleys of Appalachia, in the eastern United States. Thousands of acres of wetlands and stream miles have been filled by the "overburden" cast off into valleys and ravines by coal mining.

CPR Perspective: Mountaintop Removal

Center for Progressive Reform,
http://progressivereform.org/perspMt_top.cfm (2009)

[M]ore than 12 billion tons of Appalachian coal have been mined, primarily from West Virginia, Kentucky, North Carolina, Ohio, and Virginia. Appalachian mines currently produce over one-third of the nation's coal output ... [In] the mid-1990s, a cheaper method of surface mining, called "mountaintop removal," became prevalent throughout Appalachia. This technique involves placing explosives at various points around a mountaintop and blasting off 600 feet or more of earth. Miners then remove the loose rock and soil with draglines, which are gigantic machines, sometimes 20 stories tall, that can scoop 100 tons of so-called "overburden" at a time, allowing extraction of the exposed coal seams.... The practice literally flattens mountains and transforms densely forested mountaintops to treeless terraces and plateaus. The displaced overburden becomes "valley fill," which is pushed into valleys that typically contain headwater streams. As a result, 1,600 miles of streams have been permanently filled....

The nation's attention became focused on problems in the coalfields in 1972, when ... [f]loodwaters destroyed 500 homes, killed 125 people, and left 4,000 homeless. To counter the impacts of unregulated mining, Congress passed the Surface Mining Control and Reclamation Act of 1977 (SMCRA).... The Office of Surface Mining Reclamation and Enforcement (OSM) in the Department of the Interior oversees the implementation of SMCRA. OSM has the authority to issue regulations, approve or disapprove state permit programs, and oversee state administration. 30 U.S.C. § 1211. While states may assume the authority to implement surface mining programs, provisions for federal oversight and for citizen participation were included in SMCRA to ensure against states' tendency to prioritize economic production over environmental protection. Under SMCRA, mountaintop removal may be a legitimate mining technique, but only if it is subject to stringent regulation to protect valley streams and to reclaim mined areas to their approximate original structure and function....

Mountaintop removal is also regulated at the federal level by the Clean Water Act (CWA), which applies to a broad range of activities that affect water quality. The Act is implemented through two permitting programs: § 402, administered by the U.S. Environmental Protection Agency (EPA), and the "dredge and fill" program of § 404, administered by the Corps of Engineers. The former governs waste by-products and other pollutants discharged into waters of the United States while the latter governs dredged materials and materials used to fill waters and wetlands to convert them to dry, developable land. If an activity is regulated under § 404, it will not be required to obtain a § 402 permit. Coeur Alaska, Inc. v. Southeast Alaska Conservation Council, 77 USLW 4559 (June 22, 2009). Both programs require individual dischargers to obtain permits, but certain categories of relatively innocuous activities can be covered by streamlined, general permits. The Corps is authorized to issue these "nationwide permits" (NWPs) under Section 404, but only for activities that "will cause only minimal adverse environmental effects when performed separately, and will have only minimal cumulative adverse effects on the environment." Mountaintop mining has been allowed under NWP-21, discussed below....

The adequacy of ... the Corps of Engineers' implementation of section 404 has been challenged in several highly publicized lawsuits.... [One] case challenged the Corps of Engineers' approval of a Martin County Coal Corporation project in Kentucky under NWP-21. A non-profit group, Kentuckians for the Commonwealth, challenged the Corps' practice of permitting valley fills as a violation of the Corps' own long-standing CWA regulation that explicitly forbade issuance of a § 404 permit to dump material primarily to dispose of waste. Kentuckians for the Commonwealth v. Rivenburgh, 204 F.Supp.2d 27 (S.D.W.Va. 2002), rev'd, 317 F.3d 425 (4th Cir. 2003).

In 2002, while the case was pending, the Corps issued a new rule that allowed the dumping of waste rock and dirt as "fill." As a result, "placement of overburden, slurry, or tailings or similar mining-related materials" requires only a 404 permit, rather than a 402 permit. 67 Fed. Reg. 31129, 31133 (May 9, 2002) (codified at 33 C.F.R. § 323.2(e)(2))....
The Fourth Circuit upheld the rule and concluded that the Corps properly exercised its discretion to issue a permit to Martin Coal. Since then, the Fourth Circuit has upheld several more permits issued by the Corps to other West Virginia mining companies. See Ohio Valley Envtl. Coalition v. Aracoma Coal Co., 556 F.3d 177 (2009)....

The lawsuits described above reveal at least three fundamental weaknesses in the regulatory framework governing mountaintop removal. First, [one decision in a SMCRA case,] ... by according sovereign immunity to states, seriously undermines the important federal policy of ensuring protection for all citizens notwithstanding individual states' demonstrated tendency to prioritize economic activity over environmental, health, and safety protection....

Second, the Corps' new interpretation of "fill" blurs the long-standing and principled jurisdictional line between waste disposal activities covered by § 402 (the EPA's permit program) and fill materials covered by § 404. Allowing regulation of mountaintop removal under § 404 side-steps readily enforceable, technology-based standards otherwise required under § 402....

Finally, authorizing valley fills under § 404 makes them more likely to be covered through a blanket nationwide approval like NWP-21. As the 2009 MOU apparently recognizes, NWP-21 represents a choice that disregards health, safety, and environmental values and seriously impairs the opportunity for public participation.

Moreover, the Corps' approval of mountaintop removal through NWP-21 exceeds the Corps' authority under the law. A general permit may be issued only if the category of activities has minimal adverse effects, both individually and cumulatively. The Corps' own rules state that these permits may be used only for activities that are not controversial and that provoke little or no public comment. Mountaintop removal fits none of these criteria.... The Corps itself agreed that valley fills have the potential to cause significant environmental effects, but it claimed that mitigation and after-the-fact monitoring minimize the effects. Several courts have found, however, that these measures routinely prove unsuccessful, and the Corps conceded that there is a great deal of uncertainty with respect to the efficacy of wetland and stream mitigation to restore ecological function. Ohio Valley Envtl. Coalition v. Aracoma Coal Co., 556 F.3d 177, 218–223, 225 (4th Cir. 2009) (Michael, J., dissenting in part).

If mountaintop removal continues at its present pace and form, Appalachian residents will continue to suffer.... Individual permitting processes for mountaintop removal, along with strict enforcement by federal and state governments and private citizens, are necessary to prevent social and environmental destruction....

The extension of § 404 jurisdiction and the concomitant reduction of § 402 jurisdiction, as well as the Corps' belief that these tremendously destructive activities entail only "minimal adverse effects" and can therefore be permitted by nationwide permits, are untenable and should be reversed. In addition, EPA should take an active role in protecting the nation's waters from valley fills, and OSM should ... exercise strong oversight over states that fail to implement SMCRA's requirements.

Notes and Questions

1. How should federal environmental laws address water pollution from mountaintop mining? Should the EPA or the Corps take the lead? The Supreme Court has held that if a discharge is subject to the § 404 dredge and fill permit program administered by the Corps, it is not subject to the § 402 NPDES permit program administered by EPA. Coeur Alaska, Inc. v. Southeast Alaska Conservation Council, 129 S. Ct. 2458 (2009), citing 40 C.F.R. § 232.2 (providing definitions of "fill" and "pollutant"). Justice Ginsburg's dissent noted that the majority's holding would allow industries to gain immunity from EPA's strict pollution control standards by dumping solid material into water bodies in such a manner as to raise the bottom elevation, thereby qualifying as "fill" subject to the less onerous § 404 permit program, even if the material is in fact a type of waste that should be regulated by the EPA rather than the Corps. Id. at 2482–2483.

2. Federal law authorizes states to take delegations of authority to administer both water pollution and coal reclamation programs. Is a state like West Virginia in the best position to handle the environmental, economic, and social issues raised by mountaintop mining? Are there special circumstances in the region that justify taking a lenient approach to regulation?

3. In 2009, President Obama's new EPA Administrator announced that the EPA would exert closer scrutiny over applications filed under NWP-21 to ensure that valley fills avoid significant degradation of the nation's waters. The Corps subsequently reached a Memorandum of Understanding with the EPA and the Department of Interior, whereby it agreed to minimize the adverse consequences of mountaintop removal by requiring more stringent environmental reviews for future permit applications. The Corps also agreed to issue a public notice of its intent to preclude the use of NWP-21 for the discharge of valley fills in Appalachia. MOU Among the U.S. Department of the Army, U.S. Department of the Interior, and U.S. Environmental Protection Agency Implementing the Interagency Action Plan on Appalachian Surface Coal Mining (June 11, 2009), available at http://www.epa.gov/owow/wetlands/pdf/Final_MTM_MOU_6-11-09.pdf. Such memoranda are less formal than officially promulgated regulations, and are easier to revise or rescind than either regulations or legislation. If you were an at-

torney representing the Corps under a new, more conservative, pro-business administration in the future, what would you advise your client to do with respect to the use
of NWP-21?

4. How can affected communities best play a role in decisionmaking and enforcement? For a video clip expressing the viewpoint of a West Virginia reporter, see Cather-
ine Porter, Coal Mining Ravages Appalachia Mountains, Feb. 23, 2008, http://
www.thestar.com/sciencetech/Environment/article/306165.

5. If in doubt about the status of a potential wetland on her property, what should a
landowner do? What if the EPA hands the landowner a Clean Water Act compliance order,
telling her to get a 404 permit or stop construction, at the risk of paying a hefty fine?
When the EPA prevails against a person who has been issued a compliance order but has
failed to comply, that person may be forced to pay $75,000 ($37,500 for the statutory violation and an additional $37,500 for violating the compliance order) *per day*. 33 U.S.C.
§ 1319(a)(3), (d). In Sackett v. EPA, 132 S.Ct. 1367 (2012), the EPA asserted that an Idaho
residential lot owned by the Sacketts contained navigable waters and that the landowners' construction project violated the CWA. The Sacketts did not believe their property
was subject to the CWA so they asked the EPA for a hearing, but the EPA denied the request. In his concurring opinion, Justice Alito remarked:

> The reach of the Clean Water Act is notoriously unclear. Any piece of land that
> is wet at least part of the year is in danger of being classified by EPA employees
> as wetlands covered by the Act, and according to the Federal Government, if
> property owners begin to construct a home on a lot that the agency thinks pos-
> sesses the requisite wetness, the property owners are at the agency's mercy. The
> EPA may issue a compliance order demanding that the owners cease construc-
> tion, engage in expensive remedial measures, and abandon any use of the prop-
> erty.... And if the owners want their day in court to show that their lot does not
> include covered wetlands, well, as a practical matter, that is just too bad. Until
> the EPA sues them, they are blocked from access to the courts, and the EPA may
> wait as long as it wants before deciding to sue. By that time, the potential fines
> may easily have reached the millions. In a nation that values due process, not to
> mention private property, such treatment is unthinkable.

Id. at 1375 (Alito, J., concurring). In the end, the Supreme Court held that landowners
who find themselves facing such an order could sue the EPA in federal court to obtain a
wetlands determination, without risking penalties, because the EPA's compliance order was
a "final agency action" subject to judicial review under the Administrative Procedure Act,
5 U.S.C. §§ 701, 704.

5. Returning to the issues surrounding coal mining, an alternative to strip mining
on mountaintops is shaft mining. Shaft mining is notoriously dangerous, however. In
2006, twelve of thirteen miners were killed when an explosion trapped them in the Sago
Mine. Just a few years later, twenty-nine were killed in Upper Big Branch Mine disaster. Both incidents occurred in West Virginia. *See* U.S. Mine Rescue Assc., *Historical
Data on Mine Disasters in the U.S.*, http://www.msha.gov/sagomine/sagomine.asp (visited July 16, 2012).

Are there better ways to satisfy the quest for electricity? Consider the advantages and
disadvantages of hydropower, favored by New Zealand, Norway, Brazil, and several other
countries, and nuclear power, favored by France and a few other European Union countries (the EU gets 30 percent of its electricity from nuclear power). Nuclear power, in
particular, is said to be making a comeback in the United States. India and China have

also committed to building plants and developing reactor technology. Recent events in Spain and in Japan may curb the enthusiasm.

> With oil and natural gas prices skyrocketing and coal tarred by its image as the worst-polluting fossil fuel, Spain's power sector had been eyeing the prospect of a future in which nuclear energy would meet the country's growing electricity needs while lowering greenhouse gas emissions. But what seemed like a new nuclear dawn now risks being derailed by the events at the Ascó nuclear power station that have unfolded over the past month under the glare of an increasingly nuclear-opposed public.
>
> First, a radioactive leak that occurred at the plant near Tarragona, Valencia, last November went undetected until the middle of March. Then, plant directors attempted to cover up its severity, informing the Nuclear Security Council, Spain's atomic watchdog, ... that it was a "minor incident." Days later a study revealed that the radiation was 400 times worse than the station operators had initially claimed, ranking the "minor incident" as the second-worst nuclear accident ever in Spain. Two plant officials were fired and a probe was launched.

Emilio de Benito, *Radiation Leak Ruins Nuclear Dawn*, Diario El Pais, Apr. 29, 2008. Subsequently, in March 2011, Japan experienced a horrific nuclear accident at the Fukushima Daiichi Nuclear Power Station.

> The crisis began when an earthquake struck off the east coast of Japan, churning up a devastating tsunami that swept over cities and farmland in the northern part of the country.... Explosions and leaks of radioactive gas took place in three reactors at the Fukushima Daiichi nuclear plant that suffered partial meltdowns, while spent fuel rods at another reactor overheated and caught fire, releasing radioactive material directly into the atmosphere.... Japan's nuclear regulators and Tepco have said that the earthquake and tsunami were far larger than anything that scientists had predicted. That conclusion has allowed the company to argue that it was not responsible for the triple meltdown.... [However,] [in] 2012, a report released by an independent parliamentary commission concluded that the crisis was a preventable disaster rooted in government-industry collusion and the worst conformist conventions of Japanese culture.... [A]n internal investigation showed that the damage to the core of at least one of the meltdown-stricken reactors at Fukushima could be far worse than previously thought, raising fresh concerns over the plant's stability and gravely complicating the post-disaster cleanup.

World: Japan, New York Times, July 15, 2012, at http://topics.nytimes.com/top/news/international/countriesandterritories/japan/index.html. After the meltdown at Fukushima, all 50 of the country's functional reactors were idled for several months, and "the Japanese people have remained deeply divided on the safety of nuclear power." *Id.* Although nuclear power is billed as "clean" energy, it can impact water quality: "Japanese officials turned to increasingly desperate measures, as traces of radiation were found in Tokyo's water and in water pouring from the reactors into the ocean.... [Months later,] radioactive water may be leaking out of the reactor at a higher rate than previously thought, possibly into a part of the reactor known as the suppression chamber, and into a network of pipes and chambers under the plant — or into the ocean...." *Id.*

How likely is it that Japan and others can wean themselves off nuclear power and fossil fuels with a combination of energy conservation and renewable development? Island nations may have a slight advantage, if marine renewables catch on. The world's first community-owned tidal turbine is being developed in Scotland.

The Nova-30 (30kW) tidal turbine employs a horizontal axis, three-bladed rotor to extract reliable and predictable energy from the tides. The turbine, which will be deployed in the Bluemull Sound..., will be owned by the North Yell community, which received a grant of £150,000 from the Scottish Government to help its development. It will help regenerate the fragile economy of North Yell — one of Europe's most remote communities, providing valuable income and supporting [up to 120] local jobs.

World's First Community-Owned Tidal Turbine to Power Up, ClickGreen, Aug. 24, 2012, at http://www.clickgreen.org.uk. Company representatives said, "We see significant potential for tidal arrays for other communities across Scotland." *Id.*

4. Cooperative Federalism: State and Tribal Delegations

The CWA includes several provisions to address relationships with states and Indian tribes. It directs federal agencies to cooperate with states in developing solutions to prevent pollution "in concert with programs for managing water resources." 33 U.S.C. § 1251(g). The Act also proclaims the congressional policy that "the authority of each State to allocate quantities of water within its jurisdiction shall not be superseded, abrogated or otherwise impaired" and that "nothing in this chapter shall be construed to supersede or abrogate rights to quantities of water which have been established by any State." *Id.*

States and tribes are authorized to accept delegations from the EPA to administer permit systems and take enforcement actions under the CWA. 33 U.S.C. §§ 1342(b), 1370, 1377. This "cooperative federalism" approach requires the EPA to delegate authority for NDPES permits if the state or tribe meets certain statutorily delineated criteria. Upon delegation, the EPA's permit program is suspended, but it may still review and veto proposed permits and must periodically review overall state or tribal administration to ensure compliance with the CWA.

Some states and Indian tribes have utilized their ability to administer CWA programs to impose requirements that are more stringent than federal law. The Pueblo of Isleta provide a leading example of a tribal CWA program that benefits water quality above and beyond the norm. In City of Albuquerque v. Browner, a federal court upheld the Pueblo's stringent water quality standard for primary contact ceremonial usage in the Rio Grande River, even though it would require expensive upgrades to the City's wastewater treatment plant upstream. 97 F.3d 415 (10th Cir. 1996), cert. denied, 522 U.S. 965 (1997).

Other provisions of the CWA provide additional powers to states. Section 401 compels applicants for a federal permit or license to obtain a certification from the appropriate state that the proposed project will not impair water quality, in effect, giving state agencies a limited veto over proposed projects. 33 U.S.C. 1341(a). States have utilized this power to impose minimum streamflow requirements on hydroelectric dam projects licensed by the Federal Energy Regulatory Commission (FERC). S.D. Warren Co. v. Maine Bd. of Environmental Protection, 126 S.Ct. 1843 (2006); PUD No. 1 of Jefferson County v. Washington Dept. of Ecology, 511 U.S. 700 (1994).

5. Citizen Enforcement Measures

The successes of the CWA permit program are attributed in part to its provisions for public involvement. Before a permit may issue, the public must be provided an opportunity to comment. Once a decision is made, any interested person may request a formal hearing before the permitting agency or bring suit in federal court under the CWA's citizens' suit provision. *See* 33 U.S.C. §§ 1319, 1365. The CWA imposes strict timing requirements on citizens' suits, however, to ensure that cases are brought while pollution is ongoing and to avoid interfering with government enforcement efforts. *See* Gwaltney of Smithfield, Ltd. v. Chesapeake Bay Foundation, Inc., 484 U.S. 49 (1987). Successful plaintiffs can recoup their attorneys' fees and costs.

Citizen suits have had a significant impact on the way business is done in the U.S.

> Citizen suits provide a vehicle for enforcement where the EPA has been unwilling or unable to move forward due to lack of resources or lack of political fortitude. They are especially important to ensure the implementation of politically charged programs like water-quality standards and pollutant allocations for nonpoint sources, many of which require changes in local land use planning. For example, the TMDL requirement for addressing impaired waterbodies was virtually ignored by the EPA and the states until a series of citizen suits forced compliance. It is fair to say that, without citizen enforcement, most environmental programs would have "languish[ed] under the political constraints of the marketplace."

Zygmunt J.B. Plater, *Environmental Law and Three Economies: Navigating a Sprawling Field of Study, Practice and Societal Governance in Which Everything is Connected to Everything Else*, 23 Harv. Envtl. L. Rev. 359, 382–83 n.54 (1999).

Ironically, even while it enhanced the ability of citizens to enforce statutory requirements against polluters and recalcitrant government agencies, the CWA curtailed the development of federal common law as a tool to abate interstate water pollution. In *City of Milwaukee v. Illinois*, 451 U.S. 304 (1981), the Supreme Court held that the CWA preempted the federal common law of nuisance. While recognizing that "the Court has found it necessary, in a 'few and restricted' instances ... to develop federal common law," the Court concluded that it should be employed only when necessary to resolve issues that are not addressed by statutes. *Id.*

6. Groundwater

The CWA addresses only "waters of the U.S.," generally defined as surface waters and adjacent wetlands. Groundwater controls have been left largely to the states and local governments. As a result, underground aquifers and even some drinking water supplies remain vulnerable to contamination.

In 1974, Congress responded to reports of increased waterborne diseases and public alarm about cancer and other health risks by enacting the most comprehensive drinking water program to date, the Safe Drinking Water Act (SDWA). Pub. L. No. 93-523, 88 Stat. 1660 (1974), codified at 42 U.S.C. §§ 300f–300j-26. Although previous enactments had authorized the establishment of standards for bacteriological and some chemical contaminants, those provisions were applicable only in limited circumstances, such as water supplies on interstate carriers. The SDWA, designed to protect and ensure the safety of public water supplies, goes beyond those provisions. It regulates many types of contaminants in public drinking water supplies (both surface and groundwater) and protects certain types of groundwater aquifers. A public water system is one that has at least 15 service connections or regularly serves at least 25 individuals. 42 U.S.C. § 300f(4)(A).

The SDWA, as amended in 1986 and 1996, accomplishes its goals through four key programs: the establishment of national drinking water standards; the regulation of underground injection wells; the protection of aquifers that serve as the sole source of municipal drinking water; and the protection of areas surrounding wellheads that provide municipal water supplies. 42 U.S.C. §§ 300g–300g-6, 300h-3, 300h-6, and 300h-7. The 1986 amendments required EPA to expand and quicken the pace of the standard-setting process. Actual implementation of the standards is the responsibility of the state under a delegation of "primacy" from the EPA; in the absence of such delegation, administration is an EPA responsibility. 42 U.S.C. §§ 300g-1–300g-3, § 300g-5.

The 1996 SDWA amendments were intended to enhance the Act's effectiveness by providing federal support for state and municipal efforts to comply with drinking water standards, requiring that risk assessment and cost-benefit analysis be utilized in adopting drinking water standards, and enhancing strategies to protect source waters before they are contaminated. In addition, the amendments require that the public be informed about the safety of their drinking water. Act of Aug. 6, 1996, Pub. L. 104-182, 110 Stat. 1613–93.

Under the SDWA, the nation has made great strides in ensuring the quality of public drinking water supplies, and about 200,000 public water systems providing water to over 240 million Americans are regulated.

> Chief among the public health triumphs of this century has been the provision of safe and healthful drinking water to most of our citizens. This single measure has done more to improve the health status of the community, and at a lower cost, than any other achievement, not excepting immunization, advances in medical technology, or modern medical treatments and drugs.

Jonathan Schneeweiss, *Watershed Protection Strategies: A Case Study of the New York City Watershed in Light of the 1996 Amendments to the Safe Drinking Water Act*, 8 Vill. Envtl. L.J. 77, 77–78 (1997). Yet there is still work to be done. Most importantly, groundwater is covered only to the extent it is used as a public drinking water supply, but not if used for agricultural or industrial purposes. Moreover, the SDWA protects only public, not private, drinking water supplies. According to the EPA, even water from public drinking water supplies may contain "lead, chloroform, and microorganisms … pos[ing] relatively high human health risks." Environmental Protection Agency, Setting Priorities for Strategies for Environmental Protection (Washington, DC: EPA, 1990), 14. Lack of funding and under-enforcement have been at the root of the problems. Although the SDWA provides for civil and criminal penalties, federal and state regulators rarely impose them. Regulators find it difficult to prosecute municipalities and small system operators, "in light of the political clout of the former group and hapless ineptitude of the latter." Rena I. Steinzor, *Unfunded Environmental Mandates and the "New (New) Federalism": Devolution, Revolution, or Reform?* 81 Minn. L. Rev. 97, 221 (2006). *See* Christine Rideout, *Where are All the Citizen Suits? The Failure of Safe Drinking Water Enforcement in the United States,* 21 Health Matrix 655, 664 (2011) (stating that the maximum contaminant goal level set by EPA is not realistically enforceable).

Private litigation through both citizens' suits and common law claims may increase in an effort to fill the enforcement gap. For example, in In re Methyl Tertiary Butyl Ether (MTBE) Prod. Liab. Litig., 415 F. Supp. 2d 261, 275 (S.D.N.Y. 2005), plaintiffs successfully asserted nuisance claims against petroleum companies for "knowingly unleash[ing] massive, long-lasting and still spreading contamination of groundwater and drinking water wells" through the use of a gasoline additive. And in Baker v. Anschutz Exploration Corp., No. 6:2011 cv06119 (W.D.N.Y. Feb. 2011), plaintiffs alleged that their groundwater wells had been contaminated "with combustible gases, toxic sediments, and hazardous chemicals" as a result of improper drilling and operation of defendants' gas wells. Similarly, in City of Greenville v. Syngenta, 3:10-cv-00188-JPG-PMF (D. Ill. 2010), and Holiday Shores Sanitary Dist. v. Syngenta, 3:2004cv00688 (Ill. 2004), plaintiffs argued that manufacturers of a commonly used herbicide, atrazine, should be held liable for contaminating waterbodies used for drinking water supplies.

7. Persistent Problems in Water Quality: Non-Point Source Pollution

As the following materials from agency websites and news articles indicates, the United States shares a common problem with Canada, New Zealand, and other countries: nonpoint source pollution (polluted run-off). As you consider the materials on non-point source pollution, consider how each country is addressing its problems, and which approaches seem most effective.

Nonpoint Source Pollution: The Nation's Largest Water Quality Problem

U.S. Environmental Protection Agency, EPA841-F-96-004A
http://www.epa.gov/nps/facts/point1.htm (Jan. 23, 2007)

Why is there still water that's too dirty for swimming, fishing or drinking? Why are native species of plants and animals disappearing from many rivers, lakes, and coastal waters? The United States has made tremendous advances in the past 25 years to clean up the aquatic environment by controlling pollution from industries and sewage treatment plants. Unfortunately, we did not do enough to control pollution from diffuse, or nonpoint, sources. Today, nonpoint source (NPS) pollution remains the Nation's largest source of water quality problems. It's the main reason that approximately 40 percent of our surveyed rivers, lakes, and estuaries are not clean enough to meet basic uses such as fishing or swimming.

NPS pollution occurs when rainfall, snowmelt, or irrigation runs over land or through the ground, picks up pollutants, and deposits them into rivers, lakes, and coastal waters or introduces them into ground water. Imagine the path taken by a drop of rain from the time it hits the ground to when it reaches a river, ground water, or the ocean. Any pollutant it picks up on its journey can become part of the NPS problem. NPS pollution also includes adverse changes to the vegetation, shape, and flow of streams and other aquatic systems. NPS pollution is widespread because it can occur any time activities disturb the land or water. Agriculture, forestry, grazing, septic systems, recreational boating, urban runoff, construction, physical changes to stream channels, and habitat degradation are potential sources of NPS pollution. Careless or uninformed household management also contributes to NPS pollution problems.

The latest *National Water Quality Inventory* indicates that agriculture is the leading contributor to water quality impairments, degrading 60 percent of the impaired river miles and half of the impaired lake acreage surveyed by states, territories, and tribes. Runoff from urban areas is the largest source of water quality impairments to surveyed estuaries (areas near the coast where seawater mixes with freshwater).

The most common NPS pollutants are sediment and nutrients. These wash into water bodies from agricultural land, small and medium-sized animal feeding operations, construction sites, and other areas of disturbance. Other common NPS pollutants include pesticides, pathogens (bacteria and viruses), salts, oil, grease, toxic chemicals, and heavy metals. Beach closures, destroyed habitat, unsafe drinking water, fish kills, and many other severe environmental and human health problems result from NPS pollutants. The pollutants also ruin the beauty of healthy, clean water habitats. Each year the United States spends millions of dollars to restore and protect the areas damaged by NPS pollutants.

During the last 10 years, our country has made significant headway in addressing NPS pollution. At the federal level, recent NPS control programs include the Nonpoint Source Management Program established by the 1987 Clean Water Act Amendments, and the Coastal Nonpoint Pollution Program established by the 1990 Coastal Zone Act Reauthorization Amendments. Other recent federal programs, as well as state, territorial, tribal and local programs also tackle NPS problems.

In addition, public and private groups have developed and used pollution prevention and pollution reduction initiatives and NPS pollution controls, known as management measures, to clean up our water efficiently. Water quality monitoring and environmental education activities supported by government agencies, tribes, industry, volunteer groups, and schools have provided information about NPS pollution and have helped to determine the effectiveness of management techniques. Also, use of the watershed approach has helped communities address water quality problems caused by NPS pollution. The watershed approach looks at not only a water body but also the entire area that drains into it. This allows communities to focus resources on a watersheds most serious environmental problems—which, in many instances, are caused by NPS pollution.

John Heilprin, U.N. Says Number of Ocean 'Dead Zones' Rise
Associated Press, Oct. 20, 2006

WASHINGTON—The number of oxygen-starved "dead zones" in the world's seas and oceans has risen more than a third in the past two years because of fertilizer, sewage, animal waste and fossil-fuel burning ... Their number has jumped to about 200, according to new estimates released by U.N. marine experts ...

The damage is caused by explosive blooms of tiny plants known as phytoplankton, which die and sink to the bottom, and then are eaten by bacteria which use up the oxygen in the water. Those blooms are triggered by too many nutrients—particularly phosphorous and nitrogen.

The U.N. report estimates there will be a 14 percent rise in the amount of nitrogen that rivers are pumping into seas and oceans globally over a period from when the levels were measured in the mid-1990s to 2030. Oxygen starvation robs the seas and oceans of many fish, oysters, sea grass beds and other marine life, and the number of such dead zones has grown every decade since the 1970s. Not all of them persist year-round, as they do in the Gulf of Mexico, where the Mississippi River pours its fertilizers and other nutrients. Some dead zones return each summer, depending on winds that generate upwelling, in which nutrient-rich water is brought to the surface from lower depths. But all the dead zones pose a danger to global fish stocks, which many marine scientists say are increasingly hammered by overfishing and pollution.

Dead zones first were reported in the United States' Chesapeake Bay; the Baltic Sea; the Kattegat bay in the North Sea; the Black Sea; the northern Adriatic Sea; and some Scandinavian fjords. Others have appeared off South America, China, Japan, southeast Australia and New Zealand, according to ... [marine scientist] Robert Diaz....

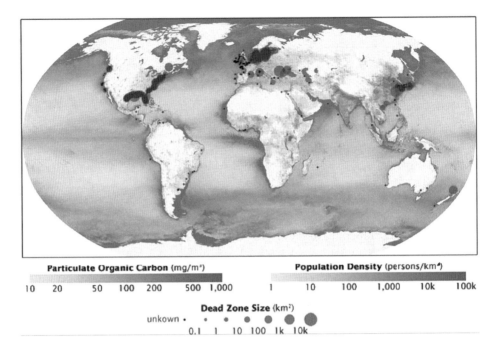

Particulate Organic Carbon (mg/m²)

10   20   50   100   200   500   1,000

Population Density (persons/km²)

1   10   100   1,000   10k   100k

Dead Zone Size (km²)

unkown ·
0.1   1   10   100   1k   10k

NASA Earth Observatory, Dead Zones (2008), available at http://earthobservatory.nasa.gov/IOTD/view.php?id=44677.

Notes and Questions

1. According to some courts, "the CWA does not require states to take regulatory action to limit the amount of non-point water pollution introduced into waterways." Defenders of Wildlife v. EPA, 415 F.3d 1121, 1124 (10th Cir. 2005). Although a few states, including New Mexico, Washington, and Florida, apply their anti-degradation provisions to *all* sources of pollution in Outstanding Natural Resource Waters, including nonpoint sources, many if not most states appear to have no restrictions on nonpoint source discharges whatsoever. This leaves water bodies in rural areas and suburban areas unprotected from the most significant sources of water pollution. *See* American Wildlands v. Browner, 94 F. Supp. 2d 1150 (D. Colo. 2000), *aff'd*, 260 F.3d 1192 (10th Cir. 2001); Michael C. Blumm and William Warnock, *Roads Not Taken: EPA vs. Clean Water*, 33 ENVTL. L. 79, 104 (2003); David Zaring, *Best Practices*, 81 N.Y.U. L. REV. 294, 326–27 (2006). The CWA includes an incentive program for states that adopt nonpoint source control policies, 33 U.S.C. § 1329, but this program has been "underfunded and underenforced." Sandra Zellmer, *Wilderness, Water, and Climate*, 42 ENVTL. L. 313, 365 (2012).

2. Should atmospheric deposition—another type of nonpoint source pollution—be addressed through water pollution laws like the CWA? If so, how? Mercury, in particular, has become a significant issue.

> *Grants Pass, Or.* — Scientists looking for fish tainted by mercury found them in every fish and every river they sampled across the [American] West, suggesting that industrial pollution generated around the world is likely responsible for at least some of it. The survey ... represents the biggest regional sampling yet of mercury in fish in the West ... [T]he low but widespread levels suggest the mercury

came from deposition — mercury in the atmosphere falling to the earth in rain
and snow ... While generally below levels considered unsafe for people to eat
from time to time, the mercury could pose a danger to fish and wildlife that depend on fish for their diet....

Jeff Barnard, *Survey Finds Mercury in Fish in West,* Associated Press, Jan. 24, 2007. According to the EPA, "[t]housands of waterbodies are listed on State Clean Water Act Section 303(d) lists as impaired due to mercury." EPA, TMDLs and Mercury (2012), http://
water.epa.gov/lawsregs/lawsguidance/cwa/tmdl/mercury/index.cfm.

In many waterbodies, mercury originates largely from air sources, such as coal-
fired power plants and incinerators that deposit in waters or adjacent lands that
then wash into nearby waters.... In some cases the presence of mercury may be
a result of past practices that used mercury, such as historic gold mining, or
from geologic deposits.... Products containing mercury may also result in releases
to water and air during waste handling and disposal processes.

Id. The EPA recognized, "Given the variety of potential mercury sources, developing and
implementing TMDLs for mercury-impaired waters may involve coordination among
multiple programs — water, air, waste, and toxics programs." *Id.* Be that as it may, who
has (or should have) the ultimate responsibility for addressing the problem? (Note that
transboundary issues related to atmospheric deposition and other forms of pollution are
addressed in Section F, *infra.*)

The EPA has attempted to regulate mercury emissions from power plants through the
Clean Air Act, 42 U.S.C. § 7412, but its initial efforts fell short:

[T]he U.S. EPA's so-called Clean Air Mercury Rule ... would have allowed dangerous levels of mercury pollution to persist under a weak cap-and-trade program
that would not have taken full effect until after 2020 ... Seventeen states and
dozens of Native American tribes, public health and environmental groups, and
organizations representing registered nurses and physicians, challenged EPA's
suite of rules in 2005. The plaintiffs maintained that cap-and-trade contributed
to "hot spots" for mercury, a neurotoxin linked to birth defects, learning dis-
abilities and neurological problems.... [T]he Court of Appeals ruling in favor of
the states and environmental groups maintained that EPA illegally removed coal
and oil-fired power plants from the list of regulated source categories under a section of the Clean Air Act that requires strict regulation of hazardous air pollutants, including mercury. New Jersey v. EPA, 517 F.3d 574 (2008). [T]he appeals
court ... rebuked the Bush-era EPA for attempting to create an illegal loophole
for the power generating industry, rather than applying the Clean Air Act's "maximum achievable control technology" standard for mercury emissions.... The
Supreme Court in effect denied an appeal, filed last year by a coalition of utilities seeking reversal of a federal court decision vacating the mercury rule.

ENN, *U.S. Supreme Court Blocks Weak Bush-Era Mercury Rule*, Env. News Service, Feb.
24, 2009. EPA went back to the drawing board and, in 2012, issued its new "National
Emission Standards for Hazardous Air Pollutants from Coal- and Oil-fired Electric Generating Units and Standards of Performance for Fossil-Fuel-Fired Utility Units — Final
Rule." 77 Fed. Reg. 9303. This rule will require power plants to reduce emissions of mercury and other toxic chemicals from their smokestacks, and it is anticipated to save 11,000
lives and prevent 130,000 asthma attacks and 4,700 heart attacks annually. "However,
these long overdue safeguards ... continue to face relentless attacks from coal heavy utilities, coal companies and their Congressional allies." Arpita Bhattacharyya and Daniel J.

Weiss, *Pro-Pollution Sen. Inofe Aims to Block Life-Saving Standards,* Climate Progress Blog, Feb. 16, 2012. The utilities have brought a lawsuit challenging the new rule, and the EPA has promised to review information provided by industry to "provide greater certainty for five planned power plants in Georgia, Kansas, Texas and Utah" that would be covered by the standards. Timothy Gardner, *EPA to Review Mercury Rule on New Power Plants,* Reuters, July 20, 2012. What's all the shouting about? When it issued the rule, the EPA predicted that the new rule will cost utilities about $9.6 billion annually, but will save $90 billion a year in healthcare costs. What reasonable grounds could anyone have to complain about a rule with projected economic benefits of $80 billion a year?

8. Oil Spills

The blowout of the BP Deepwater Horizon oil platform in the Gulf of Mexico riveted the world's attention on April 20, 2010, and revealed layers of regulatory failure in the United States' deepwater drilling program.

> Eleven workers were killed in the explosion. When the platform sank to the ocean floor two days later, oil erupted out of the riser—a 5,000-foot pipe connecting the Macondo Well at the ocean floor to the platform on the surface. Efforts to stem the flow failed when a safety device, the "blowout preventer," could not be activated. Everything that could go wrong did. Finally, after a number of attempts to stop the leak, BP capped the well on July 15. Nearly 5,000,000 barrels of oil were released over the course of 86 days, making the Deepwater Horizon spill the largest offshore oil spill in world history....
>
> Offshore drilling activities ... are regulated under the Outer Continental Shelf Lands Act (OCSLA), which establishes a four-stage oil and gas development process. 43 U.S.C. §§ 1334–1351. The program includes: (1) preparation of a nationwide five-year oil and gas development plan; (2) specific lease sales consistent with the five-year plan, identifying which areas are open to development and at what pace; (3) exploration plans; and (4) development and production plans. Each of these steps is a separate agency action subject to NEPA. [The National Environmental Policy Act is covered in detail in Chapter 3.A, *supra.*] At each step, the analysis is intended to be increasingly detailed and focused, honing in on the specific activities and areas at issue.
>
> At the time the activities related to the Deepwater Horizon were going through the these steps, the U.S. Department of the Interior Minerals Management Service (MMS) was in charge of ensuring that NEPA was carried out properly. In April 2007, MMS released a "programmatic EIS" that purported to analyze the potential region-wide impacts associated with the 2007–2012 Outer Continental Shelf Oil and Gas Leasing Program. Also in April 2007, MMS also released a final EIS (the Multi-Sale EIS) for eleven lease sales in the Gulf of Mexico Central Planning Area, which covered 80 million square miles, including the Deepwater Horizon site. A few months later, in October 2007, MMS issued an EA for Lease Sale 206 within the Central Planning Area. The EA was accompanied by a Finding of No Significant Impact, which concluded that because any potentially significant impacts associated with Lease Sale 206 had been addressed in the Multi-Sale EIS, there were no new or different significant impacts to be considered. Finally, in April 2009, MMS approved BP's drilling plan for the Deepwater Horizon project without any environmental review whatsoever. MMS stated

that the plan was categorically excluded from NEPA because the danger of a blowout, and any potential environmental damage, was minimal or non-existent....

Sandra Zellmer, Robert Glicksman, and Joel Mintz, *Throwing Precaution to the Wind: NEPA and the Deepwater Horizon Blowout*, 2 J. of Energy & Env. Law 62–70 (2011). The authors conclude that "MMS's implementation of NEPA fell far short of the statutory goals and requirements by failing to consider and plan for the worst case scenario, and by improperly relying on categorical exclusions and tiered analysis of potential environmental effects." *Id.* Although NEPA itself has not been amended, a variety of other reforms have been adopted, including the re-organization of MMS into a new agency, the Bureau of Ocean Energy Management, Regulation and Enforcement (BOEMRE). According to the federal government:

> [T]he Obama Administration launched the most aggressive and comprehensive reforms to offshore oil and gas regulation and oversight in U.S. history. The reforms, which strengthen requirements for everything from well design and workplace safety to corporate accountability, are helping ensure that the United States can safely and responsibly expand development of its energy resources....

BOEMRE, *Regulatory Reform,* http://www.boemre.gov/reforms.htm (visited July 23, 2012). Offshore drilling safety reforms include the following:

- Operators must demonstrate that they are prepared to deal with the potential for a blowout and worst-case discharge;

- Permit applications for drilling projects must meet new standards for well-design, casing, and cementing, and be independently certified by a professional engineer; and

- [T]he bureau will begin to use multiple-person inspection teams for offshore oil and gas inspections to improve oversight and help ensure that offshore operations proceed safely and responsibly.

Id.

The primary statute governing liability for, and cleanup of, oil spills from ships is the Oil Pollution Act of 1990, 33 U.S.C. §§ 2701–2761. It also requires large tanker ships plying U.S. waters to have double-hulls. It applies to incidents occurring after August 18, 1990, and covers oil of any kind, in any form, including petroleum, fuel oil, and sludge. The Act's major provisions are described below.

> *Oil Pollution Act § 1074.* The Oil Pollution Act provides that ... each party responsible for a vessel or a facility (1) from which oil is discharged, or (2) which poses the substantial threat of a discharge of oil into navigable waters or adjoining shorelines, is liable for removal costs and damages. The Act also sets limits on liability for damages resulting from oil spills ...

> *§ 1089.* Each responsible party for a vessel or a facility from which oil is discharged, or which poses the substantial threat of a discharge of oil into or upon the navigable waters or adjoining shorelines, is liable for removal costs and damages. 33 U.S.C.A. § 2702....

> *§ 1095.* A responsible party will not be held responsible for removal costs and damages if that party is able to establish, by a preponderance of the evidence, that the incident or threat was caused solely by an act of God, an act of war, or the act or omission of a third party. However, a responsible party may not invoke these defenses if the party knew about the incident and failed to report it, refused to

cooperate or assist in the removal, or refused to obey an order issued under the Federal Water Pollution Control Act or the Intervention on the High Seas Act.

Richard B. Gallagher, John Kimpflen, and Tim A. Thomas, *Discharge of Oil or Hazardous Substances into Navigable Waters or Ocean,* 61C Am. Jur. 2d Pollution Control (Database updated March 2008). For a comparative analysis, see Thomas J. Schoenbaum, *Liability for Damages in Oil Spill Accidents: Evaluating the USA and International Law Regimes in the Light of Deepwater Horizon,* 24 J. of Envtl. L. (2012) (concluding that Deepwater Horizon highlights the need for a more comprehensive international oil pollution liability regime, since the current regime, which is limited to oil spills from ships carrying oil as cargo in bulk, would not have covered the blowout).

With respect to pollution prevention or liability provisions adopted by individual states within the U.S., the Oil Pollution Act does not affect any obligations or liabilities under state law, nor does it preempt state authority to impose additional liability with respect to the discharge of oil within the state or the removal activities that occur in response to such a discharge. 33 U.S.C. § 2718. Even though the OPA does not preempt state laws, federal maritime law might. However, in general, a state may adopt such remedies as it sees fit so long as the state remedy does not: (1) contravene the essential purpose expressed by an act of Congress; (2) work material prejudice to the characteristic features of general maritime law; or (3) interfere with the proper harmony and uniformity of that law in its international and interstate relations. In re The Exxon Valdez, 270 F.3d 1215 (9th Cir. 2001).

In the *Exxon Valdez* case, fishermen and Alaskan landowners brought tort claims for economic losses against Exxon, which owned the oil tanker that ran aground in 1989. A jury found in the plaintiffs' favor in 1994, and awarded both compensatory and punitive damages. On appeal, the Ninth Circuit Court of Appeals held, among other things, that: (1) prior civil and criminal penalties assessed by state and federal governments did not bar the award of punitive damages; (2) the Clean Water Act did not preempt a private right of action; (3) a corporation could be held vicariously liable for punitive damages based on its sea captain's reckless conduct; and (4) Alaska law permitting tort damages for pure economic loss was not preempted by general admiralty law. The court remanded the case to the district court, however, to take another look at the punitive damages award of $5 billion, which it found excessive. The propriety and amount of the punitive damages award has bounced back and forth between the trial and appellate courts, and it was ultimately reduced to $2.5 billion. The U.S. Supreme Court accepted certiorari and heard arguments in 2008 on the following issue: *When Congress has specified the criminal and civil penalties for maritime conduct in a controlling statute, here the Clean Water Act, but has not provided for punitive damages, may judge-made federal maritime law ... expand the penalties Congress provided by adding a punitive damages remedy?* Exxon Shipping Co. v. Baker, Supreme Court No. 07-219 (2008). In the opinion of two law professors, the punitive damages award should stand.

Alexandra Klass and Sandra Zellmer, Exxon Should Just Pay Its Penance

Minneapolis Star-Tribune Mar. 1, 2008

The Supreme Court heard arguments last week in a case with big implications for victims of reckless corporations. At issue is whether Exxon can be made to pay punitive damages to the fishermen whose livelihoods were ruined by the 1989 Exxon Valdez oil spill. Exxon says it has already paid fines to the government under federal maritime and environmental laws, and shouldn't have to pay punitive damages, too. That may be good for Exxon's bottom line, but it's miserable public policy. Punitive damages help deter the kind of bad behavior of which Exxon is plainly guilty, so the Court should make the company pay up.

A quick review of the facts: On the night of March 24, 1989, the oil tanker Exxon Valdez hit a reef and ran aground in Prince William Sound, Alaska. Out poured 11 million gallons of crude, causing one of the largest and most damaging oil spills in history. Experts say the accident killed more birds and marine mammals than any other U.S. oil spill before or since, and the harm continues to this day, not just to fish and wildlife, but also to fishermen and others who made a living from the waters of the Sound.

The ensuing investigation revealed that the captain of the ship was a relapsed alcoholic who was drinking at sea. Even more damning for Exxon was the revelation that the company knew about his drinking, but did nothing. Rather than firing him or suspending him while he got sober, rather than demoting him or finding him a desk job, Exxon left him in command, letting him pilot its massive tanker and its dangerous cargo through the sensitive waters of Prince William Sound. Sure enough, on the night of the accident the captain reportedly put away five double vodkas, then left the bridge, leaving a junior officer to conduct the high-stakes navigation.

The government rightly pursued Exxon for violating the Clean Water Act, forcing it to pay $3.4 billion in cleanup costs. But the environment wasn't the only victim. Thousands of people lost their livelihoods that night, and they, too, deserve restitution. So they sued, and won big: $500 million in damages for their actual losses, and $5 billion in punitive damages to both punish Exxon and discourage future bad behavior. Granted, $5 billion might seem like an awful lot of discouragement, but Exxon is the biggest company in the world, with 2007 profits of $39.5 billion.

On appeal, Exxon got the punitive damage award reduced to $2.5 billion, but now it's asking the Supreme Court to throw that out as well. . . .

In actual practice, juries rarely award punitive damages and, when they do, courts conduct exacting reviews to ensure that the awards are based on the facts and the law, not passion or prejudice. Among other things, punitive damages should be proportionate to the harm caused. In this case, they are. In arguments before the Supreme Court, the lawyer for the fishermen pointed out that because so many people were harmed, the $500 million in damages for actual losses amounted to about $15,000 per person. After nearly 20 years, that's not much for having one's livelihood destroyed.

Presumably the $2.5 billion will make a difference to the people of Prince William Sound. But more than that, it's enough money to help persuade Exxon and others to take greater care in guarding against reckless behavior with potentially catastrophic consequences. . . .

Notes and Questions

1. The lower court's decision did not, in fact, stand. In Exxon v. Baker, 554 U.S. 471 (2008), the Supreme Court held that the Clean Water Act's pollution penalties do not preempt the award of punitive damages, but concluded that the award should be limited to an amount equal to compensatory damages — $500 million. *Id* at 476.

2. *Exxon v. Baker* notwithstanding, the United States is still at the forefront of punitive damages awards in the twenty-first century. What role should punitive damages play in controlling pollution and preventing environmental harm?

The institution of punitive damages appeared in England at the end of the eighteenth century (the first case dates to 1763). It then crossed the Atlantic Ocean and became an established part of the law of the United States, and at the same time, from England, it spread through all the countries of the Commonwealth. Punitive damages exist in Australia, New Zealand, South Africa, Canada. Despite the fact that they are criticized, limited, and controlled, their existence remains ... [and indeed] punitive damages play an important role, especially in the United States, where they can be exceptionally high.... However, it is fair to say that ... European countries remain impervious to this ... Americanization of their legal system ... Hence, the quantum of damages awarded by European judges remains "under control" and the concept of punitive damages itself is still nonexistent in Civil Law countries and the granting of such remedy is strictly limited in England and Wales. In addition, the introduction of this foreign concept would be contrary to the International Public Policy of most European countries.

Thomas Rouhette, *The Availability Of Punitive Damages In Europe: Growing Trend Or Nonexistent Concept?*, 74 Def. Couns. J. 320, 321 (2007).

3. Should U.S. domestic law on punitive damages apply when the harm occurs outside of the United States? U.S. corporations are occasionally sued in either domestic or foreign courts for both compensatory and punitive damages for harm occurring outside the U.S. In a hotly contested 2007 case against Dole (a California company) and Dow Chemical (a Michigan company), a California jury awarded Nicaraguan workers compensatory and punitive damages ($3.3 million and $2.5 million, respectively) for injuries resulting from the use of pesticides on Dole's banana plantations. Noaki Schwartz, Associated Press, *$2.5 million Awarded to Banana Workers,* Daily Review (Hayward, CA), Nov. 15, 2007. The case, Tellez v. Dole Food Co., No. BC 312 852, 2008 WL 744052 (Cal. Super. Ct. Mar. 7, 2008), raised significant issues of first impression regarding (1) whether multinational companies should be held accountable in the country where they are based or the countries where they conduct operations, and (2) whether punitive damages awards were allowed. The workers proved that they were made sterile by use of the pesticide 1, 2 Dibromo-3-Chloropropane (DBCP) when they were required to apply DBCP by mixing it with sprinkler irrigation water or by injecting it into the ground. The use of DBCP in the United States was generally prohibited in 1979, but it was still being used in the mid-1990s in developing countries. The jury concluded that the defendants acted maliciously by concealing material facts, *i.e.,* that DBCP caused adverse effects on male fertility and other serious harm. Dow, however, was not liable for punitive damages because the judge agreed to apply Michigan law to it, which prevented punitive damages. The judge remarked that this was a "bellwether case," and the first in a series of pending cases involving thousands of agricultural workers. *Id.* Dole is appealing the verdict.

According to Alejandro Garro, a professor of Latin American law at Columbia University, it is the verdict itself, rather than the amount, that is important. It will make corporations such as Dole "pay attention to what they do abroad," he said.

"It is worth noting that if the case had been tried abroad and [Dole] had been found liable, punitive damages would not have been an option, given the fact that in most legal systems damages can only be awarded to compensate the victims, but never to punish the defendant ..." The case was widely seen as a test of how well the U.S. legal system could respond to injuries inflicted in a globalized economy. Because the harm occurred in Central America, the defendants had argued for years that the trials should take place there, rather than in the U.S.

John Spano, *Dole Must Pay $2.5 Million to Farmhands,* L.A. Times, Nov. 16, 2007, at 3. Some of the trials have in fact taken place in Central American countries. To date, Nicaraguans suing under Nicaraguan law have obtained over $715 million in judgments against Dow, Dole, and Shell Chemical Company. Some of the awards were issued without participation by the defendants. To avoid enforcement of the various judgments rendered in Nicaragua, Dow and Shell sought a declaratory judgment against 1,030 Nicaraguans in federal court in California, claiming "that any judgment obtained by the Nicaraguans in Nicaragua is not recognizable or enforceable in the United States." Dow v. Calderon, 422 F.3d 827 (9th Cir. 2005). The case was dismissed on the grounds that a Nicaraguan statute that gave the defendants the choice of submitting to jurisdiction of U.S. courts for resolution of the DBCP cases or posting a deposit as a condition of defending in Nicaraguan courts did not confer personal jurisdiction over Nicaraguans. *Id.* Other cases involving transnational litigation for harm allegedly caused by corporations in other countries are addressed in Chapter 2.D (The Alien Tort Claims Act).

4. The impact of the Exxon Valdez oil spill, which ranks around 20th by size in international spills, with 37,000 tonnes, was magnified because it was in a narrow sound in the spring of the year, when fish and birds relied on the area for breeding, feeding, and nesting. In 2002, the breakup of the Prestige, a leaking tanker off the coast of Spain, was far larger in terms of quantity. With 77,000 tonnes of fuel oil, it ranks 14th in world tanker spills. *Disaster hits Fishing, Wildlife,* New Zealand Herald, Nov. 21, 2002, at 1. However, in terms of environmental damage, experts say the Prestige's distance from the shore helped alleviate adverse effects because the high seas broke up some oil slicks before they reached beaches. Should liability turn on the magnitude of harm under the specific circumstances of the spill? If so, would shippers take more (or less) precaution depending on their location?

5. In 2007, a cargo ship, the Cosco Busan, ran into the San Francisco Bay Bridge. Over 50,000 gallons of bunker crude oil spewed out of the ship. The spill closed beaches, coated birds with crude, and left a swath of oil for miles. The captain was charged with violating the Clean Water Act and the Migratory Bird Treaty Act, but not the OPA.

> In the San Francisco Bay Area, the Cosco Busan will live on as a symbol of environmental catastrophe. Yet the Cosco Busan is only the latest in a series of shipping accidents plaguing our trade routes.... The New Carissa broke up in 1999, spilling 70,000 gallons of fuel along the Oregon coast. The San Francisco Bay Area, the Oregon Coast and the Aleutian Islands are all part of the Great Circle Route that ships transit between the West Coast and Asia. More than 7,000 ships per year travel the route—almost 20 per day—and the number is growing. Yet the safety measures are not in place to protect the North Pacific Ocean....
>
> After the Exxon Valdez spill, the state of Alaska created an independent Oil Spill Commission. The commission issued 52 recommendations, 50 of which were enshrined in the Oil Pollution Act of 1990.... Unfortunately..., that act primarily addresses oil tankers, not cargo ships like the Cosco Busan.
>
> Gov. Arnold Schwarzenegger ... should take a page from our friends in Alaska [and] strengthen our shipping safety regulations.... Cargo ships can carry 40 times the amount of fuel reported to have spilled in this incident—the next spill could be much larger....

David Gordon & Walter Parker, *Cosco Busan Spill a Wake-up Call,* San Francisco Chronicle, Nov. 18, 2007, Open Forum.

6. The International Maritime Organization and many countries currently impose double-hull requirements similar to the OPA. Interest in international regulation was stimulated in 1967, when the Torrey Canyon hit a reef in the Scilly Isles, fouling the south coast of England and the Norman coast of France with 120,000 tons of oil.

Two main measures were taken [in Europe] — the first to address the consequences of an accident (who was liable and to what extent) and the second to prevent such accidents from happening. The former was signed in London in 1969 — the International Convention on Civil Liability for Oil Pollution Damage (CLC).... CLC was complemented in 1971 by the Oil Pollution Compensation Fund (IOPC Fund), created from the contributions of oil importers, to provide compensation to the extent that the protection afforded by the CLC Convention was inadequate ... The second main measure, a convention covering prevention of pollution of the marine environment by ships from operational or accidental causes, was adopted in 1973 — the International Convention for the Prevention of Pollution from Ships (MARPOL).... All European Union (EU) member states belong to the 1992 CLC/Fund system. They are also signatories to MARPOL....

On December 12, 1999, a Maltese tanker, the Erika, ... broke in two off the coast of Brittany, France. Age, corrosion, insufficient maintenance, and inadequate surveys were all strong contributing factors to the structural failure of the ship. Some 19,800 tons were spilled. The clean-up operations took place along some 400 kilometers of polluted coastline, and over 250,000 tons of oily waste were collected from the shoreline. The shipowner's insurer ... offered a compensation of nine million euro. Additional compensation was offered from the 1992 IOPC Fund — €172 million. As of January 1, 2004, claims amounting to 206 million euro have been submitted, exceeding the amount of compensation available. The EU had to admit "that action on maritime safety under the auspices of the IMO falls short of what is needed to tackle the causes of such disasters effectively...."

MARPOL ... seeks to bring about the gradual phasing-out of single-hull oil tankers and their replacement by double-hull tankers or tankers of equivalent design. Oil tankers built since 1996 must have a double hull or be of equivalent design, while single-hull oil tankers are to be phased out by 2026. This timetable was, however, considered too slow by the EU, and a Council and Parliament regulation concerning phasing-out of single-hull tankers was adopted.... [In addition,] in 2000, the Commission issued ... the Erika II package ... [which] included a regulation creating the European Maritime Safety Agency, a directive concerning the establishing of a monitoring and information system for improving the surveillance of traffic in European waters, and a regulation aimed at establishing a complementary European fund (amounting to one billion euro) for the indemnity of victims of oil spills....

Moreover, the European Parliament insists on addressing seriously in EU legislation the problem of human failure and flags of convenience.... [H]uman failure is a prime cause of tanker casualties (eighty percent of collisions and groundings). Flags of convenience have a very relaxed approach to the verification of qualifications before granting marine certificates, and they operate substandard and undermanned ships because it is profitable.... The ownership of the registered tonnage is largely concentrated in new flag states where the IMO conventions are either not uniformly adopted or, if adopted, not properly enforced due to insufficient controls of ships by the flag state authorities.... This allows many substandard ships to continue to operate under one of the flags of convenience where controls are not too strict....

The most important [new steps] seem[] to be further evolution of the regime of civil liability for oil pollution and developing ways to protect the coastline of the member states from the ships that merely pass nearby, without entering into ports. If the EU, being the second largest trading block in the world, can tackle this problem, it will have an input into the safety of world shipping.

Malgorzata Anna Nesterowicz, *European Union Legal Measures in Response to the Oil Pollution of the Sea,* 29 Tul. Mar. L.J. 29 (2004).

7. Individual states within the U.S. may also bring enforcement actions for dumping in territorial waters. In 2006, Washington State imposed the highest fine possible under state law ($100,000) against Celebrity Cruises for dumping more than 500,000 gallons of untreated wastewater, including untreated sink, shower, and laundry water, along with some treated sewage waste, in Washington waters. The cruise line hired a consultant to review the incident, terminated the ship's environmental-compliance officer, and agreed to invest $4 million on improved wastewater treatment for the vessel. Robert Mcclure, *Celebrity Cruises Asks for Leniency in Fine*, Seattle Post-Intelligencer, Dec. 20, 2006.

In 2001, in an effort to minimize problems with ocean dumping, members of the International Council of Cruise Lines adopted policies and procedures for recycling, onboard wastewater treatment, and separation of oil from bilge water. In 2002, Norwegian Cruise Lines agreed to pay the United States $1.5 million in penalties for dumping oily bilge in U.S. waters and for doctoring a log book to cover up the illegal discharges in previous years. The prosecution was one of several brought by the U.S. Justice Department in a crackdown on pollution by cruise ships. *Leisure Line Dumping,* Daytona News-Journal, Aug. 8, 2002, at A. The U.S. prosecutes U.S. flag ships for polluting within 200 miles of the coastline, but ships under foreign flag are referred to their own governments.

Some countries have taken other types of steps to address oil spills. New Zealand, for example, has declared certain prime diving spots, like waters around the Poor Knights Islands, off-limits to big ships in order to protect them from oil spills. Tankers must stay at least 9km off the coast. *Dive Spots Saved,* New Zealand Herald, May 19, 2004, at A1. Should the U.S. and other countries follow suit?

8. Because detection at sea is so difficult, governments sometimes provide incentives, such as bounties, to encourage citizens and employees to come forward with information. There are three basic approaches in the United States.

[A] wide variety of statutes protect internal company whistleblowers from retaliation. A handful of federal and state environmental statutes go a step further and authorize government enforcement agencies to pay rewards to individuals who furnish information leading to environmental convictions ... [Congress first authorized environmental rewards in wildlife protection statutes, such as the Endangered Species Act, where informants have proven a critical means of ferreting out individuals trading illegally in protected wildlife. Congress has since included reward provisions in Superfund and in the 1990 amendments to the Clean Air Act.] Finally, the federal False Claims Act provides citizen informants with the opportunity to collect sizable penalties through *qui tam* actions by providing information regarding a limited set of environmental violations related to governmental contracts and reporting requirements....

Barton H. Thompson, Jr., *The Continuing Innovation of Citizen Enforcement,* 2000 U. Ill. L. Rev. 185, 226–230. Provisions that provide financial incentives to citizen and employee informants can be effective, but even with incentives, employees in particular may feel bound by a "code of silence" that protects the members of their group. Kelly Saunders, *Whistle-blowing in Canada: One Step Forward or Two Steps Back?*, Midwest Political Science Assn. Annual Conference, Chicago, IL, Apr. 03, 2008, at 2, http://www.allacademic.com/meta/p268304_index.html.

> Citizen informants are arguably even more important than citizen prosecutors and monitors to the effective enforcement of modern American environmental laws ... Many environmental violations are covert and difficult to spot—regulated companies modify emission data, generators of hazardous waste engage in midnight dumping, or ships discharge contaminated ballast water out of the sight of others ... Any laws designed to encourage informants, however, trigger society's conflicting norms about "snitching." Reward programs and other financial incentives also raise concerns about the veracity and credibility of paid information.

Id. What role should citizen or employee reporting play in controlling pollution from ships? The following excerpt describes the "lay of the land."

> In recent criminal maritime environmental prosecutions, crewmembers have received significant awards for reporting illegal discharges of oil to the government. Invoking the bounty provision in the Act to Prevent Pollution from Ships (APPS), which allows courts to award up to one-half of the fine to those who provided information leading to the conviction, courts have awarded whistleblowers millions of dollars at the request of the government....
>
> The first case whereby a crewmember was rewarded under the APPS bounty provision for blowing the whistle on illegal discharges of oily bilge occurred in 1998. The reward stemmed from the conviction of HAL Beheer BV, the operator of the Holland America Line cruise S.S. Rotterdam, for APPS violations for failing to keep required records of oil discharges. HAL Beheer paid $2 million in fines and restitution ... Subsequently, two ship's officers and one corporate manager pled guilty to negligently discharging oily bilge water. The investigation was initiated after an assistant engineer reported the illegal discharges to U.S. and Canadian Coast Guard officers in Vancouver and Juneau, Alaska. The assistant engineer who provided the information was awarded $500,000 pursuant to the APPS bounty provision....
>
> [W]histleblower awards in 2004, however, surpass those in previous years combined ... In January 2004, the operator of the Guadalupe, OMI Corporation, pled guilty to preparing false documents in an effort to cover up illegal discharges of oily water ... and agreed to pay a $4.2 million criminal fine. The investigation started when a second engineer on the Guadalupe reported the illegal discharges to a local police department when the ship docked in New Jersey ... [T]he whistleblower was awarded a record $2.1 million, one-half of the fine ... This marks the largest bounty ever paid to a whistleblower under APPS.

Jeanne M. Grasso and Allison Fennell, *When the Whistle Blows, Companies Pay*, 109 Marine Log 11, Nov. 1, 2004.

B. Canada

Water quality is governed by various authorities at both the federal and provincial levels in Canada. "[T]he general rule is that provinces have primary power in most of Canada, whereas the federal government has primary power in the three territories that cover northernmost Canada, on First Nations reserves, and for trans-boundary issues." David Brooks, *Whither (or Whether) Water Policy In Canada,* 34 CA-US L. J. 279, 284 (2010).

> Specifically, the federal government has regulatory authority over: (i) water on federal lands; (ii) water that is in Canadian territories (being the other functional division of land in Canada besides provinces); (iii) water within national parks; (iv) water on Indian reserve land; (v) water that is commercially navigable, water that is inter-jurisdictional (flowing over or spanning provincial boundaries or between boundaries between provinces and the United States), and both ocean and freshwater fisheries.

Cameron Jefferies, *Unconventional Bridges Over Troubled Water—Lessons to be Learned From the Canadian Oil Sands as the United States Moves to Develop the Natural Gas of the Marcellus Shale Play,* 33 Energy L.J. 75, 85 (2012). "In addition, the Canadian Parliament has the authority to make laws necessary for peace, order and good government (POGG powers), which includes laws relating to international and interprovincial pollution." Peter Bernard and Andrew P. Mayer, *A Tale of Two Sovereigns: Canada, The United States, and Trans-Border Pollution Issues,* 13 U.S. Maritime L.J. 125 (2000–2001).

Despite these authorities, "by the mid-1990's, there was so little evidence of its role that the federal government had to create a *Where's Water?* task force to determine who was doing what." Brooks, *supra,* at 284–85. The conclusion: "Canadian government is more reluctant to intervene in water policy than central governments in other federal states or regional governments around the world." *Id.*

This section of the chapter focuses on federal water pollution and water quality-related laws, and provides an example of provincial laws in Alberta and Ontario.

1. Federal Water Pollution and Water Quality Laws

At the federal level, for fish-bearing waters, the Canadian Department of Fisheries and Oceans is said to "hold[] the 'big stick.'" Craig Pulsifer, *Settlement Pondering: Thoughts on Erosion Control,* Can. Forest Industries, Aug. 1, 1999. The federal Fisheries Act contains several provisions that protect water quality and water quantity in fish habitat. Fisheries Act, ch. LX, 1868 S.C. (31 Vict.) 177 (Can.); Fisheries Act of 1985, S.C. ch. F-14 (1985) (Can.). First, the Act prohibits the following activities by any person:

> 35. (1) No person shall carry on any work or undertaking that results in the harmful alteration, disruption or destruction of fish habitat....

> 36. (1) No one shall (a) throw overboard ballast, coal ashes, stones or other prejudicial or deleterious substances in any river, harbour or roadstead, or in any water where fishing is carried on....

> (3) Subject to subsection (4), no person shall deposit or permit the deposit of a deleterious substance of any type in water frequented by fish or in any place under any conditions where the deleterious substance or any other deleterious substance that results from the deposit of the deleterious substance may enter any such water.

> (4) No person contravenes subsection (3) by depositing or permitting the deposit in any water or place of

>> (a) waste or pollutant of a type, in a quantity and under conditions authorized by regulations applicable to that water or place made by the Governor in Council under any Act other than this Act; or

(b) a deleterious substance of a class, in a quantity or concentration and under conditions authorized by or pursuant to regulations applicable to that water or place or to any work or undertaking or class thereof, made by the Governor in Council....

Section 36 is a strict liability "zero tolerance" offense, and violators may face penal sanctions even if the "deleterious substance" is not proven harmful to fish. R. v. Kingston (2004), 70 O.R. (3d) 577; R. v. MacMillan Bloedel Ltd (1979), 47 C.C.C. (2d) 118 (B.C. C.A.).

In addition, Section 37 of the Fisheries Act authorizes the Fisheries Minister to require modifications to a project's plans or operations to prevent or mitigate adverse effects on fish habitat. The project proponent must submit plans, studies, or analyses to allow the Minister to determine whether the project will "likely" result in the "alteration, disruption or destruction of fish habitat, or in the deposit of a deleterious substance...." Fisheries Act § 37(1).

Additional protection can be found in Section 5 of the Navigable Waters Protection Act (NWPA), which prohibits any "work" from being "built or placed in, on, over, under, through or across any navigable water" unless "the work and the site and plans thereof have been approved by the Minister, on such terms and conditions as the Minister deems fit, prior to commencement of construction...." S.C. ch. N-22, § 5(1)(a) (1985). Although this appears to give the Minister broad discretion to prevent harm to navigable waters, exemptions under the NWPA have been frequently granted. Nathaniel Stevens, *Canada and the United States—Dealing With the Hydro Power Paradox: Evaluating the Environmental Effects of a Natural Energy Source*, 19 Suffolk Transnational L. Rev. 273, 290–291 (1995).

The primary federal statutes dealing specifically with water pollution are the Canada Water Act and the Canadian Environmental Protection Act, the latter of which goes well beyond water quality by regulating toxic substances and other pollutants into air, soil, and water. Selected provisions of these statutes are provided below.

Canada Water Act
R.S. 1985, c. C-11

An Act to provide for the management of the water resources of Canada, including research and the planning and implementation of programs relating to the conservation, development and utilization of water resources.

Preamble

... WHEREAS pollution of the water resources of Canada is a significant and rapidly increasing threat to the health, well-being and prosperity of the people of Canada and to the quality of the Canadian environment at large and as a result it has become a matter of urgent national concern that measures be taken to provide for water quality management in those areas of Canada most critically affected;

AND WHEREAS Parliament desires that, in addition, comprehensive programs be undertaken by the Government of Canada and by the Government of Canada in cooperation with provincial governments, in accordance with the responsibilities of the federal government and each of the provincial governments in relation to water resources, for research and planning with respect to those resources and for their conservation, development and utilization to ensure their optimum use for the benefit of all Canadians;

NOW, THEREFORE, Her Majesty, by and with the advice and consent of the Senate and House of Commons of Canada, enacts as follows:

Definitions

(1) In this Act, …

"federal waters" means, other than in Yukon, waters under the exclusive legislative jurisdiction of Parliament and, in Yukon, waters in a federal conservation area within the meaning of section 2 of the *Yukon Act*; …

"inter-jurisdictional waters" means any waters, whether international, boundary or otherwise, that, whether wholly situated in a province or not, significantly affect the quantity or quality of waters outside the province;

"international waters" means waters of rivers that flow across the international boundary between the United States and Canada;

"Minister" means the Minister of the Environment; …

"waste" means

(a) any substance that, if added to any water, would degrade or alter or form part of a process of degradation or alteration of the quality of that water to an extent that is detrimental to their use by man or by any animal, fish or plant that is useful to man, and

(b) any water that contains a substance in such a quantity or concentration, or that has been so treated, processed or changed, by heat or other means, from a natural state that it would, if added to any other water, degrade or alter or form part of a process of degradation or alteration of the quality of that water to the extent described in paragraph (a);

"water quality management" means any aspect of water resource management that relates to restoring, maintaining or improving the quality of water.…

Prescribed substances and certain water deemed waste

(2) Without limiting the generality of the definition "waste" in this Act,

(a) any substance or any substance that is part of a class of substances prescribed pursuant to subparagraph 18(1)(a)(i),

(b) any water that contains any substance or any substance that is part of a class of substances in a quantity or concentration that is equal to or in excess of a quantity or concentration prescribed in respect of that substance or class of substances pursuant to subparagraph 18(1)(a)(ii), and

(c) any water that has been subjected to a treatment, process or change prescribed pursuant to subparagraph 18(1)(a)(iii),

shall, for the purposes of this Act, be deemed to be waste.

Prohibition, Application, Agreements …

9. Except in quantities and under conditions prescribed with respect to waste disposal in the water quality management area in question, including the payment of any effluent discharge fee prescribed therefor, no person shall deposit or permit the deposit of waste of any type in any waters composing a water quality management area designated pursuant to section 11…, or in any place under any conditions where the waste or any other waste that results from the deposit of the waste may enter any such waters.…

11. (1) The Minister may, with the approval of the Governor in Council, enter into agreements with one or more provincial governments that have an interest in the water quality management of

(a) any federal waters; or

(b) any waters, other than federal waters, the water quality management of which has become a matter of urgent national concern....

18. (1) The Governor in Council may make regulations (*a*) prescribing

(i) substances and classes of substances,

(ii) quantities or concentrations of substances and classes of substances in water, and

(iii) treatments, processes and changes of water...

for carrying out the purposes and provisions of this Act.

Canadian Environmental Protection Act
1999, c. 33

Declaration: It is hereby declared that the protection of the environment is essential to the well-being of Canadians and that the primary purpose of this Act is to contribute to sustainable development through pollution prevention....

2. (1) In the administration of this Act, the Government of Canada shall....

(a) exercise its powers in a manner that protects the environment and human health, applies the precautionary principle that, where there are threats of serious or irreversible damage, lack of full scientific certainty shall not be used as a reason for postponing cost-effective measures to prevent environmental degradation, and promotes and reinforces enforceable pollution prevention approaches;

(a.1) take preventive and remedial measures to protect, enhance and restore the environment;

(b) take the necessity of protecting the environment into account in making social and economic decisions;

(c) implement an ecosystem approach that considers the unique and fundamental characteristics of ecosystems;

(d) endeavour to act in cooperation with governments to protect the environment; ...

(f) facilitate the protection of the environment by the people of Canada;

(g) establish nationally consistent standards of environmental quality;

(h) provide information to the people of Canada on the state of the Canadian environment;

(i) apply knowledge, including traditional aboriginal knowledge, science and technology, to identify and resolve environmental problems;

(j) protect the environment, including its biological diversity, and human health, from the risk of any adverse effects of the use and release of toxic substances, pollutants and wastes;

(j.1) protect the environment, including its biological diversity, and human health, by ensuring the safe and effective use of biotechnology;

(k) endeavour to act expeditiously and diligently to assess whether existing substances or those new to Canada are toxic or capable of becoming toxic and assess the risk that such substances pose to the environment and human life and health;

(l) endeavour to act with regard to the intent of intergovernmental agreements and arrangements entered into for the purpose of achieving the highest level of environmental quality throughout Canada; … and

(o) apply and enforce this Act in a fair, predictable and consistent manner.

(1.1) The Government of Canada shall consider the following before taking any measure under paragraph (1)(a.1):

(a) the short- and long-term human and ecological benefits arising from the environmental protection measure;

(b) the positive economic impacts arising from the measure, including those cost-savings arising from health, environmental and technological advances and innovation, among others; and

(c) any other benefits accruing from the measure.

(2) Nothing in this section shall be construed so as to prevent the taking of any action to protect the environment or human health for the purposes of this Act.

Interpretation

"environment" means the components of the Earth and includes

(a) air, land and water;

(b) all layers of the atmosphere;

(c) all organic and inorganic matter and living organisms; and

(d) the interacting natural systems.…

"environmental quality" includes the health of ecosystems.…

"pollution prevention" means the use of processes, practices, materials, products, substances or energy that avoid or minimize the creation of pollutants and waste and reduce the overall risk to the environment or human health.…

"release" includes discharge, spray, inject, inoculate, abandon, deposit, spill, leak, seep, pour, emit, empty, throw, dump, place and exhaust.…

Action to Prevent or Compensate Loss

39. Any person who suffers, or is about to suffer, loss or damage as a result of conduct that contravenes any provision of this Act or the regulations may seek an injunction from a court of competent jurisdiction ordering the person engaging in the conduct

(a) to refrain from doing anything that it appears to the court causes or will cause the loss or damage; or

(b) to do anything that it appears to the court prevents or will prevent the loss or damage.

40. Any person who has suffered loss or damage as a result of conduct that contravenes any provision of this Act or the regulations may, in any court of competent jurisdiction, bring an action to recover from the person who engaged in the conduct

(a) an amount equal to the loss or damage proved to have been suffered by the person; and

(b) an amount to compensate for the costs that the person incurs in connection with the matter and proceedings under this section.…

Regulation of Toxic Substances

93. (1) ... the Governor in Council may, on the recommendation of the Ministers, make regulations with respect to a substance specified on the List of Toxic Substances in Schedule 1, including regulations providing for, or imposing requirements respecting,

（a) the quantity or concentration of the substance that may be released into the environment either alone or in combination with any other substance from any source or type of source;

(b) the places or areas where the substance may be released;

(c) the commercial, manufacturing or processing activity in the course of which the substance may be released;

(d) the manner in which and conditions under which the substance may be released into the environment, either alone or in combination with any other substance;

(e) the quantity of the substance that may be manufactured, processed, used, offered for sale or sold in Canada;

(f) the purposes for which the substance or a product containing it may be imported, manufactured, processed, used, offered for sale or sold;

(g) the manner in which and conditions under which the substance or a product containing it may be imported, manufactured, processed or used;

(h) the quantities or concentrations in which the substance may be used;

(i) the quantities or concentrations of the substance that may be imported;

(j) the countries from or to which the substance may be imported or exported;

(k) the conditions under which, the manner in which and the purposes for which the substance may be imported or exported;

(l) the total, partial or conditional prohibition of the manufacture, use, processing, sale, offering for sale, import or export of the substance or a product containing it ...

95. (1) Where there occurs or is a likelihood of a release into the environment of a substance specified on the List of Toxic Substances in Schedule 1 in contravention of a regulation ... any person described in subsection (2) shall, as soon as possible in the circumstances,

(a)...notify an enforcement officer or any other person designated pursuant to the regulations and provide a written report on the matter to the enforcement officer or other person;

(b) take all reasonable measures consistent with the protection of the environment and public safety to prevent the release or, if it cannot be prevented, to remedy any dangerous condition or reduce or mitigate any danger to the environment or to human life or health that results from the release of the substance or may reasonably be expected to result if the substance is released; and

(c) make a reasonable effort to notify any member of the public who may be adversely affected by the release or likely release.

(2) Subsection (1) applies to any person who

(a) owns or has the charge, management or control of a substance immediately before its release or its likely release into the environment; or

(b) causes or contributes to the release or increases the likelihood of the release....

(5) Where any person fails to take any measures required under subsection (1), an enforcement officer may take those measures, cause them to be taken or direct any person referred to in subsection (2) to take them....

(7) Any enforcement officer or other person authorized or required to take any measures under subsection (1) or (5) may enter and have access to any place or property and may do any reasonable things that may be necessary in the circumstances.

(8) Any person, other than a person described in subsection (2), who provides assistance or advice in taking the measures required by subsection (1) or who takes any measures authorized under subsection (5) is not personally liable either civilly or criminally in respect of any act or omission in the course of providing assistance or advice or taking any measures ... unless it is established that the person acted in bad faith.

Notes and Questions

1. Note that the statutory provisions do not appear to distinguish between point sources and nonpoint sources of water pollution. What types of activities trigger regulation under the Fisheries Act, the Water Act, and the Environment Protection Act? Would the following activities be prohibited or otherwise regulated?

- Pesticides sprayed from a nozzle on a tanker truck onto a field directly adjacent to a stream.
- Pesticides sprayed from a crop duster (airplane) onto a field a mile away from a stream.
- "Deep-ripping" through saturated areas of a field to convert it from orchards to a vineyard.
- Ballast water pumped from a foreign flagged ship into a Canadian port, resulting in the introduction of zebra mussels and other nonindigenous species.
- Mountain-top mining, where coal companies push overburden into the valley below. Assume that fish-bearing streams are located in the valley.

2. What substances do these statutes regulate? Is their scope broader or narrower than the U.S. Clean Water Act?

3. What waters are protected under Canada's federal laws? Do they extend to groundwater?

4. A prosecution for violations of the Fisheries Act is provided below in the *Fletcher v. Kingston (City)* case, which also involved violations of Ontario law.

2. Provincial Approaches to Water Pollution

This section considers a few illustrative examples of water quality issues and legal responses from Ontario and Alberta. A case involving pollution in British Columbia is discussed at the end of this chapter in Section F on International and Transboundary Pollution Control.

This portrayal is not intended to be comprehensive, but rather to provide a snapshot of some of the most pressing issues and a sampling of provincial approaches to water pollution. As you read these materials, consider how other jurisdictions, especially subnational (state or local) governments, respond to similar problems.

a. Ontario

The following case demonstrates the distinctions between the federal Fisheries Act and Ontario's Water Resources Act (OWRA). In particular, it examines Section 30(1) of the OWRA: "Every person that discharges or causes or permits the discharge of any material of any kind into or in any waters or on any shore or bank thereof or into or in any place that may impair the quality of the water of any waters is guilty of an offence." It also illustrates the interplay of citizen and government enforcement efforts, along with evidentiary requirements and scientific methodology.

Fletcher v. Kingston (City)
2004 Carswell Ont 1860
Ontario Court of Appeal 2004

* * *

7 The City of Kingston operated a municipal dump site on the west shore of the Cataraqui River, adjacent to Belle Island, from the early 1950s to the early 1970s. The landfill was created in a marsh in the Cataraqui River and formed a peninsula of garbage. After its closure, the landfill site was transformed into a recreational area but little was done to address the possibility of leachate generation and migration.

8 Leachate is the term used to describe liquid that emanates from a site after having percolated through it. At a landfill site, leachate is created when rainfall percolates through the site's sandy overburden, dissolving some solids, mixing with liquids and absorbing various gases from the underlying waste materials. Leachate eventually comes to the surface in seeps and streams. Leachate can also migrate with shallow groundwater.

9 The charges in the instant case arise from alleged contaminants emanating from the landfill site and entering the Cataraqui River. Ms. Fletcher laid charges by means of a private citizen's information. The Ministry laid separate charges by means of its own information.

10 On four separate dates, Ms. Fletcher had samples taken of leachate entering the Cataraqui River from the landfill site....

11 The Fletcher samples were analysed for "acute lethality" to rainbow trout fingerlings. Rainbow trout is the standard test species for this type of analysis. Acute lethality testing normally involves the placing of test animals in progressively more dilute concentrations of a sample material in order to observe its effect upon them. It is meant to simulate what happens in the field. If the sample material kills a sufficient number of test organisms during an acute lethality test, one can conclude that the sample material is harmful to the environment, fish life or fish habitat.

12 Ms. Schroeder[1] conducted the acute lethality tests of the Fletcher samples …

13 The Fletcher samples were tested only at 100% concentration. All of the trout fingerlings that were exposed to the Fletcher samples died within twenty-four hours. Many of these fingerlings died within one hour. Ms. Schroeder testified that the effluent collected in the Fletcher samples was acutely lethal to fish....

---

1. Ms. Schroeder was qualified as an expert for the private prosecution in the testing of effluent for toxicity in a laboratory.

15 Ms. Schroeder also tested the ammonia levels of the Fletcher samples. She found that those ammonia levels were high enough to account for the mortality of the fish.

16 After being advised of the analysis results from the testing of the Fletcher samples, the Ministry took its own samples of leachate from the landfill site.... Mr. Lee testified that all rainbow trout exposed to at least a 25% concentration of the leachate samples ... died within twenty-four hours of the test.... Mr. Lee testified that based on the results from "acute lethality" testing involving rainbow trout of the Ministry leachate samples..., there was no doubt in his mind that the leachate was poisonous to aquatic life.

25 Mr. Poirier conducted the Ministry's acute lethality tests involving *Daphnia magna*.... [H]e concluded that the Ministry leachate samples ... represented leachate that was deleterious to fish. In addition, Mr. Poirier testified that only two companies have ever submitted an effluent more toxic than the Ministry leachate sample from February 10, 1997....

27 The Ministry leachate samples were analyzed for chemical parameters including pH and ammonia.... Mr. Lee testified that the total ammonia values of the Ministry effluent samples were high enough to have been acutely lethal to fish....

29 All the experts at trial agreed that ammonia was the main toxicant rendering the samples acutely lethal. Ammonia is a naturally occurring substance which, at certain concentration levels, is necessary for life. Ammonia is composed of unionized ammonia (NH_3) and ionized ammonia (NH_4^+). Unionized ammonia is much more toxic than ionized ammonia. The proportion of a solution of total ammonia that is composed of unionized ammonia increases as the temperature and/or pH of the solution increases. Further, the pH of a solution will rise as a result of vigorous shaking and/or aeration.

30 Some species of fish are more sensitive to unionized ammonia than others. Pink salmon is the species that is most sensitive to unionized ammonia; rainbow trout is the second most sensitive species. The fact that some species are more sensitive to unionized ammonia than others means that the minimum concentration level of unionized ammonia that will be toxic depends upon the species of fish concerned.

31 On the Fletcher information, the City was convicted of four counts of unlawfully depositing or permitting the deposit of a deleterious substance in the Cataraqui River, contrary to s. 36(3) of the *Fisheries Act*, and thereby committing an offence contrary to s. 40(2)(a) of that Act. Each count related to a separate day on which samples of the leachate had been collected.

32 On the Crown information, the City and Ms. Januszkiewicz were convicted of three of four counts under ss. 36(3) and 40(2)(a) of the *Fisheries Act*....

33 On appeal, the convictions and the acquittal were set aside and a new trial was ordered. The Crown and Ms. Fletcher appeal from the decision of the appeal judge....

35 The trial judge had no difficulty in finding that the City created and owned the landfill site, was responsible for the site's ongoing operation and maintenance, and had deposited or permitted the deposit of a substance in the Cataraqui River, which was water frequented by fish. As the trial judge noted, the issue that was "hotly contested" was whether the substance in question—the leachate—was deleterious.

36 In determining whether the leachate was deleterious, the trial judge adopted the test enunciated in *R. v. MacMillan Bloedel (Alberni) Ltd.* (1979), 47 C.C.C. (2d) 118 (B.C. C.A.), leave to appeal to S.C.C. refused, [1979] 1 S.C.R. xi (S.C.C.), holding that the prosecution need only prove that the substance introduced was deleterious or harmful to fish.

37 The trial judge found that the main toxicant that rendered the samples acutely lethal "was generally agreed to be ammonia" of which "the unionized form was accepted as the most toxic." He found that the samples that had been chemically analysed confirmed the presence of high ammonia concentrations.

38 At trial, the City and Ms. Januszkiewicz argued that the prosecution had failed to prove that the leachate was deleterious. Among other things, they argued that the pH of the samples had changed between the time the samples were taken and the time they were tested, with the result that the toxicity of the samples had increased when the acute lethality tests were performed. The trial judge rejected this argument on the basis that the testing methodology used by the Crown and Ms. Fletcher had "widespread scientific support", was "fair and impartial" and had been carried out objectively. He characterized the defence argument as "entirely theoretical". The court also noted that the defence had not put forward an *in situ* sample for analysis.…

40 The court rejected the due diligence defence. Relying on *R. v. Sault Ste. Marie (City)*, [1978] 2 S.C.R. 1299 (S.C.C.), the trial judge stated that the defence of due diligence involves the characterization of efforts taken to prevent the act or event, including the history of the defendants' efforts for a reasonable period before the charge dates. He found that both the City and Ms. Januszkiewicz were aware that the leachate was flowing into the Cataraqui River and that they chose to ignore the problem.

41 He concluded: [T]he Court rejects the defendants' position that they were duly diligent in respect to preventing the discharges. The Court can find no evidence of a comprehensive plan, not even one of effective monitoring of the closed landfill site to detect discharges. Certainly, no effective resources were committed to even dealing with the problems on a haphazard basis.

42 The court imposed a fine of $30,000 on each of the four privately laid counts and made one half of the fine payable to Ms. Fletcher and one half payable to the Minister of Finance for the Canadian government.…

43 With regard to the prosecution brought by the Ministry against the City, the court ordered a fine of $10,000 for each of counts two, three and four, totalling $30,000, to be paid within ninety days.

44 Ms. Januszkiewicz was given a suspended sentence in respect of her convictions on the Ministry information. The sentencing judge reasoned that a suspended sentence was appropriate because other "authors of this misfortune" were not before the court and, although Ms. Januszkiewicz was "not entirely blameless", she was "in the wrong place at the wrong time".

45 Further, the City was ordered to: Within three months provide the Ministry with a rationalized long-term site monitoring program … [and] provide the Ministry with a plan for the capping of the site.…

47 The appeal judge held that the trial judge erred in applying the test in *MacMillan Bloedel* to the question of whether the leachate was deleterious. In his opinion, the appropriate test was that set out in *R. v. Inco Ltd.* (2001), 155 C.C.C. (3d) 383 (Ont. C.A.). He reasoned as follows:

> I also see no useful policy reason to find a dichotomy exists between the interpretations given to s. 30(1) of the *Ontario Water Resources Act* in *Inco* and s. 36(3) of the *Fisheries Act* given in *MacMillan Bloedel*. The "two-tier" test offered by Chief Justice McMurtry in *Inco* assists in interpreting "a deleterious substance" in s. 36(3) since both the provincial and federal statutes deal, essentially, with "im-

pairing water quality," either *per se* or those waters "frequented by fish." Consequently unless ammonia was established to be an inherently toxic substance, it would be necessary in my view under s. 36(3) "to consider the quantity and concentration of the discharges as well as the time frame over which the discharge took place." I do not see in the trial judge's reasons that those factors were taken into account in assessing all of the evidence.

48 The appeal judge concluded that a new trial was necessary. Having allowed the appeal on convictions and concluded that the wrong legal standard had been applied at trial, he held that the Crown ought to succeed in its cross-appeal of the acquittal on count one of the Ministry information.

49 The main issue to be determined in this appeal is the proper interpretation of s. 36(3) of the *Fisheries Act*.

50 In essence, the appellant argues that the offence created by s. 36(3) is made out by proof that a substance discharged into waters frequented by fish is "deleterious" within the meaning of the Act. The appellant Fletcher relies on that argument and, additionally, asks this court to decide whether it is sufficient to show that a substance is acutely lethal to fish to be considered "deleterious" under the Act, whether or not the substance is "inherently toxic".

51 The respondents, on the other hand, maintain that to make out the offence under s. 36(3), the prosecution must also prove that the substance impairs the receiving water thereby making it deleterious to fish....

54 Subsections 34(1) and 36(3) of the *Fisheries Act* are the key provisions engaged by this appeal.... As reference is frequently made to s. 30(1) of the *Ontario Water Resources Act*, R.S.O. 1990, c. O.40 ("*OWRA*"), it is set out below....

57 Subsection 30(1) of the *OWRA* provides that:

> Every person that discharges or causes or permits the discharge of any material of any kind into or in any waters or on any shore or bank thereof or into or in any place that may impair the quality of the water of any waters is guilty of an offence....

58 With respect, in my view the appeal judge erred in applying the test set out in *Inco* to the question of whether the leachate was deleterious for the purposes of s. 36(3) of the *Fisheries Act*. The *Inco* test was established in reference to s. 30(1) of the *OWRA*. As discussed more fully below, the wording of s. 36(3) is markedly different than that of s. 30(1). Moreover, the scope and purposes of the two pieces of legislation is different. Unlike the *OWRA*, a piece of provincial legislation that focuses on Ontario waters, the *Fisheries Act* is federal legislation that applies to all waters in the fishing zones of Canada, all waters in the territorial sea of Canada and all internal waters of Canada....

60 Subsection 36(3) of the *Fisheries Act*, reproduced below for ease of reference, prohibits persons from (1) depositing or permitting the deposit of (2) a deleterious substance of any type (3) in water frequented by fish or in any place where the deleterious substance may enter such water.

> ... *no person shall deposit or permit the deposit of a deleterious substance of any type in water frequented by fish or in any place* under any conditions *where the deleterious substance* or any other deleterious substance that results from the deposit of the deleterious substance *may enter any such water* [emphasis added]....

62 In s. 34(1)(a), "deleterious substance" is defined as:

> (a) any substance that, if added to any water, would degrade or alter or form part of a process of degradation or alteration of the quality of that water so that

it is rendered or is likely to be rendered deleterious to fish or fish habitat or to the use by man of fish that frequent that water.

63 On an ordinary and plain reading of paragraph (a), a substance is deleterious if, when added to *any water*, it would alter the quality of the water such that it is likely to render the water deleterious to fish, fish habitat or to the use by man of fish that frequent the water. There is no stipulation in paragraph (a) that the substance must be proven to be deleterious to the receiving water. There is no reference to the receiving water in paragraph (a). On the contrary, the language makes it clear that the substance is deleterious if, when added to any water, it degrades or alters the quality of the water to which it has been added. The "any water" referred to in paragraph (a) is not the receiving water. Rather, it is any water to which the impugned substance is added, after which it can be determined whether the quality of that water is rendered deleterious to fish, fish habitat or the use by man of fish that frequent that water.

64 I agree with the interpretation of s. 36(3) given by Seaton J.A. in *MacMillan Bloedel* ... "What is being defined is the substance that is added to the water, rather than the water after the addition of the substance."

65 The focus of s. 36(3) is on the substance being added to water frequented by fish. It prohibits the deposit of a deleterious substance in such water. It does not prohibit the deposit of a substance that causes the receiving water to become deleterious. It is the substance that is added to water frequented by fish that is defined, not the water after the addition of the substance. A deleterious substance does not have to render the water into which it is introduced poisonous or harmful to fish; it need only be likely to render the water deleterious to fish. The *actus reus* is the deposit of a deleterious substance into water frequented by fish. There is no requirement in s. 36(3) or paragraph (a) of the definition of the term "deleterious substance" in s. 34(1), of proof that the receiving waters are deleterious to fish.

66 In *R. v. Northwest Falling Contractors Ltd.*, [1980] 2 S.C.R. 292 (S.C.C.), the Supreme Court of Canada considered the constitutional validity of s. 33(2) [now s. 36(3)] of the *Fisheries Act*. In that case, the appellant was charged with violating s. 33(2) as a result of diesel fuel having spilled into tidal waters. In the course of explaining why the provision was constitutionally valid, the Court opined both on the purpose of the legislation and the meaning of s. 33(2). It made the following six pertinent observations at pp. 300–01. (1) Fish, as defined in the legislation, are part of the system that constitutes the fisheries resource. The power to control and regulate that resource must include the authority to protect all those creatures that form part of that system. (2) The legislation is aimed at the protection and preservation of fisheries as a public resource. (3) The provision is concerned with the deposit of deleterious substances in water frequented by fish or in a place where the deleterious substance may enter such water. (4) The definition of a deleterious substance is related to the substance being deleterious to fish. (5) The subsection seeks to protect fisheries by preventing substances deleterious to fish from entering into waters frequented by fish. (6) The provision is restricted to a prohibition of deposits that threaten fish, fish habitat or the use of fish by man.

67 In my view, the interpretation of s. 36(3) given in *MacMillan Bloedel* is consonant with the reasoning of the Supreme Court of Canada in *Northwest Falling Contractors*. Accordingly, I reject the respondents' contention that the Supreme Court of Canada has, by means of its decision in *Northwest Falling Contractors*, directed the courts to consider the effect of the deposit on the receiving water by means of a consideration of the toxicity of the substance and the circumstances of the discharge....

69 The appellant Fletcher asks this court to determine whether, for the purposes of a prosecution under s. 36(3) under the *Fisheries Act*, a substance will be considered deleterious if it is shown that the substance is acutely lethal to fish. The question, as phrased, cannot be answered because it provides insufficient information — it does not speak to all of the requirements of paragraph (a) of the definition of the term "deleterious substance" in s. 34(1). Paragraph (a) requires proof that the substance, if added to water, alters the quality of the water so that the water is likely to be rendered deleterious to fish. I would add, however, that if a substance, when added to water, alters the water so that the water is acutely lethal to fish, I am of the view that the substance is deleterious.

70 The respondents argue that although the Crown does not have to prove actual harm or damage to fish or fish habitat when the substance in question is inherently toxic, when the substance is not inherently toxic the Crown must prove that the substance is deleterious at the point it enters the receiving environment. It will be recalled that the trial judge found that ammonia was the main toxicant within the leachate. Ammonia is a naturally occurring substance that can be beneficial and which dissipates quickly in water. This, they argue, necessarily leads to a consideration of the nature and circumstances of the discharge including the length of time over which the discharge occurred and the nature, quality, quantity and concentration of material discharged.

71 In my view, the essence of the respondents' argument is that the proper test to be applied where the substance is not inherently toxic is that given by this court in *Inco*.

72 In *Inco*, the defendant was alleged to have permitted effluent containing high levels of nickel and iron to be discharged into a river. Charges were laid against the defendant under s. 30(1) of the *OWRA*....

73 As can be seen, s. 30(1) expressly provides that a person who permits the discharge of material into water is guilty of an offence if the discharge "may impair the quality of the water", that is, the water into which the material was discharged.

74 McMurtry C.J.O., writing for the court in *Inco*, ... said this:

> Inherently toxic substances will always fail that test, reflecting zero-tolerance for discharging materials that, by their nature, may impair water quality. If the material in the discharge is not inherently toxic, then it will be necessary to consider the quantity and concentration of the discharge as well as the time frame over which the discharge took place.... Subsection 30(1) prohibits the discharge into water of materials that *may impair* the quality *of any waters* [emphasis in original].

75 In a prosecution pursuant to s. 30(1) of the *OWRA*, the prosecution must establish that the substance discharged into water has the potential to impair the quality of the water into which it was discharged. In a prosecution pursuant to s. 36(3) of the *Fisheries Act*, what must be proven is that a substance discharged into water frequented by fish is deleterious. The elements of the two offences are different because the language of the offence-creating provisions is different. In my view, it would be incorrect to apply a test established for prosecutions under s. 30(1) of the *OWRA* to charges brought pursuant to s. 36(3) of the *Fisheries Act*.

76 For this reason, I am of the view that the appeal judge erred not only in making the test under s. 36(3) of the *Fisheries Act* the same as that under s. 30(1) of the *OWRA* but also by holding that the trial judge should have made a finding of fact as to whether the leachate was inherently toxic.

77 Site-specific impairment is not a necessary ingredient of the offence under s. 36(3). Although the second step of the test formulated by this court in *Inco* relates to substances

that are not inherently toxic, the test does not apply to prosecutions under s. 36(3). It applies to prosecutions taken under s. 30(1) of the *OWRA*, a provision that does focus on impairment of the quality of the receiving water. It may be that one method for proving that a substance, when added to water, renders that water deleterious to fish is through an examination of the nature of the substance and the quantities and concentrations in which it was discharged. However, that does not make such considerations a necessary component of the offence under s. 36(3); rather, it provides a possible form of proof.

78 Accordingly, in my view, ss. 36(3) and 34(1) cannot be taken as requiring the Crown to prove the nature of the allegedly deleterious substance. The prohibition in s. 36(3) is against the deposit of a deleterious substance "of any type". What must be proven is that the substance, whatever it might be, is a deleterious substance within the meaning of paragraph (a) of the definition of that term in s. 34(1). In this case, it meant that the prosecution had to prove that the leachate, when added to any water, was likely to render the water deleterious to fish or fish habitat or to the use by man of fish that frequent the water. It did not have to prove which component of the leachate was responsible for the degradation or alteration of the quality of the water such that the water was likely to be rendered deleterious to fish. Nor was it obliged to show that fish living in the vicinity of the seep were harmed. . . .

80 As the appeal judge applied an incorrect legal test when considering the judgment of the trial judge, it falls to this court to determine whether the trial judge erred in concluding that the elements of the offences alleged under s. 36(3) had been made out. It will be recalled that the elements of the offence to be proven under s. 36(3) are: (1) depositing or permitting the deposit of (2) a deleterious substance (3) in water frequented by fish or where the substance may enter such water.

81 On the record, there can be no doubt that the trial judge was entirely justified in finding that the respondents had deposited waste in the dump site; that when it rained, some part of the waste or its residue combined with rain water to become leachate; that the leachate seeped into the Cataraqui River; and, that the Cataraqui River is frequented by fish. In the language of s. 36(3), the trial judge was entitled to find that the respondents permitted the deposit of leachate into water frequented by fish.

82 Did the trial judge err in concluding that the leachate was a deleterious substance within the meaning of the definition of that term in s. 34(1)(a)? That is, did the trial judge err in concluding that the leachate, if added to any water, would alter the quality of that water so that the water was likely rendered deleterious to fish?

83 The Ministry's acute lethality tests were performed on the Ministry samples at a variety of concentrations. The diluted concentrations were made by adding the leachate to a proportionate amount of water. Given the trial judge's acceptance of the protocols employed and the test results on the diluted Ministry samples, I see no error in his conclusion that the leachate contained in those samples was a deleterious substance within the meaning of paragraph (a) of the definition of that term in s. 34(1).

84 The tests of the Fletcher samples were performed only on the samples at 100 per cent concentration. In other words, the Fletcher leachate samples were not added to water. The trial judge did not directly address the question of whether the Fletcher samples, if added to water, would have altered the quality of the water thereby rendering it deleterious to fish. The evidence on that point is unclear. On the record before this court, I cannot conclude beyond a reasonable doubt that, had the Fletcher leachate samples been added to water, the water would have been rendered deleterious to fish. As a consequence, the appeal in relation to the Fletcher prosecution must fail.

85 The intervenor Pollution Probe submits that s. 36(3) must be interpreted in light of the "precautionary principle". It cites *114957 Canada Ltée (Spray-Tech, Société d'arrosage) v. Hudson (Ville)*, [2001] 2 S.C.R. 241 (S.C.C.) ("*114957 Canada*") in support of this submission. *114957 Canada* concerned the interpretation of s. 410(1) of the Québec *Cities and Towns Act*, R.S.Q. c. C-19. The Supreme Court held that this provision granted a municipality the authority to adopt a by-law that restricted the use of pesticides within the municipality's territorial limits.... [T]he Court's interpretation of s. 410(1) was consistent with the "precautionary principle", a principle of international law and policy....

> In order to achieve sustainable development, policies must be based on the precautionary principle. Environmental measures must anticipate, prevent and attack the causes of environmental degradation. Where there are threats of serious or irreversible damage, lack of full scientific certainty should not be used as a reason for postponing measures to prevent environmental degradation.

86 *114957 Canada* indicates that the values reflected by the "precautionary principle" may help inform the contextual approach to statutory interpretation. However, the meaning of s. 36(3) of the *Fisheries Act* is clear and unambiguous. As a consequence, there is no need to resort to the "precautionary principle" as an interpretive guide to the legislative text in question. I note merely that the interpretation of s. 36(3) contained in these reasons is not inconsistent with the "precautionary principle" established under international law....

101 Accordingly, I would ... set aside that part of the judgment of the Summary Conviction Appeal court that allowed the appeals against conviction of the City and Ms. Januskiewicz in the Ministry's action. The result is to restore the convictions and acquittal at first instance in the Ministry's action....

Notes and Questions

1. How does § 36(3) of the Fisheries Act differ from § 30(1) of the OWRA? As a prosecutor, which statute would you prefer to use as the basis for a charge against a defendant like the City?

2. The court found that § 36(3) of the Fisheries Act "is not inconsistent with the 'precautionary principle.'" Can the same be said for § 30(1) of the OWRA?

3. Who initiated suit against the City of Kingston? Who would receive the payment of penalties resulting from a successful prosecution?

4. What was the source of the deleterious substance in this case? What was the substance in question? Would this source and this type of substance be subject to a CWA enforcement action in the United States?

b. Alberta

Alberta is home to extraordinary environmental amenities, such as Banff National Park and the sparkling waters of Lake Louise. It also has a long history of mining, logging, and other forms of natural resource exploitation. An early legal battle over a proposal to dam the Oldman River represents "one of the longest, most bitter and occasionally bizarre episodes in the history of Alberta's conservation movement." Oliver A. Houck, *The Story of Rafferty, Oldman, and the Great Whale*, 29 B.C. Int'l &. Comp. 175 (2006), quoting Ed Struzik, Edmonton Journal 1992. Professor Houck sets the scene:

The first serious proposals to dam the Oldman River date back to the 1950s ...
In 1984, taking advantage of a crippling summer drought, Alberta Premier Peter
Lougheed announced that his government would proceed with the dam ... He
anticipated "no environmental concerns." The environmental facts of life, however, are that dams block fish runs, and irrigation return flows are notoriously
high in silt, fertilizers, pesticides, and salts and metals leached from the soil. A
federal study, completed a few years later, found that there could be significant
impacts indeed on water quality, fisheries, and the Peigan reservation downstream. The Edmonton Journal ... editorialized: "The Oldman Dam has the potential to be an ... environmental disaster."

As the proposals for the Oldman waxed, waned, and shifted locations, a fledg-
ling group of farmers and environmentalists started raising questions, then criticisms, and the battle lines slowly formed.... By spring 1989, despite harsh winter
construction conditions, the dam was 40% complete, building continued, and
the legal actions had not panned out on any front. Then, a miracle occurred.
That March, federal Judge Cullen, sitting in Saskatchewan, found the Ministry
of Transport bound by the EARP guidelines ... [And] in 1990, an appellate court
ruled ... that the federal Transport license required environmental review and ordered both Transport and Fisheries to comply.... With obvious reluctance, the
Minister convened an Environmental Review Panel for Oldman Dam. Alberta,
meanwhile, did the smart thing. It appealed the decision to the Supreme Court
and proceeded post haste towards completing the dam. The Environment Ministry—unsure of whether it had the authority to enjoin the construction, unsure
of whether, even if it did have the authority, Alberta would obey—did nothing
at all....

Finally, in 1992, the court ruled. One can usually tell how a case will turn out with
the first few sentences of any opinion. In this case, the Supreme Court of Canada
began: "The protection of the environment has become one of the major challenges of our time." ... [Friends of the Oldman River Soc'y v. Canada [1992] 1
S.C.R. 3, 16 (Can.).] The opinion moved through the statutory issues like so
much underbrush. Yes, the EARP guidelines order had been authorized by a
statute. And no, it did not conflict with the authorities of Transport and Fisheries. And no, although the dam was largely completed, it was not too late for
mitigating measures....

Id. at 199–209. According to Houck, "The effect of the opinion ... was to legitimize Canadian federal environmental law.... The provinces would have to get used to a new national
order." *Id.* at 209. With regard to the judicial role, Houck concluded, "In both systems,
but more markedly in the United States, the enforcement of environmental assessment requirements against unwilling and non-disclosing agencies depends on judicial review." *Id.*
at 241. In the end, although the construction of the Oldman Dam was eventually completed,
the case "propelled Canada into modern environmental law." *Id.* at 239.

The state of Alberta's environment, including its water resources, has once again garnered international attention as of late. The following case study explores the issues.

Case Study: Canada's Oil Sands

In 2009, for his first official foreign visit, newly-elected United States President Barack
Obama met with Canada Prime Minister Stephen Harper in Ottawa, Ontario. Sheryl Gay
Stolberg, *Obama Makes Overtures to Canada's Leader,* New York Times Online, Feb. 19,

2009. http://www.nytimes.com/2009/02/20/world/americas/20prexy.html. Trade policy, the war in Afghanistan, and Alberta's oil were among the most important topics discussed by the two heads of state. Wait a minute—oil in Alberta? It turns out that Alberta has a lot of it, and the U.S. is buying it. Unlike oil wells digging deep into the sands of Saudi Arabia to extract crude oil, Alberta's oil is bitumen—a tar-like substance that, unlike crude, does not flow freely, as it is heavier than water and more viscous than molasses—and it must be extracted by removing trees from the dense boreal forests of northern Alberta and scraping up the oil sands from the earth. Bitumen also requires relatively extensive processing to extract and refine the oil.

Alberta Geological Survey (May 9, 2012), http://www.ags.gov.ab.ca/energy/oilsands/index.html.

Alberta's oil sands cover an area the size of Florida, with the Athabasca River and the town of Fort McMurray at the heart of production. While there are 173 billion barrels of oil recoverable with 2008 technologies, the amount of potentially recoverable oil from Alberta could be around 315 billion barrels. Canadian Broadcasting Corporation Online, *Alberta's Oilsands: Black Gold or Black Eye?, By the Numbers,* http://www.cbc.ca/edmonton/features/dirtyoil/numbers.html (accessed Feb. 9, 2009).

The U.S. imports more oil from Canada than any other nation, with about half of that oil coming from Alberta's oil sands. Only 3% of accessible bitumen has been extracted from oil sands since 1970, but production has been ramped up significantly in recent years.

To say that the oil sands are big business is an understatement. "When we are looking at the tar sands, we are looking at a project that is the largest capital investment project on the face of the planet, and largest industrial project on the planet, and the ecological implications are just as great," according to Greenpeace Canada. Sarah Shenker, *Canada's 'Dirty Oil' Challenge*, BBC News Online, Dec. 11, 2008, http://newsvote.bbc.co.uk/mpapps/pagetools/print/news.bbc.co.uk/2/hi/Americas/7763365.stm.

Between 2006 and 2016 an estimated $100 billion will be invested in the extraction and processing of bitumen in Alberta. American oil tycoon T. Boone Pickens manages a $5 billion hedge fund (U.S. dollars), with oil sands as the single largest investment. Two of the Earth's two wealthiest citizens, Bill Gates and Warren Buffet, have shown interest in the area. Suncor Energy announced in 2008 that it would spend roughly $21 billion in Canadian dollars to make it Canada's largest oil sands producer. Ian Austen, *Canada: Suncor Expands in Oil Sands*, New York Times Online, Jan. 31, 2008, http://www.nytimes.com/2008/01/31/business/worldbusiness20prexy.html. Private and state-owned oil companies from Abu Dhabi, South Korea, Japan, India, France, and Great Britain have invested or have shown interest in the oil sands. Andrew Nikiforuk, Tar Sands: Dirty Oil and the Future of a Continent 22 (Greystone Books 2008).

When a monstrous three-story $5 million truck as wide as a tennis court is needed to haul the oil sand, and steam or a hot water concoction is needed to separate the oil from the earth, costs add up quickly. The energy needed for oil sands processing is at least three times as much in greenhouse emissions as conventional oil extraction. The industry is Canada's largest greenhouse gas emitter and will single-handedly keep Canada from meeting its Kyoto Protocol goal. Shenker, *supra*. Additional greenhouse gases are emitted when the forests are cut down to access the oil sands beneath them.

Left-over tailings from the production process include non-recyclable water and toxic substances such as naphthenic acids (NAs), polycyclic aromatic hydrocarbons (PAHs), arsenic, and mercury. Although many of these substances are naturally occurring, as oil sands tailings, they are in much higher concentrations, rendering the waste water untreatable, thus requiring containment in tailings ponds. The tailings ponds are so large that they can be seen from space. Syncrude's tailings pond, at 540 cubic meters in volume, is impounded behind one of the world's largest dams, second only to China's Three Gorges Dam. As one might expect, the ponds are susceptible to seepage. A 2008 report by Environmental Defense found that 11 million liters of toxic wastewater leak each day from the ponds. CBC, *Tailings Ponds*, http://www.cbc.ca/edmonton/features/dirtyoil/tailings.html, accessed Feb. 9, 2009.

A rare type of cancer, cholangiocarcinoma or bile duct cancer, has claimed the lives of a disproportionate number of citizens in a downstream community. The people of Fort Chipewan — a Canadian First Nation — have experienced cancer at a rate that is 30% higher than expected. Fort Chipewan residents have also sighted deformed fish with tumors, whitefish turning red, declining numbers of migratory birds, and the loss of wildlife species like rabbits, lynx, mice, and muskrats. Shenker, *supra*. Five hundred migrating ducks died after mistaking one of Syncrude's tailings ponds for freshwater and landing on the oily surface. Robin Kunzig, *Scraping Bottom*, National Geographic Online, March 2009, http://ngm.nationalgeographic.com/2009/03/canadian-oil-sands/kunzig-text/1.

Between the industrialized world's insatiable thirst for oil and the strained relations with many of the leading oil-producing Middle Eastern countries, Alberta may be a solution to North America's energy crisis. But it is fair to ask whether oil sands production is worth the societal and environmental risks.

Added to the costs and risks of production are the costs and risks of transportation and refining the bitumen. TransCanada, best known for operating Canada's largest natural gas network, is building the Keystone pipeline, a complex web of pipes that will move the oilsands output to refineries in the United States. The first section of the pipeline was routed under the Missouri River in South Dakota-Nebraska. In *Natural Resources Defense Council, Inc. v. U.S. State Department*, 658 F.Supp.2d 105 (D.D.C. 2009), NRDC sued the U.S. State Department, alleging that it violated the National Environmental Policy Act (NEPA) by issuing a permit to TransCanada for the pipeline without a sufficient assessment of the environmental impacts. The court found that the State Department, acting on behalf of the President in issuing the permit under Executive Order 13,337, was exercising a presidential prerogative that was not subject to judicial review under the Administrative Procedure Act. Since then, there have been nearly a dozen spills from pump stations affiliated with this pipeline. Cody Winchester, *Keystone 1 Accident Reveals TransCanada's Sneaky Side*, Sioux Falls Argus Leader, May 10, 2011. Meanwhile, TransCanada has proposed a larger, sister line — the Keystone XL — that would pass through the Great Plains to refineries on the Gulf Coast. After much political wrangling, the State Department is expected to make a decision in 2013. Dan Frosch, *New Application is Submitted for Keystone Pipeline*, N.Y. Times, May 4, 2012.

One of the potential oil refineries, the Hyperion Energy Center, will be located in rural South Dakota near Elk Point on prime agricultural land. If it proceeds, it will be the largest refinery and electric generating plant ever built in that state and one of the largest in the United States. In 2009 the South Dakota Board of Minerals and Environment approved Hyperion's application for a Prevention of Significant Deterioration (PSD) preconstruction air quality permit. The Sierra Club has appealed the permit, alleging that the refinery will release toxic air and water pollutants. Meanwhile, local residents are waging a zoning war against the project. For updates, see Sierra Club, *We Oppose Hyperion*, http://opposehyperion.com, accessed July 24, 2012.

Notes and Questions

1. To what extent should the possibility of water or air pollution from oil sands production in Canada affect the purchasing decisions of the United States and its consumers? To what extent should the environmental effects of transporting and refining the oil in the United States play a role in environmental permitting and analysis in Canada?

2. Although oil sands production contributes greatly to Canada's greenhouse emissions, those emissions are merely a drop in the bucket, relatively speaking, given that the U.S. produces nearly one-quarter of all carbon dioxide emissions worldwide. What steps, if any, should be taken to control oil sands emissions or to convince Canada to exercise greater control over them?

3. According to critics of oil sand extraction, the government of Canada has done very little to regulate the industry. *See* CBC, *Tailings, supra* ("the government has never had formal regulations on tailings management, performance, or enforcement mechanisms"). Martyn Griggs of the Canadian Association of Petroleum Producers, on the other hand, claims that the industry is one of the most regulated industries in the country. If more regulation is needed, what should the regulators focus on? Extraction processes, land use concerns, waste water treatment, air emissions from vehicles and other aspects of development, pipeline integrity, or something else entirely? For details on Alberta's approach to water pollution, see Government of Alberta, Water for Life: Action Plan 10–14 (2009), available at http://environment.gov.ab.ca/info/library/8236.pdf.

4. Canadian scientists have long sought more stringent monitoring and reporting of the environmental effects of tar sands development, and they have criticized "the often

secretive, sporadic and misleading scientific reports on the environmental impact of the oilsands industry."

> Owing to the lack of vigorous scientific monitoring and reporting on the oilsands, nobody really knows what lies beneath the surface of the land and in waters surrounding the great moving blot on the northern landscape that is the oilsands projects. Nor does anybody really know what effect this pollution has had on wildlife and humans.

William Marsden, *Scientists Win Historic Battle over Oil Sands Monitoring,* Financial Post, Feb. 6, 2012. The government's reports "have given the oilsands a clean bill of health, helping to silence critics."

> Their reports have allowed the Alberta government and the oilsands companies to claim that the high levels of pollutants in the oilsands are the result of natural seepage from bitumen deposits and not of the industry's extraction and refining processes. Therefore, politicians and industry have claimed that fears that oilsands operations are a threat to fish and other wildlife, as well as human health, are groundless.... But the tide changed in 2009 when a small group of independent scientists ... published ... peer-reviewed articles in the Proceedings of the National Academy of Sciences in the United States. The scientists claimed that each year, the oil sands companies were pumping the equivalent of a major oil spill into the environment, ... described as a "potent brew of toxic organic and inorganic chemicals." These included alarming levels of PACs [polycyclic aromatic compounds] that could only have come from the oil sands processors.

Id. In 2012, Alberta's Environment Minister, Diana McQueen, promised to create an independent commission and put it in charge of a new monitoring program that will involve "world-class," peer-reviewed science, with all data and reports to be made public as soon as they became available. In addition, the number of monitoring sites, the frequency of monitoring, and the range of chemicals and heavy metals to be monitored will be expanded.

5. Roughly 60 billion barrels of oil sands are buried beneath Utah, but the oil is deeper and is lower in quality than the oil in Alberta, deterring investment in Utahs' oil sands so far. Long time Utah Senator Orrin Hatch stated in 2006, however, that companies "are only waiting for the U.S. government to adopt a policy similar to Alberta's which promotes rather than bars the development of the unconventional resources." Nikiforuk, *supra,* at 33. The oil industry launched pilot projects to extract petroleum from tar sands and oil shale across parts of Utah and Colorado, but regulators seem uncertain how to assess the potential environmental damage of extracting this form of petroleum. "Utah regulators said they quickly concluded U.S. Oil Sands [the applicant, which is based in Alberta, Canada] couldn't possibly pollute any groundwater in a desert, and they offered the company a pro forma discharge permit without an independent or rigorous analysis." Paul Foy, *Utah Oil Sands Project Challenged Over Groundwater Pollution*, Huff. Post, May 17, 2012. In view of the experiences thus far with development in Alberta, should the U.S. allow companies to pursue oil sands extraction in Utah? If so, what constraints should be placed on development? What if the oil reserves are situated under federal public grasslands, wildlife refuges, or parks? (Laws governing development on various types of public lands are covered in Chapter 5.A.1)

6. Many investors today want a portfolio that reflects social and environmental awareness. How does investing in an oil sands company stack up?

7. If we had labels of origin so that you knew precisely where the fuel at your local gas station came from, would you choose to buy oil from the oil sands or from the Middle East? Or would you opt for ethanol derived from corn? *See* Kate Galbraith, *New Study Tallies Corn Ethanol Costs,* NY Times Blog, Feb. 5, 2009, at http://green.blogs.nytimes.com/2009/02/05/new-study-tallies-corn-ethanol-costs/ (reporting Minnesota researchers' findings that "identified corn ethanol as more 'costly' [for health and environmental impacts] than cellulosic ethanol or even regular gasoline, though the range of cost estimates was wide and dependent on a large number of variables").

3. Oil Spills

Canada's largest oil spill from a ship occurred in 1988, when the Odyssey, a ship registered in Liberia, split in two during a storm off the coast of Nova Scotia, spilling 132,000 tonnes of crude oil into the North Atlantic. All twenty-seven crewmen were lost. *See* Remy Melina, *The 10 Worst Oil Spills in History*, MSNBC, Apr. 23, 2010; Edith Lederer, *Lifeboats Found, No Survivors*, Anchorage Daily News, Nov. 11, 1988.

The U.S. and Canada have experienced at least two incidents where oil spills from ships crossed the international boundary. In 1988, oil escaped from the fuel barge *Nestucca* off Grays Harbour, Washington, and spread north to Vancouver Island. In 1991, a Japanese flag factory trawler, the *Tenyo Maru*, sunk after it collided with a Chinese flag cargo ship in Canadian waters adjacent to Vancouver Island. The U.S. Oil Pollution Act is covered in Section A.8 of this chapter. An assessment of Canadian law governing oil spills and Canada's implementation of international conventions such as MARPOL and the CLC, also described in Section A.8, *infra*, follows.

Peter Bernard and Andrew P. Mayer, A Tale of Two Sovereigns: Canada, the United States, and Trans-Border Pollution Issues
13 U.S. Maritime L. J. 125 (2000–2001)

[A]s a general rule pollution from ships falls within federal jurisdiction [in Canada] …

Canada Shipping Act—The Canada Shipping Act [R.S.C. 1985, c.S-9, §1] … is the most comprehensive legislation with respect to the business of shipping…. Part XV of the Act applies to ships within Canada's Exclusive Economic Zone ("EEZ") and deals with pollution prevention and response, but excludes a pollution discharge from ships engaged in oil or gas exploration or drilling. Part XVI provides civil liability and compensation…. Part XVI also applies to pollution damage in Canadian waters or the Canadian EEZ. In the case of oil pollution from a Convention ship, it applies to oil pollution damage in the Canadian EEZ, the territorial sea, inland waters, or EEZ of other states that are party to the [International Convention on Civil Liability For Oil Pollution Damage (CLC), Nov. 29, 1969, 973 U.N.T.S. 3, 4, reprinted in 9 I.L.M. 45 (1970), as amended]. The Act applies irrespective of the location of the actual or expected discharge of the pollutant and irrespective of the location where any preventative measures are taken. Part XV authorizes the implementation of Marpol 73/78, a protocol designed to deal with intentional pollution …

Implementing regulations include the Oil Pollution Prevention Regulations, the Garbage Pollution Prevention Regulations, and the Pollutant Discharge Reporting Regulations. The Oil Pollution Prevention Regulations implement vessel construction requirements along the same lines as those set in Marpol 73/78 and oil pollution preparedness requirements ... Requirements include the submission of plans and specifications in case of newly built ships or major refits, enclosed deck areas for bunkering operations, tanks for oily residue and sludge, double-hulls,[49] and equipment specifications for tankers or other ships. In addition, the Oil Pollution Prevention Regulations prohibit discharge of oil or oily mixtures unless the discharge is: (1) necessary to save the ship or lives, or (2) the discharge results from an accident in which the ship or its equipment is damaged and the accident is not the result of unseamanlike action....

The Garbage Pollution Prevention Regulations prohibit the discharge of garbage in Canadian internal waters, in the territorial sea south of the sixty degrees north latitude, in the territorial sea north of the sixty degrees north latitude not within a shipping safety control zone prescribed pursuant to the Arctic Waters Pollution Prevention Act, or in Canadian fishing zones described in Section 16 of the Oceans Act or its regulations.

Under the Pollutant Discharge Reporting Regulations, the master of a Canadian ship is required to report any prohibited discharge of a pollutant, actual or probable, from the ship and the master of a non-Canadian ship is required to report such a discharge in waters under Canadian jurisdiction. A report must be made to a Canadian pollution prevention officer if the pollution occurs in waters under Canadian jurisdiction, or to an appropriate official of the nearest coastal state when the discharge of a pollutant from a Canadian ship or probability thereof occurs outside Canadian waters.

Under the Canada Shipping Act both individuals and ships may be found guilty by summary conviction or indictment depending on the seriousness of the offense and conduct of the offender. In case of summary conviction an individual may be imprisoned for up to six months, individuals and ships may also be liable for a fine not to exceed CAD $250,000. In the event of indictment, an individual may be liable for a fine of up to $1,000,000 and imprisonment of up to three years and a ship may be liable for a fine of up to $1,000,000....

In addition to the CLC and Fund conventions and their focus on compensation for damage from oil tanker discharge, ... the Canada Shipping Act also addresses pollutant discharge from other ships. Section 677 makes ship owners strictly liable for oil pollution damage, for costs incurred by certain government agencies, any person in Canada, and to other state parties to the CLC for measures taken to prevent, repair, remedy or minimize oil pollution damage. This includes costs that the government or other individuals incur for reasonable anticipatory actions. Further, an owner is liable for impairment to the environment and for the costs of reasonable reinstatement measures undertaken or planned.

Section 678 makes the owner of a ship strictly liable for costs incurred by government agencies or any other persons with respect to measures taken to prevent, repair, remedy or minimize damage from a pollutant discharged from a ship. This section expands the shipowner's liability for clean-up costs in Section 677 to include the costs of clean-up associated with the clean up of pollutants other than oil. Pollutants include oil or other substances that would degrade water quality.

Section 679 allows a ship owner to limit liability for actual or anticipated oil pollution damage that did not result from the personal act or omission of the owner, or from in-

---

49. ... With respect to phase out of single hulled vessels oil tankers built since July 1993 and oil barges built since March 1995, they must have a double hull or equivalent design if they are to operate in Canadian waters. As of July 1995, existing single skinned tankers and oil barges must be retrofitted or phased out. For large vessels, the scheduled phase out is consistent to that in Marpol 73/78 and for other vessels the phase out schedule is consistent with the U.S. Oil Pollution Act of 1990....

tentional recklessness or knowledge that the oil pollution damage would likely result. These liability limitations, as amended by the 1984 Protocol to the CLC, replaced the more onerous requirements set out in the 1969 CLC which only allowed limitation as long as there was "no actual fault or privity" on the part of the ship owner....

Section 684 requires a Convention ship carrying more than 2040 tons of crude, fuel, heavy diesel, lubricating or other persistent oil to carry a certificate of insurance to enter or leave a Canadian port.... [A] claimant may take action against the guarantor of the owner of a Convention ship for pollution damage. The guarantor may raise the same defenses as the owner, and may also attempt to establish that the occurrence resulted from the willful misconduct of the owner as a defense....

The owner or guarantor may be released from liability if the illegal discharge resulted from an act of war, hostilities, insurrection, or other force majeure if it was wholly caused by an act or omission of a third party that intended to cause damage. This section also provides release if the discharge was wholly caused by the negligence or wrongful act of any government or authority responsible for the maintenance of lights or other navigational aids in the exercise of that function.

Arctic Waters Pollution Prevention Act—The Arctic Waters Pollution Prevention Act of 1970 [R.S.C., c.A-12 (1985)] ("AWPPA") was introduced to prevent pollution of waters adjacent to the mainland and islands of the Canadian arctic. The Act addresses the risk of damage to the region from resource extraction activities and to the Arctic's unique and fragile natural environment as well as the Inuit and other inhabitants. AWPPA prohibits the deposit of waste of any type in Arctic waters by ships or persons ...

Canadian Environmental Protection Act—The Canadian Environmental Protection Act of 1999 [R.S.C., ch. 33 (1999)] ("CEPA") regulates the release of certain substances into the environment, as well as the manner in which listed substances may be carried, imported and exported.... The relevant portion of CEPA ... is Part 7, Division 3, concerning disposal of wastes at sea. Division 3 implements the 1972 Convention on the Prevention of Marine Pollution by Dumping of Wastes and Other Matter ("London Convention") as well as the 1996 Protocol to that convention relating to incineration at sea. CEPA prohibits dumping of substances without a special permit, provides for inspections, and authorizes the detention of ships for violations. The Act allows for the disposal of wastes including: (1) dredged sediment; (2) fish wastes; (3) ships and platforms; (4) uncontaminated organic waste of natural origin; (5) inert inorganic geologic matter; and (6) bulky items such as steel, iron and concrete. Division 3 does not apply to disposals resulting from normal vessel operations, or those regulated by the Canada Shipping Act or the Canada Oil and Gas Act. Penalties for violation of CEPA include a fine of not more than $1,000,000, imprisonment for a term of not more than three years, or both, and on summary conviction, a fine of not more than $300,000 or imprisonment for a term of not more than six months, or both. Under Part 2 of CEPA any person who has suffered loss or damage as a result of conduct that contravenes any provision or regulation may, in any court of competent jurisdiction, bring an action to recover from the violator an amount equal to the loss or damage proved by that person.

Canada Oil and Gas Operations Act—The Canada Oil and Gas Operations Act of 1992 ("COGOA") is designed with regard to the exploration for and exploitation of oil and gas.... COGOA applies to exploration, drilling production, conservation, processing and transportation of oil and gas.... [P]olluters are strictly liable for the Canadian government's clean up costs for damage from the emission of gas, oil or related debris from oil production facilities out to the 200 mile limit or the edge of the continental shelf....

Oceans Act — The Oceans Act [R.S.C., ch. 18 (1985)] ... creates a framework for the development and implementation of a strategy to manage its coastal waters, inland waters, territorial sea, and EEZ. The strategy is to be based on policies such as sustainable development, integrated management of activities in the different waters and the precautionary approach. Further, the strategy is intended to involve broad consultation with interested groups, including other levels of government, aboriginal organizations, and coastal communities.

The Oceans Act grants the Minister of Fisheries and Oceans fairly broad powers and duties in relation to policies and programs for Canada's oceans by combining Fisheries and the Canadian Coast Guard under one Ministry. As a result, the Minister of Fisheries is now responsible for the safe and efficient movement of ships, marine communications and traffic management, ice breaking, channel maintenance, marine search and rescue, pleasure craft safety, and marine pollution prevention and response ...

Proposed Federal Legislation: Bill S-17 and the Marine Liability Act — Canada is in the process of creating the Marine Liability Act via Bill S-17 [Bill S-17, An Act Respecting Marine Liability and to Validate certain By-Laws and Regulations, 36th Parliament, Canada (2nd Session 2000)].... [T]he Marine Liability Act will combine the liability provisions previously contained in the Canada Shipping Act with some new provisions. The purposes of Bill S-17 are to: (1) adopt a new regime of shipowner liability to passengers and a new basis for apportioning liability; (2) consolidate existing marine liability regimes into one comprehensive law ... The proposed law makes no substantive changes to the general provisions relating to liability and compensation for marine pollution. Yet it does make some significant changes to the law pertaining to personal injury, general maritime tort law, the carriage of passengers and certain aspects of the law respecting the carriage of goods....

Canada/United States Joint Marine Pollution Contingency Plan — The principal cooperative agreement relevant to protection of the marine environment from spills is the Canada-United States Joint Marine Pollution Contingency Plan. *See* Environment Canada, Environmental Emergencies Branch, Canada-United States Joint Inland Pollution Contingency Plan (1994), available at http://www.ec.gc.ca/ee-ue/plans/InlandPlan_e.cfm (last modified Jan. 10, 2001). Implementation and maintenance of the plan are the joint responsibility of the coast guard in each country. The agreement provides for cooperation in response to pollution posing a significant threat to the waters or coastal areas of Canada or the United States. The Canada-United States Joint Marine Pollution Contingency Plan is limited to spills in the waters of one party that are of such a magnitude as to justify a call on the other party for assistance.... In addition, the plan deals with establishment of joint response centers and joint response teams, the appointment of the on-scene commanders by both parties, mutual obligations with respect to public information officers and the general dissemination of information....

[In addition,] ... Canada has, to a great degree, adopted the international regime ... For example, Canada has signed on to both the CLC and Fund Conventions.... The CLC deals with the compensation from the owner of a polluting ship while the 1992 Fund Convention deals with payment of compensation on behalf of cargo interests....

There are great differences between the Canadian and American damage compensation regimes but the potential for damage on the coasts of each nation is equally great. The question to be asked is, "Will the citizens living near the border be protected equally on both sides of the line?" Remedies are, of course, available even if the suit must proceed in negligence or nuisance, but will the claimant recover the damages awarded if the ship is lost and underwriters elect not to respond? There are differences depending on the origin of the oil spill; if it is from a convention ship carrying oil as cargo rather than from bunkers on board the vessel as fuel. Will the claimant recover pure economic loss? Can the governments on both sides of the border recover for environmental or non-use damages in each jurisdiction? ...

Given that the United States is not a member of the CLC or Fund Conventions, an action against the vessel owners in Canada must be based on the wording of Section 677 of the Canada Shipping Act or in tort as opposed to a claim for compensation under the CLC or Fund Conventions....

[The U.S. Oil Pollution Act] ... provides for claims by foreign persons and governments if the foreign claimant is able to show that they have not otherwise been compensated, and recovery is authorized by a comparable treaty or agreement with the United States. The claimant must demonstrate that Canada has certified to the U.S. Secretary of State that such a comparable remedy exists. In spite of all the cooperative agreements between Canadian and United States jurisdictions regarding pollution prevention and cleanup, Canada has no treaty agreement with the United States regarding mutual recovery. Canadians are, therefore, not able to file a claim under OPA '90....

Notes and Questions

1. The author asserts, in his conclusion, "The distinction between the Canadian and United States compensation regimes is significant, and difficulties which await the claimant that attempts to secure a remedy on the other side of the international border result from that diversity...." Bernard, *supra,* at 181. He continues:

> From the Canadian perspective, matters would be significantly simpler if the United States were a participant in the international compensation regime. United States participation would result in a readily accessible source for compensation in the event of an oil pollution incident that causes pollution damage to either country. Obviously, the United States has its own reasons for opting-out of the International Compensation Regime, which likely include levels of compensation available under the CLC and Fund Conventions.... As they stand, the respective compensation regimes of Canada and the United States do not address the issue of how to deal with trans-border claims for contribution. Considering the heavy tanker and oil barge traffic around Canadian/United States marine boundaries in the Pacific Northwest, this is a serious deficiency that must be addressed.

Do the discrepancies between the legal regimes of the two nations seem like a serious problem? If so, how should any shortcomings be addressed?

2. How do the two nations address pollution from cruise ships and other types of vessels? Do existing legal regimes seem adequate? Have the laws kept pace with the challenges posed by climate change and rising sea levels?

> [S]ome scientists ... predict that the Northwest Passage will be ice-free in summer as early as 2030, permitting commercial vessels to traverse the Passage without icebreaker assistance ... The accessibility of the Northwest Passage, at least in summer, could greatly reduce transit times of commercial voyages between Europe and Asia.... In an age of ever-increasing costs of vessel operation, and ever-more-stringent controls on carbon dioxide emissions, shipping lines are more and more willing to consider moving cargoes and people by water across the top of the world.

Already, more commercial vessels are entering northern Canadian waters, not only to carry out traditional winter resupplying of widely scattered villages, but also to carry cargoes from new mining developments and eco-tourists yearning for a glimpse of the unspoiled Arctic environment.

Peter G Pamel and Robert C Wilkins, 29 No. 3 J. Energy & Nat. Res. L. 333, 334–35 (2011).

3. The *Tale of Two Sovereigns* article mentions the Marine Liability Act, S.C. 2001, c.6, which was passed in 2001 and amended in 2009. Part 4 of the 2009 amendments excludes "marine adventure tourism activity" and vessels that are "manually propelled by oars or paddles" from its provisions related to liability for carriers of passengers by water. This was adopted to address industry concerns that "liability insurance was often unavailable to tourism operators, as these operators were treated the same as commercial passenger vessels." A. William Moreira et al., *Canadian Maritime Law Update: 2009*, 41 J. Maritime Law & Commerce 317, 322 (2010). But "the definition of 'passenger' was also amended to include a 'participant in a marine adventure tourism activity, [and] a person carried on board a vessel propelled manually by paddles or oars and operated for a commercial or public purpose...,' thus imposing upon adventure tourism operators the global limits of liability applicable to all passenger carriers," *i.e.,* approximately $3,300,000 CDN. *Id.,* citing Bill C-7 clause 3, amending section 24.

4. Like Canada, the U.S prevents ocean dumping by statute, 33 U.S.C. §§ 1411, 1414b, and it has specifically adopted the MARPOL Protocol in domestic legislation, 33 U.S.C. § 1907. In addition, in some instances, federal land management agencies in the U.S. have taken a role in preventing oil pollution from ships. In Clipper Cruise Line, Inc. v. U.S., 855 F.Supp. 1 (D.D.C. 1994), the court upheld Park Service regulations limiting entry into Glacier Bay National Park to three cruise ships per day. The regulations were adopted in response to a previous Clipper ship collision and resulting pollution. When the Park Service decided to allow additional cruise ships, an environmental group sued to prevent the change. *See* National Parks and Conservation Assoc. v. Babbitt, 241 F.3d 722 (9th Cir. 2001) (enjoining a plan for a 72% increase in cruise ship traffic).

5. The Canadian Environmental Protection Act, R.S.C. 1985, c. C-15.3, provides that persons who report infractions may keep their name confidential, and that no employee shall be disciplined, dismissed or harassed for reporting on the release of certain toxic substances to a federal inspector. Although the United States and New Zealand were both "quicker off the mark" to protect whistleblowers than Canada, Saunders, *supra,* at 2; *see* Robert G. Vaughn, *The Whistleblower Statute Prepared for the Organization of American States and the Global Legal Revolution Protecting Whistleblowers,* 35 Geo. Wash. Int'l L. Rev. 857, 880 (2003), Canada adopted the Public Servants Disclosure Protection Act in 2005. It protects most federal employee whistleblowers who report "serious wrongdoing," including "an act or omission that creates a substantial and specific danger to the life, health, or safety of persons, or to the environment." S.C. 2005, c.46 § 8(d). At the provincial level, Manitoba, New Brunswick, Nova Scotia, and Saskatchewan have adopted legislation to protect public service whistleblowers. Lukasz Granosik et al., *Update on Whistleblowing in Quebec and Canada,* 22 No. 1 Emp. & Indus. Rel. L. 21 (2012).

C. New Zealand

According to the New Zealand Ministry for the Environment, "Water resources and aquatic ecosystems are essential to New Zealand's economy. They are also a significant part of our natural heritage, our recreational activities, and of particular practical and spiritual value for Māori." New Zealand Ministry for the Environment, *On Water,* http://www.mfe.govt.nz/issues/water/ (2007). Water resources range from spectacular alpine lakes and waterfalls to coastal estuaries to abundant trout streams and mighty, roaring rivers. It should come as no surprise, then, that "New Zealand has enjoyed a widespread reputation for environmental consciousness." Owen Furuseth and Chris Cocklin, *An Institutional Framework For Sustainable Resource Management: The New Zealand Model,* 35 Nat. Resources J. 243, 248 (1995). It has not always been so, however.

> [T]he image of 'clean, green New Zealand' masks the problems of non-point pollution inherent in agricultural and forestry production and a growing number of individual environmental policy conflicts that emerged beginning in the early 1970s.... New Zealand was poorly prepared for dealing with long-standing environmental quality issues such as soil and water pollution, as well as an expanding set of new problems in municipal and hazardous waste disposal, water resource allocation, and the effects of increasing industrialization. The environmental ... framework ... was characterized by poorly defined pollution controls standards, weak inter-governmental cooperation and coordination ... A New Zealand Nature Conservation Council report identified three major flaws with the existing administrative framework: overlapping institutional responsibilities, conflicting mandates of government agencies, and poor coordination among agencies. When a 1983 study compared New Zealand's environmental policy and planning with other Pacific rim nations ... New Zealand ranked last, behind Indonesia, Malaysia, Australia, and Japan; and the nation's environmental protection mechanisms were assigned to the lowest level in the model.

Id. The central government performed a comprehensive statutory review of the legislative and administrative structures for environmental and natural resources and land use planning, and made the following discoveries:

> New Zealand's environmental policies and policy-making were uncoordinated and often fragmented. There was evidence that earlier governments had not shown much initiative nor leadership in developing a broadly based environmental management system. While there were over 100 statutes having "particular relevance to the environment" and various governmental organizations at the national, regional, and local levels held mandates relating to the environment, New Zealand lacked a national environmental policy.

Id. at 249. "The culmination of this process in 1986–87 was a restructuring of the local government framework and extensive legislative reforms to create a national framework for sustainable management." *Id.* at 246.

The centerpiece of these reform efforts was the 1991 Resource Management Act (RMA), which is the key piece of legislation governing the management of freshwater resources in New Zealand. A notable feature of the RMA is its focus on the *effects* of human activities on the environment, rather than regulating on the activities themselves. In other words, the RMA is "a performance based approach to regulation" that limits the adverse environmental effects of human activities in order to achieve sustainable use and management of resources. *Id.* at 259.

> Among the most fundamental reforms was the establishment of sustainable management as the guiding principle for decisions affecting the allocation and use of natural resources and the maintenance of environmental quality. The adoption

of sustainability has been accompanied by numerous changes in land use and environmental planning processes and institutions. Prescriptive planning models have been replaced by a performance based planning paradigm. Environmental impact assessment has been strengthened. There has been widespread consolidation of governmental units and the creation of new, more powerful local (regional) governments, with boundaries drawn using a hydrologic criterion. Decision making processes have been shifted from central government agencies to the local level.

Furuseth and Cocklin, *supra*, at 243. (Provisions of the RMA related to environmental impact assessment are explored in Chapter 3.C, *supra*.)

Under the RMA, regional councils are responsible for making decisions on the allocation and use of water within their boundaries and for managing water quality. Likewise, "water availability has been managed by local authorities under the RMA. They have set standards for water quality, adopted their own management system, and then allocated water more or less to whoever asked for it first...." Molesworth & Featherston, *Water World*, 38 NZ Lawyer 6, April 21, 2006.

Rather than a laundry list of "command and control" requirements, the RMA "provides a framework for environmental protection." Tim Kelley and David Slaney, *A Comparison of Environmental Legislation and Regulation in New Zealand and the United States*, 69 J. Env. Health 20 (2006).

Regional governments (councils) determine the specific requirements and associated penalties for noncompliance. In practice, it could be argued, this arrangement often works the way legislation works in the United States, since in the United States individual states do retain some latitude in the enforcement of federal environmental legislation. The N.Z. approach, however, allows significant latitude in environmental requirements and penalties related to the different topographic regions, climes, and population density of New Zealand, which may vary dramatically within relatively short distances, relative to the United States.

Id.

The RMA does, however, contain some specific prohibitions. Section 15 of the RMA prohibits the discharge of any:

(a) contaminant or water into water; or

(b) contaminant onto or into land in circumstances which may result in that contaminant (or any other contaminant emanating as a result of natural processes from that contaminant) entering water; or

(c) contaminant from any industrial or trade premises into air; or

(d) contaminant from any industrial or trade premises onto or into land—

unless the discharge is expressly allowed by a national environmental standard or other regulations, a rule in a regional plan as well as a rule in a proposed regional plan for the same region (if there is one), or a resource consent.

RMA 1991 § 15(1) (emphasis added).

Under the RMA, water is defined broadly as "water in all its physical forms whether flowing or not and whether over or under the ground." *Id.* § 2(1). "Contaminant" is also defined broadly:

any substance (including gases, odorous compounds, liquids, solids, and micro-organisms) or energy (excluding noise) or heat, that either by itself or in combination with the same, similar, or other substances, energy, or heat—

(a) when discharged into water, changes or is likely to change the physical, chemical, or biological condition of water; or

(b) when discharged onto or into land or into air, changes or is likely to change the physical, chemical, or biological condition of the land or air onto or into which it is discharged.

Id. § 2(1). To "discharge" includes to "emit, deposit, and allow to escape." *Id.*

In URS New Zealand Ltd. v. Dist. Court at Auckland [2009] NZRMA 429 (HC), the High Court illustrated the breadth of the "discharge" prohibition.

In 2007, URS ... drilled a number of bore holes to install ground water monitoring wells to investigate a partially decommissioned fuel retailing site for contamination. Unknown to URS or its subcontractor, that drilling pierced and broke an empty fuel delivery line. URS left the site following the completion of its investigations. Later that year, another fuel retailing company contracted Fuelquip (NZ) Ltd to re-commission the site. That re-commissioning involved pumping fuel through the fuel line to purge it of air. Fuelquip failed to test the line before pumping fuel through it, which resulted in 10,000 L of fuel escaping through the damaged fuel line and entering a nearby stream. Fuelquip pleaded guilty to charges of discharging a contaminant under section 15 the RMA and was sentenced.

The Auckland Regional Council (ARC) charged URS on the basis that URS, too, allowed the discharge to occur by virtue of its action that led to piercing the fuel line and failing to notice, or to investigate and take appropriate steps to prevent possible damage to the fuel line (precautions that a reasonably prudent person in the position of URS should have taken). URS submitted that to cause a discharge for the purposes of section 15 requires that a party be in control of the relevant operations or contaminants at the time of the discharge....

The High Court adopted a broad interpretation of 'discharge' in section 15 and dismissed URS's primary submission. The High Court noted that the offence does not require that a party intend to commit the offence (it is a 'strict liability' offence), and held that, on the clear wording of section 15, there was no requirement that a party be in control of a contaminant, or the operations releasing the contaminant, at the time of a discharge.

The High Court relied on the definition of 'discharge' in the RMA, which includes 'allow to escape'. That definition, the Court noted, extends potential liability to parties that exhibit a 'passive lack of interference' in respect of a discharge.... The RMA is designed in that respect to promote self regulation and the acceptance of responsibility.

The result of the High Court's decision is that a party who has a past connection to a site, and has made an act or omission that contributes to a discharge at a later point in time (albeit in combination with the acts of another party) can be held liable for allowing a discharge—even if it did not have control of the operations at the time that the actual discharge occurred.

Russell McVeagh, *The Carbon Copy Resource Management Update*, Sept. 2009, at http://www.russellmcveagh.com/_docs/rmupdatesep2009_250.html#top.

The RMA recognizes some defenses to Section 15 liability. These defenses require "that the effects of an act were adequately mitigated or remedied ... [and] impose 'an incentive on a party of potential liability to take prompt and effective steps to remedy the consequences of its acts or omissions' regardless of whether the party has control of the operations that directly created the offence. *Id.* In the *URS New Zealand* case, "URS may escape liability if it could establish that a third party (such as Fuelquip) committed an intervening act, between URS's damaging of the fuel line (and inaction to investigate and take precautionary steps) and the discharge, which severed the chain of causation between URS and the discharge — so that URS's actions no longer operated as the cause of the discharge, and were of merely historical importance." *Id.*

In addition to Section 15, Section 107 of the RMA limits the types of discharge permits that may be granted. This "effectively represents qualitative environmental 'bottom lines'" with respect to discharges. DEREK NOLAN, ENVIRONMENTAL AND RESOURCE MANAGEMENT LAW 560 (4th ed. 2011). Section 107 provides:

> (1) Except as provided in subsection (2), a consent authority shall not grant a discharge permit or a coastal permit to do something that would otherwise contravene section 15 ... allowing—
>
>> (a) the discharge of a contaminant or water into water; or
>>
>> (b) a discharge of a contaminant onto or into land in circumstances which may result in that contaminant (or any other contaminant emanating as a result of natural processes from that contaminant) entering water; or
>>
>> (ba) the dumping in the coastal marine area from any ship, aircraft, or offshore installation of any waste or other matter that is a contaminant,—
>
> if, after reasonable mixing, the contaminant or water discharged (either by itself or in combination with the same, similar, or other contaminants or water), is likely to give rise to all or any of the following effects in the receiving waters:
>
>> (c) the production of any conspicuous oil or grease films, scums or foams, or floatable or suspended materials:
>>
>> (d) any conspicuous change in the colour or visual clarity:
>>
>> (e) any emission of objectionable odour:
>>
>> (f) the rendering of fresh water unsuitable for consumption by farm animals:
>>
>> (g) any significant adverse effects on aquatic life.
>
> (2) A consent authority may grant a discharge permit or a coastal permit to do something that would otherwise contravene section 15 ... that may allow any of the effects described in subsection (1) if it is satisfied—
>
>> (a) that exceptional circumstances justify the granting of the permit; or
>>
>> (b) that the discharge is of a temporary nature; or
>>
>> (c) that the discharge is associated with necessary maintenance work—
>
> and that it is consistent with the purpose of this Act to do so.

In Marr v. Bay of Plenty Regional Council [2010] NZEnvC 347, the Environment Court of New Zealand reviewed a resource consent to discharge treated wastewater from the Tasman pulp and paper mill to the Tarawera River. It described the effects of the discharges to the river prior to regulation:

> The effect of the Tasman Mill discharges on the river was undoubtedly adverse in the extreme.... "[F]or 40 years (the mill company) was allowed to do as it pleased with the river, use it as a sewer, a rubbish dump.... 44 gallon drums used to float pass, plastic hoses, wood pulp, dioxins, furans, and the water was black." ... [F]lounder and herring no longer came up the river at all, whitebait were much less plentiful and fishing grounds off the mouth of the river were "buried under black rotting wood pulp."

Id. para. 32–33. The court observed that the discharge was a "noncomplying activity," and that "s107 only allows us to grant consent ... if there are 'exceptional circumstances' and it is consistent with the purpose of the RMA" as well as the relationship of Maori with "ancestral lands and waters, and other taonga." *Id.* para. 35–36, 40. Due to the "considerable positive economic and social benefits of the Tasman Mill," however, including direct benefits of "an estimated ... $191m and a full-time equivalent employment (FTE) level of 830," the court held that the consent should be issued, but that the applicants should be required to fund their own research into colour and clarity reductions and achieve an "inconspicuous colour discharge" by 2034. *Id.* para. 42–44, 230.

Despite its broad terms and its sustainability goal, the RMA's provisions have not been entirely successful in protecting water resources. Declining water quality is ranked by some "as New Zealand's number one environmental problem." *Hopes Rise for Water Planning*, Nat'l Bus. Rev., June 29, 2012. Consider the following two examples:

> Canterbury ... [has] one of the largest estuaries in New Zealand (700 hectares in total), home to many forms of bird life, and ... surrounded by residential housing.... [O]ver the last 15 years fragmented regulatory efforts by the regional and city councils saw the estuary's water quality significantly decline from recreational activities, surface and stormwater runoff and, most significantly, a city wastewater outflow (treated sewage)....

> [Meanwhile,] ... one of New Zealand's largest lakes and a coastal lagoon [Lake Ellesmere/Te Waihora, also in the Canterbury Region] ... had increasingly become the site of "resource use conflicts" due to declining water quality from drains and farming pollution around the lake and upstream. This degradation had "fallen through the cracks" of ad-hoc regulation and management by six government agencies, and, given its cultural significance, was of serious concern to local Māori who owned the lakebed.

Cameron Holley and Neil Gunningham, *Natural Resources, New Governance and Legal Regulation: When Does Collaboration Work?* 24 NZ Univ. L Rev. 309, 322 (2011).

The RMA is in part to blame:

> There are two problems with regional planning for water [under the RMA]: The planning process can be cumbersome, time consuming and litigious; and the cumulative effects of takes and discharges have to be managed....

> [P]lans and policies are drawn up in-house by regional council staff and then subject to consultation and notification. Where there isn't agreement, they can be subject to drawn-out, expensive and escalating appeals through the Environment and High Courts, often featuring the confrontational use of conflicting technical and scientific expertise.... Not surprisingly, plans can take a ridiculously long time to be put in place or changed. The forum's report cites two instances of plans taking 12 and a half years from start to finish and variations on two existing plans taking six years. That's way too long for effective

business and community decision making.... [In addition,] the RMA makes no provision for cumulative effects. Councils must still consider applications for consents for takes or discharges if the water in their regions is already over allocated, or its assimilative capacity is exceeded.

Id. According to some:

The RMA is poorly equipped (though not bereft) of ways to handle competing economic claims. Regional councils' approaches to solving claims vary unpredictably. There was no easy way a regional consent application in, say, Otago, could weigh the urgency of generating electricity in, say, Auckland. Meanwhile, environmentalists and developers alike found the system of determining the environmental and national heritage value of waterways seemed random. Water quality is declining, and possibly changing land use. Climate change is adding to the pressure by drying the East Coast.

Molesworth & Featherston, *supra,* at 5.

These problems have generated national attention. The National Policy Statement (NPS) for Freshwater Management, issued in 2011, identifies freshwater management as a nationally significant issue requiring central government direction. The NPS calls for a consistent national regulatory framework to ensure there are clear limits to govern the allocation of water and management of water quality. The goal of the NPS is to "help drive national consistency in local RMA planning and decision-making while allowing for an appropriate level of regional flexibility." Ministry for the Environment, *National Policy Statement for Freshwater Management* (Nov. 15, 2011), http://www.mfe.govt.nz/rma/central/nps/freshwater-management.html. "The intent is that any more than minor potential adverse effects of activities, in relation to water takes, use, damming and diverting, as well as discharges, are thoroughly considered and actively managed ..." *Id.*

Under RMA § 55, local authorities must "give effect to" national and regional policy statements. In addition, under RMA §§ 67 and 75, regional and district plans must give effect to a NPS. More specifically, all consent authorities must have regard to the NPS for Freshwater Management when considering and/or making decisions on resource consents. Ministry for the Environment, *National Policy Statement for Freshwater Management 2011: Implementation Guide* 6 (2011).

The following excerpts from the Ministry for the Environment's website highlight some of the issues and problems that led to the NPS.

New Zealand Ministry for the Environment: On Water (2007)

http://www.mfe.govt.nz/issues/water/

Water quality in New Zealand ... varies considerably. Substantial rainfall feeds an extensive lake and river system, but freshwater is distributed very unevenly across the country. In some places water is plentiful, but in other areas demands sometimes cannot be met.... The quality of our coastal marine environment is highly variable too, with less than 0.1% of our marine environment currently protected, compared with 30% of our land area.

Land-use intensification is placing even greater pressure on both the marine and freshwater environments, which support some of our most important ecosystems and much of New Zealand's biodiversity....

Ministry for the Environment:
Recreational Water Quality in New Zealand (2007)

http://www.mfe.govt.nz/state/reporting/recreational-water/index.html

New Zealand's coastal and inland fresh waters are widely used for a range of contact recreational activities such as swimming, sailing, surfing, water skiing and underwater diving. Maintaining and protecting the quality of this recreational water is therefore an important public health and resource management issue.

The quality of recreational waters in New Zealand is variable. Human health can be compromised by contaminants from sewage and storm water outfalls, septic tanks, sanitation discharges from boats, and effluent run-off from agricultural areas. Generally, concentrations of contaminants will be lower at sites on the open coastline than at inland freshwater sites. This is because the water at open coast beaches is often more rapidly diluted and flushed by tides and waves. However, during and after heavy or prolonged rain storms, contaminant levels are likely to be higher at all beaches as a result of increased urban and rural surface water runoff. Consequently, during these periods it is generally a good idea to avoid entering the water.

Intensifying land uses in rural areas and rapid urban development of coastal areas has the potential to put increasing pressure on the quality of our recreational waters.... Regional and district councils in New Zealand monitor water quality at hundreds of coastal and freshwater river and lake sites every summer. Water samples are typically taken once a week over the summer and are tested for the concentration of specific micro-organisms. These micro-organisms are indicators of human disease risk associated with contact recreation.... Water quality is defined by the number of samples taken over a bathing season that comply with guidelines for acceptable public health risk. The higher the number of samples that comply with guidelines, the better the water quality....

* * *

The following provisions of the Ministry for the Environment's NPS Implementation Guide highlight the government's new approach for safeguarding water quality.

Ministry for the Environment:
Implementation Guide
supra, at 11–16

Objective A1. To safeguard the life-supporting capacity, ecosystem processes and indigenous species including their associated ecosystems of fresh water, in sustainably managing the use and development of land, and of discharges of contaminants.

Achieving the objective of safeguarding the environmental bottom line will require consideration of all sources of potential contaminants (human and natural) holistically, including point source discharges and diffuse discharges. These include contamination from urban storm water, application of fertilisers or pesticides and effluent discharge from stock grazing.

Freshwater bodies, and the aquatic communities they support, will be variable across a region for different types of freshwater ecosystems. The level of habitat protection to safeguard life-supporting capacity will also depend on regional circumstances. Life-supporting capacity is measured through a range of indicators or parameters.

Objective A1 is a relevant consideration for all applications for resource consents, including discharge applications and land-use applications that potentially impact on freshwater quality.

The word "safeguard" requires a proactive response by local authorities determining ways to ensure, for example, "protection of freshwater ecosystems". However, the objective does not imply there would never be any change or adverse effect in a waterbody. Rather, it requires that change is proactively managed to ensure the defined objective continues to be met ...

> **Objective A2.** The overall quality of fresh water within a region is maintained or improved while:
>
> a.   protecting the quality of outstanding freshwater bodies
>
> b.   protecting the significant values of wetlands, and
>
> c.   improving the quality of fresh water in waterbodies that have been degraded by human activities to the point of being over-allocated.

Objective A2 recognises that a bottom line of at least maintaining all aspects of water quality everywhere is not possible. It does not require every degraded waterbody will be cleaned up, some will remain in their current state; the objective-setting process will determine which ones. The Objective allows for some variability in water quality as long as the overall water quality is maintained in a region....

In setting regional freshwater objectives and limits under Policy A1, and in managing discharges under Policy A3, regional councils will need to identify and protect outstanding freshwater bodies, identify and protect significant values of wetlands, and ensure over-allocated waterbodies are not further degraded.

Objective A2 will be a relevant consideration in consent and Notice of Requirement decision-making.

> **Policy A1.** By every regional council making or changing regional plans to the extent needed to ensure the plans:
>
> a.   establish freshwater objectives and set freshwater quality limits for all bodies of fresh water in their regions to give effect to the objectives in this national policy statement, having regard to at least the following:
>
>   i.   the reasonably foreseeable impacts of climate change
>
>   ii. the connection between waterbodies
>
> b.   establish methods (including rules) to avoid over-allocation

The following diagram illustrates the link between objectives, limits and methods, using examples to illustrate.

Figure 1. Objective Limits Cascade Example

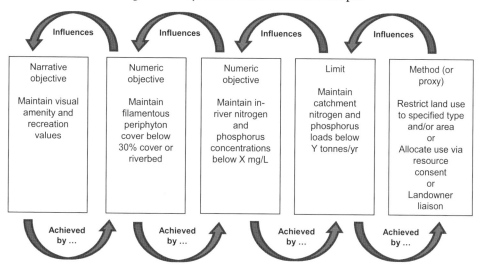

Policy A2. Where waterbodies do not meet the freshwater objectives made pursuant to Policy A1, every regional council is to specify targets and implement methods (either or both regulatory and non-regulatory) to assist the improvement of water quality in the waterbodies, to meet those targets, and within a defined time frame.

Policy A3. By regional councils:

a. imposing conditions on discharge permits to ensure the limits and targets specified pursuant to Policy A1 and A2 can be met, and

b. where permissible, making rules requiring the adoption of the best practicable option to prevent or minimise any actual or likely adverse effect on the environment of any discharge of a contaminant into fresh water, or onto or into land in circumstances that may result in that contaminant (or, as a result of any natural process from the discharge of that contaminant, any other contaminant) entering fresh water.

Notes and Questions

1. One of the hallmarks of New Zealand's RMA and complementary policy statements like the NPS on Freshwater Quality is its holistic, integrated approach, with collaboration and feedback loops between the national government and regional and local councils. When it comes to water quality and the objectives and policies of the NPS, do you think this approach is effective? How would you compare it to the Clean Water Act in the United States or the water quality programs of other nations?

2. One reform idea takes a completely different approach:

A truly economically efficient system would allow the holders of water rights to trade them as cheaply as possible. Then, water would be used for its most economic purpose. For example, if a farmer can make $100 a year from a 100 cubic metres of water, and a hydro generator could make $150 for the same water, it makes sense for the hydro generator to buy the right from the farmer. A tradeable system would make environmental protection more transparent, too, by revealing the true cost of withholding protected waterways.

Molesworth & Featherston, *supra,* at 5. Would a market-based system make sense for improving water quality and for ensuring sustainable water use in New Zealand?

3. As in Canada and the U.S., nonpoint source pollutants are a persistent problem in both urban and rural areas of New Zealand. Contaminants in stormwater run-off, in particular, can wreak havoc with the quality of streams, lakes, and estuaries.

> Sediments reduce light transmission through the water, clog fish gills, affect filter feeding shellfish, smother organisms, change habitats and fill up estuaries. Elevated levels of metals in stormwater can collect in filter feeding shellfish where they may threaten public health. Metals also affect the food chain by reducing the number and diversity of marine animals in our estuaries and harbours.... [A]ccumulation of contaminants in the estuaries are of concern because of their ecological importance. Sediment, zinc and hydrocarbons are key contaminants in the Auckland Region. Zinc primarily comes from galvanised roofs and car tyres.

Do the RMA and the NPS go far enough to address nonpoint source pollution?

4. New Zealand's coastlines are some of the most spectacular in the world. In addition to the NPS on Freshwater, the *New Zealand Coastal Policy Statement 2010* contains policies in relation to water quality in the coastal environment. It is available on the Department of Conservation's website: http://www.doc.govt.nz/conservation/marine-and-coastal/coastal-management/nz-coastal-policy-statement.

5. New Zealand's *National Environmental Standard for Sources of Human Drinking Water* (NES) is intended to reduce the risk of contaminating drinking water sources. It requires the regional councils to ensure that effects on drinking water sources are considered in regional plans and in decisions on resource consents. Explanatory materials are available on the Ministry's website: http://www.mfe.govt.nz/laws/standards/drinking-water-source-standard.html. Drinking water standards are prepared by the Ministry of Health. They are intended to "work in tandem with the NES to provide a multiple barrier approach to providing safe drinking water." Ministry for the Environment, Drinking Water Management 2.4.1, at http://www.mfe.govt.nz/publications/rma/nes-draft-sources-human-drinking-water/html/page2.html (visited July 24, 2012). The standards can apply to drinking water supplies of any size, irrespective of whether they are public or private. They assess the quality and safety of drinking water in two ways:

- *Water quality standards* define the maximum concentrations of contaminants acceptable in safe drinking water. This is done in the form of maximum acceptable values (MAVs), which apply to treated water only. A MAV is the maximum concentration of a contaminant (microbes or chemicals) in drinking water that will not make consumers ill, even if they drink the water all their lives. MAVs provide a yardstick by which the safety of drinking water can be judged. Water is safe to drink if none of the contaminants it contains exceed their MAVs.

- *Compliance criteria* specify how a water supplier is to monitor its supply to show that the water it is producing meets the water quality standards. It is the responsibility of the water supplier to show that their water supply complies with the [Drinking Water Standard].

Id. How does this compare to the laws of Canada and the U.S. governing drinking water?

D. India

Some of the world's longest rivers are found within India, including the Ganges, the Indus, the Godavari, the Krishna, and the Brahmaputra. Many of these rivers are shared with neighboring countries, particularly Pakistan, China, Bangladesh, and Nepal, and the relations over water can be quite contentious. *See Unquenchable Thirst*, The Economist, Nov. 19, 2011 ("A growing rivalry between India, Pakistan and China over the region's great rivers may be threatening South Asia's peace."). Most of the debate focuses on water quantity, but water quality is an equally significant issue for India.

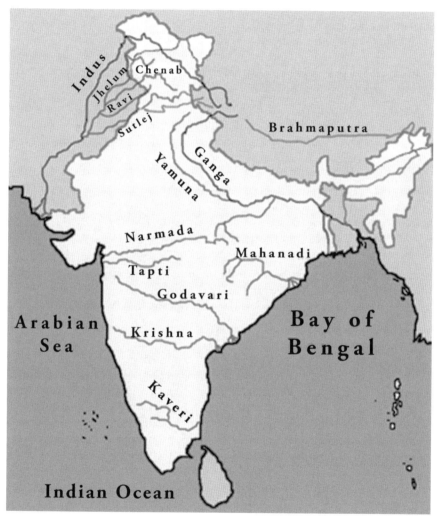

Nichalp, Rivers of India Map (June 6, 2005), GNU Free Documentation License, at http://en.wikipedia.org/wiki/File:Indiarivers.png#filelinks.

The pollution of the Ganges River, in particular, has become a matter of international concern.

One-third of India's 1.2 billion people live along the banks of the 1,560-mile-long river, many of them relying on it for drinking, cooking and washing. Millions more visit for ritual baths to cleanse themselves of sin. But untreated sewage, agricultural runoff and industrial waste have fouled its waters for decades, and hydroelectric projects and dams threaten to choke off its waters in spots ... [A] religious leader on a hunger strike over the effect of illegal mining on the state of the river, Swami Nigamanand, died after spending weeks in a coma.

Nida Najar, *To Clean Ganges, India Will Receive A $1 Billion Loan*, N.Y. Times, June 15, 2011, at A11. For details on the significance of the Ganges to India, see Vandana Shiva, Water Wars: Privatization, Pollution, and Profit 131 (2002). The international community has agreed to loan India money to help clean up the Ganges.

Indian officials signed an agreement with the World Bank ... [in 2011] to use a $1 billion loan to finance the first major new effort in more than 20 years to cleanse the revered Ganges, one of the world's dirtiest rivers.... The long-awaited loan is part of a government project that aims to halt the discharge of untreated wastewater into the river by 2020.

Najar, *supra*. Although officials are hopeful that the project will be successful, they acknowledge that past efforts have failed dismally. Untreated sewage is only one piece of the puzzle. Another is that "several glue factories in Jajmau routinely discharge toxic water" containing chromium and other poisonous chemicals into open drains flowing into the Ganges. *Glue Units Polluting Ganga in Jajmau*, Econ. Times (India), June 16, 2012. According to one report, "Many glue units dotting the river, which were sealed by the Pollution Control Board a few years back, are now functioning and discharging effluents directly into the Ganga." *Id.; see* Abhinav Malhotra, *Polluted Ganga is Unable to Provide Potable Water*, Times of India, May 10, 2012 (reporting that water levels in the river had declined and pollution had turned the water into a dark brown or black color).

Public interest litigation has had a significant impact on the way the government deals with water pollution in the Ganges and other river basins. In the 1980s and 1990s, several landmark cases were brought by renowned advocate M.C. Mehta.

Three landmark judgments and a number of Orders against polluting industries numbering more than fifty thousand ... [were issued].... [M]ore than 250 towns and cities have been ordered to put in sewage treatment plants. Six hundred tanneries operating in highly congested residential area of Kolkata have been shifted out of the City and relocated in a planned Leather Complex in the State of West Bengal. A large number of industries were closed down by the Court and were allowed to reopen only after these industries set up effluent treatment plants and controlled pollution. As a result of these directions millions of people have been saved from the effects of air and water pollution in Ganga basin covering 8 states in India.

M.C. Mehta Environmental Foundation, *Current Projects*, at http://mcmef.org/current-projects.html, quoting M.C. Mehta, In the Public Interest (2009). *See* M. C. Mehta vs. Union of India, [1987] 4 S.C.C. 463, and AIR 1988 SC 1115; R. K. Jaiswal v. State of Uttar Pradesh, No. 21552 (1997). Litigation over the Ganges is ongoing. In 2012, the Calcutta High Court issued an order to the National Ganga River Basin Authority, calling upon it "to explain what action has been taken to dredge the Hooghly (an offshoot of the Ganga in West Bengal) and keep it pollution-free." *Notice to Ganga Authority on Pollution*, Times India, Feb. 23, 2012. The court acted in response to a petition by environmental activist Subhas Datta, who argued that, although the high courts and India's Supreme Court have heard petitions on Ganga pollution for nearly 27 years, "there has been no improvement in the situation." The Calcutta High Court alone has issued over fifty orders related to Ganges pollution. *Id.*

Water pollution is by no means limited to the Ganges watershed. "[T]he Ganges is just one of many rivers that present public health problems. 'Most of India's rivers have become sewers,' said the environment minister, Jairam Ramesh." Najar, *supra,* at A11.

Not even the famed Taj Mahal is impervious to water pollution, not to mention air pollution that corrodes its marble exterior. M.C. Mehta has left an imprint there, too. During the course of his lawsuit on behalf of the Taj Mahal and the people of Agra, 511 industries were identified in the area, from oil refineries to foundries, rubber factories, and chemical plants. Mehta v. Union of India, A.I.R. 1997 S.C. 723, para. 7. Of these industries, "a whopping ninety-nine percent, had no air pollution controls at all." Oliver Houck, Taking Back Eden 103 (2010). Meanwhile, "the city of New Delhi and every smaller town between the capital and Agra were dumping nearly 300 million tons of raw sewage into the Yamuna River, which then carried down to the Taj ... squeezing human wastes into the foundations of the mosque." *Id.* at 94, citing DAVID L. HABERMAN, RIVER OF LOVE IN AN AGE OF POLLUTION: THE YAMUNA RIVER OF NORTHERN INDIA 92 (2006).

> Citing Article 21 of the Constitution, three additional articles, three statutory programs and three principles of international law [the Precautionary Principle, the Polluter Pays Principle, and Sustainable Development], the justices declared that the pollution affecting the Taj should be "eliminated at any cost." Not even a "one percent chance" could be taken when — human life aside — "the preservation of a prestigious monument like the Taj is involved." ... [The Court] ordered the conversion of some 292 industrial plants to natural gas, or their relocation from the area. It ordered ... the creation of a new agency to facilitate the process. It ordered the construction of a by-pass to funnel traffic away from the area, a green belt of protection around the monument, the removal of intruding concessions, and first steps to clean up the Yamuna River.

Id. at 104, citing *Mehta,* para. 29-51. As Mehta describes it, millions of people living along the Yamuna River were exposed to health hazards from water contamination due to the lack of sewage treatment in Delhi. The Supreme Court established strict deadlines for the Delhi Municipal Corporation to construct treatment plants in sixteen different localities in response to Mehta's petition. M.C. Mehta Foundation, *Landmark Cases* (2009), http://mcmef.org/landmark_cases.html.

Of course, wars like this are not won overnight. A report compiled by India's National Environment Engineering Research Institute in 2010 "shows that measures taken after previous scares that the 17th-century tomb was being irreparably damaged by air and water pollution are failing." Jason Burke, *Taj Mahal Threatened by Polluted Air and Water,* The Guardian, Dec. 2, 2010. There is still hope for the river, at least. By 2011, "[w]ith people from 73 villages in the district joining, the campaign [to clean up the Yamuna] has become the biggest public initiative in the region against river pollution." *Villagers Join Battle Against Yamuna Pollution,* The Hindu, Jan. 10, 2011. "Animal carcasses are not to be dumped into the river, washermen should not use chemicals to wash dirty clothes, the river bank is not to be used as a toilet.... [and] the panchayat [village council] will ban polythene bags...." *Id.*

Toxic industrial pollutants were the subject of the *Ground Water Pollution Case (Indian Council for Enviro-Legal Action v. Union of India),* which dealt with five chemical plants operating without permits in Rajasthan. Toxic effluents entered the ground water and affected the wells of fourteen villages. After six years of litigation, the Supreme Court issued an order directing the closure of the plants. The case is described below.

Indian Council for Enviro-Legal Action v. Union of India
AIR 1996 SC 1446, 1996(5) SCALE 412, 1996(3) SCC212, [1996] SCR503

In 1987, citizens of the small village of Bichhri, in the Udaipur district of the north-western state of Rajasthan, had the unfortunate luck of having a chemical complex located within village limits. To make matters worse, some of the companies in the complex specialized in the production of a highly toxic chemical known as H-acid. Because production of H-acid poses such toxic and environmental threats, H-acid manufacturing has been banned in western countries, but there is still strong demand for H-acid in those same western countries. The Supreme Court noted that "H-acid was meant for export exclusively. It's manufacture gives rise to enormous quantities of highly toxic effluents—in particular iron-based and gypsum-based sludge … It poisons the earth, the water and everything that comes in contact with it." *Indian Council for Enviro-Legal Action v. Union of India*, para. 2. Most, if not all, of the companies in the complex completely ignored all state and federal environmental laws and freely dumped the toxic sludge and wastewater wherever they chose. Two companies in particular, Silver Chemicals and Jyoti Chemicals, who sought to feed the western demand for the acid, were blameworthy for blatant disregard for the environment and health of citizens in the surrounding communities. The Supreme Court of India noted:

> Since the toxic untreated waste waters were allowed to flow freely and because the untreated toxic sludge was thrown in the open in and around the complex, the toxic substances have percolated deep into the bowels of the earth polluting the aquifers and the sub-terranean supply of water. The water in the wells and the streams has turned dark and dirty rendering it unfit for human consumption … and for irrigating the land. *Id.*

Local citizens took action and Silver Chemicals and Jyoti Chemicals both ceased production of H-acid before each was ordered closed by January 1989. However, the environmental and human damage had already been done, and that's where this litigation begins—with the suit for remedial action filed in August 1989.

Among the documented environmental ills perpetuated by Silver Chemicals and Jyoti Chemicals are:

1. Upon an order to contain effluents and wastewater, they installed an unlined holding pond on the premises but then sprayed the water on nearby hill slope, which percolated and then contaminated the groundwater;

2. They stored the toxic sludge in and around a shed, dumping the sludge onto the ground exposed to the sun and rain;

3. They turned sludge that could not fit into the pits into mounds by mixing the sludge with soil and piling it up to five meters (almost sixteen and a half feet) not far from the pits. Sample soils revealed H-acid in the leachate from these heaps. To their credit, Silver and Jyoti at least made attempts to comply with a Court order issued on April 6, 1996 that directed the two companies to entomb the sludge in lined pits under the supervision of the federal Ministry of Environment and Forests, which apparently is more that they had done towards cleanup in previous years. *Id.* at 4–9.

Silver and Jyoti cited several defenses in the remedial suit, hoping to excuse both the non-compliance with regulations while manufacturing H-acid and to avoid responsibility for the subsequent cleanup. Both stated that prior applications for permits under both the Water and Air Acts were refused, but neither offered an explanation for the rejection. Silver and Jyoti also both accused the Rajasthan Pollution Control Board, the governmental board involved in at least some of the permits, of acting hostilely in its dealings with Silver and Jyoti from the beginning. Silver filed an affidavit in which, according to the court, Silver was 'fully conscious of the need to conserve and protect environment and is prepared to fully cooperate on that behalf and ready to comply to comply with any stipulations ...' but then Silver claimed that the real culprit of all of the pollution was a different chemical plant, Hindustan Zinc Limited, and not Silver. The Court found that the Hindustan plants were located downstream of the Bichhri village, the site of the pollution, and therefore were not a contributor. Silver and Jyoti further tried to absolve themselves of liability by stating that H-acid manufacturing occurred between 1987 and 1989, therefore neither was responsible for causing pollution since they were no longer engaged in H-acid production.

The Supreme Court looked to provisions of the Water Act and the Environment Act to determine whether there was any statutory authority to force compliance and cleanup by Silver and Jyoti. The Parliament of India passed the Water (Prevention and Control of Pollution) Act in 1974, and the State of Rajasthan adopted the same resolution.

Section 24(1) of the Water Act provides:

> Subject to the provisions of this section, (a) no person shall knowingly cause or permit any poisonous, noxious or polluting matter determined in accordance with such standards as may be laid down the by the State Board to enter whether (directly or indirectly) into any stream or well.

Section 25 of the Water Act states:

> Subject to the provisions of this section, no person shall without the previous consent of the State Board, (a) establish any industry, operation or process or any treatment disposal system or an extension or an addition thereto, which is likely to discharge sewage or trade effluent into a stream or well or sewer or on land [such discharge being hereafter in this section referred to as "discharge of sewage"]; or (b) bring into any new use new or altered outlets for the discharge of sewage; or (c) begin to make any new discharge of sewage.

In light of these two provisions of the Water Act and Section 3 the Environment (Protection) Act, which allows the Central Government to "take all such measures as it deems necessary or expedient for the purpose of protecting and improving the quality of the environment" the Court concluded that Silver and Jyoti Chemicals were responsible for properly containing and storing the sludge to prevent further degradation of land and water supplies. Thus, the Central Government could properly order the removal of the sludge and require Silver and Jyoti to cover remedial measures.

The Supreme Court's order ultimately directed the Central Government to determine the remedial costs of removing the sludge stored in and around the industrial complex that formerly housed Silver and Jyoti (by this time it was 1996 and both plants had closed years earlier) and the removal of sludge from Bicchhri and nearby villages that had been polluted by H-acid toxins. *Id.* at 30. Any remaining factories in the area were ordered immediately closed and could not re-open until they had secured the requisite water and other environmental permits. The Ministry of Environment and Forest would be in charge not only of determining the cost of remediation, but for "carrying out all necessary remedial measures to restore the soil, water sources and the environment in general of the affected area to its former state." While the Court did not explicitly state that machinery and materials from the closed factories could be confiscated by the government, the Court did attach a list of assets from the companies and restated that the companies were indeed responsible for the total cost of the recovery, but provided no estimate to what these costs might be. *Id.* at 29.

Notes and Questions

1. The Supreme Court had little sympathy for the defendant manufacturers, stating:

> The units manufacturing 'H' acid—indeed most of the units of the respondents—had started functioning, i.e., started manufacturing various chemicals without obtaining requisite clearances/consents/licences. They did not install any equipment for treatment of highly toxic effluents discharged by them. They continued to function even after and in spite of the closure orders of the R.P.C.B. They did never carry out the Orders of this Court fully [e.g., entombing the sludge] nor did they fulfill the undertaking given by them to the Court [in the matter of removal of sludge and de-watering of the wells]. In spite of repeated Reports of officials and expert bodies, they persisted in their illegal course of action in a brazen manner, which exhibits their contempt for law, for the lawful authorities and the Courts.

Id. at 29.

2. Other relevant provisions of the Water Act include Section 47 (1), which states: "Where an offence under this Act has been committed by a company, every person who, at the time the offence was committed, was in charge of and was responsible to, the company for the conduct of the business of the company as well as the company, shall be deemed to be guilty of the offence and shall be liable to be proceeded against and punished accordingly." In addition, Section 47 (2) elaborates by stating that if an offense is attributed to a company or person (through act or neglect) then "such director, manager, secretary or other officer shall also be deemed to be guilty of that offence and shall be liable to be proceeded against and punished accordingly."

    a. Given the actions of Silver and Jyoti and the wording of the Water Act, what responsibility do you think individuals within the companies hold? Can they be charged personally under the Act?

    b. Do you think there should be stiffer penalties for willful or wanton pollution versus pollution stemming from neglect? If so, what penalties do you envision and how would they be enforced?

    c. The Water Act Section 28 allows persons to appeal decisions made under Section 25, *supra*, "within thirty days from the date on which the order is communicated to him." How might Silver and Jyoti's failure to appeal the permitting decisions of the Rajasthan Pollution Control Board factor into the Court's decision?

* * *

According to India's Supreme Court, India's water pollution laws are to be implemented in a manner that reflects the precautionary principle, as Surana Oils Ltd. discovered when its certificate (or permit) was rescinded in the following case. At issue were provisions of the Water (Prevention and Control of Pollution) Act 1974 and the Environment (Protection) Act 1986.

AP Pollution Control Board-II v. Prof MV Nayudu (Retd) & Ors

[2001] 4 LRI 657, CIVIL APPEAL NOS 368–373 OF 1999
Supreme Court of India

The question is whether in the event of the respondent [Surana Oils & Derivatives (India) Ltd)] being permitted to establish its industry within 10 kms of the lakes—notwithstanding the Government's policy to the contrary and the refusal of the appellant board to grant [a no objection certificate, or "NOC"]—there is likelihood of serious pollution to the drinking water in these lakes. This court referred the said question to the National Environmental Appellate Authority for its opinion. The said authority visited the site of the industry at Peddashpur village near Hyderabad and submitted a detailed and exhaustive report to this court, after receiving oral and documentary evidence. The report went against the respondent....

[T]he respondent relied upon an order passed by the appellant board [in] 1997, suggesting that if certain safeguards were provided by the industry to prevent pollution, NOC could be granted ... because of the direction of the Government of Andhra Pradesh contained in an order granting exemption from the 10 km rule ...

The Ministry of Forests and Environment ... issued a notification [in 1988] listing various industries as hazardous and included them in a red list. Item 37 of the said list is the industry which produces vegetable oils, including solvent extracted oils. The above notification was expressly stated to be issued by the Government of India in exercise of its powers vested under the Water (Prevention and Control of Pollution) Act 1974, the Air (Prevention and Control of Pollution) Act 1981, the Water (Prevention and Control of Pollution) Act 1977 and the Environment (Protection) Act 1986, directing that whenever any industry sought consent from the pollution control boards, the said boards, while processing the consent application, should decide, keeping in view the pollution-causing potential of the industry, as to which category the industry belongs.

Consequent to the directive of the Union Government, the State of Andhra Pradesh initially issued notification in GO 192 dated 31 March 1994.... and prohibited industries being located within 10 km of the two reservoirs.

... [T]he respondent purchased land of 12 acres [in 1965] in Peddashpur village situated on the outskirts of Hyderabad, within 10 km of the reservoirs. Initially, the industry applied for consent from the appellant board in 1995, through the industries department of the state government. The State of Andhra Pradesh wrote to the Government of India, recommending grant of letter of intent in relaxation of 10 km rule, subject to the industry obtaining NOC from the appellant board. [The] Government of India gave letter of intent but required the industry to obtain [a NOC] from the environmental authority of the State. At that stage, the Government re-affirmed the 10 km prohibition.... Consequent thereto, ... the application of the industry stood rejected because of the 10 km prohibition.

Undeterred, the industry proceeded to obtain permission from the gram panchayat [ed: local council] on 31 May 1996 for establishing a factory. Even though the Commissioner of Industries specifically informed the industry that it should select an alternative site, instead of heeding to the said advice, the industry obtained permission of the district collector on 7 September 1996 for change of land use from agricultural to non-agricultural use. It then proceeded to execute various civil works in spite of the 10 km prohibition.

Thereafter, the industry ... applied to the appellant board on 7 April 1997 under s 25 of the Water Act for permission to establish the factory. One of the by-products mentioned in the application was: Glycerine, spent bleaching earth and carbon and spent nickel catalysts.

The appellant board wrote to the Commissioner of Industries that the industry would be generating nickel catalyst and other pollutants which could find their way to the lakes either directly or indirectly. Even the solid waste such as activated carbon bleaching earth and sodium sulphate might find entry during rainy season from the storage yard resulting in polluting to lakes.... [T]he appellant board once again rejected the application of the industry inasmuch as the said industry was in the red list....

Confronted with the above problems, the industry approached the state government seeking exemption from the 10 km rule ... on the ground that it had invested huge amounts to establish the industry and that it had almost completed the civil works, and had purchased machinery and installed the same. The state government, in spite of the prohibitory directions issued earlier, issued GO 153 dated granting an exemption ... on the ground that ... there would be no liquid effluents and that the solid wastes would be disposable.... The Government then directed the board to prescribe conditions for treatment/disposal of aqueous/solid waste. Compelled by the above direction, the appellant board passed an order on 16 July 1997 requiring various precautions to be taken by the industry.

Meanwhile, the Society for Preservation of Environment and Quality Life (SPEQL) filed WP 16969 for quashing the exemption order and obtained a stay.... The following points arise for consideration:

(1) Whether, in view of s.2(b), 3(2) and 5 of the *Environment (Protection) Act 1986* and the 1988 notification issued by the Central Government and the further notification issued by the state government ... totally prohibiting location of following industries in an area, it was permissible for the state government to issue an exemption for an individual hazardous industry within the area, even if it be by way of asking the industry to provide safeguards?

(2) Whether, in view of s.2(e), 2(k), 17, 18 and 19 of *the Water (Prevention and Control of Pollution) Act 1974,* if the state government had issued notification totally prohibiting polluting industries in the area, and if the state pollution board had rejected the request for location of a polluting industry within the area, it was permissible for the Government to grant exemption for a single industry within the prohibited area?...

Under s 2(b) of the *Environment (Protection) Act 1986,* environmental pollution means any solid, liquid or gaseous substance present in such concentration may be, or tend to be, injurious to environment. Section 2(e) defines hazardous substance as any substance or preparation which, by reason of its chemical or physio-chemical properties or handling, is liable to cause harm to human being, other living creatures, plants, micro-organism, property or the environment.

Section 3 refers to the extensive process of the Central Government to take measures to protect and improve environment. Sub-clause (2) permits measures to be taken by imposing

> restriction of areas in which industries, operations or processes or class of industries, operations or processes shall not be carried out or shall be carried out subject to certain safeguards.

Section 5 deals with the power of the Central Government to issue directions to any person ... to comply with such conditions. Section 5 clarifies that this ... includes the power to direct:

(a) the closure, prohibition or regulation of any industry, operation or process; or

(b) stoppage or regulation of the supply of electricity or water or any other service.

The [1988] notification of the Central Government Ministry of Forests and Environment was issued ... under the Environment (Protection) Act 1986 the Water (Prevention and Control of Pollution) Act 1974 and the Air (Prevention and Control of Pollution) Act 1981. It stated that industries were being classified in lists red, orange and green, and that when an industry seeks consent from the pollution control board, as required by the above Acts, the board processing the application should decide, keeping in view the pollution causing potential of the industry, as to which category the environmental safeguards should be determined. This is a general notification. Item 37 in the red list refers to an industry producing vegetable oils including solvent extracted oil. No doubt, the subsequent notification[s] [were] ... issued under s. 3(2)(v) of the Environment (Protection) Act 1986 and s. 5(3)(d) of the Environment (Protection) Rules 1986 for the purpose of restricting industrial units in Doon Valley ... [and] Andhra Pradesh....

[T]he power to issue directions under s. 5 of the Environment (Protection) Act 1986 ... were delegated to the State of Andhra Pradesh ... as follows:

> SO No 152(E) dated 10 February 1988: In exercise of the powers conferred by s. 23 of the Environment (Protection) Act 1986 the Central Government hereby delegates the powers vested in it under s. 5 of the act to the state governments ... subject to the condition that the Central Government may revoke such delegation of powers in respect of all or any one or more of the state government or may itself invoke the provisions of s. 5 of the Act, if in the opinion of the Central Government such a course of action is necessary in public interest.

The State of Andhra Pradesh could therefore issue orders ... prohibiting the location of industries in specified areas ... [and] to impose total prohibition of polluting industries to be located within 10 kms of the two reservoirs. The notification dated 31 March 1994 prohibited any polluting industries, major hotels, residential colonies or other establishments that generate pollution in the catchment areas of these two lakes within 10 kms radius from the full tank level. The appellant board and the Hyderabad Water Supply and Sewage Board ... were directed to scrupulously protect the water in the two lakes from imminent danger of pollution. GO 111 dated 8 March 1996 (Municipal Administration and Urban Development Department) ... re-iterated the same prohibition:

> 3(i): To prohibit polluting industries, major hotels, residential colonies or other establishments that generate pollution in the catchment of the lakes up to 10 kms from full tank level of the lakes as per list in Annexure I.

> 3(e): To prohibit pollution industries within 10 kms radius (in both on upstream and down stream side of the lakes to prevent acidification of lakes due to air pollution).

> 3(f): There shall be total prohibition of location of industries in the prohibited zone.

... Item 38 thereof refers to Peddashpur Village, which is within 10 km of these two reservoirs.

As stated earlier, on 3 July 1997, the state government issued notification granting exemption from the 10 km rule ... and directed AP pollution control board to prescribe conditions for treatment/disposal of aqueous/solid wastes. The result of exemption ...

was that the respondent industry could be located within 10 km of the lakes. The question is whether this exemption can be valid?

Under s. 3(2)(v), the Central Government or the state government as its delegate could issue directions as permitted by s. 5. Now s. 3(2)(v) permits restriction specifying areas in which industrial operations or processes shall not be carried out or shall be carried out subject to certain safeguards. The notification issued by the state government in GO 111 falls within the first part, *i.e.,* where industries shall not be carried out. This is a total prohibition within 10 km of the two reservoirs. When such a prohibition was in force, the state government could not obviously grant any exemption to a specified industry like the respondent.... Nor was it permissible for the state to direct the appellant-board to prescribe conditions for grant of NOC.

Coming to the provisions of the *Water Act 1974*, it is clear that ... the fundamental objective of the statute is to provide clean drinking water to the citizens. Having laid down the policy prohibiting location of any industries within 10 kms under GO 111, the state could not have granted exemption to the respondent, nor to any other industry, from any part of the main GO 111. Section 19 permitted the state to restrict the application of the Water Act 1974 to particular area, if need be, but it did not enable the state to grant exemption to a particular industry within the area prohibited for location of polluting industries. Exercise of such a power in favour of a particular industry must be treated as arbitrary and contrary to public interest and in violation of the right to clean water under art. 21 of the Constitution of India....

Exemption granted even to a single major hazardous industry may itself be sufficient to make the water in the reservoirs totally unsafe for drinking water purposes. Government could not pass such orders of exemption having dangerous potential, unmindful of the fate of citizens of the twin cities to whom drinking water is supplied from these lakes. Such an order of exemption carelessly passed, ignoring the precautionary principle, could be catastrophic.

Therefore, [the] 1997 exemption must be held to be without statutory backing and also wholly arbitrary and violative of art. 21....

Notes and Questions

1. Do you agree with the Court's reasoning? What gives the State the power to prohibit an entire industry in a particular area? And why shouldn't the State or a local government be able to grant an exemption for one or more facilities within that industry? Does it matter that the lake was used for drinking water rather than just irrigation or industrial purposes? What does the precautionary principle have to do with it?

2. Section 42(g) of the Water Act of 1974 states that: "for the purpose of obtaining any consent under section 25 or section 26, knowingly or willfully makes a statement which is false in any material particular, shall be punishable with imprisonment for a term which may extend to three months or with fine which may extend to [ten thousand rupees] or with both." In the case above, the company, Surana, proceeded to build infrastructure and civil works subsequent to a consent rejection. The company then sought an exemption based on this capital investment. Does section 42(g) apply? If not, should there be a penalty for trying to "end run" the Act? Is the denial of an exemption, and consequently the loss of the investment, sufficient to deter this behavior?

* * *

Mangroves are the only tree species that flourishes in sea water. Mangrove forests provide vital structure to coastlines, providing protection from storm surges to vulnerable communities and habitat for a variety of coastal and ocean species. World Land Trust, Reef and Mangrove Appeal, http://www.worldlandtrust.org/projects/reef-mangrove#biodiversity (visited June 28, 2012).

Mangroves in India have undergone massive destruction as they are cut down to provide firewood and to clear the way for tourist resorts. Around 70% of Mumbai's mangroves have been destroyed by various development activities.

In 1991, the Ministry of Environment and Forests issued the Coastal Regulation Zone (CRZ) Notification 19.2.1991, under the Environment Protection Act of 1986, to provide comprehensive measures for the protection and conservation of India's coastal environment. The 1991 Notification stipulated uniform regulations for the entire Indian coastline, which includes 5500 km of the mainland and 2000 km of the islands of Andaman & Nicobar and Lakshadweep. As such, it was criticized for failing to take into account the diversity of the Indian coastline "in terms of biodiversity, hydrodynamic conditions, demographic patterns, natural resources, geomorphological and geological features." Frequently Asked Questions on the Coastal Regulation Zone Noti cation 1 (2011), http://moef.nic.in/downloads/public-information/FAQ-CRZ.pdf. The 1991 Notification requires permission, or clearance, for most types of new construction on "ecologically sensitive" land in the coastal zone. *Id.*

Despite the restrictions, the mangroves continue to face destruction. In 2005, the Conservation Action Trust filed a petition in the Bombay High Court seeking the Court's intervention to stop the destruction. The High Court issued an order that put a stop to: (1) the destruction and cutting of mangroves; (2) all construction and dumping on the mangrove areas; and (3) all construction taking place within 50m of mangroves, regardless of ownership of the land. It also provided that all government owned land would be designated as Protected Forests and handed over to the Forest Department. Based on this order, in 2011 the Supreme Court of India rejected a plea by a local developer to convert the mangroves to salt pans. The developer had already constructed new bunds to keep out the sea water and dumped thousands of truck loads of debris over a 430-acre mangrove-covered site to prepare it for private development. Shweta Bhatt, *Mangrove Conservation Amidst Land Sharks,* Conservation News, Oryx (2008), at http://www.oryxthejournal.org/index.php/news/conservation-news.html. The Indian Supreme Court exhibited little patience when developer refused to comply.

Krishnadevi Malchand Kamathia v.
Bombay Environmental Action Group
CA 4421/2010, para. 29-32 (India S.Ct. 2011)

It is evident that mangroves fall squarely within the ambit of CRZ-I [The Central Regulatory Zone Regulations 1991]. The regulations allow for salt harvesting by solar evaporation of sea water in CRZ-I areas only where such area is not ecologically sensitive and important. In the instant case it has been established that mangrove forests are of great ecological importance and are also ecologically sensitive. Thus, salt harvesting by solar evaporation of sea water cannot be permitted in an area that is home to mangrove forests. . . .

[The developer failed to comply with the order by:]

 (i) Closing the natural flow of water which has adverse effect on existing mangroves;

(ii) A large number of mangroves had been cut/destroyed while repairing the bund and a large number of mangroves were found cut manually;

(iii) Height and width of the bund had been increased to an unwarranted extent …

(vii) Breathing roots and branches of mangroves were found stucking [sic] out of the muddy area of the bund; and

(viii) A large number of mangroves died because of removal of mud and stagnation of water....

[W]e have no hesitation to hold that the appellants are guilty of willful defiance of the orders passed by this Court as well as by the District Collector and they have filed … petitions using it as a legal thumb screw to enforce their claims though totally unwarranted and unfounded on facts. It is a crystal clear case of contumacious conduct … They have knowingly and purposely damaged the mangroves and other vegetation of the CRZ-I area …

[The court found the defendants in contempt and ordered restoration of the damaged areas.] In case the appellants fail to carry out the aforesaid directions within the stipulated period, the District Collector, Suburban District shall carry out the aforesaid directions and recover the cost from the appellants as arrears of land revenue and shall ensure in future that the appellants would not act in a manner detrimental to the ecology of the area and ensure the preservation of mangroves and other vegetation.

Notes and Questions

1. Do you find the Court's order remarkable in any way? Is it an appropriate means of addressing a developer's "contumacious conduct"?

2. India's Ministry of Environment and Forests issued a new CRZ Notification in 2011, in part in response to criticisms that the 1991 Notification had "no clear procedure for obtaining CRZ clearance … and no time lines stipulated. Furthermore, there was no format given for the submission of clearance applications." The Ministry also acknowledged that the 1991 Notification "did not provide … a clear cut enforcement mechanism to check violations." Frequently Asked Questions on the Coastal Regulation Zone Noti cation, *supra,* at 1. The latter point may help explain the *Krishnadevi Malchand Kamathia* case. Failure to enforce environmental laws appears to be a widespread problem in India:

> The biggest problem facing India's environment is not a lack of environmental laws. We have dozens. Nor is it a lack of precedent to protect our environment. This has been developed incrementally in India's Supreme Court over the last twenty-five years. The single biggest issue facing India's beleaguered, yet resilient environment today is the failure of the Indian government to adequately enforce existing environmental laws.... India's executive branch of government bears the greatest responsibility and blame for India's environmental decay. Though other factors contribute, the executive branch of government has either passively allowed or actively contributed to the environmental tragedy unfolding around Indians every day....

> The reasons for the failure of the executive branch are many, but one reason stands out more than any other: corruption. While corruption is not the sole contributor to the failings of the executive branch in India, it is one of the worst and most condemnable—and the most urgent to address. According to Trans-

parency International, "India stands high in the list of the 'most corrupt' nations and virtually at the bottom of international assessments of human development." …

India has a plethora of bureaucratic rules and regulations aimed at tackling corruption and keeping bureaucrats honest. Unfortunately, these rules' effect is marginal at best. Corruption, nepotism, and apathy are still rampant in India's executive branch.… When regulators egregiously ignore their duty to care for the public, they directly encourage the spread of pollution and liquidation of natural resources.

M.C. Mehta, *The Accountability Principle: Legal Solutions to Break Corruption's Impact on India's Environment*, 21 J. Envtl. L. & Litig. 141, 141, 143–145 (2006).

Perhaps it is no surprise, then, that the Supreme Court of India has been the most significant player in environmental enforcement for the past several decades.

Over the years, the Court has evolved all the operative principles necessary for a strong environmental jurisprudence. Moreover, the Court's action has also spurred the legislature into passing a plethora of environmental laws and rules that, at a minimum, empower the executive branch to take all steps necessary to preserve India's environment. Finally, the Supreme Court has gone to exhaustive lengths to request, instruct, direct, and order the executive branch to execute its constitutional duties. In my cases alone, the Court has issued thousands of orders pertaining to environmental enforcement. To this end, the executive branch, under the Supreme Court's direction, has set up a number of administrative bodies to manage India's environment, from coastal authorities, to groundwater authorities, to river authorities. The list goes on. The Court has exercised its constitutional powers to give the executive branch all the support, all the guidance, all the direction and all the tools it needs to fulfil its duty. Our apex judicial body has put the ball squarely in the executive's court.

Yet the executive continues to fail. It is a sad opus. With each day that passes India's environment suffers ever-greater destruction. Each claim of progress that the environmental offices declare rings more hollow. Each day the goals of the environmental branches of government slip further out of reach as the environment falls into further decline. The truth is that the environment is not the government's priority. The poor are not a priority. Our international commitments are not a priority. Our public health is not a priority. Our fundamental rights are not a priority. Instead our leadership is narrowly focused on rapid, unsustainable development programmes, on expansion of nuclear energy, on exploitation of resources, and on building unviable large-scale dams.… The long-term is lost to the short-term. The government is supposed to be the glue that holds our society together, yet the public's faith in the government is disintegrating, weakening our civil bonds. The government is facing a crisis of confidence. Though problems exist in each branch of government, none are more serious than the breakdown in the executive branch. The enforcers themselves are abrogating the law. As a result, the rule of law in India crumbles. This can only lead to further destruction, disintegration, and violence.

Id. at 141–143. Mr. Mehta argues that the solution turns on public awareness and civic action. "[T]he ultimate solution to the problem is a strong grassroots movement, where each citizen understands the importance of environmental sustainability and vigilantly acts to keep a check on their public servants, demanding accountability." *Id.* at 155. What other measures might be undertaken to curtail corruption, increase accountability, and ensure enforcement of environmental laws? What role, if any, should the international community play? For details on human rights issues in India, see Chapter 6 of this book.

3. According to the Ministry, the 1991 CRZ Notification raised significant environmental justice concerns:

> The restrictive nature of the 1991 Notification caused hardships to the persons/communities living in certain ecologically sensitive coastal stretches. These included slum dwellers and other persons living in dilapidated and unsafe buildings in Mumbai, communities living in islands in the backwaters of Kerala, local communities living along the coast of Goa and other traditional coastal inhabitants.

Id. at 1–2. The objectives of the new (2011) Notification include "To ensure livelihood security to the fishing communities and other local communities living in the coastal areas; [and] To conserve and protect coastal stretches." Is it realistic to think that both objectives can be met simultaneously? A third objective is "To promote development in a sustainable manner based on scientific principles, taking into account the dangers of natural hazards in the coastal areas and sea level rise due to global warming." *Id.* To this end, a broader range of activities are allowed in urban and rural areas that are not "ecologically sensitive," including desalinization plants, storage of non-hazardous cargo, structures on the landward side of existing roads, agricultural activities, mining, and salt manufacture. *Id.* at 4–5. Regardless of designation, however, the "disposal of wastes and effluents into coastal waters is a prohibited activity." *Id.* at 9. Can these objectives be met in a manner that has less impact on impoverished coastal communities?

E. England

A dispute in England gave rise to the most famous water law tort case, *Rylands v. Fletcher* (House of Lords 1868), which set a precedent for strict liability when a millowner's reservoir flooded a neighbor's land. *Rylands* is covered in Chapter 2.B, *supra.* Although many layers of statutes, regulations, directives, and caselaw have accumulated in the years since *Rylands,* strict liability still plays a role in the modern administrative state, albeit a diminishing one.

> The control of water pollution in England is framed in terms of strict liability under a 1951 Act of Parliament. Rivers (Prevention of Pollution) Act, 1951, 14 & 15 Geo. 6, ch. 64. Causing pollution or discharging directly to watercourses without the consent of local authorities is strictly prohibited, and the Act provides for personal as well as corporate liability.

> But in practice neither strict liability nor rule making about … pollution occurs [separate from] an enforcement action.… At the core of regulating water pollution in England … are moral notions of traditional rights, considerations of economic harm, and assessments of organizational power.

Albert J. Reiss, Jr., *Compliance Without Coercion, Review of Keith Hawkins, Environment and Enforcement: Regulation and the Social Definition of Pollution,* 83 Mich. L. Rev. 813, 814 (1985). Enforcement in England—and therefore the overall control of water pollution—is quite different than in the United States.

> Administrative law enforcement in the United States is controlled by elaborate procedures for promulgating and enforcing rules. The guiding principle is that any enforcement action must be constrained by some rule.…

Quite the opposite generally prevails for administrative enforcement actions in England. Parliamentary acts giving responsibilities to administrative agencies require no such rule-making or enforcing procedures. The 1951 Rivers Act and the 1973 Parliamentary Water Act [Water Act, 1973, ch. 37] ... contain almost no detail to guide administrative action, and the Regional Water Authorities given responsibility for carrying out the Act are under no obligation to promulgate rules before taking an action. Rather than prescribing generalized standards, the Authorities grant licenses ("consents") to discharge polluting substances.... "Pollution is in effect qualitatively and quantitatively controlled by the water authorities since standards are administratively negotiated ... The pollution standards in a consent are defined locally by each water authority and are specific in application, with each consent negotiated on an *ad hoc* basis."

Here we have, then, two radically different approaches to administrative rule making and enforcement. The American model begins by establishing rules that are to be applied universally and procedural safeguards to be heeded when applying them. Enforcement is almost always discretionary with the agency, however, so that there is a risk the system will be undermined by particularistic or selective enforcement. The English model begins with case-by-case decisions out of which grows a body of standards virtually unique to a given situation—standards that the agency more or less holds to in enforcing its mandate. The English Authority always maintains the flexibility to decide matters in each case without being bound by a rule, provided only that its decisions are consistent with its mandate to control pollution.

Id. at 814–15. Flexibility—adaptive management—can be a good thing, but what does it mean for the rule of law and administrative accountability? Reiss observes that in both systems "in practice, most enforcement actions conform to rules and allow discretion and bargaining." *Id.* at 815. Why do you suppose this is so? Reiss offers a partial explanation: "both systems are bound by norms of distributive justice or fairness and by practical considerations of avoiding complaint." *Id.* Consider whether these observations still hold true in the wake of changes wrought by the European Community's Water Framework Directive, Council Directive 2000/60, 2000 O.J. (L 327) (EC), and other Community Directives related to water quality.

[W]hen the Treaty of Rome was agreed to in 1957, establishing the original European Economic Community, it did not seem to envisage that the creation of a common market had any environmental implications. However, it was not too long before the Community came to appreciate that polluting emissions did not respect national boundaries. From that realisation followed the acceptance that common environmental standards were needed to avoid distorted competition between nations that had markedly different national environmental standards....

On a conservative estimate, there are more than 400 European Community Directives on the environment, and at least twenty of these are directly concerned with water quality.... [A]doption of a Community Directive [means] it is necessary for the national laws of each Member State to implement the obligations agreed to at Community level, though some flexibility is allowed for in the way national legislation and administrative systems are used to transpose Community law.

William Howarth, *Water Quality and Land Use Regulation Under the Water Framework Directive,* 23 Pace Envtl. L. Rev. 351, 364 (2006). Professor Howarth describes the implications of the Framework for the U.K. in the article excerpted below.

William Howarth, Water Quality and Land Use Regulation under the Water Framework Directive

23 Pace Envtl. L. Rev. 351 (2006)

The Water Framework Directive ... establishes new and better ways of protecting and improving rivers, lakes, estuaries, coastal waters and groundwater. These include a single way of managing water based on river basins. The usual administrative boundaries will no longer apply. Instead we will be looking after land and water together and in a way that more effectively embraces the natural environment.[1]

The United Kingdom has a relatively long history of pollution control legislation brought about by the early onset of industrialisation.... [T]he legislature in nineteenth-century England [believed] that the water pollution problem was largely one of unregulated emissions of inadequately treated effluent from industrial "manufactories" and sewage treatment works ... [and thus] regulation is best applied at the point where effluent enters a watercourse....

However, the supposition that all instances of unsatisfactory water quality are attributable to emissions from industrial or sewage treatment activities, capable of being tackled through end-of-pipe regulation, would be a major misconception.... [T]he environmental problem has shift[ed] from end-of-pipe regulation to land-use regulation ... over recent years.... [T]he most comprehensive and powerful weapon in the armoury is the land use planning system.... [But] a more substantive approach is needed in land use planning decisions if the new water quality obligations under ... [the Water Framework Directive] are to be fulfilled....

[D]iffuse contaminants are now recognised as an increasingly large part of the water quality problem, but they require a different kind of regulatory approach [than end-of-pipe regulation.... Thus, land use regulation needs ... the progressive extension of water quality law into land use regulation [to meet water quality standards].

[Recent legislation provides] three kinds of preventative regulatory mechanisms.... First, [under the Water Act 1989] the Secretary of State was given the authority to prohibit or regulate the activities of persons having custody of polluting matter in order to prevent its entry into controlled waters. This power has been exercised to regulate agricultural activities involving silage, animal waste, and oil storage on farms, and to regulate the storage of oil more generally.... [I]nadequate storage of potentially polluting matter can be a criminal offense, regardless of whether or not any actual water pollution occurs as a result ...

Next, the Water Resources Act 1991 provided the Secretary of State the authority to establish Water Protection Zones—zones in England where land use must be strictly regulated because of the vulnerability of receiving waters. Within these zones, particular activities, such as the storage of pollutants, can be regulated; however, the approach is area-specific.... The power to establish Water Protection Zones has not been used much ... only one area has been designated for this purpose.

Finally, the designation of "nitrate sensitive areas" constituted the initial, national approach to tackling problems of nutrient enrichment and eutrophication arising from fertiliser and manure application to agricultural land. This problem was of particular concern

---

1. Barbara Young, Foreword to Env't Agency, Water for Life and Livelihoods: A Strategy for River Basin Planning—A Consultation 1, 1 (2005).

because levels of nitrate contamination in some areas in England exceeded parameters in the European Community's Council Drinking Water Quality Directive and resulted in a judgment against England in the European Court of Justice in 1992. [Case C-337/89, Comm'n of the European Cmtys. v. United Kingdom, 1992 E.C.R. I-06103.] ... The Directive provides for mandatory, rather than voluntary, controls upon farming activities where nitrate levels of surface or ground waters exceed parameters that are set both for the protection of water supplies and for more general ecological protection....

Cumulatively, these three different kinds of preventative regulatory mechanisms ... represent an evolution of water protection law through the progressive regulation of activities taking place on waterside land, at least insofar as they focus upon the most contaminating kinds of land use.... However, land use planning concerns have never been conceived of as solely concerned with environmental protection. Instead, environmental protection has been one factor ... [a] "material consideration," which must be weighed into the balance in planning decisions.[34]

The case of *Ynys Mon B.C. v. Secretary of State for Wales* tellingly illustrates the environmental limitations of the customary approach to water quality concerns in determining planning applications. In that case, the proposed development involved building six houses, from which the developer would be allowed to make a connection of sewerage pipes into the local sewerage system. The development was strongly opposed by the environmental regulatory authority because the sewerage system was already acknowledged to be inadequate in that it allowed untreated, foul sewage to be discharged into coastal waters. As a consequence, the authority had formulated a policy of opposing all developments involving further connections to the sewerage system until improvements had been made.

On appeal, the court acknowledged that the environmental duties upon the authority were of high importance in representing the public interest in the environment, and recognised that the conditions at the existing sewage outfalls in the locality were unsatisfactory. Nevertheless, the policy of a total embargo upon development, advocated by the authority, was not accepted to be finally determinative of the planning issues. Whilst the policy objectives of the authority were important material considerations, they were required to be weighed against all other relevant matters. Following this approach, it was legitimate for the court to conclude that the discharge contributed by the additional houses would not give rise to such deleterious consequences as to override other merits arising from the proposed development. Thus, as this case illustrates, increasing water pollution is not necessarily a bar to authorisation of a proposed development, provided proper consideration is given to the environmental costs.

Although progress towards, or regress from, sustainable development is helpfully informative in regional planning, as in other sectors, there is a noted absence of any specific quantifiable objectives in the sustainability appraisal process ["a systematic and iterative process undertaken during the preparation of a plan or strategy, which identifies and reports on the extent to which the implementation of the plan or strategy would achieve the environmental, economic and social objectives by which sustainable development can be defined."]. Indeed, the weighty criticism has been raised that the approach may actually serve to marginalise environmental appraisal against the more dominant role of economic criteria in the assessment of regional plans.... Another criticism has been that the kind of qualitative assessment involved in the sustainability appraisal approach is based solely upon the assessor's subjectivity.

---

34. See Town and Country Planning Act, 1990, § 70(2) (Eng. & Wales).

In summary, the processes of development planning and development control might seem to offer tremendous scope for a more broadly preventative approach towards water quality protection. However, the theoretical advantages of this approach from an environmental perspective are greatly curtailed by the practicalities of planning procedures....

The European Dimension To Water Quality Regulation—[W]ater ... arguably represents the most fully developed sector [of Community legislation].... Each of the water quality directives adopted at Community level involved significant rethinking of legislative, administrative, and environmental management approaches adopted in the Member States....

[T]he legal duty to implement Community water quality directives is an uncompromising one that requires Member States to faithfully transpose each directive into national law and notify the European Commission that this has been done by the appointed deadline.... Ultimately, the object of most directives is to meet precisely specified water quality objectives for those waters to which they apply. Meeting this substantive obligation can be extremely expensive when major improvements, such as improvements to sewage treatment infrastructure, are needed....

Failure to fulfil any of the matters referred to leaves a Member State open to proceedings brought by the Commission before the European Court of Justice.... [Moreover] the Court [may] impose potentially weighty penalty payments against Member States for repeated failure to implement and enforce legislation. As a practical result, most environmental legislation in the United Kingdom is actually made for the purpose of implementing Community measures, as is likely true amongst the other Member States as well.

The Water Framework Directive—The Water Framework Directive ... is the successor to much of the earlier water legislation and also the mechanism for introducing some quite radical new initiatives. As a consolidation of existing legislation, the Directive is based upon a general principle that its provisions should be at least as stringent as those already required under previous Community water legislation. However, in many respects, its requirements actually extend considerably beyond the requirements of previous legislation. Therefore, the diverse objectives for water quality are consolidated and extended into a single mission. Broadly, this is to secure "good status" for all waters within the scope of the Directive and within the timescale allowed.

For surface waters, two key elements are encompassed: "good ecological status" and "good chemical status." The new element of "good ecological status" is defined in terms of the quality of the biological community in relation to each category of water. "Good chemical status" is defined in terms of compliance with quality standards established for chemical substances at Community level. For groundwaters, good status involves a combination of "good chemical status" and "good quantitative status;" that is, where groundwater exploitation does not exceed the rate of recharge....

Concisely stated, "good status" means that relevant waters must not fall below what is required for the following "environmental objectives" of the Directive to be met:

1. Preventing deterioration of water quality;

2. Protecting, enhancing, and restoring waters with the aim of achieving good status (encompassing both good chemical status and good ecological status of surface waters) by 2015;

3. Protecting, enhancing, and restoring artificial or heavily modified waters with the aim of achieving good status by 2015;

4. Progressively reducing pollution by priority substances and phasing out emissions, discharges, and losses of priority hazardous substances;

5. Preventing or limiting inputs of pollutants into groundwater;

6. Reversing significant upward trends in the concentration of any pollutant in groundwater; and

7. Complying with standards and objectives for protected areas by 2015, including objectives for areas for the abstraction of drinking water.

The environmental objectives of the Directive are to be secured through a sequence of tasks, involving characterising waters according to specified categories, assessing their existing status, and undertaking a range of monitoring activities. Moreover, the Directive harmonises water management across the Community at the river basin level because it requires management by river basin, as a natural geographical and hydrological unit, rather than according to administrative or political boundaries. The Directive requires management plans to incorporate specific protection zones within river basins where more stringent requirements are needed for ecological protection or for particular uses, such as drinking water supply. River basin management plans must also encompass programmes intended to ensure that water quality within the district will meet the environmental objectives of the Directive by the required deadline. Accordingly, river basin management plans are required to be established and updated within fifteen years of the Water Framework Directive, and then every six years thereafter....

[The supervising body, the Environmental] Agency is organised into eight regions defined hydrologically according to watersheds of major rivers, rather than administrative boundaries of local authorities. The system retains a degree of integration insofar as the same regulatory body is entrusted with responsibility for enforcement of a wide range of environmental controls.... [T]he Community obligations required at river basin levels are far more extensive and complex than those previously undertaken in national practice.

Specifically, realisation of the environmental objectives of the Directive envisages programmes, encompassing "basic" measures and, where necessary, further "supplementary" measures, being incorporated into river basin management plans. The "basic" measures must address the following issues:

(a) Implementation of certain Community water legislation;

(b) Cost recovery for water services;

(c) Promotion of efficient and sustainable water use;

(d) Protection of water abstracted for drinking water supply; ...

(g) Control of point source discharges;

(h) Control of diffuse sources;

(i) Significant adverse impacts, including hydromorphological conditions;

(j) Prohibition of certain direct discharges to groundwater; [and]

(k) Elimination of pollution by priority substances....[88]

The categories of "supplementary" measures are specified, non-exclusively, to include mechanisms such as economic or fiscal instruments, negotiated environmental agreements, codes of good practice, restoration measures, and management measures.

---

88. Council Directive 2000/60, 2000 O.J. (L 327) (EC), art. 11, Ann. VI.

Although river basin management planning and the realisation of the "good status" objective are probably the key elements of the Directive, a number of other features should also be noted as important innovations. First, the Directive adopts a combined approach towards emission controls and environmental quality objectives. Second, it adopts cost recovery pricing for water, whereby Member States will be required to ensure that the price charged to water consumers represents the true economic and environmental costs. Third, the Directive requires public participation through a process of information sharing and consultation before river basin management plans are established or revised.

Finally, the most challenging aspect of the good status requirement arises in relation to securing ecological quality standards.... ... For surface waters, the Directive requires good ecological status to be achieved according to an explicit classification system. Hence, in relation to different kinds of water, the composition and abundance of phytoplankton, aquatic flora, benthic invertebrate fauna, and fish must be assessed. Essentially, the approach characterizes a paradigm of each kind of water and designates features of its biological and hydromorphological quality that must be met for waters to reach a particular ecological quality classification....

The magnitude of the challenges involved in implementing the Directive is generally accepted. However, a key question is whether the timescale for implementation is commensurate with the actions that must be taken by Member States. The following table lists the formal requirements alongside their respective deadlines.

December 2000: Water Framework Directive enters into force (by publication in the Official Journal of the European Communities on 22 December) (art. 22).

December 2003: Deadline for transposition into national law (art. 24)....

December 2004: Establish register of protected areas; characterisation reports for each River Basin District to be completed (arts. 5, 6, and 7)....

December 2006: Monitoring programmes for surface water status, groundwater status, and protected areas to be operational; commence public consultation on River Basin Management Plans and Member States are to establish environmental quality standards for surface waters (if no agreement at Community level) (arts. 8, 14, and 16)....

December 2009: Programmes of Measures and Draft River Basin Management Plans are to be published (arts. 11 and 13)....

December 2012: Programmes of measures are to be operational and Commission to publish first report on implementation (arts. 11 and 18)....

December 2015: Deadline for meeting environmental objectives and review of initial River Basin Management Plans (with review and update of Plans every six years after 2015) (arts. 4, 13, 14, and 15)....

Progress at the National Level — The first of the ... [deadlines] — formal transposition into national law — was required within three years of publication of the Directive. Initial progress towards this deadline in England and Wales seemed to be rather slow. In fact, the House of Commons Environment, Food and Rural Affairs Committee ("Committee") delivered a scathingly critical rebuke of the tardiness of the Department for Environment, Food and Rural Affairs ("Department"). The Committee urged the Government to "view the Directive positively ... rather than doing the bare minimum required at the last possible moment." In reply, the Government was understandably eager to dispel the allegations of complacency. The Department provided assurances that it was engaged in a work programme delivered by a "multi-skilled team of administrators, lawyers and economists," and that the objective was that of compliance with the Directive by the legislative deadline, and not before....

[I]nitial transposition of the Directive into national law took place under the Water Environment (Water Framework Directive) (England and Wales) Regulations 2003, which came into force shortly after the official deadline. [The Water Environment (Water Framework Directive) (England and Wales) Regulations, 2003, S.I. 2003/3242.] The 2003 Regulations impose a broad division of labours between operational matters and executive responsibilities. Operational matters are generally made responsibilities of the Environment Agency, and executive responsibilities fall to the "appropriate authority," meaning the Secretary of State in England and the National Assembly in Wales. Hence, it is for the central government to approve river basin management plans, to give practical guidance, and, where necessary, directions for the purpose of implementing the Directive. It is for the Environment Agency to undertake the practical exercises of analysing the characteristics of each river basin district; reviewing the impacts of human activity; identifying bodies of water used for drinking water abstraction; preparing registers of protected areas (designated for water protection or conservation purposes); undertaking programmes of monitoring of water status; formulating environmental objectives and programmes of measures; preparing, and consulting upon, river basin management plans; submitting such plans for approval and undertaking reviews; preparing such supplementary plans as thought fit; and providing various categories of public information....

River Basin Districts consist of a river basin or neighbouring river basins, together with associated groundwater, transitional waters, and coastal water, and include definitive maps of districts. Eleven areas were designated in England and Wales (with two of these crossing the border with Scotland: the Solway-Tweed district and the Northumbria district). Another district covers the rest of Scotland, and four districts were designated in Northern Ireland (with three of these shared with the Republic of Ireland)....

Following transposition, the next formal deadline required the characterisation of waters and assessment of pressures and impacts against the stated ecological objectives of the Directive by the end of 2004. By that time, Member States were to have accomplished the formidable task of assessing the risk that individual water bodies would fail to meet the environmental objectives of the Directive. However, at the time of the initial assessment, those environmental objectives were not fully defined.

Particular problems arose in relation to the quality specifications for groundwater, priority substances, and ecological quality. These uncertainties arose because the Directive's environmental objective of preventing or limiting inputs of pollutants into groundwater does not specify which pollutants are involved. The Directive specifies that this information is to be included in a daughter directive. The daughter directive will provide criteria to apply in determining whether a "significant and sustained" upward trend in groundwater contamination exists. Until these criteria have been established at Community level, Member States must formulate their own criteria. Similar uncertainties surround the environmental quality standards for priority substances ... [and] about the boundaries between the ecological status classes for surface waters, which are needed to determine whether good ecological status has been achieved....

[Further] much of the data on water quality pressures and impacts have not previously been gathered or analysed for the purposes of Community or national law. Even where data on the existing state of water bodies is available, the futuristic and cumulative assessment of how it is likely to change over the next decade—due to plans, projects, and implementation of other Community environmental legislation—is bound to generate a high level of speculation....

[T]he [Common Implementation Strategy document] Analysis of Pressures and Impacts ... recognises the limitations of the initial analysis of pressures and impacts that have been noted above, and acknowledges that it will be necessary for some accommodations to be made. An example of this is in the assessment of surface water bodies that are to be designated as "artificial and heavily modified" so that the environmental objective of "good ecological status" is reduced to the lesser objective of "good ecological potential." For non-artificial waters, it is advised that the first impacts analysis should concentrate upon the risks of such waters failing to meet the good ecological status requirement, leaving for later consideration the assessment of whether those bodies subsequently designated as "heavily modified" are at risk of failing to meet the "good ecological potential requirement," though this should be done "as soon as practical."

This background of uncertainty or incompleteness has also been recognised by competent authorities in the United Kingdom, who have summarised the limitations of the initial characterisation exercise and reviewed the refinements needed to improve the degree of certainty that can be achieved in future characterisation exercises.... Despite all the shortcomings of the initial characterisation exercise, the characterisation reports for each river basin district were dutifully completed by the Environment Agency and communicated to the European Commission by the deadline under the Directive.

[T]he proportion of waters that were identified as being likely to fail to meet the environmental objectives of the Directive in 2015 is alarming.... Cumulatively, the findings were that over 92 percent of rivers, 98 percent of estuaries, 75 percent of groundwaters, and 84 percent of lakes are at risk of failure.... [T]he high proportion of waters that were perceived to be at risk of failing to meet their environmental objectives because of nitrate contamination and other diffuse pollutants raises the issue of what additional land use controls are needed to address the problems thus revealed by the initial characterisation exercise.

Land Use Planning and the Water Framework Directive—As noted previously, the Water Framework Directive lists a range of "basic" measures that must be incorporated into programmes of measures under river basin management plans and further, "supplementary" measures that may also be applied to secure the environmental objectives of the Directive. [T]hese reflect "traditional" approaches to protection of water quality ... [and] land use regulation—for instance, to control diffuse sources of pollution or to prevent losses of pollutants from technical installations.... [T]here are good reasons to suppose that realising water quality objectives will only be possible through a combination of measures, including effective controls upon offending kinds of land use, applied through the land use planning system.

A central issue arising from this is the extent to which river basin management plans should influence land use policy and practice.... [The] planning system in England and Wales is "plan-led" ... individual determinations of whether a proposed development should be authorised must follow the relevant development plan, unless material considerations indicate otherwise.

Under the new planning regime, the "development plan" that must be followed in determining planning applications is a combination of the "regional spatial strategy" and the local development framework that has been adopted or approved for a locality. Local development frameworks are envisaged as a "portfolio" of documents that are relevant to planning matters and which, taken as a whole, comprehensively set out the policies of a local planning authority with respect to development and use of land in its area ... encompass[ing] ... statements or policies regarding, amongst other things, any environmental, social, and economic objectives that are relevant to encouraging development or use of land.... "Spatial planning" seeks to integrate policies for land development and ... competing land uses ... put[ting] particular emphasis upon sustainable development. Hence, supplementary planning documents could include policies relating to diverse matters including regeneration, economic development, education, housing, health, waste, energy, biodiversity, recycling, protection of the environment, transport, culture, and social issues....

National guidance requires regional planning bodies to take into account a list of European Community, central government, or central government agency national policies, guidance, research, and related material when revising regional spatial strategies. Within this list is featured the national legislation transposing the Water Framework Directive.[149] Because local planning authorities must have regard to regional spatial strategies in preparing local development documents, which constitute a part of the local development scheme, they are implicitly bound to implement the Directive. The indirectness of the planning law and guidance, however, contrasts markedly with the national legislation that transposes the Directive. It is explicitly stated that each public body, in exercising its functions so far as they affect a river basin district, must "have regard to" the relevant river basin management plan.[151] Hence, the rather circuitous obligations arising under planning guidance are effectively displaced by a more specific duty under the transposition legislation.

The inference that follows is that bodies making planning determinations must pay "regard" to river basin management plans and, in principle, this may constitute an overriding consideration unless material considerations indicate otherwise.... [P]lanning permission would have to be denied where a development project might prevent the good status of waters being achieved.

"[H]aving regard" to environmental concerns may be insufficient to allocate an appropriate weight to those concerns against other material considerations. Until river basin plans are in place and planning authorities are confronted with prospective developments that conflict with them, it is difficult to be categorical about the way in which such issues will be dealt with in practice. However, the remarkable feature of the arrangements that have been put in place is the contrast between the "procedural" obligation that is imposed upon local planning authorities to "have regard" to river basin management plans, and the numerous substantive obligations that are imposed on the Environment Agency in relation to implementation of the Directive. As has been noted, the Agency ... is legally bound to perform each of its allocated tasks, not merely to "have regard" to the need to do so.[152] Given ... that land use development has the capacity to obstruct ... environmental objectives of the Directive, it is difficult to see why the obligations upon local planning authorities should be, in comparison, so weakly formulated....

A recent consultants' report to the Environment Agency ... concluded, "planning authorities cannot be expected to know what it is that has to be done to achieve what is sought[;] ... they expect to seek expert and authoritative advice, and they are entitled to

---

149. Office of the Deputy Prime Minister, Planning Policy Statement 11: Regional Spatial Strategies 19 (2004), at 8, ann. A (citing Water Environment (Water Framework Directive) (England and Wales) Regulations 2003).

151. The Water Environment (Water Framework Directive) (England and Wales) Regulations, 2003, S.I. 2003/3242, art. 17.

152. Id. art. 3.

expect this to come from the Agency in the first instance." The firm recommendation is that development planning, development control, and now strategic environmental assessment of development plans must be used more effectively to input more precise advice about the implications of changes in land use upon water management.... [T]he problem remains ... where [fully knowing of conflict with the Directive] ... a local planning authority decided to authorise a project based on a conclusion that the developmental benefits outweighed the environmental costs....

The Directive states that Member States will not be in breach where, amongst other things, failure to achieve good status is the result of new modifications to the physical characteristics of a surface water body, and a series of cumulative conditions are met.[156] The conditions require that all practicable steps are taken to mitigate adverse effects; that the reasons for the modification are set out in the river basin management plan; that these reasons are of overriding public interest and/or benefits to the environment and to society in terms of their contribution to human health, human safety, or sustainable development; and that these benefits, for reasons of technical feasibility or disproportionate cost, cannot be achieved by other means.

In relation to these provisions for "exceptional" development, it is notable, first, that the exception only relates to developments actually affecting the physical characteristics of a surface water body. Implicitly, therefore, the provisions should have no relevance to land-based kinds of development that have adverse effects upon water quality, even though these effects might contribute to a failure to meet the environmental objectives of the Directive. Second, the exception is only available in relation to projects that are of overriding public interest or those that confer specified kinds of environmental or human benefits that cannot be otherwise provided.... [This] suggests that a relatively narrow interpretation will be applied to those projects that may qualify as exceptions.

Conclusion—[T]here is no shortage of challenges to meeting the environmental obligations of the Water Framework Directive by the 2015 deadline. The present chemical, physical, and ecological state of national waters within the scope of the Directive leaves much to be desired. Clearly, extensive programmes of measures will need to be put in place through river basin management plans to ensure that present causes of failure to meet environmental objectives are fully addressed by the deadline.

However, what remains uncertain is the role of land use regulation in these programmes, alongside traditional mechanisms for protection of water quality. In principle, the historical duty of local planning authorities "to have regard" for environmental impacts, including those relating to the aquatic environment, has much to commend it. Specifically, it has allowed local control over land use planning and control over authorisation of particular developments. This may be seen as a local democratic mandate for control over the process of balancing social and economic factors against environmental impacts in determining what kinds of development qualify as "sustainable." ... The key issue is whether allowing development that results in a failure to meet the environmental objectives of the Directive could ever be justified in Community law, whatever the local perception of the development....

Subject to the narrow exception for sustainable development provided by the Directive itself, public bodies should be required to act in accordance with the requirements of the Directive. The implication of imposing that duty upon local planning authorities would be that it would not be permissible to allow development of a kind that conflicted with the environmental objectives of the Directive. Undeniably, this would involve the

---

156. Id. art. 4(7).

loss of some local autonomy in land use decision-making; but the alternative would be worse, given the prospect of proceedings against the United Kingdom in the European Court of Justice for failure fully to implement the Directive.

Notes and Questions

1. Professor Howarth details some of the difficulties for England in implementing the Directive. Addressing the jurisdictional tension between local planning authorities and the Environment Agency is one of them. Howarth argues that local planning authorities should not be allowed to approve development that conflicts with the Directive's environmental objectives, although he admits that "this would involve the loss of some local autonomy in land use decision-making." How should England address this tension? You may recall that the U.S. Supreme Court has constrained the U.S. EPA's ability to "intrude" on state and local land use planning prerogatives in cases like *Rapanos,* 574 U.S. 715, and *SWANCC,* 531 U.S. 159, *supra,* Section A.2.

2. The U.K. is not alone in facing difficulties complying with the Directive. To combat these difficulties, the Water Directors have issued the Common Implementation Strategy for the Water Framework Directive (2000/60/EC) (CIS), *at* http://ec.europa.eu/ environment/water/water-framework/objectives/pdf/strategy.pdf. This aims to provide an overarching implementation strategy, objectives, and key activities. To facilitate aid with implementation, the European Commission established a consultative group, the "Expert Advisory Forum on Priority Substances and Pollution Control." CIS 2.5.1. This group, comprised of experts from Member States, Accession Countries, and industrial and environmental NGOS, will deal with technical aspects of Article 16 of the Directive (environmental quality standards). The CIS also suggests an advisory forum to provide guidance as to criteria for assessing good groundwater status. CIS 2.5.2. Is it likely that such consultants and expert forums will help or confuse the implementation process?

Would more individualized, country-specific forums be better suited to answering each Member State's concerns? Some Member States, the U.K. for example, have developed such forums. The United Kingdom Technical Advisory Group for the Water Framework Directive (UKTAG) is a joint effort between environmental and conservation agencies. This group aims to provide "coordinated advice on the science and technical aspects" of the Directive. UKTAG, http://www.wfduk.org/ (accessed Aug. 18, 2012).

If a Member State fails to implement a EU directive by the specified date it is considered a "clear case violation" of the Treaty on the Function of the European Union (TFEU), Dec. 13, 2007, 2007 O.J. (C 306). However, the individual countries do have some autonomy as to the how of achieving the Directive's goal. Article 288 of the TFEU states, "A directive shall be binding, as to the result to be achieved, upon each Member State to which it is addressed, but shall leave to the national authorities the choice of form and methods."

If a Member State has failed to implement a directive, the European Commission will deliver an opinion on the matter and allow the offending State an opportunity to respond. TFEU Article 258. If the State does not comply with the opinion in the requisite time, the Commission may bring the matter to the Court of Justice of the European Union. *Id.* If the Court finds the Member State has failed to implement the directive (an obligation under the Treaties), the State must comply with the judgment of the Court. Article 260(1). If the Member State fails to comply with the judgment, the Commission may bring the case before the Court again to seek a lump sum or penalty payment as punishment. Article 260(2).

How does this compare to the United States? Can you think of an instance of a state failing to accommodate U.S. federal law? What power does the federal government, particularly the U.S. EPA, have to persuade states to comply with the Clean Water Act, for example?

3. Consider the various ways in which the EU directive is more expansive than U.S. or Canadian federal law. For example, the Groundwater Directive of the EU covers all sorts of groundwater in the European Union. Richard Thomas, *The European Directive on the Protection of Groundwater: A Model for the United States,* 26 Pace Envtl. L. Rev. 259 (2009). In contrast, American courts have ruled that comparable legislation, the Clean Water Act, does not apply to all bodies of water, particularly "isolated groundwater." *Id* at 283. Another example is the Safe Drinking Water Act, which only protects groundwater used as a public drinking water system. *Id* at 284. Comparatively, the Groundwater Directive and the Water Framework Directive aim to protect water for human consumption and those of economically significant aquatic species, nutrient sensitive areas, recreational waters, and areas designated for the protection of species or habitats. *Id.* at 284; Directive 2000/60/EC art. 7(1). Moreover, the Water Framework Directive addresses both water quality and water quantity, *see id.* art. 4(1)(a)-(b), but the Clean Water Act leaves water quantity to the states. Should U.S. legislation be altered to come in line with Europe's more holistic approach?

4. Professor Howarth, *supra,* describes cases where English courts have found that "increasing water pollution is not necessarily a bar to authorisation of a proposed development." This is equally true in the U.S. under the Clean Water Act. By contrast, the U.S. Clean Air Act tightly restricts the construction of new sources of air pollutants in Air Quality Control Regions that fail to comply with National Ambient Air Quality Standards. *See* Robert W. Adler, *Integrated Approaches to Water Pollution: Lessons From the Clean Air Act,* 23 Harv. Envtl. L. Rev. 203 (1999). In brief, major new sources cannot locate in a "dirty" airshed unless they meet stringent emission limitations and obtain offsets of emission reductions from existing sources. 42 U.S.C. §7503(a), (c). Should the Water Framework Directive and the Clean Water Act be reformed to prohibit new sources in water quality impaired areas?

5. The Water Framework cross-references the Dangerous Substances Directive of 1976, 76/464/EEC. According to England's Environment Agency:

> The Dangerous Substances Directive and its 'daughter' directives control discharges that are liable to contain dangerous substances and that go to inland, coastal and territorial surface waters.... We define pollution by dangerous substances as exceedence of Environmental Quality Standards (EQSs) in the water. We base the EQS of a substance on the toxicity of the substance. It defines a concentration in the water below which we are confident that the substance will not have a polluting effect or cause harm to plants and animals. If the concentration in the water is less than the EQS then we have eliminated pollution. The 'daughter' directives set the EQSs for List I substances across Europe. Each country in the EU is required to set its own EQSs for List II substances.
>
> Dangerous substances can potentially harm our health, aquatic life and water quality. They include certain industrial chemicals, pesticides and metals. They are not only found in sewage and trade discharges, but water passing through contaminated land and old mines can wash dangerous substances out into the environment. Rainwater runoff from roads and some industrial sites can also release dangerous substances into watercourses.

Dangerous Substances Directives, http://www.environment-agency.gov.uk/business/regulation/31937.aspx (visited July 25, 2012). Under the Directive, the Environment

Agency "authorises discharges that are liable to contain any dangerous substances in order to eliminate and limit pollution from certain types of substances." The Directive affects "everybody who discharges sewage or trade effluent to surface waters such as a river, lake, estuary or the sea"; all discharges "will normally be required to have a permit from the Environment Agency." *Id.*

This Directive "has had an enormous impact on pollution control in the UK." Bell and McGillivray, *supra,* at 590. "[T]he modern EC water policy approach in relation to the most hazardous substances is one of elimination at source." *Id.* The Dangerous Substances Directive is to be repealed in 2013, however, when the more comprehensive strategies of the Water Framework Directive become operational. *See* Water Framework Directive, 2000/60/EC, arts. 16 and 22.

6. With the adoption of the Water Framework Directive, water pollution policy in the U.K. and throughout Europe "is presently undergoing fundamental change." Bell and McGillivray, *supra,* at 593. By 2013, the Directive is to be fully implemented. The goal is for "all member States to 'aim to achieve' good surface water status…, good ecological [status]…, and good groundwater status in all waters by the end of 2015." *Id.* For a critique of the Directive's approach to achieving "good ecological status," see Henrik Josefsson and Lasse Baaner, *The Water Framework Directive—A Directive for the Twenty-First Century*, 23 J. Envtl. L. 463, 475 (2011), arguing that the Directive's failure to include flow regimes (hydromorphological features) as a primary element of "good ecological status" is a significant deficit, given that dams and other impoundments are "a key pressure in riverine ecosystems in Europe."

F. International and Transboundary Resource Allocation and Pollution Control

Generally speaking, international natural resources are distributed, utilized, and protected via political agreements reflecting various eligibility criteria, including the nations' geographic location, their historical claims to the resource, and their relative military powers. International water bodies, more specifically, may be governed by a doctrine of "equitable apportionment." This doctrine reflects two bedrock principles of modern international environmental law:

(1) No state has the right to use its territory in a manner that causes injury to the territory of another, and

(2) Trans-boundary resources should be shared equitably so that each state may enjoy its fair share.

When it comes to water resources, the determination of a fair share is guided by a variety of factors, including:

- Natural physical factors — geographic, hydrological, climatic, and ecological;

- Social and economic needs of the riparian states;

- Effects of the use of the watercourse in one state on another;

- Conservation and protection of water resources; and

- Availability of comparable alternatives to a particular planned or existing use.

See Convention on the Law of the Non-Navigational Uses of International Watercourses, May 21, 1997, U.N. Doc. A/51/869, Art. VI, reprinted in 36 I.L.M. 700 (1997); Concerning the Gabčíkovo-Nagymaros Project (Hung. v. Slovk.), 1997 I.C.J. 7, reprinted in 37 I.L.M. 162 (1998); A. Dan Tarlock, *International Water Law and the Protection of River Ecosystem Integrity,* 10 Brigham Young J. Public L. 181 (1996); A. Dan Tarlock, *Water Security, Fear Mitigation and International Water Law*, 31 Hamline L. Rev. 703 (2008).

According to the Food and Agricultural Organization, there have been over 3,600 treaties related to international water resources since 805 AD. United Nations, *Water for Life 2005–2015,* http://www.un.org/waterforlifedecade/transboundary_waters.shtml. Most of these deal with boundary demarcation and navigation. Within the past century, however, the focus of negotiation and treaty-making has shifted toward the use, development, protection, and conservation of water resources. (The EC Water Framework Directive, described above, reflects this trend.) According to the U.N., existing treaties could be strengthened in several significant ways, including "workable monitoring provisions, enforcement mechanisms, and specific water allocation provisions that address variations in water flow and changing needs." *Id.*

1. United Nations Convention on Non-Navigational Uses of International Watercourses

The 1997 United Nations Convention on Non-Navigational Uses of International Watercourses is an international instrument that specifically focuses on shared water resources. Convention on the Law of Non-Navigable Uses of International Watercourses, May 21, 1997, U.N. Doc. A/RES/51/229, reprinted in 36 I.L.M. 700. The Convention embraces the two key principles described above to guide the conduct of nations with shared watercourses: "equitable and reasonable use" and "the obligation not to cause significant harm" to neighbors.

In 2012, Benin became the twenty-seventh party to the Watercourses Convention when it submitted its instrument of accession to the Secretary-General of the United Nations on 5 July 2012. U.N. Treaty Collection, Ratification, Acceptance, Accession, Approval (July 13, 2012). The United Kingdom came on board in 2012 as well, motivated in part by the Rio + 20 Conference.

Rio+20 Meeting: UK to Accede to UN Water Convention
Int'l Bus. Times, June 23, 2012

At the Rio+20 meeting, Deputy Prime Minister Nick Clegg and the UK government announced that the UK will accede to the UN Watercourses Convention to help ensure that the world's 263 international boundary crossing rivers are protected and peacefully shared.... When ratified the UN Watercourses Convention will help to protect rivers such as the Mekong which, with its tributaries, flows through six countries including China, Burma, Lao PDR, Cambodia, Thailand, and Vietnam, supplying a large proportion of the world's freshwater fish catch.

"The UK has done well to support these vital UN principles for fair watersharing between states. Nowhere is this more critical than in the Middle East, where Iraqi farmers now suffer from massive water-diversion projects built upstream on the Euphrates, and decades of denial of access to the Jordan increases the strain for Palestinians and Lebanon," Mark Zeitoun, Director of the UEA Water Security Research centre said.

The UN Watercourses Convention is a flexible and overarching global legal framework that establishes basic standards and rules for cooperation between watercourse states on the use, management, and protection of international watercourses.

Notes and Questions

1. To enter into force, the Watercourses Convention requires ratification by thirty-five countries. The sticking point appears to be Article 7 ("Obligation not to cause significant harm"), which requires member states, "in utilizing an international watercourse in their territories … [to] take all appropriate measures to prevent the causing of significant harm to other watercourse states." Professor McCaffrey poses the following illustrative hypothetical:

> Suppose … upstream State A has not significantly developed its water resources because of its mountainous terrain. The topography of the downstream states on the watercourse, B and C, is flatter, and they have used the watercourse extensively for irrigation for centuries, if not millennia. State A now wishes to develop its water resources for hydroelectric and agricultural purposes. States B and C cry foul, on the ground that this would significantly harm their established uses.

Stephen McCaffrey, *The UN Convention on the Law of Non-Navigational Uses of International Watercourses: Prospects and Pitfalls* 20–21, in WORLD BANK TECH. PAPER 414: INTERNATIONAL WATERCOURSES; ENHANCING COOPERATION AND MANAGING CONFLICT (1998). How might this conflict be resolved? McCaffrey offers insights:

> [P]resumably … if State A's hydroelectric use conflicts with State B's agricultural use, the conflict is not to be resolved solely by applying the "no harm" rule of Article 7, but rather through reference to the "package" of articles setting forth the principles of both equitable utilization and "no-harm." But in actual disputes, it seems probable that the facts and circumstances of each case, rather than any *a priori* rule, will ultimately be the key determinants of the rights and obligations of the parties. Difficult cases, of which there are bound to be more in the future, will be solved by cooperation and compromise, not by rigid insistence on rules of law.

Id. at 22.

2. Even absent ratification, the Watercourses Convention is regarded as an important step towards arriving at international norms governing water. It represents "a consensus among experts that international watercourse agreements need to be more concrete, setting out measures to enforce treaties made and incorporating detailed conflict resolution mechanisms in case disputes erupt. Better cooperation also entails identifying clear yet flexible water allocations and water quality standards, taking into account hydrological events, changing basin dynamics and societal values." U.N., Water for Life Decade: Transboundary Waters (2012), at http://www.un.org/waterforlifedecade/transboundary_waters.shtml.

3. Agenda 21 of the 1992 Rio Conference declares the following objective:

> To ensure adequate supplies of good quality water are maintained for the entire population of the planet, while preserving the hydrological, biological and chemical functions of ecosystems and adapting human activities within the capacity limits of nature and combating vectors of water-related diseases.

U.N. Conference on Environment and Development, Agenda 21, 1992 U.N. Doc. A/ CONF.151/26/Rev.1, para. 18.2. It also declares a broad, overarching goal of "satisfy[ing] the freshwater needs of all countries for their sustainable development." *Id.* para. 18.7. However, it does not provide much detail.

> [Agenda 21] ... did not set out a clear blueprint for addressing systemic prob-
> lems of hydrological disadvantage at a global scale. Indeed the reference in Prin-
> ciple 2 of the Rio Declaration to the "sovereign right" of states "to exploit their
> own resources pursuant to their own environmental and developmental poli-
> cies" is in tension with a global water ethic based on principles of distributive
> justice.

Tim Stephens, *Reimagining International Water Law*, 71 Md. L. Rev. End. 20, 39 (2011). Professor Stephens argues that "the time has come to view fresh water in global terms ... [with] acceptance at a conceptual level that the supply of freshwater resources is a com- mon concern of humankind..., even if the operationalization of alleviating hydrologi- cal disadvantage will often need to be played out on a much more localized scale." *Id.,* citing Stephen C. McCaffrey, The Law of International Watercourses 168 (2d ed. 2007). Can you imagine how administrators, politicians, and stakeholders might imple- ment a water management regime based on a view of water as a global "common concern"?

2. International Provisions on Marine Pollution

There are several international agreements in place to address marine pollution. As discussed above in Section A, *supra,* the International Convention for the Prevention of Pollution from Ships 1973 (MARPOL), as modified by the protocol of 1978 (entered into force on 2 October 1983), 1340 UNTS 61 (1978), 17 ILM 546, deals with the prevention of pollution from ships, including oil tankers, and offshore oil platforms. MARPOL im- poses monitoring and enforcement responsibilities on the flag state (the state where a vessel is registered). Cecilia A. Low, *Marine Environmental Protection in Joint Develop- ment Agreements*, 30 No. 1 J. Energy & Nat. Resources L. 45, 53 (2012).

In addition, the United Nations Convention on the Law of the Sea (UNCLOS) requires states to assess the potential effects of planned activities under their jurisdiction or con- trol that they have "reasonable grounds to believe ... may cause substantial pollution of or significant and harmful changes to the marine environment." U.N. Convention on the Law of the Sea (UNCLOS) 1982, 21 ILM 1261, Art. 206. "Pollution" is defined in Article 1 as "the introduction by man, directly or indirectly, of substances or energy into the ma- rine environment ... which results or is likely to result in such deleterious effects as harm to living resources and marine life, hazards to human health, hindrance to marine activ- ities ... impairment of quality for use of sea water and reduction of amenities."

Under UNCLOS, states must adopt laws to "prevent, reduce and control pollution of the marine environment by dumping." Article 210. UNCLOS also requires states to "adopt laws and regulations to prevent, reduce and control pollution of the marine environ- ment" in respect of seabed activities and structures subject to their jurisdiction, and to en- force such laws. Articles 208(1), (2) and 214. States must ensure that their legal systems provide recourse for damage resulting from pollution of the marine environment caused by persons under their jurisdiction. Article 235(2). *See* Low, *supra*, at 53.

A majority of coastal states are parties to UNCLOS (*i.e.,* 162 nations, including Canada, India, Great Britain, and New Zealand), making it "the bedrock legal instrument governing a wide array of ocean issues ranging from navigation to fishing to environmental protection to mining." Center for Progressive Reform, *Reclaiming Global Leadership: Why the United States Should Ratify Ten Pending Environmental Treaties* 36 (2011), http://www. progressivereform.org/articles/International_Environmental_Treaties_1201.pdf.

The United States in one of few hold-outs. Indeed, "[t]he United States is the only developed coastal state, the only large economy, and the only naval power that does not belong to the Convention." *Id.* at 37. What could be the reason for its hesitation?

> Although the United States took the lead in negotiating the LOS Convention, disagreement with one portion of the Convention (Part XI, addressing deep seabed mining) prevented the United States from ratifying the Convention.... In 1994, the United Nations completed negotiation of an additional agreement governing deep seabed mining. The new agreement, drafted with significant U.S. involvement, allayed the concerns that had prevented the United States and other developed nations from joining the LOS Convention.... The Convention has received strong bipartisan support ever since.... During [the Bush II] Administration, the Senate Foreign Relations Committee twice recommended Senate approval by overwhelming bipartisan majorities (by a 17–3 vote in 2004, and unanimously in 2007). In a 2010 executive order, President Barack Obama similarly committed his administration to pursuing U.S. ratification of the Convention. Nevertheless, the Convention has never come up for a vote before the full Senate....

Id. Critics claim that the Convention imposes severe restrictions on the exploitation of the seabed, and also that the US doesn't need the Convention's protections because it has a powerful navy. According to Center for Progressive Reform scholars, however, there are virtually no downsides to ratification and significant advantages.

> Ratifying the LOS Convention would require no changes to U.S. law.... By failing to ratify the convention, the United States diminishes its influence in global ocean governance and loses the opportunity to influence the direction of the law. As the world's largest maritime power, the United States has the most at stake from developments in the law of the sea. Yet it continues to sit on the sidelines, thereby forfeiting the opportunity to participate in the governance of virtually every major ocean interest, including: freedom of navigation; marine environmental protection; natural resource management; oil, gas and mineral extraction; marine scientific research; and the peaceful resolution of ocean related disputes. Failure to join the Convention not only prevents the United States from participating in the future development of international law on these points, but it also directly jeopardizes many significant U.S. interests.

> First and foremost, global freedom of navigation is essential for the exercise of U.S. military power.... Second, the United States has an enormous stake in the health of the world's oceans and the living resources they contain. The LOS Convention delimits state obligations to manage these resources sustainably. Indeed, the United States has already ratified the addendum to the LOS Convention, which addresses both highly migratory fish stocks that cross national boundaries and the high seas, such as tuna, and straddling stocks that move between the territorial seas and exclusive economic zones of more than one country.... Third, the Convention sets the rules for further territorial claims over marine resources. For example, it authorizes states to assert claims over the continental shelf beyond their 200-mile exclusive economic zone. As recent Russian expedi-

tions to the Arctic have shown, other states are vigorously pursuing claims to the resource-rich extended continental shelf. The international commission created by the Convention to review such claims has already received nine submissions from other states, and has made recommendations on two. As a non-Party, the United States cannot assert its own claim.

Id. at 37–39.

In May 2012, the Senate foreign relations committee, led by Democratic Senator John Kerry, scheduled hearings to discuss "national security and strategic imperatives for ratification" of UNCLOS. Secretary of State Hillary Clinton declared ratification of UNCLOS one of her top priorities. Rodney Jaleco, *U.S. Senate Mulls UNCLOS Ratification,* ABS-CBN North America News Bureau, May 22, 2012. Secretary of Defense Leon Panetta and chairman of the Joint Chiefs of Staff, General Martin Dempsey, testified in favor of ratification as well. "And yet the treaty continues to face stubborn opposition from a vocal conservative minority of purported defenders of U.S. sovereignty...." Stewart M. Patrick, *(Almost) Everyone Agrees: The U.S. Should Ratify the Law of the Sea Treaty,* The Atlantic, June 10, 2012. Why do you think ratification of UNCLOS has become such a partisan battle?

Case Study: U.S.-Canada Transboundary Pollution

Power plants, smelters, and other industrial activities emit water and air pollutants that know no political boundaries. Sulfur dioxide, in particular, can disperse over long distances and its deposition as acid rain poses significant problems for air, soil, vegetation, and water bodies. What recourse does the affected nation have against either the industries or the government of the industries' home state? International and bi-lateral agreements may come into play, but there may be domestic legislation on point as well.

> One major drawback of international law is the lack of adequate enforcement mechanisms to ensure that sovereign nations and their citizens comply with its principles. It becomes crucial for countries to use domestic mechanisms for enforcement ... to ensure that the most important international legal principles are honored.

Kathryn T. Martin, U.S. *Control Over Extraterritorial Water Pollution: The Interplay Between International and Domestic Law,* 22 J. Nat. Resources & Envtl. L. 209, 209 (2008–09).

At least two provisions of U.S. law speak to transboundary pollution. Relevant provisions of Canadian law follow.

U.S. Clean Air Act
42 U.S.C. § 7415

Whenever the Administrator, upon receipt of reports, surveys or studies from any duly constituted international agency has reason to believe that any air pollutant or pollutants emitted in the United States cause or contribute to air pollution which may reasonably be anticipated to endanger public health or welfare in a foreign country or whenever the Secretary of State requests him to do so with respect to such pollution which the Secretary of State alleges is of such a nature, the Administrator shall give formal notification thereof to the Governor of the State in which such emissions originate....

This section shall apply only to a foreign country which the Administrator determines has given the United States essentially the same rights with respect to the prevention or control of air pollution occurring in that country as is given that country by this section.

U.S. Clean Water Act

33 U.S.C. § 1320

(a) Whenever the Administrator, upon receipts of reports, surveys, or studies from any duly constituted international agency, has reason to believe that pollution is occurring which endangers the health or welfare of persons in a foreign country, and the Secretary of State requests him to abate such pollution, he shall give formal notification thereof to the State water pollution control agency of the State or States in which such discharge or discharges originate and to the appropriate interstate agency, if any. He shall also promptly call such a hearing, if he believes that such pollution is occurring in sufficient quantity to warrant such action, and if such foreign country has given the United States essentially the same rights with respect to the prevention and control of pollution occurring in that country as is given that country by this subsection. The Administrator, through the Secretary of State, shall invite the foreign country which may be adversely affected by the pollution to attend and participate in the hearing, and the representative of such country shall, for the purpose of the hearing and any further proceeding resulting from such hearing, have all the rights of a State water pollution control agency....

(f) When any such recommendation adopted by the Administrator involves the institution of enforcement proceedings against any person to obtain the abatement of pollution subject to such recommendation, the Administrator shall institute such proceedings if he believes that the evidence warrants such proceedings. The district court of the United States shall consider and determine de novo all relevant issues, but shall receive in evidence the record of the proceedings before the conference or hearing board. The court shall have jurisdiction to enter such judgment and orders enforcing such judgment as it deems appropriate or to remand such proceedings to the Administrator for such further action as it may direct.

Canadian Environmental Protection Act

S.C., ch. 33

176. (1) Subject to subsection (4), the Minister [of Environment] shall act under subsections (2) and (3) only if [s/he and the Minister of Health] have reason to believe that a substance released from a source in Canada into water creates, or may reasonably be anticipated to create,

> (a) water pollution in a country other than Canada; or

> (b) water pollution that violates, or is likely to violate, an international agreement binding on Canada in relation to the prevention, control or correction of pollution.

(2) If the source referred to in subsection (1) is a not a federal source, the Minister shall

> (a) consult with the government responsible for the area in which the source is situated to determine whether that government can prevent, control or correct the water pollution under its laws; and

> (b) if the government referred to in paragraph (a) can prevent, control or correct the water pollution, offer it an opportunity to do so.

(3) If the source referred to in subsection (1) is a federal source, or if the government referred to in paragraph (2)(a) cannot prevent, control or correct the water pollution under its laws or does not do so, the Minister shall take at least one of the following courses of action:

(a) on approval by the Governor in Council, publish a notice under subsection 56(1); or

(b) recommend regulations to the Governor in Council for the purpose of preventing, controlling or correcting the water pollution.

(4) If the water pollution referred to in paragraph (1)(a) is in a country where Canada does not have substantially the same rights with respect to the prevention, control or correction of water pollution as that country has under this Division, the Minister shall decide whether to act under subsections (2) and (3)....

179. (1) Where there occurs or there is a likelihood of a release into waters of a substance in contravention of a regulation ... any person ... shall, as soon as possible in the circumstances, ...

(b) take all reasonable measures consistent with the protection of the environment and public safety to ... remedy any dangerous condition or reduce or mitigate any danger to the environment or to human life or health that results from the release of the substance or may reasonably be expected to result if the substance is released; and

(c) make a reasonable effort to notify any member of the public who may be adversely affected by the release or likely release.

* * *

Few cases have tested these provisions. In Her Majesty the Queen in Right of Ontario v. U.S. EPA, 912 F.2d 1525 (D.C. Cir. 1990), a U.S. federal court held the EPA was not required under the Clean Air Act to promulgate endangerment and reciprocity findings to prevent air pollutants in the U.S. from causing harm in the form of acid rain in Canada when it lacked sufficient information to be able to trace such pollutants to specific sources in the United States.

Her Majesty the Queen indicates that the burden on the nation complaining about environmental harm is quite high. Should it be? When diplomacy and nation-to-nation litigation fail, what might fill the gap?

Historically, the Westphalian tradition (named after the Peace of Westphalia that ended the Thirty Years' War over three centuries ago) of international law allowed only national governments to address international matters. Citizens had no direct role, and their interests could only be considered to the extent that they were espoused by their government. Nevertheless, relying exclusively on national governments to address international environmental problems has proved to be inadequate. National governments are extremely reluctant to bring environmental claims against other nations, as every national government presides over a house with at least some glass, and the fear of retaliation or setting undesirable precedents often prevails over the interests of affected citizens.

Noah D. Hall, *The Evolving Role of Citizens in United States-Canadian International Environmental Law Compliance*, 24 Pace Envtl. L. Rev. 131, 132 (2007). Hall concludes, "Relying exclusively on national governments for compliance ... ignores the potentially powerful role that citizens can and do play in environmental law and policy."

If domestic courts can't or won't provide relief, where is the complaining party to go? Nations that consent to the jurisdiction of the International Court of Justice may find some relief there. *See* Kate Halloran, *Is the International Court of Justice the Right Forum for Transboundary Water Pollution Disputes?*, 10 Sustainable Dev. L. & Pol'y 39 (2009) (describing a dispute between Argentina and Uruguay over the construction of pulp mills on the River Uruguay). Only governments may appear as parties, however. For details on the ICJ's jurisdiction, see ICJ, *Jurisdiction*, http://www.icj-cij.org/jurisdiction/ index.php?p1=5 (accessed Aug. 17, 2012).

One of Canada's most notorious cases of water and air pollution arose in British Columbia. The EPA and the Colville Tribes sought to hold Teck Cominco Ltd. responsible in a U.S. court for violations of U.S. law governing releases and cleanup of hazardous substances from its Trail Smelter. The following two articles describe the smelter and the long-running dispute. Next, an excerpt from a case brought against the company is provided.

A Century of Slag
Chris Brown, CBC News (Dec. 15, 2003),
www.cbc.ca/ ... /environment/centuryofslag.html

There's been a smelter in Trail since 1896, not long after gold was discovered in the hills nearby. During the war years, the company accelerated its processing of lead and zinc. The complaints about pollution accelerated, too. In the 1940s, U.S. farmers downwind took the smelter owners before an international panel. It forced the company to cut poisonous emissions.

In the Columbia River though, the slag continued to pile up, practically all of it discharged with the blessing of the B. C. government. The current carried it south creating islands and beaches of black sand....

A group of Washington state residents has convinced the U.S. Environmental Protection Agency to take on a Canadian smelting giant because there could be health risks from pollution dumped into the Columbia River.... The EPA study earlier this year chronicled a century of pollution from the Trail smelter. In addition to the metals from the slag, it cited numerous other toxic spills and discharges of acids and chemicals, including mercury and arsenic....

"Canadian law is much different than the U.S. law," [Paddy] Stone [who lives on the Colville Indian Reservation] says.... "It's really amazing to think that this kind of pollution could happen for so many years and nothing is said about it. But it's a different country."

Michael J. Robinson-Dorn, The Trail Smelter, Is What's Past Prologue? EPA Blazes a New Trail for CERCLA
14 N.Y.U. Environmental Law J. 233 (2006)

Locate one of the world's largest metal smelters 10 miles north of the U.S.-Canada border and allow it to dump millions of tons of hazardous by-products, including heavy metals and mercury, into the Columbia River where they are flushed downstream into the United States. Posit that downstream is a popular National Recreation Area where over a million visitors a year come to recreate on the shores and in the waters of the Columbia River, most of whom have no idea that the beckoning black sand beaches are really contaminated slag discharged from the upstream smelter, and that these shores and the river bottom comprise one of the nation's most contaminated hazardous waste sites....

For good measure, throw in the fact that the very smelter in question was, in the 1930's, at the center of one of the most celebrated international environmental cases, the *Trail Smelter Arbitration*—a case that is heralded as having established the principle that no nation may use its land to cause harm to another nation. Add to the mix the curious fact that in the face of stiff opposition from the smelter's owner, the mining and energy in-dustries, and the Government of Canada, the Bush Administration acts forcefully to hold the smelter responsible for cleaning up the mess that its foreign discharges created in the United States. When the smelter refuses to comply, two citizens, both enrolled members of a local Indian Tribe, file a citizen's suit to enforce EPA's order, and the State intervenes in support of the plaintiffs. These are the facts underlying … *Pakootas v. Teck Cominco Metals Ltd.*, … the United States' first use of CERCLA to address the cleanup of a hazardous waste site created by discharges that originated outside the United States. In addition to [a] matter of first impression, … the *Pakootas* case … [is] a lens through which to view the larger issues of transboundary pollution, and just as importantly, the extraterritorial application of U.S. law.…

Despite the diplomatic gnashing of teeth…, the Ninth Circuit's decision is unlikely to affect our nation's close relationship with Canada. That is not to say, however, that the court's ruling is not important, far from it. Holding Teck Cominco responsible for nearly a century of discharges of slag and heavy metals to the Columbia River matters a great deal to the plaintiffs who brought the case, to the Confederated Colville Tribes to which they belong and who depend on the natural resources of the area for their "subsistence, cul-ture and spiritual well-being".… The decision also matters to the citizens of the State of Washington and the United States, who are currently footing the bill for investigation and cleanup of one of our nation's most contaminated hazardous waste sites. Citizens on both sides of the United States-Canada border have overwhelmingly supported, and their respective governments have adopted, broad strict liability schemes to ensure that polluters pay for cleanup of hazardous waste sites. They will soon learn … whether a multinational corporation with operations in the United States and Canada will be able to use the bor-der as a shield from liability.…

Joseph A. Pakootas, an individual and enrolled member of the Confederated Tribes of the Colville Reservation, [and] State of Washington v. Teck Cominco Metals, Ltd., a Canadian Corporation

452 F.3d 1066 (9th Cir. 2006), cert. denied, 552 U.S. 1095 (2008)

Citizen suit was brought under Comprehensive Environmental Response, Compensa-tion, and Liability Act to enforce Environmental Protection Agency's order that Canadian operator of Canadian smelting plant conduct remedial investigation/feasibility study of por-tion of river within United States where slag from plant had come to be located.…

Between 1906 and 1995, Teck generated and disposed of hazardous materials, in both liquid and solid form, into the Columbia River. These wastes, known as "slag," include the heavy metals arsenic, cadmium, copper, mercury, lead, and zinc, as well as other un-specified hazardous materials. Before mid-1995, the Trail Smelter discharged up to 145,000 tons of slag annually into the Columbia River. Although the discharge took place within Canada, the EPA concluded that Teck has arranged for the disposal of its hazardous sub-stances from the Trail Smelter into the Upper Columbia River by directly discharging up to 145,000 tonnes of slag annually prior to mid-1995. Effluent, such as slag, was discharged into the Columbia River through several outfalls at the Trail Smelter.… The slag was car-ried downstream in the passing river current and settled in slower flowing quiescent areas.

A significant amount of slag has accumulated and adversely affects the surface water, ground water, sediments, and biological resources of the Upper Columbia River and Lake

Roosevelt. Technical evidence shows that the Trail Smelter is the predominant source of contamination at the Site. The physical and chemical decay of slag is an ongoing process that releases arsenic, cadmium, copper, zinc, and lead into the environment, causing harm to human health and the environment.

We begin by considering how this litigation fits within the CERCLA statutory framework. CERCLA sets forth a comprehensive scheme for the cleanup of hazardous waste sites, and imposes liability for cleanup costs on the parties responsible for the release or potential release of hazardous substances into the environment.

To ensure the prompt cleanup of hazardous waste sites, CERCLA gives four options to the EPA: (1) the EPA can investigate and remediate hazardous waste sites itself under §9604, and later seek to recover response costs from the potentially responsible parties (PRPs) under §9607; (2) the EPA can initiate settlement negotiations with PRPs under §9622; (3) the EPA can file suit in federal district court to compel the PRPs to abate the threat if there is an "imminent and substantial" threat to public health or welfare under §9606(a); or (4) the EPA can issue orders directing the PRPs to clean up the site under §9606(a). In this case, the EPA chose the fourth approach....

If a party receives an order and refuses to comply, enforcement options are available. First, the EPA may bring an action in federal district court to compel compliance, using the contempt powers of the district court as a potential sanction for non-compliance. §9606(a). Second, the EPA may bring an action in federal district court seeking to impose fines of up to $25,000 for each day that the party fails to comply with the order. §9606(b)(1). Third, the EPA may initiate cleanup of the facility itself under §9604, and the party responsible for the pollution is potentially liable for the response and cleanup costs, plus treble damages. §9607(c)(3).

Here, the EPA has not sought to enforce the Order through any of the mechanisms described above. Rather, Pakootas initiated this suit in federal district court under §9659, the citizen suit provision of CERCLA. Section 9659(a)(1) provides a cause of action for any person to commence a civil action "against any person ... who is alleged to be in violation of any standard, regulation, condition, requirement, or order which has become effective pursuant to this chapter." Section 9659(c) gives the district court the power "to order such action as may be necessary to correct the violation, and to impose any civil penalty provided for the violation." Further, §9613(h)(2), the "timing of review" provision of CERCLA, grants federal courts jurisdiction to review an order issued under §9606(a) when a party seeks to enforce the order ...

Teck's primary argument is that, in absence of a clear statement by Congress that it intended CERCLA to apply extraterritorially, the presumption against extraterritorial application of United States law precludes CERCLA from applying to Teck in Canada.... So a threshold question is whether this case involves a domestic or extraterritorial application of CERCLA.

Unlike other environmental laws such as the Clean Air Act, 42 U.S.C. §§7401–7671q, Clean Water Act, 33 U.S.C. §§1251–1387, and Resource Conservation and Recovery Act (RCRA), 42 U.S.C. §§6901–6992k, CERCLA is not a regulatory statute. Rather, CERCLA imposes liability for the cleanup of sites where there is a release or threatened release of hazardous substances into the environment. CERCLA liability attaches when three conditions are satisfied: (1) the site at which there is an actual or threatened release of hazardous substances is a "facility" under §9601(9); (2) a "release" or "threatened release" of a hazardous substance from the facility has occurred, §9607(a)(4); and (3) the party is within one of the four classes of persons subject to liability under §9607(a)....

CERCLA defines the term "facility" as, in relevant part, "any site or area where a hazardous substance has been deposited, stored, disposed of, or placed, or otherwise come to be located." § 9601(9). The Order defines the "facility" in this case as the Site, which is described as the "extent of contamination *in the United States* associated with the Upper Columbia River." The slag has "come to be located" at the Site, and the Site is thus a facility under § 9601(a).... The third element of liability under CERCLA is that the party must be a "covered person" under § 9607(a). Teck argues that it is not a covered person under § 9607(a)(3) because it has not "arranged for disposal" of a hazardous substance "by any other party or entity" as required by § 9607(a)(3), because Teck disposed of the slag itself, and without the aid of another. Alternatively, Teck argues that if it is an arranger under § 9607(a)(3), then basing CERCLA liability on Teck arranging for disposal of slag in Canada is an impermissible extraterritorial application of CERCLA.

Assuming that Teck is an arranger under § 9607(a)(3), we consider whether the fact that the act of arranging in Canada for disposal of the slag makes this an extraterritorial application of CERCLA. Teck argues that because it arranged in Canada for disposal, that is, the act of arranging took place in Canada even though the hazardous substances came to be located in the United States, it cannot be held liable under CERCLA without applying CERCLA extraterritorially....

A party that "arranged for disposal" of a hazardous substance under § 9607(a)(3) does not become liable under CERCLA until there is an actual or threatened release of that substance into the environment. Arranging for disposal of hazardous substances, in itself, is neither regulated under nor prohibited by CERCLA. Further, disposal activities that were legal when conducted can nevertheless give rise to liability under § 9607(a)(3) if there is an actual or threatened release of such hazardous substances into the environment....

The location where a party arranged for disposal or disposed of hazardous substances is not controlling for purposes of assessing whether CERCLA is being applied extraterritorially, because CERCLA imposes liability for releases or threatened releases of hazardous substances, and not merely for disposal or arranging for disposal of such substances.[18] Because the actual or threatened release of hazardous substances triggers CERCLA liability, and because the actual or threatened release here, the leaching of hazardous substances from slag that settled at the Site, took place in the United States, this case involves a domestic application of CERCLA.

We hold that applying CERCLA here to the release of hazardous substances at the Site is a domestic, rather than an extraterritorial application of CERCLA, even though the original source of the hazardous substances is located in a foreign country....

Notes and Questions

1. Do you agree with the outcome of the *Pakootas* case? Should the Canadian smelter have to comply with U.S. law? Would your response be different if CERCLA were less draconian, *i.e.*, if it did not impose strict and retroactive liability for a cleanup that will cost millions of dollars?

2. While the appeal in this case was pending, the U.S. EPA and Teck Cominco entered into a settlement agreement that obligated the company to perform the remediation at the

---

18. CERCLA is a strict liability statute, and liability can attach even when the generator has no idea how its waste came to be located at the facility from which there was a release.

Upper Columbia River site. If Teck Cominco fulfilled its obligations under the agreement, the EPA agreed not to sue it for non-compliance with the unilateral administrative cleanup order that had been issued under CERCLA. In return, Teck Cominco consented to jurisdiction in federal district court in the event that EPA brought a suit to enforce the settlement agreement and seek penalties for noncompliance. Upon execution of the agreement, EPA withdrew its administrative order, and the *Pakootas* case was dismissed for lack of jurisdiction. Pakootas v. Teck Cominco Metals, Ltd., 646 F.3d 1214 (9th Cir. 2011). The saga continues, however, as the Colville Tribe and the State of Washington press to recover response costs and natural resource damages resulting from the dumping of smelter slag and effluent into the river. Pakootas v. Teck Cominco, No. CV-04-256-LRS, 2012 WL 1133656 (E.D. Wash. Apr. 4, 2012). For historic details, see Austen Parrish, *Trail Smelter Deja Vu: Extraterritoriality, International Environmental Law, and the Search for Solutions to Canadian-U.S. Transboundary Water Pollution Disputes*, 85 B.U. L. Rev. 363 (2005).

3. Why didn't the Tribes and the EPA sue Teck Cominco in a Canadian court using Canadian law? Canada embraces the "polluter pay" principle, just as CERCLA does in the United States. *See* Imperial Oil Ltd. v. Quebec (Minister of the Environment), [2003] 2 S.C.R. 624 at para. 23 (noting that the principle is "found in almost all federal and provincial environmental legislation"); Stefanie Sommers, *The Brownfield Problem: Liability For Lenders, Owners, and Developers in Canada and the United States,* 19 Colo. J. Int'l Envtl. L. & Pol'y 259 (2008) (comparing the application of the principle in the U.S. and Canada, and assessing enforcement problems in Canada).

4. With respect to Canadian water pollution laws, *see* Canadian Environmental Protection Act §§ 176, 179, *supra*. At the provincial level, the B.C. Water Act, [RSBC 1996] Chapter 483, adopted in 1909, is the principal law for managing the quantification and use of provincial water resources. It governs licensing, diversions, and use of water. The 2004 amendments to the Water Act "provided B.C. with its first mechanisms to protect groundwater and a process for watershed management planning to address or prevent conflicts among or between water users and the environment, and the protection of water quality." Ministry of Environment, *Water Act Modernization*, http://www.livingwatersmart. ca/water-act/framework.html (visited July 25, 2012). These amendments were "driven primarily by growing concerns for the protection of drinking water quality and the Walkerton drinking water tragedy in 2000 [in Ontario] when seven people died." *Id.*

Water quality in British Columbia is also addressed by the 1997 Fish Protection Act, [SBC 1997] Chapter 21, which adopted measures to strengthen the protection of fish and fish habitat from water allocations. The province also adopted an Environmental Management Act (EMA) in 2004, [SBC 2003] Ch. 53. According to the Ministry of Environment:

> EMA now provides a more flexible authorization framework, increases enforcement options and uses modern environmental management tools to protect human health and the quality of water, land and air in British Columbia. EMA also enables the use of administrative penalties, informational orders and economic instruments to assist in achieving compliance.

Ministry of Environment, *Environmental Management Act*, http://www.env.gov.bc.ca/epd/ main/ema.htm (accessed July 26, 2012). The Ministry describes the major changes brought about by the EMA:

> Under the old Waste Management Act ... *all* introductions of waste to the environment, whether from a pulp mill or a car wash, required some form of authorization such as a permit or approval. Under section 6(2) and 6(3) of EMA, only introductions of waste from "prescribed" industries, trades, businesses, op-

erations and activities require authorization. Industries, trades, businesses, operations and activities are "prescribed" in the Waste Discharge Regulation. If an industry, trade, business, activity or operation is not "prescribed" by the regulation, it does not require an authorization to introduce waste into the environment; however, the discharge must not cause pollution (EMA section 6(4)).

> The Waste Discharge Regulation (WDR) ... "prescribes" industries, trades, businesses, activities and operations for the purposes of EMA section 6(2) and 6(3).... Industries, trades, businesses, activities and operations listed on Schedule 1 require an authorization, which could be in the form of a permit, an approval, a regulation, an operational certificate, an order or a waste management plan, to introduce waste into the environment. Introductions of waste into the environment from industries, trades, businesses, activities and operations listed on Schedule 2 are eligible to be authorized by a minister's code of practice.

Id. (emphasis added). Arguably, the EMA looks like deregulation, at least to some extent. *See* West Coast Environmental Law, *Environmental Deregulation*, at http:// www.wcel.org/our-work/environmental-deregulation ("In 2001 the B.C. provincial government set a target of eliminating one third of all regulations. Between 2001 and 2005 the government repealed, amended or replaced a wide range of environmental statutes, as well as cutting funding to environment-related ministries.") (accessed July 25, 2012). How likely is the EMA, along with the other B.C. and Canadian statutes described above, to solve problems like those arising at Teck Cominco?

5. U.S. companies have been sued in Canadian courts for alleged violations of Canadian law, too. In *Waterkeeper Alliance v. DTE Energy,* an environmental group sued DTE Energy in Ontario, alleging that emissions from DTE's coal-fired power plant in Michigan were damaging fisheries in the St. Clair River in violation of the Canadian Fisheries Act. The Ontario Superior Court set a 2009 trial date, but Waterkeeper withdrew its complaint when the State of Michigan announced a new rule that requires Michigan power plants to reduce mercury emission by 90% by 2015, and DTE Energy began to make significant efforts at reducing its mercury emissions. Krystyn Tully, *Case Closed: Edwards v. DTE Energy*, Lake Ontario Waterkeeper Weekly, Apr. 13, 2010. For details on the U.S. EPA's efforts to control mercury emissions from power plants, see Section A.7, *supra* (nonpoint source pollution).

Chapter V

Biological Diversity and Land Preservation

Biological diversity—the "evolutionary variation of life, built up over the several billion years of the planet's existence, at the genetic, species, and ecosystem levels"—sustains all life processes on the planet. William J. Snape, III, *Joining the Convention on Biological Diversity: A Legal and Scientific Overview of Why the United States Must Wake Up*, 10 Sustainable Dev. L. & Pol'y 6, 7–8 (2010). In addition to biodiversity, ecosystem services provided by intact, functioning ecological systems include:

Proliferation of game species and beneficial non-game species

Air purification

Ground and surface water purification

Groundwater recharge

Flood control

Food supply (through soil fertility, pollination and other ecological functions)

Pharmaceuticals

Recreational benefits

Cultural and aesthetic features

See James Salzman, Barton H. Thompson, Jr. and Gretchen C. Daily, *Protecting Ecosystem Services: Science, Economics, and Law*, 20 Stan. Envtl. L.J. 309 (2001); Sandra Postel and Brian Richter, Rivers for Life 6–8, 170 (2003). Economists estimate that humans derive trillions of dollars worth of ecosystem services from viable populations of plant and animal species, clean water and air, productive soils, functioning wetlands, and recreational opportunities. Robert Costanza et al., *The Value of the World's Ecosystem Services and Natural Capital,* Nature, May 15, 1997, at 253–260; The Economics of Ecosystems and Biodiversity (TEEB), *Mainstreaming the Economics of Nature* (2010), available at www.teeb.web.org.

The Millennium Ecosystem Assessment of 2005, conducted by 1,300 experts from 95 countries, concluded that nearly sixty percent of the ecosystem services that support human and non-human life on Earth, including biological diversity, healthy fisheries, clean air and water, and climate regulation, "are being degraded or used unsustainably." Millennium Ecosystem Assessment Synthesis Report 20 (2005), http://matagalatlante.org/nobre/down/MAgeneralSynthesisFinalDraft.pdf. "We are losing wild species ... faster than in any geologic period since the dinosaur die-off 65 million years ago." *Id.*, *Findings*, available at www.millenniumassessment.org/documents/document.359.aspx.ppt. The Assessment warns that the harmful consequences of ecological degradation could grow "significantly worse in the next 50 years." *Id.* at 16.

The problems that stem from ecological degradation and the loss of biodiversity span political and social boundaries: "Any progress achieved in addressing the goals of poverty and hunger eradication, improved health, and environmental protection is unlikely to be sustained if most of the ecosystem services on which humanity relies continue to be degraded." *Id.* at 17. Famine is one of the most immediate and disastrous consequences of biodiversity loss: farmers lose their pastures and croplands to invasive species; fruit and nut orchards lose their harvests due to a lack of wild pollinators; and game species and fisheries collapse from overharvesting or pollution. These forces lead not only to death and disease; they also contribute to unrest and political instability. According to military experts, "anthropogenically generated changes to the Earth's climate and natural environment pose a 'serious threat to America's national security.'" John T. Ackerman (Air Force), *Climate Change. National Security, and the Quadrennial Defense Review: Avoiding the Perfect Storm*, Strategic Studies Quarterly 56 (2008).

In the past, efforts to conserve biodiversity focused almost exclusively on protecting individual species, without much thought given to the big picture—ecosystems—or, conversely, anything more discrete than species, such as population or genetic diversity. Not only that, early conservation efforts were aimed at economically valuable game species, rather than insects, amphibians, or other important keystone or indicator species. It was not until the 1970s that conservation efforts began to encompass a broader array of biodiversity concerns.

The Convention on Biological Diversity provides a definition of "biodiversity":

> [T]he variability among living organisms from all sources including, inter alia, terrestrial, marine and other aquatic ecosystems and the ecological complexes of which they are part; this includes diversity within species, between species and of ecosystems.

Convention on Biological Diversity, adopted by the UN Conference on Environment and Development, June 5, 1992, 31 I.L.M. 818, 823. The Convention was adopted at the Earth Summit in Rio de Janeiro in 1992. It entered into force in 1993. As of 2012, there are 193 parties. The Convention has three primary goals:

- Conservation of biological diversity;
- Sustainable use of its components; and
- Fair and equitable sharing of benefits arising from genetic resources.

For the first time in international law, the conservation of biological diversity has been recognized as "a common concern of humankind." *Id. Preamble.* The Convention covers all ecosystems, species, and genetic resources. It links conservation efforts to the economic goal of using biological resources sustainably, and employs the precautionary principle: where there is a threat of significant reduction or loss of biological diversity, lack of full scientific certainty should not be used as a reason for postponing measures to avoid or minimize such a threat.

The Convention enjoys wide support in both developed countries (including New Zealand, England, and Canada) and less developed countries (India, Belarus, Zambia, and Chad, to name a few). Under President Bill Clinton, the U.S. signed the Convention, but it has not yet ratified it, citing concerns about inadequate protection of intellectual property rights and an unsatisfactory financial assistance mechanism. It "languishes in the bowels of government," awaiting a more friendly political climate. How the Convention on Biodiversity was Defeated (1994), http://www.sovereignty.net/p/land/biotreatystop. htm. International observers claim that the U.S.'s failure to ratify this convention (along with the Kyoto Convention on Climate Change and several other important international agreements) has obliterated its reputation as a conservation leader. *See* Center for Progressive Reform, Reclaiming Global Environmental Leadership: Why the U.S. Should Ratify Ten Pending Treaties 2 (2012). U.S. officials counter that current domestic law (particularly the Endangered Species Act (ESA), covered below in section A.2) is sufficient to meet the obligations of the Convention, so ratification is not a significant issue.

The remainder of this chapter delves into habitat protection laws and species-specific laws, beginning with the United States and working its way through Canada, New Zealand, India, and England. A case study on a controversial endangered species—the Northern Spotted Owl—is included in Section B.3 (Canada), and is referenced throughout the rest of the chapter.

A. United States

In 1970, a concern for ecological integrity emerged as a theme in U.S. natural resources law when the National Environmental Policy Act (NEPA) was enacted. 42 U.S.C. §§ 4321–4361. In NEPA, Congress declared "a national policy which will encourage productive and enjoyable harmony between man and his environment." *Id.* § 4321. As a matter of policy, NEPA strives "to promote efforts which prevent or eliminate damage to the environment and biosphere and stimulate the health and welfare of man [and] to enrich the understanding of the ecological systems and natural resources important to the Nation …" *Id.* NEPA's policy statement is a lofty one, but its mandate is limited in that it is strictly procedural, as described in detail in Chapter 3.A of this book. The statutes described in this section build on the policy of eliminating damage to the biosphere and enriching our understanding of ecological systems and natural resources with substantive provisions that protect certain types of federal lands and federally listed species. Several of the pertinent conservation statutes pre-date NEPA by several decades, including the National Park Service Organic Act of 1916 and the Migratory Bird Treaty Act of 1918; others, such as the Endangered Species Act (ESA) of 1973 and the Wildlife Refuge System Improvement Act of 1997 joined the fray later.

1. Wildlife Refuges, Wilderness, and Parks

Conservationists generally agree that "ecosystem management" is desirable for maintaining biodiversity and ecological integrity. Reed F. Noss, *Some Principles of Conservation Biology, as They Apply to Environmental Law*, 69 Chi.-Kent L. Rev. 893, 894 (1994). "Ecosystem management emphasizes the ecological health and integrity of interacting components of ecosystems, including their resiliency, stability, elasticity, and persistence." Jan Laitos, Sandra Zellmer, & Mary Wood, Natural Resources Law 70 (West 2d ed. 2012).

Intact ecosystems within federal public lands are especially important for providing species habitat and other ecosystem services. Three categories of public lands are covered in this section. The first, wildlife refuges, are set aside and managed specifically for wildlife-centric purposes, while the other two—wilderness areas and national parks—are generally managed for conservation purposes but also for recreational pursuits.

The National Wildlife Refuge System — The National Wildlife Refuge System is known as "the world's largest biodiversity conservation network." Robert L. Fischman and Robert S. Adamcik, *Beyond Trust Species: The Conservation Potential of the National Wildlife Refuge System in the Wake of Climate Change*, 51 Nat. Res. J. 1, 2 (2011).

> A sprawling, ninety-six million acre network of reserves and easements dedicated to nature protection, the National Wildlife Refuge System is the nation's most valuable asset for ecological conservation. Though the Interior Department's other dominant-use public land system, the National Park System, is much better known, the National Wildlife Refuge System is larger and more diverse. Management of the individual units of the Refuge System, especially the 545 named national wildlife refuges, will determine how well the United States conserves its biological heritage and contributes to international efforts promoting sustainable development....
>
> The 1997 Refuge Improvement Act ... sets out a systemic conservation mission, defines dominant uses, requires comprehensive planning for each refuge, establishes substantive management criteria, and specifies avenues for public participation. One of the most noteworthy aspects of the 1997 law is the relatively rich detail of the substantive management criteria, compared to previous federal organic statutes.

Robert L. Fischman, *From Words to Action: The Impact and Legal Status of the 2006 National Wildlife Refuge System Management Policies*, 26 Stan. Env. L. J. 77, 78–79 (2007), citing National Wildlife Refuge System Improvement Act of 1997, Pub. L. No. 105-57, 111 Stat. 1252 (codified as amended at 16 U.S.C. §§ 668dd, 668ee).

The mission of the refuge system is to "administer a national network of lands and waters for the conservation, management, and where appropriate, restoration of" animals, plants, and habitat. 16 U.S.C. § 668dd(a)(2). The terms "conservation and management" are synonymous, within the purview of the Refuge Act, and they mean "to sustain and, where appropriate, restore and enhance, healthy populations" of animals and plants utilizing methods associated with "modern scientific resource programs." 16 U.S.C. § 668ee.

These goals are fleshed out in the 2006 Goals and Refuge Purposes Policy as follows:

A. Conserve a diversity of fish, wildlife, and plants and their habitats, including species that are endangered or threatened with becoming endangered.

B. Develop and maintain a network of habitats for migratory birds, anadromous and interjurisdictional fish, and marine mammal populations that is strategically distributed and carefully managed to meet important life history needs of these species across their ranges.

C. Conserve those ecosystems, plant communities, wetlands of national or international significance, and landscapes and seascapes that are unique, rare, declining, or underrepresented in existing protection efforts.

D. Provide and enhance opportunities to participate in compatible wildlife-dependent recreation (hunting, fishing, wildlife observation and photography, and environmental education and interpretation).

E. Foster understanding and instill appreciation of the diversity and interconnectedness of fish, wildlife, and plants and their habitats.

U.S. Fish & Wildlife Serv., Service Manual pt. 601 § 1.8 (2006), http://www.fws.gov/policy/manuals/. The first three goals (A–C) emphasize ecological protection and biodiversity conservation, and they are given the highest priority. Fischman, *supra,* at 89.

The goals are to be accomplished through comprehensive planning and compatibility determinations. Compatible uses are those that do not "materially interfere with or detract from" refuge purposes or the system mission. 16 U.S.C. § 668ee(1).

In administering the System, the Secretary of Interior, through the FWS, is directed to:

(A) provide for the conservation of fish, wildlife, and plants, and their habitats within the System;

(B) ensure that the *biological integrity, diversity, and environmental health of the System are maintained* for the benefit of present and future generations of Americans;

(C) plan and direct the continued growth of the System in a manner that is best designed to accomplish the mission of the System, to contribute to the *conservation of the ecosystems* of the United States, to complement efforts of States and other Federal agencies to *conserve fish and wildlife and their habitats* ... [and]

(H) recognize compatible wildlife-dependent recreational uses as the priority general public uses of the System through which the American public can develop an appreciation for fish and wildlife....

16 U.S.C. § 668dd(a)(4) (emphasis added).

The FWS screens proposals for refuge use to determine whether they are compatible and appropriate. Four categories of activities do not need to be screened for appropriateness, however: 1) uses that are reserved or mandates, such as pre-existing property rights or mineral rights; 2) refuge management activities designed to fulfill a refuge purpose or the mission of the overall system mission according to "sound professional judgment"; 3) compatible wildlife-dependent recreation, such as hunting, fishing, wildlife observation and photography, and environmental education, 16 U.S.C. § 668ee(2); and 4) compatible "take" of fish and wildlife under state law. *See* Fish & Wildlife Manual, pt. 603 §§ 1.2, 1.3; Fischman, *supra,* at 96–101.

The 1997 Act is a major improvement over past refuge management directives. The saga of Kesterson National Wildlife Refuge illustrates how the system had become broken prior to enactment:

Kesterson National Wildlife Refuge in California was established in 1968 as part of a federal water project. However, by the 1980s, Kesterson National Wildlife Refuge was in crisis. Fed solely by agricultural runoff, natural selenium in the region's soils leached and concentrated into the refuge's marshes, particularly in the evaporation ponds (about 1200 acres of the refuge's 5900 acres). By 1981, all the fish on the refuge, except for the mosquito fish, were gone. Samples of the mosquito fish revealed selenium levels 100 times greater than those found in samples from a control area not receiving agricultural runoff. Between 1983 and 1985, 1000 waterfowl were observed dead. In 1983, a study of 350 waterfowl nests found that 20 percent of the nests contained at least one deformed embryo, and 40 percent of the nests contained at least one dead embryo. In 1984, the U.S. Fish and Wildlife Service (FWS or Service) closed the evaporation ponds to public use and initiated a program to harass migratory birds to prevent them from resting and feeding on the refuge by using air guns, boats, and vehicles to keep the birds from landing.... In the end, agricultural drainage was diverted from the refuge and a clean-up plan was settled upon....

At the same time Kesterson was reeling from selenium contamination, the Refuge System was facing another crisis — incompatible uses. During the 1970s and 1980s, concerns arose over oil drilling, military overflights, motorized vehicle use, grazing, logging, and other uses that were incompatible with the stated refuge purposes. These incompatible uses resulted in congressional hearings, a General Accounting Office report, and an FWS investigation [and] ultimately compelled Congress to pass the 1997 National Wildlife Refuge System Improvement Act (Improvement Act)....

The debate over the Kesterson problem ... raised a number of questions ... perhaps most important, does the Interior Department have an affirmative duty to sustain wildlife at a national wildlife refuge ... ?

Noah P. Matson, *Maintaining the Biological Integrity, Diversity, and Environmental Health of the National Wildlife Refuge System*, 4 Nat. Resources J. 1137, 1138–40 (2004). The 1997 Act seems to respond: "yes."

Although progress has been made since the 1980s, challenges remain.

In some respects the refuges face challenges similar to other public lands. For instance, increased recreation vexes refuge managers seeking to promote public use but not invite its adverse consequences. National defense and energy policy establish priorities that refuges struggle to accommodate within their conservation mission. And, years of under-funding have created terrible maintenance backlogs and unfulfilled promises of improvement.

In other respects, though, the refuges face more difficult problems. For instance, more than other public lands, the refuges in the contiguous states seek to protect and enhance ecosystems degraded almost beyond recognition by human activities including farming and dam building. The intensive management that results from this legacy means that disking, mowing, burning, and flooding remain common practices on refuges. Though many desirable species thrive on these management activities, the level of environmental disturbance can be great. Refuges contain relatively lower elevation areas, higher soil productivity, and more wetlands than the other federal lands. These attributes, along with its broad geographic distribution, account for the high biodiversity of the refuge system. But refuges also are in greater proximity to anthropogenic lands (urban, built-up, and agricultural) than other federal lands. All this makes refuges particularly susceptible to downstream pollutants and other external threats. Further, the system's relatively low national profile makes it less able to compete for monies in this period of austere federal natural resources budgets. The refuges receive fewer budget dollars for resource management and operations than the other federal public land systems, and nearly 200 refuges are completely unstaffed.

Fischman, *supra*, at 81–82.

National Wilderness Areas — In 1964, when the Wilderness Act was passed, Congress was concerned about the anthropocentric virtues of wild lands rather than biodiversity. There were two driving forces behind enactment: "the public's desire to preserve lands for growing recreational demands and the sponsors' desire to curtail agency discretion to create or dismantle administrative preserves." Sandra Zellmer, *A Preservation Paradox: Political Prestidigitation and an Enduring Resource of Wildness*, 34 Envtl. L. 1015, 1040 (2004).

The Wilderness Act defines wilderness in terms of its undeveloped character, remoteness, and size. More specifically, wilderness is "an area where the earth and its community of life are untrammeled by man, where man himself is a visitor who does not remain." 16 U.S.C. § 1131(c). The Act's selection criteria reflect this definition by delineating a list of qualifying factors:

> [U]nderdeveloped Federal land retaining its primeval character and influence, without permanent improvements or human habitation, … which (1) generally appears to have been affected primarily by the forces of nature, with the imprint of man's work substantially unnoticeable; (2) has outstanding opportunities for solitude or a primitive and unconfined type of recreation; (3) has at least 5,000 acres of land or is of sufficient size as to make practicable its preservation and use in an unimpaired condition; and (4) may also contain ecological, geological, or other features of scientific, educational, scenic, or historical value.

Id. Since 1964, Congress has designated over 650 wilderness areas, the most protected of all federal lands.

> The wilderness system envelops 106 million acres of land in forty-four states. For the sake of perspective, total federal public land amounts to over 600 million acres, which is one-third of the nation's total land base. Nearly 35 million acres, about 30 percent of the wilderness system, are within National Forests. The BLM manages only around six percent of the system, while the National Park Service manages over 41 percent and the FWS manages about 23 percent. Although this sounds like a vast preservation system, in actuality, less than three percent of the land base in the contiguous 48 states has been given official wilderness status.

Zellmer, *Preservation Paradox, supra,* 1039–1040.

The Wilderness Act prohibits activities that would detract from the wildness of wilderness areas. Specifically, the Act forbids permanent and most temporary roads, as well as all commercial activities. 16 U.S.C. § 1133(c). *See* Wilderness Soc'y v. U.S. Fish & Wildlife Serv., 353 F.3d 1051, 1069–70 (9th Cir. 2003) (en banc), *as amended in part on reh'g en banc,* 360 F.3d 1374, 1374 (9th Cir. 2004) (enjoining salmon enhancement project introducing hatchery-reared salmon fry into lake within wilderness as an unlawful commercial enterprise).

The Act also precludes motor vehicles, motorized equipment, mechanical transport, aircraft landings, structures, and installations. 16 U.S.C. § 1133(c). In addition, the Act directs that wilderness areas be "protected and managed so as to preserve its natural conditions." 16 U.S.C. § 1131(c).

Although "the wilderness system generally protects scenic areas of 'rock and ice' rather than wetlands, grasslands and other more biologically productive but less visually spectacular areas," *id.* at 1042, by remaining roadless and undeveloped, wilderness areas advance biodiversity objectives.

Sandra Zellmer, Wilderness, Water, and Climate Change
42 Envtl. L. 313, 319–320 (2012)

[W]ilderness areas provide critical ecosystem services such as clean water. Healthy watersheds help maintain viable fish and wildlife populations.

Wilderness areas also provide undisturbed migration corridors and large blocks of contiguous habitat for climate-threatened species. Outside of wilderness and other roadless lands, roads—both paved and unpaved—have significant adverse effects on wildlife. Ecologists believe that "no single feature of human-dominated landscapes is more threatening to biodiversity (aquatic and terrestrial) than roads." Roads criss-cross natural boundaries, altering pre-existing patterns of movement and communication within and between ecosystems. The abundance and diversity of native species is diminished near roads, while opportunistic invasive species thrive in and near the clearings created by roads. Roads provide greater access for humans, contributing to direct death or injury to wildlife species from roadkill and hunting, as well as indirect effects due to air and water pollution and noise. According to biologist Reed Noss, "Experience on every continent has shown that only in strictly protected [roadless] areas are the full fauna and flora of a region likely to persist for a long time." ...

High altitude wilderness areas also provide essential elevation gradients in landscapes that have become increasingly fragmented by roads and other development. Increasing connectivity by protecting wildlife corridors, reducing human-made barriers such as roads and fences, and increasing the number of reserves, especially large protected areas connected by smaller reserves, are among the top climate change adaptation priorities recommended in the scientific literature.

* * *

A Ninth Circuit Court of Appeals case demonstrates the differences between wilderness areas and national wildlife refuges. Wilderness Watch, Inc. v. U.S. Fish & Wildlife Serv., 629 F.3d 1024 (9th Cir.2010), involved a challenge to a decision of the U.S. Fish and Wildlife Service (FWS) and the Arizona Game and Fish Department to build two tanks in the Kofa Wilderness in the Sonoran Desert.

> The Kofa Wilderness makes up 80% of the Kofa Wildlife Refuge, which was created by an executive order in 1939. The executive order explicitly declared that the Refuge was being set aside for "conservation and development of natural wildlife resources," with an understood intent to preserve desert bighorn sheep (*Ovis canadensis nelsoni*).
>
> The area is extremely arid, averaging only around seven inches of rain a year. During a period of extended drought, the FWS, in partnership with the State of Arizona, constructed water tanks and pipes in the wilderness to augment water supplies for bighorn sheep.
>
> Wilderness Watch successfully sued, claiming that, while the facilities might be useful to the conservation of sheep threatened by drought and high temperatures, they were "installations" that unlawfully trammeled the wilderness, contrary to the explicit terms of the Act. The Kofa water tanks might be perfectly acceptable to achieve biodiversity conservation purposes in the nonwilderness portion of the wildlife refuge, but that does not mean they are acceptable in wilderness areas.

Zellmer, *Wilderness, supra*, at 324–25. *See* National Wildlife Refuge System Improvement Act of 1997, 16 U.S.C. §668dd(a)(4)(A) (instructing the Secretary to "provide for the conservation of fish, wildlife, and plants, and their habitats within the System").

The National Park System—The National Park Service Organic Act of 1916 requires the Park Service to "conserve the scenery and the natural and historic objects and the wild life therein" and also "to provide for the enjoyment of the same in such manner and by such means as will leave them unimpaired for the enjoyment of future generations." 16 U.S.C. § 1. Professor Keiter describes the tension wrought by this dual mandate:

In the beginning, Yellowstone, Yosemite, the Grand Canyon, and the other early parks were viewed as remote and wild places, strongholds of the nation's wilderness heritage where wild nature held sway. The parks were regularly portrayed as wilderness settings, and there was little human presence beyond the military caretakers, some nearby Native American reservations, and a few other hardy souls. The 1872 Yellowstone legislation and the 1890 Sequoia legislation called for retaining each park's resources and features "in their natural condition," while the 1910 Glacier legislation provided for "preservation of the park in a state of nature." The 1916 Organic Act and the 1918 Lane Letter to the new Park Service endorsed a similar view by instructing that the national parks were to be managed and maintained in an unimpaired condition. But this notion of the national parks as a wilderness setting was belied from the outset by the competing notion that the new parks were "pleasuring grounds" and were "set apart for the use, observation, health, and pleasure of the people." Once roads, hotels, and other structures were built in the parks to accommodate visitors, it was apparent that they were not merely primitive, undeveloped settings....

From the outset, the Organic Act instructed the Park Service to promote "public enjoyment" of the new national parks, and that mandate has spurred the view of the national park as a playground. Since then, the Park Service has embraced recreation as a primary activity in the national parks, though it has gradually eliminated some inappropriate recreational facilities—including ski areas, tennis courts, and swimming pools—and imposed management limitations on other activities to address overcrowding and environmental degradation concerns. It has also sought to distinguish between different types of recreational activities, generally favoring contemplative and physically challenging activities over motorized or less-active forms of recreation. In doing so, the Park Service has interpreted the Organic Act's non-impairment mandate to prioritize resource protection over recreational access, thus effectively subordinating the park's role as a playground to environmental concerns. When confronted with challenges to these recreational limitations, federal courts have consistently endorsed the Park Service's "resource protection-first" interpretation of its legal responsibilities. Nonetheless, recreational controversies—such as the battle over snowmobiling in Yellowstone and mountain biking on national park trails—continue to ripple across the national park system.

Robert B. Keiter, *The National Park System: Visions For Tomorrow*, 50 Natural Resources J. 71, 74, 87–88 (2010). With regard to biodiversity, Keiter explains:

Both the original Yellowstone legislation and the 1916 Organic Act expressly provide for conserving park wildlife, so it is not surprising that national parks have long been viewed as wildlife reserves. Not only did Yellowstone, with assistance from its early military caretakers, serve as the last remaining refuge for the bison, but the park also supplied elk to several states, enabling them to reestablish decimated big game populations.

Id. at 89–90.

The National Park System has grown to 397 units since its founding. It includes:

84,000,000 acres of land
4,502,644 acres of oceans, lakes, and reservoirs
85,049 miles of perennial rivers and streams
43,162 miles of shoreline
400 endangered species

National Park System By The Numbers (Apr. 11, 2012), http://www.nps.gov/aboutus/
index.htm. It experiences 275 million visitors per year. *Id.*

Individual park units often have their own management mandates that encompass
biodiversity protection. In managing Yellowstone National Park, for example, the Secretary of the Interior is required to issue "such rules and regulations as he may deem necessary and proper for the management and care of the park and for the protection of the
property therein, especially for the preservation from injury or spoliation of all timber ...
or wonderful objects within said park; and for the protection of the animals and birds in
the park, from capture or destruction, or to prevent their being frightened or driven from
the park; and he shall make rules and regulations governing the taking of fish from the
streams or lakes in the park." 16 U.S.C. § 26. In the Everglades, the Park Service is directed "to maintain the natural abundance, diversity, and ecological integrity of native
plants and animals, as well as the behavior of native animals, as a part of their ecosystem."
Id. § 410r-7(b).

Violations of these directives, or of the Park Service Organic Act of 1916, will be enjoined. *Compare* Fund for Animals v. Norton, 294 F. Supp. 2d 92 (D.D.C. 2003) (finding
that the Park Service's adoption of final rule that allowed 950 snowmobiles to enter Yellowstone and Teton parks each day despite negative environmental impacts on resources
and wildlife was arbitrary and capricious and in violation of law), *with* Bicycle Trails
Council of Marin v. Babbitt, 82 F.3d 1445 (9th Cir. 1996) (upholding Service's regulation that prohibited bicycle use of off-road areas in order to protect park resources), *and*
Michigan United Conservation Clubs v. Lujan, 949 F.2d 202 (6th Cir. 1991) (upholding
Service's regulation prohibiting trapping in two national lakeshores in order to protect
park resources). However, when the Park Service makes specific findings, supported by
a complete administrative record, regarding the proper way to manage wildlife resources
in a park, courts tend to uphold those determinations, even if it involves culling herds to
protect park resources. In Western Watersheds Project v. Salazar, 766 F.Supp.2d 1095 (D.
Mont. 2011), the court held that the Service's Interagency Bison Management Plan did
not contravene the Yellowstone Enabling Act because the Service was charged by statute
to determine how best to cull bison herd within the park to achieve optimal results for
long-term herd demographics, in light of bison overpopulation and the risk of brucellosis
transmission from bison to cattle outside park. Similarly, in Davis v. Latschar, 83 F.Supp.
2d 1 (D.D.C. 1998), the court upheld the Service's decision that the overpopulation of
deer was detrimental to the purposes of Gettysburg National Military Park and that over-
browsing by deer depleted seedlings was needed to maintain the park's appearance, and
thus that a controlled harvest of deer in historic woodlots and cropfields at the park was
justified under the Park Service Organic Act.

Professor Keiter provides a prognosis and recommendations for future ecosystem integrity in the National Park System:

> The principles of modern ecology have replaced static conceptions of the na-
> tional parks as merely a wildlife reserve or wilderness enclave with the idea that
> national parks serve as the vital core of larger ecosystems essential to sustain eco-
> logical processes and biodiversity conservation efforts. Scientific studies reveal species
> loss in the national parks during the past century, primarily because the pro-
> tected park lands were insufficient to meet habitat and related life-sustaining
> needs. Other studies document the adverse impact that development and other
> activities on adjacent public and private lands have on the national parks, cre-
> ating external threats that could destabilize park wildlife populations and criti-
> cal ecosystem services, such as clean water and flood control.

To address these external problems, scientists and conservation organizations advocate treating national parks as critical parts of larger ecosystems. They have promoted the "greater ecosystem" concept at Yellowstone, Glacier, and elsewhere, as well as related ecosystem management concepts designed to promote coordination between the Park Service and its neighbors. For its part, the Park Service's Management Policies document notes that "ecological processes cross park boundaries" and instructs park managers to engage in "cooperative conservation beyond park boundaries," in order to "creat[e] seamless networks of parks" and "establish corridors that link together ... open spaces such as those found in parks, other protected areas, and compatibly managed private lands." The ultimate goal is to ensure connectivity across the landscape to allow migration and ecological processes to occur unimpeded. Although some have criticized this view of the national parks as vital ecosystem cores as an ill-advised expansionist effort or land grab, others acknowledge the need to begin thinking and planning at the landscape scale to sustain our biological heritage.

Keiter, *supra*, at 92–93.

2. Species-Specific Legislation

Traditionally, wildlife regulations, especially fish and game laws, have come within the purview of the states. Where does the federal government get authority to intervene in wildlife issues? Several sources of power can be found in the U.S. Constitution: the Commerce Clause, U.S. Const. Art. I, §8, which gives Congress the power to regulate commerce with foreign nations and among states and Indian Tribes, and to prohibit state laws that discriminate against interstate commerce; the Treaty Clause, U.S. Const. Art. II, §2, which gives the President "the Power ... to make Treaties, provided two-thirds of the Senators present concur"; and the Property Clause, U. S. Const. Art. IV, §3, cl. 2, which establishes federal power over federal lands by stating, "Congress shall have the Power to dispose of and make all needful Rules and Regulations respecting the Territory or other Property belonging to the United States."

The Supreme Court initially addressed this issue in 1896 in Geer v. Connecticut, 161 U.S. 519 (1896), where the Court held that a state, without violating the Dormant Commerce Clause of the U.S. Constitution, could forbid the exportation of game captured or killed within its borders. Following *Geer*, states opined that *ownership* of wildlife gave the states unlimited management rights and precluded federal intervention. Gradually, the theory that states owned the wildlife within their borders weakened, and the Court was compelled to revisit the issue in Hughes v. Oklahoma, 441 U.S. 322 (1979). *Hughes* overturned *Geer* and dispelled the "legal fiction" of state ownership of wildlife, and observed that "[t]o put the claim of the State upon title is to lean upon a slender reed." *Id.* at 332, citing Missouri v. Holland, 252 U.S. 416, 434 (1920). Yet *Hughes* leaves states "ample allowance for preserving, in ways not inconsistent with the Commerce Clause, the legitimate state concerns for conservation and protection of wild animals...." *Id.* at 335. Wildlife management has become an expression of "cooperative federalism," where federal legislation, by and large, protects endangered species and other species of national interest and state legislation, by and large, regulates hunting, fishing, and species of state concern.

One of the first major federal statutes to address the protection of wildlife was the Migratory Bird Treaty Act (MBTA) of 1918. Migratory birds are included as federally protected species under the MBTA in accordance with treaties with Mexico, Canada (through British consent), Japan, and the former Soviet Union. 16 U.S.C. §§ 703–704.

Today the Act remains virtually unchanged. It provides:

> [I]t shall be unlawful at any time, by any means or in any manner, to purchase, hunt, take, capture, kill ... sell, ship, export, import ... any migratory bird, or any product, ... of any such bird or any part, nest, or egg thereof.

16 U.S.C. § 703. The MBTA adopts a strict liability standard, imposing civil and criminal penalties on those who engage in any of the prohibited acts, whether accidentally or intentionally. *See* United States v. Morgan, 311 F.3d 611 (5th Cir. 2002) (finding that a hunter's belief that leaving another hunter's birds would constitute wanton waste was not a justification for exceeding the bag limit, and was in violation of the MBTA); United States v. Van Fossan, 899 F.2d 636 (7th Cir. 1990) (conviction upheld for defendant who inadvertently killed a protected species but intended only to kill unprotected pigeons).

Does Section 703 of the Act cover otherwise lawful activities that incidentally result in degradation of the habitat of a protected bird? Several courts have said no, *see* Newton County Wildlife Ass'n v. U.S. Forest Service, 113 F.3d 110, 115 (8th Cir. 1997); City of Sausalito v. O'Neill, 386 F.3d 1186, 1225 (9th Cir. 2004), but at least one court has answered in the affirmative. *See* United States v. FMC Corp., 572 F.2d 902 (2d Cir. 1978) (finding that the Act was violated by the accidental release of toxins into a lagoon used by migratory birds). Courts that adopt a restrictive interpretation of the MBTA focus on the legislative history, which indicates that Congress was concerned primarily with hunting at the time of enactment. *See* Seattle Audubon Soc'y v. Evans, 952 F.2d 297, 302 (9th Cir. 1991). In addition, the terms listed in § 703 (*e.g.,* hunt, capture, kill) are less expansive than those of the Endangered Species Act, which includes the broader term "harm." 16 U.S.C. § 1538(a) (described below).

It was not until the 1970s that ecosystem concerns became elevated in federal law with the enactment of the Marine Mammal Protection Act (MMPA) of 1972, 16 U.S.C. §§ 1361–1407, and again in 1973 with the enactment of the Endangered Species Act (ESA), 16 U.S.C. §§ 1531–1543.

In the MMPA, Congress declared that marine mammals are resources of great aesthetic, recreational and economic significance, and that they should be protected to the greatest extent feasible commensurate with sound policies of resource management. The "primary objective" of the MMPA is "to maintain the health and stability of the marine ecosystem" and to sustain "optimum sustainable populations" (OSP) of marine mammals. 16 U.S.C. § 1361. OSP means "the number of animals which will result in the maximum productivity of the population or species, keeping in mind the optimum carrying capacity of the habitat and the health of the ecosystem of which they form a constituent element." *Id.* § 1362(9); Florida Marine Contractors v. Williams, 378 F.Supp.2d 1353 (M.D. Fla. 2005).

To accomplish its goals, the MMPA prohibits the "take" of marine mammals, with certain exceptions. "Take" is defined as "to harass, hunt, capture, collect, or kill, or attempt to harass, hunt, capture, collect, or kill any marine mammal." 16 U.S.C. § 1362(13). Harassment means any act of pursuit, torment, or annoyance which—

> (i) has the potential to injure a marine mammal ...; or

> (ii) has the potential to disturb a marine mammal ... by causing disruption of behavioral patterns, including, but not limited to, migration, breathing, nursing, breeding, feeding, or sheltering. *Id.* § 1362(18)(A).

However, the MMPA provides little substantive protection for habitat. *See id.* § 1372(a). In Native Village of Point Hope v. Minerals Management Service, 564 F.Supp.2d 1077 (D. Alaska 2008), the court held that the United States' decision to grant oil companies' applications for permits for seismic surveys in Chukchi and Beaufort Seas did not violate the MMPA, even though the agencies had not completed a programmatic environmental impact statement (EIS) for hypothetical projections of future increased seismic survey activity in Arctic Ocean, where the agencies had implemented mitigation measures and had found that, as mitigated, seismic surveys would result in only short-term changes in behavior by marine mammals.

There are several exemptions from the taking prohibition. One allows a taking if "imminently necessary in self-defense or to save the life of a person in immediate danger, and such taking is reported to the Secretary within 48 hours." 16 U.S.C. § 1371(c). The MMPA also recognizes a "Good Samaritan" exemption, which excuses a take if "imminently necessary" to avoid serious injury to a marine mammal entangled in fishing gear, so long as reasonable care is taken to ensure its safe release. *Id.* § 1371(d). Another especially complicated exemption applies to commercial fishing operations that incidentally take marine mammals while in the course of business activities. *Id.* § 1371(a)(2).

The MMPA authorizes takings by Indians, Aleuts, or Eskimos who reside in Alaska for subsistence purposes, or for the creation and sale of authentic native articles of handicrafts and clothing, so long as the take is not accomplished in a wasteful manner. *Id.*§ 1371(b). "Military readiness activities" also receive special treatment under the Act. The National Defense Authorization Act of 2004, Pub. L. No. 108-136, 117 Stat. 1392, amended the MMPA's definition of "harassment" to exclude military readiness activities that result in minor behavioral changes, added an exemption for actions "necessary for national defense," and liberalized allowances for incidental takings that occur during military readiness activities. *Id.* § 319 (codified at 16 U.S.C. §§ 1362(18), 1371). Amendments to the MBTA included a similar provision. Pub.L. 107-314 § 315(f), 116 Stat. 2509 (2002).

In comparison, the ESA has serious "teeth" and very few exceptions. It has been called "'the most comprehensive legislation for the preservation of endangered species ever enacted by any nation.'" Babbitt v. Sweet Home Chapter of Communities for a Great Or., 515 U.S. 687, 698 (1995), *quoting* TVA v. Hill, 437 U.S. 153, 180 (1978). The ESA aims to "provide a means whereby the ecosystems upon which endangered species and threatened species depend may be conserved." 16 U.S.C. § 1531(b). Conservation includes "methods and procedures which are necessary to bring any endangered ... species ... to the point at which the measures provided ... are no longer necessary." *Id.* § 1531(3). The ESA requires that threatened and endangered species be listed solely on the basis of ecological data; economic consequences play no role in the listing decision. *Id.* § 1533(b). Key provisions of the ESA are provided below.

The Endangered Species Act
16 U.S.C. §§ 1631 et seq.
§ 2 Congressional Findings and Declaration of Purpose and Policy

* * *

(b) The purposes of this chapter are to provide a means whereby the ecosystems upon which endangered species and threatened species depend may be conserved, to provide a program for conservation of such ... species, and to take such steps as may be appropriate to achieve the purposes of the [relevant] treaties and conventions....

(c) It is further declared ... that all Federal departments and agencies shall seek to conserve endangered and threatened species and shall utilize their authorities in furtherance of the purposes of this chapter....

§ 3 *Definitions*

For the purposes of this chapter—

* * *

(5)(A) The term "critical habitat" for a threatened or endangered species means—

(i) the specific areas within the geographical area occupied by the species, at the time it is listed in accordance with the provisions of [§ 4] of this title, on which are found those physical or biological features (I) essential to the conservation of the species and (II) which may require special management considerations or protection; and

(ii) specific areas outside the geographical area occupied by the species at the time it is listed in accordance with the provisions of [§ 4] of this title, upon a determination by the Secretary that such areas are essential for the conservation of the species....

(6) The term "endangered species" means any species which is in danger of extinction throughout all or a significant portion of its range other than a species of the Class Insecta determined by the Secretary to constitute a pest whose protection under the provisions of this chapter would present an overwhelming and overriding risk to man.

...

(16) The term "species" includes any subspecies of fish or wildlife or plants, and any distinct population segment of any species of vertebrate fish or wildlife which interbreeds when mature....

(19) The term "take" means to harass, harm, pursue, hunt, shoot, wound, kill, trap, capture, or collect, or to attempt to engage in any such conduct.

(20) The term "threatened species" means any species which is likely to become an endangered species within the foreseeable future throughout all or a significant portion of its range.

§ 4. *Determination of endangered species and threatened species*

(a) (1) The Secretary shall by regulation ... determine whether any species is an endangered species or a threatened species because of any of the following factors:

(A) the present or threatened destruction, modification, or curtailment of its habitat or range;

(B) overutilization for commercial, recreational, scientific, or educational purposes;

(C) disease or predation;

(D) the inadequacy of existing regulatory mechanisms; or

(E) other natural or manmade factors affecting its continued existence....

(3) The Secretary, by regulation ... and to the maximum extent prudent and determinable—

(A) shall, concurrently with making a determination under paragraph (1) that a species is an endangered species or a threatened species, designate any habitat of such species which is then considered to be critical habitat....

§ 7. Interagency cooperation

(a) Federal agency actions and consultations

(1) The Secretary shall review other programs administered by him and utilize such programs in furtherance of the purposes of this chapter. All other Federal agencies shall, in consultation with and with the assistance of the Secretary, utilize their authorities in furtherance of the purposes of this chapter by carrying out programs for the conservation of endangered species and threatened species listed pursuant to section 4 of this Act.

(2) Each Federal agency shall, in consultation with and with the assistance of the Secretary, insure that any action authorized, funded, or carried out by such agency … is not likely to jeopardize the continued existence of any endangered species or threatened species or result in the destruction or adverse modification of [critical] habitat … unless such agency has been granted an exemption for such action by the Committee pursuant to subsection (h) of this section. In fulfilling the requirements of this paragraph each agency shall use the best scientific and commercial data available.…

(e) Endangered Species Committee

(1) There is established a committee to be known as the Endangered Species Committee.…

(2) The Committee shall … determine in accordance with subsection (h) of this section whether or not to grant an exemption from the requirements of subsection (a)(2).…

(h) Grant of exemption

(1) … The Committee shall grant an exemption … if, by a vote of not less than five of its members voting in person —

(A) it determines … that —

(i) there are no reasonable and prudent alternatives to the agency action;

(ii) the benefits of such action clearly outweigh the benefits of alternative courses of action consistent with conserving the species or its critical habitat, and such action is in the public interest;

(iii) the action is of regional or national significance; and

(iv) neither the Federal agency concerned nor the exemption applicant made any irreversible or irretrievable commitment of resources prohibited by subsection (d) of this section; and

(B) it establishes such reasonable mitigation and enhancement measures, including, but not limited to, live propagation, transplantation, and habitat acquisition and improvement, as are necessary and appropriate to minimize the adverse effects of the agency action upon the endangered species, threatened species, or critical habitat concerned.…

(i) Review by Secretary of State Notwithstanding any other provision of this chapter, the Committee shall be prohibited from considering for exemption any application made to it, if the Secretary of State … certifies … that the granting of any such exemption and the carrying out of such action would be in violation of an international treaty obligation or other international obligation of the United States.…

(j) Exemption for national security reasons Notwithstanding any other provision of this chapter, the Committee shall grant an exemption for any agency action if the Secretary of Defense finds that such exemption is necessary for reasons of national security.

§ 9. Prohibited acts

(a) (1) Except as provided in section[] ... 10 of this Act, with respect to any endangered species of fish or wildlife ... it is unlawful for any person subject to the jurisdiction of the United States to—

(A) import any such species into, or export any such species from the United States;

(B) take any such species within the United States or the territorial sea of the United States;

(C) take any such species upon the high seas; ... or

(G) violate any regulation pertaining to such species or to any threatened species of fish or wildlife listed pursuant to section 4 of this Act and promulgated by the Secretary pursuant to authority provided by this chapter.

(2) Except as provided in section[] ... 10 of this Act, with respect to any endangered species of plants listed pursuant to section 4 of this Act, it is unlawful for any person subject to the jurisdiction of the United States to—

(A) import any such species into, or export any such species from, the United States;

(B) remove and reduce to possession any such species from areas under Federal jurisdiction; maliciously damage or destroy any such species on any such area; or remove, cut, dig up, or damage or destroy any such species on any other area in knowing violation of any law or regulation of any State or in the course of any violation of a State criminal trespass law;.... or

(E) violate any regulation pertaining to such species or to any threatened species of plants listed pursuant to section 4 of this Act and promulgated by the Secretary pursuant to authority provided by this chapter....

§ 10. Exceptions

(a) Permits

(1) The Secretary may permit, under such terms and conditions as he shall prescribe—

(A) any act otherwise prohibited by section 9 of this Act for scientific purposes or to enhance the propagation or survival of the affected species ... ; or

(B) any taking otherwise prohibited by section 9 (a)(1)(B) of this Act if such taking is incidental to, and not the purpose of, the carrying out of an otherwise lawful activity.

(2) (A) No permit may be issued by the Secretary authorizing any taking referred to in paragraph (1)(B) unless the applicant therefor submits to the Secretary a conservation plan that specifies—

(i) the impact which will likely result from such taking;

(ii) what steps the applicant will take to minimize and mitigate such impacts, and the funding that will be available to implement such steps;

(iii) what alternative actions to such taking the applicant considered and the reasons why such alternatives are not being utilized; and

(iv) such other measures that the Secretary may require as being necessary or appropriate for purposes of the plan.

(B) If the Secretary finds, after opportunity for public comment, with respect to a permit application and the related conservation plan that—

(i) the taking will be incidental;

(ii) the applicant will, to the maximum extent practicable, minimize and mitigate the impacts of such taking;

(iii) the applicant will ensure that adequate funding for the plan will be provided;

(iv) the taking will not appreciably reduce the likelihood of the survival and recovery of the species in the wild; and

(v) the measures, if any, required under subparagraph (A)(iv) will be met;

and he has received such other assurances as he may require that the plan will be implemented, the Secretary shall issue the permit. The permit shall contain such terms and conditions as the Secretary deems necessary or appropriate to carry out the purposes of this paragraph....

(C) The Secretary shall revoke a permit issued under this paragraph if he finds that the permittee is not complying with the terms and conditions of the permit.

* * *

In other provisions of the ESA, interested persons are authorized to petition the Secretary for species listings and for critical habitat designations. Tight, mandatory deadlines are specified in which the Secretary must take action to grant or deny the petition and, if warranted, to list a species or to designate its critical habitat. *See* ESA § 4, 16 U.S.C. § 1533(b)(3)-(6). The ESA also authorizes citizen suits against any person, including the Secretary and other federal agencies, alleged to be in violation of any provision of the Act. ESA § 11, 16 U.S.C. § 1540(g). Violations can result in civil and criminal penalties up to $25,000 and/or six months imprisonment. ESA § 11, 16 U.S.C. § 1540(a)-(b).

One remarkable aspect of the ESA is its utter disregard for the potential economic impacts of a species listing. If the Secretary finds that the "best scientific and commercial data available" demonstrates that a species is endangered or threatened, she must publish a proposed rule identifying the species as such, regardless of potential economic impacts. ESA § 4, 16 U.S.C. § 1533(b)(1)(A). Likewise, there is no exception for economic hardship to the prohibitions against "take" (Section 9) or "jeopardy" (Section 7). In Tennessee Valley Authority (TVA) v. Hill, 437 U.S. 153 (1978), the U.S. Supreme Court recognized the national interest in prioritizing endangered species and their habitats over "business as usual." The Court held that the ESA prohibited the completion of a dam, where the dam would either eradicate a population of the endangered snail darter or destroy its critical habitat. The Court enjoined the project despite the fact that the dam was nearly completed and Congress had continued to appropriate large sums of public money to the project. According to the Court, "the plain intent of Congress in enacting [the ESA] was to halt and reverse the trend toward species extinction, whatever the cost." *Id.* at 184.

Following the *TVA* decision, Congress amended the ESA in an attempt to alleviate its potentially harsh consequences for economic development. The 1978 amendments created the Endangered Species Committee, also known as "The God Squad," and provided it with the authority to grant exemptions from ESA prohibitions for the most economically beneficial projects. ESA § 7, 16 U.S.C. § 1536(h)(1). The God Squad has issued very few exemptions since its creation.

One of the most controversial listing decisions to date involves the polar bear.

Federal Officials Agree Global Warming Threatens Polar Bears' Survival, Advancing Endangered Species Act Claim
Natural Resources Defense Council Press Archive (2006)

ANCHORAGE, Feb. 13, 2006. The U.S. Fish and Wildlife Service today announced that it is opening the formal process to list polar bears as officially "threatened" due to the unprecedented meltdown of their sea-ice habitat caused by global warming. The finding comes in response to a lawsuit filed under the federal Endangered Species Act by three conservation groups. "Federal officials have now acknowledged that global warming is transforming the Arctic, and threatening polar bears with extinction," said Kassie Siegel of the Center for Biological Diversity....

Polar bears live only in the Arctic and are totally dependent on the sea ice for all of their essential needs, including hunting their prey of ice seals. An enormous body of scientific evidence shows that Arctic ice is vanishing much faster than previously expected ... [S]ome climate models predict that the Arctic could be ice-free in summer as early as 2040....

As temperatures rise, researchers say that Arctic sea ice is forming later, breaking up earlier, and the area covered by it is shrinking. Dramatic changes have occurred in Alaska, where scientists with the U.S. Minerals Management Service documented the drowning of at least four polar bears in September 2004, when the sea ice retreated a record 160 miles off the state's northern coast. The researchers...predict increases in such deaths as global warming advances.

In Western Hudson Bay in Canada, polar bears are forced onto land for a period of fasting when the sea ice melts in the spring, and cannot hunt again until the ice freezes up again in the fall. Because of global warming, the season for bears to hunt on the ice has already become too short for the bears to build up sufficient fat stores for optimum health and reproduction. As a result, this population of polar bears has declined approximately 14 percent in 10 years, from 1,100 in 1995 to fewer than 950 in 2004....

"Listing under the Endangered Species Act will provide important protections for the bears, including a requirement that federal agencies responsible for large greenhouse gas emissions consider their impacts on polar bears and their Arctic habitat," said Kert Davies of Greenpeace ... The United States is the world's largest emitter of the heat trapping pollution that causes global warming, primarily carbon dioxide emissions from cars and trucks, power plants, and other sources....

Does the ESA seem like an appropriate tool for addressing threats to the polar bear? In response to a court order, the U.S. Fish and Wildlife Service (FWS) listed the polar bear as threatened. *See Polar Bear Endangered Species Act Listing and § 4(d) Rule Litigation,* 748 F.Supp.2d 19 (D.D.C. 2010). Dana Perino, White House press secretary at the time, stated that the court's decision was a "regulatory train wreck ... This would have the Clean Air Act, the Endangered Species Act, and the National Environmental Policy Act all addressing climate change in a way that is not the way that they were intended to." Andrew Revkin, *Court Forces Government to Move on Polar Bear Status,* N.Y. Times DOT Earth, Apr. 29, 2008.

The environmental groups were not satisfied with the "threatened" status, and they sued to force the FWS to consider listing the polar bear as "endangered." The court agreed that the FWS had improperly determined that the polar bear must have been facing "imminent extinction" in order to be listed as endangered. *Polar Bear Endangered Species Act Listing,* 748 F.Supp.2d at 26. Based on the statutory definition of "endangered," 16 U.S.C. § 1532(6), the Secretary need only determine that the species is "exposed to the harm of no longer existing" to be considered endangered.

> [T]he Court finds that the overall structure of the ESA suggests that the definition of an endangered species was intentionally left ambiguous.... Indeed, under the ESA, Congress broadly delegated responsibility to the Secretary to determine whether a species is "in danger of extinction" in light of the five statutory listing factors and the best available science for that species.[14] *See Babbitt v. Sweet Home,* 515 U.S. 687, 708, 115 S.Ct. 2407, 132 L.Ed.2d 597 (1995) ("The task of defining and listing endangered and threatened species requires an expertise and attention to detail that exceeds the normal province of Congress."). In making that determination, the agency cannot "rest simply on its parsing of the statutory language [but rather it] must bring its experience and expertise to bear in light of competing interests at stake." ...
>
> Therefore, having found that the agency wrongly relied on an erroneous plain-meaning reading of the definition of an endangered species, the Court must "remand ..." The Court therefore will remand the Listing Rule to FWS for the agency to provide a reasonable interpretation of the definition of an "endangered species," as applied to its listing determination for the polar bear ... On remand, the agency should bring its expertise and experience to bear on the question of whether its determination that the polar bear is "threatened" throughout its range is warranted....

Polar Bear Endangered Species Act Listing, 748 F.Supp.2d at 29.

On remand, the agency stood by its decision that the polar bear was merely threatened, not endangered, and the court upheld its decision. The court specifically noted that the agency properly "took into account" foreign conservation efforts to protect bears. As part of its analysis, the FWS discussed harvest management programs in each of the "range countries" (Canada, Denmark (in Greenland), Norway, and Russia), along with relevant conservation benefits of those programs, addressed conservation and economic benefits of polar bear sport-hunting programs, and enumerated the regulatory mechanisms that governed polar bears in each of the range countries, including bilateral and multilateral agreements and overarching international frameworks. *In re* Polar Bear Endangered Species Act Listing and |4(d) Rule Litigation, 794 F.Supp.2d 65 (D.D.C. 2011).

Once a species is listed, critical habitat is to be designated "to the maximum extent prudent and determinable." ESA § 4(a)(3). However, designation can be delayed due to insufficient information. 50 C.F.R. § 424.12. In determining whether an area should be included in the designation, the Services must first identify occupied or unoccupied but suitable areas, based on the best scientific data available. ESA § 4(b)(2). Unlike the listing decision itself, in making a decision on critical habitat, the Services must consider the economic and other relevant impacts of designation. Suitable areas may be excluded if the "benefits of exclusion outweigh the benefits of designation," unless exclusion would result in extinction of the species. *Id. See* 50 C.F.R. § 424.12(a)(1). According to the Center for Biological Diversity, implementation has lagged.

---

14. Although imminence of harm is clearly one factor that the agency weighs in its decision-making process, it is not necessarily a limiting factor. In many cases, the agency might appropriately find that the imminence of a particular threat is the dispositive factor that warrants listing a species as "threatened" rather than "endangered," or vice versa. The agency nonetheless has broad discretion to decide that other factors outweigh the imminence of the threat.

For roughly the first 20 years after passage of the Endangered Species Act, FWS did not routinely designate critical habitat for listed species and after that only did so when sued by conservation organizations. As a result, only 45 percent of listed species have designated critical habitat. The agency has recently begun to designate critical habitat concurrently with listing of species, as required by the law.

CBD, A Future for All: Blueprint for Strengthening the Endangered Species Act 6 (2011).

Listed species may not be put in *jeopardy* by any federal action. ESA § 7(b)-(c). This requirement entails both a procedural requirement to consult as well as a substantive duty to avoid jeopardy or adverse modification. Procedurally, federal action agencies must consult with the FWS to assure that their actions—including permitting, funding, and actions on federal lands—will not jeopardize the continued existence of the species or adversely modify their critical habitat. The latter part of this requirement is substantive— if jeopardy is found, the action may not go forward. TVA v. Hill, 437 U.S. 153 (1978). The agency may, however, identify and adopt a reasonable and prudent alternative that will avoid jeopardy to the species or adverse modification of critical habitat. Consultations and jeopardy decisions under the ESA must be based on the "best scientific … data available." ESA § 7(c)(1).

In addition, individual members of a listed endangered species may not be *taken* by any person. ESA § 9(a). The prohibition against take includes killing, hunting, harassing, or harming the species by habitat modification or destruction that causes injury. *Sweet Home*, 515 U.S. at 708.

When a species such as the polar bear is listed as threatened, section 4(d) of the ESA authorizes the agency to prohibit any conduct by regulation with respect to threatened species that the Act itself proscribes with respect to endangered species. 16 U.S.C. § 1533(d). The FWS has issued a regulation extending full protection to all threatened species unless it has promulgated a special contrary regulation. 50 C.F.R. § 17.31(a).

In the polar bear litigation, the court rejected the environmental groups' argument that a special § 4(d) rule violated the ESA by failing to effectively provide for conservation of the bear because the rule did not address global greenhouse gas emissions. *In re* Polar Bear Endangered Species Act Listing and § 4(D) Rule Litigation, 818 F.Supp.2d 214 (D.D.C. 2011). Although the FWS itself had identified increasing Arctic temperatures caused by greenhouse gases as leading to a decline in the polar bear's habitat, the court found that the FWS had reasonably determined that tools for evaluating or quantifying the endpoint impacts of such gasses had not yet been developed. The FWS had also explained that "anticipated sea ice losses as a result of greenhouse gas emissions 'would not be alleviated' by an additional overlay of incidental take provisions under the ESA." *Id.* at 231.

Notes and Questions

1. The polar bear litigation is a result of "classic American environmental action, seeking leverage in existing laws to force governments to move on newly identified problems …" Revkin, *supra*. Is prioritization of issues and decisionmaking by litigation appropriate for complex issues like extinction and climate change?

2. Do the ESA's prohibitions against "take" and "jeopardy" adequately advance its goal of "provid[ing] a means whereby the ecosystems upon which endangered species and threatened species depend may be conserved," 16 U.S.C. § 1531(b)? If not, what reforms should be adopted?

3. To alleviate the burden imposed by the ESA on developers and land owners, in 1982, Congress amended § 10 to authorize a taking by private actions if it "is incidental to and not the purpose of, carrying out an otherwise lawful activity." 16 U.S.C. § 1539(a)(1)(B). An applicant for a § 10 "incidental take permit" must provide a habitat conservation plan (HCP) to minimize and mitigate the effects of the incidental take. Between 1982–1992, only 14 incidental take permits were issued (slightly more than one per year). Edward D. Koch, *The Practice of Endangered Species Conservation on Private Lands: One Federal Biologist's Experiences*, 38 Id. L.Rev. 505, 510 (2002). To deflect the mounting criticisms of the ESA by developers, the Clinton Administration made these permits, and the attendant HCPs, a top priority. As a result, more than 300 HCPs were issued between 1993–2002, covering approximately 20 million acres and over 200 listed species. *Id.* The issuance of permits with HCPs improved relationships with developers and alleviated some of the pressure in Congress to amend and "water down" the ESA. Some say that HCPs have been "a win-win situation for imperiled species and development interests: in return for ... allowing development interests to take a limited amount of habitat, they commit ... to protect and manage other habitat areas, thus enhancing the species' overall recovery chances." John Kostyack, *NWF v. Babbitt: Victory for Smart Growth and Imperiled Wildlife*, 31 Envtl. L. Rep. 10712 (2001). On the other hand, conservationists argue that many of these HCPs allow significant habitat destruction and lack dependable measures for mitigation and monitoring. *See* A. Dan Tarlock, *Slouching Toward Eden: The Eco-Pragmatic Challenges of Ecosystem Revival*, 87 Minn. L. Rev. 1173, 1203 (2003). Could HCPs be a useful tool for power plants and developers that emit greenhouse gases that cause habitat degradation for listed species?

4. Canada has two-thirds of the world's population of polar bears, but at the time of the listing litigation in the United States, it had not yet listed them under the Canadian Species at Risk Act (SARA). As the Secretary noted, "Canadian law is different from U.S. law with respect to endangered species, both in its criteria for listing and administrative process for making listing determinations." Office of the Secretary, *Kempthorne Announces Decision to Protect Polar Bears under Endangered Species Act: Rule will allow continuation of vital energy production in Alaska*, Interior Dept. Docs., May 14, 2008. In 2008, the U.S. signed a Memorandum of Understanding with the Canadian Minister of Environment for the conservation and management of polar bear populations shared by the U.S. and Canada. *Id.* Canada finally listed the bear as a "species of special concern" under SARA in 2011. Environment Canada, News Release, *Environment Minister Declares Polar Bear Species of Concern*, Nov. 10, 2011. In addition, Canada regulates the import and export of live polar bears and polar bear hides and trophies through the *Wild Animal and Plant Protection and Regulation of International and Interprovincial Trade Act*. Environment Canada, *Conservation of Polar Bears in Alaska* (Jan. 3, 2012), http://www.ec.gc.ca/nature/default.asp?lang=En&n=A997D1CC-1. The implications of listing under SARA are described below in Section B.2.

B. Canada

Given its size and its relatively low population density, Canada might seem like a natural biodiversity haven. Canada boasts many superlative national, provincial, and territorial parks, and these parks "are a source of tremendous pride" and an "icon ... of national identity." David Boyd, Unnatural Law: Rethinking Canadian Environmental Law and Policy 168 (2003).

But "[t]here are myriad signs ... that all is not well." *Id.* at 165. Several types of ecosystems are almost completely gone from the Canadian landscape.

> Coastal Douglas fir forest covers less than 1 percent of its original area. Less than 1 percent of tallgrass prairie is still in its native state.... Many of Canada's wetlands have disappeared, including 65 percent of Atlantic coastal marshes, 70 percent of southern Ontario wetlands, 71 percent of Prairie wetlands, and 80 percent of the Fraser River delta.

Id. As of 2010, there were 614 animal and plant species listed as "at risk." Committee on the Status of Endangered Wildlife in Canada, *Canadian Wildlife Species at Risk* (Oct. 2010), www.cosewick.gc.ca/eng/sct0/rpt/dsp_booklet_e.htm. At least twelve species native to Canada have gone extinct, and 21 species have been extirpated (they no longer exist in Canada but are found elsewhere). These figures are "almost certainly an underestimate because very few species have actually been studied." BOYD, *supra,* at 165.

This section covers the various categories of land preserves in Canada, and then turns to Canadian species-related legislation.

1. Wildlife Refuges, Sanctuaries, and Parks

During the 1990s, the amount of protected land in Canada doubled, in large part because of the Endangered Spaces campaign of 1989. BOYD, *supra,* at 177. The land ownership patterns of these protected lands are quite different than those found in the United States, however, where the vast majority of protected refuges, wilderness areas, and parks are federally owned and managed. In Canada, about one-third of the protected lands are under federal jurisdiction, with the remainder under provincial or territorial control.

> Canada is a country with provincial control over large areas of natural resources and federal control over navigable waters and oceans and some lands in the north. In addition, there are a variety of different title arrangements relating to aboriginal groups and their use and ownership of lands. Thus, nature conservation is done by different levels of government, depending on where the areas are and who has jurisdiction....

Harvey Locke, *Soul of the Wilderness: Canada Increases Wilderness Protection and Policy Goals,* 15 IJW 1:4–14 (2009).

By 2000, about 10% of Canada's land had some kind of protective designation—park, wildlife area, bird sanctuary, or wetland reserve. BOYD, *supra,* at 177. This figure placed Canada "sixty-first in the world in terms of percentage of and area protected," behind the United States with around 21% protected lands. The Canadian government has announced a goal of having at least 12% of its lands in protected status. *Id.*

Just how protective are the various preservation designations? In provincial land preserves, the degree of protection "varies dramatically." BOYD, *supra,* at 169. "Many provinces lack clear legislation and policy with respect to parks and protected areas ... [resulting in] a chaotic stream of ad hoc decisions and actions." *Id.*

At the national level, Canada has designated a variety of Wildlife Areas, National Parks, and other types of protected areas pursuant to federal statutes.

Wildlife areas, bird sanctuaries, and some protected marine areas are authorized by the Canada Wildlife Act. Canada Wildlife Act, S.C. ch. W-9 § 1 (1985); ch. 23 §§ 2(F), 4.1(1) (1994). Protected areas are designated by the Canadian Wildlife Service, a division of Environment Canada. As of 2004, Canada had 51 National Wildlife Areas and 92 Migratory Bird Sanctuaries covering 11.5 million hectares of land. Within such areas, activities that may harm a protected species or its habitat are prohibited by regulation. Wildlife Area Regulations, C.R.C. c. 1609. Land use permits may be granted for activities that are compatible with the conservation mission. *Id.* §4. Hiking, canoeing, and photography are generally allowed without a permit. Generally speaking, hunting and fishing are *not* allowed absent special dispensation, *id.* §3(1)(a), in direct contrast to the U.S. Wildlife Refuge System. Moreover, the possession of firearms is prohibited in Canadian Wildlife Areas. *Id.* §3(1)(b).

Marine protected areas are also authorized by §35 of the Oceans Act. These areas are intended to protect (1) fishery resources, including marine mammals, and their habitat; (2) threatened or endangered marine species and their habitats; (3) unique habitats and/ or areas of high biological diversity or productivity; or (4) other marine resources. *Id.* §35(1). Destroying or disturbing living organisms or their habitat is prohibited. The National Marine Conservation Areas Act, assented to in 2002, adds a system of marine areas that are representative of each of Canada's 29 marine regions in the Atlantic, Arctic, and Pacific Oceans, and the Great Lakes "for the purpose of protecting and conserving" them and "for the benefit, education and enjoyment of the people of Canada and the world." S.C. 2002, c.18 §4(1). These areas are managed based on the precautionary principle and an ecosystem-based approach. *Id.* §9(3). For details, see Parks Canada, National Marine Conservations Areas of Canada Program (Apr. 30, 2008), www.pc.gc.ca/progs/amnc-nmca/system/index_e.asp.

National Parks are considered the nation's "natural jewels" that reflect "the beauty and infinite variety of our land." Parks Canada, National Parks of Canada, Introduction (2006), www.pc.gc.ca/progs/np-pn/intro_e.asp. According to Parks Canada, they are "a source of pride ... and an integral part of our identity." *Id.* The Canadian National Park System was kicked off with the creation of Banff National Park in 1866. In 1911, Canada established the world's first agency dedicated to national parks. M.I. Jeffrey, *National Parks and Protected Areas-Approaching the Next Millennium,* 1999 Acta Juridica 163 (1999). The U.S. Park Service was created five years later with the Park Service Organic Act of 1916, 16 U.S.C. §1.

In a strong parallel to the U.S. Park Service Organic Act, the National Parks Act expresses a dual mandate of conservation and recreation:

> National Parks are ... dedicated to the people of Canada for their benefit, education and enjoyment ... and the parks shall be maintained and made use of so as to leave them unimpaired for the enjoyment of future generations.

Canada National Parks Act 2002, S.C. 2002 c. 32, §4(1). Industrial activity, such as commercial timber harvest, is prohibited in National Parks. Jamie Benidickson, Environmental Law in Canada 162 (2011).

The Parks Act adds that "ecological integrity" takes first priority in consideration of all aspects of management. *Id.* §8(2). In addition, ecological integrity is listed as a responsibility of Parks Canada under the Parks Canada Agency Act, S.C. 1998 c. 31, Preamble (g). However, stating that ecological integrity is a priority and enforcing that goal as a substantive requirement are two different things. In Canadian Parks and Wilderness Society v. Canada (2003), 1 Can. Env. L. Reports 3d 20 (Fed. Ct. of Appeal), the court rejected arguments that the Minister of Canadian Heritage unlawfully failed to ensure the maintenance of ecological integrity when approving the construction of a road. According to the court, the Act "requires a delicate balancing of conflicting interests which include the benefit and enjoyment of those living in, and in close proximity to, Wood

Buffalo National Park ... [and] does not require that ecological integrity be the 'determinative factor.'" *Id.* paras. 52–53. Thus, the Minister had sufficient discretion to approve the road, which was designed to alleviate the isolation of members of two remote aboriginal communities living in Wood Buffalo National Park. *See* Stepan Wood et al., *Whatever Happened to Canadian Environmental Law,* 37 Eco. L. Q. 981, 1011–12 (2010) (citing the Wood Buffalo case and concluding, "[i]n addition to legislative inaction, Canada's poor record also owes to its failure to implement existing laws").

Unlike the U.S., Canada has no "wilderness act" of national application. There are some specifically designated wilderness areas, however, that were created through specific, place-based national or provincial laws. The wilderness concept has gained momentum in recent years, as described below.

Harvey Locke, Soul of the Wilderness: Canada Increases Wilderness Protection and Policy Goals
15 IJW 1:4–14 (2009)

[T]he years 2007 and 2008 have seen major advances in wilderness protection in Canada at the level of both policy and outcomes. Led by the Canadian Boreal Initiative and the Canadian Parks and Wilderness Society, calls for protecting at least half of Canada's public lands and waters are starting to take hold in public policy.... This target of "at least half" is materially more ambitious than previous conservation targets that were set with a view to achieving representation of natural ecosystems....

The heightened global public concern about climate change in 2006 provided a major catalyst for wilderness conservation in Canada. This is due, in part, to the fact that Canada's boreal and Arctic biomes are huge storehouses of terrestrial carbon and more significant for carbon storage than tropical forests. Leaving the wetlands, peatlands, and tundra intact is both a first order climate change mitigation and an adaptation strategy. Canada's performance on meeting its environmental targets under the Kyoto protocol of the United Nations Framework Convention on Climate Change has been very poor because it is a globally significant producer of oil and gas, has vast coal reserves, and has a very large automobile industry. Nature conservation is one way for Canada to get closer to its environmental targets.... In the 2008 federal election campaign, both the Liberals and Greens adopted the goal of protecting at least 50% of the land area, and the Conservatives committed to completing the national park system.

After years of work by NGOs, the federal government, with the agreement of aboriginal communities, moved to protect on an interim basis several very large areas in the Northwest Territories ... The most spectacular wilderness conservation event was the announcement by Premier Dalton McGuinty of Ontario in July 2008 that at least half of that province's vast Far North would be protected ...

Notes and Questions

1. Is it appropriate to leave wilderness protection to individual proclamations or enactments, or should Canada pass a national wilderness act? Once created, should wilderness areas be permanent designations or should they be subject to reassessment and re-designation? What if a wilderness area had been established to protect its unique alpine and glacial ecosystems, but over time those ecosystems were lost or dramatically altered due to rising temperatures?

2. Should the Parks Act be amended to declare that parks are a place where the preservation of natural ecological integrity comes first, with economic, recreational, and other human interests second? For an argument in the affirmative, see Shaun Fluker, *"Maintaining Ecological Integrity is Our First Priority"—Policy Rhetoric or Practical Reality in Canada's National Parks? A Case Comment on Canadian Parks & Wilderness Soc'y v. Canada*, 13 J. Envtl. L. & Prac. 131, 142 (2003).

3. In 1969, the International Union for Conservation of Nature (IUCN) adopted the following definition of a "park":

A national park is a fairly large territory:

where one or more ecosystems are not materially altered by human exploitation and occupation, where the vegetable and animal species, geomorphological sites and habitats are of scientific, educational and recreational interest or where there are natural landscapes or great aesthetic value;

where the highest official authority in the country has taken measures to prevent, or eliminate as soon as possible, exploitation or occupation in the whole area, and to make sure that the ecological, geomorphological or aesthetic features which justified its creation are respected; and

where visiting is authorized under certain conditions, for inspirational, recreative, educational and cultural purposes.

International Union for Conservation of Nature, http://www.iucn.org. *See* Jeffrey, *supra*, at 174 n.62. Do Canadian national parks satisfy this definition? For that matter, do U.S. national parks satisfy it? Although the following criticism was written about the U.S., could it be true of both park systems?

The American national park system has much to offer to other countries seeking to create a unified system of parks, but it also has much to learn from an increasingly rich international definition of "national park." Yet, ... national parks risk a steady erosion of their unique, world-class resource values in the next century unless a stronger policy is implemented that gives priority to the places that must be preserved for generations over the people who are currently here to enjoy them.

Denise E. Antolini, *National Park Law in the U.S.: Conservation, Conflict, and Centennial Values*, 33 Wm. & Mary Envtl. L. & Pol'y Rev. 851, 853–54 (2009).

4. How are the interests of aboriginal peoples expressed and accounted for in the Canadian park system? Consider the following comment, which could be said of both the U.S. and Canada:

The American [national park] model ... oversimplifies and ignores the historical facts regarding the prior existence of native peoples on lands considered by new settlers as "wilderness." Thus, exportation of the U.S. model to countries with indigenous populations is often viewed with suspicion and concern for preservation of cultural heritage and ancestral homelands.

Antolini, *supra*, at 854 n.9. How should countries with indigenous populations go about establishing and managing parks?

2. Species-Specific Legislation

Along with the United States, Canada is a party to the Migratory Bird Treaty of 1916. It implements the Convention through the Migratory Birds Convention Act 1994, R.S.C.

c-22. The original focus on regulating open and closed hunting seasons remains intact, but has been expanded somewhat to incorporate sustainability principles. Benidickson, *supra,* at 171. The Act forbids the possession and sale of migratory birds, their parts, and their nests, unless otherwise authorized by regulations. Migratory Birds Convention Act § 5. The rights of First Nations to hunt migratory birds and harvest their eggs are recognized in a 1995 Protocol Between Canada and the United States.

An alleged failure to enforce the protective provisions of the Migratory Birds Convention Act was at the heart of an environmental group's submission to the Commission for Environmental Cooperation (CEC), a body created under a side agreement to the North American Free Trade Agreement (NAFTA). Article 5 of the NAAEC requires NAFTA parties to effectively enforce their environmental laws and regulations through appropriate government action. The CEC is authorized to publicize a "factual record" of failures to enforce environmental law. Although the factual record does not result in direct sanctions or other relief, it may assist submitters, parties, and other interested members of the public in proving violations and seeking remedies before other courts or tribunals at the domestic or international level. The Secretariat's recommendation in the Migratory Bird case is provided below.

Secretariat of the Commission for Environmental Cooperation of North America Ontario Logging—Notification to Council (SEM-02-001) Article 15(1) Notification to Council that Development of a Factual Record Is Warranted
49 C.E.L.R. (N.S.) 187 (2003)

Article 14 of the *North American Agreement on Environmental Cooperation* ("NAAEC") creates a mechanism for citizens to file submissions in which they assert that a Party to the NAAEC is failing to effectively enforce its environmental law....

The Submitters assert that Canada is failing to effectively enforce s. 6(a) of the *Migratory Birds Regulations* ("MBR") adopted under the *Migratory Birds Convention Act, 1994* ("MBCA") in regard to the logging industry in Ontario. S. 6(a) of the MBR provides that "[...] no person shall (a) disturb, destroy or take a nest, egg, nest shelter, eider duck shelter or duck box of a migratory bird [...] except under authority of a permit therefor." Violations of s. 6(a) of the MBR may be prosecuted by way of summary conviction or as an indictable offence....

The Submitters claim that their research, based on statistical data, estimates that in the year 2001, clear-cutting activity destroyed over 85,000 migratory bird nests in areas of central and northern Ontario. The Submitters further assert that "despite the estimated widespread destruction of bird nests," an access-to-information request filed in 2001 revealed no investigations or charges in Ontario for violations of s. 6(a) of the MBR.

The Submitters assert that logging activity in Ontario is carried out under forest management plans ("FMPs") prepared under the supervision of the Ontario Ministry of Natural Resources ("MNR") in accordance with provincial standards and without any input from federal authorities on matters related to enforcing the MBCA, which is a federal statute....

Finally, the Submitters assert that by giving the logging industry special consideration, Canada is not following the requirement of the *Compliance and Enforcement Policy for*

Wildlife Legislation, which states that "[c]ompliance and enforcement activities must be securely founded in law and must be fair, predictable, and consistent across Canada." ...

Canada contends that it is addressing the issue of nest destruction during logging activities, mainly through compliance promotion.... Canada states that compliance promotion and education are a necessary first step in a long-term enforcement approach in the forestry context that will eventually facilitate arguments in court that a given logging company will have been aware of the impacts of its actions. Canada "is concerned that obtaining limited results in a court of law for non-compliance at this stage would devalue the offence, and would be counterproductive to conservation of migratory birds." Canada states that EC is nevertheless committed to acting on any instances of non-compliance that it becomes aware of and to pursuing the most effective remedy possible....

Migratory birds are a cherished and valuable resource in North America. The study of migratory bird populations yields clues about long-range environmental impacts of local activities. Birds play a very important role in insect pest control, plant pollination and seed dispersal.... Canada and the United States recognized the importance of protecting this shared resource when they signed the Canada-U.S. Migratory Birds Convention in 1916. In Canada, the MBCA and MBR translate Canada's commitments under the Convention into legal requirements that are enforceable against companies and individuals, under penalty of high fines and even prison time. By prohibiting the unauthorized destruction of nests and eggs of migratory birds, s. 6(a) of the MBR is potentially a powerful provision for the protection of migratory birds and for the fulfillment of Canada's commitments under the Convention. Only aboriginals are exempted from the prohibition contained in s. 6(a) of the MBR, consistent with aboriginal and treaty rights recognized under the Constitution.

Primary resource industries have always played an important role in Canada's economy, and forestry is central among these industries. In many communities, forestry is the backbone of the local economy, and because forest products are the first link in the supply chain of many other industries, the performance of the forestry sector is often used as one indicator in assessing the strength of Canada's economy....

Both the submission and Canada's response recognize that destruction of migratory bird nests is a frequent environmental consequence of logging.... The submission and the response, taken together, are insufficient to dispel central questions regarding whether Canada is failing to effectively enforce s. 6(a) of the MBR in the context of logging in Ontario. Missing from the materials provided to the Secretariat, for example, is specific information regarding how the federal guidelines are implemented in practice, in particular in connection with the FMPs covering the harvest areas mentioned in the submission. Similarly, it would be useful to obtain information regarding whether and how federal information and education sessions have resulted in changes in forestry company practices and procedures ... and whether Canada has put in place measures to ensure that its industry outreach initiatives are improving compliance rates.... A factual record would provide an opportunity to gather such information, as well as information regarding the type and outcome of actions taken in response to specific complaints, with a view to considering whether ... Canada is failing to effectively enforce s. 6(a) of the MBR ...

Enforcement necessarily involves the exercise of discretion in setting priorities and making decisions about the allocation of resources. In its response to the submission, Canada explains in part how it exercises certain discretionary powers in the context of wildlife enforcement. A factual record would provide an opportunity to gather valuable additional information regarding how Canada has exercised its discretion, thereby providing meaningful context for any individual enforcement actions documented in a factual record. This would involve, for example, gathering information used to establish current enforcement priorities; information on methods used to balance priorities; information on regional (particularly Ontario) priorities and how they are set; ... information supporting the position that compliance promotion activities are a necessary precursor to prosecution; and information on current initiatives....

For the reasons stated above, the Secretariat has determined that the submission, in light of the Party's response, warrants development of a factual record.

Notes and Questions

1. Despite the Secretariat's recommendation, the CEC initially refused to authorize a factual record. It found that, although the submitters had included factual models estimating the damage that would be caused by logging, they needed to provide data showing that the logging had caused actual environmental damage. Commission for Environmental Cooperation [CEC], Council Res. 03-05, CEC Doc. C/C.01/03-02/RES/05/final, Apr. 22, 2003, at www.cec.org/Storage/72/6574_02-1-RES-E.pdf. Subsequently, when this data was provided, the Secretariat once again recommended development of a factual record. This time, the Council agreed. *See* CEC Factual Record (2007), http://www.cec.org/Storage/75/6907_CCE_21_english.pdf. The record concluded that Canada had failed to provide information of adequate enforcement, and that "Ontario's Ministry of Environment did not adopt Environment Canada's recommendations for addressing migratory bird conservation." Moreover, "Environment Canada has stated that adequate obligations do not exist under provincial rules to require MNR to protect Environment Canada's interests in forest management activities in Ontario, including its interest in the conservation and protection of migratory birds." *Id.* at 158, 160. This is a victory for the submitters, but what effect does it have?

> After publication, the CEC makes no effort to follow up the factual record or to evaluate its effects.... While it may seem counterintuitive to suggest that a process that does not result in a legally binding decision can have much effect, increased transparency and public attention can cause governments to change their behavior, and studies have demonstrated that such changes have occurred as a result of CEC factual records. John H. Knox and David L. Markell, *Evaluating Citizen Petition Procedures: Lessons From an Analysis of the NAFTA Environmental Commission*, 47 Tex. Int'l L.J. 505, 512, 527 (2012).

2. What more can the central government do, when the provincial government refuses to cooperate? Does it make sense to leave forest management to provincial governments when treaty-protected species are affected?

3. "The CEC consists of three key actors: the Council, comprised of the environmental ministers of the three countries; a quasi-independent Secretariat of international civil servants, based in Montreal; and the Joint Public Advisory Committee (JPAC), a body of fifteen citizen representatives, five from each country." Knox and Markell, *supra,* at 507. Is it appropriate for the governments of Canada, the United States, and Mexico to submit to the jurisdiction of the CEC, a body created in a side agreement to a treaty related to trade and investment? What are the implications for national sovereignty? Or for economic development?

* * *

The Fisheries Act, described in Chapter IV.B.1, *supra,* adds an important level of federal protection for fish habitat. Fisheries Act of 1985, S.C. ch. F-14 (1985) (Can.). Among

other things, the Act prevents the deposit of "deleterious substances" in fish-bearing waters and forbids "any work or undertaking that results in the harmful alteration, disruption or destruction of fish habitat...." *Id.* §§ 35–36. In addition, developers of projects that
are likely to result in the "alteration, disruption or destruction of fish habitat, or in the
deposit of a deleterious substance" must provide plans, studies, and analyses to the Fisheries Minister, so that the Minister can determine whether the project will violate the Act.
Id. § 37(1). The Minister may require project modifications to prevent or mitigate adverse effects on fish habitat. *Id.* § 37(2).

Additional protection for fish and fish habitat might be found in the public trust doctrine. *See* Michael Blumm and Rachel Guthrie, *Internationalizing the Public Trust Doctrine: Natural Law and Constitutional and Statutory Approaches to Fulfilling the Saxion
Vision,* 45 UC Davis L. Rev. 741, 749 (2012). A trial court on Prince Edward Island
breathed new life into the doctrine by entertaining a claim that the Minister of Fisheries
breached a fiduciary duty to maintain the common right to fish in Atlantic fisheries.
Prince Edward Island v. Can. (Minister of Fisheries & Oceans), [2005] 256 Nfld. & P.E.I.R.
343 (Can.). Although the court did not reach the merits of the case, it explained that "a
beneficiary of the public interest ought to be able to claim against the government for a
failure to properly protect the public interest ... [because] [a] right gives a corresponding duty." *Id.* para. 6. *See also* British Columbia v. Canadian Forest Prods., Ltd. (Can-
For), [2004] 2 S.C.R. 74, paras. 74–81 (Can.) (noting that the public trust doctrine raised
"novel policy questions" but indicating some willingness to accept the Crown's assertion
of the doctrine to recover damages from a licensee for a forest fire).

The *Canada Wildlife Act* covers wild animals and plants that are migratory or threatened and are considered of national significance. Canada Wildlife Act, S.C. ch. W-9 § 1
(1985); ch. 23 § 2(F) (1994). The Wildlife Act does not provide for the full protection of
habitat of threatened species, however, and those species that are not found on federal land
are especially vulnerable. Karen L. Smith, *Habitat Protection for the New Millenium: An
Analysis of Domestic and International Regimes in North Americ*a, 13 Geo. Int'l Envtl. L.
Rev. 509, 524–525 (2001).

The federal *Species at Risk Act (SARA),* S.C. 2002, c. 29, protects aquatic species as
well as other endangered species that are located on federal land or are covered by the
federal Migratory Birds Convention Act. Government of Canada, *Species at Risk Act, A
Guide* 6 (2003). SARA authorizes federal intervention to protect endangered species and
their critical habitat outside of federal lands when provincial conservation actions are
deemed inadequate, SARA §§ 35, 61, but this is a discretionary power that has not been
exercised.

Key provisions of SARA are provided below. As you read them, be sure to note the similarities and distinctions with the U.S. Endangered Species Act, covered in Section A.2, *supra.*

Species at Risk Act
2002, c. 29

§ 2 Definitions

"competent minister" means

(a) the Minister responsible for the Parks Canada Agency with respect to individuals in or on federal lands administered by that Agency;

(b) the Minister of Fisheries and Oceans with respect to aquatic species, other
than individuals mentioned in paragraph (a); and

(c) the Minister of the Environment with respect to all other individuals....

"critical habitat" means the habitat that is necessary for the survival or recovery of a listed wildlife species and that is identified as the species' critical habitat in the recovery strategy or in an action plan for the species....

"endangered species" means a wildlife species that is facing imminent extirpation or extinction....

"federal land" means

(a) land that belongs to Her Majesty in right of Canada, or that Her Majesty in right of Canada has the power to dispose of, and all waters on and airspace above that land;

(b) the internal waters of Canada and the territorial sea of Canada; and

(c) reserves and any other lands that are set apart for the use and benefit of a band under the *Indian Act*, and all waters on and airspace above those reserves and lands....

"species at risk" means an extirpated, endangered or threatened species or a species of special concern.

"species of special concern" means a wildlife species that may become a threatened or an endangered species because of a combination of biological characteristics and identified threats....

"threatened species" means a wildlife species that is likely to become an endangered species if nothing is done to reverse the factors leading to its extirpation or extinction....

§ 6 *Purposes* The purposes of this Act are to prevent wildlife species from being extirpated or becoming extinct, to provide for the recovery of wildlife species that are extirpated, endangered or threatened as a result of human activity and to manage species of special concern to prevent them from becoming endangered or threatened.

§ 15 *Functions*

(1) The functions of COSEWIC [Committee on the Status of Endangered Wildlife in Canada] are to

(a) assess the status of each wildlife species considered by COSEWIC to be at risk and, as part of the assessment, identify existing and potential threats to the species and

(i) classify the species as extinct, extirpated, endangered, threatened or of special concern,

(ii) indicate that COSEWIC does not have sufficient information to classify the species, or

(iii) indicate that the species is not currently at risk;

(b) determine when wildlife species are to be assessed, with priority given to those more likely to become extinct;

(c) conduct a new assessment of the status of species at risk and, if appropriate, reclassify or declassify them;

(c.1) indicate in the assessment whether the wildlife species migrates across Canada's boundary or has a range extending across Canada's boundary;

(d) develop and periodically review criteria for assessing the status of wildlife species and for classifying them and recommend the criteria to the Minister and the Canadian Endangered Species Conservation Council; and

(e) provide advice to the Minister and the Canadian Endangered Species Conservation Council and perform any other functions that the Minister, after consultation with that Council, may assign.

(2) COSEWIC must carry out its functions on the basis of the best available information on the biological status of a species, including scientific knowledge, community knowledge and aboriginal traditional knowledge....

§ 21 Status reports COSEWIC's assessment of the status of a wildlife species must be based on a status report on the species that COSEWIC either has had prepared or has received with an application....

§ 27 Power to amend List The Governor in Council may, on the recommendation of the Minister, by order amend the List ... by adding a wildlife species, by reclassifying a listed wildlife species or by removing a listed wildlife species, and the Minister may, by order, amend the List in a similar fashion in accordance with subsection (3).

(1.1) Subject to subsection (3), the Governor in Council, within nine months after receiving an assessment of the status of a species by COSEWIC, may review that assessment and may, on the recommendation of the Minister,

(a) accept the assessment and add the species to the List;

(b) decide not to add the species to the List; or

(c) refer the matter back to COSEWIC for further information or consideration....

(2) Before making a recommendation in respect of a wildlife species or a species at risk, the Minister must

(a) take into account the assessment of COSEWIC in respect of the species;

(b) consult the competent minister or ministers; and

(c) if the species is found in an area in respect of which a wildlife management board is authorized by a land claims agreement to perform functions in respect of a wildlife species, consult the wildlife management board.

(3) Where the Governor in Council has not taken a course of action under subsection (1.1) within nine months after receiving an assessment of the status of a species by COSEWIC, the Minister shall, by order, amend the List in accordance with COSEWIC's assessment....

§ 32 Killing, harming, etc., listed wildlife species

(1) No person shall kill, harm, harass, capture or take an individual of a wildlife species that is listed as an extirpated species, an endangered species or a threatened species.

(2) No person shall possess, collect, buy, sell or trade an individual of a wildlife species that is listed as an extirpated species, an endangered species or a threatened species, or any part or derivative of such an individual....

§ 33 Damage or destruction of residence No person shall damage or destroy the residence of one or more individuals of a wildlife species that is listed as an endangered species or a threatened species, or that is listed as an extirpated species if a recovery strategy has recommended the reintroduction of the species into the wild in Canada.

§ 34 Application — certain species in provinces

(1) With respect to individuals of a listed wildlife species that is not an aquatic species or a species of birds that are migratory birds protected by the *Migratory Birds Convention Act, 1994*, sections 32 and 33 do not apply in lands in a province that are not federal lands unless an order is made under subsection (2) to provide that they apply.

(2) The Governor in Council may, on the recommendation of the Minister, by order, provide that sections 32 and 33, or either of them, apply in lands in a province that are not federal lands with respect to individuals of a listed wildlife species that is not an aquatic species or a species of birds that are migratory birds protected by the *Migratory Birds Convention Act, 1994*.

(3) The Minister must recommend that the order be made if the Minister is of the opinion that the laws of the province do not effectively protect the species or the residences of its individuals....

§ 37 [Recovery Strategy] Preparation — endangered or threatened species

(1) If a wildlife species is listed as an extirpated species, an endangered species or a threatened species, the competent minister must prepare a strategy for its recovery....

§ 38 Commitments to be considered In preparing a recovery strategy, action plan or management plan, the competent minister must consider the commitment of the Government of Canada to conserving biological diversity and to the principle that, if there are threats of serious or irreversible damage to the listed wildlife species, cost-effective measures to prevent the reduction or loss of the species should not be postponed for a lack of full scientific certainty....

§ 58 Destruction of critical habitat

(1) Subject to this section, no person shall destroy any part of the critical habitat of any listed endangered species or of any listed threatened species — or of any listed extirpated species if a recovery strategy has recommended the reintroduction of the species into the wild in Canada — if

(a) the critical habitat is on federal land, in the exclusive economic zone of Canada or on the continental shelf of Canada;

(b) the listed species is an aquatic species; or

(c) the listed species is a species of migratory birds protected by the *Migratory Birds Convention Act, 1994*....

§ 61 Destruction of critical habitat [on non-federal lands]

(1) No person shall destroy any part of the critical habitat of a listed endangered species or a listed threatened species that is in a province or territory and that is not part of federal lands....

(2) Subsection (1) applies only to the portions of the critical habitat that the Governor in Council may, on the recommendation of the Minister, by order, specify....

(4) The Minister must make a recommendation if he or she is of the opinion, after consultation with the appropriate provincial or territorial minister, that

(a) there are no provisions in, or other measures under, this or any other Act of Parliament that protect the particular portion of the critical habitat ... ; and

(b) the laws of the province or territory do not effectively protect the critical habitat....

§ 64 Compensation

(1) The Minister may, in accordance with the regulations, provide fair and reasonable compensation to any person for losses suffered as a result of any extraordinary impact of the application of

(a) section 58 ... or 61; or

(b) an emergency order in respect of habitat identified in the emergency order that is necessary for the survival or recovery of a wildlife species.

§ 73 Powers of competent minister [regarding Agreements and Permits]

(1) The competent minister may enter into an agreement with a person, or issue a permit to a person, authorizing the person to engage in an activity affecting a listed wildlife species, any part of its critical habitat or the residences of its individuals.

(2) The agreement may be entered into, or the permit issued, only if the competent minister is of the opinion that

(a) the activity is scientific research relating to the conservation of the species and conducted by qualified persons;

(b) the activity benefits the species or is required to enhance its chance of survival in the wild; or

(c) affecting the species is incidental to the carrying out of the activity.

(3) The agreement may be entered into, or the permit issued, only if the competent minister is of the opinion that

(a) all reasonable alternatives to the activity that would reduce the impact on the species have been considered and the best solution has been adopted;

(b) all feasible measures will be taken to minimize the impact of the activity on the species or its critical habitat or the residences of its individuals; and

(c) the activity will not jeopardize the survival or recovery of the species....

(6) The agreement or permit must contain any terms and conditions governing the activity that the competent minister considers necessary for protecting the species....

(9) No agreement may be entered into for a term longer than five years and no permit may be issued for a term longer than three years....

§ 83 General exceptions

(1) Subsections 32(1) and (2)..., subsections ... 58(1) ... and 61(1), regulations ... and emergency orders do not apply to a person who is engaging in

(a) activities related to public safety, health or national security, that are authorized by or under any other Act of Parliament or activities under the *Health of Animals Act* and the *Plant Protection Act* for the health of animals and plants; or

(b) activities authorized under section 73 ... by an agreement, permit, licence, order or similar document.

(5) Subsection 32(2) ... do[es] not apply to a person who possesses an individual of a listed extirpated, endangered or threatened species, or any part or derivative of such an individual, if

(a) it was in the person's possession when the species was listed; [or]

(b) it is used by an aboriginal person for ceremonial or medicinal purposes, or it is part of ceremonial dress used for ceremonial or cultural purposes by an aboriginal person....

Notes and Questions

1. As between the Canadian SARA and the U.S. ESA, which seems more science based (rather than politically based) when it comes to listing species? *Compare* SARA §§ 15, 21, and 27 *with* ESA § 4. Which seems more protective of imperiled species once they are listed? Which does the best job of protecting critical habitat? Which is more cost-sensitive and/or development-friendly? Consider these questions as you read the Northern Spotted Owl case study, below.

2. Violations of SARA can result in penalties, forfeiture of property used in the offence, and incarceration. In *Regina v. McNeill* [2007] B.C.J. No. 1178, 2007 BCSC 773, three defendants pleaded guilty to illegally taking 11,000 northern abalone, a threatened species, in violation of SARA and the Fisheries Act. It was "the largest single seizure of abalone ever to come before the courts." *Id.* para. 70. The Crown sought penalties of $100,000, six months in jail, and a 15-year prohibition on scuba diving for the ringleader, who had previously been convicted of violations of the Wildlife Act and of various fishing regulations. The court found that "the offence was planned and deliberate," and that "a very large quantity of abalone were caught … and all of them died," causing significant harm to the restoration of the abalone population in the region. *Id.* para. 61. Nonetheless, the court ordered house arrest (rather than jail) for six months, a $20,000 monetary penalty, a five-year prohibition on diving, and forfeiture of the defendant's boat, dive gear, and pickup. *Id.* para. 82-88. Should violators of SARA go to jail? And should they forfeit their vehicles and equipment?

3. The precautionary principle and an express commitment to biodiversity conservation are both found in SARA § 38. Are there equivalent provisions in the ESA? Do the other substantive provisions of SARA fulfill these goals? How would you amend the statute to make it more likely to do so?

4. Note that Canada is a contracting party to the Convention on Biological Diversity, but the United States is not. The CBD requires each party to develop plans and strategies for the conservation of biodiversity and to implement a system of protected areas. Does SARA and the other Canadian preservation-oriented statutes detailed in this section satisfy the CBD?

Case Study: The Northern Spotted Owl

Joshua Walters and Shi-Ling Hsu,
Saving the Northern Spotted Owl in British Columbia[1]

(2008)

www.law.ubc.ca/files/pdf/enlaw/SpottedOwlCase04_20_09.pdf

The Northern Spotted Owl (*Strix occidentalis caurina*) is one of three Spotted Owl sub-species in North America and among the most well known and most studied bird species in the world. In Canada, the Northern Spotted Owl (Spotted Owl) is found only in southwest British Columbia and was listed as endangered by the Committee on the Status of Endangered Wildlife in Canada (COSEWIC) in 1986. The BC Spotted Owl population was estimated to be 500 breeding pairs prior to European settlement. In 1991, the population was less than 100 breeding pairs. By 2006, the BC government announced that 22 Spotted Owls remained, and only 6 breeding pairs.

---

1. Used with permission, as adapted.

The most important factor in the decline of B.C.'s Spotted Owl population is logging activity in old-growth forests.... Spotted Owl conservation has been highly controversial in both Canada and the United States due to the high economic value of timber associated with Spotted Owl habitat.

Old-growth Forest and the Northern Spotted Owl

The Northern Spotted Owl relies on old-growth forests to survive and reproduce. Although there is evidence that Spotted Owls may forage in secondary growth forests, forest age and successful reproduction are positively correlated. For example, a study in western Oregon found 95% of paired owls in undisturbed old-growth. Another study found 84% of the nest trees used by Spotted Owls were over 300 years old. In British Columbia, Spotted Owls have been shown to prefer stands with the most complex canopy cover and widest range of coarse woody debris classes—characteristics generally found in stands over 140 years old.

Old-growth habitat is important to Spotted Owls for several reasons. Old growth provides nesting sites, home ranges, feeding activities, and predator avoidance. Spotted Owls are not nest builders and thus rely on broken trees crowns and tree cavities for nesting sites. Nesting habitat is particularly important to this sub-species as they are slow to reproduce, with monogamous breeding pairs rarely breeding every year and small clutch sizes of one or two young. They also occupy large home ranges of 2,675 to 3,321 hectares and require undisturbed forest habitat within these ranges....

Spotted Owls also depend upon old-growth forests for their most important food source, the flying squirrel. Flying squirrels are also strongly associated with old-growth habitat as they depend on an ectomycorrhizal fungi found in Douglas-fir stands. Spotted Owls use a "sit and wait" hunting technique that requires suitable perches to wait on, as well as open forest understory.

Habitat Loss and Fragmentation

In BC, the single greatest threat to the Spotted Owl habitat is commercial logging. Since the 1940s, over 80% of suitable Spotted Owl habitat has been lost as a result of logging practices. By 1995, less than 30% of historic Spotted Owl habitat remained. Commercial logging has continued in these areas. Each year, approximately 3,000 hectares of suitable habitat is logged within the British Columbian range of the Spotted Owl.

Logging affects Spotted Owl populations by reducing habitat and altering the structure and composition of the forests.... Logging also isolates individual pairs, increasing the risk of genetic and demographic unfitness in an already small population.

Increased habitat fragmentation can also indirectly influence Spotted Owl survival. Spotted Owls have a number of predators, with Great Horned Owls being the most common. As Great Horned Owls thrive in open areas, logging in old-growth forests creates the fragmentation that makes Spotted Owls more susceptible to predation.

Spotted Owl meets Barred Owl

The Barred Owl (*S. varia*), a close relative of the Northern Spotted Owl associated with younger, more open forests, has historically occupied eastern North America, but has expanded its range westward across central Canada then southward into the three western coastal U.S. states. A variety of hypotheses have been proposed to explain this range expansion, including climate change and forest management practices, but none have been proven as of yet. Nonetheless, the ranges of these two species now overlap considerably, and the more aggressive Barred Owl has displaced and out-competed Spotted

Owls for nesting habitat. Scientists believe that if the two species fail to reach some sort of equilibrium, Barred Owls may eventually displace Spotted Owls entirely....

Legislation

British Columbia lacks specific species at risk legislation. Instead, the Spotted Owl is currently afforded protection under two existing provincial statutes—the *Wildlife Act*, RSBC 1996, c. 488, and the *Forest and Range Practices Act,* RSBC 1996, c. 159.

The Spotted Owl is protected by Section 34 of the *Wildlife Act*, which prohibits the taking of eggs, or the destruction of nestlings, or nesting adults. This protection is not specific to endangered or threatened species. The Spotted Owl is also on the provincial *Red List*, meaning that it has been designated "endangered" under Section 6 of the *Wildlife Act*. In addition, sections 3 to 5 of the *Wildlife Act* provide that the Minister of Environment may acquire land, and/or timber rights, for the purposes of managing or protecting a wildlife species....

Prior to 2002, the *Forest Practices Code Act* [FPCA], RSBC 1996, c. 159, was responsible for management of the Spotted Owl. By designating the Spotted Owl as a "forest resource," the *Forest Practices Code Act* mandated that a logging company's forest development plans only be approved if they adequately manage and conserve all forest resources in the area. Whether a given forest development plan is "adequate" with regard to Spotted Owl conservation was subject to a lengthy court challenge. But in 2002, the BC government overhauled BC forest practices by enacting the *Forest and Range Practices Act*, SBC 2002, c. 69.... The Forest and Range Practices Act (FRPA) is less prescriptive than prior legislation, with most wildlife-related provisions being only discretionary in nature. Also, the Minister of Environment's discretionary powers with regards to the conservation of wildlife habitat are not permitted to go against government objectives for a given area. Even if the Minister of Environment decides to initiate Spotted Owl habitat conservation, the *Forest and Range Practices Act Regulations* stipulates that any such orders must not unduly reduce British Columbia's timber supply.

The federal *Species at Risk Act* (SARA) mandates legal protection for endangered species, but only for species that are on federal land, are aquatic organisms, or covered by the federal *Migratory Birds Convention Act 1994.*

As only one percent of BC land is federally owned, SARA affords little protection for the Spotted Owl. SARA allows the federal government to intervene and protect endangered species, and their "critical habitat," when provincial conservation actions are deemed inadequate, but the federal government has declined to use this discretionary power thus far.

The BC Spotted Owl Management Plan

... In 1995, the BC government ... approached the Ministry of Forests and the Ministry of Environment, Lands and Parks to develop a new management plan with the goal of achieving "a reasonable level of probability that owl populations will stabilize, and possibly improve, over the long term without significant short-term impacts on timber supply and forestry employment." This resulted in the institution in 1997 of the Spotted Owl Management Plan, or "SOMP."

The SOMP involves managing 363,000 hectares of land for the Spotted Owl. 159,000 hectares is drawn from new and existing protected areas (mostly parks) and 204,000 hectares are maintained within a system of Special Resource Management Zones (SRMZs). The primary goal of SRMZs is to integrate spotted owl and forest management by simultaneously considering environmental, social, and economic concerns. SRMZs are managed such that a minimum of 67% of each SRMZ will always be suitable as Spotted

Owl habitat. The B.C. government claims that this strategy would "create, enhance and maintain" Spotted Owl habitat over the long-term. The SOMP also encourages the use of silvicultural techniques such as commercial thinning in young forests (60–100 years) and partial harvesting in mature forests (100–140 years) in order to accelerate the development of suitable Spotted Owl habitat within the SRMZs....

As the SOMP was clearly a compromise among conservation, economic and social concerns, Spotted Owl populations continued to face significant risks. Recognizing these risks, the SOMP predicted that Spotted Owl populations would continue to decline during the 20 to 30 years after SOMP implementation as a result of continued timber harvest. Furthermore, the SOMP predicted that these efforts would only provide Spotted Owl populations with a 60% chance of stabilizing over the long-term. The Ministry of the Environment admits that the compromises within the SOMP led to a plan that may or may not save the Spotted Owl. SOMP drew immediate criticism from scientists and environmentalists....

Court Battles

Despite the SOMP, Spotted Owl numbers have continued to decline, producing legal challenges. In June 2001, Western Canada Wilderness Committee (WCWC) filed a petition for judicial review of a Ministry of Forests District Manager's decision to grant approval of a Forest Development Plan (FDP) submitted by Cattermole Timber. The petition alleged that the District Manager approved the FDP without receiving and considering necessary information regarding spotted owl habitat in the areas from the then Ministry of Environment, Lands and Parks.... [Ultimately,] ... [t]he Court of Appeal upheld the ... decision, finding that [the decisionmaker] applied the FPCA correctly, and that her findings of fact were not "patently unreasonable," the standard of review applicable to administrative findings of fact. *Western Canada Wilderness Committee v. British Columbia (Ministry of Forests, South Island Forest District)*, [2003] B.C.J. No. 1581, 2003 BCCA 403, (2003) 15 B.C.L.R. (4th) 229, (2003) 1 Admin. L.R. (4th) 167, (2003) 1 C.E.L.R. (3d) 185 at para 73.

In 2004, Sierra Legal Defence Fund and several other environmental groups petitioned the federal government to invoke the "safety net" provisions of SARA [§ 34], the provisions that allow the federal Minister of the Environment to intervene if the province is failing to protect species at risk. Then-federal Environment Minister David Anderson wrote BC Premier Gordon Campbell and warned that he could not avoid invoking SARA's emergency provisions if circumstances warranted.... After a federal election and change in government, ... the new federal Environment Minister Rona Ambrose formally responded to Sierra Legal's Petition. Although the BC government had recently announced that only 22 Spotted Owls remain, Minister Ambrose stated that she had "formed the opinion that the Northern Spotted Owl does not currently face imminent threats to its survival or recovery." ...

Interestingly, two of the ten most active logging companies within the range of the Spotted Owl, International Forest Products (Interfor) and Canadian Forest Products (Canfor), announced that they would discontinue logging in Spotted Owl habitat. A spokesman for Interfor stated, "New scientific information makes it appear that the problem is worse than everyone thought, and we do not really want to be in the eye of the storm over this. Loggers care about the spotted owl, too."

What Next?

In April 2006, the BC government announced that it was initiating a $3.4-million, five-year action plan to recover the Spotted Owl. The province made a number of commitments, one of which was to focus on captive breeding and release. BC has now taken steps to initiate the world's first Spotted Owl captive breeding program—two Spotted Owls had been moved to wildlife refuge facilities as of August 8, 2007. Sierra Legal Defence Fund has accused the BC government of failing to protect critical habitat and relying on a captive breeding program to avoid the embarrassment of having the Spotted Owl population die-out prior to the 2010 Olympics. Conservation groups and biologists have objected to the captive breeding program, arguing that there is little point to breeding Spotted Owls for release if inadequate habitat remains in the wild.

The U.S. Experience

The U.S. experience is highly relevant because the Species At Risk Act was drafted and passed with much awareness of how endangered species regulation has fared in the U.S. Much of what is and is not in the Species At Risk Act is a conscious inclusion or omission of what is in the *Endangered Species Act* (ESA), the U.S. legislation and the first of its kind in the world. Northern Spotted Owl populations in the U.S. have also declined considerably, despite the stringent prohibitions of the ESA.

Northern Spotted Owl conservation has taken a markedly more litigious path in the United States....

- 1987: environmental advocacy groups petition the U.S. Fish and Wildlife Service (FWS), the agency charged with administering the ESA, to list the Northern Spotted Owl as "endangered" under the ESA....

- 1988: A U.S. Federal District Court finds that the FWS's decision to not list the Spotted Owl under the ESA was "arbitrary and capricious" and ordered the FWS to "supplement" its status review. *Northern Spotted Owl (Strix Occidentalis Caurina) v. Hodel*, 716 F. Supp. 479 (W.D. Wash. 1988)....

- 1990: the FWS lists the Northern Spotted Owl as "threatened" under the ESA, but declines to concurrently designate, as required by the ESA, the "critical habitat" of the Owl. Environmental advocacy groups sue.

- 1991: Judge Lilly, who heard the initial lawsuit against the FWS, orders the FWS to designate critical habitat, giving the FWS two months.

- 1991: in a separate but related case, a U.S. Federal District Court enjoins the USFS from selling timber harvested from Spotted Owl habitat.

- 1992: the FWS finally designates critical habitat, triggering additional rules regarding any activities within such critical habitat. Logging and timber sales on federal public lands ... is curtailed but not completely prohibited.

- 1993: the new Clinton Administration assembles a Forest Ecosystem Management Assessment Team (FEMAT), a technical committee with federal, state, local and university experts, to develop an ecosystem-based approach to forest management.... Option 9 was selected, calling for old-growth forest reserves, "forest matrix reserves" for timber production, and some lands set aside for experimental silviculture.

- 2005: the Seattle chapter of the National Audubon Society sues the FWS for failing to formulate a recovery plan for the Spotted Owl.

- 2007: a draft recovery plan is released ... identifying the Barred Owl, *not* habitat destruction, as the primary threat to the Spotted Owl. The draft recovery plan continues to set aside some federal lands as habitat, but exempts 1.5 million acres of federal land from Endangered Species Act application.

- 2007: the FWS commissions independent scientific reviews of the draft recovery plan.... One study concludes that there was no scientific justification for the 1.5 million acre exemption, the FWS failed to use the best available science, and selectively cited from the available science to justify a reduction in habitat protection. The study also recommended that the Spotted Owl be uplisted from "threatened" to "endangered." ...

- 2007: public consultation for the draft recovery plan closes, and the FWS aims to release a decision on the matter by June 1, 2008.

No Answers Yet

In both Canada and the U.S., the future of the Spotted Owl remains uncertain. Populations continue to decline, and conservation plans are currently in a state of flux. BC is attempting a compromise—captive breeding to increase the number of owls in the province, while avoiding large-scale habitat protection. Although both Canada and the U.S. have adopted very different approaches to conservation, Spotted Owl numbers have continued to dwindle in both countries.

Notes and Questions

1. What do you think of the "safety net" provisions of SARA (§ 34)? How, if at all, would you change these provisions? Are these provisions within the scope of Parliament's constitutionally-granted powers vis-à-vis the Province of British Columbia? (Recall the discussion of *Friends of the Oldman River Society v. Canada* [1992] 1 S.C.R. 3, in Chapter 3.B.1, *supra*, which recognized that the provinces have primary authority over natural resources development, but held that the federal government controls the federal environmental review process.)

2. Compare the U.S. *Endangered Species Act* and the Canadian *Species At Risk Act*. List some of the comparative advantages and disadvantages of the ESA and SARA as related to the Spotted Owl dispute. SARA was enacted in 2002, twenty-nine years after the enactment of the ESA, and after the ESA had already had a long history. What do you think were the conscious decisions in drafting SARA to avoid some of the problems encountered and created by the ESA?

3. Is it likely that logging activities in BC that destroy the habitat of the Spotted Owl would violate SARA? Why, and under what conditions? What specific provisions and what sources of law would serve as the basis of the violation? Does § 61, for example, apply?

4. What is the authority for habitat conservation planning under the ESA? What is the similar mechanism in SARA? Are the problems addressed by habitat conservation planning in the U.S. also problems in the Canadian context? Does SARA have other provisions to address this type of problem?

5. Is there something glaringly missing from both the SOMP, and the U.S. Spotted Owl plans? What provisions would you include in SARA to remedy this shortcoming? What other mechanisms would you establish or tap into to remedy this shortcoming?

6. Is the Northern Spotted Owl really so important to save? What are the trade-offs?

7. You are the Honourable Peter Kent, the Minister of the Environment. Your ministry is charged with enforcing SARA and other federal environmental laws. You have many regional offices, and you have an excellent staff on the ground in mountainous Eastern BC, where the forestry industry is big business, and where there are only a few Spotted Owls. There have been some sightings of a Spotted Owl in Glacier National Park

in southeastern BC, just inside the Park's borders. Canfor, a major forestry company, has a provincial license from BC to log on some landsadjacent to the Park. If Canfor decides to log that land near the Park, it would be logging very close to the area where the Owl was spotted. What should you do? What must you do?

C. New Zealand

The islands of New Zealand are bounded on the west by the Tasman Sea and on the east by the South Pacific. The Māori, a Polynesian group that arrived some time before 1300, named the islands Aotearoa, loosely translated as *The Land of the Long White Cloud*. Professors Furuseth and Cocklin provide details about New Zealand's physical geography, its biodiversity, and its "green" reputation:

> New Zealand is a young nation, both in terms of geologic age and human settlement. Located in the South Pacific, the archipelago nation covers 269,000 sq.km [104,860 square miles], primarily on two islands stretching 1,600km [994 miles] from north to south. The nearest large landmass is Australia, located over 2,000km [1,243 miles] to the west. As a result of its isolation and island status, biodiversity is high. A very large percentage of its 50,000 native plants and animals are found only in New Zealand.

> New Zealand sits astride the boundary of the Pacific and Indo-Australian tectonic plates. As a consequence, the landscape is active and dominated by mountains, and other rugged terrain. Of the total land area, only about 6 percent is considered suitable for agricultural usage, while 44 percent is classified as being unsuited for agriculture or having severe limitations for agricultural or forestry land uses.... Compared with other nations, New Zealand's population density is low, but settlement is concentrated. Most New Zealanders live in urban areas [on the North Island]....

> Internationally, New Zealand has enjoyed a widespread reputation for environmental consciousness. Nearly 20 percent of the nation is held in national parks or reserves and the long tradition of protecting native species of plants and animals are evidence of environmental sensitivity within the nation.

Owen Furuseth and Chris Cocklin, *An Institutional Framework For Sustainable Resource Management: The New Zealand Model,* 35 Nat. Resources J. 243, 247–48 (1995).

European settlement began around 1820, when both French and British expeditions landed on the islands. The signing of the Treaty of Waitangi of 1840 marked the beginning of organized British colonization of New Zealand. In 1947, New Zealand adopted the Statute of Westminster Act, providing the New Zealand Parliament full legislative powers and extra-territorial control of the New Zealand military. This event marked its legal separation from the British Crown. Another significant event in New Zealand history came in 1973, when Britain joined the European Economic Community, causing major economic adjustments in New Zealand by dramatically diminishing exports to Britain.

> Throughout its eurocentric history, New Zealand's economy has been dependent on the development and export of natural resource-based products. During the initial European colonization phase, seals, timber, gold and flax were valuable export commodities to British markets. Later, meat and dairy products and other

agricultural commodities emerged as the dominant exports. Although the land based economy which evolved in New Zealand over the past 150 years has a propensity to generate significant pollution problems, widespread environmental disruption has generally been avoided. This has largely been a consequence of the extensive rural territory, throughout which resource development activities have been dispersed, so that polluting impacts of economic activities are "diluted" by distance from other economic operations and urban populations.

Id. at 247. By the 1980s, resource exploitation had taken its toll, and environmental quality had begun to decline. Two-thirds of indigenous forest area had been cleared, leaving few native stands of trees. *See* Derek Nolan, ed., Environmental and Resource Management Law 424 (4th ed. 2011). For a detailed assessment of forestry reforms, see Robert Fischman and John C. Nagle, *Corporatisation: Implementing Forest Management Reform in New Zealand, 16* Ecology L. Q. 719 (1989). Meanwhile, exotic trees and other non-indigenous plant and animal species had spread across the islands at an alarming rate. "When a 1983 study compared New Zealand's environmental policy and planning with other Pacific rim nations, ... New Zealand ranked last, behind Indonesia, Malaysia, Australia, and Japan; and the nation's environmental protection mechanisms were assigned to the lowest level in the model." Furuseth, *supra,* at 248.

In response, New Zealand adopted the Resource Management Act, No. 69 (1991) (N.Z.) (RMA), and redoubled its efforts to conserve land, water, and native species. For history and background on the RMA and the sustainable development principle in New Zealand, see Klaus Bosselmann and David Grinlinton, eds., Environmental Law for a Sustainable Society 2002.

In 1993, New Zealand became one of the first nations to ratify the Convention on Biological Diversity. Just a few years later, the decline of indigenous biodiversity was identified as New Zealand's "most pervasive environmental issue." Nolan, *supra,* at 427, citing I. Smith, ed., *The State of New Zealand's Environment* 10.6 (1997).

New Zealand's Biodiversity Strategy 2000, which supplements the RMA, strengthens the commitment to biodiversity conservation, and declares ambitious goals related to improving the extent and condition of natural habitats and ecosystems, ensuring effective pest management, and recovery of native species. Nolan, *supra,* at 425. The Strategy, the RMA, and other relevant provisions related to land conservation and species protection are covered in the following sections.

1. The "Conservation Estate"

Protected areas in New Zealand include outstanding landscapes, national, maritime, and forest parks, and three World Heritage Areas. Together these areas are known as the "Conservation Estate." Michael Hall and James Higham, *Wilderness Management in the Forests of New Zealand: Historical Development and Contemporary Issues in Environmental Management, in* Forest Tourism and Recreation: Case Studies in Environmental Management 143 (Xavier Font and John Tribe eds., 2000).

"*Outstanding natural features and landscapes*" are identified in RMA § 6(b) as matters of national importance, and directs that they be managed sustainably and protected from "inappropriate" use or development. Accordingly, consent authorities must provide for outstanding landscapes when considering applications for resource consents and when preparing regional or district plans. Nolan, *supra,* at 1001. In a country filled with spectacular landscapes like the Bay of Islands and the Milford Sound, what, exactly, is "outstanding"? The Environment Court has employed the common dictionary definition in sorting this out: "conspicuous, eminent, esp. because of excellence." Arrigato Investments Ltd. V. Rodney Dist. Council [2000] NZRMA 241, *aff'd* [2001] NZRMA 481 (CA). It is "an adjective of some strength," and some locally significant landscapes may not qualify; a landscape must be "quite out of the ordinary on a national basis" to come within this provision. Nolan, *supra,* at 1027. However, the Environment Court may find that an area is in fact outstanding under §6(b) even if the district does not classify it as such. Unison Networks Ltd. v. Hastings Dist. Council [2007] HC Wellington, CIV-2007-485-896.

In addition to the RMA, a variety of other conservation-oriented statutes come into play in protecting natural landscapes and habitats as well. Section 7 of the Conservation Act of 1987 authorizes the Minister of Conservation and the Minister of Agriculture and Forestry to jointly declare that any state forest land be held for conservation purposes as a "conservation area." Once a conservation area is established, the Minister of Conservation may declare it to be a park, an ecological area, a sanctuary, a wilderness, or a combination of these designations. Conservation Act 1987, §18.

National parks are managed to facilitate recreation and enjoyment, but the protection of natural and historic resources must take first priority. *Id.* §19. Once established, national parks are governed by the National Parks Act, which provides for the preservation in perpetuity of the scenery, ecological systems, or natural features of designated parks both for their intrinsic worth and for public enjoyment. National Parks Act 1980 §4(1). Specifically:

> [T]he provisions of this Act shall have effect for the purpose of preserving in perpetuity as national parks, for their intrinsic worth and for the benefit, use, and enjoyment of the public, areas of New Zealand that contain scenery of such distinctive quality, ecological systems, or natural features so beautiful, unique, or scientifically important that their preservation is in the national interest....

> Subject to the provisions of this Act and to the imposition of such conditions and restrictions as may be necessary for the preservation of the native plants and animals or the welfare in general of the parks, the public shall have freedom of entry and access to the parks, so that they may receive in full measure the inspiration, enjoyment, recreation, and other benefits that may be derived from mountains, forests, sounds, seacoasts, lakes, rivers, and other natural features.

National Parks Act 1980 §4(1), (2)(e).

> Special emphasis is given to the preservation of indigenous species:

> Except where the Authority otherwise determines, the native plants and animals of the parks shall as far as possible be preserved and the introduced plants and animals shall as far as possible be exterminated.

Id. §4(2)(b). "Extermination" of non-native species may sound somewhat harsh, but according to the Department's General Park Policy:

> Many introduced plants and animals pose serious threats to the survival of indigenous species and the functioning of indigenous ecosystems in national parks. Plant and animal pests are increasing in both number and distribution and have become a pervasive obstacle to the preservation of indigenous plants and animals and ecosystem functions in national parks.

> The Authority affirms that the immediate objective is to reduce by all available means introduced species to a level where they do not impede the preservation of the indigenous species within a national park.

Department of Conservation-New Zealand Conservation Authority, General Policy for National Parks 20 (2005).

With regard to native species in the parks, no one may disturb, trap, take, hunt, or kill any indigenous animal without the prior consent of the Minister. National Parks Act § 5(2). Any consent must be consistent with the national park management plan. The Park Policy admonishes, "The take of indigenous species is not generally consistent with the preservation ethic." General Policy for National Parks, *supra*, 21. Non-commercial customary and recreational fishing for indigenous species in national parks also require a written consent from the Minister, and may be authorized on a case-by-case basis where i) it is consistent with all relevant Acts and the purposes of national parks; ii) there is an established tradition of such fishing in those waters; and iii) the preservation of indigenous freshwater fisheries within those waters are not adversely affected. *Id.* at 26 para. 4.4(f).

Section 4(2)(d) of the National Parks Act provides that parks shall be administered so that "their value as soil, water and forest conservation areas shall be maintained." The Policy explains:

> Healthy natural ecosystems provide benefits that are not well known and often undervalued. These benefits are sometimes referred to as 'ecosystem services' and include carbon absorption, clean water, landscape stability, soil conservation, reduced flooding and sediment generation, and amenity values.

Id. at 21. Accordingly, activities "should be planned and managed in ways which avoid adverse effects on the quality of ecosystem services provided by national parks." *Id.* at 27 para. 4.6(a).

Ecological areas—are managed to protect the specific scientific values for which the area was designated. Conservation Act 1987, § 18(4).

Sanctuaries—are managed to preserve indigenous plants and animals in their natural state, and for scientific purposes. *Id.* § 22. *Marine sanctuaries* are governed by the Marine Reserves Act 1971.

Forest reserves—under the Conservation Act, over eight million forested hectares (nearly 30 percent of the country's total land base) have been set aside for conservation purposes. Approximately 83 percent of this is state-owned, and managed by the Department of Conservation as national parks, soil and water conservation reserves, forest or wildlife reserves, and/or recreational areas. Nolan, *supra*, at 424, 430. Ownership of "plantation" (non-native) forests is quite different. In 2008, around 92 percent of these forests were held in private ownership, five percent were owned by the Crown, and the rest were owned by local authorities and Maori trusts. In a landmark settlement with Maori *iwi* (tribes) of the North Island, known as the "Treelord" deal, 176,000 hectares of Crown forest land were transferred to the *iwi* in partial redress for historic grievances. *Id* at 430.

Wilderness—Wilderness areas lie at the core of the nation's conservation reserve system. Hall and Higham, *supra*, at 143. Despite the historic importance of logging to the nation's economy, "[a]s attitudes towards the wilderness have changed so the majority of native forest areas came to be protected from timber cutting." *Id.* at 144. Today, wilderness areas "comply with a highly purist legislated definition of wilderness." *Id.*

Wilderness areas are designated under the Conservation Act for the preservation of their indigenous natural resources. Conservation Act 1987 § 20(1)(a). A wilderness designation requires that the landscape have no apparent modifications, including no "huts, tracks (trails), bridges, signs or other facilities." Gordon R. Cessford and Paul Dingwall, *Wilderness and Recreation in New Zealand*, 3 Int. J. of Wilderness 35, 37 (1997).

The Department of Conservation (DOC) supervises the designation process. By 1990, three proposed areas had been designated: Raukumara; Tasman; and Hooker-Landsborough. Hugh Barr, *Establishing a Wilderness Preservation System in New Zealand*, 3 Int. J. of Wilderness 7, 9 (1997). Due to lack of funding, further designations slowed substantially. Eventually, several more proposed areas were designated, bringing the total to seven, but others still languish in the process. Les Molloy, *Forever Wild: Looking Back Over the Last 30 Years at Recreation and Conservation Highlights for Our Mountain Lands*, Federated Mountain Clubs 80th Jubilee Conference (2011).

Like the United States, New Zealand classifies areas based on use. The U.S.'s wilderness designation is similar to New Zealand's wilderness grouping, although the latter is a more stringent classification as it disallows any recreation facilities or services. Accessing a wilderness area in New Zealand often requires a half-day's walk, as no motorized (road, air, or water) access is permissible. Cessford and Dingwall, *supra,* at 40.

The Conservation Act prohibits the construction of buildings, roads, or trails, and the use of machinery, vehicles, or aircraft. Livestock is also prohibited. However, the Minister of Conservation may authorize any of these activities in a wilderness area if the activity "conforms with a conservation management strategy or plan and it is desirable or necessary to preserve the area's indigenous natural resources." *Id.* § 20(b)-(e); Nolan, *supra,* at 432.

Mining deserves special mention. Under the Mining Act 1971 § 26(2)(c), conservation areas were designated as open for mining, but a subsequent enactment, the Crown Minerals Act 1991 §§ 50 and 55, requires the consent of the Minister for "minimum impact activities" such as surveying and sampling on conservation lands. Section 61 of the Crown Minerals Act specifies that the Minister may only approve access for activities with minimal environmental impacts. Nolan, *supra,* at 433. But the debate about mining on conservation lands is far from over.

> [A] proposal which attracted little attention although it represents a significant shift from the status quo … was for decisions about access to Crown land for mining to be made jointly by the land-holding Minister and the Minister of Energy and Resources.… Access to conservation land for mining would no longer be decided by the Minister of Conservation alone, but in tandem with the Minister of Energy and Resources. Cabinet has decided to amend the legislation accordingly. This shift … cuts across the fundamental separation of functions and powers, whereby the Minister of Energy and Resources grants permits for minerals and the Minister of Conservation grants access to the conservation estate. The Minister of Conservation will remain accountable for the conservation estate but not in control. His or her core role as guardian of the conservation estate will be undermined.

> Mining already enjoys a special status above that of other commercial activities on conservation land. Applications to gain access to conservation land for adventure tourism, for instance, must pass a higher hurdle than access for mining. This makes no sense. The environmental impact of an adventure tourism operation will generally be far less than that of a mine, and will encourage people to get out and enjoy the beauty and wildness of the conservation estate.…

> [However,] [t]he greatest threat to the New Zealand's unique biodiversity on the conservation estate is not mining but introduced pests, both plants and animals. Without active pest management, kiwi chicks have a one-in-twenty chance of making it to adulthood. And many of our most precious species such as kokako and native mistletoe would face almost certain extinction.

Dr. Jan Wright, Parliamentary Commissioner for the Environment, *Commissioner's Overview, Mining the Conservation Estate* 5 (2010). Kiwis and other protected species are addressed in the next section.

2. Species-Related Legislation

As an island nation, it comes as no surprise that New Zealand has a rich diversity of coastal and marine flora and fauna.

> The New Zealand Exclusive Economic Zone, extending 200 nautical miles seaward from the low water mark around New Zealand and its offshore islands, contains approximately 100 commercially significant species, including tropical tuna, red cod, school shark, rig, tarakihi, gurnard, grouper, flounder, sole, jack makerals, trevally, barracouta, kahawai, oysters, scallops, abalone/paua, southern blue whiting, oreo doreis, ling, skipjack tuna, albacore tuna, southern bluefin, hoki, orange roughy, rock lobster, snapper, squid, and other warm temperate species on shelves around the main islands. Seaweed is also an important water resource in New Zealand. Furthermore, New Zealand's mangrove forests and other marine wetlands provide additional commercial and environmental value. Freshwater species include eel, whitebait, crayfish, salmon, trout, lampreys, graylings, chars, catfish, carps, perches and mullets. Finally, New Zealand today has developed aquaculture farming operations for green-lipped mussels, Pacific oysters, salmon, recreational trout, abalone/paua, and seaweed.

Benjamin A. Kahn, *The Legal Framework Surrounding Maori Claims to Water Resources In New Zealand: In Contrast to the American Indian Experience*, 35 Stan. J. Int'l L. 49, 57 (1999).

New Zealand's prolonged geographic isolation is responsible for an incredibly unique ecosystem.

> [I]t has no native mammals save two bat species and in the absence of these animals, bird and insect species lost their ability to fly in order to fill the typical mammal niche on the forest floor. As a result, New Zealand has an ecosystem evolved without pressures from mammal species and has flora and fauna unlike any other place in the world.

Flynn Boonstra, *Leading By Example: A Comparison of New Zealand's and the United States' Invasive Species Policies*, 43 Conn. L. Rev. 1185, 1207 (2011).

Prior to the RMA, New Zealand had adopted an array of legislation aimed at species protection. Those still in effect include the Wildlife Act 1953 and the Trade in Endangered Species Act 1989.

The Wildlife Act 1953 (W.A.) declares wild animals to be absolutely protected unless otherwise scheduled as game species or other partially protected or unprotected species. Wide-ranging restrictions are listed in § 63(1)(c), and include "disturbing, destroying or possessing a nest of protected wildlife or game." The definition of hunt or kill includes any method of taking, including catching or pursuing. What about harvesting or development activities that incidentally take wild animals by destroying their habitat?

> Potentially included in these definitions is the concept of incidental take, where wild animals are killed or taken, or their nests interfered with during a development activity or vegetation removal operation. Fortunately the average mynah,

rat or opossum and many other common introduced animals are excluded from protection by way of Schedules to the WA. If however, the intention is to destroy habitat or disturb the nest of fauna such as kokako, tui or gecko, a WA permit will need to be obtained from the Department of Conservation. In practice such permits are generally obtained in large-scale operations such as forestry applications, where the habitat of an iconic species is known to be affected. When the resource consent to fell is lodged with the council, a copy is usually provided to the Department of Conservation which can make recommendations as to procedures to follow.

Pip Wallace, *Where the Wild Things Are: Examining the Intersection Between the RMA 1991 and the Wildlife Act 1953,* Resource Mgmt. J. 21 (2009). *See* Royal Forest and Bird Protection Society v. Minister of Conservation [2006] NZAR (concluding that open cast mining that impacted *Powelliphanta* land snails could be a violation of the WA).

When all of the necessary resource consents have been obtained prior to development, what is a developer required to do when a protected species is subsequently discovered? Wallace describes a case involving the moko skink.

> Over a period of a more than a decade, the Whangamata Marina Society sought and obtained a range of resource consents to develop an extensive marina at Whangamata, Coromandel Peninsula. The consents contained extensive conditions regulating development activities in order to avoid, remedy or mitigate adverse effects. In terms of fauna, there were particular concerns relating to birds such as the banded rail and the dotterel. As a condition of one of the coastal permits..., a fauna management plan was required.... When this plan was prepared it recommended surveying a particular area ... and the presence of moko skink became known.... Although works were not to have commenced on the site prior to completion of the fauna management plan, through miscommunication, kikuyu grass and pampas vegetation associated with the skink's habitat needs, had been sprayed with herbicide in various locations within the site.

Id. at 22. When the Department of Conservation demanded a WA permit to protect the skink, proceedings before the Environment Court were initiated. In an unpublished opinion, the court concluded that the effects on the skink "would not be adverse to the point that would justify intervention of the Court." *Id.*, citing Gunson v. Waikato Regional Council [2008] Environment Court, A134/2208. Wallace concludes, "A pragmatic decision such as this may provide welcome relief to the conscientious developer ... [y]et it treads a path that may not be completely beneficial to absolutely protected species." *Id.* The hands of the authorities and the court were tied, at least to some extent, because "[o]nce consent is granted ... it confers a right upon the owner to carry out the consented activities." *Id.*

The Trade in Endangered Species Act 1989 is designed to "enable New Zealand to fulfill its obligations under the Convention on International Trade in Endangered Species of Wild Fauna and Flora (CITES) and to promote the management, conservation, and protection of endangered, threatened, and exploited species to further enhance the survival of those species." *Id.* § 2. Species are listed according to the schedules adopted under CITES. *Id.* § 3(1). The Act prohibits "trade in any specimen of an endangered, threatened, or exploited species into or from New Zealand." *Id.* § 9. The Director-General may, however, grant a permit to import or to export "any specimen of an endangered species to an applicant, if those authorities are satisfied that ... [the import or export] is not detrimental to the survival of that species...," among other things. *Id.* §§ 13–14. The Act has exceptions for species bred in captivity, scientific transfers, circuses or exhibitions, and personal or household effects. *Id.* §§ 29–33. Persons who commit offenses may be subject to forfeiture of the specimen, imprisonment for up to five years, and/or fines not exceeding $100,000. *Id.* § 44, 51. *See* R v. Nichols [2003] NZCA 206 (upholding defendants' convictions under the Trade in Endangered Species Act and the Biosecurity Act for smuggling parrot eggs by strapping them, inside strands of stockings, on a courier's body and flying them from Thailand to New Zealand).

3. Biosecurity

Unfortunately, the evolutionary adaptations that make New Zealand's indigenous flora and fauna so unique also make them especially vulnerable to the adverse effects of invasive, non-native species.

> Invasive plants and animals came to New Zealand with the first human colonizers-the Maori. European settlers came with even more non-native organisms, both intentionally and unintentionally. The effect on the delicate ecosystem has been devastating. Flightless birds and insects that specifically adapted to life without mammalian predators or competitors are out-competed on the forest floor by mice and rats and are killed by stoats and feral cats. Indigenous plant-life is also put at risk from grazing invasive species like goats, rabbits, and deer. Brushtail possum are a particular problem for forest ecosystems. These animals climb and eat the leaves off native tree species. In a particular section of the Hihitahi Forest Sanctuary, more than ninety percent of standing trees are now dead due to possum activity.

Boonstra, *supra,* at 1207. Tourists who rent vehicles in New Zealand may be surprised to see posters and signs encouraging them *not* to swerve to avoid possums on the road. Road kill may be one crude form of invasive species eradication, but the legislature has chosen several more sophisticated means through its biosecurity enactments.

"Biosecurity" has become the primary focus of New Zealand's approach to both invasive species and genetically modified species. New Zealand's biosecurity policies have been described as among some "of the boldest experiments in bringing science and the precautionary approach into policy, regulation, and operational decision-making at the domestic level." Mitsuhiko A. Takahashi, *Are the Kiwis Taking a Leap? Learning from the Biosecurity Policy of New Zealand*, 24 Temp. J. Sci. Tech. & Envtl. L. 461, 476 (2005).

> Under the Biosecurity Act [Biosecurity Act 1993 (Pub. Act 1993 No. 95)] one of the Ministers of the Crown in Cabinet is appointed as the Minister for Biosecurity. The Minister for Biosecurity takes responsibility for coordinating the implementation of the Act, recording and coordinating reports of suspected new organisms, and managing appropriate responses to such reports. However, the Minister of Biosecurity does not maintain an independent Ministry to carry out his duties, but instead relies on other central government agencies and regional councils, which hold statutory operational responsibilities.

> The central government agencies with operational responsibilities under the Biosecurity Act include the Ministry of Agriculture and Forestry (MAF), the Department of Conservation (DOC), the Ministry of Fisheries, and the Ministry of Health. Each of the four agencies bears respective responsibilities, reports to the Minister of Biosecurity and has agreed to work with the other agencies on

biosecurity matters. The MAF is the lead agency and is responsible for border control (through the MAF Quarantine Service) and biosecurity issues affecting preliminary industry—agriculture, horticulture, and forestry. DOC is responsible for biosecurity issues that impact conservation and environmental values. MOF is responsible for marine biosecurity issues including threats to both conservation and the commercial values of marine resources. The MOH is responsible for biosecurity issues that impact human health. Furthermore, the four central agencies and regional councils that have statutory obligations under the Biosecurity Act are responsible for developing national pest management strategies, proposing regional pest management strategies, and taking action in response to biosecurity emergencies....

[T]he Biosecurity Act is a comprehensive, integrated, model statute for the management of biological pollution.... The major objective of the Biosecurity Act is the management of "unwanted organisms" through quarantine and pest management strategies. "Unwanted organisms" are determined by the Chief Technical Officer of the related Ministries having responsibilities under the Biosecurity Act in their respective areas of responsibility. Once an animal, plant, or any other organism is determined as an unwanted organism, it may not be released in the field, and any cargo containing such material is defined as "risk goods" and may not be imported. For unwanted organisms that have already come into the country, pest control plans are promulgated and implemented according to their urgency and necessity by responsible Ministries or Regional Councils.

Id. at 467, 469. Persons who attempt to transport noxious species without authorization pursuant to the Biosecurity Act may be subject to criminal penalties. *See Nichols*, NZCA 106 (conviction for smuggling parrot eggs into New Zealand); *see also* NZ Waterways Restoration Ltd. v. Director-General [2006] CIV 2005 485 1824 para. 69 (applicant must obtain a permit under the Biosecurity Act, in addition to the Fisheries Act and any other applicable statute, prior to taking "unwanted aquatic life"—live koi carp—from the Waikato river system for export to the U.K. and Japan, even though multiple permit requirements are cumbersome).

"New" organisms are addressed by the Hazardous Substances and New Organism Act of 1996 (HSNO Act), Pub. Law 1993 No. 30.

The HSNO Act created a comprehensive regulatory regime for "new organisms" under a single agency, the Environmental Risk Management Authority (ERMA). The HSNO Act bans any "new organism" not approved by ERMA from being imported, field tested, or released into the field. The HSNO Act defines a "new organism" as, inter alia, a species of any organism not present in New Zealand on the date of commencement of the HSNO Act (July 1998); an organism which is in containment; an organism that has been conditionally released under the Act; a genetically modified organism which has not previously been approved for importation or release; or an organism that belongs to a species, subspecies, or variety that has been eradicated from New Zealand. Any new organism may only be imported or released in the field after approval. The approval of a new organism is issued by ERMA; however, before making its decision on importation or release, ERMA must carry out a risk assessment at the applicant's expense....

Although ERMA does not have any operational responsibilities in the Biosecurity Act, the Authority plays an important role in New Zealand's biosecurity by assessing all potential invasive species, including GMOs [genetic modified organisms], and deciding to ban or approve their introduction. ERMA simultaneously administers approvals of hazardous substances as provided by the HSNO Act. ERMA is a quasi-independent multimember agency consisting of Authority Members appointed by the Minister of Environment, and assisted by staff headed by a Chief Executive and senior executives....

The HSNO Act section seven, which may represent the first use of the term "precautionary approach" in New Zealand domestic legislation, states: Precautionary approach—All persons exercising functions, powers, and duties under this Act ... shall take into account the need for caution in managing adverse affects where there is scientific and technical uncertainty about those effects.

Takahashi, *supra,* at 469–70. For details on the Biosecurity Strategy, see Biosecurity Council, Protect New Zealand: The Biosecurity Strategy for New Zealand (2003), available at http://www.biosecurity.govt.nz/bio-strategy/biostrategy.htm.

What is the meaning of the "precautionary approach" in New Zealand? The HSNO Act does not provide a definition, but a few courts and tribunals have considered the phrase in other contexts.

The Planning Tribunal (which is the predecessor of the Environment Court) in an early Resource Management Act (RMA) case held that the lack of knowledge does not automatically lead to a phase-out: "It is not to reject the precautionary approach, but there needs to be some plausible basis, not mere suspicion or innuendo for adopting that approach." Trans Power New Zealand v. Rodney Dist. (Decision A 85/94), 4 NZPTD 35. Also, in McIntyre v. Christchurch City Council, another RMA case concerning alleged harmful health effects from a mobile phone transmitter, the Planning Tribunal struck down the case after studying the U.S. Supreme Court's decision in Daubert v. Merrill Dow Pharmaceuticals, Inc., 509 U.S. 579 (1993), and other cases from England, Canada, and New South Wales, largely on the question of the reliability of the contested scientific evidence. McIntyre v. Christchurch City Council (Decision A 15/96), 1996 NZRMA 289. Some commentators suggest that the Environment Court should follow McIntyre in this type of situation and rest its decision on the "balance of probabilities." If "reliable evidence" in support of the allegation is presented, "[t]he onus will then be on the other party to prove to the balance of probabilities that the alleged effect would not occur."

Takahashi, *supra,* at 471–72. According to Takahashi, thus far, "legislators have shown an intention to decide on cost (risk)/benefit analysis, combined with existing international obligations, and it is unclear how much the legislature intended to defer to scientific knowledge and preferences in the decision-making process." *Id.* at 472.

GMOs and genetic engineering (GE) have been especially controversial.

[P]ublic anxiety toward genetic engineering and concern about its effects upon biodiversity was overwhelming, leading to a big political debate. In 2001, after a year of protracted discussions, the Labour government announced its decision to instill a moratorium of two years, prohibiting the release of genetically modified organisms in the environment, while allowing time for further research. For this controversial issue, the government formed the Royal Commission on Genetic Modification as a forum for debate and investigation.... The Commission received over 10,000 written submissions and conducted thirteen weeks of

hearings. The ban was lifted only by the expiration of the moratorium [in] …
2003, which still provoked many protests.

Maori groups, along with environmentalists including the Green Party, are
strongly opposed to GE, while the mainstream Labour Party (currently the leading party of the coalition government) disfavors the moratorium. The political
and legal rights vested in Maori by the Treaty of Waitangi gives them a position
as important stakeholders in issues relating to natural resources and heritage,
which the government cannot ignore. The Maori community has shown deep interest in preserving the indigenous biodiversity and has considerable antipathy
toward the introduction of exotic species and genetic engineering. This unique
position of Maori is often described as a "guardianship" role for the environment, but is seen by detractors as a roadblock to the biotech industry and scientists. Some have criticized Ngai Tahu, the Maori advisory committee for ERMA,
characterizing it as "largely close mind[ed]" and suggesting that ERMA places
too much weight on the spiritual values of Maori, rather than scientific facts.

Takahashi, *supra,* at 475.

At the end of the day, even with is shortcomings, "New Zealand's comprehensive structure and the internalization of the precautionary approach, among other things, provide
a model from which other countries could learn."

New Zealand has a comprehensive structure and the responsible agencies are
relatively well staffed by scientists and professionals. The decisions are made after
risk assessments and public input. The legislature has indicated its intention to
give appropriate weight to scientific and technical data and analysis to arrive at
decisions that are neutral and unaffected by political and other influences.… In
times when public funds are scarce, the Labour government's promotion of science, along with the pursuit of minimal but effective government regulation and
intervention, is impressive.…

All things considered, the New Zealand Biosecurity Act and HSNO Act do not
provide the ultimate solution, nor is the precautionary approach the panacea it
is often made out to be. Still, the attitude of New Zealand in boldly internaliz-
ing science in legislation should provide a model in the post-modern state.

Id. at 476–77. For an assessment of ways in which the U.S. could benefit by following
New Zealand's approach to invasive species, see Flynn Boonstra, *Leading By Example: A
Comparison of New Zealand's and the United States' Invasive Species Policies*, 43 Conn. L.
Rev. 1185 (2011).

D. India

India is considered a "megadiverse" country, both in terms of its flora and fauna and
of its human communities.

Like many developing nations, India is home to many diverse ecosystems, species
and genes, as well as diverse cultures.… Its living forms represent two of the major
realms and three basic biomes of the world. The country is divided into 10 bio-
geographic regions: Trans-Himalayan, Himalayan, Indian Desert, Semi-Arid, Western Ghats, Deccan Peninsula, Gangetic Plains, North-East India, Islands and Coasts.…

With its population having crossed the one billion mark (the second country after China to do so), the country's cultural diversity is stupendous: 4635 distinct ethnic communities, 325 languages belonging to twelve language families, six 'major' religions and dozens of smaller independent faiths, three racially distinct resident populations, and ways of life ranging from ancient hunter-gatherer to modern urbanism. Thereby, in itself, India is representative of the range of diversity, both biological and cultural, found in many developing countries....

Indian civilization has long recognized the intrinsic right of nature to exist. This recognition and respect is deeply interwoven with the cultural and material dependence of the majority of its people on biodiversity. As such, in India the ethical, economic, social, and cultural aspects of biodiversity are hard to separate....

In India, as in many other cultures in Asia, all sentient beings for their living form are revered for the life they manifest. Several rituals of everyday life reflect this respect for other forms of life, for their natural beauty, or for the spiritual link provided between the human species and the natural world. These rituals, be it the worship of certain plants or animals as spiritual ancestors or the setting aside of parts of land, water or forests in the name of local deities, then become important as traditional conservation and management of biological resources. Thus, in countries such as India, conserving biodiversity is about conserving the diverse cultures that define the nation.

Shalini Bhutani and Ashish Kothari, *The Biodiversity Rights of Developing Nations: A Perspective From India*, 32 Golden Gate U. L. Rev. 587, 588–89, 594 (2002). *See* Convention on Biodiversity, India Country Profile, available at: http://www.cbd.int/countries/profile.shtml?country=in#thematic (visited Aug. 11, 2012).

India's National Policy and Action Strategy on Biodiversity recognizes these linkages. The Strategy, adopted in 1999, includes:

    i)   Conservation and sustainable use of biological diversity including regeneration and rehabilitation of threatened species;

   ii)   Securing participation of State Governments, communities, people, NGOs, industry and other stakeholders;

  iii)   Realizing consumptive and non-consumptive values of biodiversity through research and development;

  iv)   Ensuring benefits to India as country of origin of biological resources and to local communities and people as conservers of biodiversity, creators and holders of indigenous knowledge systems, innovations and practices; and

   v)   Ensuring consideration of biodiversity concerns in other sectoral policies and programmes.

India Country Profile, *supra*. The policies and programs intended to protect, conserve, and sustainably use the country's biological resources are detailed below.

1. Sanctuaries and Other Reserves

The Indian government is deemed a trustee of "all natural resources," including the seashore, forests, parklands, and other ecologically fragile lands, as well as the water and the air. Michael Blumm and Rachel Guthrie, *Internationalizing the Public Trust Doctrine:*

Natural Law and Constitutional and Statutory Approaches to Fulfilling the Saxion Vision,
45 UC Davis L. Rev. 741, 763 (2012).

> The Indian society has, since time immemorial, been conscious of the necessity
> of protecting the environment and ecology. The main moto [sic] of social life has
> been "to live in harmony with nature." [The] preachings [of sages and saints of
> India] ... are ample evidence of the society's respect for plants, trees, earth, sky,
> air, water and every form of life. It was ... a sacred duty of every one to protect
> them ... people worshipped trees, rivers and sea which were treated as belong-
> ing to all living creatures. The children were educated ... about the necessity of
> keeping the environment clean and protecting earth, rivers, sea, forests, trees,
> flora[,] fona [sic] and every species of life.

Fomento Resorts & Hotels v. Minguel Martins, (2009) I.N.S.C. 100, para. 36.

The Indian Supreme Court has been enthusiastic about drawing upon U.S. precedent
on the public trust doctrine, and has even been willing to take it further than U.S. courts
have done.

> In India, which has given the public trust doctrine the most detailed judicial
> consideration of any jurisdiction outside the United States, the doctrine has nat-
> ural law origins and an extremely broad scope.... [T]he Indian Supreme Court
> has fully embraced the doctrine over a substantial period of time. In fact, the
> public trust is now much more fundamental to Indian jurisprudence than it is
> in the United States.

Blumm, *supra,* at 748, 760 citing M.C. Mehta v. Kamal Nath, (1997) 1 S.C.C. 388 (1996);
M.I. Builders Private Ltd. v. Radhey Shyam Sahu, (1999) 6 S.C.C. 464, 466. Indian courts
have construed the Indian Constitution, particularly Article 21, to require the government to perform public trust duties. The Court illuminated its expectations in *The Majra
Singh v. Indian Oil Co., A.I.R* 1999 J & K 81, 83 stating, "there can be no dispute that the
State is under an obligation to see that forests, lakes and wildlife and environment are
protected." *Id.;* David Takacs, *The Public Trust Doctrine, Environmental Rights, and the
Future of Private Property,* 16 N.Y.U. Envtl. L.J. 711, 739 (2008). The public trust doctrine in India encourages enforcement of rights by third parties on behalf of others. For
example, in 2002 the Wildlife Trust of India filed public interest litigation to stop the
draining of wetlands considered crucial for the breeding and survival of the endangered
Sarus crane. Justices S.K. Sen and R.K. Agrawal of the Allahabad High Court ordered the
wildlife warden of the state of Uttar Pradesh to be personally responsible for protecting
the species. *In Re* Wildlife Trust of India Through Mr. Aniruddha Mookerjee Director, 0–644,
New Friends Colony, New Delhi-110065 v. State of Uttar Pradesh, Civil Misc. Writ Petition No. 3807 of 2002.

The Supreme Court has been an important player in protecting ecologically sensitive
and/or productive areas, but the legislature and the executive branch has played a significant role as well. As of 2004, protected areas of India covered 156,700 square kilo-
metres (60,500 sq mi), roughly 4.8 % of the nation's total surface area. These areas include
"94 national parks and 501 wildlife sanctuaries. Of these, 100 cover both terrestrial and
freshwater ecosystems and 31 are marine protected areas." India Country Profile, *supra.*
India also has fourteen Biosphere Reserves and several Reserved Forests, "which are part
of the most strictly protected forests outside the protected areas." *Id.*

> As per the latest report of the Forest Survey of India (2003), forests cover 23.68%
> of India's total geographic area, which includes 3.04% of the tree cover. Area
> under grasslands is about 3.9% and deserts cover about 2%. It is estimated that

India has about 4.1 million ha of wetlands (excluding paddy fields and mangroves). The marine ecosystem in India covers 2.1 million sq. km, and the total area covered by mangroves is estimated at about 6,700 sq. km.

Id.

Forest reserves are a concurrent subject that can be regulated by both the Central Government and state governments. Bhutani and Kothari, *supra,* at 608. The Forest Conservation Act, Act 69 of 1980, was enacted in order to curb deforestation. No non-forest activities (such as mining) can take place in a forest reserve except with prior approval from the Central Government. Tarun Bharat Sangh, Alwar v. Union of India, 1993 SUPP (3) SCC 115.

The creation of protected parks and sanctuaries is authorized by the Wildlife (Protection) Act, Act 53 of 1972. Under §26A of the Act, a state government, in consultation with the national government, is authorized to create a sanctuary within its forests or territorial waters if the area has ecological, faunal, geomorphological, natural, or zoological significance. Upon designation, Chief Wildlife Warden "shall control, manage and maintain all sanctuaries." *Id.* §33. It is illegal to damage the habitat of any wild animal or deprive any wild animal of its habitat within a sanctuary without a permit granted by the Chief, *id.* §29, 31, and chemicals, explosives, and other injurious substances are banned, *id.* §32. Section 35 extends similar prohibitions to national parks. When it comes to livestock, however, sanctuaries and parks are treated differently—grazing is allowed in sanctuaries but not in parks. *Compare id.* §§29 and 33(d) with §35(7).

2. Species-Specific Legislation

At the beginning of the twenty-first century, India reported the following data on its wildlife and plant species:

> Almost 70% of the country has been surveyed and around 45,000 plant species (including fungi and lower plants) and 89,492 animal species have been described, including 59,353 insect species, 2,546 fish species, 240 amphibian species, 460 reptile species, 1,232 bird species and 397 mammal species. Endemism of Indian biodiversity is significant with 4950 species of flowering plants, 16,214 insects, 110 amphibians, 214 reptiles, 69 birds and 38 mammals endemic to the country.

> One of the major causes for the loss of biodiversity in India is the expansion of agriculture in previously wild areas. Other impacts include: unplanned development, opening of roads, overgrazing, fire, pollution, introduction and spread of exotics, excessive siltation, dredging and reclamation of water bodies, mining and industrialization. In this century, the Indian cheetah, Lesser Indian rhino, Pink-headed duck, Forest owlet and the Himalayan mountain quail are reported to have become extinct and several other species (39 mammals, 72 birds and 1,336 plants) are identified vulnerable or endangered.

Convention on Biological Diversity, India Country Profile, *supra.*

The origin of India's wildlife laws can be traced back to the third century BC, when Buddhist Emperor Ashoka codified a law for wildlife preservation in his Fifth Pillar Edict. The Edict stated that all quadrupeds "which are not eaten and of no utility" could not be slaughtered. It also protected many other animals, including turtles, bats, ants, ducks, geese, swans, doves, porcupines, squirrels, deer, lizards, rhinoceroses, and pigeons. Bruce Rich, *The First Habitat and Species Law*s, Envtl. Law Forum May/June, p. 20 (2010).

In 1873, Madras adopted the first elephant protection statute. The Central Government followed suit in 1879 with the Elephants' Preservation Act. Shyam Divan and Armin Rosencranz, Environmental Law & Policy in India 31 (2d ed. 2002). One of the first wildlife laws under British rule was the Wild Bird Protection Act of 1887, which prohibited the possession or sale of wild birds taken during breeding seasons. This was followed by the Wild Birds and Animals Protection Act of 1912, which regulated the hunting of designated species in most of British India. *Id.* The Forest Act of 1927 authorized hunting restrictions in protected forests and authorized the creation of wildlife sanctuaries. *Id.* at 328.

A more comprehensive legislative package for wildlife protection was adopted in 1972. *The Wildlife Protection Act of 1972* covers wild animals, birds, and plants. It applies to all of India except the State of Jammu and Kashmir, which has its own wildlife act similar to the national law. Divan and Rosencranz, *supra,* at 328. Since the Forty-Second Constitutional Amendment of 1976, wildlife has been a concurrent concern of the states and the central government. *Id.*

Section 2 of the Wildlife Protection Act defines the following terms:

(1) "animal" includes amphibians, birds, mammals, and reptiles, and their young, and also includes, in the cases of birds and reptiles, their eggs, ...

(2) "animal article" means an article made from any captive animal or wild animal, other than vermin, and includes an article or object in which the whole or any part of such animal [has been used and ivory imported into India and an article made therefrom];

(15) "habitat" includes land, water, or vegetation which is the natural home of any wild animal;

(16) "hunting" ... includes,

(a) capturing, killing, poisoning, snaring, and trapping or any wild animal and every attempt to do so,

(b) driving any wild animal for any of purposes specified in subclause (a),

(c) injuring or destroying or taking any part of the body of any such animal, or in the case of wild birds or reptiles, damaging the eggs....

(36) "wild animal" means any animal found wild in nature and includes any animal specified in Schedule I, Schedule II, Schedule, IV or Schedule V, wherever found;

(37) "wildlife" includes any animal, bees, butterflies, crustacean, fish and moths; and aquatic or land vegetation which forms part of any habitat....

Id. The Act prohibits hunting, with some exceptions:

9. *Prohibition of Hunting*—No person shall hunt any wild animal specified in Schedule I, II, III and IV except as provided under section 11 and section 12....

11. *Hunting of Wild animals to be permitted in certain cases*—(1) Notwithstanding anything contained in any other law for the time being in force ...—

(a) the Chief Wildlife Warden may, if he is satisfied that any wild animal specified in Sch. 1 has become dangerous to human life or is so disabled or diseased as to be beyond recovery, by order in writing and stating the reasons therefor, permit any person to hunt such animal or cause animal to be hunted;

(b) the Chief Wildlife Warden or the authorised officer may, if he is satisfied that any wild animal specified in Sch. II Sch, III or Sch. IV has become dangerous to human life or to property (including standing crops on any land) or is so disabled or diseased as to be beyond recovery, by order in writing and stating the reasons therefor, permit any person to hunt such animal or cause such animal to be hunted.

(2) The killing or wounding in good faith of any wild animal in defence of oneself or of any other person shall not be an offence; Provided that nothing in this sub-section shall exonerate any person who, when such defence becomes necessary, was committing any act in contravention of any provision of this Act or any rule or order made thereunder.

(3) Any wild animal killed or wounded in defence of any person shall be Government property.

12. Grant of permit for special purposes—Notwithstanding anything contained elsewhere in this Act, it shall be lawful for the Chief Wildlife Warden, to grant a permit, by an order in writing stating the reasons therefor, to any person, on payment of such fee as may be prescribed, which shall entitle the holder of such permit to hunt, subject to such conditions as may be specified therein, any wild animal specified in such permit, for the purpose of—

(a) education;

(b) scientific research;

(bb) scientific management;

> *Explanation: ... the expression, "scientific management" means*—

> (i) translocation of any wild animal to an alternative suitable habitat; or

> (ii) population management of wildlife, without killing or poisoning or destroying any wild animals.

(c) Collection of specimens

> (i) for recognised zoos subject to the permission ... or

> (ii) for museums and similar institutions;

(d) derivation, collection or preparation of snake-venom for the manufacture of lifesaving drugs....

13. Suspension or cancellation of licence—The Chief Wildlife Warden or the authorised officer may, subject to any general or special order of this State Government, for good and sufficient reasons, to be recorded in writing, suspend or cancel any licence granted under this Chapter.... Provided that no such suspensions or cancellation shall be made except after giving the holder of the licence a reasonable opportunity of being heard.

The Wildlife Protection Act of 1972 §§ 9–13.

Species listed in Schedule I and part II of Schedule II are given absolute protection under § 9, and violators face the highest penalties. Schedule III and Schedule IV species are also protected, but penalties are lower. Schedule V lists animals that may be hunted. Plants that are listed in Schedule VI may not be cultivated and planted.

Schedule I includes Bengal tigers, one of India's most iconic species. The global tiger population has dropped to just a few thousand, and experts predict that wild tigers may be extinct in twenty years. Matthias Williams, *Tigers Endangered in Half of Indian Reserves*, Reuters (New Delhi), Dec. 9, 2009. "Illegal poaching, fueled by a thriving trade in tiger parts, and natural habitat loss drove down numbers in India from about 40,000 a century ago to 1,411 at the last count in 2008." *Id.* Project Tiger, an initiative kicked off by former Prime Minister Indira Gandhi in 1973, stimulated the creation of a number of protected reserves. But in 2009 Environment Minister Ramesh said out of 38 government-monitored tiger reserves, only twelve were in good condition. "Seventeen are in a very, very, very precarious state," he said. *Id.* Two reserves — Panna (in Madhya Pradesh) and Sariska (in Rajasthan) — lost all of their tigers to poaching. A successful reintroduction effort has taken place in Panna, but reintroduced females in Sariska have not reproduced. According to scientists with the Wildlife Institute of India, Sariska has a favorable prey density, but "human habitation inside the park surely is an obstacle." Sunny Sebastian, *A Tale of Two Tiger Reserves,* The Hindu News, Mar. 21, 2012. Also, opencast mining for limestone and marble has adversely affected habitat in and around Sariska. *See* Tarun Bharat Sangh, Alwar v. Union of India, 1993 SUPP (3) SCC 115 (enjoining illegal mining operations inside the reserve).

Between 1994 and 2009, there were 691 cases filed in Indian courts for crimes against tigers but only ten of those cases resulted in convictions. Financial Express, *No Two-Bit Crime This,* Conservation India, Nov. 14, 2010. Convictions result in fines and a mandatory prison sentence of three years, which may extend to seven years. Some of the violators are part of sophisticated smuggling rings, but others are local villagers.

> Poaching is very profitable and poor villagers often help poachers in return for much-needed cash, while villagers also often cut down forests where tigers live to use as farmland ... A special panel set up by Prime Minister Manmohan Singh said in 2006 thousands of villagers inside India's reserves would have to be relocated to protect tigers from poachers and smugglers....

> India must also strengthen policing along its borders with Nepal and Myanmar to control the illegal trade in animal parts. New Delhi also wants China to phase out tiger farms, which it says operate in violation of international agreements and fuel demand in India.

Williams, *supra.*

Enforcement against poachers and other violators often requires judicial intervention, as in the case of the Tibetan Antelope.

> The Shahtoosh wool is derived from the soft undercoat of the Tibetan Antelope (also known as Chiru), which has to be killed before its fleece is removed. Three to four Chiru have to be killed to weave only one shawl. Each shawl can cost several thousand dollars in the international market.

> In 1977, the Government of India declared the Chiru as protected under Schedule I of the Wildlife (Protection) Act of India, 1972. Killing of Chiru is also in contravention to the Convention on International Trade in Endangered Species (CITES).... Public Interest Litigation was filed in the J&K [Jammu and Kashmir] High Court seeking implementation of the provisions of their Wildlife (Protection) Act as well as CITES which prohibits the import of Shahtoosh into India. On May 1, 2000, the Honorable High Court issued a judgment forcing the government to enact and enforce its wildlife law. [I]n 2002 the manufacture of Shahtoosh shawls has finally been banned in the state of Jammu and Kashmir.

Adhideb Bhattacharya & Ankit Shrivastav, *Conservation of Wildlife in India and Relevant Laws* (2011).

Ivory has also been the subject of a number of important court cases. In Ivory Traders and Mftrs. Assn. v. India, AIR 1997 DEL 267, a trade association claimed that the Wildlife Act's ban on the ivory trade violated its members' fundamental rights to conduct their trade or business under Article 19(1)(g) of the Constitution. The Delhi High Court rejected the challenge, and found that the trade in ivory was similar to other pernicious activities, like selling intoxicants, and could therefore be lawfully banned. It reasoned, "Trade and business at the cost of disrupting life forms and linkage necessary for the prevention of biodiversity and ecology cannot be permitted." *Id.* at 286.

In Balram Kumawat vs. Union of India & Ors., 2003 AIR 3268, the Supreme Court of India was confronted with the question of whether mammoth fossil ivory imported into India was prohibited under the Wildlife Act. In 1987, the appellant M/S Unigems imported mammoth fossil ivory from an unspecified source. Section 2(2) covers "ivory imported in India," but Unigems claimed that mammoth ivory is distinct from elephant ivory and therefore is not covered by the Act. According to Unigems, if the import of the ivory in question was a violation of the Act, then the trade of plastic articles that look like ivory would also have to be penalized. *Id.* at 2. In addition, Unigems argued that, because mammoths are extinct, fossil ivory is not derived from a live "wild animal" within the meaning of the Act. Unigems further noted that CITES, of which India is a member, distinguishes between mammoth and elephant ivory.

The Court rejected these arguments, relying on both the purpose and plain language of the Wildlife Act. It explained that the object of the Act was to impose a complete ban on trade in ivory (whether imported in India or extracted by killing Indian elephants) to ensure the protection of the endangered wildlife species. The Court focused next on the plain meaning of the word ivory. The statute as written prohibits the trade and importation of *all* ivory, not just elephant ivory. The Court declined to undertake a scientific analysis to determine whether mammoth ivory could be distinguished from elephant ivory. It did, however, observe that the fossil ivory in question was the same kind of "white hard dentine substance which is also available in other animal, namely whale, walrus, hippos and warthog." *Id.* at 2. According to the court, although there may be instances where technical interpretations of statute are needed, "ivory" as used in the Act is not one of them:

> It is no doubt true that normally a technical meaning should be attributed rather than a common meaning to a word if the same relates to a particular trade, business or profession, art or science or words having a special meaning.... But we are not dealing with [such a] statute. We are dealing with a law which has been enacted in larger public interest and in consonance with Articles 48A and 51A(g) of the Constitution of India as also International Treaties and Conventions.

> As pointed out hereinbefore, the Parliament has enacted the Amending Acts of 1986, 1991 and 2003 not only for the purpose of banning a trade in elephant ivory but with a view to create a blockade of the activities of poachers and others so that a complete prohibition in trade in ivory is achieved. By reason of the Amending Acts, the Parliament was anxious to plug the loop-holes and impose a ban on trade in ivory so that while purporting to trade in imported ivory and carvings therefrom, poaching of Indian elephants and resultant illegal trade by extracting their tusks may not continue.

Id. at 10.

Notes and Questions

1. According to some estimates, "there are nearly 5,000 villages in protected areas with a population of about 250,000." Divan and Rosencranz, *supra,* at 335. The creation and

management of protected areas can "deprive forest dwellers of access to common property resources, uproot communities, halt development activities and heighten tensions between local residents and wildlife bureaucracy." *Id.* What should the government do about local villagers who "help poachers in return for much-needed cash"? Sebastian, *supra.* Is relocating villagers or otherwise taking away their traditional access to fodder, fuel, and food an appropriate conservation approach? What other strategies might be employed in lieu of or in addition to relocation? What should be done about the problem of villagers who cut down forests to use as farmland? The Supreme Court struggled with these issues in Pradeep Krishen v. Union of India, AIR 1996 SC 2040, and in Animal and Environment Legal Defence Fund v. Union of India, AIR 1997 SC 1071. While expressing concerns for villagers' procedural and substantive rights, in *Pradeep Krishen,* the Court admonished:

> We cannot … afford any further shrinkage in the forest cover in our country. If one of the reasons for this shrinkage is the entry of villagers and tribals living in and around the Sanctuaries and the National Parks, there can be no doubt that urgent steps must be taken to prevent any destruction or damage to the environment, the flora and fauna and wildlife in those areas … [G]overnment … inertia … cannot be tolerated."

Pradeep Krishen, AIR 1996 SC 2040.

2. Does the prohibition on "hunting" extend to mining, logging, highway construction, and other forms of development taking place outside of protected reserves if that development harms a protected species? *See* Wildlife Act § 2(16).

3. Biosecurity

The Environment Protection Act, Act 29 of 1986, § 3, authorizes the Central government "to take all such measures as it deems necessary for protecting and improving the quality of the environment and preventing, controlling and abating environmental pollution." The Government relied on this power to issue Rules for the Manufacture, Use, Import, Export and Storage of Hazardous Microorganisms, Genetically Engineered Organisms or Cells in 1989. These rules are at the heart of India's biosafety law, and they must be updated pursuant to the Cartagena Protocol on Biosafety to the Convention on Biological Diversity, which India signed in 2001. Bhutani and Kothari, *supra*, at 608. However, the development of new agricultural crops, in particular, has raised significant biodiversity-related concerns.

> India issued its first ever National Agriculture Policy in 2000.... This policy does little to address the problem of the economic marginalization of small-scale, diverse food production systems that conserve farmers' varieties of crops, which form the genetic pool for food and agriculture in the future. On the contrary the policy inter alia seeks to give special attention "... to development of new crop varieties, particularly of food crops, with higher nutritional value through adoption of biotechnology particularly, genetic modification...."

> There are legitimate biosafety concerns arising from this focus on the development of new crop varieties. As the Government of India itself admits in the second report to the CBD, there are not adequate mechanisms in the country to deal with this potentially hazardous technology. For instance, open field trials of Monsanto's transgenic cotton have been allowed by the Government of India's

Department of Biotechnology without proper approval of the Genetic Engineering Approval Committee of the Ministry of Environment and Forests.... In the meanwhile, transgenic Bt cotton was found to be growing in the Western State of Gujarat late last year without the Centre or the State governments having given permission for the same. With such an apparent by-pass of the regulatory system, posing risks to the natural environment and divided Centre and State opinions on the manner in which it should be dealt with, the debate on whether India should adopt transgenics in agriculture has been rekindled anew.

Bhutani and Kothari, *supra*, at 615. As the authors note, "[r]eleases of genetically engineered organisms may trigger irreversible changes with the elements of the natural environment that they come in contact with...." *Id.* India, in particular, has faced an aggressive campaign by multinational agribusiness corporations selling genetically-engineered products. Meanwhile, "several Indian public sector institutions have sponsored or are conducting transgenic research in rice, tobacco, mustard, potato, tomato, brinjal, cauliflower and cabbage." *Id.* at 617.

On the flip side of these concerns, proponents argue that GM crops can improve ecological and human well-being through more nutritious and more hardy and environmentally friendly food crops.

The Chennai-based MS Swaminathan Research Foundation is developing salt-resistant paddy, with a gene obtained from a mangrove plant in the coastal belt of Tamil Nadu. [And] the Department of Biotechnology of the Government of India and Swiss researchers have reached an agreement, that would allow Indian agriculture scientists to insert the "golden rice" gene sequences into popular Indian varieties of rice.

Id. at 617. *See* Toby J. Bruce, *GM as a Route for Delivery of Sustainable Crop Production*, 63 J. Exp. Bot. 537, 541 (2012) ("GM-based crop protection could substantially reduce the need for farmers to apply pesticides to their crops and would make agricultural production more efficient in terms of resources used (land, energy, water)."). What role should government have in responding to these developments? What are the implications for small farmers and landholders and for biological diversity?

E. England

As in most nations, the legal regimes for the conservation of lands that provide habitat for wildlife species and for the protection of the species themselves developed separately in England. Similar distinctions between species protection and protected areas provisions can be found at the European level and in international wildlife conventions. Things are beginning to change, however, as governments attempt to meet the biodiversity targets of the Convention on Biological Diversity. Lynda M. Warren, *New Approaches to Nature Conservation in the U.K.*, 14 Envtl. L. Rev. 44, 45 (2012). The desire to promote sustainable development may be behind the emerging trend toward integrated ecosystem management as well. *Id.* According to a review commissioned by the U.K. Environment Secretary:

[W]e need a step-change in our approach to wildlife conservation, from trying to hang on to what we have, to one of large-scale habitat restoration and recreation, under-pinned by the re-establishment of ecological processes and ecosystem services, for the benefits of both people and wildlife.

J.H. Lawton, et al, *Making Space for Nature: A Review of England's Wildlife Sites and Ecological Network* ii (2010), at http://archive.defra.gov.uk/environment/biodiversity/documents/201009space-for-nature.pdf. In 2011, the government responded by issuing the *Natural Environment White Paper,* billed as "a bold and ambitious statement outlining the Government's vision for the natural environment over the next 50 years." Dept. for Environment, Food and Rural Affairs, *Natural Environment,* http://www.defra.gov.uk/environment/natural/whitepaper/ (accessed Aug. 24, 2012). The White Paper embraces four goals: protecting and improving our natural environment; growing a green economy; reconnecting people and nature; and building international and EU leadership. *Id.* A recognition of the services and goods provided by a "healthy, properly functioning environment" appears to be at the heart of this new strategy.

This section highlights existing legal frameworks in England and Europe and identifies significant new developments in biodiversity conservation. Despite best efforts to organize this section, readers should proceed with one caveat in mind: "the present legal structure is 'made up of succeeding geological strata of legislation with no coherent design.'" Warren, *supra,* at 48 (citations omitted).

1. Parks and Wildlife Refuges

National Parks in England and Wales were first authorized by the *National Parks and Access to the Countryside Act 1949.* Although the Act has seen significant amendments over the years, it still provides the basic framework for national parks. The purpose of the 1949 Act was twofold: "the preservation and enhancement of the natural beauty of the areas, and the promotion of their enjoyment by the public." *Id.* § 5. *See* Stuart Bell and Donald McGillivray, Environmental Law 738 (7th ed. 2008). This was expanded by the *Environment Act 1995* § 61 to include "(a) conserving and enhancing the natural beauty, wildlife and cultural heritage of the areas ... and (b) promoting opportunities for the understanding and enjoyment of the special qualities of those areas by the public." Where conflict arises between these two purposes, purpose (a) (conservation) is given greater weight. Bell and McGillivray, *supra,* at 739.

Under the 1949 Act, the National Parks Commission had responsibility for designating the first parks. Today, this authority belongs to Natural England and the Countryside Council for Wales. There are eleven "sizeable national parks" in England and Wales, including the Peak District, the Lake District, the North York Moors, and the New Forest. The New Forest is notable as a former hunting reserve of William the Conqueror, who set it aside ten centuries ago. "As the largest remaining area of lowland heath in Europe, ... William would probably still recognize much of the Forest as the same place he hunted the 'bests of the chase': wild deer and boar." Visiting New Forest National Park (2012), www.newforestnpa.gov.uk/visiting. The New Forest and other national parks in England are distinct from the national park ideal of the United States and other countries.

> Instead of being wilderness areas with few, if any, inhabitants, they contain land on which large numbers of people live. They are effectively working environments. The aim of national park designation is to plan and manage the area so as to create a balance between recreation, amenity, wildlife, and economic development.

Bell and McGillivray, *supra,* at 738.

Parks in the UK may and often do include private, working lands. Throughout Europe, there seems to be a "re-evaluation of the traditional (American) park notion that parks are 'apart' from people and exist only for nature." Denise Antolini, *National Park Law in the U.S.*, 33 Wm. & Mary Envtl. L. & Pol'y Rev. 851, 853 n.8 (2009). Of course, there are practical reasons for including human-influenced landscapes, too. Most of Europe, including England, is "intensively humanized," and has high cultural values but few natural (undisturbed) features. *Id. See* Federico Cheever, *British National Parks for North Americans: What We Can Learn from a More Crowded Nation Proud of Its Countryside*, 26 Stan. Envtl. L.J. 247, 256, 312 (2007) (advocating protection of "mixed landscapes" such as public and privately owned lands and criticizing the "North American preoccupation with unaltered landscapes" as preventing the U.S. "from developing a coherent system for preserving public values").

English landowners have occasionally contested the inclusion of their estates. In Meyrick Estate Management Ltd. v. Secretary of State for Environment, Food and Rural Affairs [2007] Env. L.R. 26, a landowner successfully resisted inclusion of his land in the New Forest National Park on the grounds that his agricultural lands were not "natural," a requirement for designation that has since been amended by the Natural Environment and Rural Communities Act 2006. Section 99 of the 2006 Act authorizes designation of areas of "natural" beauty even if their beauty is the product of human intervention in the landscape. Agricultural lands have been included within other parks, and if the new rules had been applied, Meyrick probably would have lost his appeal. Bell and McGillivray, *supra,* at 741.

Once a park is designated, "control remains essentially local," as Natural England has no executive functions. *Id.* at 741. However, Environment Act 1995 §63 gave the Secretary of State authority to establish national park authorities, which replace county councils or other relevant local boards. Members of a national park authority are a combination of those appointed by local authorities and by the Secretary. Park authorities are charged with adopting strategic park management plans to control development in the parks. Park policy guidance cautions against "major development" except in "exceptional circumstances ... demonstrably in the public interest." National Planning Policy Framework, para. 116 (2012) (Eng.). Considerations include the national and local need for the development, the cost of alternatives, and adverse environmental effects. *See* Dartmoor National Park Authority v. Secretary of State for Transport, Local Government and the Regions [2003] EWHC 236 (upholding the approval of experimental, temporary low-impact housing known as "benders" in park woodlands). "[N]ational parks are certainly not inviolable, as the siting of Fylingdales' early warning station, Milford Haven's oil terminal, and numerous quarries in the Peak District illustrate." Bell and McGillivray, *supra,* at 742–43.

In terms of habitat protection, the primary designations in the UK are national nature reserves (NNRs), marine nature reserves (MNRs), and sites of special scientific interest (SSSIs). NNRs and MNRs are managed by the relevant division of the UK's Nature Conservancy Council—Natural England, the Countryside Council for Wales, or Scottish Natural Heritage. *Id.* at 686–87. NNRs are managed for biological, geographical, or physiographical research or for preserving features of special interest. Recreation is allowed if it does not compromise the conservation purpose. Natural Environment and Rural Communities Act 2006 § 105(1). As of 2006, there were 356 NNRs in the UK, covering over 226,000 hectares of private and public, about one-third of which are located on nationally important land managed by a wildlife trust or other approved conservation body. Bell and McGillivray, *supra,* at 689.

MNRs are located in tidal and coastal waters, and are designated under the same criteria as NNRs. Wildlife and Countryside Act 1981 §36. This authority has been used sparingly; as of 2011, there were only three designated MNRs. The power to protect MNRs is similarly limited. The relevant Nature Conservancy Council may restrict pleasure boats but not lawful passage by other vessels. Wildlife and Countryside Act 1981, § 37(3)(a)-(b).

England adopted a new framework in the Marine and Coastal Access Act of 2009, which requires any area previously designated as an MNR under the Wildlife and Countryside Act to be treated as a marine conservation zone. Marine and Coastal Access Act 2009, c. 23, sched.12, § 116 (Eng.). Going forward, "MCZs will protect a range of nationally important marine wildlife, habitats, geology and geomorphology and can be designated anywhere in English and Welsh inshore and UK offshore waters." JNCC, *Marine Conservation Zones*, http://jncc.defra.gov.uk/page-4525 (accessed Aug. 24, 2012). New MCZs are to be chosen on ecological grounds, but socio-economic factors may also be considered. They are intended to "exist alongside European marine sites ... and Special Protected Areas to form an ecologically coherent network of marine protected areas ... large enough, and close enough together, to support functioning communities of marine wildlife." DEFRA, *Marine Conservation Zones* (July 2012), http://www.defra.gov.uk/ environment/marine/protect/mpa/mcz/. The relevant authority is the Marine Management Organization (MMO), which appears to have more regulatory power than previous enforcement authorities. Restrictions will vary from site to site, and "[o]nly activities that will affect the conservation objectives of the designated MCZs will be subject to possible restrictions." *Id.* at http://archive.defra.gov.uk/environment/marine/documents/protected/mcz-factsheet-managemeasures.pdf. Under section 129, the MMO may make by-laws restricting the entry or activity of persons, animals, vessels, and anything that would "interfere with the seabed or damage or disturb any object in the MCZ." Marine and Coastal Access Act, 2009, c. 23, Pt. 5, c. 1, § 129(3)(a)-(f) (Eng.).

Under the Wildlife and Countryside Act 1981 Pt. II, SSSIs are established to maintain diversity of wild animals and plants in the U.K. SSSIs are intended to be representative of British habitats, and site selection is to be made on scientific grounds rather than recreational or amenity-based grounds. Sites that include rare habitats and species are chosen, along with the best representative examples of various habitat types based on naturalness, typicalness, diversity, and size. *See* Nature Conservancy Counsel, *Guidelines for the Selection of Biological SSSIs,* Part B: Operational Approach and Criteria, para. 2.1 (1998). As of 2003, there were 4,112 SSSIs in England, 1,108 in Wales, and 1,451 in Scotland, covering over two million hectares (seven percent of the land base). Bell and McGillivray, *supra,* at 690.

In R (Aggregate Industries Ltd) v. English Nature [2003] Env. L.R.3, a landowner challenged a SSSI designation as a violation of due process under the European Convention on Human Rights, but the court found that the notification procedures, which include the right to appeal any refusal to consent to development activities and to ask that the SSSI notification be revised or revoked, were human rights-compliant. In Boggis and Easton Bavents Conservation v. Natural England [2009] EWCA Civ 1061, landowners who wished to build and maintain sea walls to combat erosion challenged the designation of an SSSI on the Suffolk coast. The court held that the designation was a legitimate approach to the conservation of important geological features, *i.e.,* fossils soon to be exposed by the cliff erosion.

Until recently, there were few restrictions on development within SSSIs. Once designated, local planning authorities received notification and were expected to include SSSIs in their plans and to protect them from development. By the late 1990s, however, English Nature and other reports documented significant degradation of SSSIs due to the impacts of agricultural and urban development as well as expanding recreational uses and abject neglect. Bell and McGillivray, *supra*, at 691. Reforms were adopted in the Countryside and Rights of Way (CRoW) Act 2000, which moved away from voluntarism and toward regulated site management. The power of the Nature Conservancy Council to ban destructive activities has been enhanced, but the management approach still entails "constructive dialogue and partnership" with landowners and local authorities. The Council has since been split into two bodies in Scotland and one in England (Natural England) under the Natural Environment and Rural Communities Act of 2006 (c16). Despite deep agency budget cuts, something must be working; by 2007, 76 percent of SSSIs in England were either in favorable condition or at least recovering. *Id.*

The EC has adopted several policies and directives relevant to habitat conservation in the UK. The EC's overarching policy—known as "*Natura 2000*"—is to create a Community-wide network of protected conservation sites. The 1992 Habitats Directive imposes general duties on member States to monitor the conservation status of all habitats and species. Directive 92/42/EC on the Conservation of Natural Habitats and of Wild Fauna and Flora Art. 11. More specifically, it requires members to send the Commission a list of candidate sites for designation. The sites must be chosen with reference to criteria specified in Annex III of the Directive. The Commission, in turn, must draw up a list of "sites of Community importance" and a list of "priority sites" of particular importance in terms of habitat types or species' needs. If the Commission believes that a priority site has been excluded from a member's list, the Directive provides for bilateral consultations, but the ultimate decision-maker is the EC Council. *Id.* Art. 5. If a member submits a list of candidate sites that is "manifestly inadequate," the member is in breach of the Directive. Commission v. Germany [2001] ECR I-5811. The Directive has been one of the most contentious facets of EC environment law in large part because it restricts "the extent to which member States can determine how parts of their territory are used—*e.g.,* for development—which is a central aspect of state sovereignty." Bell and McGillivray, *supra*, at 705.

Another important component of *Natura 2000* is Directive 79/409/EC on the Conservation of Wild Birds (the 1979 Wild Birds Directive). Member states are required to create a sufficient number of protected areas, to maintain a diversity of habitats for all European bird species, and to designate Special Protection Areas (SPAs) to conserve habitat for rare, vulnerable, and migratory bird species. *Id.* Arts. 1–4. *See* Commission v. Netherlands [1999] Env LR 147 (finding that the Netherlands had failed to designate an adequate number of suitable sites); Commission v. Spain [1993] ECR I-4221 (finding that Spain had breached the Directive by failing to designate the Santona Marshes as a SPA). When England refused to include the Lappel Bank within the Medway Estuary and Marshes SPA in Kent because it anticipated development of the Port of Sheerness, the Court held that the duty to designate SPA sites turned on ornithological criteria alone, *not* economic considerations. Royal Society for the Protection of Birds v. Secretary [1997] Env LR 431. Before the designation order could be implemented, however, the habitat at issue was destroyed by the construction of a 22-hectare car park. Bell and McGillivray, *supra*, at 706. In 2006, new habitat was created by breaching sea walls in Essex to compensate for the loss of Lappel Bank. By the end of 2007, over 250 SPAs had been designated in the UK covering nearly 1.6 million hectares of land. *Id.* at 708.

Upon designation of an SPA or a special conservation area under the Habitats Directive, member states must take steps to ensure against significant pollution or deterioration of the habitat. Directive 79/409/EC Art. 4(4); Directive 92/42/EC §6(2). Granting licenses to shoot barnacle geese to prevent them from damaging crops may violate this requirement, Royal Society for the Protection of Birds v. Secretary of State for Scotland [2001]

Env LR 19, as does failing to reduce sheep densities within grouse habitat, Commission v. Ireland [2002] ECR I-5335. Neglectful management or inaction, such as the failure to remove invasive species, can also be a violation. Commission v. U.K. [2005] ECR I-9017. These Directive provisions amount to a presumption against development, but development may be allowed when the member state can show "imperative reasons of overriding public interest" and no other alternatives. Directive 92/42/EC § 6(4). This exception has been construed fairly narrowly. *See* R (on behalf of the Lymington River Assc.) v. Wightlink Ltd [2010] EWHC 232 (allowing a ferry operator to introduce a larger class of ferry between the mainland and the Isle of Wight violated Habitats Directive Art. 6(2)).

2. Species-Specific Legislation

The English have attempted to regulate hunting and control wildlife for centuries. "Since the Middle Ages the English have tried implementing, at one time or another, almost every law that could be imagined for the taking and harvesting of wildlife. The penalty for violations of these laws have ranged from a fine, prison, mutilation, transportation, to even death." Michael Stockdale, *English and American Wildlife Law: Lessons from the Past*, 47 Proc. Annu. Conf. Southeast. Assoc. Fish and Wild. Agencies 732, 732 (1993). Specifically:

> Following the conquest of England in 1066 by William the Conqueror, all the royal domains and hunting grounds of the Saxon kings came under William's control. Insisting that wild beast had no owner but the King, he tightened up Saxon game laws and introduced mutilation as a punishment for poaching.…
>
> Public unrest and ecclesiastical pressure against such harsh punishment reached an all time high in 1184, and Henry II removed mutilation as a punishment. In 1225 the Forest Charter of Henry III stated no one was to lose life or limb for killing the King's deer. However, he would suffer a "grevious" fine if he had any money, and if he had none he was to go to prison for a year and a day. In the 13th century each royal forest had a chief forester … and a large number of foresters to carry on the day-to-day work.… Foresters … had authority to arrest anyone found in the forest with bow, snare, or hounds; they patrolled, took special care of the deer in breeding season, and provided browse and tree-clippings in winter.… [T]hey were well paid and had valuable privileges.
>
> It is wrong to suppose that poaching was an offense peculiar to the lower orders since all classes poached the King's deer. There are innumerable cases of bishops, abbots, earls, barons, and knights entering royal forests to poach. William de Ferrers, Earl of Derby in the mid-thirteenth century, although warden of High Peak Forest, was convicted of killing, with his friends, no less than 2,000 deer in 7 years.…
>
> In 1584 Elector August of Saxony announced, "That henceforth the punishment for poachers and sharpshooters, and for those who harbor same, or knowingly give them aid in anyway, shall in all our lands be the gallows." …
>
> The Game Act of 1671 established the qualifications a person must have before they could take game.… An important facet of the Act was that it gave official status to the class of gamekeepers, who acted as a type of special police in the enforcement of the game laws. The Act now authorized every lord of a manor to appoint a gamekeeper who should have the power to confiscate all para-

phernalia of sport such as guns, dogs, or nets found in the possession of un-
qualified persons. For this purpose he was to search the houses of suspected
persons and thus, he acted somewhat as a government official … The common gamekeeper was ideally a sober, honest, industrious man, with a knack for
killing vermin, and a boldness and shrewdness which would not fail him in en-
counters with poachers. In practice he was usually some bold pugnacious la-
borer, … famed for his accurate shooting, but hardly trained in the finer duties
of his trade. Often he could not resist the temptation to sell game on the sly.
Indeed, the keepers were accused of being the greatest poachers in the country.…

Although the solitary poachers gave the keeper most of his trouble, gang poachers attracted more notice. In the early part of the eighteenth century they devoted their attention chiefly to the deer preserves in the parks and chases because
of the large quantities of game present. A gang of desperate characters known as
the Waltham Blacks so terrorized the region of Windsor and Berkshire that they
stung the government into the enactment in 1723 of the harshest game law to date.
The Black Act, as it was called for more than one reason, made it a felony with
the death penalty for anyone, while disguised with blackened faces or with
weapons to kill deer illegally.… Under this "Black Act," at a special assize in Reading, 4 poachers were hanged and 36 transported.…

Such severity proved no more successful in this than in other criminal laws. A
month after the passage of the Black Act the old offenses were being committed
as freely as ever. The ruling classes replied to this menace with more and severer
laws. In 1737, King George II implemented and enforced an Act "for the more
effectual punishing wicked and evil disposed persons going armed to hunt waterfowl or fallow deer." Violators were dealt with unmercifully, given the choice:
"Seven years beyond the seas at hard labor on His Majesty's plantations in America or death."

Id. at 733–35.

By the Georgian era of the eighteenth century, the privileged classes regarded "their"
game as "more sacred than any other class of property."

Hunting to them was a kingly sport, "to be followed only by a superior order of
men." To the confirmed fox hunter, sport was an orgy in which he rode his horse
often to the point of fatal exhaustion and roused himself to such a roaring humor
that only coarse jokes and quantities of drink, into which the fox's pad had been
dipped for added zest, could satisfy him.

Id. at 736.

Occasionally, English lords and lawmakers would undertake to protect game and fish
species from the adverse effects of industrial activities. "Damming was recognized as an
industrial peril to anadromous fish as early as 1393, and weirs were required in dams to
facilitate spawning-runs ascending the streams." *Id.* at 736.

English wildlife law has, of course, evolved since the Middle Ages. The United Kingdom is a party to the Convention on Biodiversity as well as the 1973 Convention on Trade
in Endangered Species. It has also become subject to EC Directives on species protection.
In the early 1980s, England adopted *The Wildlife and Countryside Act 1981,* 1985 Chapter 31, which consolidates and amends pre-existing national legislation on wildlife conservation and natural habitats.

The Wildlife and Countryside Act addresses the protection of wildlife (birds, and some animals and plants), the countryside, and National Parks, and the designation of protected areas and public rights of way. Various amendments have been passed since enactment, including the Wildlife and Countryside (Amendment) Act 1985; Wildlife and Countryside (Amendment) Act 1991; Countryside and Rights of Way (CRoW) Act 2000 (in England and Wales); and the Natural Environment and Rural Communities Act 2006 (in England and Wales).

Section 9 of the Wildlife and Countryside Act makes it an offence to intentionally kill, injure or take any wild animal listed on Schedule 5, and prohibits interference with places used for shelter or protection or intentional disturbance of animals occupying such places. Section 4 specifies the criteria for listing (or "scheduling") species for protection:

> *4.1 Rationale underlying scheduling.* In compliance with the purpose and provisions of the relevant Sections of the WCA, the statutory nature conservation agencies will pursue scheduling when:
>
> > i. there is an international obligation to afford legal protection to the species;
> >
> > ii. an animal or plant is in danger of extinction in Great Britain, or is likely to become so endangered unless conservation measures are taken, and legal protection is likely to improve its chances of survival.
>
> Scheduling is considered to be particularly appropriate where there is a need to:
>
> > iii. protect an animal or plant species from direct human pressure such as persecution, collection or trade;
> >
> > iv. protect elements of habitat essential for the survival of an endangered species.

See id. § 4; Joint Nature Conservation Committee, *The Wildlife and Countryside Act 1981,* http://jncc.defra.gov.uk/.

The EC Habitats Directive includes more sweeping prohibitions for European listed wildlife species. Article 12(1)(d) makes it an offense not only to deliberately capture, injure, or kill such species, but also to cause deterioration or destruction of their breeding or resting places. The focus on "deliberate" acts rather than "intentional" acts (which are the subject of the Wildlife and Countryside Act's prohibitions) may obviate the need to prove criminal *mens rea* to establish a violation of the EC Directive. *See* Bell and McGillivray, *supra,* 722. The European Court of Justice held that the actor must have "intended the capture or killing of a specimen belonging to a protected animal species, or, at the very least, accepted the possibility of such capture or killing." Commission v. Spain [2006] ECR I-4515 [71]. In Commission v. Hellenic Republic [2002] ECR 1-1147, the Court found that Greece had failed to prevent deliberate disturbance to the endangered loggerhead turtle and its nesting habitat by tourists' mopeds and boats. The Court noted that Greece had failed to prevent repeated breaches of its beach-closure notices.

Under the EC Habitat Regulations, licenses to take protected species may be obtained from the Environment or Agricultural Minister for "imperative reasons of overriding public interest," including social or economic reasons. EC Habitat Regulations 44. Licenses may be issued to farmers to prevent serious damage to crops, for example, but "it must be shown that there is no satisfactory alternative and that the authorized action will not be detrimental to maintaining the favourable conservation status of the species in its natural range." *Id.;* Bell and McGillivray, *supra,* at 724.

In addition, for species that are U.K.-listed only (not EC-listed), the Wildlife and Countryside Act provides a defense for actions that are an "incidental result of a lawful operation and could not reasonably have been avoided." *Id.* §§ 4(2) (birds), 10(3) (wild animals), 13(2) (plants). This excuses unavoidable accidents, *e.g.,* when an automobile accidentally hits a protected otter on the road (this is, apparently, "a serious problem for otter conservation," Bell and McGillivray, *supra,* at 725). The defense does not apply to development in known species' habitat, nor does it apply to EC-listed species. Commission v. United Kingdom [2005] ECR I-9017.

The strongest provisions of the Wildlife and Countryside Act focus on wild birds, which are "reverse listed." Other than listed pest species and game birds, it is an offence to intentionally:

- kill, injure, or take *any* wild bird,
- take, damage or destroy their nests while the nest is in use or being built, or
- take or destroy their eggs.

Id. § 1(1) and 2. If the bird is a rare wild bird listed in Schedule 1, it is an offense to engage in reckless behavior that disturbs the bird or its dependent young. *Id.* § 1(5). Schedule 2 of the Act allows Canadian goose, mallard duck, common snipe, woodcock, teal and several other species of birds to be killed or taken outside the closed season. Part II of Schedule 2 lists species that may be taken or killed at any time by authorized persons. These include thirteen species of common birds, including crow, dove, gull, magpie, pigeon, sparrow, and starling.

The Natural Environment and Rural Communities Act 2006 amended the Wildlife and Countryside Act to include Schedule ZA1, which protects certain birds that re-use their nests: the golden eagle; the white-tailed eagle, and the osprey. According to Biodiversity Minister Barry Gardiner, the law aims to assist "long-term breeding" and greater population numbers of species subject to re-introduction and re-establishment programs by protecting their nests year round. *U.K. New Regulations to Protect Wildlife Come Into Force,* May 2006, at http://www.bymnews.com/new/content/view/29958/82/ (accessed Aug. 16, 2012).

In addition, under the Wildlife and Countryside Act § 3 the Secretary of State may designate Areas of Special Protection for wild birds. The Act also restricts the sale and possession of captive bred birds and sets standards for keeping birds in captivity. *Id.* § 6 (1) & (5)

With respect to plants, the Act makes it an offence:

- to intentionally pick, uproot or destroy any wild plant listed in Schedule 8, or
- to sell, offer or expose for sale, or possess (for the purposes of trade) any live or dead wild plant included in Schedule 8, or any part of, or anything derived from, such a plant.

Id. § 13 (1)(a) & (2)(a). Schedule 8 protects over one hundred and fifty varieties of plant species including fungi, lichens, stonewarts, mosses, liverwarts, horsetails, ferns, and flowering plants. Certain poisonous plants, once considered noxious weeds, are protected as important to biodiversity. The Fen ragwort is one example. *See Rare Fen Ragwort Loves Ditch Life,* BBC Cambridgeshire, Jan. 27, 2011 ("Fen ragwort was believed to have become extinct in the Victorian era so there was great excitement" in 1972 when some workers clearing a rubbish-filled ditch discovered it; the ditch is now a designated SSSI).

Notes and Questions

1. The UK and Europe are moving toward "a more holistic approach in which the conservation of special sites and the protection of threatened species are just part of a wider

agenda for managing biodiversity through an ecosystems approach aimed at the delivery of ecosystems goods and service." Warren, *supra,* at 52. At the same time, the pressure to reduce regulatory burdens and to enhance development opportunities is mounting in light of Europe's financial woes. *See* Europa, *European Commission: Building Blocks Towards Economic Growth,* June 27, 2012. Is it possible to balance these disparate objectives?

2. The Welsh government has taken a step further than England with its *Vision for Living Wales,* which proclaims that Wales will "live within its environmental limits, using only its fair share of the earth's resources so that our ecological footprint is reduced to the global average availability of resources," and that it will have "healthy, biologically diverse and productive ecosystems that are managed sustainably." Warren, *supra,* at 48. The new approach is "based on the ecosystems approach and designed to deliver ecosystem services." *Id.* at 49. Legislative changes to incorporate a "Natural Environmental Framework" will likely be necessary. This could be construed as an especially bold move, given that the economic output of Wales has been historically lower than most of Western Europe; in 2002, it stood at 80% of the UK average. How might Wales and other nations, including those in the developing world, live within their environmental limits? What legislative changes would be necessary in Europe and elsewhere?

3. Biosecurity and Assisted Migration

The Wildlife and Countryside Act 1981 contains measures to prevent the establishment of non-native species that may be detrimental to native wildlife and plants. It is an offense to release a species of any wild animal that is "not ordinarily a resident in" or a "regular visitor to Great Britain in a wild state." *Id.* § 14(1). This applies to 42 species including certain fish (bass), birds (geese, ducks, and pheasants), amphibians (marsh frog and midwife toads), rodents (grey squirrel, prairie dog, Mongolian gerbil), and wallabies, to name a few. Further, it is an offense to plant or "cause[] to grow" any plant listed on Part II of Schedule 9. Only four plant species—giant hogweed, giant kelp, Japanese knotweed, and Japanese seaweed—are prohibited under Schedule 9.

All of the nations covered in this book have enacted similar provisions to combat destructive invasive species. Some scientists, however, are beginning to think that these restrictions need to be liberalized.

> A growing number of ecologists worry that conservation-as-usual won't be able to keep up with the predicted pace of climate change. To some of them, assisted migration is a more proactive tool for preserving nature's richness, and possibly the only hope for saving certain species. Others wonder whether it would amount to just the sort of meddling that infested the American South with kudzu and choked Northern wetlands with purple loosestrife. Scientific models are no match for the actual complexities of ecosystems, they argue, and humans have proven inartful at playing God. It is a debate that underlines a broader shift in ecology, as some say the field needs to move into a more activist role—away from simply protecting nature and toward reshaping it.

> "The idea that we're going to set aside land and just preserve all the stuff in it isn't tenable anymore," says Notre Dame ecologist Jessica Hellmann. "Climate change will make these systems much more dynamic, and so we'll have to think about how to meet our objectives in the face of that pressure."

Chris Berdick, *Driving Mr. Lynx,* Boston Globe, Oct. 12, 2008.

No doubt, climate change will present conservation challenges that are new and quantitatively different from those addressed in the past. A suite of conservation tools will be necessary for maintaining viable populations of wildlife and plant species. At what point (if ever) is it a good idea to translocate vulnerable species—assisting their migration out of harm's way to new areas that may be more suitable in the future, as temperatures and precipitation patterns change over time?

> Range shifts in response to climate change have been observed in birds, plants and insects, as species seek to track their suitable climatic conditions. Strong paleo-ecological evidence suggests that range shifts such as these have been the dominant biological response to climate change for millions of years. Species have moved on sub-continental scales and sometimes across or between continents, on timescales as rapid as centuries or decades. But all of these past movements have occurred in fully natural landscapes—human land uses now pose major barriers to these movements. Modeling suggests that the rapidity of future climate change, coupled with habitat destruction, may cause large numbers of extinctions. More dynamic conservation strategies may significantly reduce the risk of these extinctions....
>
> Conservation mechanisms designed specifically to deal with climate change can facilitate range shifts and reduce extinction risks. Such mechanisms include strategic additions to protected areas networks, improved management of nature in agricultural and productive landscapes, artificial translocation of species and, finally, rescue in captive breeding or other ex-situ management for species with no hope of survival in the wild. Implementing these measures can maintain recreational opportunities and other ecosystem services of fundamental importance to human welfare. Protection, management and translocation can limit the numbers of species that fall into extreme distress requiring rescue. Virtually none of these systems currently exist, so the scope for reducing extinctions and loss of ecosystem services is great. Most involve changes in or modification of land uses, which incur costs and can be controversial.

Dov Sax, et al., Rethinking Conservation with Climate Change, Science-Policy White Paper, Jan. 5, 2009 (on file with author). *See* Camille Parmesan, *Ecological and Evolutionary Responses to Recent Climate Change*, 37 Ann. Rev. of Ecology, Evolution, & Systematics 637 (2006).

Assisted migration (aka "managed relocation") raises many ethical, ecological, socioeconomic, and legal issues. Historically, land managers and wildlife experts have treated "native" species and "invasive" species quite differently, and have, by and large, strived to restore habitat for the former and prohibited the introduction of the latter.

> For years, conservationists have focused on preventing or undoing the human alteration of nature. They have lobbied to keep wilderness free of subdivisions, battled against clear-cutting forests, argued for tighter controls on invasive species, and pushed factory owners to install smokestack scrubbers. When more active measures were deemed necessary, such as restoring New England's coastal rivers for fish spawning or bringing gray wolves back to Yellowstone, the decisions were preceded by years of scientific analysis, phone-book thick environmental-impact statements, and stakeholder negotiations. In the same conservative spirit, most argued that countering global warming was a matter of cutting greenhouse gas emissions and increasing the size and connectivity of wildlife reserves.
>
> Still, ecologists understand that ecosystems aren't museums in which flora and fauna can be preserved in perpetual equilibrium. When viewed on a geologic

scale, even today's most "untouched" wilderness has been in constant flux, with species rising and falling as much as temperatures and sea levels.

Berdick, *supra.*

Assisted migration is already occurring. Mark W. Schwartz *et al., Managed Relocation: Integrating the Scientific, Regulatory and Ethical Challenges,* 62 Bioscience 732, 734 (2012). In England, climate motivated relocations have occurred with several butterfly species.

> On sunny summer days, large flocks of marbled white butterflies are a familiar sight at a disused quarry in Co Durham even though the nearest breeding colonies of this species are more than 50 kilometres south in Yorkshire. But the marbled whites are not there by accident—they have been introduced as part of new research led by the Universities of York and Durham to examine the implications of climate change for the conservation and management of biodiversity.... This is the first practical demonstration that species are lagging behind climate warming and that translocations of species are technically feasible and might be effective in the conservation of species in a warming climate....

University of York Communications Office, *Assisted Colonisation to Help Species Cope with a Changing Climate* (2009), at http://www.york.ac.uk/news-and-events/news/2009/assisted-colonisation/. According to Professor of Conservation Biology Chris Thomas, "Many British butterflies are declining because of habitat destruction. These results suggest that ... assisted colonisations might be a cost-effective tool for conservation." *Id. See* David Biello, *Deporting Plants and Animals to Protect Them from Climate Change,* Sci. Am., July 17, 2008 (describing movement of the Quino checkerspot butterfly). As of 2010, the results of the translocation were positive and new populations of the butterfly had survived. University of York Research and Innovation, Issue 4 Pg. 7 (2010), www.york.ac.uk/media/ ... /research-and-innovation4.pdf.

Notes and Questions

1. Presumably, the British butterflies that were translocated by researchers at York University are not listed under the *Wildlife and Countryside Act 1981.* Should they be? What if they were?

2. As the notion of assisted migration gains attention and possibly traction among wildlife managers and legislators, an assessment of the legal landscape is imperative. What are the obstacles? What are the vehicles? More importantly, if assisted migration is deemed an appropriate conservation tool, what legal reforms may be necessary in England and elsewhere? For analysis, see Schwartz, *supra;* Alejandro E. Camacho, *Assisted Migration: Redefining Nature and Natural Resource Law Under Climate Change,* 27 Yale J. on Reg. 171, 173 (2010); John Kostyack and Dan Rohlf, *Conserving Endangered Species in an Era of Global Warming,* 38 Envtl. L. Rep. News & Analysis 10203 (2008).

F. Science, Policy, and the Courts

Biodiversity preservation and related "conservation problems are inherently transdisciplinary ... [and] must involve not only biologists, but also geographers, sociologists, economists, philosophers, lawyers, political scientists, educators, artists, and other professionals." Reed F. Noss, *Some Principles of Conservation Biology, as They Apply to Envi-*

ronmental Law, 69 Chi.-Kent L. Rev. 893, 895 (1994). Of course, politics inevitably has a role in setting environmental priorities and in charting feasible pathways to achieve those priorities, but how much of a role should politics play?

Some scholars claim that the influence of politics could be diminished if our legislatures adopted "air tight" requirements for "sound science" in our environmental and natural resource laws. Requiring sound science, however, is no panacea. Science should be used to guide our decisionmakers to appropriate results, but it can instead be used as an obstructionist tactic, as detailed in Professor Houck's description of the evolution of environmental law in the U.S., below.

Oliver A. Houck, Tales from a Troubled Marriage: Science and Law in Environmental Policy
17 Tul. Envtl. L.J. 163 (2003)

Back in the predawn of public environmental statutes, there were private remedies for environmental harms, in tort and nuisance … These remedies proved insufficient for at least two reasons. The first is that a civil law response to harm already done is small solace for someone who has lost her livelihood, or the health of her child. The second is illustrated by the real-life saga described in *A Civil Action*, involving the contamination of drinking water from, in all probability, industrial waste sites. Children died, … and their parents suffered a grief that is impossible to describe. But their legal case failed … over the requirements of proof and causation. Which chemical, of the many toxins in the waste sites, caused these infirmities and through exactly what exposure pathway? Which waste sites were responsible? Civil law failed because the science could not make the proof.…

Beginning in the 1960s, Congress surmounted these difficulties with new statutes, each based on environmental standards. The standards would operate by preventing rather than compensating for harm. They would, further, bypass the rigors of causation and proof: once a standard was set, one had only to see whether or not it was met. The question remained, however: who would set the standard? The answer seemed apparent. Scientists would, on the basis of scientific analysis.… [But] [n]one of these … [first generation environmental laws based on scientific risk assessment] worked well, and some, after enormous investment, failed utterly. We began to realize that science, although endlessly fascinating and constantly revelatory, is rarely dispositive. And in the world of environmental policy, that which is not dispositive is dead on arrival. The reason is political: environmental policy faces a degree of resistance unique in public law …

The extraordinary degree of resistance to environmental policy brings at least two consequences.… [T]hat which is not nailed down by law is not likely to happen.… Facing these difficulties [of making a scientific determination of "unreasonable risk to human health in the environment"], and with each of their decisions subject to legal challenges, the toxic programs of the air, water, pesticide, and related laws fell into a swoon. Mountains of paper spanning decades produced only a handful of standards, against a backlog of thousands of toxic substances … For opponents of these standards, there was always an unexplored factor. That is the essence of science. Meanwhile, global temperatures are rising. Parts of the Arctic ice shelf are breaking off into the sea.… For these reasons, all approaches became necessary in cutting the Gordian knot: engineering, science, tort actions, and, more recently, economic and market incentives.… There is no longer one way, there are many; and science is no longer king. Science still, however, plays lead roles. One is to sound the alarm, as it has done for decades and done recently regarding ozone thinning, climate change, and the loss of biological diversity. It is up to science as well to provide a rationale ... for the requirement of ... [expensive standards]....

With such power and so much riding on the opinions of scientists, however, ... [several] notes of caution are in order. The first is to beware the lure of a return to "scientific management." The technology standards that brought environmental programs out of their stalemate toward success were criticized from day one, and remain criticized today, as "arbitrary," "one size fits all," "inflexible," and "treatment for treatment's sake," outmoded in today's world. What we need, goes the refrain, is "iterative," "impact-based," "localized" management focused on the scientifically determined needs of this river, that airshed, this manufacturing plant, or that community. It sounds as attractive and rational as it did forty years ago, but we have tried that for decades and failed.... [These programs] eat up heroic amounts of money, remain information-starved, feature shameless manipulation of the data, face crippling political pressure, and produce little abatement ...

The second caution is the lure of "good science." Every lawyer knows what "good science" is: the science that supports his or her case. All of the other science is bad. If you are opposed to something, be it the control of dioxins, global warming, or obesity, the science is never good enough....

Notes and Questions

1. Professor Houck explains how politicians, lawyers, and even scientists use environmental labels to obfuscate rather than enlighten.

> No one likes to be tagged with the responsibility for poisoning children or destroying the Everglades, and a small industry of euphemisms has sprung up to mask the blame. Strip mining becomes "the removal of overburden," as if the soil, grass, and trees were somehow oppressing the land; dredgers in Louisiana leave "borrow pits," as if they were going to give the soil back someday.

Houck, *supra*, at 166. He adds: "It is one thing to say that you picked up a speeding ticket or had to pay back taxes. It is another to admit that you are using the Hudson River for a sewer or that you cut loose fourteen hundred tons of toxins over Los Angeles last year." Oliver A. Houck, *A Field Guide to Important Euphemisms in Environmental Law*, 15 Tul. Envtl. L. J. 129 (2001). Houck compiled a vocabulary of environmental euphemisms, all of which were crafted "to soften the blow. Just as military experts talk of collateral damage to describe the impact of weapons gone awry, so virtually every agency and industry that whacks the environment has developed its own language of damage control." *Id.* at 129.

2. Professor Holly Doremus argues that the U.S. Endangered Species Act (ESA) "offers an excellent case study of the use of science in environmental policy" because it "embodies an unusually strong legislative commitment to science as a foundation for policy, and it has been at the center of a series of very public controversies about the use of science." Holly Doremus, *The Purposes, Effects, and Future of the Endangered Species Act's Best Available Science Mandate*, 34 Envt. L. 397, 400 (2004). Can you think of other statutes in the United States or elsewhere that provide good examples of the interplay between science and environmental policy? How do other habitat conservation and species-specific provisions covered in this chapter fare in terms of scientific integrity?

3. What scientific factors should decisionmakers consider and prioritize? As the definition provided by the Convention on Biological Diversity indicates, biodiversity entails a range of factors, including the presence and viability of populations of endemic or rare

species and their related biological communities within an ecosystem, and the geographic distribution of a rich variety of species. As for habitat, essential features vary among ecosystem types. The physical features and functions of a forest ecosystem will be quite different than those of a desert, and both are distinct from marine or freshwater ecosystems. Good information about habitat quality, as well as species' population numbers and distribution, is an essential part of any biodiversity conservation effort. Although inventories have been prepared on much of our federal, state, and provincial land, because physical conditions and species' populations change over time, keeping the existing inventories up to date is a resource-intensive challenge, to say the least. The challenge is far greater when it comes to private lands. "Information about biological resources on private lands is limited—different parties possess mere fragments of data, and have little to no incentive to centralize the data in any user friendly, readily accessible format." Sandra B. Zellmer and Scott A. Johnson, *Biodiversity in and Around McElligot's Pool*, 38 Id. L.Rev. 473, 489 (2002).

4. What role should courts play in ensuring that agencies follow appropriate scientific methodology? These questions are particularly difficult when it comes to decisions that must be made on the very frontiers (or beyond) of science. If agencies do not volunteer transparency, how might courts force them to provide it?

5. Given the extensive uncertainties about imperiled wildlife and its habitat needs, particularly with changing conditions and climate, many scientists have begun to call for "adaptive management," a type of learning by doing, where hypotheses are tested through on-the-ground experimentation and environmental outcomes are monitored, analyzed, and adjusted throughout project implementation. Is this type of strategy appropriate for managing imperiled wildlife? An environmental planner from New Zealand advises caution, and recommends alternative methods:

> Adaptive management is to some extent an ongoing experiment, with the stakes being particularly high for the vulnerable. Factor in human error and it could become a lethal cocktail. Although it is accepted that considerable financial resources and scientific expertise may be employed in order to limit adverse effects on species and achieve sound results, where undue risk to species is a possibility, the use of adaptive management techniques should be rigorously controlled.

> The better approach is for the applicant to provide a comprehensive AEE (Assessment of Environmental Effects), accounting for detailed ecological planning, at the outset of the application.... An alternative, or even additional approach, is to enable termination of the consent upon review. Such an option is being promoted in relation to proposed legislation for the regulation of Environmental Effects in the Exclusive Economic Zone (EEZ)....

> > 17. A precautionary approach that allows for the application of adaptive management tools will be used to mitigate any lack of information about the marine environment and the environmental effects of individual activities. The provision for adaptive management will not restrict the ability of the consent authority to decline any application. For example, new types of activity, if approved, could have a staged work programme, with stringent monitoring requirements and the ability to revoke permission if the environmental effects exceed set levels.

Wallace, *supra*, at 24. Do you see any obstacles to cancellation of consents, or for that matter any type of license or permit issued by a governmental entity? In New Zealand, "the opportunity to prevent the operation of the consent is limited. Pursuant to §§ 126 and 132(4) RMA, consent may be cancelled if not exercised, or upon review, where it is found that inaccurate material influenced the grant of consent." *Id.* at 23.

6. Do natural ecosystems have intrinsic values, worthy of protection independent of human interests? For human societies, this idea invokes an ethical obligation to protect the integrity of ecological systems.

> To suppose that natural communities may have intrinsic and not just instrumental value, after all, is to distinguish what may be healthy for nature from what may be healthful or beneficial for humanity.... To treasure an ecological community is to see it has a good of its own—and therefore a "health" or "integrity"—that we should protect even when to do so does not profit us.

Mark Sagoff, *Has Nature a Good of Its Own?,* Ecosystem Health: New Goals for Environmental Management 67, 70 (Robert Costanza et al. eds., 1992).

For the Maori people of New Zealand, "Kaitiakitanga" describes the "exercise of guardianship ... and includes the ethic of stewardship based on the nature of the resource itself." Owen Furuseth and Chris Cocklin, *An Institutional Framework for Sustainable Resource Management: The New Zealand Model,* 35 Nat. Res. J. 243 (1995). The Maori's relationship with their ancestral lands, waters, sites, and resources are recognized in the Treaty of Waitangi and are prioritized as "matters of national importance" in RMA § 6(e). Interestingly, "intrinsic values of ecosystems" are given lower priority in the RMA as "other matters," rather than as "matters of national importance." What does this say about the RMA and about New Zealand politics and policy?

What role might ethics play in biodiversity protection? Renowned ecologist Aldo Leopold drew upon ethics when he wrote, "A thing is right when it tends to preserve the integrity, stability, and beauty of the biotic community. It is wrong when it tends otherwise." Aldo Leopold, A Sand County Almanac 262 (Ballantine 1991) (1949). Leopold's experiences as a Forest Service employee in the American Southwest during the 1910's, along with time spent on his own Wisconsin farm, "transformed him from a conventional resource-based thinker to a proponent of the idea that humans are on an ethical continuum with all animals and plants." Sarah Krakoff, *Mountains Without Handrails ... Wilderness Without Cellphones*, 27 Harv. Envtl. L. Rev. 417, 457 (2003). His "land ethic" views humans as members of a community larger than themselves. How does a land ethic square (if at all) with the moral obligations reflected in other systems of ethics? If you agree that a land ethic is an appropriate foundation for a nation's environmental laws, how would you incorporate it? And how would it be enforced?

7. How are the observations about ethics and about the role of science, scientists, and courts relevant to the case study on the Northern Spotted Owl, *supra,* Section B.2? What about proposals for assisted migration of climate-threatened species described in Section E.3?

Chapter VI

Environmental Human Rights

The international community declared a right to a quality environment in the 1972 United Nations Conference on the Human Environment (the Stockholm Declaration):

> Man has the fundamental right to freedom, equality, and adequate conditions of life, in an environment of a quality which permits a life of dignity and well-being, and he bears a solemn responsibility to protect and improve the environment for present and future generations.

U.N. Doc. A/Conf.48/14, 11 I.L.M. 1416 (1972). The Declaration's Preamble is equally direct: the environment is "essential to … the enjoyment of human rights." Continuing this theme, the Rio Declaration, adopted at the conclusion of the United Nations Conference on Environment and Development (UNCED) (Earth Summit), proclaims, "Human beings are at the center of concerns for sustainable development. They are entitled to a healthy and productive life in harmony with nature." U.N. Doc. A/Conf.151/26 (Vol. I) (1992), 31 I.L.M. 874 (1992).

Two unique categories of environmental human rights are addressed in this chapter: rights to water and the rights of indigenous peoples. The first part of the chapter considers human rights to water within the international law context rather than limiting itself to the five nations covered elsewhere in the book. The second part returns to our selected nations for a look at the environmental rights of indigenous peoples. For further reading on the topic of environmental human rights in all of its various substantive and procedural facets, see JOHN BONINE AND SVITLANA KRAVCHENKO, HUMAN RIGHTS AND ENVIRONMENT (2008).

A. Rights to Water

Water is a uniquely essential and irreplaceable resource. Fresh water is non-renewable —we have the same amount now in the hydrological cycle as we did centuries ago; it simply changes form as it moves through the atmosphere and the earth, and as it is used and reused.

Water has many attributes. First, it is elemental. Best-selling author Barbara Kingsolver described water as "the briny broth of our origins; the pounding circulatory system of the world." Barbara Kingsolver, *Water*, National Geographic 46 (2010). The human body is comprised of up to 75% water, and our blood contains 95% water. We can go for weeks without food but only a few days without water.

Water can also be spiritual. Ancient civilizations revered gods of water and of rain. Even today, priests of different religions all around the world immerse their adherents in water to symbolize the cleansing power of a supreme being's intervention.

Water is also an economic resource. As Benjamin Franklin's old adage goes, we know the true value of water only when the well is dry. Last but not least, when the well is dry (or contaminated), water can even be a subject of war. Mark Twain allegedly said, "Whiskey is for drinkin'; water is for fightin' over." Sandra Postel, *The Looming Water Wars: Farms vs. Cities*, USA Today, Mar. 2000.

Finally, the common, undeniable need for water can also bring people together.

> The planet's hydrological cycle is a water democracy—a system of distributing water for all species—for the rain forest in the Amazon, the desert life in the Sahara.... Nature does not discriminate between the needs of a microbe and a mammal, plants and humans. And all humans as a species have the same suste-nance needs for water.

Dr. Vandana Shiva, *Resisting Water Privatisation, Building Water Democracy* 2 (2006), available at http://www.globalternative.org/downloads/shiva-water.pdf.

The following article considers the nature of water and the nature of the most ele-mental human relationship with water: thirst. Professor Salzman explores how different societies have thought about drinking water and how they have managed access to it throughout time.

James Salzman, Thirst: A Short History of Drinking Water
18 Yale Journal of Law and Humanities 94 (2006)

Nestled in the Andes, the Bolivian city of Cochabamba lies in a fertile valley astride the banks of the Rocha River. Bolivia is the poorest country in South America, with two-thirds of its population below the poverty line. As in many developing countries, over forty percent of Cochabamba's 800,000 residents lack access to a water supply network. And even those who do have pipes cannot depend on reliable service. The poor often live in squatter settlements on the outskirts of town, relying for their drinking and domestic water supplies on private vendors. In a cruel irony, the poorest end up paying much more for their water than wealthier citizens connected to the city's water mains.

As part of a nationwide project to improve provision of municipal services, the gov-ernment of Bolivia launched a major privatization reform effort in the late 1990s. Prompted by financial institutions such as the International Monetary Fund and World Bank, the Bo-livian government actively sought out private investor management for Cochabamba's water and sewage services. Treating drinking water as a priced good under private man-agement, it was widely argued, would improve the water supply system infrastructure and delivery by injecting much-needed capital, greater efficiencies, and increased attention to customer needs. A forty-year concession for water and wastewater services in Cochabamba was granted to an international private consortium headed by Bechtel and known as Aguas del Tunari. In the national law passed to facilitate this transaction, water was declared the property of the state, available for licensing to private companies for distribution.

To cover the costs of laying new pipe, digging a new reservoir, and building a hydro-electric dam, Aguas del Tunari immediately raised the price of water and waste services charged to consumers, with some residents soon spending in excess of twenty percent of their household income on water. Just four months after the privatization scheme com-menced in 2000, protests began and soon mushroomed into street demonstrations and violence. In the face of property damage approaching twenty million dollars, dozens of injuries, and mass unrest, the government terminated the privatization concession and resumed control over the water supply system in Cochabamba.

During the heady days of protest, grassroots organizations met and jointly issued the Cochabamba Declaration. Their view of the conflict was clear—drinking water should not be a market commodity. As the Declaration stated, "Water is a fundamental human right and a public trust to be guarded by all levels of government, therefore, it should not be commodified, privatized or traded for commercial purposes." The Cochabamba Declaration, available at http://www.sierraclub.org/cac/water/human_right/ (last visited April 4, 2006).

This ringing prose contrasted starkly with an international statement, the Dublin Statement, published just a few years earlier. The first major recognition of water as a market commodity, the governments represented at the 1992 International Conference on Water and the Environment declared that "water has an economic value in all its competing uses and should be recognized as an economic good." [The Statement was adopted at the 1992 International Conference on Water and the Environment, attended by government-designated experts from a hundred countries and representatives of eighty international, intergovernmental, and non-governmental organizations. The Dublin Statement on Water and Sustainable Development, available at http://www.wmo.ch/web/homs/documents/english/icwedece.html (last visited April 4, 2006).]

Cochabamba was not a unique event. Similar protests over drinking water have played out in Paraguay, South Africa, the Philippines, and elsewhere. Cochabamba, however, remains the best-known example and rallying point for opponents of water supply privatization in developing countries. According to the popular recounting of the story, the conflict in Cochabamba served as a globalization morality play of rights versus markets, human need versus corporate greed. This simple dichotomy sounds in the Declaration's ringing prose and echoes in many other fora, from international statements to popular demands.

While making for sharp rhetoric, this facile dichotomy of rights versus markets is terribly limited, shedding only a dim light on the powerful tensions unleashed on the streets in Bolivia. Nor should this be surprising, for drinking water is a dauntingly complex resource to manage. Indeed, the conflicts in Cochabamba are drawn from the pages of a much larger, much older story. From earliest times, human societies have faced the challenge of supplying adequate quality and quantities of drinking water....

[T]o understand a natural resource one must understand its many natures, and drinking water is no exception. Drinking water is most obviously a physical resource, one of the few truly essential requirements for life. Regardless of the god you worship or the color of your skin, if you go without water for three days in an arid environment your life is in danger. And water's physical characteristics confound easy management. Water is heavy—it is difficult to move uphill. Water is unwieldy—it cannot be packed or contained easily. And drinking water is fragile—it easily becomes contaminated and unfit for consumption....

As the Cochabamba experience makes clear, managing and mediating these many facets of drinking water is no easy matter. In seeking to understand better how societies manage such a complex resource, this article considers three questions: How have different societies thought about drinking water? How have different societies managed access to drinking water? And how have these changed over time? These questions are, of course, interrelated. How we think of water, whether as a sacred gift or a good for sale, both influences and is influenced by how we manage access to drinking water. When management of drinking water fails to reflect popular conceptions and expectations, pressures for transition to a new management regime increase. And, as we saw in Cochabamba, when the new management regime fails to respect popular conceptions and expectations, it will fail.

Asking such questions may seem odd to an American environmental lawyer, for we tend to assume the presence of drinking water and focus on its quality rather than its natures as a resource; we tend to think in terms of quality rather than quantity. This is not surprising for, compared to irrigation water, domestic use is a trickling afterthought. And even within the category of domestic use, much less water is used for drinking than for clothes washing, watering the lawn, or even toilet flushing. In many parts of the world and for much of human history, however, quantity of drinking water has been as important as quality. While not an obvious issue to us in twenty-first century America, management of drinking water as a resource—who gets it, when they get it, and how much they get—matters a great deal.

In what is admittedly an initial examination of a deep and complex subject, the Article presents a series of case studies, briefly exploring drinking water management in societies across five continents, from 5,000 years ago up through today. Along the route, we will find that a society's management of something as seemingly simple as drinking water is no simple matter. Examining how a society recognizes the different natures of this vital resource provides a unique lens on the society's organization, equity, and view of itself.

The Right of Thirst

[T]hroughout history, human society and economies have been predicated on ready access to sources of drinking water. Archaeological excavations since the Neolithic time have found a striking correspondence between settlements and water engineering. Cisterns and wells carved from the rock have been found in excavations at Ebla, in Syria, dating from 2350 B.C., and even earlier water storage sites have been found at Jawa, in northeastern Jordan, dating from the fourth millennium B.C. Though half a world away and much later, water storage basins with minimum storage capacities of 10,000 to 25,000 gallons of water have been excavated in the Mesa Verde region of the American Southwest. and large collection and storage structures have been uncovered throughout the Maya Lowlands....

As a scarce resource, access to drinking water has been governed by rules from the earliest times. Indeed, rules establishing access to water in arid regions may very well have predated property regimes for land....

The Old Testament is filled with references to springs and wells, their importance clearly evident from the fact that each was given a special name. Jewish law regarding drinking water has been traced as far back as 3,000 B.C. The basic rule was one of common property. As reflected in the later writings of the Talmud, "Rivers and Streams forming springs, these belong to every man."[13] Because water from natural sources such as springs and streams was "provided by God," commodification of these waters would be tantamount to desecration—selling divine gifts.

Not all sources of water were natural, however. Many important sources of water came from wells, where human labor was necessary to gain access to the water. In these cases, drinking water was managed as a common property resource, though not an open access resource. Within each community, Jewish law prioritized access according to use, with high-

---

13. Talmud Bavli Shabbat, 121b; Beitza, 391; Eiruvin, 46a and 48a; Tosephta Baba Qama, 6, 15, quoted in Dante A. Caponera, Principles of Water Law and Administration 22 (1992).

est priority given to drinking water, followed by irrigation and grazing. Importantly, however, the very highest priority access was granted to those in need of drinking water, regardless of whether or not they belonged to the well's community of owners. This Right of Thirst provides a nice example of a Rawlsian rule, since any traveler in an arid region could foresee a situation where he or she might need water from strangers for survival. The right was not absolute, since villagers' necessary drinking requirements took priority over outsiders'. But outsiders' thirst took precedence over local grazing and other uses.

Islamic water law is quite similar to Jewish water law in both substance and significance. Indeed, the Arabic word for Islamic law, "Sharia," literally means the "way to water." As the Koran instructs, "Anyone who gives water to a living creature will be rewarded.... To the man who refuses his surplus water, Allah will say: 'Today I refuse thee my favor, just as thou refused the surplus of something that thou hadst not made thyself.'" The Right of Thirst reinforced this message. Since water is a gift from God to all people, sharing water is a holy duty.... Islamic water law was largely adopted into the legal code of the Ottoman Empire. It is still followed by Bedouin in the Negev, where "water to quench thirst is an unalienable right and may not be refused from any water source," and by the Berbers in Morocco, where drinking water for humans is "sacrosanct and neither may be denied anyone for any reason at any time."

In Australia, the driest inhabited continent, the need for rules over access to drinking water is self-evident. Given the scarcity of water, no distinction is drawn between water for drinking and other purposes. Most water sources are sacred parts of the dreamscape and knowledge of their location is vital to a group's survival (a truly critical example of intellectual property).

Given the variability of rainfall, sharing has played a key role in water management. Researchers describe the dominant access system as "always ask." While not an open access resource, in practice those requesting water are given permission to drink. Indeed, as one aboriginal expert has written,

> [T]he knowledge that those with plenty today will be supplicants themselves in the future [means that] ... [s]haring is encoded and embedded within all social relations: trade, marriage, ceremony and others. The code is reciprocity. Not only is the precept "always ask" essential; so too is the fact that people are almost never refused.

Clear parallels to the Right of Thirst may also be found today in a number of rural communities in developing countries. A study of communal lands in Zimbabwe, for example, reported that wells and boreholes built for private purposes are still made available for communal drinking. The authors concluded that "Cutting across all the different tenurial systems is the notion that no one should be denied access to safe drinking water." This is not to say, however, that it is an open access resource. In times of scarcity, ... communities may restrict the amount of water gathered, banning, for example, the filling of large drums or restricting withdrawals to twenty liters per family. Moreover, people must ask permission from the owner prior to using the well....

Thousands of miles away, studies of the Bihar in the northeast region of India also reveal a Right of Thirst. Because of the complex social hierarchy, priority of access and management is much more carefully proscribed than in other cultures along social caste lines.... As a result, only upper castes may make use of sacred source waters. The rule of sharing, however, is widely observed and those in need must be given access to water. At times of water scarcity, even access to an upper caste well is allowed.

One cannot, of course, draw sweeping conclusions from such a small set of examples, but this brief survey suggests two important points. First, while the rules governing drinking water management vary from culture to culture, the examples I have found in the literature present a common twist. Whether expressed through the Right of Thirst in Jewish and Islamic law, as sharing norms in India and Africa, or as "always ask" in Australia, access to drinking water in times of need seems to have been a basic right in a wide range of societies for a very long time....

Second, these cases provide clear examples of how drinking water can be managed as a physical resource (through rules over how water sources are maintained), a social resource (rules governing which castes and communities may use particular sources), a cultural resource (with water access regarded as a religious duty) and an economic resource. It is worth noting in this last regard that, while drinking water may be sufficiently scarce that norms restrict its use, this does not mean it is a commercial good. Indeed, while there surely will be counter-examples, in the societies covered in the preceding case studies drinking water has not been viewed primarily as a priced good with allocation determined by market forces. And even in societies without money, I found no barter systems for drinking water. Perhaps it is too important a resource, too connected with divine beneficence and social identity, to be treated as a fungible item for sale or barter.

Drinking water clearly is a commercial good in many societies today, however, so how did the transition to commodification occur? There is no better place to look for clues than ancient Rome.

Rome is the first great city defined by its management of drinking water. The graceful aqueducts that carried clean water to Roman cities were among the most magnificent structures of the ancient world and some proudly survive today. The water fountains that continue to define the splendor of Rome were important parts of the city's drinking water provision over 2,000 years ago. Rome is also the first major city I have found that managed drinking water as a priced resource.

While aqueducts play a critical part in the story of Roman drinking water, that was not their original purpose. Because of Rome's high water table, there was plentiful water available from local wells and springs. The main reason for construction of the aqueducts was not hygienic but social. Bath houses were an integral part of Roman society, and they required large volumes of water. Over time, however, as the city's population grew the water of the Tiber became increasingly polluted, particularly because the city's main sewer, the Cloaca Maxima, flowed directly into it. The ready availability of a reliable source of clean water from the aqueducts spurred demands for its water to be used for drinking, fountains, gardens, and even public toilets.

The Marcia was the third aqueduct, built in 144 B.C., and much larger than its predecessors. Brought into the city at a great height, the Marcia's waters were distributed throughout the city by gravity and its sweet waters were primarily used for drinking water. Almost half of the Marcia aqueduct's prized water went to private uses and roughly a quarter went to the city's public basins, known as lacus. The lacus were used by citizens for gathering water for domestic use. Importantly for our purposes, the water in the lacus was free for the taking. Most residents of Rome collected their water in this way and the lacus provided communal meeting places, much as wells continue to do in many rural societies....

Not everyone chose to collect their water from public sources, however, and Roman water finances depended on this demand for private water. Indeed, it is estimated that 40% of all the water delivered within Rome went to private buildings ... A special water tax, known as a vectigal, was charged for people who had pipes running from the main system to their houses or baths.... Piped delivery of water to a private residence was a status symbol, and a common luxury of senators....

Aqueduct construction was obviously a major public works project, funded primarily by the emperor and private donations. The funds raised by the vectigal were used to cover the costs of system maintenance. The net effect of this water financing scheme gave Roman drinking water a dual nature. To the wealthy Roman, water in the house (whether for drinking, an ornamental fountain, or domestic uses) effectively was a priced good. To the average Roman resident, however, water in the city was available by right....

The Roman story, then, provides within the same city fundamentally different conceptions of drinking water—as a public good provided by right through imperial beneficence, on the one hand, and as a private good for domestic consumption, on the other. Yet the two depended upon one another, for it was the treatment of water as a priced good that enabled cross-subsidization to ensure its public nature. In order to assess how transferable this model proved with the rise of modern cities, we turn to New York.

Ever since Peter Minuit's celebrated purchase of Manhattan Island from the natives for beads and trinkets in 1626, the settlement has faced challenges of ensuring adequate drinking water. While New York is obviously surrounded by large rivers, they open on the ocean and are too salty for drinking. The first Europeans to live in Manhattan, the Dutch settlers of New Amsterdam, relied on basic technologies to provide drinking water—collecting rainwater in cisterns and digging shallow wells. Most of the settlement's water came from a spring-fed, deep freshwater pond covering seventy acres in lower Manhattan, known as the "Kalch-Hook." The wells in New Amsterdam were private.... [T]he lack of fresh water on the island made it impossible to defend and easy to regain.

No surprise, then, that one of the first acts of the new British masters, after renaming the city New Yorke, was construction of public wells in the city. Begun in 1667, these would remain a primary source of water for New Yorkers well into the nineteenth century....

Long into the eighteenth century, most New Yorkers relied on these wells and the "Collect" (the anglicized pronunciation of the Kalch-hook) for free drinking water. During this period, however, urbanization continued and further industrial and population growth were clearly in store. Sanitation, an ever-present problem in British cities, was becoming unmanageable. Peter Kalm, a Swedish botanist visiting New York in 1748, in a remark Rodney Dangerfield would have loved, observed that *the well water was so terrible horses from out of town refused to drink it*. The Collect, once the best source of drinking water on Manhattan, had become polluted from the tanneries and slaughterhouses on its banks.

To those with an entrepreneurial spirit, the poor maintenance of the public wells and the disgusting state of the Collect posed ... a business opportunity. People with means began to purchase water from springs outside of town and deeper wells in town. Water sold from these sources became known as "Tea Water" and was either fetched by slaves or bought from "Tea Water Men" who purchased water directly from the pump owners and then carted it throughout the city for sale in buckets and barrels. By the middle of the eighteenth century, presaging the rise of ... bottled water 200 years later, sale of Tea Water had become the best source of good drinking water in New York....

The limitations of public wells and the Collect to provide clean water, growing dependence on Tea Water sales, and general concern over the availability of water to fight fires made clear the need for a serious re-thinking of New York's water supply. Thus, in 1774 the city approved an ambitious plan for a steam engine-powered waterworks that would pump water throughout the city in aqueducts similar to those of Rome. To fund the public works, the city issued "Water Works Money," the first paper money issued by an American city. Construction commenced, but … the British occupied the city and destroyed the waterworks construction. Following the Revolutionary War, water supply plans in the city stumbled along for over fifteen years.… A yellow fever epidemic struck New York in 1795 and many blamed the disease on the city's foul water and fouler streets.…

In an alliance that would seem unthinkable years later, Aaron Burr joined with Alexander Hamilton and other prominent politicians of the day to drive through a public/private solution.… Authorized by the New York state legislature and the New York City Council, the Manhattan Company, as the new organization would be called, was mandated in its corporate charter to provide New York City with clean drinking water.… Over time, this drinking water company gave up all pretence and developed into the powerful Chase Manhattan Bank. While few people actually received Manhattan Company water, the company defended its monopoly power over water provision and, as the Manhattan Company's portfolio grew, Tea Water pumps were driven out of business. New Yorkers were thus forced to rely on the increasingly revolting Collect Pond and local wells. People with money turned to imported soda water and well water mixed with liquor.…

It took a series of disasters [namely, fire and cholera] for the government to finally address water supply head on.… [A] permanent Board of Water Commissioners was created and authorized to raise infrastructure capital and condemn land in order to supply water to the city. Surprising even today, the condemnation authority extended beyond the boundaries of the city, for the water source lay upstream of New York in Croton. By 1838, condemnation of thirty-five acres of land in the Croton watershed had been completed. The Croton Reservoir was a massive project, supplying ninety-five million gallons daily.…

The story of New York's drinking water provides an instructive contrast with Rome. From its early days, New York's drinking water came from private wells, public wells, and the Collect. Faced with declining water quality, water became commodified with the rise of Tea Water. Following the failure to provide public infrastructure after the Revolutionary War, the private supply of drinking water reached its logical next step with responsibility for management of New York's entire water supply system granted to the Manhattan Company. Only when the company notably failed to provide even the most basic services for drinking water or fire protection did the city step in and occupy the field.…

Space constraints prevent fully recounting the story of London's drinking water here, but it shares many similarities with New York's reliance on private suppliers. Through the Middle Ages, Londoners gathered drinking water from local springs, wells, and the Thames River (the Romans never built aqueducts for London). By the early nineteenth century the city's water supply was in the hands of nine private companies. When a terrible cholera outbreak occurred in 1840 (which John Snow linked back to a single contaminated water source and thus founded the field of epidemiology), unlike in New York, the government did not take over supply responsibilities. Instead, in the Metropolis Water Act of 1852, private water suppliers became regulated entities, required to provide piping into private residences. Only in 1902 did municipal water become a public service.

In a fascinating parallel to the Roman lacus and Croton Hydrants, London also provided for free water but did so through charitable acts. During the nineteenth century, the Quakers founded, and later a group of nobility operated, the Metropolitan Drinking Fountain Association. This philanthropic society built free public fountains and watering troughs throughout the city. The motivation seems to have been two-fold—in part as a public service for those too poor to purchase drinking water and in large part as a strategy of the temperance movement. Thus it is no coincidence that many of the fountains were located next to popular pubs, making the point that people could slake their thirst for free with refreshing water rather than paying to drink beer or spirits.

Drinking Water in the Developing World

... Over one billion people do not have access to even a basic water supply. Well over two billion people lack adequate sanitation. As a result, approximately half of the developing world's inhabitants suffer from illnesses caused by contaminated water supplies.... Because water supply infrastructure is not provided in the poorest urban or in many rural areas, obtaining water is regarded as an individual or domestic responsibility. In contrast to the ease of turning on a faucet, lack of infrastructure means a high labor input as someone from the household (generally women and girls) must collect each day's water, whether from a communal pond or well, a tanker, or a kiosk. One billion people do not have water within a fifteen-minute walk of where they live. The daily average time spent on water gathering in 1997 across East Africa was 91.7 minutes daily, triple the time spent three decades earlier. And in the West African country of Senegal, women spend on average 17.5 hours per week gathering water.

Where communal or free water sources are too far away or contaminated, the poor purchase their water from street vendors or tanker trucks. These prices are always higher than the price of water from municipal supply systems, often twelve times as much, with the tragic irony of the poorest in society paying the most for their water.

The resulting social and economic impacts are immense. With a significant proportion of women's time and family income dedicated to domestic water supply, opportunity for productive activities such as education or other employment get squeezed. It is no exaggeration to say that introduction of piped water can transform the social and economic fabric of a community....

In recognition of these pressing issues, in its Millennium Development Goals the U.N. has pledged by 2015 to "reduce by half the proportion of people without sustainable access to safe drinking water." [United Nations Millennium Declaration, U.N. Gen. Ass. Res. A/55/L.2 (Sept. 18, 2000).] Given the poor state of water provision in the developing world and the small likelihood of debt-burdened governments making significant public monies available for infrastructure any time soon, what can be done?

This very question was explicitly considered in the 1980s, designated by the international community as the International Drinking Water Supply and Sanitation Decade ... [T]he influence of Reagan and Thatcher policies was being felt across the globe in a fundamental reconsideration of the state's proper role in the economy, and water was no exception. Rather than the solution to water supply problems, the state had come to be seen as the problem and the private sector, many argued, needed to be part of the solution....

The privatization arguments go beyond private management, however, to the nature of drinking water itself. The failure to treat water as a scarce commodity only ensures its inefficient distribution and use. A basic axiom of economics is that we over-consume goods that are underpriced. Since the market is more efficient ... at allocating scarce goods, the argument goes, market prices should be charged for water. Indeed, the fact that the very poor do pay for water, and pay quite a bit in relative terms, suggested that they both can and will pay for piped water. Thus the principle of "full cost recovery"— charging a price to cover costs and profit—has seemed both possible and desirable.

These arguments became official international policy with adoption in 1992 of the Dublin Statement ... the first intergovernmental recognition of water as a market good. This strategy was adopted in policies of international financial institutions, particularly in the Structural Adjustment Programs pursued by the IMF and World Bank in debtor countries. In Bolivia and other countries, privatization of water supply systems was made a prominent lending condition.

Spurred by the Dublin Statement and facilitated by international financial institutions, there has been an unprecedented expansion of private sector participation in water supply over the last two decades. Water supply services have been privatized across the globe, from the United Kingdom, Poland and Morocco to Argentina, Indonesia and the Philippines. "Privatization," of course, can mean many things and these arrangements have ranged from outright privatization of water supply infrastructure to public/private partnerships, management contracts, leases, etc.

Turning a profit, however, is far from assured. Water supply generally operates as a natural monopoly. Large-scale delivery of water requires large-scale infrastructure. The initial sunk costs can be massive, not to mention the continuing costs of maintenance and upgrade. This creates a significant barrier to entry for competition and requires amortization periods that can run several decades. A return on investment also requires general economic, political, and social stability over that period; yet, in many developing countries, this is far from a given. Hence the difficult challenge privatization may hold its greatest social potential in developing countries because it can inject needed capital, yet it is in precisely such settings where investment returns are least certain.

Seeking a competitive return on investments in developing countries, privatization has often been followed by efforts at full cost recovery. The immediate problem that can arise is one of inequity. If water access is based on ability-to-pay rather than willingness-to-pay, then what are the implications for poor and marginalized communities? Does changing the management regime effectively deny them access to adequate clean drinking water?

Alert to these concerns and as part of the larger anti-globalization wave, a vocal movement has arisen to challenge the growing pressure for water privatization. Its primary demand lies in recognition of a right to water. We saw such a demand expressed . . . in the grassroots Cochabamba Declaration and its statement that "[w]ater is a fundamental human right and a public trust." Similar calls for a human right to water may be found in over a dozen international documents and proposed federal legislation. . . .

The popular recounting of Cochabamba and its fiery Declaration fit neatly into the rhetoric of the globalization debates, as does the Dublin Statement. Rights-based and market-based access to water are depicted as antithetical, while arguments revolve over whether water supply should be publicly or privately managed. If our survey of drinking water management in different societies has shown anything, however, it's that this popular discourse is both simplistic and distinctly ahistorical. While making for powerful rhetoric, treating drinking water access as a binary conflict of rights versus markets, of public versus private management, forces a false choice. . . .

Nor are these two identities mutually exclusive. In Rome, water by right and by purchase co-existed; indeed the two openly depended upon one another through cross-subsidization. . . . Indeed, these cases show that markets can actually be used to ensure fulfillment of rights. . . . From a historic vantage, then, we see a range of management regimes for drinking water — some rights-based, some payment-based, and some hybrid.

Turning to the public/private debate, skeptics are right to doubt whether purely private markets can adequately address the different natures of drinking water, but purely private markets are few and far between. Public management remains the dominant source of drinking water today and takes a wide range of forms, whether through municipally-owned waterworks, regulated private water utilities, or public/private ventures. Put simply, the fact of privatization does not, in itself, tell us whether access to water will be based on full cost recovery rates, targeted subsidies, or some other scheme. Thus the privatization question turns on the practical questions of how water supply should be supervised, how the transition should be managed, and how access should be provided ...

A key point worth keeping in mind, however ... is the significance of a right to drinking water. While there will surely be exceptions, it is striking that in every water management scheme I have come across to date one finds explicit norms for providing the essential drinking water to those in need, even if they are from outside the community or are unable to pay. It may well be that a core feature of any privatization scheme must be an explicit provision for this right of thirst.

Moving beyond the simplistic discourse of rights versus markets, public versus private provision, it is striking how little attention has been paid to the more fundamental issue the nature of drinking water, itself. Drinking water has served as a physical resource, and an economic resource, and a social resource far more often than any one of these alone ... Effectively managing access to drinking water necessarily requires management across multiple dimensions expressly recognizing the natures of the natural resource ...

Considering the facets of drinking water also frames the Cochabamba story in a different light. There were many issues underpinning the unrest in Cochabamba, but the fundamental problem surely did not lie in treating access to water as a market transaction instead of by right. Water was not free before the uprising in Cochabamba and it is not free now. By granting an exclusive water concession to Aguas del Tinari and requiring that water withdrawals be licensed by the state, the government was perceived as effectively enclosing the "water-commons." Contemporary accounts suggest that fears over possible metering of water from rain barrels, streams, and wells played a far greater role in people taking to the streets than rising water bills. This failure to consider the popular conceptions of resource access proved fatal. By treating drinking water as a purely economic resource and focusing on pricing, Aguas del Tinari ignored water's significant nature as a social resource. The mass demonstrations did call for a return to previous water rates but, more fundamentally, a return to previous entitlements....

The Right of Thirst seems to have shown a remarkable resiliency. If, in fact, this norm has endured ... over such a long period of time, it surely needs to be a core aspect of privatization strategies, but how should this right be expressed? ...

We started this Article with a story, and it's appropriate to end there, as well, because much of the public's discourse over drinking water has consisted of morality tales. Evil transnational companies will commodify our water, warn anti-globalization bards, while free marketeers smoothly recount how savior transnational companies bring hope and investment. Whether the particular story turns on rights versus markets, or public versus private management, each features good guys and bad guys. And these stories have shown a striking persistence despite the fact that they are neither particularly accurate nor helpful.... [They] remind[] us of the need to move away from simplistic dichotomies such as rights versus markets, or public versus private management.... [They] also leave[] us with an unspoken challenge: if our current stories about drinking water are inadequate, then what should the new story be for the oldest resource of all.

Notes and Questions

1. Is water different from other types of natural resources and environmental ameni-ties or features? If there is a human right to drinking water, should there also be a human right to oil and gas, for example? Or to fisheries? Or inspirational landscapes? If the an-swer to any of these questions is "yes," who is the rights holder, and who holds the re-sponsibility to provide the resource in question? Who pays?

2. Professor Salzman, *supra,* argues that "treating drinking water access as a binary conflict of rights versus markets" makes for "powerful rhetoric," but ultimately "forces a false choice." Is privatization of drinking water supplies necessarily inconsistent with a human right to water? By the same token, is the recognition of private property rights in water necessarily inconsistent with a human right to water? For an analysis of the nature of water rights in the western United States, see Sandra Zellmer and Jessica Harder, *Un-bundling Property in Water,* 59 Ala. L.Rev. 679 (2008).

3. In India, the right to water came to the forefront when the village council (known as a panchayat) in Kerala voted to cancel the license of Coca-Cola's bottling plant. The coun-cil declared: "the excessive exploitation of groundwater by the Coca-Cola Company in Plachimada is causing acute drinking water scarcity in Perumatty Panchayat and nearby places, it is resolved in public interest, not to renew the license of the said Company."

> This decision ... was challenged by Coca-Cola, and the state government stayed the cancellation and directed the Panchayat to create an expert committee to perform various environmental tests to ascertain the truth. The Panchayat ap-pealed the state government decision to the High Court of Kerala, where a sin-gle judge accepted the argument of the Panchayat on the grounds that excessive extraction of a public resource by a private actor is against the public interest.

> On appeal by Coca-Cola, the appellate bench of the High Court, consisting of two judges, reversed the ruling. The appellate court asserted that it did not find a sufficient reason to rule against the multinational's right to extract water, nor did it find the extraction of excessive natural resources to violate the law. The court further reasoned that Coca-Cola had properly exercised its property rights to extract water from its own property. As part of its decision, the appellate court noted that the Kerala High Court had imposed both impossible conditions and unworkable propositions, and thus acted unjustly against the multinational....

Saby Ghoshray, *Searching for Human Rights to Water Amidst Corporate Privatization in India*, 19 Geo. Int'l Envtl. L. Rev. 643, 646–48 (2007), citing Hindustan Coca-Cola Bev-erages Pvt. Ltd. v. Perumatty Grama Panchayat, W.A 2125 of 2003, W.A. 215 of 2004, W.A. 1962 of 2003, W.P. (C) 12600 of 2004, H.C. Ker. (2005). Ghoshray explains the sig-nificance of the litigation:

> While the Kerala High Court decided the case on statutory interpretation of ex-isting laws regarding the protection and enforcement of the right to water, the ramifications go far beyond existing legal discourse ... [a]s rampant industrial-ization devours pristine natural resources and alters an agrarian way of life.... At the heart of the case lies perhaps the most poignant legal battle of the current century: the corporate right to privatization versus the indigenous right to water. Perched at this fascinating crossroad, this particular case debating water rights in India promises to open multiple legal frontiers. While constitutional ju-risprudence in India has matured significantly in order to deal with emerging issues of environment, human rights, and competing property rights, the ap-

pellate bench of the High Court of Kerala has largely bypassed deeper issues germane to the case. The debate goes beyond property rights, as it opens up more profound issues about whether the right to water belongs in the category of human rights.

Id. at 649. Meanwhile, in Plachimada, people took the dispute out of the courtroom and into the streets:

> The protests by villagers ... have shown the strength of community-led activities, even against this global multi-national company. Through round-the-clock vigils outside the factory gates, they have managed to 'temporarily' shut down Coca-Cola's local bottling plant. As of early 2007, the factory had remained closed for a number of years and a combination of community action and legal redress was aimed at permanent closure.

WaterAid et al., The Rights to Water and Sanitation, http://www.righttowater.info/ways-to-influence/legal-approaches/case-against-coca-cola-kerala-state-india/ (visited Aug. 15, 2012). The bottling plant has remained closed since 2004, "caught in a web of high-profile people's agitations, court cases and controversies over groundwater depletion and pollution, including heavy metal toxicity ..." R. Krishnakumar, *Plachimada's Claims*, 27 Frontline (India) 15, July 17–30, 2010. The other side of the story comes from E. Neville Isdell, as Chairman and CEO of Coca-Cola:

> In India, we have been challenged to demonstrate our commitment to water stewardship.... Coca-Cola has a shared interest with the communities where we operate in healthy watersheds—because they sustain life and our business. And the last thing we would ever do is spend millions of dollars to build a plant that would run itself dry.... Accordingly, we are working with many partners across India to improve watershed management, and with the Central Ground Water Authority, local governments and communities to expand the use of simple and effective rainwater harvesting technology. To date, we have installed rainwater harvesting systems in 200 locations, including schools and farms, that are helping recharge aquifers when the rains come.

WaterAid, *supra*. Once you parse through the rhetoric, is there an equitable, sustainable solution to the dispute? For an assessment of the Coca-Cola case and similar controversies, see Nobonita Chowdhury et al., *The Human Right to Water and the Responsibilities of Businesses: An Analysis of Legal Issues* (2011), at http://www.ihrb.org/pdf/SOAS-The_Human_Right_to_Water.pdf. Impacts of resource development on tribal people in India, and India's relevant constitutional provisions on environmental rights, are covered below in Section B.3.

4. Does a right to water come with a right to a healthy watershed? A case from the Philippine Supreme Court suggests that it does. In Minors Oposa v. Sec'y of the Dep't of Env't & Natural Res., July 30,1993, 33 I.L.M. 173, 185, the court entertained a petition from a class of minors on behalf of themselves and of unborn generations. In a remarkable opinion, the court issued the following findings and conclusions:

> 14. The continued allowance by defendant of [timber license] holders to cut and deforest the remaining forest stands will work great damage and irreparable injury to plaintiffs—especially plaintiff minors and their successors—who may never see, use, benefit from and enjoy this rare and unique natural resource treasure. This act of defendant constitutes a misappropriation and/or impairment of the natural resource property he holds in trust for the benefit of plaintiff minors and succeeding generations.

15. Plaintiffs have a clear and constitutional right to a balanced and healthful ecology and are entitled to protection by the State in its capacity as the parens patriae....

18. The continued failure and refusal by defendant to cancel the [timber licenses] is an act violative of the rights of plaintiffs, especially plaintiff minors who may be left with a country that is desertified (sic), bare, barren and devoid of the wonderful flora, fauna and indigenous cultures which the Philippines has been abundantly blessed with....

20. Furthermore, defendant's continued refusal to cancel the aforementioned [timber licenses] is contradictory to the Constitutional policy of the State to ... "protect and advance the right of the people to a balanced and healthful ecology in accord with the rhythm and harmony of nature."

21. Finally, defendant's act is contrary to the highest law of humankind—the natural law—and violative of plaintiffs' right to self-preservation and perpetuation....

Note that the court relied not only on Section 16, Article II, of the Philippine Constitution, as a source of the environmental right, but also on natural law. *Id.* paras. 15, 20–21. Could this aspect of the opinion be persuasive in jurisdictions without constitutional provisions on a healthy environment?

What, you may ask, does deforestation have to do with water? "By the late 1980s, only 4 percent of the Philippines remained in native cover ... and the environmental bills were coming due in eroded hillsides, dead rivers, dying reefs, water shortages, and wasting floods." Oliver A. Houck, Taking Back Eden 47 (2010). Reforms have come about slowly, but the "Supreme Court opinion dealt timber concessions on native forests ... a legal and psychological blow from which they will never recover." *Id.* at 54. By 2006, there were only three timber leases in effect and the annual rate of deforestation had fallen to two percent. *Id.* at 55.

5. Water is significant to many groups of indigenous peoples on a number of spiritual, cultural, economic, and subsistence levels. For example, in New Zealand:

Maoris have traditionally used water for ritual and medicinal purposes. Marine deities were and are prominent in Maori religion and folklore. Maoris often use water for ritual purposes even today.

Benjamin A. Kahn, *The Legal Framework Surrounding Maori Claims to Water Resources In New Zealand: In Contrast to the American Indian Experience*, 35 Stan. J. Int'l L. 49, 59 (1999). In granting resource consents to take, use, divert, or dam water, the consent authority must take Maori interests into account. For example, in Mangakahia Maori Komiti v. Northland Regional Council [1996] NZRMA 193, the period for taking water for irrigation was reduced to minimize impacts on Maori resources.

Section 6 of the RMA identifies Maori resource values as a matter of national significance, which must be both recognized and provided for. Nolan, *supra,* at 547, citing Haddon v. Auckland Regional Council and Auckland City Council [1994] NZRMA 49 (PT). RMA 8 obligates consent authorities and other resource managers to take the Treaty of Waitangi "into account." This directive represents more than a mere passing concern, but less than an outright Maori veto. Nolan, *supra,* at 161.

The Treaty of Waitangi guaranteed Maori the full exclusive and undisturbed possession of their lands and estates, forest, fisheries, and other properties which they desired to retain. While ... this cannot exclude compulsory acquisition (with proper compensation) for necessary public purposes, it and the other statutory provisions … do mean that special regard to Maori interests and values is required.…

McGuire v. Hastings Dist. Council [2002] 2 NZLR 577. "The duties … in respect to the relationship of Maroi, kaitiakitanga [stewardship], and the principles of the Treaty, are strong directions to be borne in mind at every stage of the planning process." Living Earth Ltd. v. Auckland Regional Council [2006] NZEvnC Auckland A 126/06, at 273. These rights and other rights of indigenous peoples are covered in more detail in the next section.

B. Rights of Indigenous People

Resource exploitation in and near indigenous communities can result in severe impacts on traditional lifestyles, and sometimes even forced resettlement. The environmental interests of indigenous peoples have been asserted in the high courts of Canada, the United States, New Zealand, India, and other nations with aboriginal populations in an array of cases. At stake is the right to manage and protect natural resources located on aboriginal lands and reservations as well as the right to live in a healthful environment and to ensure that environmental policies do not disproportionately affect poor and minority communities. *See, e.g.,* U.S. Exec. Order on Environmental Justice 12,898 1–101, 59 Fed. Reg. 7629 (1994).

In recognition that indigenous peoples throughout the world face discrimination in many ways from many sources, the United Nations General Assembly adopted the Declaration on the Rights of Indigenous Peoples in 2007, with 144 countries voting in favor. The Declaration expands on the earlier Convention Concerning the Protection and Integration of Indigenous and Tribal Populations (ILO No. 157), 328 U.N.T.S. 247 (1959), which is described below in Section B.3, by affirming principles of tribal self-determination.

Although the Declaration does not have legally binding effect *per se,* it is a solemn resolution akin to other "important policy statements of the organized world community — into the vicinity of instruments such as the 1948 Universal Declaration of Human Rights." S. James Anaya and Siegfried Wiessner, *The UN Declaration on the Rights of Indigenous Peoples: Towards Re-empowerment* (2007), at http://jurist.law.pitt.edu/forumy/2007/10/un-declaration-on-rights-of-indigenous.php. Moreover, provisions of the Declaration may become binding over time if they are "reflective or generative of customary international law." *Id.*

> Beyond recognition of the right to self-determination, … [there is] an array of tailor-made collective rights, such as the right to maintain and develop their distinct political, economic, social and cultural identities and characteristics as well as their legal systems and to participate fully, "if they so choose," in the political, economic, social and cultural life of the State … [Indigenous peoples] were guaranteed the right not to be subjected to genocide or ethnocide, i.e., action aimed at or affecting their integrity as distinct peoples, their cultural values and identities, including the dispossession of land, forced relocation, assimilation or integration, the imposition of foreign lifestyles and propaganda.

> The stated rights guaranteed to indigenous peoples as groups, not only as individual persons, include the right to observe, teach and practice tribal spiritual and religious traditions; the right to maintain and protect manifestations of their

cultures, archaeological-historical sites and artifacts; the right to restitution of spiritual property taken without their free and informed consent, including the right to repatriate Indian human remains; and the right to protection of sacred places and burial sites. Further listed are the rights to maintain and use tribal languages, to transmit their oral histories and traditions, to education in their language and to control over their own educational systems. They are afforded the right to maintain and develop their political, economic and social systems, and to determine and develop priorities and strategies for exercising their right to development. Their treaties with States should be recognized, observed and enforced. Last, but not least, the Declaration supports the right of indigenous people to own, develop, control, and use the lands and territories which they have traditionally owned or otherwise occupied and used, including the right to restitution of lands confiscated, occupied or otherwise taken without their free and informed consent, with the option of providing just and fair compensation wherever such return is not possible.... The political significance of this remarkable success of the indigenous peoples' movement cannot be understated....

Id. The United States was slow to endorse the Declaration, but the Obama Administration finally did so in 2011, and issued the following press release:

Today, in response to the many calls from Native Americans throughout this country and in order to further U.S. policy on indigenous issues, President Obama announced that the United States has changed its position. The United States supports the Declaration, which — while not legally binding or a statement of current international law — has both moral and political force. It expresses both the aspirations of indigenous peoples around the world and those of States in seeking to improve their relations with indigenous peoples....

The United States recognizes that some of the most grievous acts committed by the United States and many other States against indigenous peoples were with regard to their lands, territories, and natural resources. For this reason, the United States has taken many steps to ensure the protection of Native American lands and natural resources, and to provide redress where appropriate. It is also for this reason that the United States stresses the importance of the lands, territories, resources and redress provisions of the Declaration in calling on all States to recognize the rights of indigenous peoples to their lands, territories, and natural resources....

Consistent with its understanding of the intention of the States that negotiated and adopted the Declaration, the United States understands these provisions to call for the existence of national laws and mechanisms for the full legal recognition of the lands, territories, and natural resources indigenous peoples currently possess by reason of traditional ownership, occupation, or use as well as those that they have otherwise acquired. The Declaration further calls upon States to recognize, as appropriate, additional interests of indigenous peoples in traditional lands, territories, and natural resources. Consistent with that understanding, the United States intends to continue to work so that the laws and mechanisms it has put in place to recognize existing, and accommodate the acquisition of additional, land, territory, and natural resource rights under U.S. law function properly and to facilitate, as appropriate, access by indigenous peoples to the traditional lands, territories and natural resources in which they have an interest.... The Administration is likewise committed to protecting the environment, and recognizes that many indigenous peoples depend upon a healthy environment for subsistence fishing, hunting and gathering. The Administration therefore acknowledges the importance of the provisions of the Declaration that address environmental issues.

U.S. Dept. of State, Announcement of U.S. Support for the United Nations Declaration on the Rights of Indigenous Peoples (2010), http://www.state.gov/documents/organization/184099.pdf. Like the U.S., Canada, New Zealand, and Australia voted against the Declaration in 2007, but they, too, have changed their positions and now endorse it.

1. Canada and the United States

The difficulties inherent in translating indigenous peoples' environmentally related interests and traditions into conventional forms of evidence and shaping them into legally recognized causes of action pose unique challenges for litigants and for courts, as Peter Manus describes below.

Peter Manus, Indigenous Peoples' Environmental Rights: Evolving Common Law Perspectives in Canada, Australia, and the United States
33 B.C. Envtl. Aff. L. Rev. 1 (2006)

On November 18, 2004, the Supreme Court of Canada issued a pair of opinions affirming the Canadian government's sovereign obligation to honor the environment-related rights of two native tribes of British Columbia. Taku River Tlingit First Nation v. British Columbia [2004] 3 S.C.R. 550; Haida Nation v. British Columbia [2004] 3 S.C.R. 511.... Considering the centuries-old relationships between aboriginals and northern-European-rooted sovereigns in nations such as Canada, Australia, and the United States, these recent cases have grappled with some surprisingly elemental issues....

As may be expected, high court decisions in all three countries have met with contentious popular and political responses over the years, and all three courts have reacted, with the result that current common law on the environmental rights of indigenous peoples remains unsettled in spite of recent attention. *Taku River Tlingit First Nation* and *Haida Nation*, both of which work to reassert fundamental ideals of sovereign duty and aboriginal autonomy, make the present an appropriate moment to review the evolving judicial views on the environment-related rights of indigenous peoples in nations with significant indigenous populations and common law court systems.

This Article examines decisions ... in which the rights of an indigenous people have come into conflict with property claims or the natural resource regulations of the dominant culture. [It] offers analyses of selected high-profile court cases emerging in the late twentieth and early twenty-first centuries in which ... tribes strove to find verification of their environment-related aboriginal rights in the courts of the sovereign under whose protection they dwell. Not all such cases end successfully, but neither do all support a conclusion that indigenous peoples in these countries enjoy no judicial protection or that a sovereign's acknowledgment of its obligations to indigenous peoples amounts to nothing more than political hyperbole ...

[T]he foremost factor in the survival of tribal cultures in nations with common law court systems may be the courts' willingness to accept as part of its judicial role a responsibility to both recognize and impose the sovereign obligation to understand, value, and preserve the environmental interests of native populations....

Canada: The Constitutionalization of Aboriginal Environmental Interests

Canadian law addressing its indigenous peoples' rights is unique in that Canada's Constitution Act, 1982 constitutionalized aboriginal rights; section 35 of that Act states that "[t]he existing aboriginal and treaty rights of the aboriginal peoples of Canada are hereby recognized and affirmed."[14] ... A number of cases since 1982 have examined aspects of section 35, ranging in focus from the meaning and scope of aboriginal rights to the forms of evidence that courts may require in making determinations of whether aboriginal rights exist.... [T]he Canadian Supreme Court may be perceived as having come full circle recently, both building upon and reacting to prior cases until its recent reassertion of the basic ideals expressed in the landmark case of *Sparrow v. The Queen* [[1990] 1 S.C.R. 1075].

In the 1990 case of *Sparrow v. The Queen*, the Supreme Court of Canada analyzed the environmental protection offered by section 35 in the context of aboriginal fishing rights. In *Sparrow*, a member of the Musqueam Indian Band had been charged with violating Canada's Fisheries Act and its regulations for fishing with a longer drift net than was permitted under the terms of the Band's food fishing license. The fisherman defended himself by claiming that he had been exercising an aboriginal right to fish and that the net length restriction in the Band's license violated section 35.[24] The Court agreed....

First, the Court limited the scope of aboriginal rights that enjoyed constitutional protection by pointing out that the "existing" aboriginal rights referenced in section 35 included those in existence at the time that the Constitution Act took effect, and not rights that had been extinguished prior to that time.... Instead, the Court explained, the aboriginal rights coming under constitutional protection needed to be "interpreted flexibly so as to permit their evolution over time." Acknowledging that the Musqueam had occupied their native territory "as an organized society long before the coming of European settlers, and that the taking of salmon was an integral part of their lives," the Court concluded that the Crown had failed to meet its burden of proving that these aboriginal fishing rights had been extinguished prior to 1982. Thus, regardless of any patterns of regulation, the Indians held a constitutionally protected, existing aboriginal right to fish in the area where Mr. Sparrow had been fishing at the time he violated the terms of the Band's fishing license.

Perhaps more significantly, the Court went on to examine the breadth of the Musqueam Band's aboriginal right to fish so as to draw a conclusion as to whether the net length li-

---

14. Constitution Act, 1982, 35, ch. 11 (U.K.). The section reads, in full:
    (1) The existing aboriginal and treaty rights of the aboriginal peoples of Canada are hereby recognized and affirmed.
    (2) In this Act, "aboriginal peoples of Canada" includes the Indian, Inuit and Métis peoples of Canada.
    (3) For greater certainty, in subsection (1) "treaty rights" includes rights that now exist by way of land claims agreements or may be so acquired.
    (4) Notwithstanding any other provision of this Act, the aboriginal and treaty rights referred to in subsection (1) are guaranteed equally to male and female persons.
Section 25 of the Canadian Constitution also grants particular rights to indigenous populations:
    The guarantee in this Charter of certain rights and freedoms shall not be construed so as to abrogate or derogate from any aboriginal, treaty or other rights or freedoms that pertain to the aboriginal peoples of Canada including (a) any rights or freedoms that have been recognized by the Royal Proclamation of October 7, 1763; and (b) any rights or freedoms that now exist by way of land claims agreements or may be so acquired. Id. 25.
    24. ... The fishing incident that triggered the case occurred in Canoe Passage, a water body in which the Musqueam were licensed to fish; the license limited drift net length to 25 fathoms, and Mr. Sparrow was discovered using a drift net of 45 fathoms in length.

cense limitation at issue in the underlying case breached this right. The Court expressed itself as bound by history, honor, and the nature of the Constitutional Act in question to construe aboriginal rights liberally.... includ[ing] the requirement that it interpret the historical, ceremonial, cultural, and subsistence habits of the Musqueam "in a contemporary manner." Thus, while Mr. Sparrow had been engaged in commercial fishing at the time he was found to be violating the Musqueam Band fishing license, and while commercial fisheries were introduced by European settlers and were not part of the aboriginal history of the tribe, the Court indicated its openness to the contention that the ancient Musqueam practice of bartering might be construed as a modern aboriginal right to engage in commercial fishing that could be regulated only within constitutionally protected limits.

The *Sparrow* opinion's ultimate significance, however, may have been its powerful discussion of the "recognition and affirmation" doctrine, which the Court articulated as a duty on the part of Canadian courts to sensitize their interpretations of aboriginal rights to the fact that their existence had been recognized and affirmed in the Constitution. The Court detailed a Canadian history of many years during which the rights of tribes in connection with their aboriginal lands "were virtually ignored." Characterizing section 35 of the Constitution Act of 1982 as "the culmination of a long and difficult struggle in both the political forum and the courts," the Court determined that the section's promulgation "'renounce[d] the old rules of the game under which the Crown established courts of law and denied those courts the authority to question sovereign claims made by the Crown.'" ... [T]he Court concluded that the "recognition and affirmation" demanded by section 35 invoked a fiduciary responsibility on the part of the Crown to show "restraint on the exercise of sovereign power" in its dealings with aboriginal tribes.

Thus, while the Court expressly refrained from precluding all regulations impacting aboriginal rights, it placed a heavy burden on the Crown to establish that such regulations were enacted to meet valid objectives....

[T]he *Sparrow* Court then presented a two-part test for determining the constitutionality of a government regulation challenged under section 35. First, the Court stated, courts must consider whether the aboriginal group challenging the legislation is able to establish that it interferes with an existing aboriginal right. Proof of this, under the Court's test, would constitute a prima facie constitutional infringement. The Court warned that a court's analysis of aboriginal rights must consider those rights from the perspective of their aboriginal genesis rather than in their common law form. Fishing rights, the Court explained, are "rights held by a collective and are in keeping with the culture and existence of that group," and courts considering the impact of regulation on such rights "must be careful ... to avoid the application of traditional common law concepts of property as they develop their understanding of ... the '*sui generis*' nature of aboriginal rights." In determining whether the right has been infringed, the Court instructed, courts must ask whether the regulation is reasonable and whether it imposes undue hardship; courts must also ask whether the regulation denies the aboriginal people "their preferred means of exercising that right."

Under the facts before the *Sparrow* Court, then, ... the inquiry would be whether the net length restriction caused the Musqueam to "spend undue time and money per fish caught," or otherwise resulting in hardship to them in catching fish. In short, the Court infused a traditional regulatory impact analysis with a high level of sensitivity to the aboriginal perspective on their native rights and a relatively low level of tolerance for the disruption of those rights.

Part two of the Court's test shifts the burden from the tribe to the regulator and the focus of the courts' inquiry to the question of whether the government can justify its infringement on the tribe's constitutionally protected aboriginal rights.... Rejecting the vague "public interest" justification, along with the "'presumption' of validity," which it characterizes as outdated, the Court characterized justified objectives as needing to be "compelling and substantial."

Examples of valid justified regulations the Court offered included: "[a]n objective aimed at preserving [the tribe's section] 35(1) rights by conserving and managing a natural resource," and "objectives purporting to prevent the exercise of [section] 35(1) rights that would cause harm to the general populace or to aboriginal peoples themselves." Conservation, the Court acknowledged, is a valid government objective that is consistent with aboriginal beliefs and may work to preserve aboriginal rights. However, in allocating a scarce natural resource that is threatened by modern commercial practices and the contemporary iteration of aboriginal rights, the Court demanded that regulation *prioritize* the interest of perpetuating Indian access to the natural resource over all non-Indian commercial and recreational interests [emphasis added]. The constitutional protection afforded to the Musqueam food fishing right, the Court concluded, dictated that "any allocation of priorities after valid conservation measures have been implemented must give top priority to Indian food fishing." ...

The *Sparrow* Court's assertive, sensitive approach to the indigenous interests at stake may be explained by their status as newly recognized constitutional rights. Over the decade following *Sparrow*, the Canadian Supreme Court partially undermined the landmark decision....

In *Marshall v. The Queen*, a Mi'kmaq Indian charged with fishing for eels out of season and without a license in the Province of Nova Scotia claimed that his action was protected as an aboriginal right under a 1760 Treaty of Peace and Friendship [[1999] 3 S.C.R. at 465]. Because the tribe limited its claim to an assertion of tribal rights under the treaty, the Court did not engage in a direct discussion of the constitutional protection of aboriginal rights, as it had in *Sparrow*. Nevertheless, the Court's analysis of the Mi'kmaq's treaty rights adhered to the spirit of *Sparrow* by interpreting the native rights in the context of the history of relations between indigenous Canadians and those of European descent, and also by rendering an analysis consistent with the *Sparrow* Court's charge that courts honor and uphold the government's fiduciary responsibility toward aboriginal peoples....

[The Court held] ... the Treaty "affirm[s] the right of the Mi'kmaq people to continue to provide for their own sustenance by taking the products of their hunting, fishing and other gathering activities, and trading for what in 1760 was termed 'necessaries.'" The Court defined "necessaries" to include "food, clothing and housing, supplemented by a few amenities." In keeping with *Sparrow*, the Court construed this terminology in a contemporary light, concluding that "necessaries" translated into "a moderate livelihood" that "do[es] not extend to the open-ended accumulation of wealth." Mr. Marshall had been "engaged in a small-scale commercial activity to help subsidize or support himself and his common-law spouse." Observing that the constitutional test for whether government regulation infringed upon native rights was the same for both aboriginal rights and treaty rights, the Court found a prima facie infringement of the Mi'kmaq's Treaty right to fish.

The *Marshall* decision triggered an immediate and violent public reaction, including acts of property destruction and human injury, as nonindigenous members of various natural resource industries feared that the Court's holding amounted to the Mi'kmaq tribe possessing a limitless right to harvest all natural resources from the sea and land, including minerals and offshore natural gas deposits....

Taking advantage of a motion for rehearing filed by an intervenor, the Court issued a new *Marshall* opinion later in 1999 which, while denying the motion, also attempted to eliminate what it termed the "misconceptions about what the [earlier] majority judgment decided and what it did not decide." *Marshall II* [1999] 3 S.C.R. at 537.

Although the Court reiterated earlier judgments that recognized section 35 of the Constitution Act of 1982 as affording constitutional status to aboriginal rights that had been previously vulnerable to unilateral extinguishment, the Court also reiterated its earlier statements that constitutionally protected aboriginal and treaty rights "*are* subject to regulation, provided such regulation is shown by the Crown to be justified on conservation or other grounds of public importance." The Court defined "other grounds of public importance" justifying regulation of an aboriginal right to include "*economic and regional fairness, and recognition of the historical reliance upon, and participation in, the fishery by non-aboriginal groups.*"

In addition, the Court insisted that its earlier *Marshall* decision addressed only the tribe's rights in connection with fish and wildlife, which it characterized as "the type of things traditionally 'gathered' by the Mi'kmaq in a 1760 aboriginal lifestyle." Pointing out that no evidence had been presented that trading in logging, mineral gathering, or offshore natural gas deposits had been contemplated by either party to the 1760 Treaty, the Court assured readers that these activities were well outside the purview of the case....

The United States: The Supreme Court's Aggressive Disassociation of Native Sovereignty and Tribal Environmental Interests

Through recent decades, the Supreme Court of the United States has followed as discernible a trend as those observable in the high courts of Canada ... in its opinions addressing the nature of tribal rights to land or natural resources. Rather than resorting to dramatic retreats from tribal protection after attempting to assert sovereign duties to protect tribal environmental interests, however, the U.S. Supreme Court has worked consciously and steadily to eviscerate tribal authority in traditional indigenous territories, with majority opinions building upon one another to assert that a tribe's jurisdiction exists almost exclusively over its members and not over its land, and only isolated opinions that maintain a tight focus on treaty language acknowledging the centrality of land and natural resources in tribal identity. The shift from territorially based jurisdiction to membership-based jurisdiction is important in evaluating the environmental rights of American Indians because it necessarily diminishes tribal control over its lands and the environmental resources that may both sustain the tribe and serve as a core element of its culture.

The early Supreme Court cases of *Johnson v. M'Intosh, Cherokee Nation v. Georgia,* and *Worcester v. Georgia* [Worcester v. Georgia, 31 U.S. (6 Pet.) 515, 540–61 (1832); Cherokee Nation v. Georgia, 30 U.S. (5 Pet.) 1, 15–17 (1831); Johnson v. M'Intosh, 21 U.S. (8 Wheat.) 543, 571–92 (1823)], all authored by then-Chief Justice John Marshall, have served a foundational role in the common law of various nations on several core issues in the area of indigenous peoples' rights. Indeed, the high courts of both Canada and Australia have cited these cases and claimed to utilize their logic to guide their own decisions on indigenous peoples, making Marshall's trio of opinions of global consequence in the development of juridical ideas about sovereign-tribe relations....

Like the Marshall Court, the modern Supreme Court has recognized tribal sovereignty and the centrality of the environment in tribal culture. In the 1979 case of *Washington v. Washington State Commercial Passenger Fishing Vessel Ass'n,* for example, the Court displayed its sensitivity to the tribal perspective on land and natural resources in the context of interpreting a series of treaties between various tribes and the U.S. government. Under the treaties, the tribes had relinquished their interest in their territories with the exception of their "'right of taking fish, at all usual and accustomed grounds and stations ... in common with all citizens of the Territory.'" The main issue before the Court was whether the treaties provided that the Indians merely shared with non-Indians an equal opportunity to fish in their traditional territories, or whether the treaties secured for the Indians a right to a share of fish necessary to support their subsistence and commercial needs. In deciding that treaties secured for the Indians a greater interest than the opportunity to compete for fish, the Court made extensive reference to the historical part that anadromous fish played in tribal diet, trade, and social and religious customs, thus acknowledging both the segregability of Indian land and natural resource interests, and the interdependence of environment and culture.... The aim of its discussion of the tribes' environment-based culture was on discerning the understanding that the treaty negotiators would have had as to their agreement. Thus, although the case encompassed Chief Justice Marshall's perspective on the nature of tribal sovereignty as environmentally focused, it would not serve as an obstacle to more sweeping judicial pronouncements on the nature of Indian jurisdiction that ignored or even denied the environmental element....

[I]n its 1981 opinion in *Montana v. United States*, 450 U.S. 544, ... [the Court] focused on a tribe's authority to regulate its natural environment. The case's controversy centered on whether the Crow Indians possessed the authority to prohibit hunting and fishing within their reservation by all nonmembers, or whether the state of Montana possessed the authority to regulate hunting and fishing by non-Indians within the reservation. More specifically, the tribe claimed title to the bed of the Big Horn River, and thus the right to regulate all sports fishing and duck hunting in and on its waters.

First, the Court characterized the ownership of land under navigable waters as an incident of U.S. federal sovereignty that a court will not find to have been conveyed "except because of 'some international duty or public exigency.'" Then the Court confronted the language of an 1868 treaty which guaranteed the Crow Indians "'absolute and undisturbed use and occupation'" of its Montana reservation land, and also guaranteed that "'no persons, except [federal government agents] ... shall ever be permitted to pass over, settle upon, or reside in the [Crow's] territory.'" The Court determined that these phrases could not be read literally, because a literal reading would make the Crow Indians the owners of the riverbed lying within the boundaries of the reservation. By ignoring the actual treaty language, the Court was able to conclude that the treaty contained nothing that overrode the presumption against the U.S. government's allocation of ownership of a navigable riverbed.

With regard to the Crow's claim of authority to regulate non-Indian fishing and hunting throughout the reservation, the Court again relied on treaty language to reach a conclusion against the tribe. Here, however, the Court subjected the treaty to a literal reading, noting that "[o]nly Article 5 of that treaty referred to hunting and fishing, and it merely provided that the ... signatory tribes 'do not surrender the privilege of hunting, fishing, or passing over any of the tracts of country described.'" The Court denied that this amounted to any authority to regulate hunting and fishing by nonmembers on nonmember-owned land within the Crow's territory, and pointed out that "after the treaty was signed non-Indians, as well as members of other Indian tribes, undoubtedly hunted and fished within the treaty-designated territory of the Crows." In short, regardless of language elsewhere in the treaty indicating that the Crow Indians were to exercise nearly absolute control over its land, the Court read the tribe's hunting and fishing privilege as little more than an opportunity to compete with others for game and fish.

Putting aside the dubious merits of—and inconsistencies among—the *Montana* Court's various interpretations of Crow treaty provisions, ultimately the Court relied on the assimilationist policy of the U.S. government at the time it entered its treaty with the Crow Indians to conclude that Congress could never have intended non-Indian fee holders of land within the Crow Reservation to be subject to tribal regulatory authority insofar as their hunting and fishing practices on their land. Thus, according to *Montana*, reservation land sold to non-Indians was no longer part of the land reserved for Indian use. Expanding on this view, the Court concluded by limiting tribal sovereignty generally to power over members of the tribe, except where nonmembers enter consensual relations with a tribe or where territorial regulation is required to protect against a threat to a tribe's political or economic security. Non-Indian hunting and fishing on non-Indian-owned reservation land, the Court found, had not been established to "imperil the subsistence or welfare of the Tribe," and thus was not encompassed within the Crow Indians' tribal sovereignty.

In addition to reflecting a high comfort level with ideas like assimilation and the ultimate destruction of tribal government, the *Montana* opinion revealed several clues about the U.S. Supreme Court's approach to environmental issues in the context of tribal claims. First, ... the Court supported [its] conclusion by pointing out that the Crow Indians were nomadic buffalo hunters at the time they entered the treaty allocating their Montana land rights, and thus "fishing was not important to their diet or way of life" and so was not included in the treaty's broad description of tribal rights. Here the Court demonstrated sensitivity to the relationship between a tribe's historical practices in connection with the environment and its judicially cognizable rights....

... [R]egardless of any sense of inherent tribal sovereignty or threats to tribal survival, the majority opinions appear to have relied primarily on treaties as the source of tribal power. Indeed, in a 2004 nonenvironmental case, the Court observed outright that it derived its view of "inherent tribal authority upon the sources as they existed at the time the Court issued its decisions. Congressional legislation constituted one such important source. And that source was subject to change." U.S. v. Lara, 541 U.S. 193, 206 (2004)....

Commonalities and Distinctions ... in Addressing the Environmental Rights of Indigenous Peoples

The case law emerging in recent decades ... is not consistent in terms of the legislative authority provided to the courts regarding tribal interests in land or natural resources. The most striking of these varied authorities is Canada's constitutional provision affirming the rights of its indigenous peoples.... Canada often addresses competition between natives and non-natives in regulated industries such as fishing ... and the United States frames the issues in terms of native and non-native jurisdiction over persons or territory. These differences require the exercise of caution in any attempt to draw comparisons among the ... cases, particularly about the relative social or moral values reflected in the ... judiciaries' treatment of indigenous peoples.

Nevertheless, certain observations about the role and effectiveness of the common law may be fair to elicit from a consideration of the[se] lines of cases in juxtaposition. First, it appears that an important factor in any common law court's consideration of native environmental interests is whether the court is willing to view the human-environment re-lationship from a tribal perspective. A related factor is whether the courts are willing to perceive land interests and natural resource interests as separate spheres of tribal rights. A second factor that may be outcome-determinative in the common law cases of the three nations is whether a court imposes elements of proof and evidence from an aggressively nonindigenous stance, fracturing such elements into discrete and narrowly focused questions. Finally, and perhaps most importantly, the cases can be divided on the issue of whether the courts consider themselves empowered to acknowledge an overriding sovereign duty to preserve native cultures, and whether they acknowledge a judicial responsibility to bring that sovereign duty to bear as a matter of common law....

Court decisions emerging from the high courts of ... countries that have in common their northern-European-rooted sovereignties and significant tribal populations are only one source of the evolving perspective on indigenous rights in these countries. Certainly, they are even less an indicator of global trends in the valuing of indigenous cultures and the recognition of the need to protect their environmental interests as a key aspect of their survival. Still, the case law emerging from the high courts ... serves to underscore the importance of the judiciary in securing fundamental justice for indigenous peoples, and it illustrates the vulnerability of tribal communities to the still-potent assimilationist tendencies of the dominant cultures.

Canada's constitutionalization of indigenous rights appears to have empowered that country's judiciary to assert the sovereign duty to protect aboriginal populations. The post-*Sparrow* retreat from full-scale judicial championing of aboriginal rights, however, invites a conclusion that even constitutionalization of indigenous peoples' rights cannot effectively undermine the reticence of common law courts to embrace a nonassimilative perspective when evaluating such rights as against the sovereign. But the *Taku River Tlingit First Nation* and *Haida Nation* decisions undercut such a simple conclusion. Even though these two opinions do not stand as total victories for the indigenous interests in dispute, their revival of core principles addressed in *Sparrow* indicates that the Canadian Supreme Court is maturing in its role in defining the duties of sovereignty and the rights of indigenous peoples to the lands and natural resources with which they have an historical connection.

As a final observation, it is worth reiterating that contemporary cases emanating from the high courts ... have relied in some part on the jurisprudence of former U.S. Supreme Court Chief Justice John Marshall to justify their domestic policy on tribal recognition and claims encompassing land and environmental resources. This supports an observation that judicial policy on issues like cultural identity and assimilation has advanced little, and only recently, from where it stood in the early nineteenth century. Perhaps an even stronger message ... is that the status of indigenous rights remains as heavily influenced by politics today as it did centuries ago, and that the judicial branch remains uncertain of its authority to question the political policy impacting indigenous populations.

Notes and Questions

1. What is the appropriate role for the judiciary in resolving disputes between Indian and non-Indian people over resources that are the subject of century-old treaty rights? What evidentiary rules should apply, and who should bear the burden of proof? Should claims between Indian and non-Indian people be heard exclusively, or at least initially, in tribal court rather than federal, provincial, or state court?

2. Should treaties be construed—as they would have been understood at the time they were written or as they would be understood in modern times? Federal courts in the United States have held that (1) treaties must be liberally interpreted, as understood by the Indians, Choctaw Nation v. United States, 318 U.S. 423, 431–32 (1943); Worcester v. Georgia, 31 U.S. 515, 582 (1832), and (2) tribes are entitled to use modern equipment and techniques in the exercise of their treaty rights to hunt, fish, and gather. *See, e.g.,* Mille Lacs Band of Chippewa Indians v. Minnesota, 124 F.3d 904, 911 (8th Cir. 1997), *aff'd*, 526 U.S. 172 (1999).

3. In U.S. v. Dion, 476 U.S. 734 (1986), a member of the Yankton Sioux Tribe was prosecuted for shooting an eagle. The U.S. Supreme Court held that Congress had abrogated Mr. Dion's right to hunt bald eagles, as expressed in an 1858 treaty with his tribe, by subsequently passing the Golden and Bald Eagle Protection Act, which imposes liability on those who "take, possess, sell, purchase, barter, offer to sell, purchase or barter, transport, export or import, at any time or in any manner," the species or its parts, nests, or eggs. 16 U.S.C. 668(b). The Court construed the inclusion of a provision authorizing the Secretary of Interior to issue permits for tribal religious uses of eagles as clear evidence that Congress considered the treaty rights and chose to abrogate them in the Act. *Id.* Is this result consistent with a human rights approach? How would this conflict be resolved in Canada?

4. For a description of the legal battle between Canada's First Nations and officials who planned to dam the Oldman and other great rivers, see Oliver Houck, *Taking Back Eden* 61–87 (2010). Conflict was inevitable, given that the indigenous peoples saw the Oldman River as a "religious ecosystem" while the officials saw it as merely another "water resource." *Id.* at 67. The implications of the case for environmental assessment laws and for the balance of power between the national and provincial governments are covered in Chapter 3.B.1.

5. Professors Bonine and Svitlana note that the experience of indigenous peoples is particularly relevant to an understanding of the relationship between human rights and the environment. John Bonine and Svitlana Kravchenko, Human Rights and Environment 19 (2008). Others point out that indigenous peoples have special knowledge about aboriginal lands and resources that should not only be respected but should also be incorporated in environmental law. *See, e.g.*, Rebecca Tsosie, *Tribal Environmental Policy in an Era of Self-Determination: The Role of Ethics, Economics, and Traditional Ecological Knowledge*, 21 Vt. L. Rev. 225 (1996). Do you agree? Which should prevail—indigenous rights or environmental rights—if the two come into conflict, such as when indigenous peoples want to cut trees and sell them, or to hunt for bird or fish species that may be endangered?

2. New Zealand

Maori interests in natural resources, landscapes, and the environment were explicitly recognized in the Treaty of Waitangi in 1840, and are also addressed in the Resource Management Act (RMA) of 1991. In fact, the RMA's focus on sustainability mirrors Maori cultural beliefs, at least to some extent.

> "Sustainability" is a *Pakeha* [European] concept which reflects principles at the heart of traditional Maori lore. The concept of "intrinsic values" can be related to the Maori concept of *mauri* [the life principle]; concern about the needs of future generations is an approximation of the more fundamental Maori concept of the continuity of all life, including people, over the past, the present and the future.

Furuseth, *supra*, at 271. The following excerpt explores the historical contours of Maori interests in fisheries.

Benjamin A. Kahn, The Legal Framework Surrounding Maori Claims to Water Resources In New Zealand: In Contrast to the American Indian Experience

35 Stan. J. Int'l L. 49 (1999)

Fisheries have always been important to the Maori due to the proximity of their communities to the sea and the sheer amount of coastline surrounding New Zealand. According to one Maori commentator on 1840 Treaty of Waitangi issues, "our tribal fisheries and lands were our greatest treasures," prior to the arrival of the "white goblins" whose ships "came for our whales and seals" and other water resources. Maori tribes traditionally relied on the sea for subsistence harvests. Maoris looked to the sea for mammals such as whales and seals that could provide large amounts of food. Other salt water harvests included fish, mollusks, crustaceans, and echinoderms (sea urchins and sea eggs). Maoris also historically harvested seaweed, both to create bags and other carrying devices and to dry and then boil into a jelly, with sugar or juice added.

Resources within fresh water were no less vital, and according to one scholar were "amongst the important food resources for Maori from the time of their first arrival in New Zealand." Eels are one of the most important freshwater fish to the Maori. Maoris traditionally made great use of freshwater eel harvests, with over one hundred Maori names for varieties of eels or states of eel growth. Maori tribes historically guarded these fresh water fisheries and other fresh and salt water resources from unauthorized use.

Even prior to European colonization, fishing formed one of the cornerstones of Maori culture. For example, from the outset, the Maori developed extensive fishing gear to facilitate water resource harvests. Prior to the arrival of European settlers, the Maori used seagoing canoes, or "Waka Tete," to conduct deep sea fishing. Today, one commentator documents the "widespread involvement" of Maoris in the fishing industry, especially in the owning and manning of fishing boats, catching and processing businesses, marine farming businesses, and ocean resource marketing businesses.…

Notes and Questions

1. Under Article 2 of the Treaty, Māori are guaranteed full, exclusive, and undisturbed possession of their lands, fisheries, forests, and other properties. Justice Susan Glazebrook, Natalie Baird, Sasha Holden, *New Zealand: Country Report on Human Rights,* 40 Vict. U. Wellington L. Rev. 57, 100 (2009). Section 8 of the RMA states that "all persons exercising functions and powers" under the RMA "in relation to managing the use, development, and protection of natural and physical resources, shall take into account the principles of the Treaty of Waitangi." This provision clearly applies to decisionmakers, but what duties do *applicants* for resource consents have with regard to consultation? *See Carter Holt Harvey Ltd v. Te Runanga o Tuwharetoa Ki Kawerau* [2003] 2 NZLR 349 para 55 (holding that 8 imposes no duty of consultation on applicants). A 2005 amendment to the RMA speaks to the issue of consultation. *See* RMA 36A (consultation is not required in relation to applications for resource consents unless it is required under any other enactment); Ministry for the Environment, *RMA 2005—Improving Certainty for Consultation and iwi Resource Planning,* Ref. INFO 139 (Aug. 5, 2005). For insights, see Glazebrook, *supra* at 102; Jenny Vince, M ori *Consultation Under the Resource Management Act and the 2005 Amendments,* 10 NZ J Envtl L 295, 302 (2006).

2. One of the problems in the interpretation and application of the Treaty is that "the English and Maori texts of the treaty differ...." Claire Charters, *An Imbalance of Powers: Maori Land Claims and an Unchecked Parliament*, 30 Cultural Survival 1 (2006).

> The English text speaks explicitly of a cession of sovereignty to the Queen of England and the protection of Maori lands and properties. In contrast, the Maori text speaks of a transferral of, loosely translated, governor powers to the English Crown and the retention by Maori of their chieftainship over all their treasures.

Id. If you were a judge, how would you address this particular dilemma?

3. Maori claims to the foreshore (beach land between the high and low water marks, also known as the intertidal zone) and the seabed are especially controversial. The debate over property rights goes all the way back to 1840, with the signing of the Treaty of Waitangi. In recent years, "the dispute reached a climax, first with the courts, the New Zealand's government, and finally an extra-judicial independent commission all weighing in on the debate." Christian N. Siewers, Jr., *Balancing A Colonial Past with A Multicultural Future: Maori Customary Title in the Foreshore and Seabed After Ngati Apa*, 30 N.C. J. Int'l L. & Com. Reg. 253, 253 (2004). For details, see Shaunnagh Dorsett and Lee Godden, *Interpreting Customary Rights Orders under the Foreshore and Seabed Act: The New Jurisdiction of the Maori Land Court*, 36 Victoria Univ. of Wellington L. Rev. 229 (2005). Parliament and the judiciary have been criticized for their approach to these disputes.

> New Zealand's legal system is ineffective at implementing international and domestic laws that protect the rights of Maori. This has been seen most starkly in the Foreshore and Seabed Act of 2004, which had the effect of extinguishing Maori aboriginal title to the foreshore and seabed areas and was passed despite almost universal Maori opposition.
>
> The problem lies in the structure of the country's legal system. One of the greatest impediments to the protection of human rights and indigenous peoples' rights is the fact that the Aotearoa/New Zealand Parliament retains absolute sovereignty. Aotearoa/New Zealand is one of the only countries in the world where legislation cannot be overturned for inconsistency with human rights. This inherited colonial legal principle means that Parliament can, and does, override both domestic and international human rights and indigenous peoples' rights, to Maori detriment....
>
> On the basis of their view of the treaty, the Maori staged protests throughout the 1960s and 1970s against the loss of land and rangatiratanga (self-determination/chieftainship). In response to those protests, the Waitangi Tribuna, similar to a commission of inquiry, was established in 1975. It initially had the mandate to inquire only into contemporary Crown breaches of the treaty principles (not the text of the treaty itself), but was extended in 1985 to also cover historical Crown breaches.... Waitangi Tribunal findings are not automatically enforceable, but are only recommendations to the Crown. In recent years, the Crown has rejected a number of Waitangi Tribunal reports, including one that found that some tribes in the Taranaki region have a treaty interest in oil and gas in their territory. It also rejected most of the tribunal's Foreshore and Seabed Report that was critical of the government's policy on Maori property rights in the foreshore and seabed....

Charters, *supra.* Charters ends on a positive note, however.

> But Maori are far from helpless. They now have their own political party, which gained 5 percent of the vote in the September 2005 elections, and which has proved to be an excellent vehicle for expressing Maori views. There are allocated Maori seats in Parliament, too (of which the Maori party won four). Protest is common, as well. In response to the government's foreshore and seabed policies, Maori protested by marching the length of the North Island, finishing outside Parliament. That protest failed to change the policy, but it did not go unnoticed.

Id.

4. For an argument that "Maori land claims will be bolstered through the use of existing and emerging customary international law, including principles in the Declaration [on Rights of Indigenous Peoples]," which contains broader rights than those in New Zealand's domestic law, see Sarah M. Stevenson, *Indigenous Land Rights and the Declaration on the Rights of Indigenous Peoples: Implications for Maori Land Claims in New Zealand,* 32 Fordham Int'l L.J. 298, 301 (2008).

3. India

There are 461 ethnic groups of indigenous peoples (8.2% of the total population) recognized as officially Scheduled Tribes in India. Estimates of the total number of tribal groups are as high as 635. Many indigenous peoples reside in seven states in northeast India, from Rajasthan to West Bengal. Int'l Work Group for Indigenous Peoples, Indigenous Peoples in India (2011), http://www.iwgia.org/regions/asia/india.

India is uniquely situated as an industrialized nation that straddles the divide between developed and least-developed labels. In a place like India, the right to development is a counterbalance to a right to a healthy environment. *See* 1986 United Nations Declaration on the Right to Development (DRD), adopted by UN General Assembly resolution 41/128 of Dec. 4, 1986, Preamble Paragraphs and Article.

> The ... [realization of biodiversity rights within the Convention on Biological Diversity] raises the interconnected issue of realization of the Right to Development.... [R]ecall the 1986 United Nations Declaration on the Right to Development, Adopted by UN General Assembly resolution 41/128 of Dec. 4, 1986, ... which proclaims the Right to Development as an inalienable human right. It places the human being as the central subject of development and emphasizes that the human person should be the active participant and beneficiary. It stresses the right of peoples to self-determination, by virtue of which they have the right to freely determine their political status and to pursue their economic, social and cultural development....

Shalini Bhutani and Ashish Kothari, *The Biodiversity Rights of Developing Nations: A Perspective From India*, 32 Golden Gate U. L. Rev. 587, 594, 603 (2002).

India is also unique in that environmental rights are recognized in its Constitution. Article 48A declares: "The State shall endeavor to protect and improve the environment and to safeguard the forests and wildlife of the country." Article 51A(G) imposes a duty on every citizen "to protect and improve the natural environment including forests, lakes, rivers and wildlife and to have compassion for living creatures." In addition, India's courts have construed the constitutional guarantee to a right to life (Article 21) as securing the right of every person to a "wholesome environment." *See, e.g.,* Subhash Kumar v. State of Bihar AIR 1991 SC 420, 424; MC Mehta v. Union of India 1992 (3) SCC 256, 257. For background on these provisions, see Shyam Divan and Armin Rosencranz, Environmental Law & Policy in India 41–45 (2d ed. 2002).

What happens when infrastructure development displaces tribal people? It is estimated that sixty million Indian people have been displaced by dams, highways, and other projects since the 1940s. "[O]ver 40 percent are tribals and another 40 percent are Dalits [so-called untouchables] and other rural poor." Int'l Work Group for Indigenous Peoples, *Update 2011 India*, http://www.iwgia.org/regions/asia/india (visited July 1, 2012).

> The 5th Schedule and 6th Schedule to the Constitution of India provide stringent protection of the land belonging to the tribal peoples. In addition, at the state level, there is a plethora of laws prohibiting the sale or transfer of tribal lands to non-tribals and the restoration of alienated tribal lands to them. However, the laws are either not properly implemented or they are manipulated to facilitate the transfer of tribal lands to non-tribals.

Id. Moreover, India's Land Acquisition Act specifies cash compensation for the loss of individually-owned land, but rehabilitation, the process of reconstructing the livelihood of displaced persons, is not required. *See* Land Acquisition Act, pt. III(23).

The Indian government has taken the position that rehabilitation is not a top consideration when acquiring land for a "public purpose." Pooja Mehta, *Internally-Displaced Persons and the Sardar Sarovar Project: A Case for Rehabilitative Reform in Rural Media*, 20 Am. U. Int'l L. Rev. 613, 629–30 (2005). The courts, however, have not always agreed.

In Banawasi Seva Ashram v. State of Uttar Pradesh, AIR 1987 SC 374, the Supreme Court placed conditions on the removal of tribal forest dwellers by the National Thermal Power Corporation. The court permitted land acquisition by the Corporation only after it agreed to provide court-approved facilities to the ousted people. It also ordered that the loss of income from productive lands should be included in the compensation package for oustees. Other cases have directed state agencies to provide adequate resettlement and rehabilitation services for tribal people displaced by dams. *See, e.g.,* Karanjan Jalasay Y.A.S.A.S Samiti v. State of Gujarat AIR 1987 SC 532. Obtaining favorable court orders, however, is not necessarily enough.

> Although the Scheduled Tribes and Other Traditional Forest Dwellers (Recognition of Forest Rights) Act came into force on 1 January 2009, lack of proper implementation has deprived tens of thousands of tribals of their rights to forest land.... Minister of ... Tribal Affairs Shri Mahadeo Singh Khandela admitted ... that: "Complaints have been received over a period of time concerning denial of rights and eviction of tribals from forests etc."

Int'l Work Group for Indigenous Peoples, *Update 2011-India*, *supra*.

One of the most controversial projects in India's history, from both a human rights and an environmental impact standpoint, is the Narmada Valley Project. This immense project involves the construction of 31 major dams, 135 mid-sized dams, and 3,000 smaller dams by 2040. In 1979, the project received funding from the World Bank. Local people began an unparalleled period of activism under the leadership of the Narmada Bachao Andolan (NBA). As a result, the World Bank commissioned an independent review of the project. The report substantiated allegations about the government's failure to complete a comprehensive resettlement and rehabilitation plan, and the World Bank withdrew in 1993. "The Indian government, however, opted to continue without Bank funding despite citizen protests, international condemnation, a sizeable decrease in financial support, and substantial concern over the project's impact on the environment and the health of neighboring inhabitants." Pooja Mehta, *Internally-Displaced Persons and the Sardar Sarovar Project: A Case for Rehabilitative Reform in Rural Media,* 20 Am. U. Int'l L. Rev. 613 (2005).

The Sardar Sarovar Project (SSP) in Gujarat is among the most hotly contested pieces of the Narmada Valley Project.

> [M]ost oustees, particularly as a result of the SSP, are indigenous, or tribals.... And while many of them have been cultivating their land for generations, they lack formal title to it. In other areas, land that was traditionally theirs has been designated as state-owned forest reserves, cultivation of which is illegal. Consequently, they will get no compensation for their land. They will also lose access to common property resources, including agricultural and grazing land, water, forests and fish.... [T]he issue of resettlement and rehabilitations has generated vast amounts of litigation.

Divan and Rosencranz, *supra,* at 447. The petitioners' claims before the Supreme Court allege that few of the people had been resettled or had even had lands acquired for their resettlement, and how those that had been resettled by the authorities had been placed on lands contested by other owners, non-arable lands, and lands without potable water. The Supreme Court stayed the dam construction in 1995, but in an interim order in 1999, it allowed the height of the dam to be raised to 88 meters, and in 2000, the Court allowed the SSP to proceed, with rehabilitation of the displaced peoples occurring in decreed stages. *See* Narmada Bachao Andolan v. Union of India, A.I.R. 2000 S.C. 587 (directing that the SSP be completed in compliance with conditions that mandated land-for-land rehabilitation of all affected families twelve months prior to any further increases in dam height). For a detailed timeline, see International Environmental Law Research Centre, *The Sardar Sarovar Case,* http://www.ielrc.org/india/ssp.php (visited Aug. 14, 2012). A recent report criticized the "sky-rocketing costs" of the project, and called for "a fresh review of the costs and benefits ... to convince the people of India that the financial, human, and environmental costs of construction to raise the height further are defensible." Assc. for India's Development, TISS Report on Narmada Dam: Sardar Sarovar Project (2008), http://aidindia.org/main/content/view/763/376/. Meanwhile, protests have been ongoing, ranging from "well-publicized hunger strikes, sit-ins, and instances where people block roads and drape their bodies over construction equipment in order to slow the progress of dam building projects." Rosencranz, *supra,* at 525.

Absent adequate resettlement, India is in violation of two international agreements to which it is a party: the Convention Concerning the Protection and Integration of Indigenous and Tribal Populations (ILO No. 157), 328 U.N.T.S. 247 (1959), and the Covenant on Economic, Social and Cultural Rights (CESCR), 6 ILM 368 (1967). The first of these provides: "The right of ownership, collective and individual, ... over the lands which these populations traditionally occupy shall be recognized," and requires that removal can occur only for exceptional reasons and that affected populations shall be given lands of equal quality. ILO No. 157 Art. 11-12. The latter provides a right to adequate housing. CESCR Art. 11. Accordingly, the U.N. Commission on Human Rights has declared that forced evictions are a "gross violation of human rights." U.N. Doc. No. 1993/77. Despite these international requirements:

> India lacks a comprehensive legal framework to define the rights of the displaced, the obligations of the agencies causing the displacement, and the solutions necessary for rebuilding the communities and livelihoods of the people affected by the SSP. Due to this absence of state or national laws and policies, India's efforts

to resettle its displaced repeatedly fail, and the SSP-affected communities are forced to deal with sudden evictions, insufficient compensation, and the loss of their assets and livelihoods.

Despite the fact that the SSP has produced massive displacement and associated harms, the government of India has yet to implement national and state legislation to protect those who encounter displacement against their will. Without statutory resettlement and rehabilitation laws, project-implementing authorities and state governments are under no legal obligation to integrate comprehensive resettlement or rehabilitation planning into the development of the SSP. This lack of legal responsibility on the part of the government perpetuates a system in which deplorable practices govern the implementation of the SSP in a system where the displaced person's rights are undefined and unprotected.

Mehta, *supra,* at 636–37. A lack of adequate legal infrastructure is only one aspect of the problem. What can a nation like India do if there is no available land of equal quality for resettlement? One choice is to de-designate forest reserves in order to allow settlement. Deforestation raises its own set of problems, however, and in India people often live in the forest reserves already.

 Other issues facing India's indigenous, minority, and impoverished communities involve the export of transnational industrial interests to India and the environmental harms that can result from the ensuing development. "Two widely publicized examples were the lethal 1984 Union Carbide gas leak in Bhopal, and the continuing logging of tropical rainforests for First World timber companies." Divan and Rosencranz, *supra,* 594.

The Bhopal disaster raised complex legal, moral, and ethical questions about the liability of parent companies for their subsidiaries, of transnational companies engaged in hazardous activities, and of governments caught between attracting industry to invest in business development while simultaneously protecting the environment and their citizens. In the wake of the disaster and its ineffective and inequitable compensation scheme, the central government enacted legislation designed to guard India's environment and citizens from similar disasters....

Three legislative efforts attempted to respond to the Bhopal disaster. The first act was the 1986 Environment Protection Act, which ... is neither strict nor well enforced. The second act was the 1991 Public Liability Insurance Act. Lastly, the 1992 National Environment Tribunal Act purported to create a strict liability tort for injuries arising out of hazardous activities.

Since the launch of the market reform program in 1991, the government has become more keen than ever to attract foreign investment. Fearing that Bhopal will spoil the prospects for foreign dollars, the Indian government effectively brushed aside the bitter lesson of irresponsible multinational behavior, at the expense of future Indian victims. There are already many other dangerous factories in India with more to come. Regulatory licensing has been abolished for all but eighteen industry groups. Even where licensing is retained, the government lacks data to accurately and comprehensively assess occupational health hazards and environmental safety....

A paradigmatic example of India's environmental sacrifices in its drive to develop is the "Golden Corridor," an industrial belt running from Vapi at the southern end of Gujarat to Mahesana, about 270 miles north, that includes 190 industrial complexes. Currently, most factories are Indian, but foreign investors such as Shell and General Electric have recently commenced operations. Although toxic emissions and poor waste disposal practices are common in the Golden Corridor, India's development plans call for billions of new investment dollars by the year 2000.

One of the 190 industrial complexes in the Golden Corridor is Ankleshwar, which consists of 3000 firms, about half of them chemical, operating in a forty square mile complex. Hazardous substances used in production processes and manufactured at Ankleshwar include pesticides, paints, fertilizers, dyes, and pulp and paper. The Ankleshwar Industrial Association estimates that its members generate about fifty-five to sixty million gallons of liquid hazardous wastes per day, and 50,000 tons of solid hazardous wastes per year. Although the state government ordered the Gujarat Industrial Development Corporation (GIDC) to develop solid and liquid waste treatment plans in 1988, no landfill site has yet been chosen, nor does any common incinerator exist. As a result, sludge and solid waste currently lies in the open. As for liquid wastes, about fifty of the plants, consisting of more than 500 employees, have their own waste water treatment plants. The remainder of the plants simply dump their liquid wastes into storm sewers, canals, and ditches. Some of this waste goes directly to the Amlakhari River, which provides drinking water to the villages through which it passes....

No studies have been conducted regarding the health effects on workers, the health effects on surrounding communities, or chronic occupational diseases, and no unions exist to lobby for improved worker safety conditions.

Armin Rosencranz and Kathleen D. Yurchak, *Progress on the Environmental Front: The Regulation of Industry and Development in India,* 19 Hastings Int'l & Comp. L. Rev. 489, 500–03 (1996). Although this snapshot of transnational industries in India is dated, it remains true that, despite progressive legislation, "weak enforcement ... means that the actual threat of liability and cost faced by foreign investors is negligible." For additional discussion, see Saptak Sanyal and Aditya Shankar, *Property Rights And Sustainable Development In India,* 22 Colum. J. Asian L. 235 (2009) (focusing on the environmental, social, economic and legal impact of real estate and infrastructural projects in India from the perspective of the displacement of farmers and indigenous people).

Notes and Questions

1. Could people displaced by development like Narmada, or otherwise adversely affected by development (pollution, depletion of water resources, etc.), bring suit against developers in U.S. courts? *See* Chapter 2.D, *supra* (Alien Tort Claims Act).

2. For views from a broad geographic slice of South Asia, see Parvez Hassan and Azim Azfar, *Securing Environmental Rights Through Public Interest Litigation in South Asia*, 22 Va. Envtl. L.J. 215, 246 (2004) (outlining "the critical role played by public interest litigation" in affording access to justice, and finding that "the South Asian judiciary leads the world in its role as guarantor of the legal protection of sustainable development ... [but] because public interest litigation can involve both supervisory adjudication and resolution of complex policy issues, executive and legislative organs need to be strengthened to become more responsive to emerging problems"). For stories about the need for courageous advocates and public interest litigation in environmental cases around the world, see Oliver A. Houck, Taking Back Eden (2010).

Index

Note: *f* designates figure; *n*, note; C, Canada; EC, European Community; I, India; NZ, New Zealand; UK, United Kingdom; and US, United States.